443314

Who Voted for Hitler?

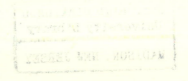

Richard F. Hamilton

PRINCETON UNIVERSITY PRESS
PRINCETON, NEW JERSEY

Copyright © 1982 by Princeton University Press
Published by Princeton University Press, 41 William Street, Princeton, New Jersey
In the United Kingdom: Princeton University Press, Guildford, Surrey

All Rights Reserved

Library of Congress Cataloging in Publication Data will be found on
the last printed page of this book

This book has been composed in Linotron Bembo

Clothbound editions of Princeton University Press books are printed
on acid-free paper, and binding materials are chosen
for strength and durability

Printed in the United States of America by Princeton University Press,
Princeton, New Jersey

To Alois Nuhn

CONTENTS

MAPS AND TABLES

BVP   Bavarische Volkspartei (Bavarian People's party: split off from the Zentrum in 1919).

DDP   Deutsche Demokratische Partei (German Democratic party, or simply the Democrats, a left liberal party; in 1930 reorganized and renamed; see the DSP).

DHV   Deutschnationaler Handlungsgehilfen-Verband (German National League of Commercial Employees: a conservative white-collar trade union).

DNVP   Deutschnationale Volkspartei (German National People's party; the Conservatives, also called the German Nationals).

DSP   Deutsche Staatspartei (German State party; successor to the DDP, organized in 1930).

DVP   Deutsche Volkspartei (German People's party; also called the People's party, a right liberal or laissez faire party).

GDA   Gewerkschaftsbund der Angestellten (League of White-Collar Unions, a moderate or centrist federation).

KPD   Kommunistische Partei Deutschlands (Communist party of Germany).

KVP   Konservative Volkspartei (Conservative People's party of Germany, a breakaway from the DNVP).

NSDAP Nationalsozialistische Deutsche Arbeiterpartei (National Socialist German Workers' party).

SA   Sturmabteilung (storm troops, the NSDAP's paramilitary organization).

SPD   Sozialdemokratische Partei Deutschlands (Social Democratic party of Germany).

USPD   Unabhängige Sozialdemokratische Partei Deutschlands (the Independent Social Democratic party of Germany, wartime split from the SPD).

WP   Wirtschaftspartei (Economic party).

ZdA   Zentralverband der Angestellten (Central Organization of White-Collar Employees, a federation with SPD ties).

Zentrum Zentrumspartei (Center party, moderate Catholic party).

The impetus for this book occurred some fourteen years ago when, in the course of a conversation, Frau Ilse Suhr lent me a book dealing with National Socialist activities in a small and elegant German resort community. Its contents—making all due allowance for its many questionable assertions (the book was written by the party's local leader)—stimulated a lot of rethinking, and even more important, some initial reresearching of the subject. My first words of appreciation, then, are to Frau Suhr who, as the saying goes, made it all possible.

It was not until 1974 that I was again able to take up work on the subject. The effort was then generously supported by the Canada Council (grant S73-1800). Some later funding came from the Faculty of Graduate Studies and Research of McGill University. Funds for preparation of the manuscript and the maps came from a grant to McGill University made by Union Carbide of Canada. My initial work on the subject, in the summer and fall of 1966, came as a byproduct of a separate research effort in the Federal Republic of Germany, one that was supported by the Social Science Research Council. To all of these organizations, I wish to express my deep appreciation. Since Canada Council funds ultimately come from the people of Canada, I wish to thank them too, the ultimate sponsors of this project.

Many people have contributed in one way or another to the writing of this book. My greatest debt, by far, is to Henry A. Turner, Jr., who provided many pages of commentary and who continued with additional details in a number of long telephone conversations. Also providing extensive comment on drafts of the manuscript were William S. Allen, Chandler Davidson, Henry Ehrmann, Peter Hoffmann, Michael Kater, and James Wright. To all of these persons I am especially grateful.

Many others have helped with technical and substantive comments or observations. It is difficult to apportion appreciation precisely, and for that reason I have resorted to an alphabetical listing. They are: Jerome Black, Werner Cahnman, Roger Chickering, Samuel Clark, Janet Doria, William Eaton, Paul Eberts, Christian Engeli, Jürgen Falter, Henry Finney, Erich Fromm, Peter Gourevitch, Carl Hamilton, Tilman Hamilton, Hanno Hardt, Peter J. Katzenstein, Veronika Kay, Jürgen Kocka,

Harold Lasswell, Anthony Masi, Peter Merkl, Anthony Oberschall, Ulrich Oevermann, Dietrich Orlow, Stanley Payne, Maurice Pinard, Allan Schnaiberg, James Sheehan, Michael Smith, Hasso Spode, Michael Traugott, Janet Vavra, Robert Vogel, Donald Von Eschen, Edgar Von Ondarza, Ernst Wagner, and Richard Willey. For all of their contributions I am deeply appreciative.

Translations from the German are, in most instances, a product of the joint labors of Irene Hamilton and myself. The ultimate responsibility for these efforts is, as with all of the text, mine alone.

I wish to acknowledge the many labors of the reference librarians of McLennan Library at McGill University. They have been most helpful in tracking down out of the way details. And I also very much appreciate the efforts of the librarians in the Inter-Library Loan Department. They have performed heroic services in obtaining out of the way publications.

Data for many German cities were made available through the efforts of persons in the following organizations: in West Berlin, the Senatsbibliothek; the Berliner Stadtarchiv; the Statistisches Landesamt Berlin; the Geheime Staatsarchiv Preussischer Kulturbesitz; the Universitätsbibliothek an der Freien Universität; in East Berlin, the Stadtarchiv; the Landesarchiv; in Hamburg, the Forschungsstelle für die Geschichte der NSDAP in Hamburg; the Staatsarchiv; in Cologne, the Historisches Archiv der Stadt Köln; in Munich, the Stadtarchiv; the Monacensierbibliothek; das Institut für Zeitgeschichte; die Bayerische Staatsbibliothek; das Munich Amt für Statistik und Datenverarbeitung; and the Bayerisches Statistisches Landesamt. Most of the information for the following cities came from the respective city archives (Stadtarchive): Essen, Dortmund, Düsseldorf, Gelsenkirchen, Duisburg, Wuppertal, Frankfurt, Hanover, Stuttgart, Nuremberg, and Mannheim. Some information was also gained from the Frankfurt Collection of that city's Universitäts-Bibliothek. Some newspapers were seen in the Stadtbibliothek of Hanover. Others were made available through the Institut für Zeitungsgeschichte in Dortmund.

More than a hundred persons have aided me in these archives, libraries, and offices. In addition to supplying books, newspapers, and published statistical materials, these people gave many hours of their time to answer questions about the character of neighborhoods, migration patterns, newspaper readership, and the like. For the many generously supplied details, nuances, and insights nowhere found in printed sources, I am very much indebted to them all. I regret that a more individual statement of appreciation is not possible.

I am very grateful to some teachers—to Gerhard E.O. Meyer and Franz L. Neumann, the first German scholars with whom I had direct contact. Two other exile scholars with whom I had more fleeting contact were Otto Kirchheimer and Paul Massing. It would take much more than a few sentences or paragraphs to express my indebtedness to them.

For Barbara Westergaard's editing of the manuscript I have both great praise and deep appreciation.

I am sure that I have overlooked some people who have been of assistance. The above expressions of thanks may not precisely indicate the actual extent of someone's contribution. I would like to ask forgiveness for any such oversight or imprecision.

Among the many typists who worked on the manuscript, three are deserving of special commendation: Carolyn Roper, Hectorine Léger, and Mohinder Massand.

Quotations from William Sheridan Allen, *The Nazi Seizure of Power* (© 1965, William Sheridan Allen) are reprinted with permission of the author and publisher, Franklin Watts, Inc. Material from Jeremy Noakes, *The Nazi Party in Lower Saxony, 1921-1933* (© 1971, Oxford University Press) is also reprinted with permission of the author and publisher.

The theories, claims, and hypotheses addressed in this book are drawn from three fields, from history, political science, and sociology. I have become very much aware of the significance of the division of academic labor while writing this volume. Some parts of the book were seen as commonplace or routine by historians; the same parts were found to be new and rather difficult by many sociologists and political scientists. Some parts that were elementary for the last two specialists were new and complicated for historians. I ask the reader to bear this in mind—some parts of the text are intended primarily for "other readers."

Montreal
September 4, 1980

WHO VOTED FOR HITLER?

MAP 1 : GERMANY — 1930

ELECTORAL DISTRICTS

1 East Prussia
2 Berlin
3 Potsdam II
4 Potsdam I
5 Frankfurt
6 Pomerania
7 Breslau
8 Liegnitz
9 Oppeln
10 Magdeburg
11 Merseburg
12 Thuringia
13 Schleswig-Holstein
14 Weser-Ems
15 Hanover-East
16 Hanover-South
17 Westfalen-North
18 Westfalen-South
19 Hessen-Nassau
20 Cologne-Aachen
21 Koblenz-Trier
22 Düsseldorf-East
23 Düsseldorf-West
24 Upper Bavaria
25 Lower Bavaria
26 Franconia
27 Palatinate
28 Dresden-Bautzen
29 Leipzig
30 Chemnitz-Zwickau
31 Württemberg
32 Baden
33 Hessen-Darmstadt
34 Hamburg
35 Mecklenburg

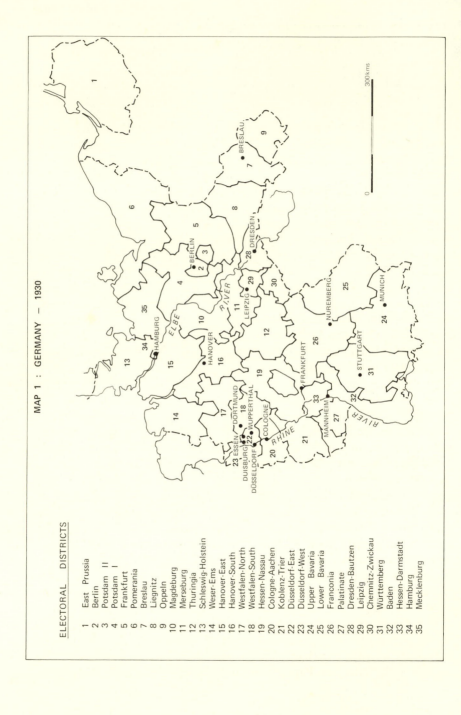

CHAPTER ONE

The Problem: Who Voted for Hitler?

How could it have happened?—that is the ever-recurring question about Germany of the 1930s and 1940s. Although the question is a simple one, the problems involved in finding a satisfactory answer seem to defy human capacities.

To deal with that question it helps to divide the history into its various episodes. There was, first of all, a series of elections in which the National Socialists made enormous gains. A briefer episode of negotiations followed, ending with Hitler being named to head the government. Then came the consolidation of power and the building of a war machine. And last, there was the war itself and the extraordinary succession of crimes accompanying that crime.

This work is concerned with the first of these episodes, with the electoral development that made the subsequent steps possible. Without that first achievement Hitler would never have come into question as a contender for the chancellorship, and, presumably, the later developments could not have happened.

As of 1928, the appeal of the National Socialists was so small that some commentators, those who recognized them at all, saw them as a minor, and declining, splinter party. But then, in state and local elections, and in the Reichstag election of 1930, they suddenly emerged as a considerable, and growing, force on the political scene. In only a little more than two years their share of the total vote increased from 2.6 to 18.3 percent (see Appendix A). The gains continued in subsequent state and local elections and also in the presidential elections in the spring of 1932. The most important election—for the National Socialists, for Germany, and for the entire world—took place on July 31, 1932. At that point Hitler's party took 37.3 percent of the vote, the highest level it achieved in a national election prior to coming to power.

That result put Hitler in a commanding position. He could, with considerable legitimacy, insist on being named to head the government. Even if not named to that position (since the constitution did not require it), he would still be a key figure, in one way or another, in almost all of the possibilities for coalition. President Hindenburg, the man with the power to name the chancellor, refused the option and continued for a while with Franz von Papen, who ruled without a parliamentary majority through the use of presidential decrees. A second Reichstag election was called for November of that year.

The National Socialists suffered a considerable reversal in this election, losing approximately two million votes. This development thoroughly alarmed Hitler and the other party leaders. The heads of the moderate parties of Germany took it as a sign that the threat was passing. But then, the brief episode of negotiations—actually an intrigue and a subsequent counterintrigue—occurred. The end result was Hitler's appointment as chancellor; the Conservative majority in the cabinet, so it was thought, would be able to prevent any excesses.[1]

There was one subsequent election, on March 5, 1933, at which point the National Socialists received the highest support they ever obtained in contested elections, 43.9 percent, a level still short of the majority for which they had hoped. One may question both the validity and the significance of this result. The Reichstag building had been set afire shortly before the elections, and the National Socialists stimulated and made use of the subsequent hysteria. They also had control of the police and of the radio for the first time and used both to further their own ends. For those reasons, little attention will be paid this last election. It came after the taking of power; the key second step in the history had already been taken.

As indicated, the basic concern of this work is with the National Socialists' acquisition of the support of 37.3 percent of the nation's voters. Many discussions of the period have focused on *the* Germans, as if they were *all* moved by the party's appeals. But with respect to these elections, in particular to that of July 1932, the question must be more specific. Since only three out of eight voters supported Hitler at that point, one must ask: *which* Germans voted for Hitler?

Even at this late date, it is possible to provide a reasonably satisfactory answer to this question. But that is only part of the problem and in many respects the less interesting part. It is much more difficult to provide an answer to the why question—*why* did they support Hitler? The question of motivation was difficult then and is even more difficult to assess now, some fifty years after the events. Most of the empirical analysis in this work is concerned with the former question. Only in Chapter 13 is the motivational question considered, and even then, clearly, the discussion must be highly speculative.

One might think, remembering what one has read or heard on the subject, that nothing more need be said with respect to the "who supported Hitler" question. The basic answer—it was the lower middle class—has long since been accepted as an indisputable fact. One of the earliest analyses declared that the National Socialist vote resulted from a "panic in the middle class"—*Panik im Mittelstand*—this in turn stemming from economic marginality and the imminent threat of "proletarianization."[2] But sometimes the facts that everyone knows prove to be the least known since the complete and utter certainty about them discourages inquiry. The status of this "fact," as will be seen, leaves much to be desired.

This explanation of National Socialism, or of fascism generally, has sometimes been referred to as the centrist position or, more simply, as centrism. The reason for this term, briefly, is that the middle classes are "at the center of" the society, that is, located between the upper-class or bourgeoisie and the working-class extremes of the class hierarchy. In some accounts they are portrayed as in the middle but vacillating, joining first the side of revolution, then later that of counterrevolution. But in another line of argument, it is claimed that the members of the lower middle class, with only few exceptions, are fundamentally reactionary. Given their "structural position," caught between big business and an increasingly powerful working class, they are predisposed to support restorationist parties or movements, such as the National Socialists, those promising to restore their previous economic well-being, social status, and political eminence.[3]

The centrist position, it will be noted, has two components, one involving structural change, the other involving social psychological reactions. Persons located in the lower middle class within the framework of advanced capitalist societies, so it is said, will lose position, either being "pushed down" to the level of the workers, or, an even worse fate, losing their middle-class positions entirely and "falling into" the proletariat. Being very much attached to their middle-class status, this being the social psychological component of the argument, a threatened loss of position is a source of considerable anxiety. In a period of economic crisis, they would, supposedly, be in a state of panic. In that condition they are easily moved by the appeals addressed to them; they are, so it is said, highly susceptible to the easy solutions put forth by clever demagogues.

This book assesses this claim using election data from several large German cities. These data, remarkably enough, have been largely unexamined even though a test of the claim would seem easy enough. All that is necessary is to locate the lower-middle-class districts and show that they gave strong support to Hitler's party. But that easy task has not been done. This means, in short, that the hypothesis has never been established in the urban context.

We will see, too, that the claim is seriously misleading when applied in the rural context, that is, when used to describe the lower-middle-class proprietors of small farms. For one important part of the farm population, for the Protestant farmers, the argument does have some initial plausibility although even there, as will be seen, it proves to be less than fully adequate. For the Catholic farmers, the explanation is hopelessly inadequate. In short, the basic answer, the conclusion that everyone knows, the explanation that the lower middle class or petty bourgeoisie provided exceptional support for Hitler's party appears to be without substantial foundation and, in some key respects, is fundamentally mistaken.

A discounting or rejection of the centrist argument requires the consideration of an alternative explanation. The alternative to be argued here, in Chapters 10 through 14, contains two major components; one is political, the other social organizational. The structural argument typically blocks off consideration of specific political contributions. Because of the presumed power or weight of the structural facts, one has little incentive to consider the responses of parties to specific political issues. Such issues and such responses would, at best, be mere epiphenomena as compared to the impact of the more "basic" social and economic structures.

But, as we shall see, the six major parties, including both the bourgeois or middle-class parties and those of the left, either had taken, or in the midst of economic crisis undertook, directions that made them unattractive to important segments of the electorate. Most important, the so-called middle-class parties all moved to the right, refusing to undertake the major governmental initiatives needed to alleviate the crisis. Under the circumstances, it is not too surprising that many voters were disposed to move away from them. And the parties of the left, for various reasons, also presented no attractive alternative to these disaffected voters. In the Scandinavian countries, voters, many of them lower middle class, turned to Social Democracy in the midst of the crisis, but in Germany the heritage of both the Social Democrats and the Communists was such as to make the left an unlikely choice for the disaffected voter. This is the negative side of the argument: the previously established parties made political choices that led to a serious disaffection of their traditional voters; those voters did not see the parties of the left as acceptable alternatives.

The positive side of the argument focuses on the actions of the National Socialists. Chosen by three out of eight voters in the key election, it is clear that they were seen by many as providing a positive option or, at minimum, as presenting the most favorable of the available options. One must raise questions about both the mechanisms leading them to make such a choice and the reasons or motives for the choice.

Many analyses of the National Socialist electoral victories have focused on the efforts of the party's top leaders, particularly on those of Hitler and Goebbels, indicating their ability to sway the tens of thousands who attended their mass meetings. But those analyses omit a key step in the argument: what led these people to go there in the first place? Their presence at these meetings, it is argued, was the result of efforts undertaken by the party's local or grass-roots activists. Hitler's party appears to have had the largest army of militants of any of the parties in Germany at that time. One should not measure that effort solely in quantitative terms, however, since the National Socialist cadres also appear to have possessed exceptional organizational and tactical abilities. One should not discount the role of their top leaders; it is necessary, however, to recognize that the efforts of the party's elite constitute only one component of the explanation for its success. A necessary precondition for those electoral victories was the sustained effort put forth by that army of political activists. It was those militants who carried the party appeals out to the general populace, who disseminated the "lessons" at the grass roots. One must, therefore, consider some social-organizational questions: why were the National Socialists able to put together this army of militants? What were the factors that made it possible? Those organizational dynamics and the substance of the party's appeals are considered in Chapters 12 and 13.

The parties provided a set of offerings (or attractions or appeals), but one must also consider the responses to those appeals. Here one enters the area of motives, and they, to be sure, are obscure, hidden, or in many cases, understandably, rather distorted. This problem is especially serious given the absence of any systematic research from the period, research designed to ascertain people's motivations. The consideration of those responses, therefore, must necessarily be the most speculative of all the topics considered in this work. In Chapter 13, for what it is worth, the reactions of the major segments of the population are discussed, indicating the considerations that led some of them to turn to Hitler's party. It cannot be stressed too much that this chapter offers only plausible guesses. In at least partial justification, however, it may be noted that the discussion there proceeds on exactly the same plane as the discussions of the centrist tradition. Lacking systematic investigations, those unequivocal claims about lower-middle-class motives also provide no more than guesses about what moved people. By way of further justification, it may be noted that the present discussion is somewhat more wide ranging, considering the outlooks of all key segments of the population. It provides, as will be seen, a more accurate focus than the nearly exclusive, and largely mistaken, emphasis on *the* lower middle class.

The "Weimar experience" is frequently cited for hortatory purposes, this in the form of warning references to the "lessons" of Weimar. But if based on faulty analysis, on an erroneous diagnosis of the illness, those lessons will not be very helpful in other times and places. They might, conceivably, even have deleterious effects. A final concern, therefore, is to make some assessment of the more general theoretical implications conventionally derived from the experience of Weimar Germany and to reassess those implications in the light of the present findings. This discussion, in Chapter 14, argues once again the need for an alternative theoretical orientation and also for some changes in research priorities. As may be gathered from the foregoing discussion, the emphasis there is on historical and political determinants and on organizational instrumentalities—or the lack thereof.

A second concern of that final chapter is to provide some explanation for this persistent focus on the lower middle class as the villain of the piece. This amounts to an inquiry into the sociology of knowledge, the question being to explain or account for this unusual and persistent preference for a given line of explanation even though the support for that position is absent or at best very weak. The basic questions to be considered are: how did this distinctive reading of the evidence come to be developed in the first place? And, once developed, why was it so stubbornly maintained over so many decades? Although rather firm conclusions may be drawn as to the research methods used by those analysts, little may be established with regard to the motives or to the psychological bases of their outlooks. In its speculative character, therefore, this discussion must closely parallel the consideration of the motivations of the general population.

The method used in this work is synthetic in character. The argument is built up step by step rather than by generating conclusions as logical products (or derivations) from some higher principles. This means that we will be examining the various "parts" of the larger picture and gradually assembling them. Only toward the end will these parts be combined to offer a sense of the totality. Among other things, it means that at times we will be dealing with very "small" concerns. The appearance of a split in the ranks of the Conservatives may affect only a small percentage of votes in the upper-class district of a given city, clearly a minor fact in the larger scheme of things. But that fact does have a place in that larger picture, and the lesson it provides is of no small importance. It is hoped that the reader will be patient with such details.

A final prefatory note: the presentation of this synthesis is not chronological; this is not a work of narrative history. The development follows instead the requirements of the synthetic argument. For those who are not familiar with the history of the Weimar Republic, it might be helpful to read Appendix A before proceeding to Chapter 2. It provides a summary of the electoral history of the period and gives a brief review of the principal events intervening between those elections.

CHAPTER TWO

A Review of the Literature

This work will make an assessment of the simple, widely accepted proposition: that the lower middle class of Weimar Germany responded to the National Socialist appeals and provided the mass electoral support for that party.[1] Statements of that position may be found in nearly all major works concerned with the rise of National Socialism. A review of some of these proves useful in order to show the precise character of the formulations. The concern is both with what has been said about support for the National Socialists and, just as significant for the present task, with what has been left unsaid.

An early formulation, that of political scientist Harold Lasswell, is typical of the many formulations that were to follow.[2] In 1933, he wrote:

> Insofar as Hitlerism is a desperation reaction of the lower middle classes it continues a movement which began during the closing years of the nineteenth century. Materially speaking, it is not necessary to assume that the small shopkeepers, teachers, preachers, lawyers, doctors, farmers and craftsmen were worse off at the end than they had been in the middle of the century. Psychologically speaking, however, the lower middle class was increasingly overshadowed by the workers and the upper bourgeoisie, whose unions, cartels and parties took the centre of the stage. The psychological impoverishment of the lower middle class precipitated emotional insecurities within the personalities of its members, thus fertilizing the ground for the various movements of mass protest through which the middle classes might revenge themselves.

The article proceeds to explain how the various themes of the party, specifically nationalism and anti-Semitism, were "peculiarly fitted to the emotional necessities of the lower bourgeoisie."

Other classes or groups in the society receive only scant mention. The aristocracy, one is told, hated "money-making by the use of mobile capital," and that led to "hatred of the Jew, the money-lender of tradition." This hatred, shared with the lower middle class, provided the basis for some limited cooperation. Lasswell also devotes two paragraphs to the position of intellectuals. For them the economic crisis meant dwindling opportunities in an overstocked market. The consequence was that Jews became the object of a mass attack led by "rival intellectuals."

At the end of the article, in the very last paragraph, a brief mention is made of the upper bourgeoisie: "Influential elements of the upper bourgeoisie of Germany have partially financed the Hitler movement in order to break up the collective bargaining system." The same paragraph contains an equally brief reference to manual workers, this to say that Hitler's "thoroughly nationalistic and demagogic" movement made "substantial inroads in the more passive elements of the wage earning class."

The major lessons are clear. The lower middle class was moved, apparently en masse, to support Hitler and his party. It was the combination of its "emotional necessities" and Hitler's shrewd use of appeals catering to these needs that stirred it to "enthusiastic action." Large numbers of workers were also moved to support him, but, as noted, this is a passing, one-sentence reference, an undeveloped afterthought. Some smaller groups, intellectuals and aristocrats, are also fitted into the picture. They obviously could not provide the mass support for the movement. At best, theirs was a helping, a facilitating effort. And finally, again apparently deserving of only a passing reference, there is the upper bourgeoisie. Unlike the other groups considered by Lasswell, here it is not the class or category as a whole offering support nor is it a question of "substantial inroads." Rather it is a matter of some otherwise unspecified "influential elements" of the class who in this case are reported to have "partially financed" the movement. Their effort, moreover, is described as rational and calculating. That of the other groups (perhaps with the exception of the intellectuals) is based on emotion, on scapegoating, on irrational linkages. It is not made clear whether these influential elements provided anything else for the movement—leadership, for example, time and effort, or votes.

In summary, were it not for the reactions of the lower middle class, Hitler's movement would never have amounted to anything. Its votes provided the necessary condition for Hitler's legal coming to power. The contributions of the other groups, while of undoubted importance, by themselves would not have made a successful political movement.

So much for the substantive claims of the Lasswell article. A note on method is in order. A question may be raised about sources: what evidence is offered to support these claims? The answer in this case is very simple—there is none. No evidence is presented in the article, and no references are made to empirical studies that might support its assumptions.[3]

There is an important substantive omission as well. If the term "upper bourgeoisie" refers to the minuscule top layer of the society, to the very rich, to the owners of the means of production, then one must note that there is no discussion at all of the condition and politics of the upper middle class. It has, somehow or other, been completely overlooked. Implicitly, at least, the suggestion is that it was not an important factor in the demise of the Weimar Republic.

The biography of Hitler by Alan Bullock, the eminent historian, also has the lower middle class figuring prominently in the development of the party. Of Karl Lueger, the anti-Semitic *Bürgermeister* of Vienna so much admired by Hitler, Bullock declares that "the strength of Lueger's following lay in the lower middle class of Vienna, the small shopkeepers, businessmen and artisans, the petty officials and municipal employees." The only statement offered in support of this conclusion is a quotation, which notes that " 'he devoted the greatest part of his political activity to the task of winning over those sections of the population whose existence was in danger.' "[4] The quotation is from Adolf Hitler's work *Mein Kampf.*

Another quotation describes the basic syndrome in classic terms: "The ditch which separated [the petty bourgeois] class, which is by no means well-off, from the manual labouring class is often deeper than people think. The reason for this division . . . lies in the fear that dominates a social group which has only just risen above the level of the manual labourer—a fear lest it fall back into its old condition or at least be classed with the labourers." Again the formulation is from Adolf Hitler, from *Mein Kampf.*[5] At another point Hitler's oratorical efforts are discussed and, again in a quotation, one is told that "he could play like a virtuoso on the well-tempered piano of lower-middle-class hearts."[6] The author in this case is Hjalmar Schacht, the banker, one of those who was instrumental in getting Hitler named to the chancellorship and, for six years, a member of Hitler's cabinet. Recognizing the statement for what it is, an unsubstantiated hypothesis, one is led to ask a simple question: how would Schacht have known what went on in hundreds of thousands of lower-middle-class hearts?

Bullock reviews the events surrounding the onset of the depression, discussing the unemployment and its consequences for the working class. He then devotes a paragraph to the lower middle class: "In many ways [the depression] affected the middle class and the lower middle class just as sharply. For they—the clerks, shopkeepers, small businessmen, the less successful lawyers and doctors, the retired people living on their savings—were threatened with the loss not only of their livelihood, but of their respectability." This is followed by a discussion of the plight of the farmers. He concludes with the statement that "in such circumstances the extravagant demagogy of Hitler began to attract a mass following as it had never done before."[7]

The linkage of the urban lower middle class and Hitler's effort is made again in a discussion of election campaign themes: "Hitler's appeal in the towns was especially to the middle class hit by the depression. . . . What Hitler offered them was their own lower middle-class brand of extremism—radical, anti-Semitic, against the trusts and the big capitalists, but at the same time . . . socially respectable; nationalist, pan-German, against Versailles and reparations."[8]

It is important to note that Bullock too does not consider the upper middle class. Again, the implicit assumption is that it was relatively unaffected by the events and did not react like the others. Presumably its members were holding to the political course they had followed previously.

Bullock does discuss the upper class, the industrial bourgeoisie. As of 1930, he says, only "a section" of this group was providing support to Hitler and the party. He lists the names and connections of a dozen or so such figures in industry and banking. There is some discussion of the various intermediaries, those who introduced Hitler into business circles and provided him with speaking engagements. The entire discussion however, is focused on the question of financial support, and even here it was not possible to make any precise conclusion. He does not go beyond the rather unspecific reference to "a section" so that one cannot say whether it is a matter of 5 or 50 percent of the class. The support grew after 1930, but what portion of the class eventually offered financial aid is not indicated.

Bullock says nothing about the *voting* tendencies of the leaders of business and finance. A tiny minority of the population, they clearly could not provide any mass support for the party. An examination of their voting in this period would provide some sense of their political outlooks and preferences. Business leaders frequently gave money to many parties. But such wide-ranging generosity was not possible when it came to voting. Unfortunately, in this matter Bullock offers neither clues nor guesses.[9]

The noted political scientist Sigmund Neumann, speaking of the "rising salaried classes," declares without any qualification that "it was in this stratum that emerging National Socialism found its most ardent recruits." In an elaborating paragraph he states:

> The extraordinary quantitative growth of the white-collar man in modern industrial society led also to a qualitative change in his social prestige. His had become a static class position, if not a castelike predicament. At the same time, the discrepancy between his now unfulfilled traditional aspirations of eventual independence and individual security made this group the frustrated class par excellence. This fate

was reemphasized in Germany by the specific experiences of a military defeat, money inflation, and radical economic depression, all of which hit the salaried employees the hardest. Thus a total crisis revolutionized this stratum. . . . National Socialism seemed to offer a satisfactory answer. . . . [The National Socialists] made themselves the proud challengers of the bourgeois world and the spokesmen for the middle class and their despair in a civic society.

There are no specific supporting data or references to such data accompanying this discussion.

Neumann identifies the "uprooted unemployed" as another group providing significant support for the National Socialists. Again there are no references. There is no specific indication of any upper-class role in the rise of the National Socialists. The closest one comes to such a reference is in the mention of the "reactionary forces of Hugenberg, Seldte, Schacht, and Papen" who, we are told, "held crucial societal positions." Otherwise the upper class is completely absent from the account as is also the upper middle class.

The same position is taken by Neumann in another source. In this second account he introduces the notion of "crisis strata." Under this heading he refers only to the salaried employees and the unemployed workers. The latter appear once again as the "rootless" unemployed. There is no discussion of the farm populations and again none of the upper class or of the upper middle class. No specific supporting references are offered.[10]

These works are by no means exceptional in their treatment of the rise of National Socialism. Were one at all interested, it would be possible to list dozens of sources that make the same sweeping assertions about lower-middle-class propensities without offering so much as a single word of supporting evidence.[11]

There are, to be sure, works that do cover the subject in greater detail and that do refer to relevant studies. A review of these proves instructive.

The sociologist William Kornhauser, in his influential book *The Politics of Mass Society*, offers many of the same claims that have just been reviewed. His supporting references, however, as we shall see, prove to be exceptionally weak. Unemployed German white-collar workers, he reports, "went Nazi," unlike their employed peers "who stayed conservative or moderate." By way of support, he refers to the very important and much-cited master's thesis by Samuel Pratt.[12] This is a work whose importance and complexity are such as to deserve special consideration. That discussion is deferred to a later point in this chapter.

The National Socialists, Kornhauser reports, gained working-class support from among the "permanently unemployed." This claim bears a reference to a frequently cited work by Evelyn Anderson. But that work offers only two sentences of text that merely state the point. It provides no evidence, and no further references are given.[13] Kornhauser says also that the National Socialists "further gained a middle-class following from the dispossessed small businessmen, along with the unemployed salaried workers. . . . The . . . widespread and deep economic insecurity destroyed the lower-middle-class faith in the prevailing social order, and made for high vulnerability to Nazi appeals. The German peasants were the first to feel the depression."[14] For support of these claims, reference is made to an article by Arthur Schweitzer.[15] This article, however, presents no data showing the lower-middle-class tendency. In all cases the linkage is made either by simple assertion or by delineation of lower-middle-class economic problems followed by the assertion. Drawing on some early publication of Heberle's data (to be discussed), Schweitzer makes clear the extent of peasant support for the party, at least for some areas of Schleswig-Holstein. The only observation required here is to note that Kornhauser's claim is a general one—it is about "*the* German peasants." As is shown below the tendency occurs among the Protestant farm populations; Catholic farmers remained firmly in the ranks of the Zentrum (Center party).[16] The question of the urban vote for the party—whether it came exclusively from the lower middle class, whether from some other class or classes, or whether from all classes in equal proportions—is not answered in Schweitzer's presentation. As a reference in support of Kornhauser's point, therefore, it is little more than a blind. The small-business theme comes up again at a later point in his work, this time in a chapter on "marginal middle classes." The only new source added here is the previously discussed and dataless article by Harold Lasswell from 1933.[17]

In the course of this discussion of the marginal middle classes Kornhauser shifts ground, now counting the lower white-collar employees as supporters of the National Socialists (unlike his earlier statement that the employed white-collar workers remained conservative or moderate). This tendency, he says, was "evidenced by the growth of antidemocratic and pro-Nazi organizations of white-collar people, and the concomitant decline in white-collar organizations that favored democracy."[18]

Germany at that time had three major white-collar union federations. One was aligned with the Social Democrats, one was democratic or moderate centrist, and the third, the largest of the three, was conservative and nationalist. For support of his claims about the political changes then in process, Kornhauser cites a work by Peter Gay. The latter does in fact indicate that the conservative federation "became Nazi" and that the democratic federation "contained many National Socialists." Both of these organizations were said to be growing in numbers while the federation linked to the Social Democrats was declining.

For his claim about the political tendencies, Gay depends on a little known account by Rudolf Küstermeier. The latter does affirm—by assertion only—the dominant National Socialist influence in the conservative federation. He does not say it "went Nazi," only that it in no small way "helped to prepare the way for Hitler." Gay does not accurately represent Küstermeier with respect to the democratic federation. The latter's formulation reads as follows: "Within the [federation] the political front goes from the Communists to the National Socialists. At the same time, the leadership of the federation is, as before, oriented toward the Democratic-State party, while the members, in increasing measure, lean toward a socialist outlook. The National Socialist influence has remained relatively small." The claims about the membership trends are also open to some question.[19] The examination of Kornhauser's sources, in short, indicates that the argument is not quite as compelling as first appears. The role of these white-collar unions is considered again later in this chapter.

At another point Kornhauser has an extended discussion of big business and the National Socialists. Basically his position is that the party "received little big business support in its initial period, but picked up considerable aid from this source during its rapid growth following the depression." In line with his general focus on rooted versus uprooted populations, he makes a distinction between the old and the new rich: "Newer sections of big business, having less at stake than the old industrial families, rallied to Hitler's side once his ascendancy became apparent. An old and rooted upper class, with established traditions, tends to strike an attitude of *noblesse oblige* toward the disinherited, and to seek accommodation via amalgamation rather than subversion of the system. The new rich, on the other hand, when faced with great pressures on their position in the existing order, more often will support extremist movements."

In a summary that lays out the relative "vulnerabilities," Kornhauser makes explicit mention of upper middle classes. Since such mentions and such summaries appear so infrequently in the literature it is useful to quote the entire passage:

> In conclusion, the middle classes are not uniformly vulnerable to the appeal of mass movements. The *old* middle classes, both urban and rural, are more vulnerable than the *new* middle classes; and the *lower* middle classes are more vulnerable than the *upper* middle classes. Mass theory helps to account for these differences by adding to the eco-

nomic factor of poorer market opportunities for the small entrepreneur and peasant, the social factor of their loss of social ties and status in the larger society. As the situation of the small entrepreneur continues to deteriorate in the face of the growing rationalization of the economic order, we may expect new mass movements to gain adherents from the old middle classes, and especially their lower sections.[20]

The upper middle class, Kornhauser claims, provides a distinctive core or center of moderation in the society. The explanation implicit in his discussion is that this class has not suffered serious financial or status losses. Regrettably he makes no estimation of the quantities of moderation (or alternatively, of vulnerability) present in these classes. Other than the rather unspecific phrase "more vulnerable," nothing is said. Presumably, however, this class factor is not trivial. One is not speaking of ten or fifteen percentage-point differences. His categoric formulations would suggest differences of much greater magnitude. Another cause for regret is his failure to locate the upper classes in this summary. However, following his reasoning about economic and social causes, the upper class ought to be even more moderate than the upper middle category. No estimate is made as to the size of the vulnerable new-rich segment present within this upper class.

Kornhauser's conclusions rest on a very thin line of supporting evidence. Many of his references provide no direct evidence at all, consisting either of assertions or of statements of what is merely a plausible case. In the single instance in which reference is made to statistical evidence, that is, to the Pratt thesis, it is not, as we shall see, of a compelling character.

Another authority on the subject, possibly the leading contemporary student of National Socialism, is the political scientist Karl Dietrich Bracher. In his book *The German Dictatorship*, under the heading "Toward a Middle-Class Mass Party," he states that the "re-emergence and subsequent growth of the NSDAP [National Socialists] cannot be understood without an examination of its connections with middle-class organizations." These organizations provided the link to the middle class, the "essential base" of the party. These groups, the "petty-bourgeois, middle-class, and small landholding groups," one is told, "had been hardest hit by the outcome of the war, the economic crisis and the structural changes of modern society."[21]

The distress of the middle class is assumed by Bracher. The main direction of his argument is to show the role of the middle-class organizations in facilitating the movement to the National Socialists. For this purpose, he selects, as "a typical case in point," the German National

League of Commercial Employees (Deutschnationaler Handlungsgehil-fen–Verband or DHV).[22] The organization was right wing, anti–Marx-ist, and anti–Semitic. This "large" organization, he says, "offered nu-merous points of contact and made it easier" for the party "to gain a foothold in industry and trade groups." In the end, we are told, the DHV "substantially furthered and accelerated the drift of the middle-class white collar workers to the NSDAP." Beyond the statement that it was a "large" organization and that it "substantially" furthered the movement to the National Socialists, we have no other specification of the magnitude of its impact.

Bracher supports these claims by reference to the memoirs of Albert Krebs. Krebs, for a time the *Gauleiter* (National Socialist district leader) of Hamburg, was simultaneously an employee of the DHV. A very important source on the relations between local and top party leaders, Krebs provides no evidence on the drift of DHV members to the Na-tional Socialists. Krebs actually stresses the division of labor between the work of the party and the work of the union. Hitler and other top leaders, moreover, complained of Krebs's using the party for union pur-poses rather than vice versa. The reference, in short, does not support Bracher's argument.[23]

Bracher argues the same process with respect to agricultural organi-zations. In this case no supporting evidence is presented with respect to the organizational dynamics. He gives figures on the vote for the Con-servatives in Schleswig-Holstein, noting that their decline was parallel to the rise of the National Socialists. But as for the takeover of farm organizations, that remains only a plausible argument, an unsupported possibility.[24]

Another theme stressed by Bracher is the *lack* of a working-class fol-lowing: "The NSDAP did not succeed in making like inroads among the workers and the trade unions. Despite all efforts of the 'left' wing, the NSDAP claim to being a 'socialist workers' party' remained a prop-aganda facade. . . . The conversion of the organized socialist workers to 'national socialism' was one of the early aims of National Socialism. But the workers did not come to their meetings; the membership of the NSDAP was composed of the lower middle class, of merchants, arti-sans, white-collar workers, military adventurers, and youthful romantic activists." No evidence or references are offered to support these claims about the working-class aversion or the middle-class attraction to the party.[25]

One other quotation is of relevance here. It was, Bracher says, "the rural and urban 'middle class,' in the broad sense of the term, which started and carried out the breakthrough of the NSDAP. The 'panic of the middle class,' which set in with the outbreak of the economic crisis, was sharpened by the fact that the middle class felt threatened not only economically but, more important, socially as well."[26] Reference is made here to Theodor Geiger's impressive work.

The title of Geiger's work might be translated as *The Social Stratification of the German People: A Sociographic Attempt on a Statistical Basis.* In this book he analyzes the detailed occupational categories of the German census and regroups them in a more meaningful way. The original census categories were so problematic that they provided one of the most important obstacles to the analysis of Weimar developments. What is impressive about Geiger's work is his attempt to resolve those difficulties. In addition to defining the classes more precisely, he provides some quantification of the redefined classes.

Having accomplished those tasks, Geiger then turns, in the remainder of the work, to a description of the "mentalities" of the groups he had delineated. These descriptions, however, with rare exception, are based on nothing more than personal assertion. In this section of the book he has a thirteen-page excursus on the middle classes and National Socialism. This contains the standard assertion about the petty bourgeoisie (*Kleinbürgertum*). In support of this claim he points to the disappearance of the Wirtschaftspartei in the state elections of Prussia (April 1932). He concludes by saying that the National Socialist gains came from the middle-class parties and from the politically indifferent (that is, the previous nonvoters). This discussion, a matter of a few sentences in Geiger, is the best supported one in his analysis of mentalities. A more detailed criticism of this line of argument is made later in this chapter. For the moment, one may merely note that Geiger's evidence is at best rather sketchy. At a later point, discussing the civil servants, Geiger finds it significant that it is the lower and middle civil servants who leaned to the National Socialists rather than the higher civil servants. No support is offered for this claim. In summary, therefore, one must note that this much-cited source provides only assertions about the lower-middle-class propensities. Once again the claims that are offered with such unqualified confidence prove to have very little foundation.

Geiger himself prefaces this discussion with some cautionary remarks about his method. "There remains," he says, "only the judgment based on the impression that the conscientious observer wins from the style of the movement, from the behavior of its journals [*Organe*], and from the development of its following." His impressionistic method appears later on, when he notes that the National Socialists campaigned successfully among the long-term unemployed. This conclusion was based on personal observation; as he put it, "one sees it where the National Socialist masses show themselves on the street." Given the limitation of the method, greater caution might be anticipated—especially when the object of study, the voting behavior of entire classes, is not as easily seen as are unemployed masses in parades or demonstrations.[27]

Bracher also refers to his own earlier and more detailed study, *Die Auflösung der Weimarer Republik*. This work covers the themes discussed here in great detail. The condition of the lower middle class is reviewed, with extensive reference to supporting literature. As with the previous works, however, one looks in vain for a presentation of *evidence* establishing the fact of a lower-middle-class reaction.[28] Once again, it must be concluded that the argument, while plausible, has not yet been supported. Put somewhat differently, one may note that much information is available on the independent variable of the lower-middle-class hypothesis, information purporting to show the lower middle class in very difficult circumstances. It is easy to draw the obvious conclusion about the reaction to such stress. But that easy procedure assumes an answer rather than investigating and establishing it.[29]

Possibly the most influential presentation of the basic thesis, at least in English-speaking countries, is that of Seymour Martin Lipset in his work *Political Man*. His approach, an indirect one, involves two steps, the first of these being a stipulation or designation of the "social bases" of the various parties. A second step presents the overall voting results for Germany from 1928 to 1933 showing the virtual disappearance of the parties previously identified as those of the middle class. Given the corresponding rise of the National Socialists, the conclusion is both easy and convincing: it was the middle class that went over to the National Socialists. Because the argument has been so influential and so compelling, it is important to review the case in some detail.

In most democratic countries, Lipset states, one finds a "fairly logical" relationship between ideology and social base. Manual workers and the rural poor support the left parties. The "owners of large industry and farms, the managerial and free professional strata" support the "conservative right." And the middle classes, especially the "small businessmen, white-collar workers, and the anti-clerical sections of the professional classes," support the "democratic center." An extended discussion of the middle class follows together with consideration of its problems under advanced capitalism. This discussion is supported with quotations from various scholars, from David J. Saposs, André Siegfried, Max Weber, Karl Polanyi, Talcott Parsons, and, once again, from the previously reviewed analysis by Harold Lasswell. Then, making a link to his discussion of the conditions creating a "working-class authoritarianism," Lipset summarizes as follows:

The [working-class authoritarianism] thesis . . . suggested that a low level of sophistication and a high degree of insecurity predispose an individual toward an extremist view of politics. Lack of sophistication is largely a product of little education and isolation from varied experiences. On these grounds, the most authoritarian segments of the middle strata should be found among the small entrepreneurs who live in small communities or on farms. These people receive relatively little formal education as compared with those in other middle-class positions; and living in rural areas or small towns usually means isolation from heterogeneous values and groups. By the same token, one would expect more middle-class extremism among the self-employed, whether rural or urban, than among white-collar workers, executives, and professionals.

The major conclusion, based on reference to the aggregate voting patterns over the last years of the Weimar Republic reads as follows: "As the Nazis grew, the liberal bourgeois center parties, based on the less traditionalist elements of German society—primarily small business and white-collar workers—completely collapsed."[30]

A major parallel stress in this chapter is that the traditional right, with its different, its upper- and upper-middle-class base, proved relatively resistant to the National Socialist infection. This is indicated by the persistence of "its" party, the German National People's party (DNVP), in contrast to the various middle-class parties. In the second of the 1932 elections, the DNVP appeared with 60 percent of its 1928 strength as opposed to the two leading middle-class parties, which retained only one-fifth of their 1928 total. This conclusion, however, is only as good as the original stipulation. And for that reason one must ask a simple question: was the German National People's party the party of the upper class?

Were there a close correspondence between class and party, the question might allow an easy yes or no answer. But the relationship is by no means so simple. In a brief summary description it would be necessary to note that the DNVP was the party of landed, Protestant, and Prussian conservatism. This point is to be seen in terms of its history, the DNVP being a successor to the German Conservative party. And the German Conservative party, in turn, was a successor to the Prussian Conservative party which had dominated Prussian affairs prior to the 1871 unification.[31]

The Prussian and landed character of this party may be seen with unusual clarity in the voting patterns of the Weimar Republic. The nation at that point was divided into thirty-five election districts (*Wahlkreise*), these providing the basic units for most of the available analyses of election results. In all of the elections from April of 1924 through March of 1933 the DNVP had its greatest strength in Pomerania, frequently referred to as the heart of conservative Prussia. Nearly half of the votes in this district went to the DNVP in the two elections of 1924. In November of 1932 this party still received one-fifth of the area's votes in contrast to an 8.3 percent figure nationally. Taking the December 1924 election as a reference point, one may note, first of all, that the German Nationals received roughly a fifth of the votes (20.5 percent), that being their high point in the short life of the republic. The nine leading districts in descending order of strength were: Pomerania, 49.1; East Prussia, 39.2; Frankfurt an der Oder, 38.3; Schleswig-Holstein, 33.0; Potsdam I, 31.3; Merseburg, 29.7; Liegnitz, 28.9; Breslau, 28.8, and Potsdam II, 27.8. These districts were all Prussian, and, except for the Potsdam districts, all were predominantly rural.

The other side of the picture involves the southern and western areas of Germany. Some of these, to be sure, were also Prussian from the time of the Congress of Vienna, but they were largely Catholic, unlike the heavily Protestant east. The lowest DNVP percentages were found in the Palatinate, 4.4; Lower Bavaria, 5.5; Cologne-Aachen, 7.1; Hesse-Darmstadt, 7.7; Koblenz-Trier, 8.5; and Baden, 8.9. These are all southern and western districts.

The Elbe River cuts diagonally across Germany flowing from the Czechoslovakian border to the North Sea. To the east of the Elbe, in "traditional" Prussia, DNVP strength was well above average, especially in the rural areas. To the west, the party's strength was below average. The party supporters, in summary, are better described in terms of region, religion, and rural small-town settings than in terms of class. It is clear also that the party's base in the regions of its strength must have extended well "down" into the social structure. It must have included many very traditional small farmers as well as the members of the aristocracy. When those small farmers left the land and moved to the city, it seems likely that many of them would have carried their politics with them. As we shall see, much of the German National strength in the cities, in Berlin for example, appeared in working-class districts.

It seems likely that some of the support for the DNVP as of the December 1924 peak was a protest vote, a vote against the parties that had managed German affairs up to that point. Many of the people who had come to the party at that time were also destined to leave it just as quickly. The losses appear to have been greatest where the 1924 vote was a protest vote and, by contrast, to have been smallest in those areas where conservatism had roots extending back over decades. Pomerania and Schleswig-Holstein were both Prussian provinces, the former a part of the Prussian heartland and the latter a late (1866) and somewhat reluctant addition to the Prussian nation. The character of the protest vote in Schleswig-Holstein has been made very clear in Heberle's analysis.

In Pomerania as of 1930, support for the German Nationals had fallen to 50.5 percent of its 1924 peak. In Schleswig-Holstein by comparison, it had fallen to 18.5 percent of the former level.

One other point should be noted before leaving the statistical analysis. As of July 1932, the low point in the DNVP's fortunes, the party still retained its regional character: six of the nine highest districts of 1924 were still among the nine highest in 1932.[32]

The major conclusion is that the relative strength of the Conservatives as compared to the People's party and to the Democrats, may *not* be taken as prima facie evidence showing the political tendencies of the urban upper or upper middle classes. The prima facie lesson is one of the persistence of a regional, landed, and Protestant party.

If the upper and upper middle classes, particularly outside traditional Prussia, did not favor the DNVP, which party or parties did they support? Speaking generally, they supported the German People's party, the party of Stresemann. This party, the right liberals as they are sometimes called, was the successor to the prewar National Liberals. Lipset's use of Heberle's book on Schleswig-Holstein did not include Heberle's description of the parties and their social bases. On the first page Heberle explains much of what has been indicated in the previous paragraphs. The nobility and landowners of the north German plains, he tells us, formed the "backbone" of the prewar Conservative party, and wealthy farmers from "all over Protestant Germany were in the same camp." Some urban business interests, those in manufacturing, mining, and heavy industries, had formed a separate party, the Freikonservative party. The rest of the business classes, he reports, were linked to the Liberal party, that is, to the Nationalliberale party. It had become "a party of rich merchants, shipowners, bankers, and the well-to-do among the professional classes. Its main stronghold was in northwestern Germany, particularly in the cities."

At a later point, discussing postwar developments, Heberle again notes the *divided* loyalties of the top business class. As he puts it: "Those parts of the middle classes which were more conservative, more imperialistic, but which still adhered to the principles of liberalism formed the *Deutsche Volkspartei* . . . which was also supported by the large export industries and commercial and shipping interests, as well as by the banking interests. . . . On the extreme right, a new Conservative party was formed under the euphemistic name of *Deutschnationale Volkspartei*. It was not so much a people's party as a coalition of the agrarian and big business interests . . . and a rally of the counter-revolutionary forces."[33]

A study of Hamburg, the second largest city in the Reich, has shown that prior to the war, the upper class supported the National Liberal party and, in the best years of Weimar, favored the Deutsche Volkspartei. In this setting the German Nationals were more of a middle-class party which stood in opposition to the German People's party of the upper class.[34]

A regional study reports very little support for the Conservatives in Baden in the kaiser's time. What support they had there, in the Heidelberg area, was very much owing to the efforts of the Bund der Landwirte (Farmer's League). This dependence made the party very much an agrarian party taking votes in the rural areas from the dominant National Liberals. Something of the same constellation appears to have developed in the Weimar period. These authors quote a 1924 election report which refers to the Deutsche Volkspartei as "essentially a party of city voters." Baden, located in the southwest, was noted for its liberalism; almost the opposite of the east elbian Prussia, it never, as we have seen, gave much support to the DNVP in the Weimar period.[35]

The German National People's party underwent some important transformations in the course of its relatively short life. Like most parties of the period, it was rent by internal factional struggles. There was the division between the rural and the industrial segments of the party and just as important, a division between extreme and moderate rightists. In the last phase of its history, the party came under the leadership of Alfred Hugenberg, the overseer of a monumental press empire and former chairman of the Krupp directorate. Largely because of the link to Krupp, many have assumed that his takeover of the party represented a victory for its industrial wing. That, however, was definitely not the case. Hugenberg's intransigence had alienated his former associates in industrial circles, and they, accordingly, had shifted their loyalties and support elsewhere. In short, in the final phase of the party, it was even less of an urban upper-class party than before. Turner, basing his conclusion on documentary evidence, summarizes the relationship as follows:

> Contrary to the widespread belief that [Hugenberg] was one of the foremost spokesmen of big business throughout the republican period, most of the industrial backers of his party had opposed his election as its chairman in 1928, rejecting him as too inflexible, too provocative, and too highhanded for their tastes. In the summer of 1930 a large segment of his party's industrial wing took issue with his opposition to Heinrich Brüning's cabinet and seceded to join the new Conservative People's party. Even among those who did not take that step, there was a strong movement to replace Hugenberg with a more moderate man. As a result, Hugenberg, who had enjoyed wide support from big business during the first decade of the republic, was

forced, during its last years to rely increasingly upon the backing of agricultural interests.[36]

The German National People's party under Hugenberg's stewardship had an on-and-off relationship with the National Socialists. They formed an alliance in 1931, called the Harzburg Front. When Hitler was given the chancellorship in January 1933, the agreement involved a coalition government with the DNVP. As one might suspect, there was little difference between the two parties in terms of their issue orientations. The major difference, a point recognized quite early on, was in the means they were willing to use. The Conservative press frequently adopted an avuncular attitude toward the NSDAP, seeing the party as rather obstreperous but, nevertheless, a valuable addition to the nationalist ranks.[37]

The equation of the DNVP with the upper class and of the DVP and DDP with the middle classes, in short, amounts to an unacceptable oversimplification. The class bases of those parties were different from region to region. They were also different in the cities and the countryside. The disappearance of the DVP and DDP in some of these circumstances might well tell us more about upper- and middle-class propensities than about the lower middle classes. This is not, however, a question to be solved by pronouncements. It is one that is addressed with some evidence in the following chapters. The realities turn out to be somewhat more complex and somewhat more unexpected than even this discussion would suggest.

Another study discussed by Lipset is the much-cited master of art's thesis by Samuel Pratt. This work examines the voting patterns in 193 cities of Germany in the July 1932 election. Using census materials for data on the occupational composition of the cities, Pratt correlated those figures with the vote for the NSDAP and for the Communists. Some difficulties with this procedure require a more detailed consideration of method than has been necessary in any of the foregoing discussion.

The German census divided persons in the labor force into the following categories:

A. *Selbständige*   The self-employed or independents
B. *Mithelfende*   Helping family members (i.e. in an
   Familienangehörige   independent enterprise)
C. *Beamte*   Civil service employees
D. *Angestellte*   White-collar workers in private
                              employment
E. *Arbeiter*   Blue-collar workers

On first sight, the categories seem clear and uncomplicated. Closer inspection, however, reveals some problems. The first of these, a relatively minor and remediable concern, involves the independents. Mixed in the one category are both farm and nonfarm proprietors. Some farm proprietors, as we shall see in later chapters, are found even within metropolitan cities (a result of exuberant annexation programs). The numbers involved, however, are so small as to pose no major problem in the subsequent analysis. The "helping family member" category is closely related to the first. Most of these helpers were engaged in farm enterprises. The portion within any city's occupational structure was very small, and hence they also present no major problem for the subsequent analysis.

A more serious problem appears in connection with the three main white-collar categories. The highest level (*leitende*, or managerial) civil servants and white-collar workers were classified with the independents. The original purpose of that combination, apparently, was to create a distinctly advantaged category. This category could then be contrasted with the remaining civil service and white-collar categories, both of which would be lower on the scale of advantage. Category A, presumably, would be upper and upper middle class, and categories C and D would be lower middle class. That, in fact, is how Pratt has classified them.[38]

But that procedure runs up against the immediate objection that the independent category is a very mixed one. Under one heading, it links magnates such as Stinnes, Krupp, and Hugenberg with every small shop proprietor in Germany. In fact, the entire petty bourgeois population (other than the helping family members) would fall into category A. The mixture is such as to make this classification of the middle class into upper and lower segments a rather hazardous one.

To indicate more precisely what the transfer of managers means, it is useful to examine some statistics. The 1933 census reported that 1.5 percent of all white-collar workers (*Angestellte*) were managerial employees, as were 1.9 percent of the civil servants (*Beamte*). When added to the category of independents they formed 1.1 percent and 0.5 percent respectively of their new category. This means that a very tiny portion of the salaried were transferred. Both of the salaried categories would contain a population ranging from the lowest of the lower middle class to the top of the upper middle class, including those just below the top managers in the hierarchy of command. And the independent category has a similar but even more sweeping range, in this case extending from the lowliest shopkeeper all the way to the owners and managers of the largest enterprises in the society. Since most of these proprietors are likely to have been "small" rather than "large" and since moreover there may have been a fair-sized middle group contained in the category, this means that the easy equation of independents as upper and the salaried as lower is unjustified.[39]

For purposes of the Pratt thesis, this problem is a formidable one: the census categories do not allow the separation of the nonmanual population into distinct upper and lower subgroups. But the implications reach far beyond the conclusions of one M.A. thesis. The problems posed by the census procedures seriously hinder *any* use of the census data in providing definitive answers to the questions being discussed here. The only valid purpose these data might serve is for a comparison of the tendencies of the old (or independent) and the new (or salaried) middle classes.[40]

The correlations for both segments were positively related to National Socialism. Pratt's initial presentation of findings, however, indicates no sharp differences between the two. Another line of analysis, one that divides the cities by region rather than by size, does show some differences with his upper-middle group (i.e. the independents) having the stronger correlations with the National Socialist vote. There is a question as to how much weight one should give this result. Some of the initial differences are small, and with additional controls they become even smaller. On the basis of this result Pratt concludes that "of the two elements of the middle class, the upper seemed to be more thoroughly pro-Nazi and anti-Communist than the lower."[41]

Lipset, taking the same finding, argues that Pratt's lower middle class (categories C and D) is in fact the upper middle and that the results therefore actually confirm his claim about the lower middle class. Even if that were the case, these results would provide only weak support for his claim because the differences in the correlations are so small. If the occupational data provided an accurate measure of the lower middle and upper middle classes, these results would better warrant a stress on the *lack* of difference rather than the emphasis on the distinct tendencies of the one segment. Given the difficulties of the measures, however, an even more appropriate conclusion would be that these results provide no conclusive evidence one way or the other.[42]

Lipset's argument about the National Socialist orientations of the lower middle class is supported also by reference to two regional studies, those of Rudolph Heberle for Schleswig-Holstein and Günther Franz for Lower Saxony. Lipset presents quotations from both authors which refer to the class-party linkages in the cities. Heberle refers to the small farm proprietors as "very much the rural equivalent of the lower middle class or petty bourgeoisie (*Kleinbuergertum*) which formed the backbone of the NSDAP in the cities."[43] And Franz is quoted as follows: "It was the bourgeois middle-class in the cities, and the farm-owners on the land who supported the NSDAP."[44] Both of these studies, it should be noted, are based on rural and small-town conditions. Neither author presents any evidence on the voting patterns by class within the cities.

There is a problem with the categoric formulations. Heberle has demonstrated, Lipset tells us, "in a detailed study of voting patterns in Schleswig-Holstein that the conservatives lost the backing of the small property owners, both urban and rural . . . while they retained the backing of the upper-strata conservatives." That sounds very convincing. Closer examination, nevertheless, provides ground for doubt. What Heberle has done is to show the voting patterns in selected rural districts of the regions of the province. The area of small holdings, the Geest, does indeed show a dramatic shift away from virtually all the other parties (including the Socialists) to the National Socialists. The latter end up, in July of 1932, with 78.8 percent of this area's total. The Hill Zone, an area of large farms and estates, ends up with a lower level of support than the Geest, but this is still a rather formidable 57.1 percent. Most of the remaining voters were not Conservatives but Socialists (21.4 percent) and Communists (6.6 percent). The point about the Conservatives' retention of the upper strata is based upon their 10 percent figure in the Hill Zone as compared to 3.8 percent in the Geest.

There is no evidence moreover that the people of the Hill Zone who voted for the Conservatives were all, nearly all, or even largely members of the "upper strata." The 10 percent might have included persons who were Conservative by family tradition but who were not among the leading or upper strata of the local society. It might well have included older populations, particularly older women, with the younger upper strata voters largely within the National Socialist camp, that is, among the 57.1 percent. The unambiguous categoric formulation—Class X voting for Party X—is not justified by the data at hand.

It is worth noting the parallels between the areas rather than the contrasts. Both started the Weimar era with very limited support for the Conservatives. The Geest gave 3.9 percent of its vote to that party in the election of 1919. This rose to 49.9 percent in December of 1924 and fell again to 3.8 percent in July of 1932. In the Hill Zone the equivalent percentages are 15.8, 40.9, and 10.0.[45]

The sense of contrast as opposed to parallelism has its basis, to some extent at least, in a methodological peculiarity in the use of correlations. Still citing Heberle, adding his own emphasis in this case, Lipset reports that in 1932: "*The Conservatives were weakest where the Nazis were strongest and the Nazis were relatively weak where the Conservatives were strong.* The correlation in 18 predominantly rural election districts between percentages of votes obtained by the NSDAP and by the DNVP is negative (minus .89)." Ordinarily one would be inclined to pay a lot of attention to a correlation of such strength. As stated it would suggest that just about all of the variance in NSDAP voting is to be explained in terms of the relative strength of the Conservatives; it is a very powerful *contrasting* statement. The statement, however, is rather misleading. One must know how much variation occurred between the eighteen districts. If the range of variation were from, let us say, 4 to 10 percent for the Conservatives, one could have a very high correlation, but it would not mean very much because all of the districts were so much alike.

Another difficulty was suggested in the previous discussion of Heberle's findings; one is not dealing with a simple two-factor relationship. These "other factors" are discussed in some sentences Lipset omitted from the previous quotation. After the word "strong" in the emphasized sentence, Heberle's original contains the following: "On the other hand, the Social Democrats and Communists had their greatest rural following where the Conservatives were also strong. This would indicate that, where the actual social conditions in the rural areas came close to the Nazi ideal of 'community,' the NSDAP obtained a stronger support than in those rural areas where a sharp distinction existed between landlords and laborers. In fact, a correlation of the votes obtained in 1932 by the conservative DNVP and of the combined SPD and KPD respectively in eighteen predominantly rural *Kreise* . . . results in a strong positive coefficient (plus .91)."[46] The lower support for the National Socialists in areas of relative Conservative strength in short, results from the strength of the left parties as well as that of the Conservatives.[47]

Most of the previously discussed evidence involves voting returns. Another kind of evidence presented by Lipset involves party membership data. From the outset it must be noted that this kind of evidence is not directly relevant to the present concern which is the sources of mass *electoral* support. Voters and members constitute two different sets of the population, and while it is easy to assume similarity or overlap, it ought to be noted that complete or nearly complete exclusivity is also possible. One might remember in this connection the case of traditional conservative parties with their aristocratic and upper-class membership and their masses of farm, small-town, and deferential working-class voters. In *any* case the question of similarities or differences is an empirical one.

The study cited by Lipset, that of Hans Gerth, analyzes the occupational distribution of the National Socialist party membership as of January 1, 1933, before the party took power.[48] Lipset's presentation shows civil servants, white-collar workers, and independent businessmen to be overrepresented in the party (that is, as compared to their representation in the gainfully employed population). Also overrepresented is a category primarily composed of helpers in family-owned businesses. The greatest overrepresentation is found among the independents and this category of helpers in family-owned businesses. Manual workers and farmers, on the other hand, are underrepresented.[49]

One must note, however, that studies everywhere have shown that membership in organizations generally varies directly with class level. Some obvious exceptions to this rule appear with trade unions and left-wing political parties. Since all empirical studies agree that manual workers had a limited affection for the National Socialists, the membership pattern of this party would also conform to the general rule. The basic problem with the Lipset and Gerth arguments is that *all* of the middle-class parties probably had a membership pattern similar to the one reported here. The Democrats, the People's party, and the Conservatives, in other words, would probably have had memberships "largely drawn from the various urban middle-class strata." Without equivalent studies of the membership of those other parties, one cannot be sure that the National Socialist pattern was in any way distinctive. It might be the case, for example, that civil servants have less representation than independent businessmen in all parties because they are under some pressure to maintain a nonpartisan stance.

One additional difficulty with these data for the present purpose is that they provide no further specification of this middle class; in fact, the appropriate term in this case would be "nonmanual" since the categories include all groups from the upper class down to the lower middle class. But this study provides no differentiation along this dimension—the party members might be concentrated among the upper middles, the lower middles, or the middle middles.

It is to be noted also that the voting patterns yield a different picture from this portrait of the membership. Farmers were underrepresented among the members of the party. But when it came to voting, farmers in Protestant areas were very much overrepresented. This, too, indicates that membership is subject to a different, class-biased set of determinants, which might not provide an adequate index of sympathy. Put differently, a relatively costless mode of support, such as voting, yields a somewhat different picture from that provided by the membership figures.

Lipset's presentation of Gerth's data appears under the heading that reads in part: "The Ratio of the Percentage of Men in the Nazi Party." Gerth's original, however, has no breakdown by sex. He presents simply "party membership" and the "total gainfully employed." Gerth gives two columns of figures under the latter heading. In the first, agricultural wage workers are classified with manual workers, and in the second, they are classified with the "peasants." Lipset's calculations, based on the first of these options, yields a working-class ratio of 68 percent versus a peasant ratio or 60 percent. Calculating on the basis of the second option, one finds an urban working-class ratio of 82 percent as opposed to a peasant ratio of 44 percent. This would suggest a greater affinity of the urban working class for the National Socialists than many authors have implied.[50]

Returning again to the question of electoral support, Lipset, like most of the other writers reviewed thus far, has no explicit statement about upper-middle-class political tendencies, although presumably they would mirror the pattern of the upper class; that is, they would show consistent support for the Conservatives. Lipset's position with regard to the upper class is that

> with the exception of a few isolated individuals, German big business gave Nazism little financial support or other encouragement *until* it had risen to the status of a major party. The Nazis did begin to pick up financial backing in 1932, but in large part this backing was a result of many businesses' policy of giving money to all major parties except the Communists in order to be in their good graces. Some German industrialists probably hoped to tame the Nazis by giving them funds. On the whole, however, this group remained loyal to the conservative parties, and many gave no money to the Nazis until after the party won power.

The position, in short, is that upper-class support for the National Socialists was partial, exceptional, the work of "isolated individuals" rather than the class as a whole. It was, moreover, largely tactical as opposed to convinced or ideological. As for voting, the suggestion is that this class "remained loyal" to its former allegiances.[51]

Another Lipset argument involves the regional autonomist parties. Again one has a stipulation as to the character of their support, primarily lower middle class and small business. These parties also largely disappeared as the National Socialists grew; hence, once again the easy conclusion is that the middle classes made the shift. The decline of these parties is indisputable. The character of their original support, however, is open to question. Lipset's stipulation is based on some fragments from the programs of these parties involving appeals to the small proprietors. Whether or not the parties in fact were so closely aligned with this narrow occupational segment is a subject that remains to be researched. In any event, their impact on the overall outcome of the elections in Germany would be relatively small.

Lipset's analysis, in summary, is by far the best and most detailed of those available. But here too, one must observe, the case is far from convincing. The most compelling evidence involves the argument by stipulation, the argument that begins by *declaring* the class base of the parties suffering the greatest losses. This declaration, at the outset, as we have seen, is open to considerable question. There is, in fact, a wide agreement in the literature that one of these parties, the People's party (DVP) was *the* party of Germany's industrial bourgeoisie and that the DNVP, the so-called upper-class party was actually based in rural Prussia. The declines of these parties, in short, had meanings that were quite different from those Lipset has assigned to them. The actual bases of these parties are explored in some detail in later chapters.

Lipset's argument based on the Pratt thesis, initially at least, may also seem a convincing one. But that argument depends on another stipulation, one concerning the meaning of the key census categories. That stipulation also has a doubtful basis, one that seriously limits the usefulness of that approach to the problem. If, nevertheless, one were to accept the premises of his argument, the correlations of National Socialist voting with the two relevant categories, those presumed to represent the upper and lower middle classes, are so similar that the conclusion of a specifically lower-middle-class propensity again seems unwarranted. Once again, then, the lower-middle-class argument appears to be based on plausible speculation or on a general agreement among authorities rather than on specific and compelling evidence.

Before proceeding to review the arguments of still another author, it is useful at this point to make some further observations about some of the points touched on in the preceding pages. The first of these involves the character of the party membership. The Gerth analysis, as noted, is based on a listing as of January 1933. Since the publication of his findings in 1940, similar analyses based on membership lists from the twenties and early thirties have appeared. All of them are fragmentary and unfortunately do not allow a precise comparison with Gerth's figures. The best of these accounts, although methodologically a step backward from Gerth's accomplishment, does allow some impressionistic judgments. This analysis is based on an incomplete listing of the members who joined in the fall of 1923 just before the *Putsch* attempt. It is clear that the working-class presence in the party was lower in 1923 than in 1933, the respective percentages being 18.0 and 31.5.

It also appears that the National Socialists had greater success in recruiting persons from the higher ranks of the social structure, from the upper and middle classes, in 1932 than was the case earlier. Hitler certainly made systematic efforts in this direction. Some data point to a shift away from a relatively narrow membership base in the lower middle class with the party becoming more representative of the population as a whole.[52]

A second side comment involves the Heberle work. Not mentioned by the writers reviewed thus far is a bit of "harder" evidence on the lower-middle-class theme. Taking eighteen minor civil divisions (excluding cities of 10,000 or more) he presents correlations between the percentage employed in the category agriculture, forestry, and fishery and the percentage supporting the NSDAP. He then repeats the operation for that occupational category *plus* those employed as helping family members. The presence of persons helping in the family enterprise, he argues, provides a measure of economic marginality; it would indicate lower-middle-class status. Accordingly, one should find the latter correlations to be greater than the former. This does in fact prove to be the case.

There are two points to be made with respect to this operation. Like the basic Lipset presentation, it too depends on a stipulation, in this case that the presence of family members working in the firm is a sign of marginality. One might argue just the opposite, that the *marginal* farm enterprise is one that cannot support additional family members. The sons and daughters on those farms are the ones who have to leave and find employment elsewhere. The presence of helping family members might well be an indication of middling or possibly even better-off farm conditions.

The other point to be noted is the limited impact of this added factor. In the 1930 election the correlation increases from .37 to .43. In 1932 the equivalent figures are .76 and .79. This indicates only a very marginal increase in explanatory power, one that would not ordinarily be viewed as providing a powerful explanation even if the original stipulation were completely adequate. It should be noted, too, that this analysis is based on small-town and rural conditions. It tells nothing about the relationship of class and politics in the German cities.[53]

All of the writers reviewed up to this point might be classified as being in the liberal tradition. It is instructive to add the account of the Communist writer R. Palme Dutt. In attempting to come to a definition of fascism, Dutt notes that it is commonly presented as a middle-class (i.e. petty bourgeois) movement. In assessing this commonplace claim he states that there is "an obvious measure of truth in this in the sense that Fascism in its inception commonly originates from middle-class (petit-bourgeois) elements, directs a great deal of its appeal to the middle class, to small business and the professional classes against the organised working class and the trusts and big finance, draws a great part of its composition, and especially its leadership, from the middle class, and is soaked through with the ideology of the middle class, of the petit-bourgeoisie under conditions of crisis. So far, there is a common agreement as to the obvious facts."[54] The major difficulty, Dutt says, is in the frequent presentation of this middle-class movement as a third party, independent of capital and labor and working in opposition to both those groups. He proceeds to cite various liberal, social democratic, and misled leftist commentators who have subscribed to this position.[55]

His point is that the "open and avowed supporters of Fascism in every country are the representatives of big capital." Fascism, he says, "although in the early stages making a show of vague and patently disingenuous anti-capitalist propaganda to attract mass-support, is from the outset fostered, nourished, maintained and subsidised by the big bourgeoisie, by the big landlords, financiers and industrialists. . . . Fascism, in short, is a movement of mixed elements, dominantly petit-bourgeois, but also slum-proletarian and demoralised working class, financed and directed by finance-capital, by the big industrialists, landlords and financiers, to defeat the working-class revolution and smash the working-class organisations."[56]

Except for this key difference in the portrayal of the bourgeoisie, the similarity of the analysis to those reviewed previously is striking. The mass support is provided by the lower middle class. There is also some support provided by unemployed workers. But rather than it being a matter of segments of the bourgeoisie belatedly supplying financial support, this account puts the entire class in a facilitating and directive role from the beginnings of the enterprise.[57]

The similarities extend beyond substantive matters to the character of the analyses. No evidence is presented nor are references given to support the "obvious facts" of lower-middle-class involvement. The same holds with respect to the claims about the limited working-class involvement. There is no discussion or mention made of an upper middle class. Dutt does offer some supporting references to buttress his claim about the involvement of the German bourgeoisie, but his method, like that of the liberal and left authors, rests in most instances on mere assertion (for a detailed discussion of the role of the German bourgeoisie, see Chapter 13). The best case involves the argument by stipulation, but that too is based on a questionable assertion.

It is perhaps useful to quote one other author who has summarized the accumulated knowledge on the subject, this being Wolfgang Sauer, a leading authority on National Socialism. He writes that "it is now established beyond doubt that the lower middle classes, both rural and urban, were at least one of the major components of fascist movements."[58]

In the previous pages, some of the leading sources on the subject of National Socialism have been reviewed. One characteristic of all these sources is a heavy emphasis on the role of the lower middle class. But for all the emphasis and for all the certitude about lower-middle-class tendencies, the supporting evidence is either lacking entirely or, where present, of a rather tenuous character.

The argument of class is most appropriate for the urban context. Implicit in that notion is the belief that divisions in the society exist such that the various categories of people have separate and distinct life conditions. In the rural context, except for large-scale farm enterprises with their managers and farm workers, the situation of independent farmers does not allow an easy division into lower middle and upper middle classes. The difference between twenty-three and twenty-seven hectares does not allow the distinctions that are possible in the cities. But the more or less obvious task of sorting out city areas into those having working-class, lower-middle-class, upper-middle-class, and upper-class populations has been almost completely neglected. Without studies of this sort it is not possible to state that the lower-middle-class support of the National Socialists is a fact established "beyond doubt." Until that evidence is in, there is considerable reason for doubt. The presence of a substantial consensus on the part of commentators is by itself no more than an *agreement* as to the facts of the matter. Such an agreement could, certainly, be consonant with "the facts." Sensitive observers, relying on their casual observations, might independently arrive at a conclusion that could later be confirmed by more systematic investigation. On the other hand, it might be that an initial misimpression is being passed on and reinforced through processes of group dynamics rather than scholarly analysis.[59]

A second feature of the analyses reviewed here is their almost unanimous failure to give any consideration to the upper middle class. Discussion of a lower middle class would normally imply an upper-middle-class counterpart. And a complete accounting of sentiment in the society would have something to say about all its major classes or segments. The omission of the upper middle class from the analysis is all the more surprising since this class is usually portrayed as having power and importance far out of proportion to its numerical strength. The omission implies that this class did not play an important role in the coming of the National Socialists. Kornhauser has expressed this position directly, indicating that the upper middle class continued to vote for its traditional party, the Conservatives. As indicated, there is some reason for doubting this claim.

A third difficulty concerns the role of the upper classes. In the liberal accounts they are said to be traditional conservatives throughout the period, only a small segment of the rich and the big business interests going over to support Hitler. In the left accounts the upper classes are portrayed as early and convinced supporters of Hitler and his party. Evidence on the voting behavior in upper-class districts is missing from both accounts. The possibility was mentioned earlier that big business frequently offered financial support to several parties. Such behavior would obscure their preferences. Analysis of the voting records, however, ought to clarify that question.

A fourth point to be made about the received analyses involves the treatment of the working class. One account says the workers were not at all moved to support the National Socialists. Others claim that the unemployed workers provided them with support. Here again no supporting evidence is presented. The aggregate voting data should allow some clarification of this question.

A related difficulty with the received literature is the failure to make any attempt at definition. The term "lower middle" is in constant use; definition of the term, however, is virtually absent. It is difficult to see how anything could be lost by the addition of some precision to what has been a very loose and diffuse discussion.

The basic point, to summarize these summary conclusions, is that the claims made with such apodictic certainty about the classes of German society, about their political orientations and behavior, appear to be much less sound, to have much less support, than the formulations and the broad consensus would suggest. The major task of this work is to bring evidence to bear on these questions.

A rule-of-thumb definition may be of use at this point. When speaking of the lower middle class, the literature reviewed here refers to the less well paid segments of the middle-class or white-collar population. It is as if one had taken the three census categories discussed above, the independents (which includes artisans), the civil servants, and the salaried white-collar employees, and had separated them into well off (or better off) and not very well off segments, the last being the lower middle class.[60] Since there is no precise line in this case, any such division is rather arbitrary, a fact that no doubt explains the lack of definition in the literature. It should be noted that the usage throughout this work follows this tendency in the received tradition. Some effort is made in the next chapter to specify the boundaries of this class, but, as will be seen, there are limits to what can be done.

Some recent accounts have shifted away from this traditional usage by including skilled workers within the lower middle class. But that is a definitional practice reflecting thought and experience of the fifties and sixties. It was not the position taken in the earlier discussions of National Socialism nor is it typical of most contemporary analyses. In the 1930s skilled workers were counted as members of the working class; they were workers (*Arbeiter*). From time to time one found writers who described them as "bourgeoisified" (*verbürgerlicht*) but even then, it will be noted, the term is used as an adjective modifying the word "worker" (or the expression "working class"). Most writers stressed the gulf or chasm separating workers and middle class rather than, as in this latter-day reformulation, their similarities.[61]

The next chapter provides an initial description of the National Socialist support as it appears in previously available studies. The subsequent chapters then present new evidence on the tendencies of the various classes in the late Weimar period. This evidence is referred to as "new" although, to be sure, it dates from 1930 and 1932 or thereabouts. It is new in the sense that this is the first time in some decades that this evidence has appeared outside the walls of municipal archives.

CHAPTER THREE

A Reconsideration of Previous Evidence

In Chapter 2, the dominant claims about the bases of National Socialist support were subjected to review. The most important of the received claims, those focusing on the class bases of that party's support, were shown to be without serious empirical foundation. That review did not reject those claims; it merely indicated that they were unproven.

The present chapter reviews previous *research* to show what it has indicated about the bases of National Socialist support. These studies, as will be seen, yield a markedly different picture of the republic's demise. The previous chapter presents the negative side of the argument; it shows the inadequacies of the traditional line of argument and indicates what is *not* contained there—convincing supporting evidence. The present chapter carries the argument forward and provides a first positive formulation of the alternative case. The evidence to be presented in this chapter, however, merely sets the stage for the basic contribution of this work; it provides an alternative framework, indicates the gaps where information is needed to support that framework, and points out what kind of evidence is needed to fill those gaps. The subsequent chapters provide some of that evidence.

There are perhaps some three dozen detailed empirical studies of the late Weimar elections. These studies are in substantial agreement with respect to some of the major characteristics of the National Socialist voting support. Two of these characteristics are so striking that it is important to consider them at length. The first of these involves size of place: *the vote for the National Socialists varied inversely with the size of the community.*[1]

The definitive presentation of data for the entire nation divided into community-size categories has yet to appear. One may obtain an adequate picture, however, by piecing together evidence from Pratt's study and from the official statistics. The accompanying table shows the results for the key election, that of July 31, 1932.

It should be noted, first of all, that over half of the valid votes were cast in communities of less than 25,000.[2] Despite the stress on urban and industrial society (with its concomitant impersonality, with its alienation and anomie), more voters lived in the Diedesfelds and Schifferstadts of Germany than in the Düsseldorfs and Stuttgarts. Although

City Size (in thousands)	Valid Vote (in thousands)	Percent NSDAP
Over 100	11,633	32.3
50-100	1,989	35.4
25-50	1,863	38.4
Less than 25	21,397	41.3
Germany	36,882	37.3

industrialization touched these smaller communities in many ways, it seems unlikely that impersonality and anomie were features of those settings. If anything, the opposite characteristics were more likely to have prevailed there.

The NSDAP support fell from 41.3 percent in the smallest communities to 32.3 in the largest. This difference of only nine percentage points may not appear to be very substantial. This picture, however, hides much of the actual variation because of the grouping in broad categories. The very largest cities gave the National Socialists less support than the others in the category. Only six of the fifteen largest cities were above the overall 32.3 percent figure for the fifty-two cities in that class.[3] At the other end of the community-size continuum, we have evidence showing enormous NSDAP percentages in small towns and villages. In many of these, the figures reached into the eighties, and in some of the very smallest villages, there were instances of 100 percent National Socialist voting.

The second key feature of the National Socialist electorate cuts across and, especially in the smaller towns and villages, obscures the community-size pattern: *the vote for the National Socialists was very disproportionately Protestant.*

Pratt, summarizing his urban data, states that "in all sizes of city, as the proportions of Catholics in the population increased the proportion of votes for the National Socialists decreased. These correlations are as strong as any that have been found in the whole study."[4] Another study, this one focused on smaller communities, yielded the following conclusion:

The larger the proportion of people who belonged to the Catholic faith in the *Kreise* as of 1933, the smaller the Nazi vote in 1924 and 1932. For the rural *Kreise* of the Provinces of Hannover and Bavaria, the correlation coefficients which describe the relationship between the percentage of Nazi votes cast in July, 1932, and the percentage of Catholics in the population are minus .89 and minus .90, respectively. For all communities of the Reich, the corresponding coefficient based on larger election districts is minus .72. These coefficients . . . indicate that the Catholic segment in Germany resisted the rise of Nazism more than any other group.[5]

As will be seen, these studies do misrepresent things as far as the cities are concerned. The basic tendency, however, seems to be unquestionable.[6]

The NSDAP had its beginnings in Munich, the capital city of Catholic Bavaria. Given that "fact," it seems plausible to link Catholicism and National Socialism. But this is misleading. After the assassination of Rathenau in 1922, Prussia and most of the other states of Germany outlawed organizations of the extreme right and left. Bavaria, then under rather unusual government, one with autonomist, rightist nationalist tendencies, refused to follow this policy. Thus rightist movements were free to continue their operations there. Munich had always been a receiving station for drifters, adventurers, and other assorted bohemian types.[7]

The NSDAP did, for the reasons just indicated, show early strength in Bavaria. But then, in the period of the party's sweeping electoral victories, that southern "free state" was surpassed by all of the heavily Protestant election districts of Germany. In July 1932, 20.4 percent of the vote in Lower Bavaria went to Hitler's party. In the rural and Protestant districts of northern Germany, in East Prussia, Frankfurt and der Oder, and Pomerania, for example, the respective percentages were 47.1, 48.1, and 48.0.[8] The Protestant tendency also shows up clearly within Catholic Bavaria. One part of this state, Franconia, to the north and west of Nuremberg, is heavily Protestant. There, one found a pattern that was strikingly at variance with that of Lower Bavaria. The Franconia percentage was 39.9. The percentages in the smaller communities there were much higher, for example: Uffenheim, 81.0; Rothenburg, 83.0; Neustadt (Aisch), 79.2; Ansbach, 76.3; Dinkelsbühl, 71.2; and Gunzenhausen, 72.5.[9]

The highest percentage of all the thirty-five election districts came in Schleswig-Holstein, 51.0 percent. This area was studied by Rudolf Heberle in one of the best and most detailed of all the accounts of National Socialist electoral support. Dividing the area into urban and rural communities (the latter referring to those with less than 2,000 inhabitants), he found for the July 1932 election the results shown in the accompanying table. Again one finds an overwhelming NSDAP percentage associated with the rural communities of a Protestant region. That 63.8 percent is of course an average. In one area, in the Geest region of Norderdithmarschen for example, the figure in July 1932 was 87.3 percent. In some very small communities Heberle found 100 percent support for the National Socialists.[10]

	Urban	Rural
NSDAP	44.8%	63.8%
SPD	29.9	18.6
KPD	13.1	5.8
DNVP	5.2	9.2
Other	7.0	5.8

Presentation of NSDAP voting by size of community obviously averages very diverse Protestant and Catholic patterns. To the best of my knowledge, no studies have systematically examined the separate patterns for all of Germany. The best available data are for the smaller communities in Hesse (Darmstadt) for the key 1932 election.[11] The researcher in this case sorted out 118 Hessian communities with a Catholic population of 75 percent or more. These were then divided by size, and the vote in each of the resulting categories was contrasted with the vote in the other communities, those with populations that were less than 75 percent Catholic.

The resulting pattern may be summarized rather simply: in the heavily Catholic communities, NSDAP voting was very low and increased with size of place (Table 3.1). In the other communities, the NSDAP vote was relatively high and varied inversely with size of place. Correspondingly, the vote for the Zentrum, of course, was very high in the Catholic communities. It was by no means a constant, however, but varied inversely with size of place. In the smallest Catholic communities more than two-thirds of the voters favored the Zentrum.

Since many accounts have argued the susceptibility of "the farmers" to NSDAP appeals, it is important to stress the awesome gap between

TABLE 3.1. NATIONAL SOCIALIST AND ZENTRUM SUPPORT IN HESSIAN COMMUNITIES, JULY 1932

(in percent)

Size of Community	Catholic Communities[a]		All Other Communities	
	National Socialists	Zentrum	National Socialists	Zentrum
Under 500	12.3[b]	68.2	73.9	3.3
500–999	15.1	63.6	65.1	4.9
1,000–1,999	13.9	56.0	50.8	6.8
2,000–4,999	19.0	41.2	44.4	7.1
5,000–19,999	21.3	44.7	36.9	10.4

SOURCE: Hessischer Landesstatistisches Amt, *Die Ergebnisse der Landtagswahl am 19. Juni 1932 und der Reichstagswahl am 31. Juli 1932 im Volksstaat Hessen*, Darmstadt: Hessischer Staatsverlag, 1932

[a] Those with a population that was 75 percent or more Catholic.

[b] A complete listing of the percentages when read across the rows adds to 100. In this case, the 12.3% plus the 68.2% plus 19.5% for all other parties (omitted from the table) add to 100.0%.

the two categories of farm communities; in the smallest Catholic communities 12.3 percent voted for the National Socialists while elsewhere the figure was 73.9 percent. In short, the formulations that speak of *the* farmers or *the* peasants are grossly inaccurate.[12]

The results in Table 3.1, as noted, cover only the smaller communities of one small state. All of the variation shown here would be contained within the smallest size category of the presentation based on Pratt's data, a category that, as noted, contained more than half of the voters in the July 1932 election. There is reason to believe, however, that the basic findings reported for Hesse would also hold for the nation as a whole.[13] The higher National Socialist voting in the larger Catholic communities is indicated by the vote in Cologne (75.3 percent Catholic and 24.5 percent NSDAP) and in Munich (81.1 percent and 28.9 percent respectively). The NSDAP vote in the eleven cities of Germany with 100,000 or more persons and 75 percent or more Catholic populations amounted to 26.1 percent, as compared to Pratt's overall figure of 32.3 percent for the large cities.

The basic lesson, then, is one of a very sharp division in the countryside, with Catholic areas voting for the Zentrum and Protestant areas voting National Socialist. Catholic and Protestant cities, on the other hand, are not as sharply differentiated in their support for the National Socialists. Although the Zentrum was also important in Catholic cities, there it took only a small part, in most cases a minority, of the Catholic vote. There is, in short, clear evidence of defection from the Zentrum ranks in the larger cities. As we shall see, much of that loss involved workers who had turned to the parties of the left. But some part of that loss ultimately benefited the National Socialists. The overall inverse relationship between National Socialist support and size of community hides this differing Catholic pattern. The size of the Protestant majority overwhelms the Catholic voting pattern. That average of the two patterns, moreover, accounts for the initial rather modest relationship with city size.

One conclusion comes through very clearly at this point: a large part of the National Socialists' electoral support came from the Protestant countryside. The discussion to this point allows a rejection or, at minimum, a discounting of some kinds of arguments. The National Socialist infection, for example, may not be explained in terms of some characteristics of "the Germans." In the more or less free elections up to and including those of 1932, five Germans out of eight steadfastly resisted the blandishments of Hitler and his party. A more specific argument is required since some segments of the German population proved susceptible while others were unmoved.

The argument in terms of a unique pernicious culture also appears doubtful, unless one wishes to argue that Protestants were that much more influenced by German culture than were Catholics or that Protestants in the countryside were more influenced than those in the cities. Similarly, the argument in terms of the disintegration of society, the focus on impersonality and anomie, appears a doubtful one. One could argue with at least some plausibility that impersonality or anomie was more frequent in Protestant communities. The eminent French sociologist Emile Durkheim in 1899 offered some evidence consonant with that thesis. But, then, still another difficulty arises; one would have to argue a greater degree of impersonality and anomie among *rural* Protestants than among those in the cities. The evidence reviewed to this point suggests the need for a different kind of argument, one that would focus on the factors present (or not effectively countered) in those locations where the National Socialists gained their greatest mass support, that is, in the Protestant countryside.[14]

There is another, a peripheral lesson, to be learned from Lind's study of Hesse. He notes that Hessian workers were disproportionately located in the middle-sized communities, which in this case means those between 1,000 and 20,000 persons. The highest vote for the Communist party in that state, accordingly, did not appear in the cities but rather came in communities having from 5,000 to 20,000 inhabitants. The Social Democrats were strong in all classes of community with 1,000 or more inhabitants. That distribution of left votes was not typical of Germany, however; it is mentioned merely to give some idea of the complexities that existed. One other point is worthy of some note: the Communist percentage in Hesse *declined* between 1930 and 1932. The Social Democratic percentage also declined, despite the economic crisis and widespread unemployment.[15]

Many of the larger German cities were commercial, financial, and administrative centers with relatively large white-collar populations. More often than in North America, manufacturing establishments were located on the outskirts of such cities. And the working-class populations also lived on the outskirts, in the now transformed farm communities. Or they commuted from outlying communities that contained both industrial workers and farmers. Many industrial workers engaged in part-time or seasonal farm work, and many farmers found industrial work after the harvest. It is only at the far removes, in the Geest region of Schleswig-Holstein or in parts of Lower Bavaria, that one found the pure farming community. And it was there too that one found the most distinctive politics, the near uniformity of political direction.

Many studies provide only truncated accounts of the election results; they dwell on the massive support for the National Socialists and fail to report the remainder of the vote. In this connection Heberle's account yields another fact of considerable importance: the largest segment of those *not* voting for the NSDAP were voting for the left, for the Social Democrats or the Communists. In that rural Protestant context, in other words, the party struggle had been greatly simplified, to the point where most voters chose either Hitler's party or the left.[16]

It is useful at this point to consider a third factor, the class question, the central concern of this work. In most analyses, the farmers, apart from those with sizable holdings, are classified as petty bourgeois, as lower middle class. Nearly the entire population of many farm communities would be petty bourgeois since no significant internal differentiation would have existed in the economic functions the inhabitants performed. Within any such community, however, one would ordinarily have found differentiations based on local prestige. To the extent that such prestige had an economic basis, it would probably depend on differences in the size or quality of landholdings (some farmers having twelve hectares, some having twenty, or some having twelve hectares of good land while others had twenty of not-so-good land). Those differences in local prestige would undoubtedly affect patterns of association in the local community. For the present purpose, however, such divisions would have no importance whatsoever since, given the homogeneity of the voting in those communities, it is clear that the difference in prestige did not lead to differences in party choices. It is not as if the "best people" of those communities had voted for one party and the rest of the citizenry had chosen another.

An immediate problem is posed for the conventional lines of class analysis by the voting in rural Germany. If one assumes that the Catholic countryside, Lower Bavaria and the Eifel, to cite two examples, was comparable to the Marsch and Geest regions of Schleswig-Holstein and that the farmers in both areas were either all or nearly all lower middle class, then it is clear that class explains next to nothing in this context. This Catholic petty bourgeoisie voted one way, for the Zentrum, while the Protestant petty bourgeoisie voted another, for the National Socialists. Since they had a common class position and faced the same catastrophe, one must account for the nearly diametrically opposite responses of the two lower-middle-class segments.

In the more differentiated communities, those with small farms mixed in among some larger ones and with both farm workers and industrial workers present, a straightforward class analysis might be more justified. Only guesses are possible in such cases, but it does seem likely that the Social Democratic and the Communist votes in such communities came from the industrial workers and the farm laborers. It is doubtful that either small or large farmers would have been supporting those parties. If that guess is correct then the heavy emphasis placed on *marginal* middle-class support for Hitler's party would be seriously misleading. Where the National Socialist strength was so overwhelming, it seems likely that *both* the impoverished small farmers and the better-off middle and large farmers were supporting that party.[17]

The only other alternative would be to assign all of the DNVP (Conservative) vote to the local upper or upper middle classes and to argue that the proportion of lower to upper was sharply imbalanced—for example, that the National Socialist 67.2 percent in the Schleswig-Holstein Marsch districts came from the small farmers and the Conservative 6.1 percent came from the large farmers. It would be a mistake, without further information, to make such an assignment of the vote. While the tendency is likely to have been in that direction, nowhere did the support for the parties show such a precise alignment with class. Conservative support extended into the ranks of small farmers and, some large farmers supported the National Socialists, in such cases setting the direction for the entire community.[18]

What about the political correlates of class in the German cities? There, in the most appropriate context for a class analysis, one might find a less ambiguous result.

One may conceive of the class structure of the nonfarm population as consisting of the manual rank (*Arbeiter*), a lower middle class (small businessmen, minor clerical employees, and low-level civil servants), and upper middle class (middle- and high-level managers, professionals), and an upper class (owners of the means of production).[19] The basic question being asked is: how do these segments vote?

Had the cities of Weimar Germany been neatly divided into upper-, upper-middle-, lower-middle-, and working-class communities, each with separate and distinct territories, ascertaining the respective political tendencies would be easy. In fact, there would be no excuse for not having done so long ago. One would simply have to obtain data on the class character of the various areas of Berlin, Hamburg, Cologne, Leipzig, Munich, and so forth and assemble the voting statistics for each of them. If the tendency were as clear as has been alleged, there should be no problem in showing a pronounced edge of National Socialist support in the lower-middle-class communities.

Before proceeding further with the immediate line of exposition, it is useful to ask what one might reasonably expect if the purely qualitative statements of the previous chapter were "translated" into numbers and percentages. The most extreme case, an obviously unreal one, would show no National Socialist votes in the "responsible" upper and upper middle classes, no such votes in the "Socialist" working classes, and 100 percent of the lower-middle-class votes going to Hitler's party. Another unlikely extreme would be a pattern of no difference. In the July 1932 election, for example, all four classes in a city would have given 33.3 percent to the NSDAP. In between those extreme positions would be the complete range of intervening options—10 percent figures versus a lower middle class 90 percent, or twenties against eighties. Or, one could find 25 to 30 percent support from the other classes in contrast to 35 to 40 percent from the lower middle class.

If the last were the case, if one were speaking of a ten-percentage-point difference, class would have very little impact on the result, or, to put it in technical language, class would explain only a small part of the variance. If such were the case, an adequate account would also have to provide some explanation for the upper- and upper-middle-class National Socialist vote and some further explanation for the working-class support. Most important, the nearly exclusive focus on the lower middle class would not be justified.

One may easily conclude, judging from the quotations offered in Chapter 2, that these commentators are claiming class to be much more powerful than this last hypothetical example would suggest. The sheer volume of the emphasis and the absence of attention to other considerations are evidence of the weight assigned to this explanation. A reasonable possibility then, again were one to give numbers, might have the upper middle class providing 20 or 25 percent support for the National Socialists versus 60 or 70 percent in the lower middle class.

Before leaving this discussion, it is worthwhile noting another possibility. All the accounts reviewed thus far ask the extent of support for the NSDAP within a given class. One might also legitimately ask the separate but related question: what part of the NSDAP support came from a given class? A class might have given overwhelming support for a party; 90 percent of those in the upper class, for example, might have supported the Conservatives. At the same time, however, because that class formed such a small part, say 1 percent, of the total population, the Conservatives might gain only 5 percent of their total vote from that rank.

The first concern involves a causal question; some characteristics of (or some features in the situation of) a category of persons cause (or give rise to) a given result. For that purpose we wish to compare persons having the characteristics in question with those who do not. The second concern is with the *composition* of a category. In this case we are asking what percentage of the NSDAP support came from the upper, upper middle, lower middle, and working classes.[20]

The points being made here may become clearer if one considers some hypothetical percentages. The accompanying table provides some illustrative figures for NSDAP support. Following the implicit line of argument of the authors reviewed in the previous chapter, the affinity of

Class	Support for NSDAP (in %)	Composition (Percentage of Nonfarm Labor Force)
Upper	15	1
Upper middle	25	14
Lower middle	60	25
Working	25	60
		100

the lower middle class for the National Socialists has been indicated by showing a much larger amount of support coming from this class than from the other classes. The column to the right provides an estimate of the relative size of these groups within the nonfarm population. A simple arithmetic calculation reveals that the *absolute* contribution of the working class to the total NSDAP vote is exactly equal to that of the lower middle class. (If one assumes a vote of 1,000,000, then 60 percent of the lower-middle-class 250,000 would be 150,000, and 25 percent of the working class 600,000 would also be 150,000.) Thus, although the lower middle class shows the greater affinity, the working-class segment is of equal importance in determining the result. Some attention is paid to both questions in the following chapters. But since the major problem addressed in the literature has been the causal question, that is where the emphasis will be placed.

What can one say about the voting tendencies of the lower middle class? Some answers are contained in the published literature. The explosive growth of the Social Democratic party, beginning in the 1890s, stimulated some very instructive research in the area. In 1905, one researcher had already discovered the "very heterogeneous nature" of the Social Democratic electorate. In the election of June 16, 1903, the party had gained 66.8 percent of all valid votes in Berlin. In Hamburg the figure was 62.2 percent, and in neighboring Altona the party received 70.1 percent of the total. All of these figures far exceeded the percentages of industrial workers in the populations of those cities. The party, in short, must have been gaining votes from other classes, specifically from the ranks of the middle class. Since the working class would not have given a unanimous vote for the SPD, those results indicate that even larger portions of the party's vote came from the middle class than the initial comparison of occupational structure and vote would suggest.

This study, by an R. Blank, covered the elections of 1893 and 1897 as well as that of 1903. In a summary by Hans Speier it was reported that 25 and 26 percent of the total SPD vote in the earlier elections came from the nonmanual population.[21] Giving more detail and projecting the findings into the later Weimar period, Speier notes that "according to Blank's calculations, the middle classes amounted to one third of the social democratic vote in the large cities, and to no less than one half in some of them. Since in the Weimar Republic the SPD has become socially acceptable and politically available for coalition governments, it seems safe to assume that the non-proletarian percentage of the total number of votes cast for both social democrats and communists is considerably higher than it was before [World War I]."[22] Blank does speculate as to which segments of the middle class had come to support the SPD. Part of his answer is foreshadowed in the previous discussion; that is, it was the middle class, specifically the Protestant middle class, of the larger cities. He adds a further specification: "artisans, small businessmen, low ranking civil servants, sales clerks, and in general small independent tradesmen of the most diverse kinds, here and there also members of the higher social classes."[23] His answer, it will be noted, focuses on the lower middle class. His analysis, it will also be noted, is concerned with a compositional question—how much of the party's vote came from the nonmanual (or white-collar) ranks? The alternative question, what part of the middle class (or of the lower middle class) supported the SPD, is not directly answered. In the larger and heavily Protestant cities, the percentage must have been considerable.

Blank offers very little in the way of support for this claim of lower-middle-class SPD support; he states merely that "it is known that" and adds a footnote reference to August Bebel who once declared, in a Reichstag address, that now "all artisans" were Social Democrats. Although direct evidence is lacking, one many still make some inferences. The options are very simple: first, that vote came predominantly from the lower middle class (as opposed to the upper middle or upper class), or, second, there was no difference in the Social Democratic support received from the various nonmanual categories, or third, there was greater SPD support in the upper middle or upper class, or both. One might wish to argue the last two options; it does seem more likely, however, that the upper middle and upper classes supported the Conservatives, the National Liberals (the right liberal predecessor of the German People's party), or the Zentrum. And that would leave the first option as the most plausible.

Blank's study does not provide the precise datum required for our purposes—the portion of the lower middle class voting for the SPD. And it tells us nothing about the pattern later in the century, specifically in the late Weimar period. Fortunately, a similar analysis is available that does both, this being the work of Hans Neisser. His estimate is based on the 1930 election, the one in which the NSDAP scored its first major victory. The findings of this analysis have been summarized in several sources. Sigmund Neumann, for example, reports the following in a footnote reference: "Interestingly enough, even in the empire around one-fourth of the SPD electorate was recruited from nonproletarian sources. Neisser assumed in 1930 (that crucial year of the Nazi rise) a 40 per cent middle-class vote for the SPD, representing under a proportional system an even more direct declaration of sympathy on the part of the voters than in the prewar majority system."[24] This footnote appears on the very same page as Neumann's discussion of the National Socialist propensities of the white-collar workers (discussed in Chapter 2). Although, to be sure, the note appears in a different context, in a discussion of the "bourgeoisification" of the Social Democrats, Neumann shows no recognition of the implication of Neisser's estimates for his claims about the white-collar class as the "frustrated class par excellence."

A second footnote reference to Neisser's work appears in Lipset's *Political Man*. He presents even more detail: "An analysis of the source of the vote for the Social Democratic party in 1930 estimated that 40 percent of the SPD voters were not manual workers, that the party was backed in that year by 25 per cent of the white-collar workers, 33 per cent of the lower civil servants, and 25 per cent of the self-employed in artisan shops and retail business." In this case too, no consideration is given to the implication of those estimates for the claim of lower-middle-class susceptibilities. Lipset even seeks to negate the impact of these estimates by adding the following sentence: "But the core of the SPD support was employed, skilled manual workers, while the core of the Nazi strength was small owners, both urban and rural."[25]

In this case, it will be noted, the figures have been given both ways, on the one hand, as a percentage of the SPD who were nonmanual workers, and on the other, as a percentage of the various middle-class segments who supported the SPD. Speier, incidentally, notes that Neisser's analysis understates the middle-class involvement with the left by assuming that *all* the Communist vote came from industrial workers. That was not likely to have been the case.

One must also note that a considerble part of the lower middle class would have voted for the Center party. In general, the Catholic percentage in Germany decreased as one ascended the class hierarchy. At the same time the degree of allegiance to or involvement with the church increased with class level.

This means that one must also add an estimate for the Zentrum voters to the figures Lipset has cited. Beginning with the figure for the lower civil servants, for example, one might have something like the following: support for the SPD (Neisser estimate) comes to 33 percent; support for the KPD (unbased estimate) to 5 percent; support for the Zentrum (unbased estimate) to 20 percent; and support for all other parties to 42 percent.[26] Among the supporters of those other parties one would find some DNVP voters, some supporters of the DVP and DDP (right and left liberals), and some supporters of various minor parties. Not all of that remaining 42 percent, in other words, can be counted as National Socialist.

Still another consideration is deserving of attention. Neisser's estimates do not take community size into account. The support for left parties increased with size of city. For that reason, the 33 percent and 5 percent estimates for the Social Democrats and Communists should be taken as minimum estimates. The higher figures found in the larger cities would further reduce that residual 42 percent, the only segment available to the National Socialists.[27]

There is still another step one ought to consider. The Neisser estimates are based on the September 1930 election. But what about the July 1932 election, when the NSDAP more than doubled its 1930 vote? The most important observation one may make in this connection is that the vote for the left was relatively stable. The KPD increased slightly in July 1932 while the SPD lost three percentage points of its 1930 standing, most of that loss occurring in the countryside.[28] The estimates given here, then, would still be more or less valid—as minimum figures for the voting of the urban lower middle class. The same may be said about the Zentrum, its strength increasing slightly over September of 1930.

In the cities at least, support for the three parties focused on here was *not* eroded by the rise of National Socialism. The only change that could have occurred in that context was for the NSDAP to have increased its share of the estimated remainder available for the other parties. In the cities that remainder must have been well below the 42 percent overall figure given here. The traditional center and right parties did suffer serious losses to the National Socialists; that is unquestionable. But the Neisser argument, together with the extensions noted here, makes it unlikely that the urban lower middle class gave especially pronounced support to the NSDAP. It seems unlikely that the National Socialists gained a majority of the urban lower-middle-class votes.

The basic conclusion, if all these assumptions are accurate, is that only a minority, possibly as low as three out of ten, of the urban lower-middle-class civil servants voted for the National Socialists. The proportion would have been somewhat higher among the salaried workers in private employment and among the shopkeepers, but still it is doubtful (again based on these assumptions) that the NSDAP would have gained a majority of these other segments of the urban lower middle class.

There is a clear and obvious need for some actual figures to take the place of the estimates offered here. For the moment, however, one must remain with speculation and hypotheses. If only a minority of the urban lower middle class voted for the NSDAP, was that minority much larger than the equivalent segments of the working class or the upper middle class? If it was greater, what was the order of magnitude? If it was only a matter of a few percentage points, one evident possibility, then clearly the entire emphasis on lower-middle-class susceptibilities would be misplaced.

Even without precise measurement the emphasis seems misplaced. One lower-middle-class segment (Protestant farmers) voted overwhelmingly for the NSDAP. Another segment (Catholic farmers) voted overwhelmingly against them (for the Zentrum). And a third (the urban categories) gave the NSDAP some kind of minority support (the remainder going to the left and the Zentrum). The question arises as to the value of a general argument about the reactions of *the* lower middle class when three major kinds of response are discernible, only one of which conforms to the requirements of the argument. Even in the conforming case, the focus is doubtful since in the Protestant countryside all groups (except sometimes the workers) were giving the NSDAP very heavy support. The marginal middle class in that setting was not particularly distinctive in its support for the National Socialists.

The argument offered here is largely hypothetical in character. It depends on Neisser's estimates and on some inferences both about the later 1932 election and about the tendencies of various groups in those later elections. One may enhance the plausibility of the argument by making a more detailed analysis of the middle class. For this purpose it is necessary to review another range of available evidence.

As was noted in the previous chapter, Weimar Germany had three white-collar trade union federations. One was rightist and nationalist in orientation, one was centrist, and one was leftist, the last being aligned with Social Democratic trade unions and cooperatives. From time to time the federations undertook studies of their members, and these give us some indication of the backgrounds of the white-collar workers and some suggestion as to their political orientations. The most important of these studies, done by the Gewerkschaftsbund der Angestellten (GDA), the centrist federation, surveyed some 100,000 members of the organization. It found that 25 percent of its sample came from working-class families. The percentage from working-class backgrounds moreover, varied inversely with age, such that among apprentices (for clerical positions), the figures were 34.0 percent for males and 42.5 percent for females. Understandably the percentages also varied with the region, being higher in industrial areas such as Upper Silesia, Thuringia, and

Rhine-Westphalia. In the industrial regions of Saxony, half of the apprentices came from working-class homes.

As for income, Speier notes that "the income of the salaried employees is in many cases lower than that of the average worker's wage, and this is particularly true of those salaried groups in which proletarian antecedents are more frequent than in other salaried groups, i.e., of the lower age groups in general and of the salaried workers who perform simple and mechanized functions in particular. From an economic point of view the transition from manual to office work is therefore not necessarily a case of ascent."[29]

It must be remembered that these findings came from a study of GDA members. There is some reason to believe that the members of this organization were middling in terms of their social backgrounds and current condition. The better-off white-collar workers tended to join the rightist federation, and those of poorer circumstances tended to join the leftist one. Speier, in a note, states that "older commercial employees in the small and medium-sized cities" tended to join the GDA while the poorly paid tended to join the leftist Zentralverband der Angestellten (ZdA). In the latter organization, the working-class backgrounds should be even more frequent, that is, higher than the 25 percent figure indicated in the large GDA study. A study undertaken in Swabia in 1927 by the Deutschnationaler Handlungsgehilfen-Verband (the dominant organization of the rightist federation) found 18.8 percent of its male apprentice members were children of manual workers. The GDA study found 36.6 percent of its equivalent members in that region to be working-class children. A limited study by the ZdA gives a 50 percent figure.[30]

The foregoing adds up to a conclusion that the marginal middle-class populations, those most likely to be earning less than manual workers, those most likely to be burdened with uninspiring routine work, and those most likely to be touched by unemployment in a crisis, came disproportionately from working-class backgrounds. They were also likely to be young, and, moreover, one is likely to be speaking of working-class daughters rather than working-class sons. Given those characteristics, it is useful to raise a correlated question: what about their motivations? Or as it is frequently put, what about their world outlooks?

Virtually all of what has been reported in the preceding paragraphs comes from Speier's brief summary of the trade union studies. He proceeds from the discussion of background and current condition to an *assertion* about the world outlooks of the salaried. Although his data very strongly suggest the need for a differentiated viewpoint, one that would give separate consideration to white-collar workers of middle-class and those of working-class background, he nevertheless proceeds to speak of an undifferentiated type. After noting that some moves from manual to nonmanual ranks do not represent economic ascent, he proceeds to reject the alternative line of speculation and inquiry. His very next sentence reads: "There are nonetheless enough weighty differences in career, form of life and social consciousness between manual workers and salaried employees so that the shift from the former stratum to the latter may still be regarded as social ascent and adaptation to middle class life." Whether that is or is not the case, however, must be established by some kind of inquiry.

There is little one can offer at this point since the studies of the period did not inquire about outlooks. One may, nevertheless, raise some questions about the position that, for short, may be referred to as the argument of conversion—namely that persons of working-class background adopt a new and different style of life in the course of their ascent into the middle class, one that involves rejection of former beliefs and ways of living.

Speier reports on a study done in Fürth, a Bavarian industrial city, in 1925. Among the children of workers still living with their parents or with relatives, the study found 6,411 who were themselves workers, journeymen, or apprentices in industry or handicraft and 1,387 who were salaried employees or apprentices. Of the latter one must ask: were they engaged in an adaptation to middle-class life? Does it seem likely that they were rejecting their working-class backgrounds, including their parents, relatives, and brothers or sisters who were working in industry or handicraft? Is it not more likely that they would maintain the family ties and loyalties? And, would it not seem likely, especially given their low earnings, low seniority, and low job security, that they would have little inclination to change their self-conceptions and their politics? And would it not also seem likely, under those circumstances that they would maintain a proletarian outlook toward social and economic matters? Would they not, like their parents, be favorably disposed toward unions?

Looking at the question another way, one might consider the consequences of adaptation to middle-class life under those circumstances. The costs of such a change, of such a putting on of airs, under those circumstances would be awesome. One might imagine the son or daughter returning to the working-class household after a day in the office and announcing the newly discovered allegiances, the disdain for working-class ways, and the attraction of right-of-center politics, say of the German People's party. Effectively the only persons willing to undertake such initiatives would be those who had decided to reject their backgrounds, including their families, friends, schoolmates, and everything else associated with their previous life. There are few people in any setting interested in or capable of such behavior. And that suggests a conclusion opposite to Speier's, namely that the newly arrived children of the working class may not have been in the process of adapting to middle-class life.[31]

The Fürth study focuses on a special case, working-class children still living with their families. But it might be argued that *adults* who were in the process of ascending would move to a "better" area. The change in community context would be the necessary prerequisite for the development of the new and separate consciousness. Several underlying assumptions are contained in this argument: that these persons would wish to move to a new area; that they were in a position to make such a move; that the population of the new area would possess markedly different social and political outlooks; and that the newcomers would in fact adopt these outlooks.

The first of these assumptions has already been discussed in a speculative way. There can be no doubt that there were (and are) *some* people willing and capable of rejecting their entire heritage. It would seem a doubtful claim, however, to attribute such motives to the hundreds of thousands of working-class children who just happened to have white-collar jobs.[32]

What about the second of the assumptions, that they were in a position to make a move? If they were earning less than manual workers, they clearly would not be able to afford a more costly residential area. It should also be kept in mind that the marginal middle class was, in great measure, made up of younger persons. Were they going to move off into other areas, competing for housing against persons further along in their careers, against persons likely to be at the peak of their earning powers? In the case of young women of working-class families, they might move on the occasion of marriage. But if such a move occurred, it would be conditioned by the earnings and social circumstances of the husband. And then one must ask about the occupation of the husbands. Wouldn't most of them be employed in working-class occupations? And if that were the case, are they, husbands or wives, likely to adopt a different consciousness?[33]

The third implicit assumption of the conversion argument involves the notion of sharp contrasts between the old and the new lives of the upwardly mobile individual: working-class life has characteristics and values A; middle-class life has characteristics and values B. The former, in most analyses, is seen as consisting largely of pain, deprivation, and punishment; the latter involves attractions and rewards. The move into Context B, not too surprisingly then, is believed to generate sweeping changes in outlook. When spelled out in this way, the argument seems rather questionable.

Is it a question of night and day differences? Is there not a likelihood that some characteristics and values would be shared by both ranks? And where differences exist, would they not be ones of degree, there being somewhat greater support for the Conservatives or for the right liberals in the lower-middle-class rank and somewhat less support for the Social Democrats and Communists? Discussions that focus on *the* middle class, moreover, average together the attitudes of a very conservative upper middle class and a somewhat more leftist (as Neisser has suggested) lower middle class. One must raise a question as to the end point in this mobility process. Did the mobile person "arrive" in the urban lower middle class or in a small-town upper middle class? In the former case the correlate of an upward move might be continued contact with working-class values and outlooks.

Lacking relevant data, one must speculate about the character of the new middle-class job. Are these white-collar employees of working-class parentage located in the central offices of major firms? Are they members of the sales staff in the leading department stores and the most elegant shops? In short, are they located in places where they will have contact with the conservative and status-conscious upper-middle-class populations? Or does some sorting out occur, with the upper-middle-class children staffing those positions and the working-class children finding their middle-class employment elsewhere, for example, in the offices next to the factories, or in the transport and warehousing firms outside of the downtown areas, or in the smaller stores in the working-class districts of the cities? And in these contexts, would not their co-workers also be of working-class backgrounds and likely to share the same values as their parents? Were that the case, such mobility would not provide the basis for a conversion. For all of these reasons, the fourth assumption spelled out above, that the mobile populations would adopt middle-class values, must be viewed as a hypothesis, rather than as an established fact.

This all leads to another largely unexplored range of considerations, the question of the geographical location of the lower middle class. Most accounts and commentaries have been indifferent to this question, giving no consideration to where the lower middle class lives. Implicitly there is a strong *suggestion* of a separate base or territory, of separate lower-middle-class communities, which provide a context allowing these people to sustain their distinctive outlooks.

That implicit assumption proves to be mistaken. As best one can tell on the basis of census materials, German cities were not divided into a series of neatly graded subcommunities. The basic pattern is one of relative homogeneity at the extremes of the class hierarchy and much mixture in the middle area. In the typical city one found a villa quarter (*Villenviertel*), that is, an area of large detached houses, some of them mansions. This would be *the* upper-class area. Next in the hierarchy, again in the typical case, would be two or three areas of elegant row or apartment houses, these being upper-middle-class areas. At the opposite extreme one could usually find a distinct poorest area of the city. Most of the remaining areas would be working-class districts. Significantly, there appear to be no districts that are overwhelmingly or even largely lower middle class. In between the working-class districts and the upper-middle-class districts one finds mixed areas, that is to say, areas with both middle-class and working-class populations present, the proportions varying from fifty-fifty to sixty-forty in either direction.

None of these areas would be pure in composition. Even the villa quarter would have a small working-class contingent. The portion of male workers in such an area, typically, was the smallest of any of the city districts. Such areas had a much larger percentage of working-class women, most of these being domestic servants. As we shall see, they form a rather large minority of the population in such districts. Many of the other workers in such areas may well have been in service occupations of one kind or another, attending to the routine work of the mansion and the community. It is less likely that lower-middle-class populations would have lived in such an area. Other than a few clerks caring for community business and some teachers in the primary schools (some of whom might well have lived elsewhere), it seems unlikely that either need or possibility would have allowed any significant lower-middle-class presence in such an area.

At the other extreme of the class hierarchy, some middle-class populations, that is to say, clerical employees, civil servants, and shopkeepers, were (and still are) to be found in *all* of the working-class areas of the cities. Few of these persons would have been upper middle class. Given the relatively large number of working-class districts together with a typical high population density, one is led to a rather important conclusion. Adding together the middle-class minorities from each of the working-class districts, one finds that a significant percentage, in some instances over half, of the lower middle class was located in working-class areas of the cities (see Chapters 4 and 5 for Berlin and Hamburg).[34] This part of the lower middle class, in short, was located in a setting where most daily social contacts would be with workers. If these people had grown up there, it would mean that their neighborhood friends and schoolmates had come from working-class families, and many of them, no doubt, would have gone into working-class occupations. And, a point touched on earlier, they would obviously have many kinship links within such neighborhoods.

The results of the white-collar trade union studies indicate that this segment of the lower middle class, this segment having such close contact with the working class, was also the most economically marginal segment of the middle class. One may also assume a rather important correlate: this group was not likely to have had a fetishistic attachment to its middle-class status; it was not likely to have had this extraordinary fear of proletarianization; nor was it likely to have suffered a status panic. It was not likely that it had felt any of these things because, for it, "falling into" the proletariat would not have meant entry into a new and completely different world. Unemployment, for these workers, as for blue-collar workers, would have meant economic stress, but socially, it would have meant a continuation of their current condition rather than the threat of a new and distinctly less desirable one.[35]

The third variety of urban community lies in between these extremes. But these are not lower-middle-class communities; they are not preponderantly made up of lower clerical workers, civil servants, and shopkeepers. No such communities were found in any of the cities studied. The closest approximation was in a small and very exceptional area of Hamburg with over 70 percent in white-collar occupations (see Chapter 5). Otherwise, the in-between districts are composites of manual and nonmanual populations. For that reason it is virtually impossible to isolate the voting tendency of either segment. That being the case, one might well ask: how can one reject the hypothesis of *middle-class* susceptibilities? The answer, strictly speaking, is that one cannot. There is an antecedent question however that also needs to be put: on what basis was the hypothesis originally offered and accepted?

One can only speculate about the populations living in these mixed districts. It seems likely that the white-collar or nonmanual segments there were somewhat better off than their peers living in the working-class districts. As for the workers in those areas, it seems likely that they too were better off economically than the workers in the working-class districts. They may have been the skilled workers, the "working-class aristocrats," and those in the working-class areas may have been the unskilled and semiskilled. Another possibility is that they were working-class populations of farm backgrounds, these districts on the whole tending to be recently annexed territories outside of the old city centers.

Respecifying the original claims in the light of these reconsiderations, one should anticipate a National Socialist attraction in these districts. This would be the segment of the middle class with the fetishistic attachment to its class position. The conventional or received wisdom has erred in focusing on the marginal, on the most poorly paid white-collar workers who, as has been suggested, probably had outlooks that would not fit with the requirements of that analytical framework. The middle-class segment having the outlooks described in that framework would be this better off or middling group. They are the ones who, presumably at least, had something to lose.

Something similar might be hypothesized of the workers living in these mixed districts. If they were better-off workers, those aspiring to bourgeois status, those concerned with maintaining their achievement, and with keeping their distance from the peers they had left behind, then maybe here too one should anticipate the same kind of status strain as presumably existed among their middle-class neighbors.[36]

Summarizing these points, we may note that in the typical German city, one found an upper-class district, a few upper-middle-class districts, mixed lower-middle- and working-class districts, and a large number of working-class districts. These were not clear-cut distinctions. Working-class populations were found in all districts. And the same was no doubt true of the lower-middle-class populations. On the basis of the reconsiderations offered here, if the marginality and panic hypothesis had any validity, it should be indicated in the voting patterns of the mixed districts.

One of the most important questions likely to arise in this connection, that is, whether the middle-class and working-class populations of the mixed districts had similar political orientations or whether they diverged significantly cannot, unfortunately, be tested in any way. In a district that was divided fifty-fifty in terms of occupation, a given result, say a 60 percent vote for the NSDAP, could represent 60 percent coming from each of the segments, or, alternatively, that figure could be an average of a 90 percent from the middle-class segment and a 30 percent from the working class. This is an important problem, one considered again in later discussions. For the moment, it can only be noted, a point made previously, that the difficulty works both ways. If it is impossible to establish a similarity of outlook, it is also impossible to establish a difference.

Since the question of lower-middle-class outlooks is of such importance, a further, more detailed exploration of the subject will prove useful. Some white collar workers, it will be remembered, were organized into the three trade union federations, one rightist, one centrist, and one leftist. If the lower middle class was given to the tendencies so often asserted of it, if, for example, it was intent on avoiding proletarianization, it would be difficult to explain the presence of any trade union involvements, let alone membership in a leftist union. This union was, to be sure, the smallest of the three, but it was by no means minuscule. Speier, as we have seen, discounts this possibility in favor of the standard claims. He states that "only about 12% of the salaried employees were members of the socialistic trade union organizations," and proceeds from that *fact* to the unsupported conclusion that the "great majority of the white collar workers in any case did not support the democratic institutions of the Weimar Republic."[37] The 12 percent figure sounds small, but it takes on a different meaning when one notes that only 45 percent of the salaried employees were organized into trade unions. In other words, approximately one-quarter of the *organized* salaried workers were in Socialist unions and another slightly larger block was in democratic centrist unions. The unorganized salaried workers might have been more conservative than the organized, and they might have been somewhat more opposed to the Weimar regime. But to assume that the failure to join a union indicates antidemocratic tendencies on the part of all or even a large part of them seems a rather sweeping and largely unwarranted judgment.

Much discussion of the white-collar unions and their significance is premised on the assumption that membership in a given union is based exclusively on political preference. That assumption is unrealistic at any time and in any place. One determinant of membership is the sheer fact of availability. If there is a union present in the office, people will be more likely to join than if there is not. The alternative is to maintain a largely expressive individual corresponding membership. Which organizations happen to be present, moreover, might reflect differences in organizational ability or aggressiveness in recruiting. Then, too, there might have been differences in the ability of the various organizations to win economic benefits, that payoff presumably being their principal purpose.

A related payoff, union insurance programs, might have led people to choose an affiliation that ran counter to their politics. Better insurance arrangements might, with greater frequency, have been decisive for the politically uninvolved. While many commentators have taken the growth of the DHV as evidence that salaried workers were turning to the right, another easy possibility is that they were choosing a superior insurance program.[38]

The impressive, but largely unnoticed, work by Heinz Hamm comments as follows on this possibility:

> A further important self-help arrangement of the unions—especially of the middle-class ones—were and are the medical funds. An employees' medical fund, of course, has better risks than a regional medical fund which takes in mainly workers and has to take every bad risk no matter what. The difference also shows up in the rates of contribution and in the remuneration of the doctors. . . . The free unions [i.e. those linked to the SPD] are opponents of these special funds because they violate the principle of solidarity of all workers.

The competition of the middle-class unions forced the free white-collar unions to accept this position.

In addition, Hamm reports efforts by the white-collar unions to create old age and life insurance programs. This was especially the case with the DHV, "which operate[d] an extensive general insurance business under the name 'German Ring.' " One small study of employee expenditures undertaken by the DHV discovered 9.4 percent of its members' incomes going for insurance premiums.[39]

Hamm's study also provides us with a wide range of additional information about these white-collar unions. In many respects the three had very different clienteles. The DHV took only male members. The percentage of women in the GDA ranged between 18 and 24 in the early Weimar years and even later never seems to have gone above the latter figure. In the leftist ZdA the figure in 1925 was 46.1 percent. In 1929 it rose even higher, to 48.8 percent.[40]

The location of the members followed a distinctive pattern, the DHV tending to be pronouncedly small town and the ZdA tending to be very much a big-city organization. One fragmentary bit of information on the location of members within the cities can be drawn from employees' insurance election results for Berlin in 1927. Hamm has given us results for some selected bourgeois (bürgerliche) and working-class districts of the city. With some necessary recalculation one finds the results shown in the accompanying table.[41] The most important aspect of this result appears in the second row. Two-fifths of the white-collar workers in the proletarian districts of Berlin who were unionized had voted for the candidates of the leftist union, a union affiliated with the free (leaning toward the Social Democrats) blue-collar trade unions. Another two-fifths favored the centrist GDA, the members of which, so Küstermeier reports, were turning to socialism as the depression deepened. Making due allowance for the motivational complexities in the choice of slates, this evidence suggests a similarity of orientation on the part of white-collar and blue-collar workers in the working-class districts. If one were to go by the voting in those districts and assume that it was the DHV segment that "went Nazi," then most of the GDA members would have voted for the left or would have remained with the various centrist or middle-class parties.[42]

District	DHV	GDA	ZdA	Total
Bourgeois	34%	42%	24%	100%
Proletarian	21	39	40	100

This suggested similarity of outlook would reinforce the view put forth above that the *most* marginal segment of the middle class was not identified with the middle class and, as a consequence, would not have suffered a status panic. The middle-class segment to which this notion might apply would have been located elsewhere, most probably in the mixed districts.

The discussion to this point has focused on the lower middle class, the principal thrust of the present argument being that the accounts of the lower middle class, of its problems and propensities, are seriously misleading. The evidence reviewed here, the evidence of general elections and of union affiliations, casts much doubt on the assumption that the urban lower middle class gave massive, or even majority support to the NSDAP. This conclusion, to be sure, rests on a rather limited empirical base.[43]

The same conclusion is also suggested by an observation made in the previous chapter. The argument by stipulation, it will be remembered, *defined* two of the parties, the Democrats and the People's party as middle-class parties and, furthermore, held the Conservatives to be a party of the upper classes. A question was raised as to the adequacy of those stipulations. The DNVP, it was argued, was a party of the Prussian countryside. The People's party, a right liberal party, would be more appropriately characterized as the party of the urban upper classes. The left liberal Democrats may have had more upper-middle-class support than is generally suspected, given the Social Democratic and Zentrum strength in the lower middle class. The near complete demise of the DVP and the DDP, then, would say more about the behavior of the urban upper and upper middle classes than about the lower middle class, the suggestion being that the upper and upper middle classes turned to the National Socialists. Still a suggestion at this point in the presentation, this could mean that the differences between the upper and upper middle classes on the one hand and the lower middle class on the other were not as sizable as has been suggested in the received literature. Or, alternatively, it could mean that the relationship is reversed, that the better-off classes gave *greater* support to the National Socialists than the lower middle class. There is no point in carrying this speculation farther since relevant evidence is available. That evidence is presented in the subsequent chapters.

The analysis of the Weimar parties has characteristically been made in terms of class. This is most clearly the case in the argument by stipulation. But most such presentations involve only very crude shorthand accounts. The support for the various parties is rarely as precisely class based as some of these accounts would suggest. This has already been seen in the case of the Social Democrats. The Center party too, following a very explicit intent, cut across class lines to achieve its support. And, as will be seen in later chapters, some of the so-called middle-class parties also managed, with considerable success, to reach across class boundaries.

Men and women had somewhat different voting tendencies. In general women tended to vote for religious parties or, alternatively, in a conservative direction; men tended to vote for the left, the left liberals—and for the National Socialists. Put another way, fair-sized majorities of both the Zentrum and the Conservative voters were women. And a fair-sized majority of the Communist voters were men. The Social Democrats, the Democrats, and the National Socialists generally received somewhat more modest male majorities. Some fluctuation occurred in the sex ratios of the party support from election to election, most especially in the case of the Conservatives. To some extent therefore, the focus on class must involve a misplaced emphasis. Some part of what has been treated as a class effect was probably a sex effect.[44]

One must also consider the question of electoral participation. Much has been made of the increasing participation in the elections, the level rising from 74.6 percent in 1928 to 81.4 in 1930 and then to 83.4 percent in July of 1932. There has been some controversy with regard to the political choices of the previous nonvoters. Some have argued that these votes, at all times, went directly to the National Socialists, this being a pure mass-society view. One important variant argument has held that the new voters of 1930 went to traditional parties; it was the subsequent increase in participation, that of 1932, that drew the previous nonvoters, the know nothings, to support the demagogic National Socialists. More recent works, these based on comprehensive reviews of the statistical evidence, have indicated that although the NSDAP drew disproportionately from among the previous nonvoters, only a minority—estimated at between one-fifth and one-third—of its votes came from that source. The rest were cast by people who had previously voted for some other party.[45]

It is useful to pursue the nonvoter question one step further with a simple query: who were the previous nonvoters? The answer, basically, is that they were older persons. Looking at the pattern by age, one finds a curvilinear relationship: average participation in the youngest years, a rise to a peak in middle age, and a precipitous falloff with advancing age. Because of differences in life expectancy (and to some extent because of the wartime casualties), the largest single reservoir of nonvoters consisted of elderly women. The next largest group consisted of elderly men.[46]

One very surprising finding appears in the work of both Pratt and Childers. Although almost all observers have stressed the youthfulness of the National Socialists, the entire enterprise being viewed by many as a youth movement, the evidence presented by these researchers indicates a positive relationship between age and voting for that party. In Pratt's study the correlations are substantial and exist even with controls for size of city, region, and occupation (census categories). "The pattern of relationship," he writes, "between the proportions of vote to the Nazis and the proportions in each age grade was negative until age 40, then a steadily increasing positive as age increased from 40 years on." Childers, who found the same pattern, also found strong positive relationships with the occupational category *Berufslose* (largely pensioners and the retired).[47]

This age relationship suggests still another conclusion about the class support for the NSDAP. Particularly within the nonmanual rank, age and class standing tend to be positively related. In the typical case, especially for males, careers begin at the lower levels of private or public bureaucracies, the plan being that one move from there to higher and more rewarding positions. While obviously not a perfect correlation (since some people are not promoted and some lose their positions), this means that the upper middle class would, on the whole, consist of older persons and the lower middle class of younger ones. And given the age relationship, the suggestion is again of an upper-middle-class propensity for National Socialism rather than a lower-middle-class one.

Many of those younger salaried white-collar employees would have been located in the large cities, and, as suggested above, they appear to have given considerable support to the moderate left SPD. This would reflect influences in their immediate environments, and, at one remove, possibly, it would also reflect the transformations occurring in the previous decades, those that gave rise to the Social Democratic party. One would expect political continuity in the upper and upper middle classes, with both parents and offspring supporting traditional bourgeois parties. Another pattern, however, seems likely in the lower-middle-class ranks. Either through personal conversion or through changing patterns of recruitment (many now coming from working-class backgrounds), a substantial gap between the young and the old appears likely. If so, the defections from traditional bourgeois parties to the National Socialists, a shift characteristically attributed to the lower middle class, would have markedly different implications. In the urban milieu it would tell instead something about the upper and upper middle classes together with the older cohorts of the lower middle class. It would also, we know from other sources, indicate something about the independent proprietors, that is, about the old middle class.[48]

It should be clear that no single generalization (or set of generalizations) about the lower middle class can satisfactorily account for National Socialist electoral support. At the very least, three lines of analysis are needed to account for lower-middle-class voting in the late Weimar elections, one for the Protestant countryside, one for the Catholic countryside, and another, a more complex discussion, for the urban segment of this class. The diverse patterns in the countryside appeared, unambiguously, from 1930 on. The pattern in the cities, as indicated, was more complicated. The conclusion about the lower middle class in the cities, that only a minority of them supported the National Socialists, must at this point be a tentative one. It is largely speculative, and based on a series of inferences. For this reason, the following chapters focus on the cities. A more direct approach to the questions raised here is clearly in order.

CHAPTER FOUR

Berlin

The City and Its People

Berlin may be described rather simply in terms of the administrative districts (*Verwaltungsbezirke*) used in both census and election reports.[1] There were twenty such districts first created in the early Weimar years. The geographic center of the city, an area containing government buildings, the Wilhelmstrasse, the famous avenue Unter den Linden, the department stores of the Leipzigerstrasse, and last but not least, the royal palace, was appropriately named the Mitte. Surrounding this center was a ring of five districts—Tiergarten, Wedding, Prenzlauer Berg, Friedrichshain, and Kreuzberg. Together these six districts formed the old city, that is, the city as it existed in the first decades of the twentieth century. (See Map 2.)

By act of the Prussian legislature, Greater Berlin was created on April 27, 1920. In the process the city annexed seven formerly independent towns, some fifty-nine smaller communities, and twenty-seven country estates. The territory of the city was increased to more than thirteen times its former size, going from 6,572 hectares in 1915 to 87,810 after annexation. Incorporating numerous lakes, waterways, forests, and green spaces, the boundaries of the city now extended some twenty-five kilometers to the southwest and southeast and fifteen kilometers to the north and south. The 1925 census reported a population of just over four million; it was by far the largest city in Germany.

It is to be noted in passing that a part at least of modern urban growth occurs through such annexations, as opposed to the uprooting and relocation of individuals and families. The populations of Reinickendorf and Köpenick, one may assume, had the same patterns of employment before and after the annexation. Their social relations, one may also assume, were not affected by the change. It is not as if they were made instantly anomic or, overnight, had become alienated by virtue of this change from being small-towners to becoming members of the metropolis. Many of these previous small-towners had worked in the old city prior to annexation, commuting there on a daily basis. One of the major incentives for the consolidation was to facilitate the planning and administration of the sprawling interdependent complex. Many of the new citizens of Greater Berlin, in short, had long since been urban; the

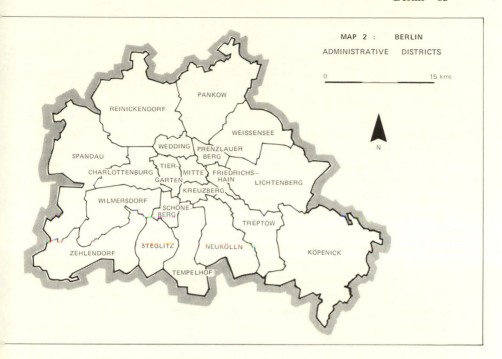

MAP 2 :   BERLIN
ADMINISTRATIVE   DISTRICTS

0   15 kms

new arrangement belatedly recognized the fact for purposes of improved government and administration. As a consequence many small-
towners now came to be classified as urbanites in the federal and state
statistical offices. Were one to forget this growth through annexation,
it would be easy to misinterpret the trends indicated in the census figures, thus exaggerating the extent of uprooting and providing spurious
support for the mass-society theory.[2]

The movement of the population within the city during the Weimar
period had a pattern that may also be rather simply described. The densely
settled districts of the old city were losing population, and the newly
annexed areas were gaining population. The movement, a slow one to
be sure, might be described as one of internal suburbanization.

As for the social composition of the city, one may note that the entire
eastern half and much of the northwestern quarter of the city was working class. The Mitte had a rather heterogeneous population, reflecting the
diversity of tasks performed there. It had some upper-class populations,
a small minority of the total, but on the whole the tendency here was
also one of working-class dominance.

Beginning with the Tiergarten, however, immediately to the west of
the Mitte, one found the upper-middle-class and upper-class districts of
the city. To the west of the Tiergarten was the famed Charlottenburg.

And to the southwest were the better-off areas of Schöneberg and Steglitz, and, the best of the city, Wilmersdorf and Zehlendorf. Tempelhof,
located between the elegant areas of the southwest and the working-
class southeast had a mixed character. And the same may be said, although to a lesser degree, of the districts of Spandau and Reinickendorf
to the west and northwest.

These brief characterizations of the city's subareas are of course very
sweeping and necessarily overlook many important internal differentiations. One could, following popular usage, refer to Zehlendorf and
Charlottenburg as well-off areas, as among the "best districts" of the
city. But that is deceptive; specifically it means that those districts contained some of the best residential areas of the city. But they also contained tens of thousands of people who were neither upper nor upper
middle class.

The smallest of the twenty districts, Zehlendorf, had a population of
65,948 persons in 1933. Charlottenburg, the most populous district with
340,596 persons, was larger than many of Germany's large cities. Zehlendorf contained some very elegant communities; one of them, Dahlem, was probably either the first or second best-off community in the
entire metropolis. But it also contained a huge housing project, called
Onkel-Toms-Hütte (Uncle Tom's Cabin), erected between 1926 and
1931, which has been described as a lower-middle-class settlement. The
Wilmersdorf district contained Grunewald, Dahlem's rival for the title
of best-off community in the metropolis. But Wilmersdorf also had a
considerable working-class population. An informant who had been active in the Wilmersdorf section of the Social Democratic party remembers constant tension between its bourgeois and proletarian members.

Steglitz was not uniformly upper middle class. One informant described the area as containing the "better lower middle class." Another
informant described it as definitely upper middle class in character with
a large number of villas. This informant compared Steglitz with a very
affluent North American suburban community. Schöneberg, described
here as better off, still contains, one informant notes, a large number of
drab working-class tenement buildings.

It is not as if one source is right and the other wrong in the case of
these conflicting judgments. They are both pointing to known facts, the
difference in overall assessments stemming from the heterogeneous
character of the districts. Schöneberg did have some elegant areas. A
majority of its population, as we shall see, was middle class, and a wide
range of incomes no doubt was to be found there; it also had a working-
class minority, more than a fourth of the population being so classified
by the census. That would mean some 55,000 persons, many of whom
were to be found in those tenement buildings.

It would be helpful to be able to explore the voting patterns within the various subareas of these larger districts. Unfortunately, the possibilities proved very limited. The only detailed figures found came from local newspapers. They allow consideration of the results for Dahlem, Grunewald, and some Wilmersdorf subcommunities. In another instance, a more detailed look at areas within the Steglitz district was possible.

SOME METHODOLOGICAL PROBLEMS

The following discussion is intended to serve two purposes: first, to establish with census data the above claims as to the character of the districts, and second, to indicate some of the complications that have to be considered in the later analysis.

The best *approximate* picture may be gained from the census classification by social strata (*Soziale Schicht*). This categorization put all employed persons into one of six broad occupational classes with retired persons providing a seventh category. The unemployed (32.4 and 25.3 percent respectively of the economically active males and females at the date of the census, June 16, 1933) were classified according to their last previous employment. Dependents without a full-time occupation (that is, wives, children, in-laws, etc.) were classified according to the occupation of the head of the household. The city's entire population, from newborn infant to aged pensioner, was thus included in the figures to be used in the following analysis.

For several reasons these figures can give only an approximate picture of the electorate. They include children, that is, persons below the legal voting age which was then 20 years. Just over a quarter of the population fell into this category. As may well be expected, there were variations in the size of the youthful segment, the proportions being somewhat larger in the working-class districts.

There is also the problem (discussed in Chapter 2) of the heterogeneity of the categories. The first of the census categories includes all persons in independent business together with top-level (*leitende*) managers and high-level civil servants. The independent business segment, by far the largest of the three segments, includes everyone from the owner of the small shop to the owner of the giant enterprise. It mixes in the same category the butcher, the baker, and the tobacconist of working-class Wedding with the factory owners of Zehlendorf. Little can be done about this problem at present. It is necessary, however, to keep in mind that part of the overlap or similarity suggested in the following figures is spurious. The independents of Wedding and the Mitte were likely to have been small shop owners; those living in Dahlem and Grunewald would have commanded middle-sized or large enterprises.

A similar problem arises with the white-collar employees in private firms (*Angestellte*) and the civil servants (*Beamte*), a category that includes teachers and professors. The range here extends from the poorly paid clerks and typists to those who would ordinarily be counted as professionals and middle management. It seems likely that here too one would have found some division by city district, with the clerks living in the working-class and mixed areas and the middle managers and professionals tending to be located in the southwestern sector. The figures for employees and civil servants, in short, may also suggest a similarity between districts that is misleading. Again there is little one can do about the problem except to keep it in mind. It is possible that a parallel division was to be found among the workers (*Arbeiter*), with the skilled being located in the better-off or mixed districts and the semiskilled and unskilled concentrated in Wedding and Friedrichshain.

A third problem stems from the initial focus on economically active *persons*. A family could contain persons falling into two or more categories. The husband might be classed as a worker, the wife as a white-collar employee, the son as a civil servant, and the grandmother as a pensioner. If the wives and daughters of manual workers had been disproportionately in white-collar occupations, that might have resulted in some significant distortions, the most important being an overestimate of the middle-class representation in working-class districts. This potentially serious problem, however, developed in later decades; during the period in question it appears to have made only a relatively small difference. Fifty-five percent of the economically active males were classified as workers in the 1933 census. By comparison, 38.5 percent of the active females were workers. To this latter group should be added another 18.9 percent who were employed as domestic servants (*Hausangestellte*) thus yielding a total of 57.4 percent.[3]

A fourth problem with the statistics to be used here involves the domestic servants. The overwhelming majority of the 169,933 persons so employed were women, only 953 of the total being male. Most of these women were young, single, and without dependents. Domestic servants therefore will be underrepresented in the subsequent tabulations, which include dependents. This may best be seen by considering one of the more affluent of the districts, Zehlendorf. Table 4.1 shows 8.9 percent of the population to be in the domestic servant category. When, however, one considers only the economically active and retired populations, the domestic servant percentage is 17.6.

The presence of domestic servants provides a useful index of class standing; compare, for example, the Zehlendorf figure with that of working-class Wedding, 1.1 percent. The presence of domestic servants in the better-off districts poses a largely insurmountable problem for the analysis of election results. Was it the Zehlendorf bankers, industrialists, and professionals who voted for a given party? Or was it perhaps their cooks and their maids? No ecological analysis can adequately answer the question. Some consolation perhaps may be found in the results of two studies done in this period showing that domestic servants had the lowest level of electoral participation of any major occupational group.[4]

A fifth problem also deserves at least a passing mention. The census dates from the middle of 1933. The first of the elections to be discussed occurred in May of 1924. This does not, however, appear to present serious difficulties. No dramatic changes in the characteristics of concern here occurred in any of these districts during the Weimar regime.

Despite the problems, we will use these 1933 census statistics. They show the economically active population with dependents classified according to the occupation of the head of household.

THE SOUTHWEST SECTOR—BERLIN'S MIDDLE-CLASS AREAS

The twenty administrative districts of Berlin have been arranged, with the single exception of the Tiergarten area, in order of the percentages in nonmanual occupations. Six of the twenty districts have been classified as middle class (Table 4.1).

The first point to strike one about the middle-class areas is the mixed character of even these districts. All of them, as already noted, are rather large, and each contains diverse urban arrangements or, in the outlying regions of the city, diverse villages. A sixth of the population in the two leading districts, Wilmersdorf and Zehlendorf, were from working-class families. Elsewhere, obviously, the working-class percentages were even larger. These districts do, nevertheless, provide the basis for a useful first view of the subject. In some key cases, moreover, it has proved possible to specify the voting results in greater detail.

The most problematic placement involves the Tiergarten. Lying just to the west of the Mitte, on the other side of the Brandenburg Gate, was a large park and forest area, once a royal park and hunting ground. To the south of this park one found elegant villas, embassies, and apartment houses. But to the north, on the other side of the Spree, was Moabit with its docks, warehouses, and working-class dwelling areas. It seems inappropriate to put the Tiergarten together with the mixed districts that follow in the table since the latter probably contained a mixture of lower-middle-class and upper-working-class populations. The Tiergarten district, by contrast, contained upper- and upper-middle-class populations in the one area and workers (probably semiskilled and un-

TABLE 4.1. BERLIN'S POPULATION BY DISTRICT AND SOCIAL STATUS, 1933[a]

District	Independents, Managers, etc.[b]	Civil Servants[c]	White-Collar Employees[c]	Total Nonmanual	Workers	Domestic Servants	Retired	Population
Middle-class districts								
Wilmersdorf	20.7%	9.8%	26.7%	57.2%	17.4%	7.5%	16.7%	196,573
Zehlendorf	18.6	14.0	24.1	56.7	18.5	8.9	15.1	65,948
Steglitz	13.6	13.8	27.7	55.1	23.1	4.1	16.6	194,795
Tempelhof	10.9	11.8	30.1	52.8	31.5	2.3	12.2	315,632
Schöneberg	16.7	8.4	25.7	50.8	26.9	4.7	16.3	221,111
Charlottenburg	15.0	7.0	23.4	45.4	31.6	5.0	16.7	340,596
Tiergarten	13.0	6.2	20.2	39.4	40.2	3.9	15.2	251,924
Mixed districts								
Treptow	8.1	8.7	23.7	40.5	44.5	1.3	12.6	124,534
Pankow	8.8	10.3	21.2	40.3	39.2	1.7	17.8	141,333
Reinickendorf	8.6	8.4	21.7	38.7	43.9	1.5	14.8	164,319
Köpenick	10.5	10.3	17.4	38.2	44.0	1.9	14.1	88,517
Working-class districts								
Lichtenberg	8.4	7.8	18.1	34.3	48.2	1.2	15.0	241,186
Mitte	14.2	3.9	16.0	34.1	48.0	2.8	13.3	266,137
Spandau	7.1	6.7	20.3	34.1	48.3	1.4	15.1	146,472
Prenzlauer Berg	9.9	6.0	17.9	33.8	48.7	1.4	14.7	312,981
Neukölln	8.5	6.5	18.2	33.2	51.9	1.1	12.5	315,632
Weissensee	10.6	6.0	16.3	32.9	52.4	1.4	11.4	81,565
Kreuzberg	11.3	4.9	16.5	32.7	48.5	2.1	15.3	339,198
Wedding	7.4	4.4	14.4	26.2	56.8	1.1	14.7	332,146
Friedrichshain	9.0	3.8	12.6	25.4	56.6	1.4	15.2	303,149

SOURCE: *Mitteilungen des Statistischen Amts der Stadt Berlin*, no. 18, pt. 10, p. 11.

NOTE: Percentages do not add to 100. There is a small group of "helping family members" (*Mithelfende Familienangehörige*) who make up the difference. In no district do they constitute more than 1.9 percent of the total.
[a] Classified according to the occupation of the economically active population plus the retired. Dependents not gainfully employed are classified according to the occupation of the family head.
[b] Includes all independent businessmen (regardless of the size of the business), plus high-level employees (managers) and high-level civil servants.
[c] Does not include those of the highest level, i.e. those in top management or official positions.

skilled) in the other. Far from being mixed together, these two segments occupied very distinct and separate territories.

Charlottenburg, also popularly known as a wealthy part of the city, contained a fair-sized working-class population, three of ten being workers. This district, too, had a diverse character. It was not an area of villas (*Villenviertel*) but rather contained elegant apartments, a typical structure in the district having shops or apartments on the ground floor and apartments left and right of the stairs on each of the upper three or four floors. An ornate facade was an absolute necessity for a Charlottenburg building.

One feature of Berlin housing deserves special consideration. Many apartment houses were divided into three sections, the front, middle, and rear house. The first of these faced the street while the others were built around an inner court. The best apartments were those on the street, and the least desirable ones were on the court. The desirability of an apartment (and the rents) varied by floor, the upper level walk-ups being less attractive. This range of housing opportunities led to a fair amount of occupational or status differentiation within a given neighborhood, something that would not occur, at least to the same extent, in London or New York.

The placement of Tempelhof is also open to some question. It had more white-collar employees, fewer independents, and fewer domestic servants than the other six districts in this category. As previously noted, this district provided the boundary between the more elegant areas to the west and working-class Neukölln to the east. It appears, in short, to have had more of a lower-middle-class character than the other better-off districts.

The other four districts provide less ground for doubt. Zehlendorf and Wilmersdorf contained areas of detached single-family dwelling units, ranging from bungalows to mansions. These were clearly the most elegant areas of the city. But here, too, one found significant internal differentiation. The older municipality of Wilmersdorf, once a separate town, had a character similar to that of Charlottenburg. Its typical housing style, for example, was also the five-story apartment house. In the western end of the district, by contrast, one found the famous Grunewald. As described in a Baedeker, it is a "colony of well-to-do detached residences laid out on Bismarck's initiative in a forest area in 1889."[5] Zehlendorf begins with the *Villenviertel* of Dahlem on the east, includes the town of Zehlendorf, and extends out to the village of Wannsee in the southwest on the lake of the same name.

Another measure of the character of these districts, one confirming the judgments based on occupation, involves the size of the dwelling units. Zehlendorf had the largest homes, 43.1 percent having six or more rooms (not counting kitchens or bathrooms).[6] Wilmersdorf follows closely, and then there is a gap with Steglitz, Schöneberg, and Charlottenburg being on approximately the same level, that is, with large homes, ones well above the city average, but not so large as those in the two richest districts. The problems mentioned in connection with Tempelhof and Tiergarten are indicated again here. The former would appear to be more of a lower-middle-class area; the latter, it will be remembered, was a divided district.

The presence of domestic servants in the districts also confirms the assessments made on the basis of employment in nonmanual occupations. Wilmersdorf and Zehlendorf are high on the list; the others come after at some considerable distance.[7] Tempelhof again appears to be questionably located. If the lower-middle-class tendency is as has been claimed, one should find greater National Socialist support there than in the other middle-class districts.

THE LOWER-MIDDLE-CLASS PROBLEM AND THE MIXED DISTRICTS

One of the problems observed in the received literature, the failure to define the lower middle class, appears at this point. An analysis of contexts and usage makes clear that the reference is to white-collar populations—both independents and salaried employees—who have low or unstable earnings. This would mean the not-so-well-to-do independent businessmen, the salaried employees, and the civil servants. Another closely related problem, noted in Chapter 3, involves the failure to give any consideration to their residential location. Did they live on the edge of upper-middle-class districts? Or did they have communities of their own, that is, areas in which the majority of the population was lower middle class? Or, still another possibility, were they located in the working-class areas of the cities? As noted, explicit discussions of the matter are difficult to find.

As far as Berlin is concerned, the figures in Table 4.1 suggest that pure lower-middle-class communities did not exist. The districts with nonmanual majorities were not, by and large, *lower* middle class. And those districts containing relatively large middle-class minorities, ones that might well have been lower middle class, also had large percentages of workers in them. For this reason the four districts of this variety have been referred to as mixed rather than as lower middle class. It might well be the case that these districts contained the well-off workers, the so-called bourgeois workers, the worker aristocrats, those aspiring to middle-class status.[8]

The basic problem many be seen from still another perspective. If one were to take the white-collar category (*Angestellte*) as roughly equivalent to this lower middle class, one would find 41.0 percent of the category living in the middle-class districts. Only 13.2 percent lived in the mixed districts, and the remainder, 45.8 percent, lived in the districts designated as working class. In all likelihood, it was the last segment, constituting just under half of the total, that suffered from economic deprivation and uncertain employment. The census category, it will be remembered, included both middle-level and lower-level white-collar workers. It seems likely that the former would have been located in other sections of the city, not in working-class areas.

The middle class that, presumably, was both losing status and desperate to maintain it, as noted in Chapter 3, would most likely be found in the mixed districts. One should, therefore, find the attraction to National Socialism to be especially pronounced in those areas. These populations, it should be emphasized, did not form the *lower* middle class; that is, they were not the poorest and least secure of the nonmanual populations.

THE WORKING-CLASS DISTRICTS

The remaining nine administrative districts of Berlin have been labeled working class. Roughly half of the population in these areas were classified as workers, and equivalent portions of the retired were probably also at one time engaged in those occupations. In all of these districts the working-class populations had a fair-sized edge over the nonmanual populations, whereas in the mixed districts the proportions were closer to fifty-fifty.

From the table, it might be assumed that these districts were all more or less alike. There are, however, some important differences in composition and circumstance that ought to be noted. The Mitte, as observed above, contained both department stores and small shops as well as most of the government buildings. It was, in short, somewhat more heterogeneous than the other districts, and the workers living there were more likely to have been linked with commerce and government than with factories and manufacturing.

Wedding, Prenzlauer Berg, Friedrichshain, and Kreuzberg, surrounding the Mitte on three sides, were classic urban working-class quarters. Otto Friedrich describes Wedding in the twenties as "a bleak jumble of brown stucco tenements."[9] Other areas, those further out from the center, such as Lichtenberg, Spandau, and Weissensee, had lower population densities and somewhat more attractive living conditions. These areas were more diverse in composition, some housing consisting of newer apartments and some being the more traditional structures of the recently annexed towns and villages. In Spandau one also found a planned city, the Siemensstadt, built to house the workers of the giant Siemens factory complex.

In Berlin (and in the other cities considered in later chapters) it is important that one recognize the differences within the working class. It would be a mistake to speak simply of "the workers" and to assume that the conditions of Wedding typified the circumstances of the entire class.

THE REICHSTAG ELECTIONS IN BERLIN: 1924 TO 1932

The first election of 1924 provides a useful beginning point, that being the first national election in which the National Socialists made an appearance. As may be seen in Table 4.2, they took just under 5 percent in the city. The largest parties at this time were the German National People's party (usually called the Conservatives in English-language works), the Social Democrats, and the Communists. The two liberal parties, the German People's party (right liberals) and the German Democratic party (left liberals) together had a strength that roughly equaled that of the Communists. In the heart of Protestant Prussia, the Catholic Zentrum took only 3.8 percent, even though Catholics, according to the 1925 census, made up 10.0 percent of the Berlin population. The remainder of the vote was scattered among minor parties.

The left at this point was divided into two large segments and one small one, and together they represented approximately two-fifths of the city's voters. On the right, or rather among the so-called middle-class parties one found another threefold division, this time into one larger and two smaller segments; they also represented approximately

TABLE 4.2. REICHSTAG ELECTION RESULTS FOR BERLIN, 1924-1932
(in percent)

	Election					
	May 4, 1924	December 7, 1924	May 20, 1928	September 14, 1930	July 31, 1932	November 6, 1932
SPD	20.4	30.3	32.9	27.2	27.3	23.3
USPD	2.6	0.6	—	—	—	—
KPD	17.9	16.3	24.6	27.3	27.3	31.0
Zentrum	3.8	3.9	3.3	3.6	4.9	4.4
DDP	8.9	10.9	7.8	5.4	1.6	1.4
DVP	8.4	6.5	6.4	3.7	0.7	1.1
DNVP	22.6	23.9	17.8	13.0	8.3	11.4
NSDAP	4.8	2.0	1.5	14.6	28.6	26.0
Others	10.6	5.6	5.7	5.2	1.3	1.4
Total	100.0	100.0	100.0	100.0	100.0	100.0
Participation	76.6	78.0	78.9	81.4	81.6	81.0

SOURCE: *Statistisches Jahrbuch der Stadt Berlin*, editions for indicated years.

two-fifths of the city's electors. The remaining fifth consisted of the National Socialist voters, those voting for the Center, and those voting for one of the minor parties.

The problem with the Weimar Republic, as has been frequently noted, was that none of the pieces fit well enough with any of the others to allow an effective coalition. Berlin is unrepresentative in that the combined forces of the left were larger than elsewhere, and the Center party was considerably smaller. Business circles found the situation especially frustrating in that they had to govern or deal with four parties (the two liberal parties, the Center, and the Conservatives) in order to, in some measure, achieve their aims. Some of them wished to see the creation of a unified party out of these four pieces, a party that could then be directed against the left. The formal possibility would have given them a slight edge over the left. Outside of the capital the relationship was much more favorable. But the Bürgerblock, as it was called, never came about. In Berlin, the parties that were to have formed its core were to dwindle from their 44 percent level of 1924 down to only 15 percent in the July election of 1932. It is useful to trace the process.

In the second, the December election of 1924, the most important changes took place on the left wing of the political spectrum. The Communists declined slightly, and the fragment of the Independent Socialists all but disappeared. The left splinter parties also suffered considerable losses. Most of these losses appear to have benefited the Social Democrats; it was as if those who had broken away in earlier years were now coming home.

Some loss was suffered by the German People's party, Stresemann's party, but this loss seems to have yielded a benefit to the liberal sister party, the German Democrats. The National Socialists lost over half of their May strength, and this would appear to have gone to the Conservatives. The December election, coming after all the turbulence of the first years of the republic, appeared to be one in which something of the prewar equilibrium was being reestablished.

The so-called good years of Weimar followed, the years of peace, stability, and economic improvement. The National Socialists fell to their lowest point in Berlin in the 1928 election, 1.5 percent of the total. Ironically, the good years which, presumably at least, reduce the incentives to support left parties, were correlated with the opposite development in Berlin and elsewhere in the nation. Both the Social Democrats and the Communists increased their strength, the former by 2.6 and the latter by 8.3 percentage points. This gain appears to have come at the expense of middle-class parties, particularly, of the Center, the German Democratic, and the German National People's parties. The most serious losses were suffered by the last two. This shift to the left reflects the internal dynamics of the center or middle-class parties. They were moving to the right, in effect pushing out their more liberal supporters. The stage was then set for the next step. Reacting to their reduced strength, right-wing supporters of those parties were then inclined to look for a new and more effective option.[10]

Between the 1928 and 1930 elections the worldwide economic crisis set in. The correlates are not entirely as one might expect. There was some shifting from the Social Democrats to the Communists, but the relative strength of the left declined rather than increased. The tiny Center party managed a slight gain. The other middle-class parties, however, suffered considerable losses, these varying between one-third and one-half of their 1928 strength. The votes lost by the middle-class parties appear to have been picked up by the National Socialists who now had 14.6 percent of the total. The role of the splinter parties in the 1930 outcome appears to have been small. Some part of the result may be attributed to the participation of previous nonvoters; the total increase between 1928 and 1930 amounted to only 2.5 percentage points, however, and not all of the new participants would have been voting for the National Socialists.[11]

Between 1930 and the July election of 1932 one finds remarkably little change on the left. Two years of disastrously high levels of unemployment yielded neither an increase in the combined strength of the left nor an increase in the relative strength of the Communists. The Center party, once again, remarkably enough, showed a modest gain. But the most important change was the serious erosion of support for the other three middle-class parties. The German People's party took less than 1 percent, and the German Democratic party took only a little more than 1. The Conservatives did somewhat better, but even they were down to approximately one-third of their peak strength for the period. The minor parties all but disappeared.

Most of the attention in this work, as noted previously, is focused on this July 1932 campaign, in which the NSDAP reached its peak in free elections. In the city, over a period of a little more than four years, Hitler's party had gone from 1.5 to 28.6 percent of the total.

The second election of 1932, that of November, yielded some sharp changes on the left and some minor changes on the right. In the three months between the two elections the long anticipated radicalizaton occurred, putting the Communists clearly ahead of the Socialists. Otherwise little was changed by the election. There was a slight reversal of the radicalization process on the right; the National Socialists lost some votes, and two of the middle-class parties, most notably the Conservatives, gained some. None of these changes, to be sure, was very large. The gains provided little consolation for the leaders of the gaining parties. The losses were, however, a source of considerable concern to the leaders of the National Socialists.

THE SUPPORT FOR THE NATIONAL SOCIALISTS

The National Socialists made their first appearance in German elections in May of 1924. At that point they were running on a joint list with another party. In most parts of the country the ballots bore the name Deutsch-völkische Freiheits-partei. Officially, the listing read Deutsche-völkische und National Sozialistische Arbeiter Partei–vereinigte Liste (German People's Freedom party and National Socialist Worker party–United List). the word *"völkische"* has always been a difficult one to translate. It means "people" in a racial or ethnic sense. It is a positive way of indicating anti-Semitism.

The result in Berlin shows five of the middle-class districts giving the United List above average support (Table 4.3). The level of support in the well-off Zehlendorf district was more than twice the Berlin average. Tiergarten, the divided district, was exactly at the average. And the one questionable placement, Tempelhof, which as noted might more appropriately be counted as lower middle class, was slightly below the average. Three of the four mixed districts came in below the city-wide average, only Köpenick being above. And all but one of the working-class districts were below the city-wide average, that one being Spandau.

Except for some minor variations, essentially the same pattern appears in the December election of 1924 and in the 1928 election. In both of these elections, it will be remembered, NSDAP support in Berlin was very low.

The 1930 election provided the takeoff for the National Socialists. In Berlin one again finds that the middle-class districts gave them the strongest support of any areas in the city. All seven of these districts were now above the city average with Steglitz leading the rest. The lowest percentage for these districts, surprisingly, appeared in Tempelhof. The mixed districts present a mixed picture. One, Pankow, was slightly above the average; the other three were below average although in none of the four cases was the variance a sizable one. The remarkable fact about these districts, the ones most likely to have contained those populations anxious about their social position, is that their vote for the National Socialists was so unremarkable.

In March of 1932 came another national election, this to select the president of the republic. One had the choice of the current president, the aged military hero Paul von Hindenburg; of Theodor Duesterberg,

TABLE 4.3. SUPPORT FOR THE NATIONAL SOCIALISTS IN BERLIN BY DISTRICT, 1924-1932
(in percent)

				Election			
	May 4, 1924	December 7, 1924	May 20, 1928	September 14, 1930	March 13, 1932	July 31, 1932	November 6, 1932
Berlin total	4.8	2.0	1.6	14.6	23.0	28.6	26.0
Middle class districts							
Wilmersdorf	**6.7**	**2.5**	**2.1**	**18.8**	**28.7**	**35.1**	**29.3**
Zehlendorf	**9.8**	**4.2**	**1.8**	**17.7**	**29.8**	**36.4**	**29.4**
Steglitz	**9.5**	**3.8**	**2.9**	**23.3**	**35.2**	**42.1**	**36.1**
Tempelhof	4.7	2.0	**1.8**	**15.6**	**27.5**	**33.9**	**30.3**
Schöneberg	**5.8**	**2.3**	**2.1**	**19.9**	**29.0**	**35.7**	**31.7**
Charlottenburg	**8.6**	**4.0**	**2.0**	**18.5**	**26.6**	**33.1**	**29.4**
Tiergarten	4.8	**2.2**	**1.7**	**16.5**	**23.9**	**29.7**	**27.1**
Mixed districts							
Treptow	3.1	1.1	1.0	12.5	22.6	27.8	25.8
Pankow	4.0	1.3	1.3	**15.3**	**25.0**	**32.4**	**29.8**
Reinickendorf	4.0	1.4	1.3	13.8	22.7	28.9	**27.0**
Köpenick	**6.0**	**3.1**	1.5	14.0	**26.1**	**30.5**	**29.5**
Working-class districts							
Lichtenberg	4.1	1.5	1.5	13.9	20.9	26.1	24.3
Mitte	4.4	1.9	**1.8**	**14.9**	22.2	28.4	25.9
Spandau	**8.7**	**3.2**	**2.3**	**15.0**	**28.1**	**34.9**	**33.0**
Prenzlauer Berg	3.1	1.4	1.2	11.9	18.5	23.8	22.1
Neukölln	3.0	1.3	1.1	11.1	19.0	23.9	22.2
Weissensee	4.1	1.4	0.9	14.2	**24.8**	**29.8**	**27.8**
Kreuzberg	4.0	1.8	**1.7**	14.0	21.0	26.6	23.7
Wedding	2.4	0.9	0.8	9.0	15.2	19.3	18.0
Friedrichshain	3.3	1.3	1.2	11.6	17.0	21.6	20.0

SOURCE: *Statistisches Jahrbuch der Stadt Berlin*, editions for indicated years.
NOTE: Figures in bold type indicate results above the city-wide NSDAP percentage.

a Conservative; of Ernst Thälmann, the Communist; of Adolf Gustav Winter, a minor figure; or, last but not least, of Adolf Hitler.

The southwestern area of the city gave above average support to Hitler in all districts with Steglitz again leading the list. Two of the mixed districts were now above average, and the other two were just below. Again the striking fact was the lack of distinctiveness in an area that one might expect to have had a very distinctive reaction. The working-class districts, with two exceptions this time (Spandau and Weissensee), were still below the average.

There was a runoff election in the presidential race. In the first presidential election, that just discussed, five candidates had presented themselves. In the runoff election a month later (April 10), the field was reduced to three, Hitler, Hindenburg, and Thälmann. The level of participation fell off somewhat, from 85.1 to 80.9 percent. Some of this abstention may have involved former Thälmann voters who thought his chances were rather small. Some evidence in support of this possibility may be seen in the absolute fall in Communist strength, Thälmann's Berlin vote going from 685,411 to 573,099. This suggests, incidentally, that a part of the Communist vote was not as committed or as disciplined as some commentators would have one believe.[12]

A significant lesson may be learned through examination of the Duesterberg vote. What does a Conservative voter do when his first-choice candidate is removed from the race? If Kornhauser and Lipset are correct, these traditionalists should have supported a nonextreme candidate with the obvious choice being Hindenburg. Unlike 1925, in his first campaign for office, this time he was the candidate of the democratic parties. Given his very obvious roots in the Prussian conservative tradition, he would be the best, the most appropriate candidate for the traditionalists' purposes. Almost all of that Conservative support, however, went to an extremist candidate, to Adolf Hitler. In all seven upper- and upper-middle-class districts the support for Duesterberg in the first round had been above the city average. In the second round, Hitler's vote was only slightly below the combined Hitler-Duesterberg vote of the first. In Steglitz, for example, one finds 35.2 percent voting for Hitler and 12.3 percent for Duesterberg in the first round. And that combined total, 47.5 percent, is only a little higher than the Hitler second-round vote of 46.2 percent. Hindenburg's percentage by comparison increased from 42.6 to 45.7. Put somewhat differently, Hitler gained 12,252 votes in the course of the month as opposed to only 1,580 gained by Hindenburg. These Conservative voters, it would seem, did not vote "responsibly." In this instance they had come out strongly in favor of a very extreme candidate.

One other observation is in order here. That Conservative tendency in the second round was not restricted to the upper- and upper-middle-class areas. Some Conservative vote appeared in all sections of the city. In Zehlendorf, 14.7 percent of the voters favored Duesterberg. In Wedding, he received 5.2 percent. In both areas the Duesterberg vote appears to have gone to Hitler in the second election.

There were five major elections in 1932. First came the two presidential elections, those of March 13 and April 10, and then, two weeks later on April 24, an election for the Prussian Landtag (legislature). This election showed that the National Socialists had made substantial gains since March, their Berlin total, 765,909 votes, being nearly 100,000 greater than in the first of the presidential elections. The pattern of support by district in the Prussian state election was approximately the same as in all the elections reviewed above. The National Socialists were again strongest in the upper-middle-class districts. Their support was average in the mixed districts. And it was below average in the working-class districts.

The election of July 31, 1932, was the decisive one for National Socialist fortunes. It was the point of peak strength prior to taking power, the strength that gave the party immense bargaining power in negotiating for the chancellorship. And here again all middle-class districts provided Hitler's party with support that was well above the city average. Steglitz, again the leader, was 47 percent above the city average. And upper-class Zehlendorf was 27 percent above the average. The mixed districts, where the National Socialists might have been thought to be strongest, were again not distinctive. Three of them were above average, but again the variance is rather small. In the working-class districts one again finds Spandau and Weissensee to be above average, the former being well above and the latter only slightly so. The pattern in the November election, apart from the general falloff in the NSDAP vote, closely matches that of the July election.

A comparison of the April Landtag (state) election with the July Reichstag election reveals a little noticed fact about this key election. Although participation was up slightly, 81.6 percent versus 80.5 percent, the number of valid votes cast was *down* by over 100,000. The explanation for this seeming paradox lies in the date of the election, July 31, one that found many people on vacation—even in the midst of the economic crisis. The official participation figure was calculated after making allowance for the votes of travelers. It excludes from consideration those Berliners who cast their votes elsewhere and includes non-residents who cast votes in the city.

The peculiarities of this July election may be seen by comparing it with the 1930 election (in September) and the second election of 1932 (in November). A person expecting to be away at the time of the election could request a ballot (*Stimmschein*) which could be deposited wherever he or she happened to be on the day of the election. The Berlin election statistics include a statement of such ballot forms given out and those taken in. The figures for the three elections appear in Table 4.4.

It will be noted that nearly 10 percent of Berlin's eligible voters intended to cast their ballots somewhere outside of their home precinct in that key election. They could have been cast somewhere else within the city, but in most cases they would probably have been deposited elsewhere in the Reich. There is good reason to assume that the vacationers of 1932 were upper or upper middle class. That being the case, the portion of those classes escaping our attention in these Berlin figures must be considerably larger than 10 percent, possibly being more than double that figure. To appreciate their voting patterns it is necessary to examine the voting elsewhere, in the German resort areas. This is undertaken in Chapter 9.[13]

In absolute numbers, the Berlin vote for the National Socialists in the July election was below their figure in the April state election. Looking at the detailed results one finds that the National Socialist vote in July was down in every middle-class district except Tempelhof. The party's vote was up in all the mixed districts, while the working-class districts were mixed: four were up, and five were down. On first sight it might appear that the upper and upper middle classes had begun to come to their senses and were moving away from the NSDAP while the masses were still moving toward the party. As we shall see later, that appears to be a doubtful hypothesis.

The increase in Tempelhof and in other mixed districts might be taken as an indication that the strains and stresses felt by the middle class were finally having their predicted effect. But other information makes that hypothesis appear questionable. The increase in Tempelhof amounted to only 61 votes out of some 68,000. The greatest proportional increase came in Köpenick where the number of National Socialist votes increased from 18,124 to 21,044. This result, however, is confounded by

TABLE 4.4. PARTICIPATION FIGURES FOR BERLIN IN THREE REICHSTAG ELECTIONS

	Election		
	September 1930	July 1932	November 1932
Eligible voters	3,402,673	3,445,936	3,461,229
Ballots given out prior to election	107,345	303,999	77,506
Ballots received from travelers	50,195	110,264	63,115
Valid votes	2,709,257	2,641,497	2,775,221
Participation	81.4%	81.6%	81.0%

SOURCE: *Statistisches Jahrbuch der Stadt Berlin*, editions for indicated years.

the presence of large numbers of vacationers. Köpenick, located at the extreme southeast of Greater Berlin, has many parks, lakes, and streams, thus providing something of a vacation area within the city. It was the only city area that received more ballots than were given out under this arrangement, the respective figures being 15,123 and 3,414. Those 15,123 ballots of the district's visitors, if significantly different from the local population, could have had a fair-sized impact since the total number of valid votes cast there amounted to 69,019. Over a fifth of that district's ballots, presumably, were cast by outsiders. Something similar appears to have occurred in the other mixed districts although, to be sure, not to the same extent.

It is worthwhile examining these results in more detail. From the point of the breakthrough in September 1930, the strongest support for the National Socialists was found in Steglitz, a district that *on the whole* might be best characterized as having a well-off population. In the July 1932 election, the second highest level of support appeared in an even more affluent district, Zehlendorf, and that was followed by Schöneberg in third place and first-ranked Wilmersdorf in fourth place. The crucial point to be noted about this result is the linkage of National Socialist strength with well-off districts, with districts that might best be described as, again on the whole, *upper* middle class.

In contrast, the districts that would have had a lower-middle-class predominance are all relatively undistinguished in their support for the NSDAP. Tempelhof ranks seventh among the twenty districts. The mixed districts, where strong support for the NSDAP might be anticipated, approximated the city-wide average. The Mitte, which had a relatively high petty bourgeois component, especially for a working-class district (see Table 4.1), has a National Socialist percentage that was close to the city-wide average.

Except for Spandau (which in July 1932 was well above the city average) and Weissensee (which was slightly above), all of the working-class districts showed some degree of aversion to Hitler's party. The poorest districts, those most likely to have contained the so-called lumpenproletarian elements, Wedding and Friedrichshain, gave the party the least support of all.

The main finding indicated here is a pronounced tendency for the National Socialist vote to vary directly with class level. It was lowest in the solid working-class districts. It did increase, relatively, in the areas most likely to have contained a status-conscious middle class. But NSDAP support increased once again in the better-off or upper-middle-class districts.

This finding can be expressed in a summary way with correlation coefficients. The rank order correlation between the districts as ranked in Table 4.3 and the ranking by National Socialist support in July 1932 was .81. The Pearsonian correlation between the percentage of non-manual workers in the districts and the percentage supporting the National Socialists was .85. Those results indicate a very close correspondence between the two factors.

The correlations for the entire period are presented in the accompanying table.

Correlations	May 1924	Dec. 1924	May 1928	Sept. 1930	March 1932	July 1932	Nov. 1932
Spearman r (between districts as ranked in Table 4.3 and rank order of NSDAP support, N = 20)	.69	.63	.64	.81	.82	.81	.68
Pearson r (between percentage non-manual and percentage for NSDAP, N = 20)	.67	.63	.66	.83	.85	.85	.74

It will be noted that the relationship between the class level of the district and NSDAP support was strong from the very beginning. It became considerably more pronounced in September of 1930 and remained high in the July 1932 election. There was some resurgence of "leftism" within the party prior to the November election, and that, apparently, stimulated some upper-middle-class disaffection thus weakening the correlations somewhat but still leaving them strongly positive. These results, it will be noted, go sharply against the received tradition.

The findings reported thus far could be misleading since all the administrative districts under consideration are large and have some mix in the composition of the population. A more detailed examination of some of these districts was possible. The first to be considered is Wilmersdorf. The Wilmersdorf district (*Bezirk*) contained the elegant *Villenviertel* Grunewald. It also contained a smaller better-off community, Schmargendorf, and the larger, older, and more heterogeneous former town of Wilmersdorf. The last contained apartment houses of the Charlottenburg variety. One might easily conclude that the educated and responsible upper-class population of Grunewald would have avoided the National Socialists and would have tended to remain with its traditional parties and that the more heterogeneous Wilmersdorf must have provided the votes for the National Socialists.

Detailed figures for the three communities of the Wilmersdorf district did prove to be available in a local weekly newspaper, the *Grunewald-*

Echo.[14] The NSDAP percentages for the July 1932 election were Wilmersdorf, 35.3; Schmargendorf, 35.5; and Grunewald, 32.7. There is, to be sure, a difference in the anticipated direction, but the variation is only a matter of a few percentage points.

The *Grunewald-Echo* also contained figures for another *Villenviertel*, upper-class Dahlem in the neighboring Zehlendorf district. In Dahlem too the National Socialist strength was considerable, 33.6 percent, only three percentage points below the figure for the district as a whole.

Steglitz, the scene of the NSDAP's greatest success, was also heterogeneous, and again one might assume that the NSDAP support came from its lower-middle-class sections. The district contains the former city of that name, a mixed community with more than half of the district's population. It also contains Lichterfelde, a community that might easily be described as upper middle class. Like Grunewald and Dahlem, it too had a predominance of single-family dwelling units. There was also a tiny subcommunity of some 5,000 persons called Südende. Judging by the housing and by the occupations given in a local address book, this too was a very well-off community. And finally, there was a medium-sized community, Lankwitz, which is perhaps best described as average middle class. The NSDAP percentages as of July 1932 in these subareas of the Steglitz district were as follows: Steglitz, 44.3; Lichterfelde, 39.5; Südende, 41.4; and Lankwitz, 38.8.[15] It is clear that there is little systematic differentiation between the subareas.

The fact that the very best-off areas, Grunewald, Dahlem, and Lichterfelde, gave slightly less support to the NSDAP than did the next best areas would suggest that the Berlin upper classes, by a small margin, were less enchanted by Hitler and his party than were the city's upper middle classes. Even here, as will be seen immediately, there is some ground for doubt.

The results considered thus far are given without any correction or adjustment. In some cases, it will be noted, the "research procedure" consists of reporting the results found in local newspapers. Some reconsideration or adjustment of those results is useful, however, since it allows a more detailed picture of what was happening within upper- and upper-middle-class circles.

It is reasonable to assume that no Jewish voters would be supporting the National Socialists. It therefore makes sense to recalculate the results for the Berlin districts since the Jewish percentages vary significantly from a low of 0.5 percent in Spandau to a high of 13.5 percent in Wilmersdorf. Zehlendorf, with 3.5 percent, is below the city-wide average (3.8 percent in 1933) as is also Steglitz (1.6 percent). If one assumes that 13.5 percent of the Wilmersdorf vote was cast by Jewish voters, one can subtract that portion from the total and recalculate the percentages, assuming, in short, that all of the NSDAP vote came from non-Jewish voters. In the case of Wilmersdorf this yields a figure of 40.6 percent for the NSDAP in July 1932 (as compared to the original 35.1 figure). It also shifts the rank order giving Wilmersdorf now the second highest NSDAP percentage (after a corrected figure of 42.8 for Steglitz). This procedure also increases the original correlation slightly, the rank order correlation for the July 1932 election now being .84.

This adjustment does little to alter the rankings of districts or sub-communities. The basic effect, of course, is that the figures are increased in all districts, those with relatively large Jewish populations obviously showing the largest increases. In Grunewald, for example, with an 11.5 percent Jewish minority, the NSDAP percentage goes from 32.7 to 37.5. The adjustment tells us something about the extent of Hitler's support within the non-Jewish population of these upper- and upper-middle-class communities. In the Wilmersdorf district, two out of five persons in the population were supporting Hitler. In Grunewald, it was three out of eight, a figure equal to the national average at that point.

A still more detailed specification of the initial results proves useful. One does not ordinarily anticipate Socialist, let alone Communist, voting in upper- or upper-middle-class communities. Yet in both Wilmersdorf and Zehlendorf, a significant minority of the vote went to the left, 35.6 percent in the former case and 29.7 percent in the latter. It seems reasonable to assume that much of that vote would have come from the workers living in those districts although, as Table 4.1 indicates, they could not, even with 100 percent left voting, provide all of that Social Democratic and Communist support.

For this more detailed specification, it will help to make some assumptions. These are that (1) no Jewish voter supported the National Socialists; (2) all Zentrum voters were Catholics; and (3) two-thirds of the combined Socialist-Communist vote came from the working-class population. In addition to these judgments about the voting tendencies, one may make some assumptions about the social location of the Jews and Catholics in these districts. These are: (4) all Jews are in nonmanual occupations; and (5) Catholics are distributed randomly by class.

As formulated, these assumptions are obviously untrue. It would be rare, for example, for *all* Zentrum voters, every last one of them, to be Catholic.[16] But as approximations reflecting what information we have on the social and political landscape of the era, they are as realistic as one can hope for. Some of these assumptions introduce a bias that increases the NSDAP estimates, but some work in the opposite direction. In any event, the procedure is intended to serve a heuristic purpose, that is, to provoke thought on a subject rather than be a dogmatic statement of how things were.

Zentrum Voters	Jewish Voters	A		Nonmanual
	Two-thirds of the Socialist or Communist voters		B	Manual

One may summarize the implications of these assumptions, with the accompanying diagram. The only segments from which National Socialist votes could have come are those labeled A and B.

In the July election of 1932 there were 114,173 valid votes cast in the Wilmersdorf district. Working with the initial assumptions those votes would be distributed as follows: 15,413 would be Jewish voters, 9,256 would be Zentrum voters, and 20,491 would represent working-class left votes (or two-thirds of the SPD-KPD total). This gives a subtotal of 45,160, which means segments A and B thus equal 69,013. Given the initial assumptions, all of the 40,086 NSDAP votes would have come from these segments A and B.[17] Seen as a percentage of segments A and B combined, one would have an NSDAP figure of 58 percent.

Even this probably underestimates the support for the National Socialists in the traditional upper and upper middle classes since it leaves the remaining one-third of the left votes unaccounted for. They would come from the Jewish voters and from Segment A. (By definition, Segment B contains the voters of parties *other* than the left and the Zentrum.) If one assumes some variation within Segment A, with left voting diminishing as one moves from the lower middle class upward in the social structure, then the NSDAP percentage for the higher-status populations of the district would probably have been even higher than the 58 percent indicated above.

Working with the same assumptions, one arrives at equivalent figures for the Zehlendorf and Steglitz districts of 52 and 58 percent. In the upper-class communities of Grunewald and Dahlem, the respective figures are 58 and 55 percent. As indicated, because of the left support in the lower-middle-class ranks, it seems likely that the percentages would be somewhat higher in the upper and upper middle classes. This would mean that at least three out of five of the Protestant voters (together with a small number of Catholic voters) in those ranks were supporting the National Socialists. This portrait of traditional upper- and upper-middle-class propensities is sharply at variance with the representations offered in much of the scholarly literature.

THE ARGUMENT BY STIPULATION RECONSIDERED

The most persuasive argument regarding the lower-middle-class attraction to National Socialism, as was noted in Chapter 2, is the indirect one. This argument assumes a specific class base to the parties that all but disappeared in the course of the years 1928 to 1932. Possibly the most widely disseminated statement of this position is Lipset's: "As the Nazis grew, the liberal bourgeois center parties, based on the less traditionalist elements of German society—primarily small business and white-collar workers—completely collapsed. . . . An inspection of the shifts among the non-Marxist and non-Catholic parties suggests that the Nazis gained most heavily among the liberal middle-class parties."[18] The validity of this argument depends on the adequacy of the initial stipulation, on the assumption of a close linkage between the middle-class parties and the middle-class electorate. That assumption, as far as Berlin is concerned, is subject to considerable question.

The second election of 1924 provides as good a base point as any for purposes of this discussion. As noted previously, conditions had returned to as close to normal as was ever to be achieved in Weimar. It is useful to examine the location of the support for those parties at that point and then to explore the subsequent decline.

In Chapter 3 it was noted that one can analyze election results in different ways, depending on the question being asked. To this point we have been considering the question: what percentage of a given class supported the National Socialists? Now we turn to the other kind of question: what percentage of support for a party came from a given class? It is the latter question that one has in mind when referring to a "middle class" party, as in the typical formulation of the argument by stipulation. The assumption is that a substantial majority of the party's vote comes from a middle-class constituency. The implication in this context is that the decline of such a party can have only one meaning, that the middle-class clientele had shifted its loyalty elsewhere, in this case, obviously, to the National Socialists.

Some recalculations of the Berlin election figures show that in the December election of 1924 the Conservatives, who are sometimes seen as the traditional upper-class party, gained nearly half (49.1 percent) of their votes from the working-class districts of Berlin. And the same held for the middle-class Democrats, their percentage in working-class districts being only a fraction lower, 48.4, than the DNVP's. The right liberal German People's party had a smaller base in the working-class districts, but even here it was a substantial 42.0 percent. And over half of the Zentrum votes, 56.0 percent, came from the working-class districts. Only the German People's party received more votes from the middle-class districts of southwest Berlin than it received from the working-class areas of the city. The rather unexpected conclusion, then, is that the so-called middle-class parties appear to have possessed substantial working-class support. Without that working-class support these middle-class parties would already have been splinter parties by 1924.[19]

It would be easy to claim, but difficult to establish except by assertion, that this support came from the middle-class populations in the working-class districts. Another hypothesis—that there was no sharp differentiation between the middle-class and working-class voting patterns in those districts—is equally plausible. If one raises the question as to where Berlin's working class came from, the answer is that it came from the surrounding countryside which was heavily Conservative (*Deutschnationale*) or, before the war, *Deutschkonservative*. It seems likely that migrants brought much of that orientation with them into the working-class districts. Many workers too, before socialism achieved its dominant status, had supported the liberal parties, in particular the left, or social, or civil libertarian liberals. It seems likely that the working-class supporters of these parties in the 1920s would be in the older age categories. Their children, many of them, would be supporting the Socialists or Communists. All of this, to be sure, must remain in the realm of speculation. At this late date, it would be difficult to establish that the division in the working-class districts was along class lines or alternatively, along lines of background and age. The latter *seems* plausible in the light of both historical studies of the transformations of the parties in the nineteenth century and survey data derived from the later experience of the Federal Republic and elsewhere.[20]

In the light of this discussion of the social bases of the middle-class parties, one may turn now to the question of the relative losses. If the claim of lower-middle-class susceptibilities were accurate one should find the greatest losses in the mixed districts. As it happens, however, the losses suffered by both liberal parties and by the Conservatives through to July 1932 were *smallest* in those districts, and the gains of the Center were greatest. It would appear as if the "less traditionalist elements" of German society mentioned by Lipset were most prone to maintain their traditional direction, or, in the case of the Zentrum, to reestablish what might have been a previously held tradition.

The losses suffered by the middle-class parties were *greatest* in the working-class districts. The differences between the three sectors, to be sure, were rather small since the losses were substantial everywhere.[21] The dynamics of the change, nevertheless, were quite different from those suggested in the literature. The losses by the middle-class parties were disproportionately in *working-class* districts. Two of the three parties in question appear to have lost almost all their working-class support between 1924 and 1932, while the DNVP lost "only" two-thirds of its initial support. In 1928, the losses went to the parties of the left. It was only later, in 1930 and 1932, that the losses went heavily to the NSDAP.

One implication of this finding will be immediately obvious: the decline of the so-called middle-class parties has implications for working-class as well as for middle-class voters. More specifically, it tells us that a large part of the National Socialist vote in Berlin came from Germany's equivalent of the Tory workers. It came from those who, whether simply for reasons of family tradition, or because of belief in liberal, nationalist, or conservative principles, had avoided the parties of the left. Those voters represented only a minority in the working-class districts. But, since those districts were so populous, those minorities added up, as we have seen, to form close to half of the support for the parties in question. With the shift to the National Socialists, as of July 1932, the same was true of their support. Almost half, 48.4 percent, of the NSDAP vote in Berlin at that time came from the nine working-class districts of the city.

As a note of incidental intelligence, one might consider two events that intervened between the July and November elections of 1932. The first involved the killing of a Communist in the Silesian town of Potempa, an act of more than usual brutality on the part of the Sturmabteilung, the victim being kicked and trampled to death. Convicted of murder, five SA members were sentenced to death. True to his previous practice, Hitler came out with a defense of the murderers and condemned the injustice of the state that would deal out such a punishment. Some commentators have argued that this public position cost him votes. Presumably, given the claims of upper- and upper-middle-class responsibility and of the authoritarianism of most others in the society, the rate of defection ought to show a clear increase as one moves up in the class hierarchy.

A second event involved National Socialist support of a Berlin transport workers' strike. It was thought that this resurgence of "left" National Socialism would gain the party some working-class votes, but cost it votes elsewhere in the society.

Comparing the results of the two Reichstag elections of 1932, one finds that the NSDAP lost in all of the Berlin districts. Because of the vacationers, however, that comparison is not the most appropriate one. A better possibility is to compare the November result with the performance in the Landtag election of April. Making this comparison one does find that the NSDAP losses were most severe in the upper- and upper-middle-class areas. National Socialist losses were modest in the mixed districts and middling in the working-class districts. This last result hides a lot of variation. There was a slight increase in Weissensee and Lichtenberg. Spandau and Neukölln were more or less constant. In all other working-class districts the party suffered losses, the most serious being in Kreuzberg, the largest of the Berlin districts.

The support of the strikers does not appear to have gained the National Socialists any significant numbers of working-class voters although it might possibly have reduced their losses. Whether the losses in the upper and upper middle classes resulted from revulsion against the SA violence or from dislike of the National Socialist support for the strikers is a question that may never be satisfactorily answered. It is impossible, in other words, to say what the underlying motives of those defectors were. In any event it should be noted that the changes being discussed were all very small ones. The overall support for the National Socialists in Berlin was 27.9 percent in April of 1932 and 26.0 percent in November. The SA violence and the defense of that violence were not sufficient to move the three persons in ten in the upper- and upper-middle-class districts who were still supporting them.[22]

SOME CONCLUSIONS

What can one say by way of conclusion? First, the highest levels of support for the National Socialists in Berlin came from the upper- and upper-middle-class districts. At their peak, in the first election of 1932, their best performances came in Steglitz (42.1 percent), Zehlendorf (36.4 percent), Schöneberg (35.7 percent) and Wilmersdorf (35.1 percent). These figures probably underrepresent the extent to which the traditional Prussian upper and upper middle classes offered support to the NSDAP. Estimates taking account of the workers, the Zentrum supporters, and the Jews in these districts suggest that the National Socialist support among those remaining probably exceeded 60 percent.

Second, the closest approximation one can make to the lower middle class is in the mixed districts, those that contained a significant portion of manual workers. The voting patterns in those districts are not especially distinctive. Contrary to the frequently asserted claims, these districts had levels of National Socialist voting that were more or less equal to the city-wide average. Had the lower middle class played the decisive role so often attributed to it, the level of support there should instead have been well above the city average. The populations in these locations, moreover, were latecomers to the new faith, unlike the upper-middle-class districts where National Socialist support was above average from 1924 on. Even in the late elections the level of NSDAP support in the mixed districts was about the average for the city. Looking elsewhere—at Tempelhof or the Mitte, districts that may have had large lower-middle-class concentrations—one again finds a lack of distinctiveness. Tempelhof ran at about the city average from 1924 to 1928 and eventually went somewhat above the average. The Mitte, with two minor exceptions, was persistently below the average.

Third, the working-class districts provided strong support for the parties of the left throughout the period in question. There was, however, a fair-sized minority in those districts who had originally supported the Conservatives or one of the liberal parties. The losses suffered by these parties in the working-class areas were considerable, the highest in the city. Their voters, some of them, turned to the left in 1928, the rest going to the NSDAP in 1930 and 1932. With two exceptions these districts gave less than average support to the NSDAP. At the same time, it should be noted, support for the National Socialists was not minuscule in those districts. It ran between a fifth and a quarter of the total. Put another way, almost half of Berlin's NSDAP vote came from the nine working-class districts of the city.

The fourth conclusion involves the dynamics of change. There has been a strong focus in the literature on the losses of the middle-class parties with the clear suggestion that these were middle-class losses—hence the claim about the middle-class susceptibilities. But the evidence presented here indicates that all these parties originally had significant support in working-class districts and that their losses were greatest in those areas of the city. Their losses, by comparison, were smallest in the mixed districts, those most likely to have contained populations with the anxieties usually attributed to the lower middle class.[23]

There is still another question to be considered: why did the various groups react as they did? Specifically, what accounts for the peculiar propensity of the Berlin upper and upper middle classes? Some suggestions may be considered immediately. A more comprehensive discussion of the motives of urban voters is found in Chapter 13.

THE QUESTION OF LINKAGES

Where did the voters of the Weimar period get their information about the National Socialists? How did they, especially in the 1924 beginnings, form an image of the party upon which to base a judgment, either for or against?

The answer to these questions, especially for the beginning period, appears to be a rather simple one: through the newspapers. Hitler first gained national renown when he and his associates attempted a *Putsch* in Munich on November 9, 1923. Among his associates were the former leader of the German armies, General Erich Ludendorff, and one Hermann Goering, who at this time was best known as a much-decorated fighter pilot, the one-time head of the Richthofen squadron. The event itself brought Hitler to national attention. The presence of these associates probably gave him some legitimacy, at least in nationalist circles, that he would not have gained otherwise.

In late February 1924, Hitler, Ludendorff, and a number of others were brought to trial. Reporters from the major German newspapers and from the international press were present to cover the trial. Hitler used the occasion to advertise his undertaking. His defense consisted of an attack: "I alone bear the responsibility. But I am not a criminal because of that. If today I stand here as a revolutionary, it is as a revolutionary against the Revolution. There is no such thing as high treason against the traitors of 1918." He was in a good position to make an attack because the leaders of the Bavarian government (who were bringing the charges against him) were also implicated in plotting against the republic and because the judges, chosen by the minister of justice, a friend and protector of Hitler, allowed the speeches and could be expected to be lenient in sentencing.[24] Sentence was rendered on the first of April; the May election campaign was already in progress.

Since the distant trial could not be appreciated directly by the voters of Dahlem or Grunewald, it is instructive to examine the press handling of the outcome and its comments on Hitler's party. One of the city's leading newspapers was the eminently liberal (*left* liberal, German Democratic) newspaper, the *Vossische Zeitung*. Its front-page headlines on the first of April read: "Ludendorff Acquitted"; " 'Probationary Term' for Hitler, Poehner, and Comrades"; "Ludendorff Ridicules the Court"; "Police against Mass Meetings"; "Demonstration March of Hitler's People." In the following weeks the *Vossische* carried dozens of items linking Hitler and Ludendorff to the Deutschvölkische party. The newspaper also carried stories reporting on the ideological character of the party, making clear what it stood for. These included accounts of its anti-Semitic orientation. An entire first-page column was given to this theme under the headlines: "*Deutschvölkische Heidentum*" (German People's Paganism) and "*Das Neue Testament ein Judenbuch*" (The New Testament a Jewish Book). Another account quoted a Völkische party leader who stressed that the party's program called for the removal of Jews from all public office. There were reports of street fighting and, shortly before the election, of a murder that was said to be the work of the party's activists. One Hitler follower was quoted as follows: "We do not want peace for the German people, but turmoil!"[25]

Conservative papers reported things somewhat differently. In the arch-conservative *Neue Preussische Zeitung*, otherwise known as the *Kreuz-zeitung*, the attitude toward Hitler and the Deutschvölkische party was clearly rather friendly. This was already evident in its comment on the court decision of April 1: "The judgment against Hitler [and the others] is hard."[26] On the second of April it reported in great detail on the national meeting of the Conservative party, at which one of the speakers had kind, almost fatherly, words to say about "the *völkische* movement." This speaker, however, was concerned that nationalist youth would be led astray and the forces of the right split.

An editorial on the third of April was very positive in its comments about the Deutschvölkische party. It reviewed the party's program beginning with its opposition to the Treaty of Versailles and touched also on its effort to make Germany "free from unfruitful parliamentarianism, free from the domination of international Jewry and finance capital, free from every exploitation of labor, free from Marxism and bolshevism."

The editorial comment is sympathetic but also notes by way of objection, that the party "is too much oriented to fighting." The writer feared that "a fragmentation of the national will" might result from its effort. A final comment in this editorial is worth noting. Comparing the positions of the Conservatives and the Deutschvölkische party, the editorial observes that "aside from specifics that might exist in the not yet discussed social question, we cannot find any fundamental difference in outlooks."

The *Kreuzzeitung* also noted the acts of violence that occurred in the course of the election. Unlike the *Vossische Zeitung*, however, its focus was on violence directed against the Conservatives and the Deutschvölkische party.

One final point about the content of this newspaper deserves mention. In a highly editorialized discussion of the election result, it was suggested that the gain by the Democrats of a few thousand votes in Berlin might have been a result of the "East Jewish immigration in the last years." Speaking of the competition, of publishers Wolff, Mosse, and Ullstein, the *Kreuzzeitung* referred to them collectively as "the Jewish democratic press." Elsewhere it spoke of "Jewish capital."[27]

Another conservative newspaper of some prominence was the *Berliner Börsen-Zeitung*, the stock exchange newspaper. Its comment on the sentencing was simple. It did not want to see Hitler and his associates "behind fortress walls" but rather, "just like Ludendorff, in freedom."[28] At a much later point, in 1932, Goebbels noted in his diary that the party received consistently favorable treatment from this newspaper. The operations of the *Börsen-Zeitung* would have been no secret or surprise to him. Its business editor, Walther Funk, gave up that position in 1931 and joined the National Socialists to work for them as a contact man with business and industrial interests.[29]

This same sympathy for Hitler and the NSDAP was also evident in Berlin's conservative press in the period 1929-1933. The approval was generally tempered with some concern over program and direction, and there was a continuous demand for clarification of the party's position. A brief review of the content of these newspapers is useful.[30]

The *Deutsche Allgemeine Zeitung (DAZ)* had had links with the National Liberals prior to the war, and, for much of the postwar period, it was generally favorable to the DVP. For a while the *DAZ* was secretly owned by the government and served as an outlet for Stresemann, Germany's foreign minister from 1924 to 1929. But Social Democratic opposition forced its sale, the journal then being picked up by a consortium of businessmen. (This history is discussed in more detail in Chapter 13.) Its May Day issue in 1930 contained a positive report on Mussolini's Italy, under the headline "What Can Europe Expect from Fascism?"

Prior to the September election, the *DAZ* expressed concern about the NSDAP position. Noting that the "sound of the drum is not pure," it demanded clarification of such issues as what the NSDAP meant by "socialism" and what it meant by a "legal revolution." The newspaper rejected the party's expansionist notions, its demand for *Lebensraum*. After the election, it argued the need to "direct the people's movement in reasonable channels." A later commentary, summed up the many pluses and minuses of the party, and concluded, as one of the pluses, that "no one in public affairs fights the Communist overthrow attempts in the same manner as the NSDAP."

In 1931, the newspaper continued its sympathetic but concerned reporting and comment. Pfeifer, the source of this review, characterizes the newspaper's attitude as showing the "well-meaning watchfulness of an older brother." In 1932, the attitude was still generally approving, but the paper specifically recommended Hitler for some lesser position, not for the chancellorship. In the presidential election that year it could see Hitler as a minister but not as a president. A headline reproved the party: "Not Sole Domination [*Alleinherrschaft*], but Cooperative Effort." The only sensible solution it saw was to "bind the movement to the state." This thrust, which is discussed in more detail in later chapters, was based on the notion that Hitler and the party could be "tamed" by allowing him to share power. Accordingly, after the Prussian state election, the newspaper advocated replacing the SPD-Zentrum coalition with an NSDAP-Zentrum coalition.

It is of special significance that this newspaper, which in early 1932 was in the hands of the business consortium and in mid-year came into the possession of Hugo Stinnes, Jr., should welcome the government of Franz von Papen. While many Marxist writers see business as favoring Hitler, the striking thing about the editorial position of much of the conservative press, in Berlin and elsewhere, was its enthusiasm for Papen, this in the middle of 1932. The newspaper's solution to the political crisis at that point was to strengthen the DNVP and to include the NSDAP, in a subordinate position obviously, in the Papen government. The accounts of this period, it should be noted, were embellished with references to the KPD-NSDAP street fights, with the National Socialists being portrayed as valiant defenders against Communist outrages.

Later in the year, the *DAZ* found cause for concern in Hitler's defense of the Sturmabteilung defendants in the Potempa case. His reaction, which on the one hand they found understandable, was on the other "so strong" as to be "hardly useful." The increased use of "socialist" themes in the November election also caused them "regret" and "concern."

In mid-November 1932, however, the newspaper conceded: "We are not National Socialists and much that a Hitler-led government might plan fills us with the deepest concern. But we see no other solution now than to charge Hitler with the solution of the crisis."[31]

The *Deutsche Tageszeitung*, a Conservative journal, was, of course, generally favorable to the DNVP. Oriented, in part at least, toward farmers, it appears to have had some audience outside of Berlin. In national politics of the period, the newspaper was favorable to Brüning and later to Papen. It was bothered by the vagueness of the NSDAP program, especially with regard to agriculture, and wanted specification of concrete plans. It was opposed to the party's "socialism" and even referred to the National Socialists as National Marxists.

In 1932, it expressed its satisfaction with the election of Hindenburg. Like the *DAZ*, it favored a National Socialist-Zentrum coalition in Prussia and again the guiding notion appeared to be one of taming Hitler and creating a bourgeois government in Prussia.

It took a very strong stand against Hitler in the Potempa case. It was disappointed that none of the long-desired moderation had appeared; it also saw his statement as damaging the possibility of coalition with the Zentrum. Its recommendation in the November election was rather open; under the heading "Bolshevism or Germany?" it argued simply for a "national" vote. Unlike the *Deutsche Allgemeine Zeitung*, the *Tageszeitung* opposed the change of chancellor in January 1933, a change that meant the naming of Hitler.[32]

In the *Kreuzzeitung* one finds still another variant on the themes reviewed thus far. It too commented on the KPD-NSDAP street fighting, and it too portrayed the KPD as promoting those struggles and the NSDAP forces as reacting in self-defense. It faulted the Berlin police for its onesided actions vis-à-vis the NSDAP. Invariably, as the *Kreuzzeitung* saw it, the police excused the left.

The *Kreuzzeitung* picked up an important theme that was overlooked or played down by other conservative newspapers. From an early point it recognized that the NSDAP effort was detrimental to the DNVP. In a comment on the 1930 election, the paper argued that the NSDAP would be all right if it brought workers into the national ranks. If, however, it only captured middle-class voters, it made no sense.

It too pressed for clarification, for specification of program. It particularly wanted a statement of position on the monarchy, on the possibility of restoration. There was some difference of opinion indicated in the statements of prominent Conservative spokesmen. Elard von Oldenburg-Januschau, a leading figure in their ranks, expressed his uncertainty about the party, but, nevertheless, called for NSDAP participation in the government. The difficulties seen by others he found to be based on exaggerations.

The newspaper's disapproval and concern continued throughout 1931 and extended into 1932. It opposed Hitler's presidential candidacy objecting to, among other things, his "all or nothing" attitude, his attacks on the DNVP, and his lack of governmental experience. It opposed the NSDAP-Zentrum coalition in Prussia, feeling that Hitler was "not ready." After the July 1932 election, it favored NSDAP participation in the national government but did not favor Hitler as chancellor. When the possibility of coalition government broke down, it found fault with the NSDAP for not supporting the Papen government. The party was putting its own interests ahead of the requirements dictated by the national emergency.

The *Kreuzzeitung* disapproved of the NSDAP-KPD alignment in the Berlin transport workers' strike in November. At the same time it saw the need for the NSDAP in a possible armed defense of the Papen government. After the November election it published a summary article entitled "Why Hitler Cannot Become Chancellor." It expressed full appreciation for his national efforts but complained of his failure to appreciate the efforts of others. It opposed his demand for sole domination complaining of the NSDAP's "absolute onesidedness."

At this point an internal split threatened the NSDAP. Gregor Strasser, who is frequently described as leading the party's left wing, came into a confrontation with Hitler. Eventually he withdrew, giving up all his party offices. In this struggle the *Kreuzzeitung*, significantly, favored Strasser. (Strasser's role as the party's "left winger" is discussed more fully in Chapter 13.)

It was only on the day of Hitler's accession, January 30, 1933, that the *Kreuzzeitung* conceded, finding the result a "thoroughly positive" accomplishment. Papen, named as vice-chancellor, had served as a valuable mediator; in the process, by accepting coalition with the Conservatives, Hitler had given up his "all or nothing" demand.[33]

Der Tag was a property of the Hugenberg concern. Alfred Hugenberg, an arch reactionary, the organizer of a massive press empire, was at this point also head of the DNVP. While much of his empire was aimed at a mass audience, *Der Tag* was a more respectable offering, one with a "good middle class" following.

In 1929, Hugenberg had organized the anti–Young Plan campaign against the plan that revised the schedule of reparations payments. Into this broad coalition of conservative forces, Hugenberg had brought Hitler and the NSDAP. It was, possibly, the party's most significant achievement since Hitler's trial in 1924, because it gave the National Socialists both attention and legitimacy. Not too surprisingly, the reports about the NSDAP appearing in *Der Tag* were very positive. The paper was especially enthusiastic about the NSDAP's fighting capacities and its readiness to counter the KPD provocations.

The newspaper welcomed the early electoral victories of the NSDAP, seeing them as "strengthening of the right front." It noted that this strengthening meant losses for the DNVP but, unlike the *Kreuzzeitung*, *Der Tag* expressed little concern. The National Socialist electoral success in Thuringia led to participation in that state's government, Wilhelm Frick becoming minister of the interior and thus gaining control of the police. This was greeted with sympathy and approval. The newspaper also indicated its approval of the results of the state election in Saxony, the only regret expressed being that only one-quarter of the NSDAP gains had come from the left parties, the rest coming from various bourgeois parties.

There were occasional modest hints of disapproval as, for example, in the 1930 election when the paper asked for clarification of the party's policies. Still, by the end of 1930, unlike other conservative journals, it had reached the conclusion that the party in fact was giving precedence to its national as opposed to its socialist emphasis.

In October of 1931, Hugenberg put together another national coalition, the Harzburg Front. It again included the NSDAP, and again *Der Tag* gave Hitler's party both attention and favor. A front-page account of October 11 listed Hitler first among the Front's members. The relations within the Harzburg Front coalition became severely strained in 1932. The presidential election, with both Hitler and a DNVP candidate competing, caused unavoidable conflict. Relations deteriorated in midyear and became even more problematic later on, in the course of the November election, when the NSDAP sharply attacked DNVP "plutocrats." *Der Tag* objected to this treatment by its supposed ally but did what it could to maintain good relations, apparently still having in mind the possibility of a rightist coalition government. It saw the November election, with its slight increase in DNVP support, as a victory. In January 1933, it approved the Hitler government with its strong DNVP representation. For the Enabling Law of March 1933, which granted Hitler dictatorial powers, it offered "unqualified approval."[34]

The preferences of the *Grunewald-Echo*, which served two of the richest communities of the city, Grunewald and Dahlem, are also of interest. Its issue of July 31, 1932, the day of the election, leaves little doubt as to the object of its affections. Pictures of National Socialist leaders and formations appeared on pages two and three. One headline read: "Disciplined and Unrestrained, Despite Hatred and Terror the SA Marches." Another read: "Everywhere National Socialist Mass Demonstrations." Its editorial was devoted to the subject of the NSDAP and unemployment.[35]

This limited review of those city newspapers most likely to have been read by citizens living in the "best" districts strongly suggests that the conservative press did much, unwittingly perhaps, to aid Hitler on the road to power. It gave him considerable publicity which, even when it came accompanied by reservations, can only be described as favorable. Whatever qualms the reader might have had, given the uncertainty of the NSDAP's positions on many key issues, may well have been assuaged by the sense of urgency about the situation which was stimulated, in part at least, by the same newspapers. Recognizing the imminent crisis, seeing "evidence" in the pages of these newspapers of the developing leftist threat, those readers would have felt alarmed, and the question of effectiveness would have become of ever greater importance. Put simply, that question was: who could effectively counter the Marxist threat? And since it became increasingly obvious that the traditional parties, being in disarray and, moreover, without any serious fighting forces, could not, those alarmed readers would have turned, in ever greater number, to the National Socialists. As the conservative press so amply testified, the NSDAP did have the fighting forces; it had repeatedly demonstrated its ability to counter the threat. As the economic crisis worsened and the sense of urgency felt by these voters increased, the shift became relatively easy—even if the National Socialists were not seen as entirely satisfactory allies.

The point has often been made that the National Socialists themselves had only a small press and that much of that press's readership would have been limited to the most devoted of the party faithful. This friendly support in the conservative press, however, probably did much, as the cliché has it, to prepare the ground.

One other point is worth noting, this being the asymmetry in the reporting of violence. The *Vossische Zeitung* emphasized National So-cialist attacks on liberal and left parties; the conservative press empha-sized Communist (or "Marxist") attacks on Conservatives and National Socialists. If readers read only one side, they would have had, one may assume, sharply differing views as to who was the instigator of the street fighting and who the innocent victim.

A second linkage between the party and the public would occur through the political efforts of the party, through circulars, parades, meetings, and the like. Goebbels's diaries report meetings throughout the city in 1932. There were meetings in Wedding and Friedrichshain and in Pan-kow and Reinickendorf. There were also meetings in the "better" areas—in Wilmersdorf, Schöneberg, and Zehlendorf. Given the stress on the lower-middle-class base of the party, one might not expect to find an *Ortsgruppe* (local group) in Grunewald, but there was one in that elegant community too. The National Socialist message, in great measure, was taken to the general public through this direct and personal medium. It did with cadres what other parties, particularly the liberal parties and the Conservatives, ordinarily accomplished with the printed word.

Some of the findings reported previously in this chapter may be ex-plained in terms of this organizational effort. Spandau, it was noted, gave consistently greater support to the National Socialists than other working-class areas. The various party histories point out that it had a better organization there than elsewhere. When Goebbels took over as Berlin *Gauleiter* in 1926, he scheduled the first mass meeting in Spandau to take advantage of the party's one special reservoir of strength. In his retrospective account he writes that "Spandau was at that time one of the first solid bases of the political organization and the SA. From here, the movement reached out, in an irresistible development, into Berlin itself.[36] The greater electoral support for the party in Spandau may have resulted from the activities of this larger and, possibly, more adept local organization rather than from some unique feature of the local social or occupational structure.

The accounts of National Socialist writers provide some sense of their basic strategy. Local groups were formed and meetings were held in all areas of the city. But singled out for special attention were the meetings held in the working-class centers of Berlin, such as Goebbels's first meeting in Spandau or, even more important, a meeting held shortly thereafter in the heart of working-class Wedding in a building the Com-munists viewed as "their" hall. Such meetings do not appear to have been intended for "meaningful communication" since they quickly turned into demonstrations of fighting capacity. Since, however, these strug-gles were then reported in the newspapers, this might have provided important indirect communication.[37] Many members of the Berlin bourgeoisie would have read of the SA's audacity and fighting ability. Conceivably, as their own parties declined in strength, they would have seen the National Socialists as providing a combination of party and army that they could adopt as a substitute. This possibility is discussed at greater length in Chapters 12 and 13.

What has been shown, so far, with supporting data, is an extraordinary and hitherto largely unsuspected attraction to the National Socialists on the part of the upper and upper middle classes of the capital city. The following step in the analysis, to explain *why* they were so attracted, must necessarily be much more tentative. It has been suggested that the conservative press played a role in vouching for and legitimating this party. The demonstration projects undertaken by the party in the working-class districts, in the heart of "red" Berlin, may also have had an effect in leading these affluent and supposedly responsible members of the community to support Hitler's party. This shift became easier for them when their own first-choice parties had been undermined. Even then, it will be noted, if one still held to the responsibility thesis, it would have been necessary for those persons to overlook or excuse a lot of ethical seaminess in the behavior of the party.

The motivations of the various segments of the electorate must have been quite diverse. The Grunewald bourgeoisie would have voted National Socialist for reasons quite different from those of the worker in Friedrichshain. And the motives of the cadres would have been quite different from those of the ordinary voter. One obvious question that must be considered is why the National Socialists had such large numbers of active and devoted party workers at their disposal. An attempt is made to deal with these questions too in Chapters 12 and 13.

CHAPTER FIVE

Hamburg

THE CITY AND ITS PEOPLE

In the twenties, Hamburg had a population of just over a million persons. This made it Germany's second largest city, well behind Berlin with its four million and somewhat ahead of Cologne, Munich, and Leipzig, the next largest cities of the nation.[1] Unlike Berlin, it had acquired most of its 1920 territory in previous centuries. Actually a city-state, its lands included a second city, Cuxhaven, downstream at the mouth of the Elbe, an island in the North Sea, Neuwark, and several other properties outside of the city proper. These acquisitions reflected the needs—and the power—of a leading commercial city, Hamburg having been the most important member of the Hansa League of the late Middle Ages. Cuxhaven was the site of a fortress for protection against marauders; Neuwark was the site of a lighthouse.

Hamburg conducted trade in two directions, upriver into the heart of central Europe and downriver to ports throughout the world. Its strategic location made it one of the largest port cities in the world.

The original city, now called the Altstadt (old city), was located east of the smallish Alster River at the confluence with the Elbe. In the fourteenth century, the Alster was dammed to form a small lake. In later years, the lake was divided by a roadway and bridge yielding the present lakes, the Inner Alster and the Outer Alster. In the course of the religious settlements of the sixteenth century, the church lands to the west and north of the Alster came to be properties of the city. The eighteenth, nineteenth, and early twentieth centuries saw the movement of population out from the old city into these areas.

The present analysis will be concerned with the populations of the city proper, not with those of the outlying territories. The only exception involves a few suburban communities containing some of the city's upper- and upper-middle-class population.

Most official statistics provide detailed census and election figures for the twenty-seven subareas of the city. There was a wide range in the size of these districts, going from the tiny community of Klein Borstel, with its 873 inhabitants, to Barmbeck, a giant working-class community, the scene of a Communist uprising in 1923, with its 150,590 inhabitants (1925 census figures). The districts in the massive port area

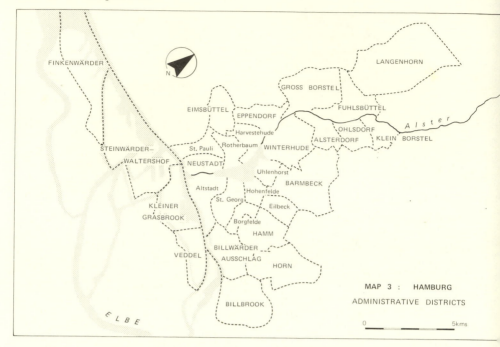

MAP 3 :   HAMBURG

ADMINISTRATIVE DISTRICTS

0   5kms

had relatively small populations, and some of them had rather unusual characteristics.

The geography of the city may be described as follows: the Altstadt, which was similar to the Mitte of Berlin, contained the major shops, the offices of the major firms (some shipping firms excepted), and the offices of government. Like the Mitte, it had a large working–class population. The districts immediately to the east and west of the Altstadt (St. Georg to the east, Neustadt to the west across the Alster, and further west the famous St. Pauli) also had large working–class populations. (See Map 3.)

Not too surprisingly, all of the areas along the Inner and Outer Alster were (and still are) very elegant ones. To the north of St. Georg, the streets immediately adjacent to the Alster in Hohenfelde, Uhlenhorst, Winterhude, and Alsterdorf all contained luxurious housing. Inland, however, the quality of the housing declined, the neighborhoods there being mixed middle class and upper working class. Behind the three last-named communities was Barmbeck, the largest working–class area of the city.

On the other side of the Alster, north of St. Pauli and Neustadt, were the "best" sections of the city. Moving north of those communities, one came first to very well off Rotherbaum and then to the best of them all, Harvestehude. Still further to the north was a middle-class area, Eppendorf, and then some thinly settled areas whose populations ranged from middle class to mixed (as that term was used in the previous chapter).

Some well-off communities were located beyond the city limits, further up the Alster or upstream along the Elbe. Downriver, beyond working-class Altona, which lies to the east of St. Pauli, one found the most affluent communities of the entire metropolitan area. There, on the bluffs overlooking the Elbe and looking across over Lower Saxony, one found Klein Flottbek and, the most elegant community of all, Blankenese.

METHODOLOGICAL CONSIDERATIONS

The same general procedure was used to classify the districts of Hamburg as was used for Berlin. That procedure, however, could not be reproduced exactly since precisely equivalent census results were not available. The present analysis will be based on the 1925 census (as opposed to the 1933 census used in Berlin) and will be based on the occupations of employed persons as opposed to "employed persons plus dependents" used for Berlin.[2]

Some districts have been combined so as to reduce the number of small or thinly populated ones. Three adjacent communities upstream along the Alster—Klein Borstel, Ohlsdorf, and Alsterdorf—have been combined. In terms of occupational composition and housing patterns they were very much alike. They were also similar in their levels of support for the National Socialists. In the following presentations they will be referred to as the Northeastern Districts.

The relatively small community of Gross Borstel (3,152 persons) to the west of the Alster has been combined with its larger neighbor Eppendorf (85,948). Again the two have similar occupational structures and housing characteristics.

Five districts in the harbor area have been combined in most of the following presentations and are listed simply as the Harbor Districts. In this case there are some significant variations in occupational patterns and political choices. For this reason, they are separated later in the chapter for a detailed examination.

The ordering procedure used here is also different from that used in Berlin. The districts have been arranged in terms of the working-class percentages, going from the lowest, in Harvestehude, to the highest, in Billwärder Ausschlag (Table 5.1). The only exception occurs with the Harbor Districts which, because of their unique characteristics, have been put at the end of the table. Harvestehude, it will be noted, does

TABLE 5.1. OCCUPATIONS OF EMPLOYED PERSONS BY DISTRICT: HAMBURG, 1925

District	Occupation				Total Population
	Independents, Managers, High Civil Servants	Other White-Collar Employees and Civil Servants	Working Class[a]	Domestic Servants	
Harvestehude	28.8%	28.6%	11.4%	29.2%	29,460
Rotherbaum	25.2	39.1	17.3	15.5	31,252
Hohenfelde	25.2	38.1	24.0	10.9	33,891
Fuhlsbüttel	13.9	51.9	26.7	6.1	8,884
Northeastern districts	17.1	39.7	29.5	10.7	5,538
Eilbeck	17.5	43.5	32.7	4.6	60,951
Eppendorf and Gross Borstel	17.1	38.5	35.9	6.7	89,100
Hamm	15.4	41.6	37.2	4.0	73,628
Borgfelde	14.9	37.4	42.7	3.2	33,960
Langenhorn	8.1	43.6	43.1	3.1	7,708
Eimsbüttel	15.0	36.0	44.3	2.6	129,664
Uhlenhorst	16.6	29.2	44.4	8.1	44,785
Winterhude	15.1	28.8	44.5	9.8	47,586
St. Georg	16.4	29.6	48.5	2.6	96,411
Altstadt	18.5	23.7	51.4	3.6	19,420
Barmbeck	11.5	32.4	52.6	1.5	150,590
Horn	11.7	28.5	54.7	2.7	9,258
Neustadt	16.5	21.1	56.8	2.9	65,136
St. Pauli	13.7	23.3	59.8	2.4	69,220
Billwärder Ausschlag	7.7	25.1	63.5	0.8	52,903
Harbor Districts	10.8	34.0	50.5	1.0	15,679
Hamburg	15.8	32.6	44.5	5.0	1,075,024

SOURCE: Statistisches Landesamt, *Statistik des Hamburgischen Staates*, pt. 33, "Die Volks-, Berufs- und Betriebszählung vom 16. Juni 1925," pt. 2: "Die Berufszählung." Hamburg: Otto Meissners Verlag, 1928.

NOTE: The percentages do not add to 100. The difference (2.1 percent) consists of "helping family members" (*Mithelfende Familienangehörige*).

[a] Includes some domestic servants who do not live in.

not have the highest percentage of nonmanual workers of all the districts. Because of the large number of domestic servants present, nearly three out of every ten employed persons, it would fall well down on the list were one to follow the Berlin procedure.

The order in Table 5.1 is consistent both with general assessments of the social standing of the districts and with other statistical measures. It puts Harvestehude first on the list of the twenty-one districts that result after the combinations. This community is generally conceded by local experts to have been the number-one area of the city. That standing is indicated also by the low percentage of blue-collar workers and the corresponding extremely high percentage of domestic servants. Harvestehude also had the largest average size of dwelling of the city's districts.[3] Harvestehude was closely followed by Rotherbaum which in all these respects occupied a clear number-two position. Large portions of the residents of these districts would best be described as upper class. In addition, no doubt, on the streets away from the Alster, there were also populations that would be better described as upper middle class (see the rough guideline definitions in note 19, Chapter 3).

Across the Outer Alster, just to the north of St. Georg, was the Hohenfelde district, which occupied a clear number-three position. It was third in its low working-class percentage, in its high domestic servant percentage, and in the high average size of its dwellings. This district was very solidly upper middle class in character.[4]

After Hohenfelde in the social hierarchy came Fuhlsbüttel, located in the northern part of the city to the west of the Alster. Then came the Northeastern Districts, across the river opposite Fuhlsbüttel. These areas were also upper middle class in character although clearly not quite so affluent as those previously discussed.

A very gradual increase in the working-class percentages occurs in the next eight districts listed in Table 5.1. There is, in other words, no sharp break such as would allow one to make categoric distinctions. One can only describe them, as in the Berlin case, as mixed. Although middle-class populations were dominant in those districts, there was also a significant working-class presence, ranging from 32.7 percent in Eilbeck to 44.5 percent in Winterhude.

Some additional comment is necessary in the case of Uhlenhorst and Winterhude. One might, because of their location in the rank order, count them as clear mixed cases, that is, as consisting of lower-middle-class populations and perhaps of the better-off workers. But these districts were also divided, much like Berlin's Tiergarten district. They both front onto the Outer Alster, and as noted above, all the river- and lake-front neighborhoods were elegant. The streets directly on the Alster and for one or two blocks inland contained upper and upper middle classes, a thin edge of very well-off populations. Beyond them, moving inland, one found the mixed areas where middle-middle- and lower-middle-class populations lived alongside working-class neighbors. That thin edge is indicated by the relatively high percentage of domestic servants in those two districts and also by the presence of some unexpectedly (had they been mixed districts) large dwelling units. Because of the peculiar mixture in these districts, a more detailed analysis, making use of precinct data, is undertaken later.

The remaining districts may be referred to as working class, which in this case means that approximatley 50 percent or more of the employed population was engaged in working-class occupations. Although the districts are being labeled working class, it ought to be noted that a large portion of the working population in these districts were in nonmanual (or white-collar, or middle-class) occupations. Again, following the arguments made in Chapter 3, it is assumed that they came from backgrounds similar to those of the workers. They probably went to the same schools (which means primary schools); they were probably kinsmen and friends as well as neighbors. The assumption is that they ordinarily shared the outlooks of the workers rather than standing in opposition to them. A considerable portion of the white-collar employees in these areas must have been wives and daughters of workers. It seems unlikely that they would have attempted to maintain a separate and distinct class position.[5]

The middle class that would feel threatened, suffering a status panic and desperately searching for some means to maintain its position, would probably be found living in Hamm, in Borgfelde, in Eimsbüttel, in Uhlenhorst, or in Winterhude. And if that were the case, one should find the reaction, the support for the National Socialists, to be especially concentrated in those districts.

It is useful to keep in mind some difficulties with the figures just given. They show the occupations of employed persons. Some of these employed persons were not of voting age. This would have been the case for many workers (who began their occupational careers at an earlier age than did the nonmanual workers), in particular domestic servants. A second problem arises in that these figures do not distinguish heads of families from second earners; hence, for the reasons noted in the previous chapter, they may not give a precise statement of the working-class strength in the districts. If wives and daughters of workers, for example, tended to be employed in white-collar occupations, that would lead to an underestimate of the working-class presence.[6] And a third difficulty is that these figures do not include retired persons. Their previous occupations, in most cases, however, would probably be similar to those of the currently employed persons so this factor would not cause any serious distortion.

All three considerations suggest that it would be unwise to place too much emphasis on any particular figure as giving a precise representation of a district's character. These figures are intended to establish the rank ordering of the city's subareas. The problems mentioned here are not likely to affect that result seriously. St. Pauli is not likely to end up in the same position as Winterhude or Eimsbüttel to be ranked next to Hohenfelde.

One additional observation about the social characteristics of the districts is in order. Religion, as has been noted repeatedly in previous chapters, had a strong effect on voting patterns. Catholics gave strong support to the Zentrum. And Jews, clearly, would not be among the supporters of the National Socialists or, at most times, of the Conservatives. Both religious groups were only tiny minorities in Protestant Hamburg. The 1925 census shows the Catholic population forming only 5 percent of the total, and it was distributed rather evenly throughout the city in a way similar to that noted in Berlin.

The pattern is quite different with the Jewish population who formed 1.8 percent of the city's 1925 total. Jews were heavily represented in Harvestehude (15.9 percent) and in Rotherbaum (15.2 percent). Eppendorf, immediately to the north of Harvestehude, was next with a total of 3.5 percent. The other districts had only trace representation, most having less than 1 percent.[7]

ELECTORAL PATTERNS IN HAMBURG: 1924–1932

The Social Democrats increased their strength regularly from May of 1924 through 1928. Here too, as in Berlin, one finds this unexpected pattern of growth on the left during the good times of Weimar. With the onset of the depression, one finds a reversal of the trend, the Social Democrats suffering a five-percentage-point loss as of 1930. The SPD held that position in the first of the 1932 elections but then lost once again in November of that year.[8] (See Table 5.2.)

The Communists had an even more unexpected history. They too gained in the good years of Weimar. This gain was not achieved, as is usually the case, at the expense of the Social Democrats although there may have been some two-step shifting. The onset of the depression, remarkably enough, had very little impact on their fortunes; they improved their position by only 1.4 percentage points. The subsequent two years of extremely depressed conditions, even more remarkably, did not change this pattern. In July 1932, the Communists actually took a slightly smaller share of the vote than they had in 1930. The widespread expectation that the economic crisis would radicalize, that it would force people, especially the workers, to move to the left was not supported. Only in the last episode, in the three months between the elections of 1932 did that kind of shift occur. This would appear to have been a pure exchange, with voters leaving the Social Democrats for the Communists.[9]

Because of the frequency with which the argument of "economism" appears (that workers become conservative in good times and radical in bad), it is useful to take a glance at the combined left vote. This amounted to nearly half of the total, 47.0 percent, as of December 1924, a point at which economic and political affairs had achieved some stability. That level increased to 54.1 percent in the course of the good years and *fell* with the onset of the depression, to 50.5 percent in 1930. The level declined again in July 1932 after two more years of depression, this time to 49.9 percent. The events between July and November did little to change the overall level, the total at the latter point coming to 50.9 percent.

One other point is worth stressing. The left gains achieved in May of 1928, those achieved in the good years, would appear to have come at the expense of the Conservatives! The reality, no doubt, was much more complicated than this statement would suggest. Young first-time voters may have gone disproportionately to the left. Former Conservatives may have shifted to the liberal parties; in working-class Barmbeck, for example, the DNVP lost votes while both the DVP and DDP gained. That is a net result, it should be noted. While some former

TABLE 5.2. REICHSTAG ELECTION RESULTS FOR HAMBURG, 1924-1932
(in percent)

Party	Election					
	May 4, 1924	December 7, 1924	May 20, 1928	September 14, 1930	July 31, 1932	November 6, 1932
SPD	27.5	32.1	36.8	31.8	31.5	28.3
USPD	0.5	0.2	—	—	—	—
KPD	18.8	14.7	17.3	18.7	18.4	22.6
Zentrum	1.6	1.8	1.6	1.5	2.1	1.8
DDP	13.1	12.7	11.8	8.7	6.2	5.5
DVP	11.7	12.7	13.2	9.0	1.9	3.2
DNVP	19.4	21.4	12.6	4.0	5.0	9.0
NSDAP	6.1	2.3	2.6	19.0	33.3	27.0
Others	1.3	2.0	4.1	7.4	1.7	2.5
Total	100.0	99.9	100.0	100.1	100.1	99.9
Participation	79.0	76.5	80.1	84.6	86.5	84.4

SOURCE: *Statistische Mitteilungen über den hamburgischen Staat*, nos. 14, 20, 23, and 25, Hamburg: Otto Meissners Verlag, 1924-1930; nos. 29 and 30 (same title), Hamburg: Lüteke & Wulff, 1932.

DNVP voters moved to the liberal parties, some former liberals may have shifted to the left.

In contrast to their Berlin counterparts, the Socialists of Hamburg were always in a dominant position vis-à-vis the Communists. In Berlin the two were close in May of 1924 and were equal in 1930 and in July of 1932. In November, the Communists there surpassed the Social Democrats. Although some radicalization was indicated in Hamburg in November, the Social Democrats still had a fair-sized edge over their competitor on the left.

Little need be said about the Zentrum. In Protestant Hamburg, that party was a very minor force at all times during this period.

The Democrats (left liberals) experienced a relative loss in every single election of the period. These losses were not particularly serious through 1928, but in 1930 and July 1932 the rate of decline increased sharply. The German People's party, Stresemann's party, increased its strength through 1928 and then suffered serious losses in 1930 and again in the first election of 1932. The Conservatives, as already noted, suffered their first serious loss in 1928 and experienced another devastating one in 1930. In their case, however, a slight recovery occurred in July of 1932, and another gain was made in November of that year. The meaning of that recovery is considered at a later point; there is a question as to whether Conservatives were returning to the party or voters from other middle-class parties were looking for an alternative, their first-choice option having disappeared.

A comparison of Hamburg and Berlin shows the liberal parties to have had greater initial strength in the former city. Their combined total in May of 1924 was 24.8 percent versus 19.4 percent for the Conservatives. In Berlin, the respective figures were 17.3 versus 22.6. This again indicates the distinctively Prussian character of the Conservative party as discussed in Chapter 2. In commercial Hamburg, by contrast, liberalism was dominant, and the Conservative vote as of 1924 appeared to be more of a protest vote.[10]

The National Socialist development follows a pattern noted earlier in Berlin. There are some slight variations in that here the party already showed a slight gain in 1928, which was typical of western and southern Germany. And, another difference, it suffered a more pronounced decline in November 1932 than was the case in Berlin. The only other observation of note is that in every election the level of National Socialist voting in Hamburg was higher than in Berlin. At its pre-1933 peak, in July of 1932, Hitler's party took exactly one-third of the vote.

In National Socialist literature, as well as in the writing of the party's opponents, much attention has been given to the masterly demagogic efforts of the Berlin *Gauleiter*, Joseph Goebbels. Showing an extraordinary appreciation of crowd psychology, so it is said, he manipulated audiences with unequaled skill. Goebbels's accomplishment, however, as measured by these voting results, was at all times inferior to that of his less well known colleagues in Hamburg.

THE PATTERN OF NATIONAL SOCIALIST SUPPORT

Given the claims and assumptions of the literature reviewed in Chapter 2, and given the specification of them in Chapter 3, one should expect to find National Socialist strength concentrated in the so-called mixed districts, in those districts between Eppendorf and Winterhude in the listing of Table 5.1. There should be more limited support for Hitler's party in the upper- and upper-middle-class districts. And there should be very little NSDAP support in the working-class districts.

The pattern of support for the National Socialists, however, does not conform to those expectations.[11] The most striking finding in Table 5.3 is the consistency with which above average National Socialist voting appears in upper- and upper-middle-class districts. With only a single exception, National Socialist support exceeded the city-wide average in all districts from Harvestehude to Eilbeck in all seven elections. These best-off districts gave the NSDAP above average support in it first appearance in national elections, in May of 1924, just after Hitler's conviction for his activities in the Munich *Putsch*. The above average support continued in the next two elections when the overall support for the party declined to minuscule levels. Then, in the election of 1930, in the party's first major national success, those well-off districts gave substantial percentages, ranging from 20 to 30, to the National Socialists. And in the key election, that of July 1932, the percentages in the well-off districts were over 40. That must be contrasted with the city-wide figure of 33.3 percent. Hohenfelde, a very affluent upper-middle-class area, leads all the rest with the National Socialist vote there amounting to 47.9 percent of the total.

The somewhat lower percentages in Harvestehude (40.9) and Rotherbaum (43.4) do not result from any special moderation or responsibility on the part of the traditional upper-class populations. Both of those communities had fair-sized Jewish minorities, it will be remembered, which means that the level of National Socialist support among the remaining members of those communities must have been close to the level in upper-middle-class Hohenfelde. If we assume that all of the NSDAP votes came from the non-Jewish population, following the initial estimating procedure used in discussion of the Berlin results, we get considerably higher percentages, the respective figures for Harvestehude, Rotherbaum, and Hohenfelde now being 48.6, 51.2, and 48.7.

It was from the three "best" areas of the city that the NSDAP received its strongest support. Approximately half of the non-Jewish voters in those districts supported Hitler's party in July 1932.

The levels of National Socialist support in the mixed districts of Hamburg tend to run at approximately the city-wide average. They do not show the pronounced enthusiasm for Hitler's party that would be required to support the received claims. In this respect, it will be noted, the Hamburg experience is very much like that in the mixed districts of Berlin.

National Socialist support in the working-class districts was generally below the city average in all of these elections. To that extent the received hypothesis does gain support. This was not uniformly true, to be sure, the most striking exception occurring in the Altstadt which

TABLE 5.3. SUPPORT FOR THE NATIONAL SOCIALISTS IN
HAMBURG BY DISTRICT, 1924-1932
    (in percent)

	Election					
District	May 4, 1924	December 7, 1924	May 20, 1928	September 14, 1930	July 31, 1932	November 6, 1932
Harvestehude	**7.0**	**2.9**	**2.7**	**22.0**	**40.9**	**30.6**
Rotherbaum	**9.4**	**3.4**	**4.5**	**25.5**	**43.4**	**36.2**
Hohenfelde	**8.8**	**3.5**	**3.6**	**29.7**	**47.9**	**38.0**
Fuhlsbüttel	**8.7**	**2.7**	**3.3**	**22.1**	**45.8**	**36.4**
Northeastern Districts	**9.9**	**3.4**	2.2	**21.8**	**43.9**	**32.4**
Eilbeck	**8.6**	**3.6**	**3.3**	**25.4**	**43.1**	**35.7**
Eppendorf and Gross Borstel	**6.5**	**2.7**	**3.0**	**21.0**	**37.2**	**29.5**
Hamm	**7.7**	**3.1**	**3.2**	**21.8**	**37.1**	**30.2**
Borgfelde	**6.3**	2.2	**2.8**	**20.6**	**34.5**	**27.9**
Langenhorn	3.1	1.1	1.1	12.5	25.5	20.5
Eimsbüttel	**7.1**	2.3	**2.9**	**19.6**	**33.6**	**28.0**
Uhlenhorst	5.8	2.2	2.3	18.9	32.7	24.9
Winterhude	4.6	1.7	2.0	18.9	**34.9**	**27.5**
St. Georg	5.6	2.1	2.6	18.9	31.7	26.1
Altstadt	5.4	2.2	**3.5**	**25.2**	**42.0**	**33.7**
Barmbeck	4.9	1.9	2.0	15.0	28.0	22.9
Horn	5.6	2.5	1.5	13.1	29.9	24.2
Neustadt	4.4	1.6	2.5	16.8	27.0	21.5
St. Pauli	5.1	1.9	2.6	17.3	28.7	23.5
Billwärder Ausschlag	2.7	0.9	1.3	8.8	19.3	14.4
Harbor Districts	4.7	1.7	1.6	12.5	25.4	19.2
Hamburg	6.1	2.3	2.6	19.0	33.3	27.0

SOURCE: *Statistische Mitteilungen über den hamburgischen Staat*, nos. 14, 20, 23, and 25, Hamburg: Otto Meissners Verlag, 1924-1930; nos. 29 and 30 (same title), Hamburg: Kommissionsverlag von Lüteke und Wulff, 1932.
NOTE: Figures in bold type indicate results above the city-wide NSDAP percentage.

was above average in 1928 and continued to be well above the city average in all subsequent elections.

A point deserving special consideration in this connection involves the absolute level of the NSDAP vote in the working-class districts. In Barmbeck, 28 percent of the July 1932 votes went to the National Socialists. That level is more or less typical for the other major working-class districts of the city. Even in the Harbor Districts, the level was not much different; there, one voter in four supported Hitler's party. Only in the Billwärder Ausschlag was the level significantly below this typical working-class level; there it was "only" a matter of one voter in five.

The Billwärder Ausschlag was an unusual district. More than any other, it contained those who might easily be referred to as lumpenproletarian. In sharp contrast to the frequent claim about lumpenproletarian susceptibilities, this district responded least to the National Socialist appeals.

To summarize these complex results as simply as possible, one may note that the National Socialist percentages tended to increase with the class level of the district. In general, the more affluent, and, presumably, the more educated the population, the greater the likelihood that it supported the National Socialists. At the same time it is to be noted that National Socialist support in the working-class districts was not minuscule although, to be sure, it was below the average for the city. The mixed districts, those most likely to contain the desperate and anxious middle-class populations were, contrary to the received claim, not at all distinctive.[12]

The results contained in Table 5.3 may be summarized economically with correlation coefficients. Very briefly, whether one looks at the Spearman or the Pearson correlations (which focus on rank order and percentages respectively), the result is a pattern of very strong associations throughout the period.

Correlations	May 1924	Dec. 1924	May 1928	Sept. 1930	July 1932	Nov. 1932
Spearman r (between disticts as ranked in Table 5.3 and rank order of NSDAP support, N = 21)	.82	.80	.62	.81	.84	.83
Pearson r (between percentage working class and percentage for NSDAP, N = 21)	−.78	−.77	−.59	−.71	−.81	−.77

THE PRESIDENTIAL ELECTION

The pattern indicated in the Reichstag elections also appeared in the 1932 presidential elections. In the first round, it will be remembered, there was a choice of Hindenburg, the republican candidate at this point; of Duesterberg, the Conservative; of Thälmann, the Communist; and of Hitler. In the best-off districts of Hamburg, Duesterberg came in above his city-wide average although in no case did he gain more than a tenth of the vote. Thälmann came in well below his city-wide average in those districts. Hindenburg's vote there approximated his average. Last but not least, Hitler's vote in these districts was substantially above the city average. In the city, 24.3 percent of the voters chose Hitler. In Harvestehude Hitler gained 29.7 percent, in Rotherbaum it was 31.1, and in Hohenfelde it was 35.8.

The experience in the second round of the presidential election paralleled that of Berlin, the Duesterberg vote apparently going to Hitler. Hitler's vote in the second round was roughly equal to the combined Hitler-Duesterberg vote of the first round. Once again the thesis of upper- and upper-middle-class responsibility appears open to some question.

Although the fortunes of the KPD are not the central focus of this work, it is worthwhile examining the vote for Thälmann. He succeeded in gaining 15.6 percent of the city's votes in the first round. In the second round, his share fell to 12.8 percent of the total. Put in other terms, he had lost more than one-fifth of his first-round votes. As already noted in the Berlin case, a part of the Communist vote proved to be neither solid nor committed. Hamburg, it should also be noted, was Thälmann's home city. He had worked on the ships and later was employed there as a dockworker before becoming a leader of the local KPD.

One other observation deserving of note involves the relative standing of Thälmann in the various districts of the city. One would anticipate, especially given the concern evidenced in some circles, that he would show enormous strength in working-class districts. In the first round he received 30.5 percent in the Neustadt, his highest figure, and 27.8 percent in St. Pauli. In the largest working-class district, Barmbeck, his share amounted to only 17.9 percent, not very much above his city-wide average. In fact in that area he took fewer votes than did Hitler, who gained 20.1 percent of the total. In the second round of elections Hitler increased his vote in every district of the city but one, that being the down-and-out Billwärder Ausschlag. Again the assumption of the easy or natural attraction of workers to the Communists appears to be open to some doubt. The sources of this working-class reluctance are considered in greater detail in Chapter 11.

Some of the "better" communities of the metropolitan area, it will be remembered, were located outside of Hamburg State, that is, in the surrounding Prussian territories. It is useful to examine the voting patterns in those areas.

Up the Elbe lies the tiny suburban community of Reinbek. In July of 1932, the National Socialist vote there was 39.9 percent. Up the Alster, to the north of the city, one found the well-off communities of Poppenbüttel and Wellingsbüttel. The respective National Socialist percentages there were 45.8 and 47.3. Down the Elbe, beyond working-class Altona and lying somewhat inland was an elegant community, Gross Flottbek. Its National Socialist percentage was 47.4. To the south, and facing on the river, was the much more elegant sister city, Klein Flottbek. Its National Socialist percentage was 51.1. And the most affluent of them all, a neighbor to Klein Flottbek, was Blankenese. There, 53.8 percent of the voters chose the National Socialists in July 1932. That figure was the highest found anywhere in the Hamburg metropolitan area.[13]

SOME PRECINCT DATA

A more detailed examination of the city districts is made possible by the availability of voting results for the precincts (*Stimmbezirke*). This examination allows more insight into the voting patterns, and, as shall be seen, provides further confirmation of the previous findings.

Hohenfelde, it was noted, had the highest National Socialist percentage in the July 1932 election of any district in the city, the figure being 47.9. There was very little differentiation within the district. Of the nineteen reporting districts, twelve were above 50 percent, and another two were very close to the area average.[14] One district was slightly below the average, two others were further below it, and two others were well below the average at 27.7 and 19.2 percent. The slightly below average precinct was well inland from the Alster; it included the dwellings on a well-traveled street. The two somewhat below average precincts were adjacent to the St. George General Hospital. The lowest "precinct," with a 19.2 percent National Socialist vote, was the Marienkrankenhaus (St. Mary's Hospital). This was the city's largest Roman Catholic hospital; the vote there would have been that of the institution's patients (one could vote in hospitals in Weimar Germany). The other very low district, that with a 27.7 percent National Socialist vote, was adjacent to this hospital. It seems likely that a large portion of the population in that precinct was Catholic. Given the location (next to the S-Bahn tracks and the streetcar yards), it was likely to have contained lower-middle- and working-class populations rather than medical professionals.

Uhlenhorst, with a July 1932 National Socialist average of 32.7 percent, was a peculiarly mixed district. It had some very elegant upper-class housing facing the Alster. But as one moved inland there was a shift to lower-middle- and working-class housing, the district eventually meeting with working-class Barmbeck. If the twin hypothesis of upper-class responsibility and lower-middle-class irresponsibility were valid, one should find low National Socialist percentages in the Alster precincts and an increase as one moves inland. That expectation is not supported. Instead, the National Socialists did very well in the Alster precincts, and their percentages fell as one moved inland. In one "row" of precincts, their percentage fell from 50.9 on the Alster, to 37.8, and then to 22.6. In an adjacent row, the equivalent figures were 53.4, 31.9, and 20.3.

Uhlenhorst's northern border is formed by the Osterbeck Canal. The canal is rather wide there where it flows into the Alster, and the housing at that point, too, consists of elegant mansions. There too the National Socialist percentages were high, 41.2 and 42.9. The precincts just to the south of the canal, those directly facing the Alster (or facing the lake-front park there) had percentages ranging from 38.8 to 45.7. In sharp contrast, the highest percentage in the seven immediately adjacent inland precincts, all of which had much less elegant housing, was 22.6. Most were around 20 percent although one was a very low 11.4.

Winterhude, north of Uhlenhorst, presents a similar picture. Only the south edge of the district touches the Alster Lake. The rest of the western boundary, however, follows the Alster River and was also an area of very good housing. The districts along the Alster again provided above average support for the National Socialists. The district average in July 1932 was 34.9 percent. Five precincts along the river had averages of 39.7, 41.7, 39.6, 41.6, and 37.6. The precincts immediately adjacent to these faced onto a large city park, and these too had high National Socialist percentages, 48.1, 42.8, and 40.5. The precinct touching the Alster Lake had a percentage of 41.2. Winterhude's interior precincts appear to have had heavy working-class percentages. Accordingly, the National Socialist percentages are very low. In one cluster of eight, the range was from 15.2 to 27.4.

This account presents perhaps too tidy to picture. Cutting diagonally across the district was a well-traveled street, the Barmbeckerstrasse. Some interior precincts along this street also had high National Socialist percentages. It is not as if all of the high percentages were found in the most elegant areas.

SOME SPECIAL CASES

The Harbor Districts, as mentioned earlier, present a rather mixed picture. Most curious of all was Steinwärder-Waltershof. Four of these five districts (in 1925) had fair-sized working-class percentages. In Steinwärder, however, only 29.1 percent of the economically active population was engaged in blue-collar occupations. A small number, 39 out of the total of 787 economically active persons, was listed as independents. Most, 62.3 percent, were reported as white-collar workers and civil servants. It seems reasonable to assume that these white-collar workers and civil servants were *lower* middle class—what other middle-class populations would reside in such a location? Steinwärder, in short, would appear to be a majority lower-middle-class district, the only one of its kind to be found in the course of this study.[15]

Given the setting, one might assume an unusual population, possibly a community of single males. That did not prove to be the case. There was a roughly balanced sex ratio, 775 males to 703 females and roughly the same proportions of single, married, widowed, and divorced persons as were found in the other districts of the city. In short, the area appeared to have a normal residential population.

According to the received theories, this district should have voted heavily for the National Socialists. In the July 1932 election, 23.2 percent of the district's voters supported that party. The support, in other words, was ten percentage points *below* the city average. Rather than voting National Socialist, most residents voted either Socialist or Communist. This finding is clearly in line with the position argued in Chapter 3, that middle-class populations living in close proximity to workers would tend to share the working-class political outlooks rather than standing in opposition to them.

One of the districts, Finkenwärder, at the extreme west end of the harbor, was exceptional in another way. Despite its working-class majority (56.2 percent) it had a high level of National Socialist support, 41.1 percent. The reasons for this deviation are not easily discovered. It might have been due to the influence of some charismatic local leaders. There was some farm population in the district; the docks were on one side of the area, and on the other side of the tracks there was farm land. Some of the conservative farm influence might have persisted in that community and provided the raw material for the National Socialist activists who came along later.

One should not make too much of any of the results from the harbor area. All the districts had small populations, the largest having only 5,445 persons in 1925. The number of voters, of course, was much smaller.

Another clue to the voting tendencies of the various population segments is to be found in the voting tendencies in the various hospitals of the city. These may be divided into three broad categories: public (i.e. state owned), religious, and private. The Catholic Marienkrankenhaus, as already noted, had a very low National Socialist percentage, 19.2 versus the city average of 33.3 in July 1932. The public institutions also had relatively low National Socialist percentages, and, as might be expected, they had relatively high Socialist and Communist percentages. For example, in precinct 277a at the Eppendorf General Hospital, the percentage voting for the National Socialists was 26.0; in precinct 277b it was 30.8. In precinct 466a at the Barmbeck General Hospital, the percentage was 23.5; in precinct 466b, 24.6; and in precinct 466c, 19.4.

Three Protestant hospitals had surprisingly low National Socialist percentages. They were: Elim Hospital, precinct 195a, 23.0; Jerusalem Hospital, precinct 196a, 27.8; and Elim Old People's Home, precinct 281b, 4.5.

The first two are reported to have been extremely religious institutions, their voters providing something of a Protestant counterpart to the Catholic Zentrum voters. They gave heavy support to a religious splinter party, the Christian Social People's Service, the respective percentages being 52.1 and 35.4. The old people's home showed the same tendency, in this case the percentage being 80.9, possibly the high figure in the nation for that party. No votes, incidentally, were cast for either Social Democrats or Communists in that institution. One other possibility is that these three institutions contained relatively large numbers of women; this splinter party was especially attractive to women voters.

Still another religious institution was the Israelite Hospital. Nineteen votes were cast there (of a 132-vote total) for the National Socialists, and 3 went for the anti-Semitic Conservatives. A likely explanation for this unexpected finding is that many of the patients were not Jewish. The 1925 census found only 38 Jews there out of 78 patients.[16] The largest block of votes cast in the hospital that day was for the Social Democrats (58). They were followed by the Communists (30) and then, after the National Socialists, by the German Democratic party (16).

A very crude indication of the shifts in voting of the city's Jewish population may be gained by contrasting the results in the *Bürgerschaft* (city government) election of April 24 with those in the Reichstag election of July. It should be kept in mind that the same people are not likely to have voted in the two elections, but rather that these are two erratic samples drawn from a similar subpopulation. There seems here to have been a break to the left, the German State party (formerly the Democrats), who gained fifty votes in April, lost to the Socialists and Communists. The April results made it clear that the DDP had all but disappeared; a vote for the Democrats in July would have appeared to be wasted, and so, as a consequence, its supporters shifted to a next best alternative.

This leaves the private hospitals. Those able to make use of the services of these institutions in 1932 would have been well off, either from the upper class or at least from the upper-middle category. The National Socialist percentages follow: Siloah Hospital, 62.0; Free Mason Hospital, 44.1; Vereins Hospital, 48.4; Bethanien Hospital, 55.7; Ebenezer Hospital, 47.8; and Bethesda Hospital, 58.1. These results are consistent with the pattern evidenced in the voting of the city districts and therefore clearly reinforce the earlier conclusions.

Another institution listed in the published voting records was the Abendroth House. There, some forty of forty-nine persons (81.6 percent) voted for the National Socialists. This institution was supported by a foundation that had been created over a century previously by a former *Bürgermeister* of the city. Its task was the rehabilitation of prostitutes.

The impact of summer vacations noted in the July result in Berlin may also be seen in Hamburg. In April, 11,229 ballots were given out prior to the state election. For the national election of July, 57,439 were given out. The proportion varied with the economic standing of the district; if ballots given out prior to the election are expressed as a percentage of eligible voters, in Harvestehude, for example, the percentage was 12.8; in Rotherbaum, 10.6; in Hohenfelde, 9.6; in Fuhlsbüttel, 7.4; and in Hamburg as a whole, 6.5.

Many of the voters in these best-off districts, then, did not vote in Hamburg in July. As in Berlin, it will be necessary to locate their votes elsewhere.

Some Estimates

Like Wilmersdorf and Zehlendorf in Berlin, even the best-off districts of Hamburg are occupationally mixed. There was some working-class population in Harvestehude, in Rotherbaum, and in Hohenfelde. And there was some vote for the left parties in those districts, which probably came largely from their working-class minorities. And that likelihood in turn means that the vote for the National Socialists among the remaining population must have been higher than what has been indicated by the previous figures.

One may estimate the National Socialist support among the traditional upper and upper middle class of Hamburg through use of the assumptions elaborated in the previous chapter. By traditional upper and upper middle class, we are referring to the Protestant segment of those classes. The basic assumptions are: no Jewish votes for the National Socialists; Zentrum votes are those of Catholic voters; and two-thirds of the combined left vote comes from the working-class populations of the district. The basic estimate then involves exclusion of these three segments and a calculation of the National Socialist votes as a percentage of the remaining votes (see Chapter 4 for the detailed discussion). This yields a percent National Socialist figure for a population segment that is largely (but not entirely) Protestant and nonmanual.[17]

This procedure yields the following estimates. In Harvestehude, 64 percent of the remaining population segment voted National Socialist, in Rotherbaum, 70 percent, and in Hohenfelde, 63 percent. These figures do not give a precise estimate of the voting of the upper and upper middle classes. The population segment in question does include some lower-middle-class populations and a tiny working-class segment. By the terms of the initial assumptions the other third of the left voters would be located in the nonmanual segment. It seems likely that they would be lower middle class rather than upper middle class. Were that the case, the National Socialist percentages in the upper middle and upper classes of those districts would have been even higher than these estimates indicate.

THE ARGUMENT BY STIPULATION

The argument by stipulation (see Chapter 4) can also be assessed with the Hamburg data. One can recalculate the basic election results to find out what percentage of a given party's vote came from upper-class districts, what from middle-class districts, and so forth.

This has been done for the three key parties usually discussed in this connection, the Conservatives and the right and left liberals. The second election of 1924 has been taken as the base point for this analysis and the districts of the city have been divided into three categories. The first, the upper- and upper-middle-class districts, includes those from Harvestehude to Eppendorf and Gross Borstel as listed in Table 5.1. The second, the mixed districts, includes those from Hamm to Winterhude. And the third, the working-class districts, includes those from St. Georg down to and including the harbor areas.

The situation as of December 1924 does not accord with the assumptions of this argument. All three middle-class parties gained approximately one-third of their votes from each of the three categories of district. The German People's party gained a few more percentage points from the better-off districts. The German Democratic party had a slight edge in the working-class districts. The German Nationals (Conservatives) occupied an intermediate position between the two. In short, all three parties cut right across the class spectrum to achieve their 1924 strength. As in the Berlin case, we have taken the votes for the respective parties in July 1932 and calculated them as a percentage of the December 1924 totals. This procedure allows one to see where the losses of so-called middle class parties occurred and where they were most serious.

The results of this inquiry show, as in Berlin, that it was the mixed districts, those most likely to contain threatened middle classes, that maintained the highest levels of party loyalty.[18] In the face of considerable social and economic stress, they proved *most* resistant to the National Socialist enchantment. The differences, it must be noted, are not very large. They must, nevertheless, be seen in comparison to the received expectations which argue a massive defection here and, by contrast, a disproportionate upper- and upper-middle-class loyalty to their traditional parties.

Those discussions, as we have seen, typically overlook the support these parties received in working-class districts. For the Conservatives and the right liberal German People's party, the losses were *most* serious in these districts. This finding raises several questions for further consideration. Did the losses result from the attractions offered by the National Socialists? Or was there perhaps more of a push, the politics of these parties themselves having repulsed working-class voters? Did the losses, which weakened the parties, then stimulate upper- and upper-middle-class voters to look elsewhere? These questions are discussed at length in Chapters 10 and 13.

One other point may be noted. These results from Germany's second largest city are very similar to the pattern noted in Berlin. They provide additional testimony in favor of the arguments made there, in particular that the middle-class parties originally had considerable working-class followings and that a large part of their respective losses involved just those supporters.

Three additional points deserve attention. The conventional lines of analysis have focused on what we might call class-specific processes. The lower middle class, for example, suffers a specific set of strains and reacts, en masse, by turning to the National Socialists. The working classes face a different set of strains, and they turn from the SPD to the KPD. Those emphases fail to recognize that in both Berlin and Hamburg, the same process appears to have been occurring in middle-class, working-class, and mixed settings. Conservatives and liberals in all three areas were abandoning their traditional parties and shifting to the National Socialists. The underlying motives may have been different (as is argued in Chapter 13). But the behavior to be explained is not that of *the classes* (in their entirety), but rather of those *segments* of the classes that had once been either conservative or liberal. This means that an explanation of the development of the National Socialist constituency must take into account a cultural factor (the bases of these loyalties) as well as the structural factor (the class position).

A second point deserving at least some notice concerns the differences between Berlin and Hamburg. In Berlin, the DNVP was the most successful of the three in retaining voter loyalties. In Hamburg, the left liberal German Democrats were the most successful.[19] In both cases, the DVP was the big loser. These differences make it clear that the deterioration of the established parties varied somewhat from one community to the next. The differing patterns also show that some of the movement was determined by local, not national, factors.

Behind these differences was a little-noticed regroupment process. While most supporters of these parties were moving to the National Socialists, others were seeking out a next best option. In Berlin these voters appear to have gone to the DNVP and, to a much lesser extent, particularly in the well-off communities, to the Zentrum. In Hamburg, they appear to have remained with the DDP, only later, in November of 1932, shifting to the DVP and, with greater frequency, to the DNVP.

One final observation needs to be made in this connection. The loss of votes by the middle-class parties is correlated with National Socialist gains. Their losses in the working-class districts mean corresponding NSDAP gains there. And that means, considering now the compositional question, that a significant part of the National Socialist vote came from these working-class districts. For Hamburg this means, taking the areas from St. Georg down to and including the Harbor Districts as listed in Table 5.1, that nearly two out of every five NSDAP votes (actually 38.0 percent) came from the predominantly working-class areas of the city.

SOME CONCLUSIONS

The findings of this chapter very closely parallel those drawn from the Berlin experience. The highest levels of support for National Socialism in Hamburg came from the upper- and upper-middle-class districts. When the votes of the working-class and the Jewish minorities in these districts are discounted, the estimated levels of National Socialist support among the remaining segments, largely well-off Protestants, indicate that roughly two-thirds of them were supporting Hitler's party at its peak in July 1932.

The mixed districts, the closest approximation to the lower middle class that we can make, do not show any distinctive voting pattern. The support there for the National Socialists was not exceptionally high;

rather, these districts tended to hover more or less around the city-wide average. If they possessed the tendencies attributed to them, one should have found pronounced National Socialist voting patterns in just these areas.

The working-class districts generally fall below the city-wide National Socialist percentage. As with Berlin, however, the support for the party in those areas was not minuscule. The levels of support at the pretakeover peak were above 25 percent in all cases but one. That single exception was the very poor Billwärder Ausschlag.

Worker support for the National Socialists appears to have come from those who previously, for one reason or another, had supported a liberal or conservative nationalist direction, in other words, *not* from those who had supported the Marxist parties. This would mean that the claim of unemployed workers as most vulnerable is open to much question. Unemployment is unlikely to have been concentrated among these workers. If anything the opposite would have been the case; these workers would probably have been older and would have had somewhat greater job security. Employer hiring and favor, in many instances, were linked to political considerations. Such favor would have been more likely to fall to conservative workers than to Socialists or Communists.

A fourth conclusion also parallels the Berlin findings. The demise of the so-called middle-class parties is ordinarily taken as an indication of shifts in the middle-class ranks. But in Hamburg, as in Berlin, these parties reached across the class spectrum, and losses were suffered in all contexts. The greatest losses, however, were in the working-class districts of the city. By itself, then, the decline of those parties has wider implications; it points to more than just the reactions of the middle class.

These findings have some obvious methodological implications. To explain the shift to the National Socialists, one must explore not just the responses of the much-discussed lower middle class, but those of the upper, the upper middle, and the working classes as well.

Little else may be said by way of conclusion at this point. One can, however, raise again some more speculative considerations. It will be noted that in Hamburg, as in Berlin, it is virtually impossible to isolate lower-middle-class populations in a way that allows acquisition of compelling evidence establishing their voting behavior. There is, however, less excuse for the uncritical acceptance of standard dogma in the Hamburg case than in the other cities discussed in this work. As was noted earlier, studies of voting patterns within German cities are very infrequent. In Hamburg, however, a study was done of the voting pattern in the 1930 Reichstag election. It was published a year later. It was, to be sure, not much of a study, consisting merely of two columns of comment accompanied by a series of colored maps showing the levels of support for the major parties in the various precincts of the city. There was no discussion of the social composition of the populations living in these precincts. For those not familiar with the city, therefore, the maps themselves would have little meaning. The map showing National Socialist strength, appropriately, was colored in various shades of brown. In all but two of the precincts surrounding the Alster, the National Socialist percentages were shown to be above the city average. Considerable NSDAP strength was indicated in nearly all Rotherbaum districts, and even greater support was found in Hohenfelde. National Socialist strength appeared in other areas of the city as well, scattered in a seemingly meaningless pattern. But the strength in the well-off areas of the city was such that one could hardly miss it.[20] And yet, such is the force of an unchecked idea, most commentators have done just that—missed the lesson of upper- and upper-middle-class attraction to Hitler and his party.

THE QUESTION OF LINKAGES

Thus far the focus of this chapter has been on results. Only very peripherally has it dealt with the question of why various groups turned to the National Socialists. Without going into motives, which, of course, are effectively beyond the reach of contemporary research, one can, nevertheless, consider the role of the facilitating agencies. Here, too, one finds some striking parallels to Berlin in that the key linking agencies, those connecting the party and the voters, appear to have been the party cadres and the city's newspapers.

Like Grunewald in Berlin, well-off Rotherbaum had a National Socialist *Ortsgruppe* (local group), one whose territory extended to include Harvestehude. This was not just one *Ortsgruppe* among many. The one-time *Gauleiter* of Hamburg, Albert Krebs, reports that because of the capacities of its members, many of whom were active as speakers, this unit exerted a large influence throughout the entire state organization. The tactics used by the party in Hamburg were similar to those Goebbels used in Berlin. This was particularly the case with the provocative march into working-class districts. The resulting conflicts gained them sympathetic headlines and news stories in at least a part of the city's press.[21]

There is good reason to believe that a good part of Hitler's success in Hamburg resulted, directly or indirectly, from the recommendations or positions taken in the local press. Like Berlin, Hamburg had a range of bourgeois newspapers reflecting the principal political orientations of the day. Possibly the most influential of these, the one most likely to be read by good bourgeois citizens was the *Hamburger Nachrichten*. It was generally conservative and monarchist in orientation and hence closely linked to the DNVP. There was also the *Hamburgischer Correspondent*; it had a smaller circulation, and was close to the DVP. Then there was the *Fremdenblatt*, which was generally right liberal in orientation, close to the National Liberals before the war and to the DVP afterward. While a passable journalistic enterprise, the *Fremdenblatt* did not have the niveau of the *Nachrichten*. It was, so people report, read by an average middle-class audience. Finally, there was a mass circulation newspaper, the *Hamburger Anzeiger*. It was unusual for a newspaper of this type in that it had a pronounced political direction; it favored the German Democrats, or, as they were known following a reorganization in 1930, the German State party.

In addition, there were the usual journals of the left and an NSDAP entry, the *Tageblatt*. For explanation of the political changes of the period, however, one must look at the role played by the bourgeois journals.

During the September 1930 election the *Nachrichten*, the preeminent quality newspaper, conducted what might best be described as bourgeois coalition politics. An editorial summed matters up under the heading: "*Der Feind steht links!*" (The Enemy Stands to the Left!). Instead of fighting the SPD, it observed, the bourgeois parties were fighting each other. In particular it referred to the struggle between the DNVP and a defecting splinter group, the Conservative People's party (KVP). This same coalition theme had been stressed earlier in an advertisement inserted by some local potentates. Its recommendation was: "Avoid illusions. Think soberly and vote for one of the bourgeois parties." The newspaper reported the activities of all groups on the right, stopping short of the DDP and the Zentrum. Because of their persistent coalitions with the "Socialists," these parties were denied any favor, including even the simple granting of attention. The choice, as the *Nachrichten* saw it, was very simple: bourgeois versus socialist.

It was within this framework that the *Nachrichten* gave supportive attention to the NSDAP. Interior Minister Joseph Wirth issued a report during the 1930 election campaign charging the NSDAP with treasonous activities. The *Nachrichten* carried a long story that cast doubt on Wirth's claims, saying that Wirth's report was no more than an election tactic. A week before the election, the Sunday edition reported rather positively on a speech Hitler gave in Hamburg.

Continuously embellishing the reports on election meetings and speeches were the accounts of street fighting. These had a consistent direction; they stressed the provocations of the left and the "understandable" National Socialist response. The NSDAP cadres were typically portrayed as innocents, as the victims both of Communist attacks and of unfair official reactions. One major headline, for example, reads: "Thirty-four National Socialists Arrested, the Communist Murderers in Freedom?"

An editorial a few days before the election listed five acceptable rightist parties with the DNVP, DVP, and KVP leading the list, followed by two splinter organizations. It then added a sixth, appending its recommendation: "And at the extreme right appears the National Socialist German Workers' party, which intends to bring about a rejuvenation and renewal of our collective national existence. The choice of one of these electoral options is more or less a matter of temperament. *All six of these parties are trustworthy* [and] *nationalist*. [They] struggle *against* the internationalist Marxist parties, the Social Democrats and Communists, who would destroy people and nation, family and German spirit" (emphasis in the original). The day before the election the *Nachrichten* ran an editorial entitled: "For Whom Should You Vote?" This account again discusses the rightist parties, again finding them all acceptable. It ends up with another very positive description of the NSDAP, noting that the party had picked up the lower-middle-class vote. The editorial argued that successful national policies would bring well-being and work to all strata and occupations of the German people. When that happened, National Socialism would "lose its socialistic tendencies." The editorial's final recommendation was: "Vote National!"

The *Nachrichten* accounts in the July 1932 election follow a similar pattern, but with different emphases. The most important change is the sense of urgency communicated on almost every page. There were daily reports of Communist attacks and insurgency. "The Flags Are Lowered" reads one headline, this accompanying a story on the burial of a National Socialist, who was "murdered," the paper claimed, by a Communist. One issue reports on "Communist preparations for civil war." Another account in the same issue contains rather positive reports on two National Socialist meetings. Another deals with the question of "how the red front murders."

At the same time as this alarm about the left was being communicated, the newspaper's attacks on the Zentrum were extremely hostile, one editorial for example being devoted to "the red Zentrum." Hugenberg, then leader of the Conservatives, gave a speech which was reported under the headline: "The System Must Now Die!" The reporting on National Socialist meetings in this period was both extensive and enthusiastic. Gregor Strasser, who addressed a meeting in Harburg, across the river from Hamburg, was given three columns of space.

As for the specific political choices at the moment, the *Nachrichten* offered unambiguous approval of Papen (who had replaced the Zentrum's chancellor, Heinrich Brüning). For Papen's overthrow of the SPD-Zentrum government in Prussia, the *Nachrichten* had rich praise. The task, as this paper saw it, was to provide a strong national front behind the Papen government. In that collective effort, the National Socialists would be one unit, a fighting force. Its final recommendation proved to be a rather open-ended one. The editorial declared that "the Papen government embodies again the Prussian ideal," and it issued a call for support of "the national wave."

It should not be too surprising, given the sense of the imminent Communist uprising that was being communicated, given the sense of urgency, and given, too, the nearly complete condemnation of the republic and its supporting parties, that many upper- and upper-middle-class readers of the *Nachrichten* should have made an "appropriate" reaction, that they should have voted for Hitler's party, a party that had been approved, vouched for, and made acceptable by this newspaper.[22]

The *Hamburgischer Correspondent* was a less important journal, and by most accounts had less influence in upper- and upper-middle-class circles. In the 1930 election, it was clearly opposed to the National Socialists. Unlike the *Nachrichten*, the *Correspondent* did not view the NSDAP as a worthy member of the bourgeois coalition. It supported the DVP and, wherever possible, denigrated the NSDAP's aspirations. It quoted a Communist speaker, to give just one example, who claimed to be working "shoulder to shoulder" with the National Socialists. It also pointed to the anomaly of members of the Sturmabteilung, many of whom were unemployed, spending money for streetcar travel in the service of the party while Goebbels purchased a Mercedes. It shared the world view of the *Nachrichten*, seeing a polar choice between bourgeois and socialist governments. Its explicit option, however, was for the DVP.

In 1932, this focus had lost something of its clarity. The *Correspondent* favored Hindenburg in the presidential election. But in the Reichstag election of July, its prescription, expressed in a simple slogan was: "Vote bourgeois and national!" An editorial on election day indicated approval of Papen and Hindenburg; its explicit recommendations at this point extended only to the DNVP and DVP. It expressed concern over the National Socialist violence. The most positive statement about the NSDAP, almost an aside, was the suggestion that these excesses could best be controlled by bringing the NSDAP into the government to work jointly with the other national parties.[23]

Only limited holdings of the *Hamburger Fremdenblatt* were available; all copies from 1932 were missing. The *Fremdenblatt*'s position in the period of the 1930 election might best be described as "bourgeois democratic." It favored the left liberal DDP (Staatspartei) and offered approval to the Brüning government (unlike the *Nachrichten* and the *Correspondent*). Like the *Correspondent*, the *Fremdenblatt* undercut NSDAP claims. It published the minister of interior's report on the National Socialists under the headline: "The Party of High Treason." It offered an ironic, sarcastic report of Hitler's speech in Hamburg. And an editorial declared that Hitler meant the destruction of the German economy. It also claimed that National Socialists, on the whole, were authentic (*waschechte*) socialists. The socialists within the party, it declared, were the "core of the movement." Its final editorial (in an issue containing full page advertisements for the Staatspartei), recommended votes for the "parties of the center." Its most explicit statement had a negative character: it recommended that no votes be cast for the Communists, Social Democrats, National Socialists, or supporters of Hugenberg.[24]

It is difficult to establish influence with any degree of certitude; it seems likely, however, that these more moderate journals, the *Correspondent* and the *Fremdenblatt*, were simply overwhelmed by events. Because of their small circulation, any influence they had on the election results would have been limited.

The *Hamburger Anzeiger*, a popular journal tending to spectacles and scandal, was in a position to exert much greater influence. According to one informed source, it had the largest circulation of the four bourgeois newspapers. Most such general papers tended to be politically neutral so as not to offend any segments of their readership. Filled with chatty news stories and moderately sensational content, they made their way through the sale of advertising. The *Hamburger Anzeiger*, however, had a very clear position. It was for the Staatspartei—in September 1930, in July 1932, and again in November of 1932. In the presidential election it was very much in favor of Hindenburg and opposed to Hitler. Its position with respect to the NSDAP was unambiguous at all times; it was sharply opposed.[25]

The orientations of the most influential of these newspapers may explain at least part of the voting result delineated earlier. The *Hamburger Nachrichten*, which, as we have seen was very sympathetic to the National Socialists, seems to have played a key role in making that party acceptable to its upper- and upper-middle-class audience. The *Hamburger Anzeiger* would have had an impact on the broad middle classes. It would have countered much of the National Socialist attraction and, more specifically, it would have aided the DDP-Staatspartei. It seems likely that the *Anzeiger*'s support explains the relative success of the Staatspartei in Hamburg, that is, in contrast to its nearly complete failure in Berlin. We will have occasion to return to this question in later chapters where again, in many instances one finds evidence of a mass media influence.

One final point is deserving of some note. The analyses of the left, as was noted in Chapter 2, treat *the* bourgeoisie as an undifferentiated category, and see it as favoring National Socialist aspirations from an early point. This review of the bourgeois press in Hamburg yields a different picture. The four bourgeois newspapers each provided a distinct political option; in other words, they did *not* have a common outlook. And none of them, moreover, preferred Hitler's party. Even the *Nachrichten*, which was clearly the most sympathetic, envisaged a lesser role for Hitler and his party. They were to be foot soldiers in a broad national coalition. At best, the NSDAP was to be one party among the many in the nationalist ranks.

CHAPTER SIX

Cologne and Munich: A Second Pattern

Cologne and Munich were the third and fourth largest cities of Weimar Germany. One cannot consider them in as much detail as was possible for Berlin and Hamburg because statistical evidence is lacking, the main difficulty being the absence of adequate census data for the subareas. The ranking of the subareas in these cities must therefore be largely judgmental.

These two cities can be considered together since they both had sizable Catholic populations. As a consequence there was considerable support for the Catholic Zentrum in Cologne and for the Bavarian People's party in Munich. This Catholic dominance made these communities exceptional among the large cities of Germany; they were the only ones among the republic's twenty-five largest cities in which three-quarters or more of the population were Catholics, the respective percentages for Cologne and Munich being 75.3 and 81.1. The next city with such a high Catholic presence was Augsburg, twenty-ninth in size and like Munich, located in Bavaria. The other large cities with Catholic majorities were in the Ruhr area and because of the special features of that region were different from Cologne and Munich in their politics. Those cities, Essen, Düsseldorf, and Duisburg, are considered in Chapter 7.

The trio of middle-class parties, the Conservatives, the People's party, and the Democrats, which generally received their support from Protestant voters, occupied only a minor place in the electoral affairs of Cologne and Munich. For this reason, among others, the pattern of support for the National Socialists had a somewhat different character from that observed in Berlin and Hamburg.

COLOGNE

The city of Cologne, as of 1933, had a population of 756,605 persons. Located on the Rhine approximately midway on that river's course between Switzerland and the North Sea, it was the Rhineland's largest city. From the time of the Congress of Vienna, it had belonged to Prussia.

The city's Altstadt, centered on the famous cathedral, forms a half-circle on the west bank of the river. This was surrounded by a larger half-circle, an area called the Neustadt; it was located between the "old" or medieval city wall and the "new" walls, the latter being maintained down to the 1920s. At that time, the walls, fortifications, and moats were removed and replaced by a semicircle of parks.

A series of annexations, most of these occurring before the war, had led to the incorporation of vast surrounding territories. This expansion reached over fifteen kilometers to the northwest along the Rhine and there took in farm areas and industrial satellite communities. The city extended also over onto the right side of the Rhine and there included both populated areas and sizable forest and park districts. In terms of its territory, the city was second only to Berlin.

Possibly the most important characteristics of the city's population, for the present purposes, is its religious composition. The 1933 census, as already indicated, found 75.3 percent of the population to be Roman Catholic. This figure stands in marked contrast to the 10.4 percent for Berlin and 5.3 percent for Hamburg. Less than a fifth, 19.6 percent, were Protestant; 2 percent were Jewish; and 3.1 percent were listed as without religion. The remaining fragment was listed as "other Christian religions."[1]

One district—Marienburg—stands out among all the others for its wide variance from the city-wide average. The Catholic percentage there was 53.7, the lowest of any of the fifty subareas for which data are available. The Protestant percentage, 35.1, was the highest of the fifty districts. And the Jewish percentage, 8.4, was also the highest in the city. Marienburg, located on the Rhine at the southern edge of the city, was the richest community, the *Villenviertel* of Cologne.[2]

A report based on the 1927 census of housing indicates that 78.3 percent of the 452 dwelling units of Marienburg were single-family units. Over half of the remaining 21.7 percent were two-family houses. The report notes further that these housing characteristics set Marienburg apart from all other areas of the city.[3]

The available statistics, unfortunately, do not allow anything more than a judgmental assessment of the occupational composition of the city districts. Bayenthal, immediately to the north of Marienburg, is reported to have been very much upper middle class. And Lindenthal, to the west of the older city between the broad park areas surrounding the inner city and the forest lands on the western outskirts, also had an upper-middle-class character. It contained the university as well as some hospitals and clinics; many professionals employed there also lived in the immediate area.

The old city, the Altstadt, contained the cathedral, the main railroad station, government buildings, stores, and hotels. It was, obviously, a very heterogeneous area, one that would have resembled the Altstadt of

Hamburg and the Mitte of Berlin. This semicircle was divided into three administrative districts, north, center, and south. The last had a considerable working-class percentage.

A wide avenue had long since taken the place of the old fortifications. It separated the Altstadt from the Neustadt, the latter forming the next ring in the semicircle. New fortifications, as noted, had once surrounded this ring. One of Konrad Adenauer's many accomplishments— he was Cologne's *Bürgermeister* from 1917 to 1933—was to replace the new fortifications with a broad ring of park land, which surrounded the entire inner city. In the Neustadt one found newer, more elegant housing dating from the 1880s, the basic style being the four-floor apartment house similar to those found in Berlin's Charlottenburg and Wilmersdorf. While not as elegant as those communities, the Neustadt, particularly the north and center segments, is said to have had a fair-sized upper-middle-class presence. The southern segment, matching the Altstadt, was more working class.

Much of the area to the north of this inner city and much of the area across the river were working class. The remaining areas must have contained some mix of working-class and middle-class populations similar to what has been seen elsewhere.[4]

The political developments in Cologne during the early Weimar years were different in many respects from those in Berlin and Hamburg. The 1918-1919 revolution touched Cologne as it did all major cities. But unlike Berlin's, Cologne's revolution was largely imported—a trainload of sailors from the northern port cities arrived one day. Control of the city government, however, was never seriously challenged by the forces of the left. The city, as a result, was spared the ravages of the Freikorps pacification.

Cologne was occupied by the British under the terms of the Armistice and the later Versailles treaty. Under the terms of the same treaty the French occupied the Rhineland to the south of Cologne. In 1923, French troops occupied the Ruhr valley to the northeast of the city. The resulting struggle had an impact, both direct and indirect, that spilled over into Cologne affairs. The French during this period also sponsored a separatist movement intended to create an independent buffer state out of the western provinces of Germany. This too, like the Ruhr occupation, led to armed struggle, assassinations, and sabotage. The struggle in Berlin and Hamburg, from the beginning, was one of left versus right. In Cologne, on the other hand, two struggles were carried on simultaneously, the national conflict, initially at least, overshadowing the class conflict. Both struggles were damped to some extent by the dominance of the moderate Zentrum party and by the equally moderate British occupation.[5]

The Electoral History: 1919-1933. Whereas in Berlin and Hamburg, the Center party gained only a tiny fraction of the vote, in heavily Catholic Cologne, it was the largest party in every election until March 1933, at which point the National Socialists took the lead. The dominance of the Center in turn meant that both the left and the middle-class parties took a smaller share of the vote. This fact would ordinarily suggest that the base for National Socialist gains was smaller. That assumption is not entirely warranted, however, largely because its base in Cologne was somewhat different from that in Berlin and Hamburg.

The original constellation of forces on the left was dramatically different from that in Berlin (Table 6.1). In Cologne, virtually all of the left vote in January 1919 went to the Majority Social Democrats with only a tiny fraction going to the Independents, the respective percentages being 38.6 and 1.4. In Berlin, not only was the left vote considerably larger (64.0 percent versus Cologne's 40.0 percent), but the division was quite different, the Majority Socialists there having 36.4 percent versus the Independents' 27.6 percent. The situation in Hamburg was closer to Cologne's experience than to Berlin's, the respective percentages for the Majority SPD and Independent SPD being 51.3 and 6.7. Among other things, these results show the difficulties that stem from depending on Berlin-centered histories.[6]

The dominance of the Majority Social Democrats on the left was maintained in the municipal election of October 1919, but some increase in Independent strength had already appeared. The leftward trend continued in the Reichstag election of June 1920 at which time the Independents were a significant minority. The Prussian state election of February 1921 showed the Majority holding its position, but at this time most of the former Independents were now voting for the Communists. A dramatic shift occurred in the Reichstag election of May 1924; the Communists gained a clear majority of the left votes. This result is all the more remarkable when it is remembered that the Social Democrats still retained most of the left votes in Berlin and Hamburg. The volatility of Communist voting is indicated, however, in the December election of that year; at that point the majority was once again with the Social Democrats.

The Cologne development matched the experience of Berlin and Hamburg in the following years in that both left parties increased their share of the total vote. Between December 1924 and May 1928, in the "good years," left voting increased from 31.6 to 39.6 percent. In Berlin and Hamburg some of this shift to the left appeared to have come from a rather unexpected source, from former Conservatives. In Cologne the Conservatives did suffer a slight loss, but the most obvious source of new votes for the left in this city was from among former supporters of the Zentrum. The decision taken within the higher councils of the party at that time to play down the interests and concerns of the left or working–class wing of the party appears to have triggered an exodus of working–class supporters. The modest gains for the Zentrum in the upper- and upper-middle-class areas of the city by no means compensated for these losses.[7] This shift to the right is discussed at greater length in Chapter 10. The new party leaders, it should be noted, did not abandon their new direction with the onset of the depression. If anything, they became even more committed to it.

In the final stage, in the last years of the republic, the Communist vote showed a continuous increase. This was the case in all elections up to and including that of November 1932. Unlike the situation in Berlin and Hamburg, where the KPD percentage was stable between 1930 and July 1932, in Cologne the party showed a gain of 5 percent. The Social Democratic percentage showed a corresponding decline in all of these late Weimar elections. The overall percentage for the left, moreover, declined in 1930. In both of the 1932 elections it was only slightly above the precrisis level of 1928.[8]

Two points deserve to be noted here: first, the radicalization in Cologne, as in the two previously discussed cities, occurred within relatively fixed boundaries, within that segment of the population that had been supporting the left all along. And second, the fact of Cologne's being a Catholic city provided only a modest check on the growth of Communist support. In July of 1932, the Communist vote there was 22.0 percent as compared to 27.3 percent in Berlin. The Cologne figure is higher than the 18.4 percent the Communists gained in Protestant and working-class Hamburg.[9]

In the January 1919 election to the Constituent Assembly the Zentrum gained 40.8 percent of the votes, an achievement that appears to have depended on the unusually high level of participation in that election.[10] It was also one of the few occasions in all of modern electoral history that the participation of women exceeded that of men. In subsequent elections the Zentrum percentage fell off, to 35.9 in 1920 and again to 32.7 in May of 1924. There was a slight recovery in December of 1924, but then the decline continued, to 29.1 percent in May 1928 (when working-class supporters switched allegiances), and finally to the low point, 24.9 percent in September 1930. The hold of party and church on the Catholic voters of this city appears to have been a fragile one. As of 1930 the Zentrum had lost nearly 40 percent of its 1919 percentage share, a figure that contrasts with a 25 percent loss in the nation as a whole. This points once again to a conclusion put forth in Chapter 3, that Zentrum loyalties were weak in the cities and that the party's basic strength was found in the Catholic countryside. The Zentrum's rightward shift in the face of such soft commitments was to have very important consequences. Some gains were achieved in July of 1932. There

TABLE 6.1. REICHSTAG ELECTION RESULTS FOR COLOGNE, 1919–1932
(in percent)

Party	Election							
	January 19, 1919	June 6, 1920	May 4, 1924	December 7, 1924	May 20, 1928	September 14, 1930	July 31, 1932	November 6, 1932
SPD	38.6	26.3	12.6	20.0	24.8	19.4	18.4	17.4
USPD	1.4	11.8	1.1[a]	—	—	—	—	—
KPD	—	—	17.1	11.6	14.8	17.0	22.0	24.5
Zentrum	40.8	35.9	32.7	35.2	29.1	24.9	28.2	27.3
DDP	11.0	4.9	3.4	4.8	4.2	4.4	0.3	0.4
DVP	5.4	14.5	10.5	11.9	12.0	6.7	1.4	2.8
DNVP	2.8	2.8	6.6	7.2	5.5	1.7	3.1	5.5
NSDAP	—	—	3.0	1.0	1.6	17.6	24.5	20.4
Others	—	3.7	13.0	8.3	8.1	8.2	2.1	1.7
Total	100.0	99.9	100.0	100.0	100.1	99.9	100.0	100.0
Participation	70.2	56.9	59.3	59.5	60.4	74.0	76.9	68.7

SOURCE: *Kölner Statistisches Handbuch*, 13. 1 (1958): 272–273.
[a] Subsequently 0.5 percent or less and located with Others.

is a suggestion in the available data, however, that this late gain came from the not very reliable ranks of the previous nonvoters. Even then the party did not achieve the percentage strength it had had in May of 1928.[11]

Looking at the trio of center right parties, one finds, from 1920 through 1930, a relative dominance of the right liberals, that is, of the German People's party. The Conservatives had only a minuscule percentage at the start of the republic. They managed to increase their share to 7.2 percent in December 1924, a pale reflection of the surge that came elsewhere in the Reich. At no point prior to July 1932, however, did they gain more than the People's party. The People's party, as we shall see, was the leading party through 1930 in Marienburg, the best-off district of the city.

The Conservatives suffered a serious loss in 1928 and were almost eliminated in 1930. A major part of the latter loss, however, was due to a split within the party, the defecting People's Conservatives appearing in the "others" category.[12] There seems to have been some regrouping in the two 1932 elections, with some rightist voters choosing the DNVP as their best option.

The People's party showed a slight increase in 1928, but it lost nearly half its strength in 1930 and was nearly eliminated in July of 1932. It made some gains in the November election, but the party still had only a trivial share of the total vote. The DDP, never strong in the city (apart from the exceptional 1919 election), held its modest strength even in September 1930. It was eliminated in July of 1932.

The National Socialist development in Cologne shows some initial similarities to the developments in other cities. The party had a modest success in May 1924 but lost two-thirds of that accomplishment in December that year. As in most areas of southern and western Germany, it had already showed some increase in 1928, and then, in September 1930, it achieved its massive breakthrough. The second massive gain came in July of 1932, that being followed by the decline in November.

Some accounts rather seriously misrepresent the National Socialist development. A former city official, for example, one who certainly should have been well informed about the city's affairs, was quoted, in the early fifties, as follows: "One cannot talk about a rise of National Socialism in Cologne. Our good Catholic population showed itself immune to the temptations of a political messianism in a way that the population of no other large city of Germany did. . . . although Cologne had to suffer especially hard from the effects of the economic crisis after 1929."[13]

As of September 1930, however, the National Socialist percentage in Cologne exceeded the percentage in Berlin and was less than two percentage points below the equivalent figure for Hamburg. In July of 1932, both cities overtook Catholic Cologne, but even then the differences between them were not sizable. In Berlin, Hitler's party received 28.6 percent as compared to 24.5 percent in Cologne. These results once again raise questions about the effectiveness of Goebbels's demagogy, the percentages in Berlin being not that different from those achieved in less auspicious Cologne.[14]

The Support for the National Socialists. As indicated, precise data from the census such as would allow us to establish the standing of the city districts, were unavailable. For that reason the assessments made earlier, except for Marienburg, have a rule-of-thumb character. Some evidence confirming those judgments appears in the voting patterns of the districts. The data from December 1924, that convenient reference point election, show two-thirds of the voters in upper-class Marienburg supporting the three middle-class parties, the DVP, DDP, or DNVP. One-third of the community's voters supported the German People's party, strongly suggesting that it, not the conservative DNVP, was the favorite of the leading elements in the city, a result that parallels the experience in the upper-class areas of Hamburg.

The other better-off areas, Neustadt-North, Neustadt-Center, and Lindenthal, all had support for this trio of parties that was well above the city average. The Bayenthal results, unfortunately, are combined with the votes from several other more heterogeneous communities, the actual listing being "Bayenthal etc."[15] Many of the other city districts have been lumped together, and this, combined with the lack of information on occupational composition, means that little can be done by way of analysis. The results (shown in Table 6.2), therefore, are considerably simplified. We have shown the National Socialist percentages for the inner-city districts (including both the old and the new cities), for three of the better-off districts, and for one relatively large mixed district ("Nippes etc."). All of the other districts, which would have been working class or mixed in character, have been combined. While that means the loss of much detail, the lessons to be learned there may be easily summarized.[16]

In the 1930 election, the year of the breakthrough, one finds a pattern that is strikingly different from those observed in Berlin and Hamburg. The best-off areas, Marienburg and Lindenthal, were *not* above the city average; the former community in fact was well below that average. All of the areas of the inner city, upper middle, middle, and working class alike, were above average, the first providing the NSDAP with its greatest support. The mixed Bayenthal district was slightly above the city's average. Except for one minor subarea, all of the other districts,

TABLE 6.2. SUPPORT FOR THE NATIONAL SOCIALISTS IN COLOGNE SUBAREAS, 1930-1932

(in percent)

| | | Election | |
	1930	July 1932	November 1932
Inner city			
Neustadt-North	**23.0**	**33.8**	**28.1**
Neustadt-Center	**24.0**	**34.4**	**29.3**
Neustadt-South	**20.8**	**28.0**	**23.9**
Altstadt-North	**21.0**	**27.8**	**23.4**
Altstadt-Center	**23.9**	**31.2**	**26.5**
Altstadt-South	18.5	22.9	19.9
Outer city			
Marienburg	12.1	24.5	16.1
Lindenthal	17.2	**27.7**	**20.6**
Bayenthal etc.[a]	**19.1**	26.4	**22.6**
Nippes etc.[a]	16.3	24.8	21.0
All other districts	14.6	20.7	17.3
Cologne total	17.6	24.5	20.4

SOURCE: Lorenz Huber, "Die politischen Wahlen in Köln in den Jahren 1919 bis 1926," *Kölner Verwaltung und Statistik*, 6: 1/2; Huber, "Die Reichstags und die Landtagswahl in Köln am 20. Mai 1928," *Kölner Verwaltung und Statistik*, 6: 3; "Die Ergebnisse der 5. Reichstagswahl am 14. September 1930 in Köln nach Stimmbezirken," *Beilage zum Monatsbericht des Statistischen und Wahlamts der Stadt Köln für August 1930*; "Die 6. Reichstagswahl am 31. Juli 1932 in Köln," *Beilage . . . für Juli 1932*; "Die 7. Reichstagswahl am 6. November 1932 in Köln," *Beilage . . . für November 1932*; and "Die Wahlen vom 5. und 12. März 1933 in Köln," *Beilage . . . für März 1933*.
NOTE: Figures in bold type are above the city average.
[a] Includes other communities.

most of them working-class and mixed communities, were well below the city average.

A similar pattern may be observed in the July 1932 election. The "good middle class" areas of the inner city again gave Hitler's party the highest percentages received anywhere in the city. The working-class district Altstadt-South at this point fell just below the city-wide average. Lindenthal and Bayenthal were now both slightly above the city average, and at this point Marienburg was exactly at the average. Nippes, the mixed area, was also very close to the average. All other subareas of the city were below the average.

In the November election, the NSDAP lost in all areas although the same general relationships remained. The only finding of note involved the rate of decline. Whereas the NSDAP vote in the city fell 16.7 percent below the level of July, in Marienburg its vote was down by 34.3 percent. In Lindenthal the decline was 25.6 percent. In Cologne, there appears to have been a sharp reaction against the National Socialists, perhaps because of the leftward course they adopted at this time or perhaps because of revulsion over the Potempa affair.

The contrast with Berlin is especially striking. The upper-class and upper-middle-class districts in that city gave above average support to the National Socialists from the very beginning and continued to do so until the end of the republic. In Cologne, on the other hand, the National Socialists' greatest strength came in the upper-middle-class districts of the inner city while the populations in the best-off areas of the city resisted the temptation to support that party. Some support did come belatedly, in July 1932, but then much of it disappeared again as rapidly as it had come.

Although there was considerable mixing of populations in the inner-city districts, the persistent strength of the party in Neustadt-North and Neustadt-Center, the strongest districts in both 1932 elections, suggests upper-middle- as opposed to lower-middle-class support. Admittedly, this is no more than a suggestion. The data on this particular matter are the weakest of any for the three cities discussed thus far.

Some of the statistical corrections undertaken in the previous chapters may be made here also. Significant Jewish minorities appeared in Marienburg (8.4 percent), in Neustadt-Center (7.8 percent), and in Altstadt-Center (4.6 percent). If one assigns all the NSDAP votes to the non-Jewish populations, the figures in those districts increase somewhat; Neustadt-Center goes from 34.4 to 37.3 percent, Altstadt-Center from 31.2 to 32.7 percent, and Marienburg from 24.5 to 26.7 percent. The last adjustment would put Marienburg slightly above the city average. Even with these adjustments, however, the original pattern is only very slightly changed.

The fact remains, therefore, that Marienburg showed a political development that was very different from those seen in Zehlendorf and Wilmersdorf or in Harvestehude. A second pattern is clearly indicated in the votes of this city's upper class. This alternative pattern is all the more unexpected since in Marienburg, with what for Cologne was a high Protestant percentage, one would have anticipated relatively high support for the National Socialists. Marienburg's modest levels of support take on added meaning in the light of this compositional factor.[17]

As with the other cities reviewed thus far, in Cologne, too, it was not possible to sort out homogeneous lower-middle-class communities. And none of the areas likely to have had lower-middle-class clusterings gave especially strong support to the NSDAP. In fact, other than Nippes, all of the mixed districts were below average, and Nippes, in both 1932 elections, was very close to the city average. Once again, we do not find support for the lower-middle-class hypothesis.

The Question of Linkages. One possible explanation for this Cologne exception is that the bourgeois newspapers had different orientations from those of Berlin and Hamburg. The options for the "good middle class" reader in Cologne may be very simply described. Leading the list as the undisputed quality newspaper was the *Kölnische Zeitung*, a journal with a long liberal tradition, one reaching back to the eighteenth century. Also of some quality was the *Kölnische Volkszeitung*, a journal that was unmistakably devoted to the interests of the Zentrum. And then, of distinctly lesser quality, were two newspapers for the general public, papers that specialized more in sensationalism than in serious political news; these were the *Stadt-Anzeiger* and the *Kölner Tageblatt*. The *Stadt-Anzeiger* was put out by the same organization—DuMont Schauberg—that put out the highly respected *Kölnische Zeitung*.

As for the voters of elegant Marienburg, the consensus among the local experts is that they would have read the *Kölnische Zeitung*. If they had strong Catholic commitments they would probably have read the *Kölnische Volkszeitung*, either as an alternative or in addition to the *Kölnische*. One local expert thought there would also have been some readership of the left liberal *Frankfurter Zeitung*, and that some may have read the *Vossische Zeitung* from Berlin. The former had a good financial section which may have been read to the exclusion of the news and editorials. In all likelihood, however, the *Kölnische Zeitung* was the most widely read newspaper in Marienburg, Bayenthal, and Lindenthal.

The upper- and upper-middle-class newspaper readers in Cologne, in short, did not have a local conservative newspaper at their disposal. The *Kölnische* was very much a liberal newspaper. While generally supportive of the German People's party, a free enterprise party with some similarities to the Republicans in the United States, the *Kölnische* was distinctive, nevertheless, in that within the liberal framework it was very much open to reform. It was not, in other words, a reactionary newspaper. This is perhaps best indicated by its political preferences— it favored or was open to both right and left liberal parties. Unlike some of the Berlin newspapers and unlike the *Nachrichten* of Hamburg, this journal, at the time of the 1930 election, was decisively opposed to the National Socialists. There was none of the avuncular support for the "exuberant" nationalism of the NSDAP; its position was one of sharp and unambiguous condemnation. In reporting on violence, it talked in terms of Communists versus National Socialists; both were counted as extremists, both seen as rowdies. There was no tendency evident to excuse the NSDAP as a victim of Communist attacks or to portray its members as heroic fighters in the struggle against Communism.

The newspaper reported on the meetings of all parties although, to be sure, those of the DVP and DDP (at this point, the Deutsche Staatspartei) predominated. The newspaper was unusual for the analytical detail it offered. Whereas the *Vossische Zeitung* and the *Berliner Tageblatt* had what one might term a mass-society emphasis, stressing the demagogic and irrational character of the NSDAP offerings, the *Kölnische* provided detailed accounts of the internal dynamics of the party and its use of the "organizational weapon." It provided detailed reports, for example, on the Stennes mutiny (an uprising of the Berlin SA against Goebbels's leadership there) and on Hitler's interventions to stabilize the situation.

An editorial of September 3, 1930, provides the best statement of its position. Entitled "Defense against National Socialism," it pointed to the party's attacks on both communism *and* capitalism. It complained of a general refusal to recognize the party's attitude toward capitalism and objected to the belief that the NSDAP represented nothing more than "harmless play." Then, in a theme that remained more or less constant with the *Kölnische* to the end, it argued that both the right and the left had a common trait, "the will to destroy private property, through a party dictatorship to carry out socialism in its crudest form." The conclusions drawn were that the democratic parties must conduct a unified struggle against both extremes, they must announce a clear rejection of any coalition with the NSDAP, they must guarantee the control of their meetings (*Hausrecht*), and they must demonstrate that they will not capitulate.

One also finds, in the days following, rather detailed accounts of the affairs of most major parties. Gustav Stolper of the Staatspartei gave speeches in Cologne and in Aachen. An NSDAP attempt to disrupt was thwarted. The paper provided details on the split within the DNVP. There was a report on an open letter Catholic supporters of the DNVP had directed to the leaders of the Zentrum. The incongruity of the coalition of Zentrum and Social Democrats in Prussia was pointed out: parish priests condemned the SPD from the pulpit, and yet the Zentrum continued the alliance. There was an analysis of left, center, and right factions within the NSDAP. And there was a report on the DNVP which opened with the headline: "Hugenberg Counts on Hitler."

An editorial on September 6 called on women to get out and vote. After an initial recommendation for the DVP, the final conclusion was somewhat more open-ended, asking "that all women vote, that they vote bourgeois."

On the same day, the paper carried a report from the SPD press service, this under the heading "Communists and National Socialists." A Communist speaker was quoted as follows: "Yes indeed, we admit that we stand allied with the National Socialists, that we, in union with the National Socialists want to destroy the existing capitalist system, that we, together with the Nazis want to introduce national bolshevism. . . . if the Nazis have helped us in the fight, we will settle accounts with them ourselves . . . with the fascists we want to free the German working class. Bolshevism and fascism both have a common goal; the destruction of capitalism and the Social Democratic party. To attain this goal, we will use any means."

The Marienburg reader, in short, was given cause to believe that National Socialists and Communists, if not exactly blood brothers, at least were pursuing very similar aims. Put differently, unlike the readers of Berlins's *Börsenzeitung* or Hamburg's *Nachrichten*, these readers were not being told that the National Socialists were acceptable members of a bourgeois coalition. The final editorial recommended a vote for either the German People's party or the German State party. This recommendation came under a headline calling for a strengthening of the "liberal center."[19]

The same basic position was put forward prior to the July 1932 Reichstag election, although here, late in the campaign, there was a decisive shift in position. An editorial, two weeks before the election, one concerned with "bourgeois consciousness," dealt with left and right socialism. Its summary conclusion was simple enough: "Against socialism left and right!" On the following Wednesday, the paper published an editorial entitled "The Two-Facedness of National Socialism," arguing that the party would not protect private property.

But on the Friday before the election, the new note was sounded: "After the thirty-first of July the National Socialists must bear responsibility and be drawn into the work of political reconstruction. . . . On the thirty-first of July it is important to vote for those parties that have recognized the necessity that the National Socialists be drawn into responsibility now, who, nevertheless are resolved *not to abandon the indispensable essence of the bourgeois ideals.*" On the day of the election the editorial elaborated on this theme, its point being that otherwise the two socialist fronts, right and left, might join together. To prevent that eventuality, it recommended bringing the National Socialists into a bourgeois coalition, so as to achieve a "burdening with political responsibility." This solution, taming them with power, as we shall see, was one with wide currency in the late Weimar years.

On the day after the election, the editorial writers proceeded to digest the lessons. Their continued lack of enthusiasm for the NSDAP was indicated by their reference to that party, along with the KPD and the SPD, as the "three socialist parties" that, together, now had more than two-thirds of the seats. Their immediate recommendation was for a continuation of the Papen government; the immediate practical implication was for the Zentrum to tolerate his government. The alternative, as they saw it, was some kind of left coalition.[19]

Later in August, five death sentences were handed down in connection with the Potempa murder. This act of bestiality by Sturmabteilung members (see Chapter 4) obviously required further reflection on the acceptability of Hitler and his party. The SA members were given the death sentence under an emergency decree that was intended to halt the mounting political violence. The *Kölnische Zeitung* editorial frankly admitted the brutal character of the murder but then reminded its readers of the Ohlau incident (see note 22, Chapter 4), a complicating consideration that is absent from most subsequent accounts. The newspaper recommended that the death sentence be changed to a prison term.

The newspaper provided a review of press comment on the sentence, which indicated a wide consensus that prison was the appropriate punishment. In the aftermath of Hitler's statement defending his men, the newspaper provided another review of press reaction. This indicated an equally strong consensus; even the *Börsen-zeitung* condemned his remarks.

This proved bitter medicine for the editorialists. As they put it: "All of the reservations that thus far have been raised against the granting of important office to National Socialists have been considerably strengthened by Hitler's behavior in response to the Beuthen judgment—they have become almost insurmountable." They then proceeded to recommend the medicine nevertheless, it being justified by the otherwise hopeless political situation. Where should Germany turn "if the effort is not made to harness their radicalism and to give the National Socialists responsibility and thereby the opportunity to demonstrate their true abilities? A government [such as Papen's] that has nine-tenths of the people against it, cannot keep itself in the saddle in the long run." Their conclusion (given emphasis with heavy type) was that "it is the task, in the Germany of today and tomorrow, to bring National Socialism to the point that it bears responsibility within the framework of the constitution."[20]

This conception of "the political task" disappeared completely in the course of the November election. The key factor was the National Socialist involvement in the Berlin transport workers' strike along with the Communists. The *Kölnische* carried reports of National Socialist financial support for the strike. One NSDAP party member ended a speech with the appeal to the *Volksgenossen* (people's comrades)—"Show that you are Socialists of the act." An editorial by Alice Neven DuMont called for support of the government (i.e. Papen) and Hindenburg. The recommended parties at this point were the DVP and the DNVP, it being left to the voter to choose. Her editorial strongly opposed Hitler.

The Sunday (election day) editorial called for a strengthening of the "bourgeois right." The recurrent ambiguity of the paper's editorials was indicated in a paragraph well down in the piece, one intended to provide proper balance: "As for the difficulties made by the National Socialist party for the bourgeois elements, one should not, however, forget the larger danger that threatens from the extreme left."[21]

The shifts in position of the *Kölnische Zeitung* are broadly consonant with the shifts in voting seen in upper-class Cologne. When the newspaper was solidly opposed to the National Socialists, in September 1930, those districts gave the party below average support. In mid-1932, when there was a limited, tactical acceptance of the party's aspirations, those districts gave support that was slightly above average. But in November 1932, when the newspaper again sharply opposed the NSDAP, the support for Hitler's party in those districts fell off precipitously.

The *Kölnische Volkszeitung*, as indicated, was a firm advocate of the interests of the Zentrum. As such, the newspaper was also, obviously, a defender of the Brüning government and an unambiguous opponent of National Socialism. To the extent that it was read by upper- and upper-middle-class populations, it would also presumably have helpd to limit the growth of the NSDAP and, simultaneously, helped maintain or even increase Zentrum strength.[22]

The other two newspapers that might have been read by at least some middle-class citizens were the *Stadt-Anzeiger* and the *Kölner Tageblatt*. Both of these were well below the previously discussed newspapers in quality. The *Stadt-Anzeiger* reported crimes, fires, and auto accidents. In a period when most newspapers concentrated on political violence in Germany, this newspaper picked up nonpolitical murders and, reaching far afield, reported Mississippi lynchings. It also had a large sports section and carried many advertisements. Politically it was about as neutral (or indifferent) as one could possibly be. In the 1930 election, aside from encouraging participation ("The Nonvoter Sins against the Fatherland"), it offered little discussion or direct recommendation. At that point a brief editorial favored "a strong center."

In the July 1932 election, its contribution was even more limited. Ten days before the election a brief back-page editorial declared that "the *Stadt-Anzeiger* is a nonpolitical paper" and, to ensure its neutrality, announced it would not accept political advertisements. On the day of the election it published a very noncommittal editorial; it opposed the "brutalization" of the political scene and expressed appreciation for those who had to bear the burden. This thoroughly depoliticized performance was all the more amazing when one remembers that the *Stadt-Anzeiger* was published by the same firm as the *Kölnische Zeitung*.[23]

The *Kölner Tageblatt* was also a general or popular newspaper, and it too was basically a scandal sheet. It had a larger sports section than the *Stadt-Anzeiger*. It had had some links to the DDP in previous years, and some signs of this connection were still found in its pages in the early thirties. It published an editorial written by the leading district candidate of the Staatspartei in its morning edition the day before the election. On the day of the election its editorial recommended that people get out and vote. The argument, a rather indirect one, was that nonvoters strengthened the radicalism of the right and left since the "fanaticized and those led astray by radicalism will all go to the polls." This issue contained three advertisements for the Staatspartei and one for the DVP. This restrained enthusiasm for the moderate parties was offset by a rather unexpected news item, this being a story on the murder of Horst Wessel, a National Socialist hero and martyr. The account was rather long and detailed for this paper and also was generally sympathetic.

A similar mixed performance accompanied the July 1932 election. A couple of stories attacked National Socialist lies and misrepresentations. The final editorial was also clear and unambiguous, if lacking a specific focus: "Voters! Don't forget! Your freedom is at stake! Vote for the parties of the bourgeois center." A few days before the election, however, the paper published a picture of Prince August Wilhelm, one of the kaiser's sons. The single line of comment read: "Prince Auwi in the first row of the NSDAP." One wonders what lessons the *Tageblatt*'s readers would have drawn from this.[24]

The best newspaper of Cologne, in short, discouraged support for the NSDAP. This performance stands in sharp contrast to that of some equivalent newspapers in Berlin and Hamburg, where, as we have seen, the papers' positions would certainly have made it easy to shift allegiance. The general newspapers of Cologne, on the other hand, probably affected few political decisions one way or another, certainly not through direct influence. Their refusal to supply either anchorage or direction, however, would have left their readers open to other influences. In normal times, there would not have been any systematic, that is, any concerted direction to those other influences. But at this point, with NSDAP cadres dominating the streets and meeting halls, neutrality would allow a considerable drift away from traditional loyalties.[25]

MUNICH

With its 1933 population of 735,388, the city of Munich was the fourth largest city of Germany. It was similar to Cologne, as already noted, in having a large Catholic population, and, as will be seen, its electoral development, particularly in the end phase of the republic, also showed similarities to that of Cologne.

So much for the parallels. The city was different from all other German cities in many ways. It was the capital city of Bavaria, which, after Prussia, was the largest state in the Reich. And Bavaria, a somewhat reluctant participant in Bismarck's Reich, had a history of opposition to the control and domination of the Prussians. After the assassination of the foreign minister, Walther Rathenau, in 1922, the Berlin government forbade extremist movements, both left and right, a *Verbot* that included the National Socialists. The Bavarian government, still traumatized by the revolutionary events of 1918-1919, refused to follow the government decree. A similar federal-state crisis arose a year later over the question of banning paramilitary organizations with Bavaria again refusing to comply. Not too surprisingly, Bavaria became a haven for rightist activists who arrived there from throughout the Reich. It was this freedom that allowed Munich to become, as NSDAP spokesmen later phrased it, the "capital city of the movement."

The city had an important musical, literary, and artistic tradition, and a large colony of Bohemians—artists, intellectuals, journalists, and assorted literati—had been drawn there from throughout the nation. Some members of this Bohemian colony had led the first or moderate phase of the 1918 revolution. Munich's postwar history was more tumultuous than anywhere else except possibly Berlin, and the revolutionaries' party, the Independent Socialists, suffered a disastrous defeat in the election for the Bavarian Constituent Assembly. Their leader, Kurt Eisner, was assassinated in February 1919 on his way to the parliament where he was to offer his resignation. This event stimulated another uprising that eventually resulted in a more ruthless left government, the so-called Bavarian Soviet, this under leaders recently returned from Russia. The Freikorps "liberated" the city on May 1, 1919. An estimated 600 deaths followed.[26]

The next five years brought an extraordinary series of difficulties, ending with Hitler's *Putsch* attempt and his subsequent trial and conviction. The governments of Bavaria, as indicated, posed no end of problems for the government in Berlin. Stressing the autonomy of the Bavarian Free State, they refused to implement Berlin laws and decrees. They rejected the Berlin demand that the NSDAP's Sturmabteilung be disbanded, this paramilitary force having attracted the attention of the French who viewed such formations as violating the Versailles treaty obligations. The Bavarian precedent in turn had implications for autonomist (or insurgent) tendencies in other states. The Bavarian government under Gustav von Kahr, moreover, toyed with the idea of a complete break with Germany and later flirted with various rightist movements, their intent being to "clean up" the entire Reich. The involvement of this government with Hitler and his movement made it difficult for them, to say the least, to conduct a serious prosecution after the failure of the 1923 *Putsch*. As was noted in the Berlin chapter, this trial in Munich gave Hitler a stage from which he could for the first time dramatize his movement before a national audience.

The constellation of parties in Bavaria was somewhat different from that found elsewhere in Germany. A first and key difference involved the presence of the Bavarian People's party in place of the Zentrum. Dissatisfied with Zentrum policies—ostensibly with the Zentrum's neglect of Bavarian interests—the Bavarian People's party had split off to form an independent party. In the Weimar regime the Zentrum had a significant center of gravity among the workers of the Ruhr and Rhineland, and under the new proportional representation electoral system it was forced to pay attention to the workers' interests. This in turn meant some corresponding neglect of conservative business interests, of the Catholic aristocracy, and of the small farmers. In Bavaria, however, the People's party allowed the prewar coalition of these various conservative groups to continue. This meant that the Catholic members of Munich's upper class had an adequate vehicle for the representation of their interests throughout most of the republic's history. The strength of their party, unlike that of their Protestant peers in Berlin and Hamburg, was not eroded. And unlike the party of their Catholic peers in Cologne, theirs had no long standing coalition with the Socialists. For this reason, among others, they had little incentive to shift to another party in the final years of the republic.

The converse of this upper- and upper-middle-class link to the BVP was a general weakness of the so-called middle-class parties in Munich, particularly of the DVP and the DDP. Given the small representation of Protestants in the city, the segment from which those parties drew most of their support, and given the loyalty of the upper- and-upper-middle-class Catholics to the BVP, this weakness will come as no great surprise.

One other respect in which the city was different has serious implications for our analysis. Unlike the Hamburg city fathers, who provided more than ample funds to document the community's accomplishments, the city fathers of Munich proved rather indifferent to such matters. In 1914 the budget for the collection and publication of statistics was drastically reduced, and adequate funds were not restored until 1954. Only four yearbooks were published during that forty-year period which means that there are no easily accessible data for the elections of the Weimar period. The only detailed information available was the original typed copies of the precinct results. No aggregations of these 700 or so units exist for the various districts of the city. Any consolidation of those results would require painstaking work with the voting results, with the volume describing precinct boundaries, and with city maps for that period. Moreover, no data were discovered showing the social composition of the different subareas of the city. Hence all judgments made about the city's subareas depend on the assessments of informants. Because of these many difficulties, only a very limited presentation of results is possible.

The Electoral Developments. In such a heavily Catholic city, one might expect little support for the left, for the Marxist parties, but that expectation, as in Cologne, is mistaken. As of May 1924, 31.8 percent of the voters favored one or the other of the two Marxist parties (Table 6.3). The vote for the left is well below that of Hamburg (46.8 percent); it is somewhat lower than the Berlin figure (40.9 percent) and is roughly equal to that of Cologne (see Table 6.1).[27]

In Munich too one finds an unexpected growth in leftist strength during the period of economic stability. The left vote increased by 4.5 percentage points in the December 1924 election and again by nearly five percentage points in the May 1928 election. An important variation on the pattern seen elsewhere occurs in Munich: Communist strength declined steadily in this period while the fortunes of the Social Democrats showed continuous improvement. The overall increase in the strength of the left meant that the SPD was drawing not just from the Communists, but from other parties as well.

With the onset of the depression, two contrasting developments occurred on the left. There was, as seen elsewhere, a decline in the total vote for the left parties.[28] Within the left, however, there was a pro-

TABLE 6.3. REICHSTAG ELECTION RESULTS FOR MUNICH, 1924–1932
(in percent)

Party	Election					
	May 4, 1924	December 7, 1924	May 20, 1928	September 14, 1930	July 31, 1932	November 6, 1932
SPD	16.6	25.2	32.6	28.6	22.2	20.6
KPD	15.2	11.1	8.5	10.1	15.4	19.7
BVP	20.6	23.7	23.1	22.9	26.9	24.9
DDP	} 2.7[a]	4.5	3.5	2.3	0.5	0.5
DVP		—	5.4	1.6	0.8	0.9
DNVP	12.3	21.5	9.1	2.4	3.2	6.7
NSDAP	28.5[b]	9.1	10.7	21.8	28.9	24.9
Others	4.1	4.9	7.1	10.3	2.1	1.8
Total	100.0	100.0	100.0	100.0	100.0	100.0
Participation	68.6	79.3	75.0	82.3	76.9	74.4

SOURCE: *Statistisches Handbuch der Stadt München*, Munich: Carl Gerber Verlag, 1928, p.302; and *Statistisches Handbuch der Stadt München*, Munich: R. Oldenbourg, 1954, p. 243.
[a] The DDP and the DVP formed a coalition for the May 1924 election.
[b] The Völkische Block.

nounced shift away from the Social Democrats to the Communists. Unlike Berlin and Hamburg, here the shift to the Communists was continuous, occurring in all three Reichstag elections prior to Hitler's coming to power.

The total vote for the left increased slightly in November of 1932, to 40.3 percent, a figure that was still below the 41.1 percent achieved in 1928. Such details, however, were not likely to have been seen by alarmed rightists. The shifts within the ranks of the left would, no doubt, have provided them with considerable cause for alarm.

Another more or less constant factor was the strength of the Bavarian People's party, this conservative organization gaining approximately one-quarter of the city's votes in all elections of the late Weimar period. It suffered no dramatic loss of support such as occurred with the Zentrum in Cologne in 1928 after its turn to the right. Because of the persisting conservative character of the BVP, its support showed little change up to the July 1932 election. At that time it showed fair-sized gains, some voters from the so-called middle-class parties no doubt having shifted into its ranks.

Bavaria was not an auspicious setting for the liberal parties at any time. The anticlericalism of the liberal parties worked to their disadvantage in this Catholic milieu. Their history, ideologies, and current programs were such as to limit their chances in Munich as compared, for example, to their sitiuation in commercial Hamburg. Hence one finds them in a series of mutually supportive coalitions in the early Weimar years. When they finally appeared as independent parties in the 1928 election, they gained a total of 8.9 percent, as against their 14.2 percent in Berlin and 25.0 percent in Hamburg. But this support fell off in 1930 and declined even further (to 1.3 percent) in July of 1932. The liberal parties did not have much initial strength to lose to the NSDAP in 1930, the NSDAP already having eaten into their support in May of 1924.[29]

The Conservatives, as noted repeatedly, were a Prussian, landed, and largely Protestant party. Their following in the Bavarian capital therefore proves rather surprising, 12.3 percent in May 1924, and even more surprising, 21.5 percent in December of that year. The first figure is well below the Berlin level at that time (22.6 percent), but the second is not far from it (23.9 percent). Most of the Conservative strength of December 1924 was lost in the May 1928 election, and those losses continued in the 1930 election. In Munich, it appears that the vote of December 1924 was determined more by tactical considerations than by fundamental loyalties. Many Conservatives appear to have voted for the NSDAP front organization, the Völkischer Block (a right-wing alliance put together early in 1924 to contest elections in Bavaria), in the May election of 1924 and drifted to another base in December. In the 1928 elections defections from the conservatives went in unexpected directions. Some, to be sure, went to the right liberals. Some went to a plethora of splinter parties that appeared at that point. Some of the former Conservative voters would appear to have gone to the Social Democrats who, as we have seen, peaked at that time. It is not possible to establish that point with certainty since there is, once again, the possibility of two-step flows (the one-time Conservatives voting for a moderate or center party and former supporters of such parties shifting to the Social Democrats).

The May election, it will be remembered, came not quite six months after Hitler's *Putsch* attempt, and only a little more than one month after his conviction. The Völkischer Block gained just over one-quarter of the votes cast in Munich at that point, high treason having done little to damp enthusiasm. There is, indeed, some evidence that Hitler's actions had just the opposite effect.[30] The May 1924 level of support in Munich, it will be noted, is far above that discovered in any of the cities discussed thus far.

A precipitous falloff in support for the Völkischer Block occurred in the December 1924 election, the largest part of the losses, as already noted, apparently going to the Conservatives. That decline still left the Block with 9.1 percent of the total vote. The National Socialist vote in 1928 amounted to 10.7 percent, up slightly from December 1924, which again parallels the experience elsewhere in southern and western Germany. The party then doubled its strength in the 1930 election and made another sizable gain in July of 1932. Its rate of advance, however, was lower in Munich than elsewhere in the nation. The 1930 figure was still somewhat higher than the figure for the Reich. The July 1932 figure, by contrast, was well below the 37.3 percent the NSDAP gained in the nation. At that point the Protestant countryside had overtaken this Catholic city.[31]

Voting in the City's Subareas. The difficulties involved in any analysis of voting in Munich have already been mentioned. The following discussion, accordingly, can only be fragmentary.[32]

The "best" area of the city, the *Villenviertel* of Munich, was the Bogenhausen district. Comparable to Harvestehude and Marienburg, it was the home of leading business and government figures. It was also the home of Germany's leading author, Thomas Mann, and of the noted conductor Bruno Walter. Another resident author, at least that is how he was listed in the city directory, was Adolf Hitler.

The older and most elegant part of the Bogenhausen district fronted on the Isar River. In the early twenties, that segment was all there was to Bogenhausen. But later in that decade, some blocks away from the

river, new houses were constructed, and, still further inland, some mul-
tistoried structures with spacious apartments were built. For the earliest
of the relevant elections, the focus is on the two precincts of the old
Bogenhausen area.

In the May 1924 election those precincts showed a level of support
for the Völkischer Block that was roughly equal to that of the city as
a whole. The support for the coalition, in short, was not unusual; the
best-off populations were neither especially attracted nor especially repelled by Hitler's movement.

At that point, the strongest party in Bogenhausen was the DNVP,
something of a surprise for the Bavarian capital. In both precincts, the
DNVP together with the Block took a majority of the vote. One possible explanation could be that Bogenhausen, like Marienburg, had a
disproportionately Protestant population, which was now voting for the
appropriate party. Rejecting the clericalism of the BVP, such voters had
not found an adequate party on the Bavarian scene in the turbulent first
years of the republic. But in 1920, the BVP had formed the rightist
government in the aftermath of the Kapp *Putsch*, and shortly thereafter
its coalition was enlarged by the inclusion of the DNVP. In 1924, it
was clear that this party was experiencing a nationwide surge; the enhanced viability of the party nationally could also have motivated a shift
to the DNVP.

A sizable increase in the number of Bogenhausen DNVP votes appeared in December 1924. There can be little doubt that most of these
new DNVP voters had previously voted for the National Socialists
(specifically, for the Völkischer Block). The Block had taken 34.9 percent of the city's vote in the Landtag election of April 6, 1924. A month
later, in the Reichstag election its total fell to 28.5 percent. And in December it fell again to 9.1 percent. A coalition of rightist parties had
been organized for the municipal elections in December, the BVP, the
DNVP, and the DVP being the major partners. Their aim was to break
the "red domination" of city hall. Clearly a regrouping of conservative
forces was in process, and the DNVP, at this point, was the major
beneficiary of the shift.

A vote for the DNVP, it should be noted, did not indicate sharp
opposition to the National Socialists, most especially in Bavaria. It was
not, as some have argued, a vote for responsible conservatism as opposed to the irresponsible National Socialist variety. The DNVP generally was favorably disposed to the NSDAP. In Bavaria, its supporters
saw the National Socialists as having a reliable army, an important agency,
as they saw it, to help fend off a possible Communist thrust. The memories of the Munich Soviet of 1919 had not faded, and as a consequence,
much of the city's middle-class population lived with a continuous siege

mentality. The vote for the DNVP could easily be seen as a vote for a conservative nationalist *protector* of National Socialist interests. The DNVP representative in the Bavarian government was a Dr. Franz Gürtner. He had been minister of justice since 1922, and it was under him that Hitler and his associates had been prosecuted. It was felt that he "had been instrumental in procuring [the] light sentences," and members of the BVP tried hard to have him removed. But the DNVP refused to withdraw his name, and he was again named to that office after the state election in 1924.[33] This shift to the DNVP was not to last, however. In 1932, as we shall see, the party had lost much of its new-found support in Bogenhausen, part of the loss going to the BVP and the rest to the NSDAP.

Because of the expansion away from the river, a somewhat larger area comprising eight precincts (nos. 360 to 367) was examined in connection with the July 1932 election. The results for this election, when 28.9 percent of the city's votes went to the NSDAP, show Bogenhausen to have voted more like Cologne's Marienburg than Hamburg's Harvestehude. The average for these eight precincts was 29.7 percent, a result that is only marginally different from the figure for the entire city.

A fairly wide range of results was found within this area; one district gave only 18.8 percent of its votes to the NSDAP while another gave 43.1 percent. The remaining six precincts ranged between 24.5 and 36.5 percent. Unlike the Hamburg experience where the "best" precincts, those facing the Alster, gave the highest support to the NSDAP, in this case the best precinct (no. 366), which faced directly onto the Isar, gave the party 26.3 percent. Another very good area, just inland from this precinct gave the low percentage, the 18.8 figure.

In most of these precincts the strongest party was the Bavarian People's party. The DNVP, in most of these subareas, now held a very distant third position. It is not possible to say with any certainty what was operating here. Upper-class Catholic voters may have been returning to a home base. Or Protestant voters may have been turning to a more viable option as their previously favored party lost strength. If in a pattern similar to that found in Berlin, Hamburg, and Cologne, the city's Jewish population was concentrated in Bogenhausen, it too may have abandoned losing parties (as, for example, the Democrats) in favor of the best available option.[34]

Another *Villenviertel*, Grünwald, was located outside the city. Regrettably, the only figures obtained were for the November 1932 election. The NSDAP percentages in the area's two precincts at that time were 30.1 and 32.6. The percentage for the city at that point was 24.9, which means NSDAP support there was well above the level for Munich as a whole. Since there had been a general falloff from the July peak, one may assume the NSDAP vote at that time to have been in the neighborhood of 35 to 40 percent. Grünwald, in short, appears to have been different from Bogenhausen. It would have matched Harvestehude in its tendency rather than Marienburg.

There is little one can say to explain these differences. At this late point it would be difficult to obtain useful information even through interviews. Possibly there was a local newspaper in Grünwald that offered support to the party. Or maybe there was some especially active local unit of the party there. Or, still another possibility, some of those who were influential in the community may have informally supported that political direction.

One may note, in any case, how misleading it is to speak simply of *the* upper class (or *the* bourgeoisie) and to assume that the class acted on the basis of some clear and unambiguous interest. Within the same metropolis, different segments of the class showed some rather unexpected divergent tendencies.

To the west of the old city one finds the Nymphenburg Park which contains an elegant baroque palace, once the possession of the Wittelsbach family, until 1918 the royal house of Bavaria. The areas surrounding the palace grounds, particularly those to the south and to the east, were generally upper middle class in character.

An examination of the vote in three precincts of this area (nos. 107-109), showed support for the Völkischer Block that was slightly above the city average in May of 1924. In addition, there was strong support for both the Bavarian People's party and the Conservatives. The July 1932 election showed these precincts to be slightly above the city's NSDAP figure (they were, respectively, 31.1, 35.6, and 28.0 percent). In November of that year, two of them had fallen below the level of the city, and one remained, even with the falloff, well above that level.

About all one can say on the basis of this very limited sampling of Munich's upper-middle-class areas is that they too were not sharply different from the city as a whole. These districts do not stand out as did Steglitz in Berlin or Hohenfelde in Hamburg. The sense that one gets from both the Bogenhausen and the Nymphenburg results is that Munich did *not* show the same differentiation by class that was discovered in Berlin and Hamburg. Rather than higher NSDAP support appearing in the better-off districts, in Munich support seems to have been fairly even throughout the city. The only exception is Grünwald, the suburban upper-class community in which the pattern was more like that of Harvestehude. In short, it appears that both Cologne and Munich differ from Berlin and Hamburg.

Some Possible Explanations. Two explanations for this Munich exception appear likely. The first, already considered at some length, is that the upper and upper middle classes of Munich had a functioning viable party, the BVP, available to represent their interests. The traditional parties of those classes located in the cities outside of Bavaria had either been wiped out or were seriously decimated causing those voters to seek out a next-best alternative.

Another possibility is that here too, as in Cologne, there was a different media impact. The city's leading newspaper was the *Münchner Neueste Nachrichten*. In the late Weimar period, it, like the *Kölnische Zeitung*, provided serious opposition to the NSDAP, at least until the owners, in the course of the presidential election, enforced a degree of neutrality vis-à-vis Hitler's party. This would mean that Munich's upper and upper middle classes had been receiving a different message from that received in most other cities. The BVP organ, the *Bayerischer Kurier*, would have had a similar impact; it would have stabilized the support for the BVP and limited any possible NSDAP gains among its readers.

The possibility of a media effect may be seen through an examination of events over a longer period. In the earlier period, as we have seen, the NSDAP had gained considerable support in the city, its popularity dwindling rapidly in the course of 1924. That early popularity reflects, among other things, the enthusiasm of the city's press. One historian reports that the *Münchner Neueste Nachrichten* "had been democratic in the early years of the Republic but leaned towards Hitler early in 1923 and supported Kahr during the fall." Another journal, the *Münchner Zeitung* "was also pro-Nazi early in 1923 but [it] cooled off markedly in the course of the year." Another source reports the same dramatic shift of the *Neueste Nachrichten*, from early republicanism to later Hitler enthusiasm, following a change in ownership. This source indicates that the favor shown the NSDAP continued up to the date of the *Putsch* and even included some favorable commentary on the occasion of Hitler's trial in the spring of 1924.[35]

Some personnel changes occurred within the publishing house in 1930. The new director, Anton Betz, demanded a considerable grant of power as a condition for taking the position. The newspaper provided general support to the Brüning regime in this period although its specific recommendation in the 1930 Reichstag election was for the Konservative Volkspartei, a responsible offshoot from Hugenberg's DNVP and a member of Brüning's coalition. The newspaper's enthusiasm for this party appeared in almost every issue, this favor being shown especially for General Paul von Lettow-Vorbeck, its leading candidate in Munich. The KVP made its best showing in the entire Reich in this district, suggesting once again a likely media impact. The *Münchner Neueste Nachrichten*, it should be noted, had the fifth largest circulation in the nation.

From 1930 to the spring of 1932 the newspaper was very decidedly opposed to Hitler's aspirations. In the first round of the presidential election, its editorials were sharply opposed to Hitler and very much in favor of Hindenburg, this position being reflected also in its handling of other news and comment. A series of editorials in the week prior to the election dealt with the following questions: Why not Hitler? Why not Duesterberg? Why not Thälmann? This series ended, in Friday's issue, with an editorial entitled: "Why Hindenburg?" The Saturday issue declared (in a five-column heading): "Hindenburg Must Win, Because Germany Must Live!" A copy of the ballot, properly marked for Hindenburg, was described as *"Der richtige Zettel"*—the correct or proper ballot. And on Sunday, the election day edition, a page-one declaration stated: "We vote Hindenburg!"

Given this unquestioned enthusiasm, it comes as something of a surprise that in the second round of the presidential election the recommendation and comment were so tepid and limited. This election even prompted an editorial entitled "Neutrality?" which explained that the case for Hindenburg had been presented in the first round of the campaign. The reduced attention and concern reflected a behind-the-scenes struggle within the newspaper, which was under considerable pressure from one of the owners to temper its opposition to the NSDAP. It was now to follow a policy of taming the National Socialists. It was hoped that they could be brought into the Bavarian government where they would be "saddled" with some serious "responsibility."[36]

This new direction was very much in evidence in the issues appearing prior to the Bavarian state election of April 24 and also in those prior to the Reichstag election of July 31. In the former instance the newspaper argued the viability of the NSDAP as a coalition partner in the state government. Its final recommendation was a rather weak statement for the BVP. In the Reichstag election, it concentrated on the technicalities of the election rather than on the substance. The Saturday editorial, again a lukewarm performance, called for support of the "large bourgeois parties." The Sunday editorial, under the heading *"Nun aber Schluss!"* (roughly, Now an end to it!) recommended a range of conservative parties and, after considering the pros and cons of National Socialism also found it to be an allowable option. The newspaper's internal struggle had been solved by ignoring the election; a close reading was necessary to find any relevant news and comment.

It is conceivable that this late neutrality tipped the balance of forces for some wavering voters in favor of the NSDAP. The media were not, of course, operating in a vacuum. Interpersonal influences were also at work. With the newspaper no longer strongly opposed to NSDAP aspirations and with the party's activists sedulously pushing the line, some marginal voters may have responded to the new influence.

CHAPTER SEVEN

Cities of the Ruhr

This chapter will be concerned with Essen, Dortmund, Düsseldorf, Duisburg, and, in less detail, Wuppertal, the five largest cities of the Ruhr. The Ruhr, of course, was the leading center of heavy industry in Germany. Within a relatively small territory, approximately fifty by thirty kilometers, there were some two dozen cities, half of which had populations of over 100,000. Those to be discussed here were all over 400,000. The major activities in the Weimar years were coal mining, steel manufacturing, and steel fabrication. In contrast to the blue skies and green spaces found elsewhere in Germany, the dominant color of the cities in this region (until the depression shut down the mines and mills) was an ashen gray. Except for Düsseldorf, the provincial capital and therefore an administrative and cultural center, the entire area had a very large working-class percentage.

One might anticipate the presence of a militant left working class in this area. Such an expectation, while not entirely without foundation, would miss the complexity of the actual situation. The cities had *relatively* large Catholic populations, reflecting the agreement reached following the Thirty Years' War and the patterns of migration in the nineteenth and twentieth centuries. Catholic populations migrated into the region from across the Rhine. And Protestant populations came there from the farm regions in the east of Germany. In addition, in the twentieth century a fair-sized Polish population migrated to the region.[1]

The politics of the region, to some extent at least, still reflected these origins. The Zentrum, not too surprisingly, was strong in the region although as was indicated in previous chapters, this support had suffered considerable erosion, especially in these industrial cities. Some of the Protestant workers continued to support the bourgeois parties, that is, to vote the traditional loyalties brought with them from the countryside. Many of the Polish workers, those who were citizens, did not support either the left or the Zentrum but rather voted for the Polish party, an ethnic splinter organization.

In the recent past, the people of the Ruhr had experienced a series of bloody conflicts, which began with the revolution of 1918. In the first years of the republic, Communist insurgency was followed by the appearance of the Freikorps. Many workers were caught up in a struggle they would have preferred to avoid. They nevertheless became the victims of the Freikorps onslaught, an effort that in its scope and ruthlessness, brought down insurgents and innocents alike. One result, it would appear, is that the Social Democrats lost support and the Communists, for the moment at least, were the beneficiaries.[2]

Then, overlaying that struggle, came the national struggle in 1923 when French and Belgian troops occupied the Ruhr. The initial response of the national government was to support a general strike (called passive resistance). The end result of this resistance was the runaway inflation which figures so prominently in the history books. A less well known feature of the struggle was the appearance of nationalist paramilitary groups in the Ruhr to conduct active resistance against the occupiers. The French forces, as might be expected, fought back, and among other things executed some of these fighters, thus providing martyrs for the nationalist cause. In the end, however, it was Germany rather than France that was broken by the effort. Stresemann, at that point serving as chancellor, abandoned passive resistance and began negotiations. Steps were taken at the same time, in late 1923, to substitute a new currency. Some years of relative quiet followed, but then, with the onset of the depression, the struggle began again with violence escalating steadily to 1933.

The elements of this history were to be found in the consciousness of all adult citizens; it could scarcely have been otherwise. And that history would have provided the background against which the new options were assessed. There was little working-class solidarity to be seen in the Ruhr cities of the early 1930s. The loyalties and passions generated in the earlier struggles did not allow much in the way of a unified opposition to the emerging National Socialist threat. Some of the initiatives in the thirties, particularly those of the Communists, accentuated the divisions rather than bridging them. As for the bourgeoisie of the region, it must have felt it was standing on the edge of the precipice.

Such feelings would probably have moved many upper- and upper-middle-class citizens to support the National Socialists. Sensing the weakness of their own parties in the face of the "Marxist threat," many of them, probably, would have felt the need for a more effective defense of their interests. Perhaps with some qualms and some reluctance, they eventually chose the National Socialists with its fighting arm, the Sturmabteilung, as the appropriate means for this purpose. These feelings or predispositions would have stemmed from the events in the early years of the republic or, perhaps more specifically, from the events occurring within their own city, each having a somewhat different experience with revolution and counterrevolution.

The events of 1928 to 1932 would not have been experienced directly, at least not in the typical case. The lives of most adult males, then and now, are largely circumscribed by the home and the work place with only occasional outings to see friends and relations or, perhaps, to attend political meetings. The lives of most adult females in that age would have been even more limited, their activities being largely restricted by the requirements of the home. There was no significant proliferation of the mass media at that time so that for most people the key medium, the basic source of information about the events of the outside world, would have been a local newspaper. A fair range of possibilities existed in any large city, ranging from Communist and Socialist journals, to the bland middle-of-the-road general newspapers, to journals of the right, the so-called bourgeois newspapers. And then too there would ordinarily be a small circulation National Socialist entry. A Zentrum-oriented newspaper would be found in cities with significant Catholic populations. Except for the general papers, these sources of information were very much party oriented; hence one would not ordinarily receive an unbiased portrait of the day's events. Few families would have subscribed to a broad range of local newspapers so as to obtain a balanced perspective. Most would have subscribed to one, or at best two, usually those most closely linked to their own political persuasions.

Given the resulting near-monopoly position of these new sources, it is appropriate that one consider the possibility of media effects. It is for this reason that in this chapter we again explore the content of the leading journals. Attention will be focused on the bourgeois journals and on the general press since they are the sources that would have been read by the key groups, those who changed political loyalties in this period. It is important to remember that, initially at least, *two* factors are assumed to be operating, initial predispositions and media impact. We can offer no hard evidence with respect to the predispositions, and some of the media effects appear to be more complicated than this first discussion would suggest. It should be clear that these attempts at explanation must be viewed as speculative or hypothetical.

ESSEN

With its 654,461 persons, Essen was the sixth largest city of the nation.[3] Located almost in the center of the region, in some ways it was the area's most important city. Among other things, it was the home of the Krupp family and the center of its many activities.

As for the basic geography, there was, once again, an Altstadt at the center of the city. In the four decades prior to 1933 the city had seen extensive annexations in all directions, the last of these occurring in 1929. The Ruhr River winds through the southern side of the city and, for approximately five kilometers of its course broadens out to form the Baldeney Lake. North of this lake the land rises sharply forming a bluff from the top of which one has an impressive view of the countryside to the south. The bluff is covered with forests; here one found the Krupp family estate, the Villa Hügel. Not too surprisingly *the Villenviertel* of Essen adjoins this forest in the Bredeney district. All of the other better areas of the city were to be found in immediately adjacent areas.

The areas to the east, west, and north of the Altstadt all contained substantial working-class majorities. On the southwest edge of the city one found some rural areas in which farming was still being carried on. Some of the people living there were full-time farmers; many more were factory workers who engaged in farming as a part-time (or as a depression) occupation.

Before the war the city was characterized by a three-cornered political pattern with the National Liberals representing the "better" classes, the Zentrum drawing support from across the class spectrum, and the Social Democrats representing the less well off. Other parties, such as the Conservatives and the left liberals, were present, but they played distinctly minor roles. In the first elections of the republic, the Conservatives and the German People's party, because of the general hopelessness of their position in this city, formed an electoral coalition. The parties first ran separate slates in the 1920 Reichstag election and at that point the People's party was definitely the larger of the two. With the growth of the Conservatives in 1924, their positions were more or less equal, a condition that lasted to the end phase of the republic.

The voting preferences of the upper class of the city may be seen by examining the vote in the city council elections of 1929, at which point the respective DNVP and DVP percentages in Bredeney were 10.7 and 15.5. In Rüttenscheid, an upper-middle-class district, the figures were 9.7 and 15.0. The DNVP predominance was to be found in some rural and Protestant districts, for example in Schuir (29.5 and 3.6) or in Haarzopf (11.3 and 8.2).[4] In Essen as elsewhere, the favored party of the upper class was the right liberal German People's party. The conservative German Nationalists, clearly, drew their greatest following from less exalted ranks. The preference for the DNVP over the German People's party also appeared in some sections of the working class. It was striking, for example, in the western section of the city where many of the Krupp workers were housed.

This pattern reflects the party's roots in the Prussian countryside. The suggestion, once again, is that many of these workers brought their politics with them to the city and successfully maintained those loyalties in the new context. There is no evidence available on the point, but it seems likely, if this migration hypothesis is valid, that the German Nationalist workers would have been older than most of their class peers.

Essen's statistical office published rather detailed accounts of the elections. For the July 1932 Reichstag election, the key election of the period, it presented results for the city as a whole, and for forty subareas.[5] The NSDAP received 24.0 percent of the city's vote in that election. Thirteen of the forty districts gave above average support to Hitler's party. In order of their support they are: Schuir, 44.1 percent; Südviertel, 38.7 percent; Rüttenscheid, 37.4 percent; Heide (Stadtwald), 36.1 percent; Stadtkern, 34.3 percent; Südostviertel, 32.8 percent; Bredeney, 32.6 percent; Huttrop, 32.4 percent; Haarzopf, 31.7 percent; Holsterhausen, 30.3 percent; Fulerum, 29.9 percent; Westviertel, 26.1 percent; and Ostviertel, 25.3 percent.

Schuir, leading the list, was a thinly populated rural area with a largely Protestant population. Its voting tendency approximates that of rural Protestant areas elsewhere in the nation, the only difference being that this one happened to be located within a large city. Given that only 238 valid votes were cast in this district, its contribution would obviously not weigh heavily in the 375,097 vote total. Haarzopf, just to the north of Schuir, was similar to it with a small population (1,304 votes), a Protestant majority, and rural characteristics. Fulerum, another thinly populated area (1,143 votes), was immediately to the north of Haarzopf. Together the three formed the southwest border of the city. All three had Protestant majorities; all three had a rural appearance although it should be noted that two of them, Schuir and Haarzopf, had working-class majorities.

The Stadtkern was the old city center and the districts with "viertel" (quarter) in the name are the immediately surrounding areas. All of these districts contained substantial working-class majorities, although some, in particular the Südviertel, also contained a rather well-off middle-class minority. Were one to draw an isosceles triangle with the Stadtkern at the apex and the two legs reaching down to the Baldeney Lake, it would include all of the "better" districts of the city, those districts that contained the upper and upper middle classes of the city. Included as one moved south from the Stadtkern, would be the Südviertel (second on the list); Rüttenscheid (third); Heide (fourth); and Bredeney. Of the remaining districts on the list, the Südostviertel and Huttrop lie just to the east of this triangle while Holsterhausen borders it on the west.[6]

The districts that gave the National Socialists above average support were, in short, of two varieties: the thinly populated rural Protestant districts and the better-off areas. The levels of support in these areas showed some variation, to be sure, but in areas most likely to have had relatively large lower-middle-class populations, Huttrop or Holsterhausen, they were below the levels in districts that would have had upper-middle-class populations. Two other districts that, according to Kühr's data, had mixed populations (in the sense used in previous chapters), Rellinghausen and Bergerhausen, were both below the city average, their respective NSDAP percentages being 17.9 and 22.4.

To make clear what groups we are dealing with, it is helpful to consider the districts in more detail. Knowledgeable informants agreed that Bredeney was, without doubt, the number-one area of the city. Its voters gave the NSDAP a level of support that was 35.8 percent above the average for the city. That level, it will be noted is only slightly below the levels in the best areas of Berlin, in Zehlendorf and Wilmersdorf. Unlike the Berlin districts, Bredeney had a considerable Zentrum vote (32.4 percent versus 30.7 percent in Essen as a whole). The Conservative vote in Bredeney was also well above the city average (10.5 percent versus 4.0). The significance of this Conservative vote will be seen below. Approximately one-fifth of the vote in this elegant quarter went to the Social Democrats and Communists, a fact that points to the presence of some working-class populations in the area. Again, were one able to make the corrections allowed by the Berlin and Hamburg data, the NSDAP percentage among the well-off Protestants must have been considerably higher than the figure given here would suggest.[7]

A part of Rüttenscheid (Haumannshof) contained villas, but for the most part, the area contained upper-middle-class populations (*gehobenen Mittelstand*). Heide, which borders on both Bredeney and Rüttenscheid, also had single-family houses and a socially elevated population. This area, which is now called Stadtwald (city forest), also had a mixture of population in that some rural and working-class settlements remained from a previous era. In the center of the Südviertel one found the Stadtgarten (city garden) and the city's concert hall. The housing in the immediately surrounding area was reported to have been rather elegant. The major lesson, it would seem, is that two of these areas, Bredeney and Rüttenscheid, were by no means *lower* middle class in character.

A difficulty discovered in other cities may be noted once again here, namely, that of locating *the* lower middle class. The only available census with a breakdown by subareas came in 1939. From Kühr's account one can see a pattern roughly similar to that observed in Berlin and Hamburg. Much of the middle class (white-collar workers and independent businessmen) was spread thinly throughout the many working-class areas. And many others from the middle class were found in mixed districts, where they lived with large numbers of workers, so that it was, and is, impossible to separate out the votes of these "petty bourgeois elements."

All one can do is to indicate that the mixed districts of Essen, those coming closest to a fifty-fifty middle-class–working-class split, are not especially distinctive, some being slightly above the city-wide level and some slightly below it. The only way that the familiar lower-middle-class hypothesis could gain support would be if the middle-class populations in those districts had voted overwhelmingly for the National Socialists while their working-class neighbors had voted overwhelmingly against them. There appears to be no definitive way of either establishing or denying this possibility. That observation holds both for the present and for the past. One can only suggest, for the reasons discussed in previous chapters, that it is unlikely such a sharp cleavage along class lines would exist within these neighborhoods, that is between people who had grown up together and gone to school together, and who were friends and kinsmen.[8]

Again, as in Berlin and Hamburg, one finds that the National Socialist vote in the working-class districts of the city was below average, but by no means minuscule, amounting here to approximately one-fifth of the total vote. When one asks the related question—what percentage of the National Socialist vote came from the various classes?—one must, however, note that in Essen a majority of that vote came from working-class districts.

In previous chapters it has been suggested that newspapers played a role in determining the electoral outcomes. For the bourgeois audience of Essen, the options were rather limited. The leading newspaper for the educated middle-class audience was the *Rheinisch-Westfälische Zeitung*. The same publisher also put out, for a more general audience, a publication called the *Essener Anzeiger*. Those aligned with the Zentrum could read the *Essener Volkszeitung* which was similar in character to the *Kölnische Volkszeitung*. Also available was a smaller and more neutral paper, the *Essener Allgemeine Zeitung*. The Communists, Social Democrats, and National Socialists also put out newspapers, but they certainly were not significant factors in the better areas of the city.[9]

Kühr describes the *Rheinisch-Westfälische Zeitung* as an extreme right journal. It was antirepublican and German nationalist throughout the Weimar period, a basic direction already apparent in its attitude toward the Kapp *Putsch* of March 1920. The insurgents, the paper declared, were acting out of "the most honest of convictions" and because of a "deep love of the fatherland."[10]

It is useful to consider the reporting and commentary (the two are not easily distinguished) of this newspaper at greater length since it would have been a leading source of information for the affluent classes of the city, particularly for those not committed to the Zentrum. Here is, first of all, a brief summary of its reporting of the events over the two weeks preceding the Reichstag election on September 14, 1930.

A report on a meeting of Conservatives which was addressed by Hugenberg appeared under the following headlines: "The Task: To Confront the Zentrum with the Decision—'Right or Left.'" For the Conservative press, this theme was—next to the Marxist threat—the one most ardently discussed. The Zentrum did occupy a pivotal position. The presence of "the Socialists" in both national and Prussian governments was made possible only by the support of the Zentrum. Had the Zentrum joined with the right, the conservative (*bürgerliche*, bourgeois) forces would have been able to control the government, and the Social Democrats would have been out. (The political struggle is discussed in more detail in Chapter 10.)

This account also discussed (and approved) the possibility of a coalition with the NSDAP. The key passage reads: "The assertion that one cannot make bourgeois politics with the National Socialist German Workers party, is one that is born out of fear of the opposition. The party leader [Hugenberg] believes it possible to ensure that the National Socialists together with the German Nationals will no longer allow the fence-sitting politics of the Zentrum."

When Wirth's position paper on the NSDAP appeared, the *Rheinisch-Westfälische* belittled it, arguing that the case was not proven. The NSDAP was vouched for in many other ways.

A very factual account of the Stennes insurgency appeared early in September. A later edition contained a discussion of Hitler's settlement of the affair. In an aside, there was a brief report of Communist infiltration in some party units. These units, it was reported, "had been immediately dissolved."

The morning issue of September 5 contained a letter written by some "national" Catholics arguing the necessity of a vote against the Zentrum and for the conservative German Nationals, this because of the Zentrum's persistent link with the Social Democrats. The same theme was discussed in an editorial on September 9, the focus there being on the Brüning-Braun link and the "contradictions" this involved for the Zentrum. Again the stress was on the need for a joint effort of the DNVP and NSDAP against the SPD-Zentrum coalition.

On September 10 the paper gave considerable space to an NSDAP meeting in Essen addressed by Wilhelm Frick, the NSDAP minister of interior in Thuringia (where a DNVP-NSDAP coalition already existed). The report described Frick as "an unusually calm, sober, and matter of fact observer of the situation . . . a man for day-to-day work." The rest of the account contains his listing of the NSDAP's accomplishments in that state. As an aside, Frick noted the difficulties the coalition had encountered from the Social Democrats and the Zentrum.[11]

Mixed in with the political themes just summarized were brief notes reporting the day's events. The reader was treated to a running commentary on the violence that was occurring throughout Germany. These accounts had a clear pattern to them: day after day they reported on violence and criminality originated by the forces of the left. SPD groups, it was said, broke into villas, destroying and vandalizing. A note appeared on the forthcoming trial of those accused of killing Horst Wessel. Communists were present at the previously mentioned Hugenberg meeting; they attempted to disrupt the meeting and caused some violence. Under the heading "Communist Excesses" there followed a story about an NSDAP group that was "attacked from the rear" by Communists, sending one of them to the hospital. This phrase—attacked from the rear—recurs continuously in these accounts; the practice would have outraged many, particularly former members of the military. In one issue there were two reports of Communist attacks on the police. From Hamburg there was a report, without comment, of fighting between National Socialists and Communists. Another report told of a Communist attack on National Socialists with some of the attackers being taken off to jail. A National Socialist was killed in Essen by an unknown attacker. From Düsseldorf came a report: "Communists against the Police." The day before the election one read "Bloody Election Struggles in Schwerte and Dortmund," "2,000 Persons Attempt an Attack on a National Socialist Meeting." And from Chemnitz came the report: "Communists Shoot at Police."

The recommendations made by the *Rheinisch-Westfälische* were open-ended, indicating only a direction rather than a specific party. Their Sunday (election day) edition carried the headline: "Out of the Crisis! Vote Right!" This editorial opened with an extended discussion of the "youth revolution" and expressed satisfaction that it would bring in "new men." "This onslaught of youth, in itself, brings with it something indiscriminate and unfeeling . . . on the other hand, this party [the NSDAP] does nevertheless have a negative merit; the large number of new representatives that it sends to the Reichstag will take the seats of old hacks. In some cases that might be a shame, but for most of them no one will shed a tear."

Then, under a subheading, "New Times Demand New Men," it notes that "the regrouping has begun: one feels it most actively among the National Socialists and the Conservatives, but the waves have been felt even in the democratic camp." Although the newspaper left the choice open to the reader, it is clear that through the previous news-editorializing, it had defined the NSDAP as a reasonable or plausible option.

In the two rounds of the 1932 presidential election, the *Rheinisch-Westfälische Zeitung* once again avoided a direct recommendation. Its recommendation on the day of the first-round balloting, however, was such as to allow an easy inference in favor of Hitler's candidacy. Under the headline "Make the Right Wing Strong!" the editorialist reviewed the seven years since the last presidential election, years in which this extraordinarily devastating crisis had appeared. The times called for "unity of the nation" and made necessary "energetic, single-minded leadership [*Führung*]." Reviewing again the enormous tasks facing the nation, the editorial argued the need to lead (*führen*) the "mighty awakened national will to resistance." The final recommendation was: "Therefore vote right!" This does not sound like a recommendation for the 84-year-old Hindenburg. In the second round of balloting the newspaper made no recommendation.

This hesitation had disappeared by the time of the 1932 legislative elections. An editorial in April 1932 discussed and rejected one of the options open in the Prussian state election, this being a vote for the right liberal German People's party. A front-page editorial dismissed the nationalist "words" of DVP party spokesmen, expressing doubt that the national forces within the DVP could carry the day; they inevitably would have to compromise with the left. The final conclusion reads: 'In these difficult times in which we live, and in the still more difficult times to come, only sharp and ruthless national fighters come into consideration—and today those are only the *German National party* and the *National Socialist party*.'

The day before the Prussian election, the paper reported a Hugenberg speech given in the Westphalia Hall in Essen. Hugenberg said: "This system that has ruined us must be *destroyed*. [storm of applause] This overthrow cannot be achieved by the National Socialists alone. For this the German National opposition is also necessary."

At the moment of the July Reichstag election, "the system" had in fact been destroyed. The Weimar coalition was out of power having been replaced by Papen's presidential regime. And the black-red coalition was also out in Prussia. There, the National Socialists had joined with the Communists to provide the votes necessary to carry the latter's motion of no confidence. No satisfactory alternative coalition had been found, and so the Braun government continued in office. Taking as a pretext the events of "bloody Sunday" in Altona (where Communists had fired on SA formations), Papen removed the Braun government and substituted people of his own choosing. His government, in short, had accomplished two of the principal long-run aims of German conservative forces. Not too surprisingly, his government was viewed with much approval in bourgeois circles. In fact, as Turner has shown, Papen, not Hitler, was the favorite of the industrial elites of Germany (see Chapters 10 and 13). This preference was clearly indicated in the editorials and news stories of the *Rheinisch-Westfälische Zeitung*.

The basic problem for the paper was that Papen at this point was a man without a party. Persons wishing to support him directly had no means of doing so. The conception offered by the *Rheinisch-Westfälische* was that Papen would govern with the support and backing of the two national parties, the DNVP and the NSDAP.

Otherwise, little else in the newspaper's coverage had changed. It continued to give extensive approving coverage to the National Socialists. In the morning edition of July 25, it reported a Hitler speech in Duisburg (see below). It accepted the NSDAP's report that 100,000 attended, although the figure was considerably discounted in police reports. It covered most of Hitler's speech dealing largely with reparations, and it also included the final sentence: "For once, think of Germany, on July 31." This account was followed by three briefer ones reporting a Hitler speech in Gladbeck on July 24, another one in Bochum on the same day, and a third in Wuppertal, also on the twenty-fourth.

The day before the election it published a two-column, page-one, account entitled "The NSDAP Program" (a Strasser radio address), and on election day it had two large features: "Why National Socialist?" and, for the DNVP, an article entitled, "Above All Stands Germany!" The pages of the issues prior to the election were again embellished with accounts of violence instigated by the left. The final recommendation was that the sensible voter could only vote for "one of the great national parties," and this vote was immediately linked to Papen's future plans.

The same arrangement was recommended in the November election although this time it was tempered by the hostility existing between the NSDAP and DNVP. The paper also noted the NSDAP's support for and involvement in the Berlin transport strike, a fact it regretted since, as the paper put it, nothing was more important than national unity. Its recommendation was that Papen should continue and that he should attempt to gain the support of the DNVP and the NSDAP. The editorial ends on a note of concern: "For us, the question for the future reads: will the National Socialists and German Nationals get together? Will they be in a position to march together?"

The basic picture of German society gained from this paper was one in which the Social Democratic-Zentrum governing coalitions in nation and state were undermining and destroying the country. Members of those parties, at the same time, were lining their own pockets. Germany faced insurmountable and completely unjust demands placed on it by the Versailles treaty, by the provisions of the Dawes Plan, and later on by the Young Plan. Against these demands the coalition did nothing. And finally there was the daily struggle for control of the streets as Communists attacked police, authorities, and the parties loyally defending the nation.[12] From this perspective it followed that a new government was needed, one that was strong enough to clean up the entire mess.

In summary, this conservative newspaper provided continuous approval for Hitler and his party; this does not mean, to be sure, exclusive and unambiguous backing. The recommendation and support were more limited; the NSDAP would move in tandem with the Conservatives. More specifically, together with the Conservatives, it would supply the much-needed backing for Papen. Regardless of the specific arrangements envisaged, the paper's dramatization of events was such as to encourage votes for Hitler's party. Given the consistent approval, it is not surprising that the areas of the city where the *Rheinisch-Westfälische Zeitung* was likely to have been read gave strong support to the NSDAP. This pattern in Essen should be contrasted with the voting in Cologne's *Villenviertel*, Marienburg, where readers were following the rather intelligent and moderate *Kölnische Zeitung*.

It should also be noted that those readers who accepted the newspaper's alarming portrayal and who voted for the Conservatives were *not* supporting an option that was separate and distinct from the National Socialist offering. In the plans of the *Rheinisch-Westfälische Zeitung*, the DNVP would work with the NSDAP to accomplish a common end, the destruction of "the system." That, to be sure, was the newspaper's definition of the program; the actual motivations found among the DNVP's voters were likely to have been more diverse. This review, however, casts some doubt on the casual suggestions that DNVP voting represented the sentiments of responsible upper-class conservatives reacting *against* the National Socialist threat.

The *Rheinisch-Westfälische Zeitung* had a following that reached beyond the city limits. Kühr says that the paper's circulation increased in the course of the nationalist wave that finally swept away the republic. The owner, as noted above, also brought out the *Essener Anzeiger* which, although declaring itself to be politically independent (*parteilos*), did not, according to Kühr, "differ from the *Rheinisch-Westfälische Zeitung* in anything in its nationalist tenor." It should come as no great surprise to learn that the editor and publisher of the *Rheinisch-Westfälische*, Theodor Reismann-Grone, was viewed with great favor by the National Socialists, so much so in fact, that he was chosen by them to be the first *Bürgermeister* of the city under the Third Reich, a post he held until the coming of the war.[13]

As a minor postscript to this history, it is useful to note another option written up with obvious approval in the pages of the *Rheinisch-Westfälische Zeitung*, the experience of Mussolini's Italy. In August 1930, the readers were treated to a page-one account entitled: "Political Travel—Reflections on Fascism." This generally positive account of a trip to Italy ends with the statement that "Mussolini is making for all of Europe the enormous attempt of constructing a unitary organic state and out of its authority, striving for a renewal of political content. This experiment, which has been ventured by a state-creating genius in Italy, will not be spared any people that does not wish to see economy and culture collapse in the class struggle."

On the day before the July election of 1932 it carried another approving story: "Moscow Once Agitated in Italy Too." Referring to "the Communist blood bath in Sarzana," the account ends with this elegiac note: "Today, only a white marble tablet on the front of the Sarzana city hall, where now for years a fascist podesta has ruled alone, reminds one of the 1921 blood bath. The seed from that time has blossomed a hundredfold; ten years of fascism have brought peace and well-being to the land, and a new generation has learned discipline and obedience."[14]

Because, as noted, more than half of the National Socialists' vote came out of working-class districts, it is important to explore the patterns there in greater detail. Prior to the NSDAP upsurge, the working-class vote for the most part split into Social Democratic, Communist, and Zentrum components. But also present in the working-class districts were some voters who supported the DNVP, the DVP, and other rightist options. As has been discussed, these unlikely linkages probably stemmed from the rural roots and conservative political socialization of many workers. Another source of working-class conservatism involves the Krupp family which, prior to the war, had been National Liberal or Free Conservative in its loyalties. The Free Conservatives of the prewar era were a party of practical conservative industrialists (as opposed to the ideological conservatives of the Prussian-based and aristocratic *Deutschkonservativen*. Kühr notes that "the National Liberal and Free Conservative tradition of the Krupp house also obligated a large part of its workers and white-collar employees. . . . The class identification of the 'Kruppians,' whose pride in being members of the firm and of the house of Krupp was well known in Essen and beyond, influenced their vote for the DVP more than their actual occupation." In conversations with one-time employees of the firm, Kühr picked up reports that people were employed (and dismissed) not only on grounds of their occupational qualifications but also "according to the religious confession and the political position of those in question, who could sympathize with the DVP or also with the DNVP."[15]

The western section of the city, sometimes referred to as Krupp City, contained eight districts which otherwise were collectively known as Borbeck. In the 1929 city council election Borbeck provided above average support for the Zentrum, some modest support for the DNVP and the DVP, and a remarkable vote for a collection of splinter parties. The vote for the Communists was exactly equal to that in the city as a whole, and the vote for the Social Democrats was below the city average. Between the 1929 election and the July 1932 election support for the left increased (going from 30.6 to 38.3 percent), most of that going to the KPD. A small decline in the Zentrum percentage was registered (from 42.3 to 37.4). And the NSDAP went from 1.4 to 19.3 percent, which mirrored a decline in the DNVP, the DVP, the DDP, and the splinter parties (whose combined percentage went from 25.7 to 5.0). The NSDAP built its strength in this area by gaining the support of the conservative workers and thereby undermining the rightist parties.[16] The tendency toward polarization in the area is very clear. A basic question arises as to why there was any polarization at all: why didn't all those votes go to the left? To answer that question it is necessary, once again, to refer to the events of the earlier struggles in the Weimar history.

There was little support for a left or revolutionary direction in November of 1918. The immediate response to the revolution by the Majority Social Democrats was the formation of a joint organization (Aktionseinheit). As Kühr puts it, "The representatives of both [Majority and Independent Socialists] went energetically to work for the maintenance of peace and order." In the process they worked together with the then *Oberbürgermeister*, Hans Luther. There was no Spartakus group in Essen at that point; it was first formed later in the month.

This Spartakus unit triggered off a series of activities that embarrassed the working-class leaders of the Workers and Soldiers' Council. The unit broke into the offices of the *Rheinisch-Westfälische Zeitung* early in December. The leaders of the other Socialist parties were thus put in a position in which they were obliged, as defenders of peace and order, to attack an "ally" on the left. In that role they were made to appear as defenders of the reactionary press. There was much strike activity in December, but the strikes were settled before the year's end. A streetcar workers's strike broke out, with Spartakus support, on the fifth of January. And then came a more general strike, with the initial support of all three Socialist organizations, beginning on January 9, to back the socialization of the mines. This strike, it will be noted, occurred in the same week as the leftist uprising in Berlin. This strike was settled on the thirteenth, but then some local Spartakus people undertook to keep it alive. They successfully closed one mine and attempted to impose their will on the workers in another. In the process they attacked the soldiers acting on behalf of the Workers and Soldiers' Council, and in the shooting that followed, seven people were seriously injured.

The next episode involved the entry of the army, sent into the city by the revolutionary government in Berlin. The city's Workers and Soldiers' Council met to discuss a general strike as a response, but the Majority Social Democrats and, with some reluctance, the Independents decided against the effort. The four major segments of the trade union movement also opposed a strike. Only about 10 percent of the workers went out at this point, and the only organized group on the left supporting the action was the Communists.

Before this strike was broken, in mid-February, there was again a wide range of violence. The miners in one area fought the left insurgents who were attempting to shut them down. There was shooting and one death in this case. In another setting, a fight occurred between Spartacists and members of the workers' Security Force with ten wounded and two deaths. At three pits the radicals threw mine cars (*Steinwagen*) down the mine shafts trapping the miners.

The left forced the issue once again in late March of 1919. This time, according to Kühr, "the demands were so formulated as to make it impossible for the government to fulfill them. The left radicals thus created the condition for a permanent strike." The military were moved in once again, strike leaders were arrested, and the strike was broken.

In March 1920, the trade unions called a general strike to combat the Kapp *Putsch*. In Essen, the left followed the strike call but then also moved to create a "dictatorship of the proletariat." On March 19, a Red Army occupied the city in a "confused and disorderly" takeover. On April 7, the troops of the Reichswehr entered the city. Executions followed in an equally confused and disorderly takeover as the troops "cleaned up" the city.

The KPD continued to play a provocative and manipulative role in events until the stabilization of the regime in late 1924 and early 1925. Although it profited in the sense of gaining votes from the Social Democrats, later elections showed that the new support was not all that stable. Kühr indicates that although the KPD continued to press political strikes in this period, these efforts gained little response from the now somewhat wary workers. The party line changed at this point, and up to 1928 its initiatives were generally rather moderate in character.

In November 1928, the local party leaders received word of a new change in the party line, this announcing the introduction of the so-called ultraleft tactic that was to characterize events to 1933. The key features of the new direction were the reintroduction of violence and a focus on the SPD, now defined as "social fascist," as a prime target.

Some increase in KPD votes did occur simultaneously with the appearance of the economic crisis and the new tactic. And that growth, the most visible sign of Communist strength, figured prominently in the minds of the bourgeoisie—a prime source, no doubt, of its rising fears. The actual state of affairs within the party, however, bordered on disaster. The number of new members increased, but so did the number leaving the party. Those taken in by demagogy could just as easily take themselves out again. The financial condition of the party was precarious. To cover up a lack of success or actual losses, lower level cadres passed false information up to higher levels of the party. In May 1932, 41 of the 216 shop cells of the party in the Ruhr were struck from the party records for the simple reason that they had never existed.

In the end, Kühr reports, it was recognized that "the party's physical terror had brought rejection rather than sympathy from the workers." As a bitter final note, Kühr reports that many of the party members noted for their "lust for terror" changed the color of their shirt with no evident difficulty once the National Socialists were in power.[17]

The situation of workers, their wives, and their children, must have been one of bitter frustration. Those who, for decades, had promised an all-embracing this-worldly salvation called socialism, once in power did not socialize anything. And those who now spoke of communism, it became increasingly clear, drew workers into dubious ventures through manipulation and force. Where the Communists were successful, the workers' traditional party, the Social Democrats, would unleash the army. The result was highly predictable—uncontrolled violence directed largely against workers.

The workers of a rightist or nationalist persuasion, Germany's equivalent of England's Tory workers, had some grounds to hate both of the left parties. At the same time, their own parties, the traditional parties of the right, did less and less for them. They, however, were the only group of workers who had what they could see as a genuinely positive option. The National Socialists were clearly an active and powerful party that championed national values and at the same time at least talked a "social" line. Unlike the Conservatives and the People's party, who merely talked against "the Marxists," the National Socialists had an army present in the field, an army actively engaged in the struggle against "the Marxist enemy." In no small measure the working-class support for the National Socialists would appear to have been generated by this history of rather dubious initiatives on the left.

DORTMUND

The second largest city of the Ruhr was Dortmund, located on the eastern edge of the industrial region. The city's population growth was similar to that of Essen, going from 4,289 persons in 1818, to 10,532 in 1849, and then to 142,733 at the turn of the century. Later growth and a series of annexations produced Gross-Dortmund in 1928.[18] According the the 1933 census it had a population of 540,875 persons, making it the tenth largest city in the nation. Like Essen, most of its numerical growth occurred in the first decades of the twentieth century.

The city was distinctive in this region in having a Protestant majority. The actual proportion fluctuated with the migrations of the century, but during most of the Weimar period the level stabilized at approximately 60 percent.[19] As for industry, the city was dominated by coal and steel works and by breweries.

Dortmund's geographic core was known as the Innenstadt (inner city). The best areas of the city were located to the east and to the south of this core, the three most important districts being referred to simply as Osten, Südosten, and Süden (east, southeast, and south). A district to the southwest (Südwesten) also seems to have had an above average middle-class population, but the further away from the center one moved, the greater the percentage of workers. The areas in the north of the city were all heavily working class as were the recently annexed areas to the south of this semicircle of "good" districts.

The political history of the city is summarized by Graf as follows: "The development in the Dortmund-Hörde election district up to the First World War was characterized by a dominance of liberalism up to the nineties, by an equally strong position of the Zentrum, and by a steady growth of the Social Democrats to become the strongest party. . . . The past history as a Reich city, the late annexation to Prussia, and most especially the industrial structure of the city, are all shown in the fact that conservatism of the Prussian variety could never play a decisive role during the Kaiserreich."[20] In the election of 1884 the Prussian Conservatives gained only twenty-eight votes in the entire city. They ran no candidates thereafter.

The liberalism of the period came in a left and a right variety. The former, represented by the Fortschrittspartei (or the Progressives) once had considerable representation in the city. Graf states that it was once "supported by an appreciable portion of the Protestant workers." With the rise of the Social Democrats, however, working-class voters shifted to the new party which reduced the Dortmund Progressives to insignificance.

The subsequent struggle in the city was between the right-wing National Liberals and the Social Democrats. The minority Zentrum remained on the sidelines, at one point admonishing its followers to practice "strict abstention from voting" in the runoff elections between the two leading parties. The Social Democrats, after some very hard struggles, achieved electoral dominance in the city. Once that dominance was established, the National Liberals underwent a decline as did also the Zentrum. Graf gives the following calculations of Catholic loyalty to the Center party: in 1877, there were 901 Zentrum voters per 1,000 eligible Catholics; in 1893, there were 727; and in 1907, there were 550.[21]

Two observations are of note. The upper classes of this city, as in the other west German cities reviewed to this point, favored the right liberals, that is, the National Liberals, the forerunner of Weimar's Deutsche Volkspartei. And again one sees that the Center party was not the stable monolith some have suggested. The loyalties of the Catholic voters were subject to erosion, especially in the industrial working-class centers where contact with the church dwindled, and the influence of fellow workers, by comparison, was much more insistent.

The postwar period opened with a substantial SPD victory, mirroring the pattern elsewhere. On the occasion of the Kapp *Putsch*, the Communists took over the city, and conditions were rather chaotic in the brief period of their rule. Units of the Reichswehr and the Freikorps "restored order." A reaction against both Communists and Social Democrats followed this episode. In the Reichstag election later that year the Communists gained only 1.0 percent and the Social Democrats found their strength reduced from 46.5 to 19.6 with most of their vote going to the USPD. Following the demise of the USPD, most of its voters, in May of 1924, went to the Communists. Some sense of the volatility, of the indecision of the working-class voters, may be seen by contrasting that vote with the December 1924 election result. At that point the KPD figure fell from 30.8 to 15.5 percent, most of the losses stemming from a shift back to the SPD. The KPD lost once again in 1928 and, correspondingly the SPD gained. From 1928 to November 1932, the trend reversed once again with the SPD suffering steady losses to the KPD. From a 38.3 to 12.6 relationship in the Dortmund of 1928, the respective percentages changed to 20.3 and 31.2.

As for the other parties, until 1930 the Zentrum lost strength, after which, perhaps as a result of increased participation, it showed modest increases. The Democrats were a tiny minority party throughout the period and suffered erosion of even that limited strength. The conservative DNVP was also a tiny minority party throughout the period, never going over 7 percent.

The party of the upper and upper middle classes in this city, as indicated, was the German People's party. Graf speaks of the DVP and of "its dominant position in the socially elevated areas of the southern inner city."[22] Once again, the decline of that party (from 13.6 percent overall in 1928 to 1.3 in July 1932) tells us something about the politics of those classes rather than about the politics of the lower middle class.

Unfortunately, Graf gives only limited and indirect comment on this development. Speaking of the municipal elections of November 17, 1929, in which the National Socialists first showed signs of growth, he reports that "the main base of support for the NSDAP was the Innenstadt district with 3.8 percent [versus the city-wide figure of 1.8 percent], but the bourgeois residential districts of the southeast, south, and east also gave it over 3 percent of the vote while in the pure working-class areas in the north of Dortmund, the National Socialists were very weak."[23]

The only exception to this pattern occurs in the northwest of the city in an area called Mengede. There, in a district that combined miners and farm populations, the NSDAP took 3.6 percent. In 1922 this area provided the first NSDAP *Ortsgruppe* in Westphalia and later gave rise to the first SA unit and still later, to the region's first SS unit (Schutzstaffeln, originally the party's elite bodyguard formations). "In this area of the city," Graf tells us, "the NSDAP had its base in the farming and middle-class strata; however it did succeed in making breakthroughs in the ranks of the miners."[24] In the other mining areas of the city, the party took between 0.4 and 0.5 percent. Mengede would appear to have had a development similar to that of Berlin-Spandau, possibly because of the efforts of some especially talented local leaders. Graf does not give any further details on the voting in the different areas of the city. His account ends with that 1929 election.

The National Socialists took 20.7 percent of the vote in the April 1932 Prussian state election, that being their highest percentage. In the Reichstag election of the following July they fell back slightly, to 19.6 percent and, as elsewhere, fell once again in November of that year. The National Socialists were described as being "very shocked" by the July loss. It occurred everywhere in the city, even in Mengede, their stronghold. The loss of momentum which elsewhere occurred in November came early to Dortmund. The party's showing here throughout the late Weimar period, was a poor one. In all elections from 1928 to 1933, Dortmund gave the lowest support to the National Socialists of all the cities over 200,000. This is especially striking given the Protestant majority in the city. It is a fact very much in need of an explanation. One suggestion is offered below.

In the 1930 Reichstag election, the National Socialists took 8.3 percent of the city's vote. Looking at the distribution within the city one finds the Innenstadt again leading the list and the better-off districts to the east and south following closely. Among the remaining areas of the city Mengede is again highest.[25] The percentages in order were: Innenstadt, 16.6; Süden, 16.1; Südosten, 15.7; Südwesten, 14.0; Osten, 12.2; and Mengede, 11.1. The Innenstadt had a very mixed population at that time, and Mengede was working class, but the other four districts would have contained effectively all of the city's upper class and upper middle classes.

The lower-middle-class populations, here as elsewhere, would have been located throughout the working-class districts and in the few mixed districts of the city. Lacking any census data on the character of the districts, it is impossible to establish with any certainty which ones would have had large lower-middle-class populations. For the present purpose, however, the significant fact is that *none* of the other districts had percentages higher than the six given on the above list. The best evidence in support of the lower-middle-class hypothesis would be found in the figure for the Innenstadt. That could reflect the voting of small shopkeepers who, presumably, would be found there in greater number than elsewhere in the city. Even if the lower middle class of the Innenstadt was providing those votes, one would have to account for the very small differences between the vote in that district and that in the others on the list. Some considerable emphasis would have to be given to the motives and voting of the upper and upper middle classes of the city. The only other point of note in this connection is that the vote in these "better" districts at this time was well below the level found in the equivalent districts of Berlin and Hamburg.[26]

The only detailed information found for the later elections, those of 1932, was for the Prussian state election of April and the Reichstag election of July. The reports, which appeared in the city's leading newspaper, the *Dortmunder Zeitung*, were limited in that they only gave the votes for nine of the parties, omitting any account of the others. There was, moreover, no total vote figure given for the various subareas. The results were presented, however, for all 390 precincts. Only the recently annexed areas appeared under headings indicating the subareas. The precincts of the old city appeared in serial order with only very brief descriptions (e.g. no. 112. Pestalozzi School, Essen Street 7). With some help from local informants and through the use of old city maps it was possible to get some approximate grouping of these precincts. A cluster of 44 precincts was discovered that appeared to be coterminous with the three southern districts on the previous list (i.e. Süden, Südosten, and Südwesten). In these precincts, the NSDAP vote in July 1932 amounted to 27.8 percent of the nine-party total. That figure contrasts with 19.9 percent of the same nine-party total in the city as a whole. One informant stated that the very best area of the city, the *Villenviertel*, was in the eastern district (Osten). A cluster of ten precincts covering the streets indicated showed an equivalent NSDAP percentage of 31.9.[27] These figures once again indicate that it was the upper and upper middle classes that gave strongest support to Hitler's party.

There were three bourgeois (*bürgerliche*) newspapers in Dortmund.

The *Dortmunder Zeitung* is generally acknowledged to have been the city's leading newspaper, at least in terms of prestige and reputation. As such, it would have had an audience similar to those of the *Rheinisch-Westfälische Zeitung* and the *Kölnische Zeitung*. Also present on the Dortmund scene was the *Tremonia* which was aligned with the Zentrum and thus had a position similar to the *Volkszeitungen* of Cologne and Essen. A third newspaper, the *General Anzeiger*, was more for popular consumption. There were also the usual publications associated with the SPD, the KPD, and the NSDAP. On the surface the range of offerings would appear to have been very similar to the range available in Essen. There were, however, as we shall see, some important differences in content.

The *Dortmunder Zeitung*'s news columns provided straight unemotional factual accounts of political meetings across the range of what one may refer to broadly as the center parties. It did not, as a rule, report the meetings of Social Democrats or of Communists, or for that matter, of National Socialists. Its editorial favor generally went to the parties of the traditional right although its commitment, one might note, was rather limited and the recommendations rather lacking in specificity.

The targets of its hostility were more clearly delineated than the persons or parties it favored. In the days leading up to the 1930 election, for example, it ran an editorial "Civic Duty" that was very much opposed to the Social Democrats. It ran a later article on the "SPD-Konzern" (the SPD Combine). And still another article on the same theme was entitled "Indifference of the Bourgeois." A later article dealt with "discouragement," its subhead lamenting the "lacking energy in the center camp." The newspaper's treatment of the political scene is indicated by its handling of Interior Minister Wirth's indictment of the National Socialists. Under the heading, "The Aims of the National Socialists," it merely gave a brief summary of the report without any comment. The nonspecific character of its election recommendations may be seen in the 1930 election day issue in which it called on "German men and German women" to "do your duty." The duty in this case amounted to voting for "our civic parties" against the radicals. The idea was to make the former parties strong enough so they would not have to compromise with "the extremes."

There was little change in the handling of the 1932 elections. In some instances, to be sure, National Socialist speakers were given more space than before. The thrust was still largely against the left, as for example in the issue prior to the Prussian state election in which the headlines for the editorial read: "The Reconquering of Prussia: In the Name of the People, Tomorrow There Will Be a Calling to Account." The actual recommendation called for a "strengthening of the right Center . . . to bring about a strengthening of reason and of political tolerance." That would seem a recommendation against the NSDAP, although again there is clearly a lack of precision in the formulation.

In an editorial comment prior to the July Reichstag election it declared that a Reichstag "of reconstruction must be elected." In this editorial it now announced that "we are prepared for practical joint effort with the National Socialists." That willingness, however, was tempered by some concern over their use of Marxist themes. Again the negative direction is clearer than the positive; the SPD-Zentrum combination must be prevented. Even a National Socialist-Zentrum combination would be unacceptable. The recommendation on Sunday, the day of the election, was again remarkably nondirective: "We will encounter better times— if on Sunday every voter does his duty." In smaller print the paper again declared its opposition to the extreme left and right parties (mentioning no names) and again failed to make any specific positive recommendation. Its election day editorial in November posed the problem as one of "right or left" but again made no specific recommendation. At that time, it was clear that it liked Papen's government.[28]

In summary, then, one may conclude that the *Dortmunder Zeitung*'s position with respect to National Socialism was midway between the reasoned opposition of the *Kölnische Zeitung* and the general support provided by the *Rheinisch-Westfälische*. This paper did little to stimulate support for the NSDAP, but it also did little to damp enthusiasm.

Were one to consider the analysis of Germany's problems contained in its news and editorial columns, the portrait would be closer to that of the *Rheinisch-Westfälische* although, to be sure, it lacked the sense of urgency found in the pages of that paper. The upper-class and upper-middle-class readers may have paid more attention to the world view contained in those pages, and they may well have responded in terms of their own felt sense of urgency. They may, in other words, have paid little or no attention to the rather dim guidance offered in the election day editorials. It is possible too that some of Dortmund's *bürgerliche* population would have been reading the *Rheinisch-Westfälische Zeitung* which, as indicated, had a regional following, one that was increasing in those years.[29]

The *General Anzeiger* had a markedly different character. With a circulation of 250,000, it was the largest newpaper in Germany outside of Berlin. The subhead described it as a newspaper "for Dortmund and the entire Rhine-Westphalian industrial region." It is not clear how much that expressed a wish and how much was reality. With a circulation of that size, however, some considerable part of it must have spilled over into surrounding communities.

The *General Anzeiger*, in contrast to the usual apolitical general paper, was an active advocate of a left liberal position. On another dimension the paper has been described as pacifist republican. It was strongly opposed to the National Socialists.

Opposition to the NSDAP by the SPD, KPD, and Zentrum press was constant in all cities. What is unique in Dortmund was the degree of serious and committed opposition found in this large general circulation newspaper. It is conceivable that the *General Anzeiger*'s opposition in this Protestant city was the decisive factor that contained or discouraged the enthusiasm that otherwise would have been aroused in support of the National Socialists.[30]

The *General Anzeiger* continued its opposition even after Hitler's accession to office. Its publication of a very unflattering charcoal sketch of *"der Führer"* led to a quick reaction. The newspaper was taken over and amalgamated with the local NSDAP organ.[31]

The argument of media impact, it should be emphasized, can only be a partial one. The upper and upper middle classes in this city did, without benefit of the media, vote disproportionately for the NSDAP. Something else was operating although what, specifically, that might have been is not clear. It might have been more direct forms of communication, such as National Socialist speakers campaigning in the better areas. Or these voters may have been reacting against a perceived threat, the "specter of communism." The Communists organized Sunday marches through the streets of the better districts that summer. Their audience may have reacted against what they saw as a very ominous development.

Böhnke says the events of March 1920, the Communist takeovers of Ruhr cities, remained in the memory or the region's population. The National Socialists, he says, rarely referred to those events in their propaganda, but those events may, nevertheless, have provided the basis for the area's upper and upper middle classes' reactions. Another closely related factor was the disappearance of the so-called center parties. Graf comments about the election of 1930 as follows: "The surprise of the election campaign was the fact that the democratic parties . . . with little resistance, let themselves be pushed onto the defensive and left the field of struggle to the extreme parties." Describing the events of 1931, Böhnke notes that when the National Socialists pulled out of the Reichstag in February, they launched a wave of meetings that continued until the autumn. He refers, by contrast, to the "submission" of other parties.[32] The reasons for these sharply contrasting political efforts are considered in more detail in Chapters 12 and 13. Many voters of the center must have sensed the weakness of their traditional parties and thus have felt a need to search for a more effective alternative. Their feelings of alarm and their sense that the Communists were on the verge of a takeover may have led them to vote for the National Socialists.

One other point deserves emphasis. Although the highest percentages for the NSDAP appeared in the best areas of the city, here as elsewhere that support made up only a small part of the party's total vote. The three best districts, Osten, Südosten, and Süden, for example, provided only one-fifth of the NSDAP's 1930 total. Even when one adds the more mixed Südwesten and the very heterogeneous Innenstadt, those areas still provided only a minority, roughly three-eighths of the National Socialist total. Although the available data do not allow a precise delineation of the districts with heavy working-class majorities, it does appear that here too, as in Berlin and Essen, a majority of the National Socialists' votes came from such areas. Although a relatively small minority in any given working-class district, because there were so many such districts, those minority votes added up to yield the most significant total contribution to the National Socialist electoral success. Once again it seems incumbent on us to provide some explanation of the motives leading people in this context to give up their previous political loyalties. This question is considered in more detail in Chapter 13.

DÜSSELDORF

Düsseldorf was the third largest city of the Ruhr at this time, the eleventh largest in the nation. As of 1933, it had just under one-half million inhabitants. As the provincial capital it was the site of many government buildings, as well as of many splendid park areas. It was graced also by several city and hunting palaces. Located on the right side of the Rhine a short distance below Cologne, it was, without question, the most attractive city in the Ruhr area. For these reasons, it had a somewhat different character from the other cities of the region. Of the five cities being considered in this chapter, Düsseldorf had the highest Catholic percentage, 61.2 (see note 5, this chapter). Much of the city's growth too had occurred in the twentieth century, in part through massive annexations in the late 1920s.

This city too began with its Altstadt, that district containing most of the historic buildings of the city. In the nineteenth century, the famous Königsallee was contructed along the eastern side of the old city. The moat was preserved and the area made into a park. On one side were the banks, the government buildings, and the Park Hotel. On the other, was the most elegant shopping avenue of the entire region. To the north, a broader park area contained, on one side, an art gallery, museums, and the congress hall, all of which were constructed in the 1920s. On the other side, the park extended out to include another smaller museum and, at a greater distance, the Jägerschloss (hunting palace). The Zoo-Viertel (containing the zoological gardens), farther to the north, contained one of the leading upper-class residential areas of the city. The late incorporations added some other elegant areas to the city such as Benrath to the south with its palace and gardens. And to the north, on the Rhine midway between Düsseldorf and Duisburg, a rather diverse community, Kaiserswerth, was added. Elsewhere in the city one did find working-class areas. Düsseldorf did not lack manufacturing; it was simply less extensive than in Essen or Dortmund.

There was an understandable tendency for the better-off classes of the surrounding cities to move to the Düsseldorf area. Some of the best-off citizens of neighboring Duisburg, for example, lived in Düsseldorf. This tendency is well illustrated by the dilemma that faced the United Steel Works, the giant combine formed in the mid-twenties, when it had to decide on the location of its head offices. As Albert Vögler, the head of the company, wrote the Düsseldorf *Bürgermeister*, Essen had distinct technical advantages. It was, after all, located in the center of the Ruhr district and provided easy access to the company's units in Dortmund to the east and to those in Düsseldorf to the west. On the other hand, Frau Vögler, and apparently other executives' wives too, preferred Düsseldorf. The final decision was for Düsseldorf.[33] Because of its different history and because of this attraction, Düsseldorf had a higher nonmanual percentage than other cities of the area. More specifically, it had more upper- and upper-middle-class subcommunities than did the other cities of the region.

Prior to World War I, the city had a triumvirate of political forces present, one very much like that observed in other Ruhr cities. But in Düsseldorf there was a difference in that all of the forces of the Protestant upper classes were organized into a Liberal Association. The Zentrum regularly took the Reichstag seat, but, because of the different local suffrage arrangement, the Liberal Association had a firm majority in the city council. This arrangement dissolved in the aftermath of the war as the old parties and the old electoral arrangements fell by the wayside. The Deutschnationale Volkspartei organized very quickly in the city as did the left liberal Deutsche Demokratische Partei. The right liberals were not able to organize in time; hence, in the first of the elections of the period, the *bürgerliche* vote went almost entirely to the Conservatives and to the left liberals. That accident of organization seems to have had a lasting impact since the Conservatives continued to show relatively greater strength in Düsseldorf than elsewhere in the Reich.[34]

The postwar events in Düsseldorf had similarities to and differences from those of the other Ruhr cities. The revolution began there in the evening of the eighth of November 1918, insurgents having arrived on the train from Cologne. The city had a stronger Independent Socialist group and a stronger Spartakus organization than was to be found elsewhere in the Ruhr. The first Spartakus actions occurred in early January, coinciding with the Berlin events. In February they interfered with the conduct of municipal elections, and government troops were brought in to allow a second try. Spartakus people later suppressed the bourgeois newspapers and still later encouraged strikes. The troops reappeared once again in April to restore order.

The Versailles treaty provided for French occupation of some cities on the right side of the Rhine, Düsseldorf and Duisburg among them. This occupation, complete with confiscation of government buildings and private homes, began in March of 1921. In January 1923, these cities were used as the bases from which the rest of the Ruhr area was occupied. Düsseldorf city histories contrast the French occupation of their city with the more benevolent English occupation in Cologne. While Cologne thrived, Düsseldorf essentially stood still, the population even undergoing some decline. It had certainly lost much of its prewar attractiveness.

The French withdrew from the rest of the Ruhr in December of 1923 and later, in August of 1925, from Düsseldorf. President Hindenburg visited the city in a great national holiday of celebration. A general upswing of business occurred in the following years. Prior to the war Düsseldorf had been known as a center for meetings and congresses. All such events had been in abeyance since 1914. A large exposition was arranged in 1926 to herald the revival of the city, and permanent buildings were constructed for this purpose. It seemed that good times had returned.

But within only a very few years, the depression made its appearance bringing massive unemployment and foundering city budgets. The same electoral shifts occurred here as elsewhere. And the violence committed by parties of the left and right mounted with each month of crisis. Before considering the voting patterns in the different areas of the city, it is useful to consider one episode of the history in greater detail.

Düsseldorf was the scene of one of Hitler's greatest triumphs—or at least so it has been characterized in many histories. The industrialists of the city and region were organized in an Industrieclub. Through the efforts of the steel magnate and Hitler supporter Fritz Thyssen, it was arranged that Hitler speak to the club. This occurred in the Park Hotel on January 26, 1932. Alan Bullock, accepting National Socialist writings at face value, notes that the industrialists' initial reception of Hitler was "cool and reserved." But he gave "one of the best speeches of his life," and at the end, the audience, "whose reserve had long since thawed, rose and cheered him wildly." Hitler's press secretary, Otto Dietrich, is quoted as saying, "The effect upon the industrialists was great and very evident during the next hard months of struggle."

The account given by the city's *Oberbürgermeister* Robert Lehr is somewhat different. He was asked to introduce Hitler and did so, with two short sentences. More than two decades later he wrote his account of both the speech and the response to it:

> The entire first part of the speech, in my judgment, was a sounding out and showed no especially striking train of thought until Hitler came to speak of the master-of-the-house standpoint in the management of the economy and, by attacking the Versailles treaty, created an atmosphere that appealed to many. Nevertheless, the expressions of approval and the applause were meager. . . .
>
> From my conversations with club members that evening and in the following days I was able to establish that the evening had not left an overwhelming impact on any of those with whom I spoke. They had also all noticed the uncertainty in the first part of the speech with its platitudes and continuous repetitions and were moved only by some sentences in the second half of the speech.
>
> That evening Hitler was unable either to bring in any significant number of convinced members or to move them to any exceptional contributions."[35]

Another point of note in Lehr's account is his description of the political orientations of those present: "The industrialists of the club belonged predominantly to the German People's party, a smaller part to the German National People's party, and a few very influential gentlemen to the Zentrum. Clearly taken by Hitler at that time were Privy Councilor Kirdorf and Fritz Thyssen." This account, in short, also indicates that the DVP party was the preferred party of the industrial bourgeoisie which means, once again, that linking the bourgeoisie with the DVNP and the middle class with the DVP is a mistake.[36]

The Düsseldorf statistical office published results for the city as a whole and for twenty-two subareas for all elections but one, regrettably that of July 1932. Fortunately, however, the detailed results for the precincts are to be found in the pages of the *Düsseldorfer Nachrichten*. For the initial presentation, however, the aggregated results of the Prussian Landtag election of April 1932 will be used.[37] They closely parallel the results of the later Reichstag election. In the city at that point, 29.7 percent of the vote went to the National Socialists. The highest percentages were found in the following subareas: Kaiserswerth, 40.0 percent; Mittelstadt, 39.7; Oestliche Friedrichstadt, 38.5; Volksgarten-Krankenhaus, 37.6; Zoo-Viertel, 36.9; Ständehaus-Floraviertel, 35.6;

Mörsenbroich, 33.3; Hofgartenviertel, 32.7; and Derendorf-Golzheim, 32.7.

Two of the areas on the list have already been mentioned, Kaiserswerth, a rather diverse community to the north of the older city, and the Zoo-Viertel, the leading *Villenviertel* of the older city.

No communities are homogeneous throughout. Within any given overall figure for a subcommunity there might be, and usually is, considerable variation, and the lower-middle-class tendency may be hidden within that overall figure. With this possibility in mind, one can explore the seven precincts of Kaiserswerth (two of them actually were from an adjacent community, Lohhausen). The community contained a large Catholic hospital and a Catholic old people's home. It also contained the mother house of a Protestant religious order for the training of sisters and a Protestant hospital. The rest of the population ranged from the well-off families living along the Rhine, many of them pensioners, to some lower-middle-class populations located inland.

There was a wide range of support for the National Socialists in the seven precincts, from a low of 7.6 to a high of 70.2 percent.[38] The low figure appeared in a district that appeared to contain some rather committed Catholics. The voting took place at an address on the Suitbertus-Stiftsplatz at a point opposite the Marienkirche in the center of the older, the Catholic part of Kaiserswerth. The commitment of this area's population is indicated by an 86.3 percent vote for the Zentrum. Another low figure for the NSDAP appeared in a second precinct in which the Zentrum was rather strong with 51.8 percent.

It is difficult to interpret the result in one of the polling places, this being a Diakonissen Institute. The Diakonie was an order of Protestant sisters that was run in much the same way as a Catholic order. The sisters also ran the hospital there. The result in this case probably included the votes of the sisters and their patients, and may also have included those of the populations in the surrounding neighborhood. This precinct gave the 70.2 percent vote to the NSDAP. The four remaining precincts ranged in their support between 32.2 and 48.5 percent, all of which were above the city-wide figure.

The precincts were rearranged somewhat for the July Reichstag election. The voting in the Suitbertus-Stiftsplatz still showed a very low level of support for the National Socialists (7.1 percent) and massive support (82.0 percent) for the Zentrum. The vote of patients in the Diakonissen Hospital was now presented separately, and it would appear that the vote of the sisters was now mixed in with that of the general population. The remaining five precincts ranged from 31.3 to 46.8 percent. Were one to judge from the voting pattern, the last district would appear to have been the best off of the lot. This judgment is based on the low percentage for the left, the SPD and KPD receiving respectively 3.4 and 4.1 percent. The second-strongest party in this precinct was the DNVP which picked up 20.9 percent.[39]

The picture for the other districts on the above list is not as clear as one might wish, in part at least, because of the heterogeneity of some of the areas. The best-off areas of the city appear here. The Zoo-Viertel, with its factory owners, businessmen, managers, and civil servants, was probably the best-off area of the city, and there the National Socialists received 36.9 percent of the vote. Another well-off area, the Hofgartenviertel, also had doctors, lawyers, and managers among its population. Not quite so affluent as the Zoo-Viertel, it is reported to have had high- and middle-level civil servants. It was slightly above the city-wide average in its level of NSDAP support.

The other areas on this list of preeminent NSDAP districts appear to have been rather mixed. The Mittelstadt is described as predominantly middle class and the Oestliche Friedrichstadt as definitely lower middle class. The Volksgarten-Krankenhaus district had doctors and some professionals in the neighborhood of the hospital but otherwise was lower middle class and, elsewhere, had a working-class area. The Ständehaus-Floraviertel was a mixed middle-class and working-class area. Mörsenbroich, an area with a small population forming the northeast corner of the city, was still very much agricultural. The last district, Derendorf-Golzheim, the second largest of the city, was also rather diverse. One street, the Cecilienallee fronted onto the Rhine and, of course, housed a very well-off segment of the city's population. But as one moved inland one found first mixed areas and then an area of plain working-class apartment houses.

A seemingly contrary case involves a recently annexed community, Benrath, generally counted as a well-off area. It does not appear on the above list, actually having given less than average support for the NSDAP (26.7 percent versus the city's 29.7). But this community was not uniformly upper or upper middle class. Only the streets in the immediate neighborhood of the palace were better ones. Elsewhere one found a small business area which was bordered by railroad tracks. And, on the other side of the tracks, one found a working-class subcommunity. In short, Benrath had a divided population, some well off, some lower middle class, and some working class, the three tending to have separate territories rather than being mixed in the same neighborhoods. An examination of the Landtag results in the two "best" precincts showed National Socialist percentages of 38.0 and 45.0. Here again it was the best-off areas, not the lower middle class that gave the strongest support to Hitler's party.

The Düsseldorf results appear to differ from the basic pattern found in Berlin, Hamburg, Essen, and Dortmund. One does find clear evidence of strong upper- and upper-middle-class support for the National Socialists, but here one also finds some middle class or mixed districts to be equally high in their support. This may result from their heterogeneity; an otherwise clear pattern, in other words, may be hidden in the district average (as, for example, in the case of Benrath). Or the result may be genuine, in which case it would constitute evidence of middle-class support for the National Socialists; in fact, it would be the most substantial support for the received claim to be discovered thus far in the present research.

There is little to be said with respect to the many other areas of the city. One may assume the presence of a lower middle class mixed in with working-class populations elsewhere in the city. All of these other areas gave significant minority support to the National Socialists. The lowest level in the 1932 Landtag election was 17.8 percent. Six other districts ran around 20 percent.[40]

Again there is little that one can offer to explain the dynamics of these developments. There is little information available on the grass roots political activity of the party and of course none on the motivation of the voters. Again one can examine the content of the leading bourgeois newspaper to obtain at least some idea of what this audience was reading, and from there one can speculate as to what might have been moving it.

The *Düsseldorf Nachrichten* was reputedly the city's leading *bürgerliche* newspaper. In character it resembled the bland *Dortmunder Zeitung* more than the *Kölnische Zeitung* or the *Rheinisch-Westfälische Zeitung*. That is to say, it was rather apolitical in tone. It had developed out of a purely commercial journal (as opposed to a political one), and this was still reflected in the 1930s, the publishers obviously not wishing to trouble any advertiser. On the few occasions that the newspaper did indicate a preference, it did so in a very restrained manner, without use of dramatic headlines or stirring editorials. The tepid character of this newspaper's politics is shown by its position with respect to the 1932 presidential election—it made no recommendation. Only on the day after the election did it take some kind of stand; it urged its readers to accept the result.

In the course of the Prussian state election, the paper again manifested its remarkably apolitical character. It is striking just how little political news was contained in its pages compared to other newspapers of the period. It gave brief accounts of the meetings of the nonsocialist parties and included NSDAP meetings among those covered. One National Socialist speaker was reported as speaking on the subject "Prussia awakes," a variation on one of the party's national slogans. "It is necessary to destroy the parties," he said.

Most of the political content of this paper was carried in the advertisements. The DNVP, for example, had an advertisement recommending that the voters "rally with Hugenberg" and, in a parallel message it offered a threat; "Zentrum People! There Will Be an Accounting for Your Ruinous Politics." The Zentrum responded in its advertisement a few days later. A DVP advertisement stressed Hitler's left-wing commitments, offering a Hitler quotation: "I am a Socialist!"

The *Düsseldorfer Nachrichten*'s Sunday morning issue on the day of the Landtag election left its readers with a very modest recommendation: "Vote Well!" Three months later, just before the Reichstag election, its editorial reminded the readers of the "need to vote."

The *Nachrichten* was reputed to be a DVP, that is, a right liberal newspaper. In its news and editorial comments in this period, however, it made almost no attempt to defend that position. Most studies of media impact have focused on positive effects, that is, on the addition of new content to a prior orientation, which caused some modification of behavior or outlook. In this case, a new external influence appeared while this journal failed to defend the prior position. The absence of any defense may have left upper- and upper-middle-class readers vulnerable to the appeals of the demagogue.[41]

An adequate understanding of their response would require some additional information. One would need to know about the initial dispositions of the city's upper and upper middle classes and also something about the means or channels through which they learned about National Socialism. Possibly a few hundred influential members of this community had heard Hitler directly in the Park Hotel, and it could be that they had passed their conclusions on informally, to family members, to friends, and to acquaintances within their immediate circles. Or it could be, especially in view of *Bürgermeister* Lehr's doubts about the immediate reactions, that they were moved by other National Socialist activists, by some local figures campaigning within their midst. One thing appears certain. The *Düsseldorfer Nachrichten* had reduced its possible influence to zero. By doing so, it left the political field open to some other agent or agencies.

DUISBURG

In 1933 Duisburg was the thirteenth largest city in the nation, the fourth largest in the Ruhr. Located at the confluence of the Ruhr and Rhine, it was the largest inland harbor of Europe. Because of its strategic location, it was also a major steel-manufacturing and processing center. The Rhine flowed along the western side of the city with nearly the entire frontage occupied by smelting and processing plants. The most important enterprises were those of the August Thyssen and the Mannesmann firms. To the northeast of the city were more factories, those of the Ruhr Chemie Holten lying just over the boundary in neighboring Oberhausen. East of the central and southern parts of Duisburg was the city forest which joined, without a break, the city forest of neighboring Mühlheim. To the east of Mühlheim, only a short distance away, was the city of Essen. Düsseldorf was immediately to the south of Duisburg. As one might expect, a very large portion of Duisburg's population consisted of industrial workers.

Just over half of the population was Catholic (51.7 percent); there was a large Protestant minority (42.7 percent), and most of the rest were listed as without religion. The religious composition of the city reflected its historical settlement. Duisburg, like all the cities we have considered, was constructed out of villages and rural areas that were added on in the course of the nineteenth and twentieth centuries. The various parts of the 1930 city had been subject to many different authorities in previous times. The district Wanheim-Angerhausen had belonged to Protestant Cleve, and it still had a Protestant majority in the late 1920s. Meiderich, the district immediately to the north of the Ruhr, had also been under Protestant authority, and it too had a Protestant majority 260 years after the Treaty of Westphalia. Hamborn, just to the north of Meiderich, had been under Catholic rule and was, nominally at least, Catholic in the 1920s. All three areas had significant working-class populations.[42]

No data were discovered that allowed precise demarcation of the class composition of the city areas. The experts, however, locate the city's upper class in Duissern, to the east of the Altstadt on the edge of the city forest. A low hill, called the Königsberg, is located there; on its west side were some rather handsome villas. The streets of the Duissern area were known for their villas, bungalows, and elegant apartment houses. The Dellviertel was also a "good" area and probably contained an upper-middle-class population. The Altstadt, the old city, also contained some better-off populations, but the majority there probably consisted of lower-middle-class commercial and artisan populations plus a considerable working-class contingent. The district to the south of Duissern, Neudorf, is also said to have had some "good" areas, especially in the streets facing the city forest.

The political character of these districts may be seen in the results of the 1928 election, shown in the accompanying table. This picture does tend to confirm the expert judgments about the character of these districts. In Duisberg, as in so many other cities, the party of the dominant

District	DVP	DNVP	Zentrum	DDP	Total
Duissern	24.3%	17.4%	22.8%	5.4%	69.9%
Dellviertel	20.5	13.0	29.9	4.2	67.6
Altstadt	15.9	13.5	22.6	3.7	55.7
Neudorf	13.9	11.3	26.2	3.7	55.1
Duisburg (city)	11.3	12.5	23.9	3.0	50.7

social groups was the Deutsche Volkspartei. And, accordingly, one finds the greatest strength for that party in the areas just mentioned, with Duissern leading the list.[43] Except in Neudorf, one finds above average support for the DNVP in these districts. Above average support for the DDP also appears in all four districts. The picture of the Zentrum is more mixed, but then that party tended to take votes from across the board, its intention being to bridge, not stress, class differences. It did moderately well everywhere except in the Protestant working-class areas.

The bourgeois DNVP was not exclusively an upper-class party. Its best showings came from the Mittelmeiderich (28.7 percent) and Obermeiderich (18.3 percent) districts, which were perhaps better described as Protestant and as containing a mixture of lower-middle-class and working-class populations. In Obermeiderich there was also some farm population present. Once again the depiction of the DNVP as an *upper-class* conservative party proves to be mistaken.

The only data found that allowed a breakdown by subarea were for the 1930 Reichstag election. At that point the National Socialist percentage in the city had jumped from 1.5 (the May 1928 figure) to 18.0, a figure that, since it is just under the national average, is rather unexpected for a Catholic and working-class city. The three Protestant bourgeois parties had lost approximately half of their former strength.

In terms of NSDAP support the leading districts were: Altstadt, 26.1 percent; Duissern, 24.6 percent; Dellviertel, 24.3 percent; Wasserviertel, 23.9 percent; Neudorf, 23.2 percent; Kasslerfeld, 22.7 percent; and Meiderich, 22.3 percent.[44]

As was the case with some of the cities previously reviewed, the Altstadt leads the list. It would be easy to assume that this represents the vote of lower-middle-class shopkeepers, the Altstadt at that time being so closely associated in people's minds with small stores, artisans' shops, and so forth. That association could well involve an ecological fallacy, since the Altstadt, here as elsewhere, had a very mixed population, some upper- and upper-middle-class families for example, still being located there. A more detailed exploration was not possible since precinct results were unavailable.

The best areas of the city follow on the list, in second, third, and fifth rank. The presence of the Wasserviertel (harbor area) and Kasslerfeld (also in the harbor area) on the list is difficult to explain. They both had relatively small populations, and it is conceivable that strong Protestant clusters were located in the area. The results for Meiderich were not broken down for the three subareas of that community. It is possible that two factors, Protestantism and the rural character of one of the districts, affect the result.

There is little else that can be said about Duisburg. It appears, making all due allowance for the limitations of the data, to provide a close parallel to Essen, where the NSDAP strength also came from rural Protestant areas, from the better districts of the city, and from the mixed Altstadt. The best support for the lower-middle-class thesis is found in the Altstadt result, but, as indicated, that evidence is ambiguous.

Even if one were to grant that the Altstadt result represented lower-middle-class votes, and if one also were to be generous in definition and grant that the votes from the Wasserviertel and Kasslerfeld were lower middle class, that would amount to 3,504 National Socialist votes. At the same time, however, the three better areas of the city, Duissern, Dellviertel, and Neudorf, provided 10,065 votes for Hitler's party. It would, therefore, be necessary to give considerable attention in any analysis to the vote from the city's upper- and upper-middle-class areas. The conclusion drawn by Duisburg's historian and archivist, that the National Socialists "appealed more and more to the strata of the middle class and the petty bourgeoisie," overlooks a significant source of the party's support.[45] Those better areas together with the lower-middle-class or mixed districts still provided only one-third of the votes cast for the National Socialists. Here as elsewhere a signficant portion of that vote, probably at least half, came from working-class districts. The motivations of these voters must also be considered in any satisfactory analysis.

Some of the dynamics observed elsewhere also appear here although with slight variations. Under the French occupation, which, as in Düsseldorf, dated from 1921, nationalist organizations were prohibited. Hence the first NSDAP *Ortsgruppe* dates from July 1925, the date of the French evacuation. And in a pattern similar to that found in Hamburg, the first group was provocatively located, in "red Hamborn," a working-class area. The unit held the usual meetings, and the Communists were regularly present, in most cases apparently making up the majority of the audience. Up to 1928, it would also appear that the NSDAP was always bested in these struggles. On the ninth of November 1928, a double anniversary of the 1918 revolution and the Munich *Putsch*, all of the Ruhr units of the party convened in the city for a march through the "red" Hochfeld district. This was the party's big demonstration up to this point. It seems to have been its Pharus Hall battle.[46] The membership is said to have grown rapidly in the following years, to 3,800 in the summer of 1931 and to 5,000 in March of 1932. The party took 29.7 percent of the vote in the Prussian state election of April that year, its peak performance prior to Hitler's coming to power. In the July Reichstag election, its support fell off slightly, to 27.5 percent.

Most ordinary citizens would have seen the events of those times through their local newspaper. For the well-off citizens of Duisburg, the most likely sources would have been the *Rhein und Ruhrzeitung* and the *Duisburger General-Anzeiger*. For the concerned Catholic reader, there would also have been the *Echo vom Niederrhein*.[47]

The *Rhein und Ruhrzeitung*, like the *Dortmunder Zeitung* and the *Düsseldorfer Nachrichten*, is best described as a weak defender of the political center. Its most obvious opponents were found on the left. During the 1930 Reichstag election, scarcely a day went by without an editorial attacking the SPD or, on occasion, the SPD and the Zentrum combined. The Communists, not being a governing party, seemed not worthy of its attention. The newspaper's positive contribution was expressed in an editorial entitled "Citizens to the Front." There the paper complained of a splintering in the bourgeois ranks and, another important theme, that ten million people had not voted in the previous election, seven or eight million of them being *Bürger*. Therefore, it was argued, the need was for "the winning of a bourgeois united front." In this connection, almost as an afterthought, it mentioned another danger, this from some unnamed "bourgeois radicalism." In another editorial, this again directed at the threat from the left, mention was made of the problem posed by "radical fanatics of the left and right." The paper reported on the meetings of the bourgeois parties. It published next to nothing on the meetings of the left parties, and similarly, had little to say about NSDAP meetings.

The final recommendation made in the 1930 election day issue was simple: "Everyone Must Vote." A page-one editorial carried the following headline: "Wake Up! And Vote! Citizens! Should the Radical Parties Become Ever Stronger Simply Because You Are Sleeping?" The assumption being made here is that the nonvoters were disproportionately oriented toward the moderate parties of the political center. The belief was that the radical parties would have had all their loyal supporters mobilized in any case. Those remaining would be the politically indifferent moderates. This assumption was widely shared by the moderate and right press at the time, and the concern with maximizing participation was therefore a constant theme at election time.

The difficulties of the centrist direction are indicated in the *Rhein und Ruhrzeitung*'s position with respect to the elections of 1932. In the presidential election it clearly favored Hinderburg. To make the choice more palatable, it denied that he had become a left candidate. In the Prussian state election it was still campaigning against the Social Democrats and their "party dictatorship" in Prussia. The editorial had a clear negative aim but an unclear and open-ended positive recommendation: "Against the Weimar Coalition, against Radicalism, for a Majority of the Rightist Parties. For a New Prussia." And it offered an extra reminder for the nonvoters: "He Who Does Not Vote, Votes Left!" The editorial on the following day expressed satisfaction over the result: "The attack on the Weimar coalition has been an indisputable success." The positive side of the result is again less clear: "The National Socialists will now have to show what practical work they can accomplish."

In the Reichstag election, the newspaper again appeared embarrassed by the absence of an unambiguous positive option. Were one to judge preferences by reports of party meetings, one would conclude that its heart was with the DVP and DNVP. It is remarkable how little space was given to NSDAP meetings, even at this late point. The final recommendations included a reminder that "the right to vote is the duty to vote" (*Wahlrecht ist Wahlpflicht*). The key editorial concluded that "the thirty-first of July can and must, therefore, bring the parliamentary confirmation for the change of course initiated by President von Hindenburg through his creation of the Papen government. We remind [our readers], in this last hour, of their duty to help in this work by voting on Sunday for the parties of the right!" The "parties of the right" were not named.

In November, it again gave strong support to Papen. This support, the paper's strongest statement on the subject, appeared in the context of opposition to the National Socialists: "The Papen government took office with the hope that all national circles of the German people would stand behind it and support it with all their strength in disposing of the black-red system. National Socialism has attacked [this government] from behind. . . . It needs support from the people." The recommendation was summarized with the slogan: "With Hindenburg for Germany!"[48]

The columns of the *Rhein und Ruhrzeitung*, then, show weak and ineffectual opposition to the National Socialist option. One cannot be sure how this stimulus was interpreted by its readers. The newspaper may well have contributed to the alarm and concern over the rottenness of "the system." And by generating such disgust and alarm, it may have prepared readers to support the extreme option. After all, in the face of the exceptional threat, exceptional measures would seem clearly justified. Then, too, by failing to specify the solution to the problem, by failing to support and reinforce a traditional political direction, it left the path open for this new alternative.

The *Duisburger General-Anzeiger* had a similar character, that is, one of lukewarm support for a right center direction. If anything, it was even less political than the *Rhein und Ruhrzeitung*. Most of the politics in the paper appeared in the advertisements, all of the major parties from the DNVP to the Staatspartei being regularly represented. Prior to the 1930 election this newspaper offered no editorials and no clear recommendations. All the news stories were very brief summary items. Its unconcerned tone is evidenced in an editorial on the Monday morning after the election, one entitled "And Now What?" With regard to the National Socialists, all it could offer was the suggestion that they "would not likely come into question for a joint effort with the parties of the center."

The same tone is evidenced in the issues preceding the Prussian state election in 1932. It should be noted that this was a family newspaper. Much attention was given to household whimsy, to fashion, to furniture and design, and, for the men, to sports. Much attention was also given to sensational news stories occurring beyond the nation's borders, a practice referred to in the trade as "Afghanistanism." In line with this preference for the "interesting" and the sensational, it picked up Hitler's airplane campaign across Germany, a remarkable innovation at the time. It also reported the words of Prince August Wilhelm, the kaiser's son, who preceded Hitler at one NSDAP meeting. The prince declared that "today Hitler wishes to break the chains of slavery."

Some reports of violence were found in these pages. The National Socialist Robert Ley attacked Social Democratic leader Otto Wels in a Cologne restaurant. There were thirty-five wounded in a beer hall brawl in Munich. And, amid this action the paper gave its attention to the meetings of the DVP and DNVP.

The July 25, 1932, issue reports on Hitler's appearance in the Duisburg stadium. The speech, touched on earlier in this chapter, was given considerable attention. Most striking, if for no other reason because of its being given a separate paragraph and heavy type, was the following quotation: "We solemnly swear it: yes, certainly, it is our will, our resolve, to do away with these thirty parties in Germany." The newspaper made no comment on this quotation. It simply recorded "the fact" that it had been said.

The *General-Anzeiger* gave space to other party leaders, for example, to Wirth of the Zentrum and to Eduard Dingeldey of the DVP, and just before the election it published an interview with Papen. The Sunday editorial recommendation was rather weak. Coming under the familiar heading, "The Right to Vote Is the Duty to Vote," it proceeded to a very vague recommendation. Germany, it said, "must have a Reichstag that can work hand in hand with a strong government." A cautionary "within the framework of the constitution" is included there, and if one thought hard and was convinced of all the steps of the argument, one could say that that excluded the NSDAP. On the other hand, the lesson was not made specific, and the reader could easily judge the elements differently, concluding that the urgency of the matter was such as to require steps outside the constitution.[49]

The readers of the bourgeois newspapers in this city, then, would have read sources that did not strongly oppose the National Socialists. In fact, the prestige newspapers of Dortmund, Düsseldorf, and Duisburg, as we have seen, were all remarkably restrained in their political orientations during this period. While they did not champion the National Socialist option, the arguments for their favored parties, those of the right, were rather weak and lacking in clear direction. The National Socialist voting advantage that appeared in the upper- and upper-middle-class districts of these cities clearly did not require or depend on outright newspaper support. All that was required was a kind of neutrality (or indecisiveness) with respect to that party's merits. Strong newspaper opposition could eliminate that advantage, as was seen in Cologne and possibly in Munich.

The sources of that National Socialist advantage must be looked for elsewhere, possibly in some predisposition found among the upper and upper middle classes generally or in the personal face-to-face efforts of NSDAP militants. These newspapers would appear to have provided the facilitating conditions for the NSDAP advances. Because they failed to reinforce traditional loyalties, these newspapers left their readers available to the demagogues who were active throughout these communities during this period. By communicating a sense of alarm, by dramatizing the Marxist menace, and by making clear the weakness of the bourgeois parties, they made it easy for their readers to conclude that more drastic measures were required, measures that could only be provided by the National Socialists. Put simply, the lesson communicated, perhaps inadvertently, was that exceptional conditions require the use of exceptional means.

WUPPERTAL

Directly to the east of Düsseldorf and to the southeast of Essen lies the city of Wuppertal. It is different in some key respects from the other cities considered in this chapter. It had, first of all, a very high Protestant percentage, 70.1 percent, a figure well above that for Dortmund, the next highest city with its 53.6 percent. The Protestantism of this city, moreover, was not Lutheran but Reformed, that is, Calvinist in character. In the common parlance of the city, a "mixed marriage" was one between Calvinist and Lutheran. The later immigrant Catholics are reported to have mediated in the struggles between these two hostile branches of Protestantism. It is not entirely clear what the consequences of this Reformed presence were for the later politics of the city. It is reported that the Christian Social party was strong there, this being a "social" anti-Semitic party begun in the 1880s by the court preacher, one Reverend Adolf Stöcker.[50] One possible consequence, a lasting effect, perhaps, is that the National Socialists were very strong in this city; in fact, they gained the highest percentage in Wuppertal of any of the fourteen cities being considered in this work. Hitler gained 43.0 percent of the vote in the second round of the presidential election of April 10 (outdoing Hindenburg who only took 41.1 percent). His party took 43.4 percent of the total in the Prussian state election of April 24. In the Reichstag election in July, the NSDAP took 42.7 percent.[51]

The city's geography and history are also somewhat different from the other cities considered in this chapter. Local citizens are quick to point out that Wuppertal is not a Ruhr city. It lies in the valley of the Wupper River, to the south of the Ruhr. It is only the careless outsider who lumps all cities of the area together as falling into the Ruhr pot.

The city called "Wuppertal" resulted from the amalgamation in 1929 of two predecessors: Elberfeld, lying to the west in the valley, and Barmen, lying to the east. Barmen's most famous son was Friedrich Engels. Joseph Goebbels was the NSDAP district leader in Elberfeld from 1924 to 1926.[52]

Wuppertal might be described as a string city, for it stretches along the narrow Wupper valley. The proletarian and lower-middle-class populations were housed in the low lying areas, and the well-off populations lived on the heights. Another point of special note is that this city drew its population from a different *Hinterland* than the other cities considered in this chapter. Duisburg and Düsseldorf drew from the Rhineland and from Westphalia. Dortmund drew from Westphalia, and from the Prussian provinces east of the Elbe. Wuppertal's reach was more restricted; it drew its population from the hill country immediately to the south in the Westerwald.

Precinct results for the July 1932 election were available, but unfortunately analysis of the internal differentiation proved next to impossible.[53] For this reason, only the global result and its implications are discussed.

Possibly the most appropriate comparison is with Dortmund, which also had a Protestant majority. Both cities were heavily industrial, and consequently both had large working-class populations. But there the similarity ends; one had the lowest NSDAP percentage of all the cities considered in this work, and the other had the highest.

One could explain the difference in terms of differing histories, that is, in terms of the differing Protestantisms of the two cities. Or, one could offer a cultural explanation in terms of the cosmopolitanism or openness of the one city and the closed character of the other, the one drawing populations from a wide area, the other from a more restricted, more provincial area. Another possibility would be differences in the effectiveness of the respective National Socialist local organizations. None of these hypotheses can be easily assessed, it being difficult to get any adequate measure of the variables in question.

Another explanation is, however, more accessible, this again being the possibility of a media effect. Dortmund, it will be remembered, had a mass circulation newspaper that was strongly opposed to National Socialism. Wuppertal, it happens, had a newspaper that was very favorably disposed toward Hitler's party. A review of its coverage of events proves useful.

The newspaper in question, the *Bergisch-Märkische Zeitung*, was a leading bourgeois journal.[54] It was clearly both nationalist and rightist in its direction. In the early days of September 1930, there were articles and editorials dealing with all the standard themes of the rightist repertory. There were calls for revision of the Versailles treaty; there were alarms over the role of Marxism in the Austrian military (the lesson being that Marxism's impact was the same everywhere); there were reports on DNVP meetings ("Take down the Red Flag!") and on NSDAP meetings. An article reminded readers of the sixtieth anniversary of the battle of Sedan. The paper published extensively from the open letter of Catholic clergymen with regard to the Zentrum: "By putting the Social Democratic party in the saddle, the Center party, especially in Prussia, has made an enormous contribution to the de-Christianization of our public life." The lesson was that "national Catholics" should vote for the DNVP.

The paper objected to Minister of Interior Wirth's position paper indicting the NSDAP, the objection being to such use of his office in the midst of an election campaign. Another story, under the heading "Germany Is Being Drained!" reported the views of United States Senator James Reed (as given in the *Chicago Tribune*) on the "true state" of German affairs.

There was a steady run of reports on violence. In its pages the violence was always perpetrated by the left: "Reichsbanner Attack," "Marxist Stabs National Socialist," "Attempted Attack by Communists." And by comparison, another headline speaks of the "exemplary discipline of the SA."

One finds the standard claims made about the nonvoters: "These ten million nonvoters are not Marxists. They are deserters from the front of loyal citizens. Marxism has long since mobilized its reserves of voters." Under the heading, "If National Socialism Has a Success," one finds a very positive account given by the Thuringian National Socialist minister, Wilhelm Frick. Among other things, he promised a considerable reduction in the number of civil servants.

The newspaper's position was very clear in this election. It was opposed to Marxism and its clerical collaborators. Its voting recommendation was also clear. As indicated in the preelection editorial—"How Does the Front Stand?"—it was for Hugenberg and the DNVP. At the same time, it regularly reported NSDAP meetings, and these reports were unambiguously positive. The NSDAP street fighters were portrayed as a group of honorable and disciplined fighters against the Marxist menace.

Hitler and the National Socialists were viewed with even greater favor in 1932. This is most striking in the three-cornered run off election for the presidency. The front page of the election day issue carried a large headline: "No Vote for Hindenburg." This was followed by a smaller headline, "No Vote for Our Opponent!" And this in turn was followed by a story (actually more of an editorial) entitled "Hitler in Essen." Some sense of the newspaper's vehemence on the subject may be gained from the other front-page stories. There was a picture of a mass street meeting complete with red flags which was accompanied by the following provocative questions and explanation: "Revolutionary Demonstration in 1918? No! A Hindenburg Election Meeting in 1932." And to finish off the field marshal, a column was devoted to "Ludendorff: The 50th Anniversary of His Service." This account indicated that all the famous Hindenburg-Ludendorff victories were to be credited to the adjutant, not to the field marshal.[55]

In the course of the Prussian state election, the *Bergisch-Märkische Zeitung* was again very favorable to the NSDAP. It complained about prohibiting the NSDAP's Sturmabteilung without a corresponding prohibition of the republican Reichsbanner. It continued to report favorably on NSDAP meetings. A tendency also appeared at this time to mix the reports on the DNVP and the NSDAP as, for example, in a story "Hugenberg and Hitler in the Electoral Battle." To refresh memories, it ran a series of articles on the 1918-1919 history of Spartakus under the headline, "Should It Again Come to This?"

The editorial recommendation was for the Harzburg Front, that is, for the front formed by the DNVP and the National Socialists. The election day editorial ends with the following: "Save Prussia! Declare yourself for the Harzburg Front. There is only one choice: Harzburg Front or system." The day after the election, the newspaper hailed the achievement: "Victory of the National Opposition" and "DNVP and NSDAP Beat the System by 30 Seats."[56]

Its position in the July Reichstag election was exactly the same. The election day editorial reads: "To vote national means to liberate Germany. . . . In the darkest hour of our history, providence has given the German people two men . . . Hugenberg and Hitler. Around them is gathered the freedom-fighting national-revolutionary movement of Germany." At this point the paper even found some good words to say for Hindenburg because he had brought Papen into office. The basic lessons to be remembered on that election day were summarized in slogans scattered throughout the newspaper: "He Who Loves Germany Declares Himself for the National Movement. The Enemy Stands on the Left!" And there is also a ditty: "Black and Red—Germany's Dead!" And another slogan reads: "Against Zentrum and Bolshevism. Vote National!" With evident satisfaction, the newspaper's headlines on the day following the election announced: "Free Road for National Renewal; Burial of the System."[57]

The *Bergisch-Märkische Zeitung*, in summary, was very strongly opposed to the republic and all those identified with it, including Hindenburg. It and the *Fränkischer Kurier* (considered in the next chapter) were the most hostile of any of the newspapers in the cities studied here, outdoing even the *Rheinisch-Westfälische Zeitung* of Essen. Both the *Bergisch-Märkische Zeitung* and the *Fränkischer Kurier* were strongly supportive of Hugenberg and the DNVP. Although not properties of the Hugenberg press empire, they were clearly within the same spiritual family.

Wuppertal had the usual range of newspapers, from KPD and SPD offerings on the left to a National Socialist offering on the right. The official and apolitical *Täglicher Anzeiger* carried advertisements for both the DNVP and the SPD. The *Barmer Zeitung* was described as liberal, but was in fact also apolitical. In its preelection issue (July 30, 1932), it gave only factual accounts and provided no recommendations. The newspaper with the largest circulation (approximately 90,000) was the *General-Anzeiger*. There was also a Catholic newspaper, the *Bergische Tageszeitung*. The center journals, by remaining neutral with respect to the struggles of the period, left the *Bergisch-Märkische Zeitung* unchallenged in the city's bourgeois circles.[58]

The electoral and census data for these five Ruhr cities were not as rich as those for Berlin, Hamburg, and Cologne.[59] For that reason the presentation has been less detailed, and it has not been possible to address some of the questions raised in previous discussions. In Berlin and Hamburg, support for the National Socialists increased with the social standing of the district. This pattern was found in Essen and Dortmund and also, to a lesser degree, in Duisburg. In Düsseldorf, although the "best" districts gave the National Socialists above average support, some middle class and mixed districts also gave high levels of support. This may be an exception to the rule of NSDAP support varying with class, or it may result from the diverse composition of some of the subareas. Wuppertal, as far as one can tell, presents another exception. The overall level of NSDAP support was very high, and the one area that was clearly better off gave the same high (42.7 percent) support as was found elsewhere in that city. Because of the city's complicated geography, there is little more one can say.

The specific character of these two uncertain cases, however, deserves some emphasis. The findings there are similar to the Berlin, Hamburg, Essen, Dortmund, and Duisburg results in that the "best" districts gave high levels of support to the NSDAP. They differ from those cases in that some middle-class or mixed districts appear to have given the NSDAP equally strong support. The lesson is not that the lower middle class is distinctive, but rather that no difference exists between that segment of the population and the groups higher up in the nonmanual ranks.

There is little one can say with certainty to explain these results. In a very general way they do appear to reflect press orientations. Dortmund, with a major anti-NSDAP journal, had the lowest level of support for that party, and Wuppertal, with a warmly enthusiastic journal, the highest. Some of the press made no clear recommendation (apart from opposition to Marxism) and thus effectively rejected the possibility of exerting influence. They may have thereby left the political field to other agents or agencies. At this point the trail of evidence gives out. One can only speculate about the activity of those other agents, about where they campaigned and with what effects. And the same holds for questions about voter orientations, about their predispositions, and about their reactions to the various political stimuli offered them during the last years of the republic.

CHAPTER EIGHT

Five Other Cities

This chapter deals with an assortment of five cities. Nothing in particular ties them together; they simply provide five additional occasions to explore the relationship between class and voting. The five cities are Frankfurt am Main, Hanover, Stuttgart, Nuremberg, and Mannheim.

FRANKFURT

Frankfurt, Germany's ninth largest city in 1933, had at that time a population of 555,857. One of the oldest cities in central Europe, it was both an administrative center and a leading commercial town throughout the Middle Ages. For most of its history it was a free city, but after the Austro-Prussian War in 1866 it was annexed by Prussia and joined to the new province of Hesse-Nassau.

In the 1920s it was still a leading commercial center. One should not, however, overlook the equally important fact that most of its employed population was engaged in industry—in printing, in brewing, in the production of chemicals and pharmaceuticals, electrical equipment, machine tools, leather, and last but not least, frankfurters. Immediately to the west of the older city was the city of Höchst, annexed in 1928, which contained the giant chemical works of one unit of I.G. Farben.

A Protestant city at the time of the Westphalian settlement, it still had a Protestant majority of 57.2 percent in 1933. Approximately one third (33.1 percent) of its population was Catholic. The city had the highest Jewish percentage of any German city, 4.7. The next highest figures were 3.8 percent in Berlin, 3.2 percent in Breslau, and 2.3 percent in Mannheim.

The support for the National Socialists in Frankfurt was below the national average in both 1924 elections. But then, in 1928, in 1930, and in both 1932 elections it exceeded that average. The available evidence might suggest that Frankfurt also constituted an exception to the pattern observed in Berlin, Hamburg, and elsewhere in that its leading upper- and upper-middle-class area did *not* provide above average support for the National Socialists. Closer examination reveals, however, that certain segments of the population in this area gave overwhelming support to the National Socialists.[1]

The city had a large medieval Altstadt. Across the Main River was a smaller extension of the old city called Sachsenhausen. The old city wall was torn down in 1333, and the new wall added a larger territory, called the Neustadt (new city). The new wall came down in 1806, and the area of fortifications and moat became a park. The housing facing this park was of an elegant upper-middle-class variety. Beyond this park area came a ring of outer-city districts. And beyond them came the more recently annexed ex-farm communities. In the West End, a district embracing the western and northwestern outer-city districts, one found the most elegant villas in the city. They were within walking distance of the downtown businesses and, for evening entertainment, of the opera house. There was a large middle-class area to the south of the Main River called Outer Sachsenhausen. Within this district, which incidentally bordered on the city forest, was another villa quarter containing a small segment of the city's upper class. Most of the rest of the Outer Sachsenhausen population was middle class.[2]

No official election results with consolidated figures for the various subareas appeared after 1929. That last official accounting was for the municipal election of November 17, 1929, at which point exactly 10.0 percent of the city's voters chose the National Socialists.[3] The highest NSDAP percentages appeared in the northern Neustadt (17.2), the western Neustadt (15.5), the eastern Neustadt (14.9), and the Altstadt (13.7). The remarkable feature of this result is that the four highest districts (of thirty-seven) were the four districts of the older city.

Looking at the better-off outer-city districts, one finds the western outer-city district, the best of the city, to have had the lowest percentage in this part of Frankfurt, 6.7, a figure well below the overall average. And the second most elegant district, the northwestern outer-city district also had a low figure (8.4), again below the city average. Regrettably only a single figure was given for the entire Outer Sachsenhausen area, which, at 11.6 percent, was somewhat above the city's average. Several other districts were above the city average at this time, most of these being mixed ones to the north and east of the older city. The recently annexed rural subcommunities to the north and northeast gave fairly strong support to the NSDAP, but only one, Eschersheim, was above the city average. The working-class areas were all very low. Nied and Sossenheim, for example, had the lowest percentages in the city, 2.2 and 1.3 respectively.

It will be remembered that Frankfurt had the highest Jewish percentage of any German city. The distribution within the city was very irregular, with some districts, the West End for example, having just over 20 percent and some, mostly the newly annexed areas, having less than 1 percent. One can assume that few Jews voted for the NSDAP and that a correction would therefore be in order. As expected, the correction led to an increase in the NSDAP percentages in the districts with sizable Jewish populations.[4] Otherwise, there was little impact on the rank ordering. The center-city districts were still highest. They were still followed by the northern and eastern outer districts. And the West End was still relatively low. The figure for Outer Sachsenhausen showed little change.

The *Frankfurter Zeitung* published a detailed statement of precinct results for the July 1932 Reichstag election.[5] At this point, the NSDAP percentage for the city was 38.7. The newly annexed working-class districts in the Höchst area were generally well below that figure (although they still provided the NSDAP with significant minorities, giving it approximately one-quarter of the votes cast there). Elsewhere, the most striking initial impression is the lack of differentiation, with most districts falling within five percentage points of the city average.

Within the old center city, two districts were slightly below the average, and two, the northern and eastern area of the Neustadt, were well above the average. As for the districts of the outer-city ring, three were below the average and three were above. Two of those below the average were the "best" areas of the city, the western outer city having a relatively low figure of 31.2 percent and the second best district, the northwestern outer city, being just below the city's figure with 36.0 percent. Outer Sachsenhausen now had a relatively high figure of 49.0 percent. This is especially striking because, at least in the popular imagination, it would be Inner Sachsenhausen that would have the distinctive petty bourgeois character, but there the National Socialist percentage was slightly below average at 37.2.

One striking new development found in the 1932 pattern is the remarkable strength of Hitler's party in the more rural (or small townish) subcommunities to the north of the city. Three of these, on the northernmost border of the city, gave well over half of their votes to the NSDAP (Niederursel, 61.1 percent; Bonamos, 57.1 percent, and Berkersheim, 57.8 percent). Neighboring Escherheim, already high in 1929, now gave close to half (47.4 percent). One can only speculate about the causal dynamics in these areas. They were more rural and heavily Protestant, conditions favoring the NSDAP elsewhere. It seems likely that the party's campaigners were very active there.

Assigning all of the NSDAP vote to the non-Jewish populations puts the more proletarian eastern Neustadt and the eastern outer-city districts somewhat above the city average (with 43.6 and 42.9 percent respectively). It raises the figure for the elegant western outer-city district to 39.9 percent, slightly above the city-wide figure and puts the NSDAP percentage for the second best area, the northwestern outer-city district, at 46.7, eight points above it.

There was a fair-sized Catholic minority in the western outer-city district, it forming 25.2 percent of the total. One might assume, following the previous estimating procedure, that all Zentrum votes there, 28.6 percent of the July 1932 total, would be those of the district's Catholics. However, in this instance, it seems likely that many Jewish voters had chosen the Zentrum as their best available alternative, that party's 1932 figure being well above the 11.4 percent registered in 1928. A similar development appeared in the northwestern outer-city district. This phenomenal growth of the Zentrum did not occur in districts with small Jewish percentages. If this did signify a shift in Jewish voting, following the estimating procedure used in previous chapters would entail some significant double counting. If, however, one assumed that only half of the Zentrum vote was from Catholics and assigned the NSDAP votes to the remaining population, the percentage for this largely Protestant segment would be 47.6. Approximately one-quarter of the district's votes, moreover, went to the left (25.8 percent, most of that to the SPD). That would put the NSDAP percentage among the district's nonmanual Protestants well up in the sixties. The best conclusion then is that Frankfurt too followed the pattern found in the best areas of Berlin and Hamburg. What looked like an exception on the basis of the overall figures results from the relatively large Jewish and Catholic minorities present in Frankfurt's best areas.

In summary, one may note that, as elsewhere, the working-class districts provided fair-sized minority support for the National Socialists although, again as elsewhere, the figures for most such districts are below the city average. The pronounced support for the NSDAP in Protestant and rural areas of the city also appears here. The other areas of the city, both the mixed ones and some better off ones provided above average support for Hitler's party. This city's results do differ from those observed in most other cities in that its "best" district proved to be "merely" average rather than outstanding in its support for the National Socialists. But that, as just indicated, is deceptive; that result hides the high NSDAP support found among the district's well-off Protestants, the level there being similar to that found in most other German cities.

This result is a puzzling one. One might assume that the Protestant upper and middle classes would have had more contact with Jews than was the case in most other cities discussed here. The West End contained the university which, at least in terms of its faculty, provided a center of social, political, and cultural liberalism.[6] Another factor that should have limited the development of upper-class support for National Socialism was the character of the city's leading *bürgerliche* newspaper, the *Frankfurter Zeitung*. It was one of the most active opponents of National Socialism in all of Germany. Another bourgeois newspaper, the *Frankfurter Nachrichten*, gave steadfast support to the right liberal DVP.[7]

If one examined the distribution of the vote in this city and observed the high NSDAP percentages in the central city, and if one assumed that the central city housed petty bourgeois populations, one could easily take that result as providing support for the traditional hypothesis. The relatively high figures in the northern and eastern outer districts would also serve to confirm that conclusion.

The Jewish population of Frankfurt had a different social composition from that of Hamburg or Cologne. In the last two cities, it was overwhelmingly upper or upper middle class. In Frankfurt there was a large segment in the West End, but there was an even larger Jewish population in the eastern parts of the city. Some of these would have been shopkeepers and independent businessmen, and some undoubtedly would have been in competition with non-Jewish tradesmen. It is possible that some anti-Semitism had its origins in that context. And that anti-Semitism may have been accentuated and exploited by National Socialist activists as the economic crisis deepened. In other words, Frankfurt may have been a key context for the development of this focus on the grievances and political reactions of the lower middle class. The only difficulty, were that the case, is that Frankfurt's experience was not typical of other German cities, and the strength of the support for the National Socialists in some upper-middle-class circles has been overlooked.

Another possibility worth considering is a migration hypothesis. The city recruited its population from the surrounding rural areas of Hesse. And in the immediately preceding decades, this region, particularly to the north of the city, had been a major center of anti-Semitic activism. One of the leading political anti-Semites, Otto Böckel, operating out of the University of Marburg, had spread his message and built a movement through the use of extensive interpersonal contacts and small meetings.[8] The later migrants to Frankfurt may have already been disposed toward some elements of the National Socialist position before arriving in the city, before any competition and strain had occurred there. Those anti-Semitic migrants then came to be located in Frankfurt neighborhoods where they had many Jewish neighbors.

High support for the National Socialists would be consonant with both explanations. The experience of the mixed districts elsewhere, however, suggest that the lower middle class–National Socialism linkage is a contingent rather than a necessary one. The contingency in this case is that this city drew its new populations from what was probably the most anti-Semitic area of all Germany.[9]

HANOVER

Hanover, with 443,920 persons in 1933, was the twelfth largest city of Germany. Located in the northwest, it lies midway between Hamburg and Dortmund. It was once the capital city of the Hanoverian monarchy, but then, with the incorporation of Hanover into Prussia following the Austro-Prussian War, the city was reduced to the status of a provincial capital. With its many elegant government buildings, it resembled other smaller capital cities, Munich, Düsseldorf, and Stuttgart. All of these communities also had much manufacturing and therefore large working-class populations. Unlike the cities of the Ruhr, however, in these cities the manufacturing was less visible.[10] For the casual visitor, it was overshadowed by the parks, the lakes, the museums, and the many government buildings.

One feature of the city especially deserving of attention is its religious composition; 80.9 percent of the population was Protestant, and only 10.6 percent was Catholic. There was a tiny Jewish minority of 1.1 percent, and the remainder was without religion (*Gemeinschaftslose*). The surrounding countryside, the *Hinterland* from which the city drew its population, was also heavily Protestant.

The city's voters initially showed only a limited interest in the NSDAP.[11] But then, beginning in 1930 and continuing in the subsequent elections, the party regularly gained support that was above the national average. In the May 1924 election, the NSDAP's percentage was 8.7; in December 1924, it was 2.7; in May 1928, 2.3; in September 1930, 20.7; in July 1932, 40.2; and in November 1932, 34.9.

An official publication gave a breakdown of the 1930 election results for twenty-eight subareas of the city.[12] The subareas giving the strongest support for the NSDAP were the following: Georgstrasse, Lavestrasse, 30.7 percent; Südstadt, Maschviertel, 29.6 percent; Südstadt, Bahnseite, 28.9 percent; Königstrasse and Bödekerstrasse, 28.3 percent; Lange Laube, Königsworth, 27.9 percent; List, 27.2 percent; Waldhausen, Waldheim, 26.3 percent; and Kirchrode, 25.5 percent. For Hanover as a whole, the percentage was 20.7.

The first of these districts was essentially the Altstadt of Hanover. Unlike the equivalent areas in other cities, however, this Altstadt contained government buildings, the Finance and Cultural ministries, for example, as well as various museums and schools. The Georgstrasse, a wide and elegant street reminiscent of Haussmann's avenues in Paris, cut through the entire district, passed in front of the opera house, the dominant structure of the Altstadt, and to the east, contained many elegant shops similar to those of the Königsallee of Düsseldorf. Unlike most such old cities, which probably had large numbers of lower-middle-class persons, this one tended more toward the upper middle class. Local informants say the area housed prosperous businessmen, doctors, and lawyers.

Immediately to the south of the Altstadt was another dominant landmark of the city, the new city hall. This structure was located in a park area which contained a small lake and gardens. A few hundred meters farther to the south was a cluster of ponds that later were to become the largest of the city's lakes, the Maschsee. To the east of these ponds was the Südstadt (south city) area, a recently built up district, most of which is best described as solidly middle class in character. One side of the district lay along the row of ponds, the other bordered on the railroad lines. These were the second and third areas on the above list, the Südstadt, Maschviertel and the Südstadt, Bahnseite. The former area was described as "good middle class." Its housing was reminiscent of Charlottenburg in Berlin. The latter area was described simply as middle class. No one referred to it as a lower-middle-class district.

The next district, the Königstrasse and Bödekerstrasse area, was located to the northeast of the Altstadt and bordered on a large park area called the Eilenriede. This area is described by local informants as very elegant, with populations ranging from upper middle class to very wealthy.

The Lange Laube-Königsworth area was a rather heterogeneous one. Many printing establishments and newspaper publishing houses were located there. Informants said it had rather mixed populations, some middle class and some workers. It also had a fair-sized Jewish population, 5.6 percent.

List was also a peculiarly mixed area. It bordered on the Eilenriede Park, being immediately to the northeast of the Königstrasse-Bödekerstrasse district. There were villas facing immediately onto the park, but elsewhere it was largely working class. A separation of the votes in the two areas was not possible, but the experience of other working-class districts would suggest relatively low NSDAP support there.

The Waldhausen-Waldheim district lay to the south of the Südstadt. It was *the Villenviertel* of Hanover at that time. It is perhaps of some interest to note that the NSDAP's *Gauleiter*, Bernhard Rust, lived in this district.

The last community on the list, Kirchrode, was at that time largely rural. It contained some better-off populations, but it was only later that it was destined to become one of the better areas of the city.

There were two other better areas in the city in the early thirties. To the west of the Nordstadt, near the Technical University, were some villas. Unfortunately the available data did not allow examination of voting in this segment. A subcommunity to the east, Kleefeld, which also bordered on the Eilenriede Park, also contained some villas. The support for the National Socialists in this area was below the city average at 16.3 percent. It seems to have been a divided community, one part of it heavily working class (indicated by an SPD vote of 50.3 percent) and the other, a smaller segment on the park side, the area of villas.

Allowing for the difficulties posed by these peculiarly mixed communities, one is struck by the character of the districts giving strongest support to the NSDAP. The list contains the best districts of the city. With the exception of the two mixed cases and rural Kirchrode, the range extended from average or good middle-class districts all the way up to the very best district of the city. The lower middle class does not figure prominently in this result.

There was one other very good area of the city, the Zooviertel. It was located next to the Zoological Garden, the Eilenriede Park, and the concert hall. Hindenburg was living there in 1914 when he was called out of retirement. Unfortunately, the available figures for the 1930 election combine the results for the Zooviertel with those of adjoining Bult, just to the south across the railroad tracks and adjacent to the city's slaughterhouse.

It will be noted that Hanover, like Düsseldorf, has many park areas and many smaller upper- or upper-middle-class areas. In most other cities the "better" classes were more congregated.

It was possible to obtain some comparable figures from the precinct results reported for the July 1932 Reichstag elections.[13] At a time when the city as a whole gave a 40.2 percent vote to the National Socialists, a Bödekerstrasse precinct gave over half, 54.6 percent, of its votes to that party. And two precincts in the Südstadt provided the NSDAP with 53.6 and 55.7 percent of their votes. The Waldheim-Waldhausen *Villenviertel* was divided into two precincts. The respective percentages there were 53.5 and 59.4. The better-off areas, in short, were again well above the city average.

The high overall percentage for the National Socialists in the city and the very high percentages in the better districts suggest, following the earlier discussion, the possibility of some media influence. Two bourgeois newspapers, the *Hannoverscher Anzeiger* and the *Hannoverscher Kurier*, seem to be of special importance in accounting for the voting in these circles.

The *Anzeiger* was one of those general newspapers that tried to be all things to all people—except for people on the left. It provided weak support for right center parties. But by virtue of the weakness of its support in that crisis period, it made it easy for traditional right voters to choose another alternative. In the September 1930 election, it reported on meetings of all center and right parties. Its reports also included the NSDAP, in most instances the accounts being straightforward and matter-of-fact.

The "all things" character of the paper may be seen in an article in the Sunday feuilleton section entitled "Mussolini Receives Me," a positive account of that dictator's activities in Italy. The paper was running a series on von Bülow's memoirs at that point, and for another taste, there was an article bearing the tantalizing headline: "Mata Hari's Daughter in Hollywood?"

A dim sense of its preferences appeared in an editorial urging everyone to vote, although a specific recommendation was absent. One should vote, it said, for the party doing the best by both the owning and the nonowning classes, the party "that does not wish the cataclysm but rather development for the common good." Finally, the day before the election, in an editorial entitled "State and Party" it announced its preference for the republican parties over those parties opposed to the state. In an unusual gesture for a paper of this kind, it credited the Social Democrats for their willingness to compromise on reforms for the sake of the republican coalition. The voters, it declared, should nevertheless support the *bürgerliche* parties that were open to reform.

In the Prussian state election of April 1932 it continued the generous approach to all but the extreme left. On the Friday prior to the election, it ran statements by leaders of all but one of the major parties. Hitler was included; it was the Communists who were excluded. An article by a Staatspartei (formerly DDP) member of the legislature appeared on Saturday. Otherwise there was no editorial recommendation. There was no editorial recommendation on Sunday, the day of the election, either. Instead, the paper provided a couple of paragraphs describing each of the parties; grouped under appropriate headings, it considered first "the right center," then "the national opposition," and then, on page two "the Weimar coalition."

In the course of the July Reichstag election it again provided a blurred picture. Goebbels spoke in Hanover, and that event was duly reported, all in a very factual manner without any comment. On the twenty-ninth, it gave much space to a Papen interview, this under the heading "Germany Must Live!" The paper again supplied single-paragraph statements from party leaders; in this instance it began with Hitler in Berlin. On election day it gave considerable space to another Papen statement under the heading: "Last Warning: The Right to Vote Means the Duty to Vote." Although paying attention to Papen's statements, it made no clear recommendation. For diversion, it was now serializing Bismarck's memoirs.

The *Hannoverscher Anzeiger*, in short, gave weak initial support to the center right parties. That support became even less visible in later elections. Its straightforward noncommittal reporting in fact carried the messages of National Socialist spokesmen to a wider audience. The *Anzeiger* made no clear attempt to discount any such impact, let alone to oppose it.[14]

The *Hannoverscher Kurier* had an even more curious position. It was solidly committed to Hindenburg in both rounds of the presidential election. In the Prussian state election, however, it made no specific recommendation. It was clearly against the Weimar coalition, but in its editorial "About Prussia," it ended up declaring itself merely to be "for the true Prussian spirit in German nationality!" The editorial comment the day following the election, however, sounded a rather different tone. The editorial entitled "The Weimar Coalition Beaten" regretted the lack of a majority to the right of the Zentrum but at the same time noted that "the hour for the National Socialists has come. It now depends on them."

The *Kurier*'s position in the Reichstag election was similar to that seen in other conservative newspapers. It was for Hindenburg, liked his choice of Papen, and was for "national" backing to support his government. This is clear in its election day issue which featured the Papen radio address "For the New Germany." An editorial by a Walter Jänecke, entitled "Convalescence," saw the problem as one of a divided nation, with the SPD, which led one of the divisions, refusing to recognize the "decisive transformation of the people." His account speaks approvingly of the young generation and its "readiness for collective cooperation." "What could be more beautiful," he wrote, "than for this youth, openly and strongly committed to the fatherland, from its ruins to make the German state powerful again?" The hope expressed in the conclusion of this piece was "that on the evening of this day, the will to recovery will be revealed in the victorious declaration of the people's majority—to a mighty fatherland and to its leader Hindenburg."

The editorial on the day *after* the election stressed again the paper's approval of Papen. The editorial also approved or legitimated the National Socialists.

> The vote confirms the assumption in the highest government positions was correct. When a party, in barely two years, more than doubles its number of seats, there can be no clearer proof of the need for this election. If a peaceful improvement of conditions were de-

sired, then one could not forcibly suppress this development of a movement and of a party. One has to let it come into its own.

Also strange in this election was the fact that the Papen government, which at this moment is at the helm, could not be elected. Nevertheless, despite that fact, one can say that its course is confirmed.

Prior to the November election, this paper ran a rather enthusiastic story under the heading "Hitler in Hanover."[15] One other aspect of this paper's content is deserving of attention. Just prior to the July election the paper carried a half-page advertisement for the National Socialists. This was a rather unusual occurrence. Some indication of what may have been happening appears in Noakes's work on Lower Saxony:

From 1930 onwards the local press came under increasing financial pressure. Many small towns had two rival bourgeois papers, quite apart from the inevitable SPD paper. The economic crisis intensified rivalry for subscribers, while their source of income from advertisements dried up. In this situation, many papers turned more and more towards support for the NSDAP as a means of acquiring new subscribers, though this was also of course an adaptation on the part of the paper to the changed views of its readership. By the Summer of 1932, a large number, in fact probably a large majority, of the bourgeois papers in Lower Saxony were, if not entirely committed to the NSDAP, at least very sympathetic to it. Perhaps the most notable example of this trend was the old-established *Hannoversche Kurier*, which before 1918 had been the leading National Liberal paper in the province of Hanover. By 1932, the paper was in serious financial difficulties and, after negotiations at the highest level involving Hess, Keppler, and Rust, it agreed to follow an NSDAP line in future and presumably received some sort of financial guarantee in return.[16]

Most accounts of the rise of National Socialism have little to say about the role of the media, or, specifically about the newspapers. These accounts assume a direct relationship between manipulator and manipulated. The party and its agents purvey the line, the general populace directly, somehow or other, "hears" or otherwise comes to apprehend that line. The experience in German cities reported thus far indicates that the relationship was somewhat more complex; the conservative nationalist press in many cases played a key role in passing the words of National Socialist "agents" on to the ultimate "consumers." In addition to passing on the lessons, some newspapers also played a role in vouching for or accrediting the party's speakers.[17]

STUTTGART

Stuttgart, located in the southwest of Weimar Germany, was the capital city of the state of Württemberg. Like Hanover, it had been the capital city of a monarchy which accounts for the palaces and general elegance that contrast so strikingly with the commercial monuments of Hamburg and Frankfurt. With 415,028 persons in 1933, it was the fourteenth largest city of the nation. Three-fourths of its population was Protestant.

The city has an unusual geography. At the center one finds the Altstadt which in this case is dominated by palace, gardens, and theater, thus making it different from the equivalent districts in most other cities. Eleven other administrative areas surrounded this Altstadt, and together they were known as the inner districts. The Neckar River formed their northeastern boundary. This center was surrounded by a semicircular or horseshoe-shaped hill. The city, in short, had the appearance of a large stadium with the older city districts forming the playing field, the Neckar running along one end, and the heights rising in all other directions. As one might well expect, these heights were populated by the city's better-off populations. In recent decades, the city had annexed areas beyond the Neckar and beyond the heights. Many of these new additions were one-time farm communities and many of them, in the late twenties and early thirties housed commuting workers.

The NSDAP vote in the city ran somewhat below the national average, a finding that matches the experience of most other cities. In 1928, the NSDAP took 2.5 percent; in 1930, it gained 9.8 percent; in the April 1932 Landtag election it was up to 23.7 percent, and in the July Reichstag election it took 27.2 percent.[18]

The statistical office of the city published election results both for the city as a whole and for the forty-five administrative subdistricts. These in turn were aggregated into six larger groupings, for the inner-city districts, for the heights, and for various outlying sectors. In the July 1932 election, the inner-city districts were slightly above the city average in their support for the National Socialists, the actual figure being 30.0 percent. The heights districts provided the greatest support for Hitler's party, with 33.0 percent. The outlying districts were all below the average.

There was, to be sure, considerable variation within each of these larger areas. In the inner districts, for example, one found a high figure of 39.9 percent in the Altstadt and relatively high figures of 35.6 in the Obere Stadt (upper city) and in the district containing the palace garden, the railroad station, and the city garden. Again it would be easy to say "petty bourgeoisie" with respect to the Altstadt, but in this case, more than in most other cities, that area was likely to have contained better-off populations including many higher civil servants. Something of the same may be suggested for the other two strong NSDAP areas of the inner district. The lowest support here for the National Socialists came in the Inner and Outer Prag districts which housed railroad workers; there the National Socialists took approximately one-fifth of the total.

All of the eight heights districts were above the city average in support for the National Socialists, the percentages going as high as 37.4 in the Weinsteige district. There was also, as one might expect, a fair-sized vote for the bourgeois parties in these districts and also some vote for the Zentrum. While the percentages for the Social Democrats and Communists in these areas were below the city average, they were not nonexistent.

There was some variation also in the more recently annexed areas. The best summary, however, would stress the range noted in working-class areas elsewhere, between 20 and 25 percent. A few went well above that range, the most notable instance being in a tiny district called Rotenberg which had an NSDAP percentage of 50.5. The other extreme was found in another tiny area, Hofen, where 5.4 percent of the electors voted for the NSDAP. It was not left voting that kept the level so low, but Zentrum support, the figure here being 61.9 percent. Both areas were rural, the one strongly Protestant and the other, obviously, strongly Catholic.

The pattern of National Socialist support in Stuttgart is similar to that found in most of the other cities reviewed here. The highest level of support occurred in the upper-class districts. No other districts in the city consistently exceeded these districts in their support for the NSDAP, as would have had to be the case were one to give credence to the lower-middle-class theory. The only possibility in this connection would involve the three districts of the inner city, that is, the Altstadt, the Obere Stadt, and the gardens and railroad station district. But it is more likely that they had upper-middle rather than lower-middle-class populations although, to be sure, that is a judgment, relevant evidence not being available.[19]

In summary, one can say that the pattern was for National Socialist support to increase from a 20 to 25 percent level in working-class districts to the 33 percent level in the best districts of the city. This level in the best areas, it should be noted, is low relative to that in the better areas of some other cities reviewed here.

Part of the explanation for this relatively low level of support may be found once again in newspaper recommendations. Stuttgart's leading bourgeois newspaper was the *Schwäbischer Merkur*.[20] Its position was one of consistent support for liberal or moderate conservative options.

In the 1930 election it recommended support for Theodor Heuss, the leading candidate for the Unity List of the DVP and the Deutsche Staatspartei. It also published a critical article on the Conservatives, "The Tragedy of the German National People's Party." And it published, without comment, Interior Minister Wirth's position paper on the National Socialists. It was also rather steady in its support of the "Right to Vote Means the Duty to Vote" slogan. In the 1932 presidential election it unambiguously favored Hindenburg's candidacy, the election day issue proclaiming, "The Entire People behind Hindenburg." In the Landtag election it again favored a United List; this time, however, it was that of the DVP and the moderate People's Conservatives. This newspaper's influence may have served to damp the enthusiasm that elsewhere, with the support of a sympathetic press, gave the NSDAP even more of a following in upper-class districts.

NUREMBERG

In 1933, Nuremberg, with its 410,438 persons, was the fifteenth largest city of Germany. Located in the Protestant corner of Bavaria, in Franconia, it differed sharply from Munich in that roughly five-eighths of its population was Protestant.

The city archive, fortunately, had among its collections two post–World War II seminar papers that dealt with the voting patterns in subareas of the city. Offering only selected precinct results, these studies yield illustrative, as opposed to complete, findings for the city subareas. The handful of precincts covered do show a picture similar to that found in most of the cities reviewed previously, that is, one in which there is strong upper-class support for the National Socialists. That part of the result is clear and unambiguous.

The NSDAP was strong in this city from the time of its earliest electoral activity. In May of 1924 it took 26 percent of the total. In 1928, when the party was being counted out elsewhere, it gained 11 percent in Nuremberg. In the municipal election of December 1929, it increased its share to 15 percent and in the process brought one Julius Streicher into the city council. In the September 1930 Reichstag election it gained nearly one-quarter of the city's vote. To this point, it will be noted, the party had done consistently better in Nuremberg than in the nation as a whole. The results in later elections, by comparison, were very close to the national averages. Even then, however, the result was exceptional since most cities fell below the national average, the great strength of the NSDAP, it will be remembered, being concentrated in the Protestant countryside. In 1932, in the first round of the presidential election the NSDAP garnered 33.9 percent of the votes and in the second round,

39.2 percent. In the April election for the Bavarian Landtag, the party had 37.3 percent of the vote, in the July Reichstag election, 37.8 percent, and in the November Reichstag election, 33.0 percent.

The first of these seminar papers focused on the July 1932 Reichstag elections.[21] It sorted out five city precincts, three of which, St. Johannis, Gibitzenhof, and Gartenstadt, were described as working-class and two, Stadtpark and Luitpoldhain, as better-off subcommunities. The results from the working-class precincts are of interest only in showing the internal differentiation within the working class. Although the SPD dominated in all three districts—its vote was more than twice the KPD's in two of them—its strength varied considerably, the percentages ranging from 35.6 to 72.1. There was also a considerable variation in the NSDAP vote, its percentages going from 7.7 to 28.5.

The Stadtpark precinct was described as a "better quarter" whose population was largely middle class. In July just over half of these middle-class voters supported the National Socialists. Somewhat surprising, perhaps, is the considerable falloff in that vote in the second Reichstag election, the shift evidently benefiting the conservative DNVP.

The fifth district, Luitpoldhain, was described as "a typical mansion district in which only independent businessmen, lawyers, doctors, and also some Jews lived." As can be seen in the accompanying table, a majority (51.2 percent) of the votes in this very well-off district went to Hitler's party. This pattern closely approximates that of upper-class Blankenese in the Hamburg area or Waldheim and Waldhausen in Hanover. This percentage is also approximately the same as the figure (52.0 percent) for the middle-class Stadtpark precinct. On the basis of this limited comparison, there would be no justification for a nearly exclusive focus on the tendencies of the middle class since both the middle and upper classes of Nuremberg appeared equally susceptible to the NSDAP appeals. Looking at the second of these elections, one is struck by the fact that the NSDAP percentage in Luitpoldhain *increased* (to 55.8 percent) while virtually every place else in Germany the National Socialists suffered losses. As of November, Luitpoldhain was well ahead of middle class Stadtpark (41.7 percent) in its support for Hitler's party.

The second of these seminar reports followed a similar design.[22] Er-

District	NSDAP	DNVP	SPD	KPD
Stadtpark				
July 1932	52.0%	7.9%	21.0%	4.3%
November 1932	41.7	16.1	19.3	5.3
Luitpoldhain				
July 1932	51.2	7.2	19.1	2.5
November 1932	55.8	4.9	25.5	4.4

lenstegen, for example, is described as a *Villenviertel*. The NSDAP took 50.3 percent of this district's vote in the July 1932 Reichstag election. Some of the difficulties of relying on informants' judgments appear here, since the St. Johannis district which was listed simply as working class in the first study is described in this one as having a mixture of "lower middle class and workers."

One might note some additional considerations. The statement that Luitpoldhain contained "only" businessmen, lawyers, and so on, is clearly mistaken. There must have been manual workers there too, as in all other districts. The vote for the Social Democrats and the fraction for the Communists attest to this likelihood. There was some support for the Bavarian People's Party (BVP), the Catholic offshoot of the Zentrum, in all districts. And at least Luitpoldhain is described as having had some Jewish population. Again, if one lays aside this working-class support for the left, the Catholic support for the BVP, and the Jewish vote, then the NSDAP percentage among the remaining largely Protestant and largely upper- or upper-middle-class population must have been well above the 50 percent levels indicated in the initial results.[23]

The city had the usual array of newspapers. The leading *bürgerliche* newspaper was the *Fränkischer Kurier*, which was said to have been close to the DNVP. In addition, there was the politically neutral *Nürnberger Zeitung* which had a somewhat wider circulation. Then there was the popular, sensational even, *Acht-Uhr Blatt* which was "somewhat right" and moved even more in that direction during the last years of the republic. Then too there were newspapers linked to Social Democrats, Communists, National Socialists, and the Bavarian People's party.

Of special importance as a possible cause of the upper-class voting patterns seen in two of the city's *Villenvierteln* would be the position of the *Fränkischer Kurier*. A sample of its coverage and recommendations appears in the first seminar report. Its issue on the day of the Bavarian state election contained a report of an address by Hermann Goering which offered the following directive: "Save the German people, destroy the system!" The newspaper's front-page recommendation was directed against the threat of an SPD-BVD coalition (the actual government was made up of rightist parties). Its slogan read: "Against black and red the only help is black-white-red!" Black, white, and red were the colors of the Kaiserreich and of the monarchical DNVP. They were also the colors of the National Socialists.[24]

MANNHEIM

Mannheim, a middle-sized industrial city, is located at the confluence of the Rhine and Neckar rivers. The 1933 census reported a population of 275,162 persons, which made it the twenty-third largest city in Germany.

Two areas stand out clearly as the most affluent sections of the city, these being the Oststadt (east city), and, somewhat further to the east, a smaller community, Neuostheim, located along the Neckar River. The 1939 census, the only one available for this purpose, showed both districts as having very high percentages of middle-class populations and correspondingly low working-class percentages. The 1925 census of housing indicates that these two were exceptional areas, both for the high average size of the housing units and for the low person-per-room ratios. The personal judgments of old-timers in the city also confirm the conclusion that these two areas were clearly upper and upper middle class.[25]

There was a third such area. Mannheim, founded in 1606, was from the start a planned city. A large Versailles-like palace dominates the city and from both ends of the palace grounds a wide street (the Ringstrasse) sweeps around to form a giant horseshoe. Within this area the streets are arranged in a grid. Those nearest the palace, in an area once referred to as the Oberstadt (the upper city), also contained larger dwelling units and were inhabited by upper- and upper-middle-class populations.

The Conservatives, the DNVP, had only a limited following in these districts. In Mannheim, the largest city of the traditionally liberal state of Baden, the Conservatives gained only 3.5 percent of the city-wide total in the 1928 Reichstag election. In the election of 1919, the upper and upper middle classes of Mannheim had voted heavily for the left liberal German Democratic party. Soon thereafter, the thrust was to the German People's party.

The National Socialist fortunes were at a low ebb in the 1928 Reichstag election. In Mannheim the party gained only 1.9 percent of the total vote. On the twenty-seventh of October 1929, however, a state election was held in Baden, and it was clear at that early point, before the onset of the economic crisis, that the party's fortunes were improving. At that time it took 6.1 percent of the total vote in the city.

Two observations with respect to the differentiation of the vote within the city are of special interest. First, the upper- and upper-middle-class areas were above the city-wide average in their support for the National Socialists. The figure in the Oststadt was 8.2, in Neuostheim it was 8.8, and in the Oberstadt it was 9.2. Second, there was little clear differentiation within the middle class areas of the city. The mixed population in the Mannheim Unterstadt provided the greatest support for the National Socialists with 9.5 percent, a fraction more than in the better-off Oberstadt. A divided community, Lindenhof, was also above the city average with 7.2 percent. The same figure, however, was also found in the working-class area of Jungsbusch/Mühlau. This was exceptional, however, since all other working-class areas were well below the city average.

In the Reichstag election of 1930 the National Socialists took 13.5 percent of the total vote, a sharp increase from their 1.9 percent of two years earlier and their 6.1 percent a year earlier. In Neuostheim the National Socialist percentage was 16.8. In the Oststadt the figure was 17.2. In divided Lindenhof the figure was 16.6 percent.[26]

In the election for city councilors in November 1930, the National Socialists increased their vote again, this time taking 16.9 percent of the total. In order of NSDAP support, we have the following percentages: Neuostheim, 28.0; Oststadt, 23.4; and Oberstadt, 23.0. These were now followed closely by two middle-class communities, Lindenhof with 21.3 percent and Feudenheim with 21.0 percent. These two communities are discussed in greater detail below.[27]

The first Reichstag election of 1932, that of July 31, was the decisive election of the period. In Mannheim at that point, Hitler's party received 29.1 percent of the total, a figure that is roughly eight percentage points below the national average. In upper- and upper-middle-class Neuostheim, however, the party gained 43.8 percent of the total, a figure that is 50 percent above the city's average.

It is worthwhile noting some details. Twenty percent of the family heads in Neuostheim were workers. The combined vote for the Socialists and Communists there amounted to 18.3 percent of the total. A majority of these votes probably came from working-class voters, but some would also have come from lower-middle-class voters in the area. Another 15.5 percent of the voters chose the Catholic Center party. This would mean that the vote for the National Socialists among the remaining upper- and upper-middle-class Protestants of the area would probably have been well over the 50 percent level.[28]

The overall percentage for the nine precincts of the Oststadt, 34.6, was well below the figure for Neuostheim but still above the city-wide average. The Oststadt had a slightly larger vote for the left parties. The support for the Center party was also somewhat larger, reflecting the presence of a slightly larger Catholic population. Also in the Oststadt was a fair-sized Jewish minority, 6.9 percent of the area total. Again, were one in a position to consider separately the components of the district vote, one would probably find the support for the National Socialists among the remaining upper- and upper-middle-class Protestants to be considerably higher than that indicated for the district as a whole.

It was not possible to make a precise assessment of the voting of the Oberstadt (for the reason given in note 26 of this chapter). Nevertheless, an examination of the voting pattern of the precincts in the general area also showed National Socialist support running above the city average.

In short, the upper- and upper-middle-class areas of the city of Mannheim gave Hitler and his party support that was consistently above the average for the city as a whole. The difficulty posed by the lower middle class being widely scattered throughout the city arises once again in this city. The best one can do is to work with the divided or mixed districts, those having considerable middle-class populations living together with large working-class minorities.

Two such areas have already been mentioned in passing, Lindenhof and Feudenheim. The middle class, as indicated by the 1939 census, formed 52.6 percent and 46.3 percent respectively of the populations of these areas, and the respective percentages of workers were 32.4 and 39.4. The remaining population in these areas was retired. It seems reasonable to assume that the distributions of the retired persons' former occupations were similar to those of the employed persons.

Lindenhof, located just to the south of the older city, was bordered on one side by the Rhine River, and on the other, approximately four blocks inland, by an area of factories. This was actually a divided district with well-off populations living on the river front (on the park edge) and workers living inland.

In the first of the 1932 elections Lindenhof gave the National Socialists 34.1 percent of the vote. This figure, it will be noted, is very close to the percentage found in the Oststadt. There is some differentiation within this subarea, with the precincts near the factories tending to have lower support for the National Socialists. The precinct containing streets directly on the Rhine and facing the park next to the Rhine had the highest level found in the upper- and upper-middle-class areas, 47.6 percent.

Feudenheim at that time must have had more of a lower-middle-class population. An outlying farm village, it was annexed in 1910. Even today, although its character has changed considerably, it is still surrounded by open fields. In 1939, two-fifths of its population were workers. It had more Protestants than the rest of the city, a circumstance that would ordinarily work to the advantage of the National Socialists. In the 1932 election being discussed, 36.9 percent of the Feudenheim vote went to the National Socialists. There was, as would be expected, a smaller vote for the Center (12.3 percent) and a larger vote for the left (42.0 percent). Only a small number of Jews lived in either Lindenhof or Feudenheim.

The claim about low National Socialist voting in working-class areas is generally but not completely supported. Wallstadt, for example, a neighbor of Feudenheim, was another of the recently annexed villages, this one joining the city in 1929. Nearly two-thirds of the Wallstadt population were workers or in working-class families. The National Socialist percentage there was 29.4, a figure that was actually slightly above the city average. This comes as a bit of a surprise since the Catholic percentage in the population was also somewhat above the city average.

One might argue that village conditions were exceptional in an industrial city and that it is important to examine the experience of more typical Mannheim workers. An area that was more likely to contain a typical industrial working-class population was the Waldhof-Gartenstadt area, this consisting of two neighboring communities to the north of the city. These were not isolated communities like the villages. Rather than being surrounded by fields, they were surrounded by factories, harbors, and railroad yards. In Wallstadt, the annexed working-class village, the Socialist vote was considerably stronger than the Communist vote. In Waldhof, on the other hand, the Communists had the edge over the Socialists. In the Gartenstadt, the same relationship obtained, although the Communist edge was less pronounced. In Waldhof, the National Socialist percentage was 16.8. In the Gartenstadt, it was even lower, at 10.2.

Some indication of the complexities involved appears in the consideration of still another Mannheim working-class community. Sandhofen had a National Socialist percentage of 27.8, just under the city average. The difference between the results in Wallstadt and Sandhofen and those in Waldhof and Gartenstadt point to one of a difficulties of the pure class analysis, namely the significant variations in the tendencies within a given class. The point may be illustrated more sharply by noting the variation among the precincts of Sandhofen, where support for the National Socialists ranged from 16.9 percent to 52.3 percent.

Chapters 4 through 8 of this work have reviewed evidence on the voting patterns found in fourteen of the twenty-three largest cities of Weimar Germany. Omitted from the review are the following cities in the east: Leipzig, Dresden, Breslau, Chemnitz, Königsberg, and Magdeburg. These were all heavily Protestant cities, all but Breslau having a percentage exceeding 75. Lacking information on these cities one can only speculate. One may infer that unless some special newspaper influences were present, they would show a pattern similar to the heavily Protestant cities of the west, such as Hamburg, Hanover, or Stuttgart (for the NSDAP percentages, see Appendix B). Also omitted in this review were two smaller cities of the Ruhr, Gelsenkirchen, for which no adequate data were found (see note 59, Chapter 7), and Bochum. The city of Bremen, which was being studied by another researcher, was also omitted.

In none of the fourteen settings reviewed did results consonant with the lower-middle-class hypothesis appear. As noted, it was next to impossible to discover a pure lower-middle-class urban district such as is necessary to establish the voting tendency of this segment. No exceptional vote for the NSDAP was discovered in the mixed districts of these cities, the districts most likely to have contained threatened lower-middle-class populations. Instead, in eleven of the fourteen cities examined, one found a striking propensity for upper- and upper-middle-class districts to favor the National Socialists. The principal exceptions, in Cologne and Munich, appear to stem from the efforts of rather committed and capable prorepublican bourgeois newspapers. Frankfurt was only an apparent exception, the low initial NSDAP support in the West End being an artifact resulting from the large Jewish and Catholic minorities there.

In Wuppertal, there appeared to be no clear differences between one of the best districts and the various middle-class districts. NSDAP support there was high in all such districts. The analysis, however, was hindered by flukes of geography and resulting inadequacies of the available data. A similar result appeared to be the case in Düsseldorf although again the available data did not allow an unambiguous conclusion.

The finding of upper- and upper-middle-class National Socialist tendencies, from the perspective of the received literature, is an unexpected one. Given the focus in that literature on the lower middle class, the discussion of motivations, understandably, has been centered on the circumstances of that class. And accordingly, the motivations of the upper and upper middle classes have been largely overlooked. It is clearly necessary, therefore, to shift the focus of the motivational analysis. Before considering such matters, however, one may add some additional confirming evidence in support of the case presented thus far. It is useful to consider the voting of those who were traveling or who were on vacation on July 31, 1932, the day of the crucial election.

CHAPTER NINE

The Summer Election: Travelers and Vacationers

With the suffrage restrictions of prewar Germany still very much a part of recent memory, the authors of the Weimar election law proceeded in a sharply opposed direction, making every possible provision to facilitate participation. People who were traveling on election day (Sundays, it will be remembered) could cast their ballots in railroad stations. People on vacation or visiting friends or relatives could cast their ballots in the district they were visiting. And those who where in hospitals, as we have seen, could cast their votes there.

Persons who anticipated being away from home on the day of the election indicated that intention to local authorities and were given a ballot (*Stimmschein*) that could be deposited elsewhere on election day. In the ordinary election, the percentage of such absentee ballots was minute. But the key election of 1932 fell in the middle of the summer, on July 31. And at that point, as we have seen, up to one-tenth of the population in some urban districts had signified its intentions and been given absentee ballots. It is worth reviewing some of the evidence on the absentee ballots since it too, as we shall see, tells us something about the class character of the voting at that time.

The first of the cities for which we have data is Hamburg, again thanks to the extraordinary detail in the published results for that city. In the Hauptbahnhof, the main railroad station, the travelers passing through that day cast a total of 1,184 valid votes. Of that total, 551, or 46.5 percent, were cast for the National Socialists. It is hard to know what figure to take for purpose of comparison. In the city of Hamburg as we have seen, 33.3 percent of the voters supported the NSDAP. The votes in the Hauptbahnhof could have been cast by lower-middle-class populations from the surrounding countryside, from Schleswig-Holstein or Lower Saxony. If so, one would have to explain how persons in such desperate financial straits would have found the money for Sunday travel. Because of the economic crisis, it seems very unlikely that the mid-summer travelers that year would have been lower middle class or that they would have been workers. It is more likely that they, overwhelmingly, were upper or upper middle class.[1]

In the Cologne Hauptbahnhof one finds a similar result. There, the

National Socialists received 33.1 percent of the votes as opposed to 24.5 percent within the city. Indicative of the social standing of the travelers are the vote for the DNVP, 10.9 percent versus the city's 3.1 percent, and the vote for the DVP (3.6 and 1.4 percent). In this case, given the heavily Catholic and heavily pro–Zentrum character of the surrounding countryside, the possibility of this NSDAP vote being a lower-middle-class farm vote is very definitely excluded. This finding would also, presumably, have some relevance for Hamburg.

There is no reason to assume that the absentee ballots were cast by voters from Cologne itself. More likely, the voters came from other cities and were passing through Cologne, either on their way south to a vacation area or on their way home from such an area. Most travelers from the Ruhr cities would have passed through Cologne and would have changed trains there.[2]

In Munich on that day, a much larger number of votes were cast in the Hauptbahnhof, the total there being 5,067 in contrast to 1,184 in Hamburg and 1,433 in Cologne. Although Munich was a smaller city, much of the summer tourist travel would normally flow through there, either going from the north of Germany to Bavarian resort areas, or en route to Austria or Switzerland. Of the total, 37.3 percent were cast for the NSDAP, a figure that is well above the 28.9 percent for the city as a whole.[3] This would not appear to be the vote of populations from the countryside since in the Upper Bavaria election district (including Munich itself), the National Socialist percentage was 27.1. In the surrounding *Hinterland* the party received only 23.3 percent. In neighboring Lower Bavaria, the equivalent figure was 20.4. A more likely possibility is that this vote was cast by persons coming from outside the immediate region. And again, one must raise the question: what kinds of people were able to make such a journey in the midst of the worst crisis in decades?

This pattern of high National Socialist voting on the part of travelers, incidentally, was not limited to the July 1932 election. In Hanover in the September 1930 election, when the city as a whole gave 20.7 percent to the NSDAP, the travelers gave that party 28.7 percent. In Augsburg, also in Bavaria, a predominantly Catholic city located in the center of a very Catholic *Hinterland*, the NSDAP received 32.6 percent of the railroad station vote in the November 1932 election. That compares with the city's average of 23.0 percent. In Munich's Hauptbahnhof, the number of valid votes cast in November 1932 fell from the summer's 5,000 plus to 1,292. Still, the percentage for the National Socialists was high at 32.6, compared to the city's 24.9. Not all such results showed this striking support for the National Socialists. In the tiny community of Lauingen in Bavaria (in the district Dillingen), only 3.9 percent of the 179 votes cast in the railroad station in November 1932 went to the

National Socialists. By contrast, 87.7 percent went to the Bavarian People's party. This community contained a theological academy and accordingly attracted a unique set of visitors.[4]

Returning again to the July 1932 election, we have evidence for another group of travelers, those on board ships. For them, provision was made for a *Bordwahl* (an on-board vote). Results from seven such "precincts" are reported with the Hamburg results.[5] They are shown in the table below.

Five of these percentages are above the national average, two of them obviously well above that figure. The two below average figures are only marginally below the national level, and, as we shall see, some exceptional circumstances account for these results.

The first of these ships, the *Monte Rosa*, normally traveled between Hamburg and Buenos Aires. It sometimes was used for pleasure cruises. The *Resolute* normally was engaged in pleasure trips, in cruises to the Mediterranean or to the Caribbean. The *Deutschland* was the flagship of the Hamburg-American Line, and it ordinarily sailed between New York and Hamburg. The *Oceana* was a pleasure ship; it too sailed the Mediterranean and the Caribbean. The *Wangoni* ordinarily traveled between Hamburg and West Africa. Its passengers may well have included businessmen and plantation owners. Both the *Tacoma* and the *General Artigas* were freighters that also carried a few passengers.

It seems likely that the votes of the ships' officers and men were included in these results, the men's inclusion being indicated by the support for Social Democrats and Communists, both of which were represented in varying proportions in these results. Roughly one-fifth of the votes on the *Monte Rosa* went to the left parties, another fifth went to the DNVP, and the remaining fifth was scattered among the other bourgeois parties. The presence of this left vote, in all likelihood cast by the ship's workers, by the ordinary seamen, would mean that the NSDAP support among the passengers would be somewhat higher than is indicated in the figures given above. The pleasure ship, the *Oceana*, had the highest left vote of the seven, with roughly one-third of the ballots cast there going to the Social Democrats or Communists. The

Ship	Percentage NSDAP	Votes Cast
Monte Rosa	41.0	713
Resolute	47.6	437
Deutschland	43.2	303
Oceana	36.0	292
Wangoni	35.5	107
Tacoma	62.3	61
General Artigas	57.1	28

National Socialists took a majority of the *Oceana*'s nonleft votes. The *Wangoni* had only a small vote for the left (14 of the 107 votes cast). Its passengers were more likely than those on the other ships to have been living abroad, and they would have been less influenced by recent events in Germany. One bit of evidence supporting this hypothesis is that the *Wangoni*'s voters provided the highest percentages for the traditional bourgeois parties.

It seems likely that the German passengers on these ships, by and large, would have been from the nation's upper and upper middle classes. Except for the *Wangoni*, a special case, the passengers on these ships appear to have given substantial support for the National Socialists; the adjusted figures (that is, those excluding the votes of crew members for the left parties) are all above the 50 percent level. Just over half of the nonleft votes on the *Monte Rosa* went to the National Socialists. Hitler's party gained more than three-fifths of the nonleft votes cast on the *Resolute*. And on the *Deutschland*, more than four-fifths of the nonleft votes went to the National Socialists.[6]

Germany's lower-middle-class citizens, those facing financial ruin, those desperately clinging to their middle-class status in the midst of the worldwide economic crisis, were not likely to have been able to afford ship travel of any kind, whether for intercontinental visits or for summer vacations. These results, accordingly, may be taken as providing a very strong indication of upper- and upper-middle-class voting propensities.[7]

Meinrad Hagmann has called attention to and provided some evidence of the connection of National Socialist voting and the tourist trade. He also noted some additional complicating factors: "In Upper Bavaria we see that areas with a strong tourist trade . . . [stood] in the forefront of the National Socialist movement. . . . There were numerous settlements of nonnative persons in the Bavarian tourist areas after the First World War, and this also was not without influence. . . . a large number of the party leaders had made themselves at home there, as in the Berchtesgaden area, and from there conducted their propaganda. Tölz is known because of its SS-settlement."[8]

It is useful to begin this discussion with a consideration of the September 1930 election. One finds an overall National Socialist figure of 13.1 percent in the twenty-seven administrative districts of Upper Bavaria (omitting for the moment the seven cities). Ten of those districts were above that average, the leaders being Miesbach with 23.5 percent followed by Garmisch-Partenkirchen with 21.4 percent. Five of the six southern border districts, Garmisch-Partenkirchen, Bad Tölz, Miesbach, Rosenheim, and Berchtesgaden (only Traunstein being excepted), were above average. These districts, located at the foot of the Alps,

provide some extraordinary scenery and, not surprisingly, are among
the most attractive of Germany's vacation areas. Aibling and Wolfratshausen, resort areas immediately to the north of these border districts,
were also above average. Southwest of Munich is a very elegant community, Starnberg, located on the lake of the same name. It would
certainly qualify as one of the nation's leading resort areas, and it too
was above average in its support of the National Socialists. The striking
feature of this result is that only two or the ten above average districts
in 1930 were *not* prominent resort areas, these being districts just to the
east of Munich.[9]

One might think that the September election would be uncontami-
nated by the vacationers' votes. But unlike the pattern in North America, where summer typically ends with the Labor Day weekend, the
European vacation period extends well into September.[10] Part of that
result, therefore, is due to the votes of vacationers. There was also, as
Hagmann notes, some year-round settlement of non-Bavarian populations in these districts, as can be seen in the above average Protestant
percentages in some of them. Elsewhere in Upper Bavaria the Protestants generally made up less than 3 percent of the population.[11]

In the July 1932 election, the linkage of National Socialism and the
elegant resort areas was even more striking. The NSDAP average for
Upper Bavaria's administrative districts was 23.3 percent, with the following districts leading the list: Berchtesgaden, 34.9; Miesbach, 34.6;
Bad Tölz, 34.3; Garmisch, 34.3; Wolfratshausen, 33.2; and Starnberg,
32.8. With one exception, Traunstein again, all of the resort areas showed
above average support for the NSDAP. One difference between the
September election of 1930 and the July election of 1932 is that the
former came toward the end of the vacation season. The latter, however, was at high season, and accordingly there were sizable increases
in the number of votes cast. In Berchtesgaden the total number of votes
increased from roughly 11,200 to roughly 17,500. In Garmisch the respective figures were 18,300 and 26,300, and in Starnberg they were
16,600 and 20,000.[12]

The number of votes cast for the NSDAP more than doubled in Upper Bavaria between 1930 and 1932, and, significantly, the greatest increases were in the resorts. In Berchtesgaden, the number of NSDAP
votes went from roughly 2,100 to roughly 6,100 (an increase of 290
percent). In Garmisch the respective figures were 3,900 and 9,000; in
Miesbach 5,800 and 10,600; in Tölz 2,400 and 5,200; in Traunstein
1,800 and 5,400. The city of Bad Reichenhall, located in the Berchtesgaden district, also showed a sharp increase in NSDAP votes, going
from 900 to 2,500. The city of Bad Reichenhall, located in the Berchtes-
Another way of portraying the vacationers' vote is to contrast the

pattern in these resort districts with that in Upper Bavaria as a whole. Whereas the NSDAP vote in Upper Bavaria increased by 53 percent during the period in question, in the southern tier resort districts (including also the city of Reichenhall), the increase was 123 percent.

This relocation of the urban votes is also shown by the unusual increase of DNVP voting in these districts. Nationally, the DNVP suffered a loss in the July 1932 election, falling from 7.0 percent in the previous election to 5.9 percent. That loss was general throughout Prussia where the respective percentages were 9.2 and 7.0. In Bavaria, however, not ordinarily a fertile field for the DNVP, a small increase was registered, the respective figures being 2.2 and 3.4 percent. The percentages were particularly striking in these resort areas, for example, in Berchtesgaden (7.1 and 11.9), Garmisch (6.7 and 11.9), Miesbach (3.2 and 7.8), and Tölz (3.9 and 7.5).

There is still another way in which the relocation of votes is indicated. The vacationers eventually left the resorts and returned home. One should therefore anticipate an above average drop in participation in the November Reichstag election in these vacation areas. This was, in fact, the case. Although there was some decline in participation throughout Germany at this time, the declines in the resort areas were precipitous, in some instances falling, as might be expected, below the level of September 1930. This was the case, for example, in Berchtesgaden where the number of valid votes cast in the three Reichstag elections were roughly 11,200, 17,500, and 8,800. The equivalent figures for Garmisch are 18,300, 26,300, and 14,100.

The November voting results would provide the best indicator of the tendencies of the resident populations in these areas. Since they were more likely to have been lower middle class than the well-off visitors, those results should also be of some interest for the present purposes. If the July NSDAP vote was cast by the vacationers rather than by the resident population, one ought to see a disproportionate fall of that party's strength, and that does happen to be the case. In Berchtesgaden, the number of votes cast for the NSDAP in November was only slightly above the number cast in September of 1930, the rounded-off figures for the three elections being 2,100, 6,100, and 2,300. The pattern in Garmisch was very similar, the equivalent figures being 3,900, 9,000, and 4,000. The NSDAP vote in Upper Bavaria declined by some 22 percent between July and November that year. In the southern tier districts the decline amounted to 44 percent. In Garmisch, 56 percent of the NSDAP's summer vote disappeared. In Berchtesgaden, the loss amounted to 62 percent.[13] These results strongly suggest that the National Socialist votes cast there in the summer of 1932 were those of affluent upper- and upper-middle-class populations; they were not cast by an economically strained lower middle class.

In the November election the resort areas continued to have the highest NSDAP percentages of the Upper Bavarian administrative districts. Given the high initial levels, even the disproportionate fall left the resort areas ahead of the Bavarian Catholic farm areas. It should be remembered too, that the recent migrants remained and that they tended to have values quite different from those of the indigenous populations.

To the west of Upper Bavaria was Swabia. It contained three administrative districts on the Austrian border, and these too were prominent vacation areas, all of them having fair-sized absentee voting percentages. They all show the same sharp increases in the number of valid votes cast in July and equally sharp declines in November of 1932. And they also show the same increases in the numbers of NSDAP (and of DNVP) votes that have been seen in Upper Bavaria.

These areas, although among the highest and well above the district's average, did not, however, provide the highest NSDAP percentages in Swabia. In Upper Bavaria, the comparison was between resort areas and what were largely Catholic farm areas. In Swabia, however, the highest NSDAP support was found in Nördlingen, a Protestant (56.6 percent) farm area. Some of the other leading districts also had nonminuscule Protestant minorities.[14] In Swabia then, strong NSDAP support appeared in two contexts, among rural Protestants (as in Schleswig-Holstein, Lower Saxony, and elsewhere) and among the vacationers.

Some of these results may be specified in greater detail. An administrative district (*Regierungsbezirk*) is still a large and heterogeneous area. That of Füssen, for example, contained the city of the same name (with six precincts and a hospital reporting) plus sixteen other communities, some of them having more than one precinct. Overall, 24.2 percent of Füssen's votes in July 1932 were cast through absentee ballots. Within the precincts, the range was from 11.0 percent in Füssen IV to 58.4 percent in Füssen II. Aside from the hospital, where only 7.2 percent of the votes were cast for the NSDAP, the lowest percentage found was in Füssen IV, the figure there being 16.3. The highest NSDAP percentage appeared in Füssen II where a majority of the votes cast were absentee, the NSDAP figure there being 37.0.[15]

In this case we have results for the Bavarian state election of April 24. That was before the influx of visitors, thus allowing a before and after comparison at a time when there was little overall shifting of voting tendencies. In Füssen IV, where 103 absentee ballots were cast, the NSDAP votes increased from 102 to 151, suggesting that nearly half of the new votes went to Hitler's party. In Füssen II where 682 absentee ballots were cast, the NSDAP vote went from 153 to 429, suggesting that nearly two-fifths of these added votes were for Hitler's party. There was also, as might be expected, a substantial increase in DNVP votes (from 52 to 160), and, some of the visitors being Bavarians, there was an increase in votes for the Bayerische Volkspartei (from 130 to 302).

There appears to have been a peculiar mix of political activity within this small territory. Some of the smaller communities appear to have been devoted exclusively to farming, and there the total vote in April and July was remarkably stable. The major struggle in those communities appears to have been between the Bavarian Farmers' and Middle Class League, which lost close to half of its votes, and the Bayerische Volkspartei, which appears to have gained them. The NSDAP vote in these areas, minuscule to begin with, showed either little change or in a couple of cases, absolute and percentage declines.[16]

One may examine the pattern of voting in the vacation places elsewhere in Bavaria and elsewhere in the nation. In the northwestern corner of Bavaria, one finds the heavily Protestant region Franconia, Nuremberg being the area's largest city. Given the rural and Protestant character of the three administrative districts, Upper, Middle, and Lower Franconia, the area had, as one would expect, rather high NSDAP percentages. Among these agricultural communities, however, one finds some towns that are not ordinarily thought of as having a lower-middle-class character.

The highest NSDAP percentages in the cities of this area were found in Coburg (58.6) and Bayreuth (52.6). Coburg was a year-round resort, which had attracted many retired army officers. It provided the highest support for the NSDAP of all the cities of Germany. Bayreuth, of course, had been the home of composer Richard Wagner and was the setting for the Wagner festival (which however, was not held in 1932). Similar high percentages were found in the rural areas surrounding Coburg and Bayreuth. Some rural districts in the area provided even higher support for the NSDAP, these being Protestant farm areas.

In Middle Franconia, Rothenburg ob der Tauber, one of those cities where many absentee ballots were cast, was first among the nine cities of the region in NSDAP support (58.5). And in Lower Franconia, the highest percentages were registered in Kitzingen (45.2) and in Bad Kissingen (39.5), two resort areas. Among the rural administrative districts, Kitzingen was second highest in NSDAP support. Lower Franconia had a strong Catholic majority with only some communities, Kissingen and Kitzingen, for example, being Protestant.

Bavaria at that time also possessed the Palatinate (Pfalz) an area on the left side of the Rhine, just north of Alsace and Lorraine. Two cities of the area, Landau and Neustadt/Haardt, would ordinarily be counted as resort areas. The respective NSDAP percentages, 54.9 and 51.1, were the highest of the region. The immediately surrounding areas were also high in their support for the party, but they were outdone by some of the region's Protestant farm areas. The Bergzabern district contained another smaller summer resort community. The NSDAP received 55.5 percent of the vote cast in the district in the summer of 1932.

The Bavarian resort areas have been given such attention because much of the vacation traffic, then and now, involves north to south movement, with people from Berlin, Hamburg, and Cologne, for example, journeying south to Bavaria (or to Austria, Switzerland, and points beyond). Given the heavy Catholic dominance in Old Bavaria and the closely related dominance of the Bavarian People's party, the votes of those visitors stood out in very sharp contrast to the local pattern. The presence and tendencies of those visitors were indicated by the high number of absentee ballots, and by the specific choices—by the votes for the National Socialists and, to a lesser extent, for the DNVP and other bourgeois parties.

Not all of the vacationers went south. There was always Bad Pyrmont in Hanover. In Hesse there was Bad Homburg. Bad Ems and Münster were possibilities. In the Rhineland there was Bad Kreuznach, and there were also possibilities on the North Sea—Helgoland has already been mentioned—or on the Baltic—Travemunde, for example.

A moment's reflection would suggest that a different pattern would obtain in the northern resort areas. The local populations in those communities would follow very closely the political tendencies of the region, which is to say that by the spring of 1932 they would already have given substantial majorities to the National Socialists, like the neighboring Protestant farm areas. The appearance of the summer visitors, who gave "only" 40 to 50 percent of their votes to Hitler's party, would have reduced the NSDAP percentages in these resort areas.[17]

What can one say about these findings? It is clear that the 1932 summer vacationers gave relatively strong support to the National Socialists. It is also clear, given the circumstances of the moment, that anyone able to go on vacation, especially to the best resorts of Germany, would have been at least upper middle class. The absence of populations from the upper- and upper-middle-class areas of German cities plus their evident presence in such places as Starnberg and Berchtesgaden, strongly support the conclusion offered throughout this work, namely, that the upper and upper middle classes of Germany gave disproportionate support to Hitler's party. Any doubts caused by the urban data presented in the previous chapters should be alleviated by these findings.[18]

CHAPTER TEN

The Parties of the Right and Center

The view that we have been criticizing throughout this work, the centrist position, has two major components, one social structural and the other social psychological. Basically the theory says that the social structures of advanced capitalist societies change in such a way as to worsen, absolutely or relatively, the position of the lower middle class. That is a constant feature of these societies; in the downswings of the economic cycle, moreover, those stresses are sharply accentuated. The social psychological component of the theory deals with the responses of lower-middle-class persons experiencing these routine or aggravated strains. They reject their traditional parties and turn to the parties or movements that promise a restoration of their former position.[1]

If one takes this theoretical position as providing the rudiments of an acceptable explanation for the rise of National Socialism, then certain lines of research will be stimulated while others will tend to be neglected. One would presumably be inclined to research and document the initial assumption, the claim of an objective loss of position by the lower middle class. Since at this late point, little can be done to establish the character of personal reactions (for example, that the members of the lower middle class did feel the strain, that they were anxious, and so on), the second feature of the argument tends to be merely assumed.[2] Or, one states the initial claim (worsening position) together with data showing the presumed consequence (a vote for the National Socialists) and simply asserts the character of the intervening motivation. As has been seen, the studies dealing with the voting tendencies of the lower middle class have been less than adequate; a simple assertion, moreover, is an untested hypothesis.

Another line of research called for by the centrist theoretical orientation would consist of an account of the various offerings made by the National Socialists. This would tie down another link in the argument, showing how the NSDAP played on the nervous anxieties of the lower-middle-class voters. And therewith, one would have a complete analysis, or as complete as is possible at this late date, the analysis covering all four points, economic stress, the assumed reaction, the National Socialist offering, and the political response to that offering.

The initial argument, it was noted, is structural in character. That term is rarely defined, certainly not with any precision. If one were to construct a definition on the basis of current usage, it would have to contain reference to a binding or constraining framework, one that, because of its compelling or limiting character, would have to be treated as a fundamental (as opposed to peripheral) cause. People are located within these frameworks or contexts (typically within classes or occupations) which are then treated as having a powerful determining impact on behavior and outlooks. So powerful are these structural causes, in fact, that they outweigh or overwhelm any lesser-order causal factors. One's class position, for example, is viewed as a much more substantial determinant of behavior than a mere attitude. Members of the lower middle class might have personal commitments to progress, human decency, love of their neighbor, and so forth. But the strains induced by their structural position in the society are viewed as so powerful as to overwhelm any of these concerns. As a result, they will become political reactionaries, because they are so vulnerable to the appeals of those who promise a way out of their dilemma.

One consequence of this ranking of the causal variables is that some variables are emphasized, and others are slighted. If a variable has no significant weight, then clearly the only reason for studying it would be aesthetic. For this reason, a wide range of nonstructural variables tend to be given short shrift.

It is useful to note some of these limitations. Structures are treated as fundamental, as givens. It is a rare occasion when they are treated as the product of human will, or, what amounts to the same thing, as the product of positive policy. The characteristics of advanced industrial societies "unfold." They are, to use William Graham Sumner's words, unplanned or crescive developments. Or, perhaps more appropriately, in the terms of the Marxian perspective, structures develop "independently of human will." Because they are independent of will, the entire area of policy and policy making tends to be neglected. The lower middle class will be crushed, no matter what policy makers do.

When put this way, the claim is obviously subject to some doubt. Policy makers may do nothing at all, that being a legacy of the laissez faire tradition. Or they may undertake programs that yield an unexpected and horrendous catastrophe. Or, since failure is by no means in the cards, their policies might yield positive results. The general neglect of policy, in other words, is not justified.

In addition to the failure or the refusal to examine policy matters in any detail, one finds a correlated unwillingness to consider the positions of the various parties in any detail. The original framework makes this too a pointless, an unnecessary, labor.[3] Typically one finds what amounts to good guy–bad guy simplicities. The good parties, the virtuous parties of the democratic center, do what they can in the troubled situation. But given the structure of that situation, there is little they can do. In the words of the famous phrase (or cliché), there are no easy solutions. And while the good parties are dealing with the complexities of the situation, the parties of the demagogues are offering (or more precisely, proffering) these easy solutions. Since the parties of the center cannot, or will not, offer the same questionable political merchandise, they come to be the losers in this game wherein one or more of the players is engaged in unfair play.[4]

An important result of this procedure is that the analysis of the political struggle comes to be one-sided. One demonstrates at length the demagogy, the dishonesty, the "dramaturgy," and the cunning of the National Socialist manipulators. There is little said, by comparison, about the parties of the center other than to indicate their good intentions and, at the same time, their helplessness. One would not ordinarily describe a military campaign in such a way, that is, exclusively in terms of one contender's initiatives. (Nor, for that matter, would one describe hockey, boxing, or tennis in such one-sided terms.) For this reason, it is worthwhile examining the responses of the major parties both to the economic crisis and to the developing political crisis.

Since in the structural analysis the basic problem is all of one piece, the basic responses are too. The National Socialists are consistent manipulators, and the liberal parties of the center consistently work at their complex solutions. The same lines of analysis serve as well for 1930 as for 1932. But if one takes an interactive view, it is apparent that this abstract and general analysis makes unwarranted simplifications. With the coming of event A, the parties make appropriate adjustments of position. Event B then follows, and the parties make what they take to be necessary readjustments. Then comes event C which stimulates further readjustments.

The voters in each instance make their own decisions with respect to each of these changes in circumstance. Where event A was an election in which the voter's preferred party suffered a major loss, he (or she) had some incentive to seek out a second-best alternative in the next election. Whereas the structural argument has a key segment of the electorate responding to a set of structurally induced strains, this alternative reading of the evidence has that segment responding to the changing positions and relative standings of the parties.[5] A review of that history from such an interactive perspective will shed some light on the data presented in the foregoing chapters.

The parties will be considered in the following order: first, Hitler's sometime ally, the German National People's party; then, the moderate parties of the center, the right liberal German People's party, the left liberal German Democratic party, and the Catholic Zentrum. Also among the moderate or centrist forces, an integral part of their continuing coalition, was the Social Democratic party which will be considered in the following chapter along with the German Communist party. The activities of the National Socialists are explored in Chapter 12.

THE DEUTSCHNATIONALE VOLKSPARTEI

This party, called simply the Conservatives in most English-language publications, was a new formation dating from 1919. As indicated earlier, it was a successor to the prewar German Conservative party, which in turn was a successor to the Prussian Conservative party dating from before the Franco-Prussian War. In this new formation an effort was made to transcent its former limits. As a consequence it initially embraced a broad collection of rightist forces. Included were remnants of two prewar conservative parties, the German and the Free Conservatives, the Völkische (anti-Semitic) movement, the Christian Social movement, the Pan German Association (Alldeutscher Verband), and some prewar National Liberals. It did extend, therefore, beyond the Prussian limits of the main prewar Conservative party. In addition to its agrarian support, it had some representation of industry, some of cultural interest groups, and some of urban occupational interest groups, these representing nationalist-oriented manual workers and white-collar employees. In some ways the party was a Protestant analogue to the Zentrum although it obviously lacked the history and background that gave that party its cohesiveness.

As a consequence of its diverse base, the party proved to be a rather fragile enterprise. Almost all of the important splinter parties of the Weimar Republic were initially part of this coalition. The first of the defections involved the anti-Semites, who left to form the Deutsche-völkische Freiheitsbewegung (The German People's Freedom Movement), the NSDAP's coalition partner in the May 1924 election. One of the largest of the splinter parties, the Wirtschaftspartei, was an important beneficiary of individual defections from the DNVP. And in the last years of the republic, the "practical conservatives" broke away to form the short-lived Conservative People's party, and the Christian Social group left to form a party called the Christian Social People's Service.[6]

The party had a deceptive electoral history. From a modest beginning in 1919 with 10.3 percent of the .vote, it climbed to 15.1 percent in 1920, then to 19.5 percent in May of 1924, and again to 20.5 percent in December of that year. It was a heady experience after an inauspicious beginning. The sense of growth, the feeling that history was with them, led the party's leaders to make demands far exceeding their real bargaining strength. They overlooked the vulnerability of their coalition, and they failed to recognize that newly gained voters could leave the party just as quickly as they had come. What could easily have been a tactical choice at a given moment was mistaken for a permanent commitment.[7]

The party stumbled continuously over matters of policy. A conservative, nationalist, monarchist, and antirepublican party, it still had to deal with the day-to-day issues that affected both the interests of its voters and the institutions of the republic. It kept up a brave front of opposition and made much of its ideological purity. But like the prewar oppositional Social Democrats, it too was forced into compromise. Sometimes it was caught in very embarrassing positions of conflict between its rhetorical pronouncements and its subsequent behavior. It made much of its "fundamental opposition" to everything connected with the Versailles treaty. But when it came to the vote on the Dawes Plan (which specified the terms and the implementation of reparations payments), the party divided with roughly half of its Reichstag faction voting for the measure. The plan could not have been implemented without those DNVP votes.[8]

That vote pointed up one of the most important lines of division within the party. One segment consisted of nationalist ideologues, the other of more pragmatic, issue-oriented conservative politicians. The latter, who had provided the votes for the Dawes Plan, knew that the German economy needed "clarity" on this matter and furthermore, that American loans were contingent on this settlement. The intransigent ideologues either did not see this, or, not being closely tied to those economic interests, simply did not care.

In this period of incipient decline, the party was led by Count Kuno Westarp, who was identified with the pragmatic wing of the party. Arrayed against Westarp were the intransigents, the ideological conservatives, their leader being Alfred Hugenberg. As indicated earlier, because of his previous links to the Krupp firm he has sometimes been viewed as an agent of, or spokesman for, heavy industry. But the facts were otherwise. The leaders of heavy industry had dropped him; his rigidity and intransigence stood in the way of their practical needs.[9] At this point, however, with his immense press empire and aided by his new allies in the countryside, he was able to chart an independent course.

The practical wing of the party had pressed for participation in the government, something the party had achieved for the first time in 1925 in the Luther government and again in the third Marx (Zentrum) government, which lasted from January 1927 to February 1928 and which, for convenience, was extended to June 1928. Participation in the government, of course, had forced concessions and compromise.

A Reichstag election was called during May 1928. The Conservatives lost nearly a third of their former votes and, of course, an equivalent number of seats. This loss, understandably, led to a heated discussion of party policy, each faction blaming the other for the disaster. In July of that year, after having received a unanimous vote of confidence, Westarp resigned as party leader. Hugenberg and his allies took this as the occasion to force a change of direction. It is significant that they saw the influence of the working-class and white-collar groups within the DNVP as the source of the party's recent problems since these groups too had pushed for participation in the government. Accordingly, the express concern of the intransigents was to reduce the power of the occupational groups within the party.[10]

Shortly after the May election, Walter Lambach, a leader of the Deutschnationaler Handlungsgehilfen-Verband, published an article questioning the commitment of the party to the monarchy and recommending that appeals be made to attract nationalistic republicans into the party. The Hugenberg group made an issue of this "revisionism," the end result of which, on October 20, 1928, was Hugenberg's election as the new leader of the party. This choice, it will be noted, involved a very clear message for the working-class and white-collar supporters of the party. As we have seen, they were not inconsequential segments among the party's regular supporters. But at this point, just before the depression broke, the Conservatives made a move that could only have alienated its own wage-earning and salaried supporters.

Hugenberg announced his new program under the slogan *"Block oder Brei"* (bloc or mush). He was soon to achieve his aim although the cost paid for that uniformity was the loss of many members from the other more moderate factions. The most important internal move undertaken by Hugenberg was the undoing of party democracy, it being replaced with his own *Führerprinzip*. These efforts, rather understandably, brought him into conflict with the Reichstag representatives who were not about to agree to the demand that he alone should determine the position of the parliamentary faction and that his decisions should be binding on all representatives.[11]

The most important struggle, both for the party and for the nation, involved the initiative and referendum on the Young Plan. This plan specified and improved on the terms of the previous settlement, the Dawes Plan. On the ninth of July 1929, Hugenberg and some associates announced a national committee to oppose the new proposal. It was a flagrant bit of demagoguery since rejection of the Young Plan left the less favorable Dawes Plan in force. Their point was that acceptance of *any* plan meant acceptance of the Versailles terms including the war-guilt clause. Hugenberg had at his disposal his formidable press empire which included some directly owned newspapers and a news agency and wire services that supplied news and filler material to a wide range of daily and weekly newspapers. The national committee was intended as a broad coalition of national forces and included, in addition to the Conservatives, the nationalist and expansionist Pan German Association, and the Stahlhelm, a nationalist veterans' organization. And, of much greater significance, it also included Adolf Hitler and his party.

The campaign involved a series of events, each providing an occasion for agitation and propagandizing. The committee published its Freedom Law (the full title was The Law against the Enslavement of the German People) in September of that year. The last and most controversial of its four paragraphs directed that members of the government be charged with treason for implementing any aspect of the Young Plan. After some struggle, this was accepted by the party, and the committee proceeded to the collection of signatures, 10 percent of the electorate being required to bring the law to the Reichstag. This was accomplished (barely, with 10.02 percent) on the second of November. The Reichstag then took the matter up, and, by overwhelming majorities, voted down each of the paragraphs on November 30. Significantly, even some of the DNVP deputies voted against the proposals. That set the stage for the referendum which took place on December 22, 1929. Approximately twenty-one million votes were needed for the effort to succeed; less than six million were obtained. The Young Plan was accepted by the Reichstag and signed into law by President Hindenburg on March 13, 1930. The whole campaign, from beginning to end, provided eight months for agitation.[12]

The refusal by some DNVP Reichstag deputies to support the Freedom Law precipitated an internal struggle and led to the exodus of twelve moderates on December 4, 1929. Hugenberg's effort to achieve a bloc was thus aided, but the loss of an important segment of this tenuous coalition of course made the party somewhat smaller.[13] In the first fifteen months of Hugenberg's leadership the party lost forty-three of its seventy-eight Reichstag deputies.

Perhaps the most decisive impact, however, was made on the general public, or at least, on its nationalist conservative segment. In the Hugenberg press, the largely forgotten Adolf Hitler now reappeared as an equal partner in this nationalist coalition. The Hugenberg apparatus gave him and his party both attention and legitimacy. For the first time since the 1923 *Putsch* and 1924 trial, he had, as Bullock puts it, succeeded "in breaking into national politics and showing something of his ability as a propagandist. . . . Every speech made by Hitler and the other Nazi leaders had been carried with great prominence by the Hugenberg chain of papers and news agencies. To millions of Germans who had scarcely ever heard of him before, Hitler had now become a familiar figure, thanks to a publicity campaign entirely paid for by Hugenberg's rival party."[14]

The resurgence of the National Socialists is typically linked with the September 1930 election. That was the occasion on which they exploded onto the German scene. If one dates this new beginning from that visible sign of strength, it is then "obvious" that the economic depression was *the* salient cause. But this new growth of the party began earlier, before the onset of the depression.

The 1928 election is generally taken as the low point in the party's fortunes; those results, however, are deceptive. In western Germany, the party was already on an upward road. It was in the eastern and central districts that it suffered losses vis-à-vis the December 1924 election. The average of the two tendencies in the overall result suggested across-the-board losses.[15] But something was clearly already happening in large areas of Germany in May of 1928, before the depression and before Hugenberg's Freedom Law campaign.

An examination of state elections in this period shows a very close connection between the anti–Young Plan campaign and the takeoff of the National Socialists. Three state elections took place during the campaign, one in October, another in November, and the third in December of 1929. Another election occurred a few months after the law was signed, just three months before the September 1930 Reichstag election. In Baden, Thuringia, and Saxony (Lübeck did not have National Socialist candidates in the 1926 state election), one finds a slow growth of NSDAP strength prior to the campaign efforts of Hugenberg and his associates. And, the decisive fact here, one finds a considerable advance indicated in all four of the elections that came during or immediately after the campaign (Table 10.1).[16]

This first big step forward appears, on first sight at least, to have been the result of a media impact. It would be a mistake, however, to emphasize only this factor; in the years since the refounding of the party in 1925, the National Socialists had had fairly continuous success in recruiting new members. Dietrich Orlow, discussing the Saxony election of May 1929 (prior to the anti–Young Plan campaign), explains the result solely in terms of the agitational efforts of the party's militants. That agitation alone, however, yielded only the small increase from 2.7 percent in the 1928 Reichstag election to 4.9 percent in the state election (the levels of participation were almost the same, 79.9 and 78.4 percent respectively). This modest gain from organization alone stands in marked contrast to the gain achieved by activism in combination with media

TABLE 10.1. SUPPORT FOR THE NATIONAL SOCIALISTS AT THE TIME OF THE ANTI-YOUNG PLAN CAMPAIGN

State	Election	NSDAP
Baden	Landtag, October 25, 1925	1.2
	ₐ Reichstag, May 20, 1928	2.9
	Landtag, October 27, 1929	7.0
Lübeck	Landtag, October 11, 1926[b]	[c]
	ₐ Reichstag, May 20, 1928	1.6
	Landtag, November 11, 1929	8.1
Thuringia	Landtag, January 30, 1927	3.5
	ₐ Reichstag, May 20, 1927	3.7
	Landtag, December 8, 1929	11.3
Saxony	Landtag, October 31, 1926	1.6
	Reichstag, May 20, 1928	2.7
	ₐ Landtag, May 12, 1929	4.9
	Landtag, June 22, 1930	14.4

SOURCE: *Wirtschaft und Statistik*, 9 (1929): 976, and 10 (1930): 36, 359; and *Statistik des Deutschen Reichs*, vol. 372, pt. 2, p. 78.
[a] The lines drawn across the table signify the beginning of the anti-Young Plan campaign (July 9, 1929).
[b] In Lübeck the state election was referred to as a Bürgerschaftswahl.
[c] The NSDAP did not run candidates.

support as suggested by the June 1930 election result. Orlow reports that attendance at party rallies picked up during the campaign, and a National Socialist memorandum from October 1929 reports that membership rose sharply in all parts of Germany.[17]

It seems likely, therefore, that both factors made independent contributions to the NSDAP election successes. It also seems likely that the two factors interacted. Hugenberg's campaign justified and legitimated Hitler and his party. The local organizations and activists were present to recruit those for whom the party had now become acceptable. The media justification may well have brought them to party meetings, thus making personal contact and influence easier for the activists. And the end result, of course, would be that the party had a much larger cadre available for the next effort, for the September 1930 Reichstag election campaign.

It is worth stressing this point about a media effect. In the social science literature, there exists what amounts to a school position on the subject; the media, so it is said, do not change people's party choices. The argument, put simply, is that most people have fixed party identifications which, in effect, anchor them and keep their political loyalties from wandering. People then select out media content that reinforces and supports their original dispositions. For these reasons, the dominant effect of the media has been viewed as one of reinforcement, of stabilization.[18]

But that view is largely based on experience in the United States, where the two major parties have a century and more of history and tradition behind them. Party identifications there have been passed on, in relatively stable times, for three, four, or more generations. But in Weimar Germany, only two of the parties, the Social Democrats and the Zentrum, had such long-term continuity. And the Weimar era, beginning with war and revolution and continuing with border struggles, putsches, inflation, and much instability of government, was not such as to encourage the formation of stable identifications. Identifications, particularly with the parties first formed after the war, were likely to have been weak and tenuous, and Hugenberg's activities in 1929 and 1930 could easily have facilitated changes in affiliation.[19]

Hugenberg's intention was to break the left, to take votes away from Social Democrats and Communists. But his press empire, on the whole, did not reach the voters of those parties. To the extent that his empire touched workers at all, it probably reached those who were conservative or nationalist in outlook, particularly those living in smaller communities. When Hugenberg advertised, justified, and legitimated the efforts of his competition, he made possible a shift that came at *his* cost, and that of the right liberal DVP, not that of the left. Given the boundaries within which his press network operated, the campaign could scarcely have had any other consequence.

This displacement on the right was aided by some other features of the struggle. Hugenberg's attack on working-class, white-collar, and farm segments within the DNVP provided those voters with a push to encourage a move. Not all of them defected to the National Socialists, however. Some split off and supported the newly formed Konservative Volkspartei. Others supported the Christian Social movement. The growth of the splinter parties, which became such an issue in the late elections, was also stimulated by Hugenberg's effort. Many of those who initially supported the splinter parties later turned to Hitler. Some of them may have returned to the DNVP, despite Hugenberg, when their other options disappeared or proved ineffectual.[20]

In undertaking the alliance with Hitler and his party, Hugenberg was entering into a campaign that he could not win. No matter how tough Hugenberg talked, he could hardly outdo the ever-resourceful, ever-ruthless National Socialists. His argument for forceful and exceptional measures within the context of the anti–Young Plan campaign, could do little else but advertise the superiority of his ally and competitor in the use of such means. Although this peculiar dynamic was apparent from this early point in their relationship, Hugenberg continued the alliance, with only one serious interruption, up to and including their formation of the final government of the Weimar regime.

Normally a coalition is based on some shared goals and some mutual respect. One lays aside the minor differences and proceeds toward the common goal. But the National Socialists continuously violated these rules of coalition; they continued their attacks on their new allies. As Bracher puts it, "even now their campaign against reaction, against the Stahlhelm and the DNVP, was scarcely moderated."[21] Hugenberg, nevertheless, continued the arrangement.

On February 12, 1931, the DNVP and the NSDAP made a joint demonstrative exodus from the Reichstag (in protest against Chancellor Brüning's use of a presidential decree). The Hugenberg-Hitler-Stahlhelm coalition was reaffirmed once again in the formation of the Harzburg Front at a large public rally with uniformed formations, flags, and regalia, which took place on Sunday, October 11, 1931. Hitler again trumped his partners in this venture. He did, with some reluctance, participate in the effort, but he also made clear his disdain for the whole enterprise. The following Sunday, Hitler and the National Socialists held their own demonstration on the same spot. Some 100,000 SA and SS men were brought in by 40 special trains and 5,000 trucks. The effect far surpassed that of the previous Sunday. The NSDAP show of numbers, organizational capacity, and dedication made the DNVP-Stahlhelm group appear as hopeless dilettantes.[22]

These meetings took place in the tiny state of Brunswick. The reason for this choice was very simple: that small and largely Protestant state had a coalition government made up of Conservatives and National Socialists. It was one of the few places the National Socialists could congregate because uniformed formations were prohibited elsewhere. It was this coalition government that arranged for Hitler's citizenship, thus making it possible for him to run for the presidency in 1932.

The presidential campaign caused some strain in the coalition when the Conservatives and the National Socialists both presented candidates. That put them in direct opposition, the implications of a plurality (or majority) in the presidential election being quite different from the legislative elections in which proportional representation prevailed. The Hitler-Hugenberg coalition, nevertheless, was continued intact, for what it was worth, through the July 1932 Reichstag election. There was a falling out later that year, and in the November election both partners went their own ways. The NSDAP made a left turn at this point and, among other things, conducted sharp and bitter attacks on its former allies whom it now "recognized" as hopeless reactionaries. The DNVP gained some votes in this election, as did also the DVP although in neither case were these enough to make much difference. Some of that return was probably tactical. It was not that the voters had discovered anything especially attractive in Hugenberg's politics; it was just that they had no other place to go.

The remainder of the party's history may be described very briefly. Hugenberg and the DNVP formed the coalition with the National Socialists that brought Hitler into the government on January 30, 1933. And a few months later, Hugenberg undertook, at Hitler's behest, the dissolution of the DNVP.

It provides little consolation to learn that Hugenberg had a sudden insight on January 31, the day after he had made Hitler's rule possible. At that point he is reported to have said, privately to be sure, that "yesterday I committed the biggest blunder of my life. I allied myself with the biggest demagogue in the history of the world."[23]

DIE DEUTSCHE VOLKSPARTEI

The German People's party was, supposedly at least, one of the classic middle-class or center parties of the Weimar regime. Actually, it was neither of those things. It was, more than any other, *the* party of the industrial bourgeoisie. As for its politics, it might best be described as a classic laissez faire free enterprise party with rather strong national emphases. It was a center party only in that its votes came from across the class spectrum, the votes of an industrial upper class alone being insufficient to produce a viable political party. A significant minority among its following, as we have seen, was working class.

The party had some difficulties in the early months of the new republic. Its one outstanding leader, Gustav Stresemann, had been very much at the forefront of the war effort, most especially as a supporter of unrestricted submarine warfare and as an annexationist. As a consequence, in the discussions on the possibility of a united liberal party, one that would join the prewar National Liberals and the Progressives, the latter objected to his presence and went their own way to form the German Democratic party. The DVP, as a consequence, had a late start and, accordingly, an inauspicious beginning in the 1919 election to the Constituent Assembly (4.4 percent). It experienced a considerable upsurge in the 1920 election, gaining 13.9 percent of the total, its peak strength in the fourteen years of the republic. It fluctuated in the subsequent elections with 9.2 percent in May 1924, 10.1 in December of that year, and 8.7 in May of 1928. Like the Conservatives, it suffered some decline in that year, but for the DVP it was not an unquestionable disaster. The loss could easily be taken as a normal one at a time when there was a general shift to the left. It was, however, the last moment of even qualified success experienced by the party.

The People's party faced serious internal divisions, ones that, to some extent at least, paralleled those of the Conservatives. In its case, however, the constellation of forces was somewhat different, and the center of gravity could be located more easily. The major contending factions within the DVP were almost all occupational and hence were very practical (as opposed to the more ideological thrust of the Hugenberg forces).[24]

At the risk of simplification, one can say that *the* problem of the DVP was that the industrial-big business faction had made steady gains within the party and was threatening to squeeze out the other interests. After the election of 1928, Stresemann complained that at least twenty-five of the party's forty-five Reichstag deputies were directly or indirectly connected with German industry.[25] Stresemann was so occupied with foreign affairs (he was Germany's foreign minister, it will be remembered, from August 1923 until his death) and coalitional struggles of the various governments that he was, understandably, forced to neglect the organizational problems of his own party. As the party's single outstanding charismatic leader, he was, nevertheless, able to hold the dominant faction in check.

The party's catastrophe began with Stresemann's death in October 1929. His death, it will be noted, came in the midst of the Hugenberg-Hitler campaign against the Young Plan, a plan that was the product of Stresemann's negotiations; no party was more closely identified with it. The plan was not, as its opponents claimed, a disaster for Germany. It did, as has been noted, scale down the yearly contribution for reparations. And in the negotiations, Stresemann had succeeded in gaining the removal of foreign troops from the Rhineland some five years prior to the original plan. But at that point, with the Social Democratic government of Hermann Müller under heavy attack, realities counted for little. Stresemann's successor as foreign minister, Julius Curtius, was also a member of the People's party. The party had no press adequate to respond to the attack and no leader as capable as Stresemann.

There was a movement within the party, sponsored in part by its white-collar employee segments, to check the growing influence of big business. The Deutschnationaler Handlungsgehilfen-Verband had some representation within the party and supported this movement. In fact, the Lambach declaration that was used by Hugenberg as the occasion for a war to the death against the DNVP's practical wing was intended also for DVP members. Lambach's idea was for the white-collar groups to gain more power in both parties and, in the longer run, to merge the two rather pointlessly divided parties of the right. This particular struggle, like the conflict within the DNVP, was also a struggle of generations. The support for this reform within the DVP came from its youth group, founded by a DHV spokesman within the party in the spring of

1929. The aims were simple: to "build a bridge between the DVP and the younger generation" and ultimately to create "a united middle party." The death of Stresemann was an important setback for this movement.[26]

One other aspect of Stresemann's politics is deserving of attention. He generally opposed the idea of a right coalition that would include the conservative DNVP and shut out the Social Democrats. His position on this point was very simple. It would sharply polarize the German party system into right and left. And, as important, it would lead the Social Democrats to seek an opening to the left; that is, they would be forced to attempt coalitional relationships with the Communists. A center coalition, extending from the People's party to the Social Democrats, would motivate the latter to engage in and support moderate and responsible government measures. An additional consequence, of course, was that in such a coalition the People's party would have to be more social (that is, favorable to welfare state measures) than it would otherwise have been. It was a difficult course for him to steer given the growing pressure within his own party to form a right coalition and to break the connection with the left.[27]

Two months after Stresemann's death, the party chose Ernst Scholz to succeed him as party leader. A one-time cabinet minister, now in retirement, he "had always stood close to the DVP's industrial wing."[28] The party's votes helped to bring down the Müller cabinet in March of 1930, the specific issue being the question of social insurance payments which, with growing unemployment, were becoming an awesome problem. The party then joined in the *"sozialistenreine"* (clean of socialists) government of Heinrich Brüning.

In this same period the DVP began to suffer disastrous losses in state elections. There was cause for alarm in all but the Baden election of October 1929. The party fell there from 9.5 in the previous Reichstag election to 8.0 with approximately the same level of participation. In Lübeck, the bourgeois coalition, the Hanseatischer Volksbund, took 35.5 percent in November 1929 compared to 44.4 percent three years earlier. And in Thuringia, in December of that year, the party fell from 11.2 to 8.8. In the Saxony election of June 1930, it gained only 8.7 percent, a serious falloff from the state election a little more than a year previously, when it had received 13.4 percent (that figure represented an *increase* over its performance in the 1928 Reichstag election, 11.6 percent). In a period of one year it had suffered four electoral losses, each increasingly serious.[29] One factor that would have had some effect in these elections was the steadily rising level of unemployment which, by the spring of 1930, was already clearly of exceptional proportions. It is next to impossible, of course, to sort out the specific sources of the defections. Many commentators from that period, including many party leaders, spoke of bourgeois defections as if the evidence on that point was clear and unambiguous. Some bits of evidence, however, indicate that the pattern was not all that clear.[30] The shift from Stresemann˙to Scholz, after all, should have been attractive to bourgeois voters and should by contrast, have encouraged working-class and white-collar voters to look elsewhere. Another possibility, however, since important losses occurred in all classes, is that the Hugenberg press campaign was the decisive factor, moving susceptible nationalists to vote for some other party. The selection of Scholz did signal a shift to the right. But on matters of foreign policy, with a DVP foreign minister present in the government, the party was highly vulnerable to the attacks of Hugenberg and the National Socialists.

The September 1930 Reichstag election brought an indisputable disaster. The party's strength fell from 8.7 percent to 4.5. The result, quite naturally, stimulated a most urgent discussion, similar to that of the Conservatives following the 1928 election. The conclusions drawn were simple and straightforward: the DVP had to expand, to broaden its base, and become a genuine *People's* party. And, an instrumental concern, it would have to centralize the party structure to provide effective competition for its more bureaucratically organized competitors. It was recognized that Scholz was not up to these tasks. He retired in November of that year making room for Eduard Dingeldey, a young lawyer who had only gone into national politics in 1928 after having been active in the Hessian state government. His choice was viewed with favor by the party reformers and renovators; the youth group approved.

But things did not turn out well for the reformers. The party had no trained cadres. The attempt to centralize and restructure the party ran up against the opposition of well-entrenched notables. Members of local party committees were not about to yield their places, nor were they about to undertake the activities necessary to change the party so as to make it an effective competitor in the new and more demanding struggle they now faced.

Another, more ominous, aspect of Dingeldey's policy involved saddling the NSDAP with the responsibilities of office. Closely related to the idea of "taming" the radicals was the notion of the corrosiveness of office; nothing, presumably, could reduce the attractiveness of a party more than holding office. In repeated conversations, it is reported, Dingeldey attempted to awaken Hitler's interest, and on the other side, to move Brüning to take the National Socialists into the cabinet.[31] This effort was undertaken, not because of any faith in the NSDAP, nor because of any attraction to its leaders or policies, but to lessen the pressure on the DVP from its demagogic propaganda.

These involvements with the NSDAP did not remain merely subjects for discussion. The National Socialist success in the Thuringian Landtag election in December 1929 gave the NSDAP a key position in coalitional negotiations. Out of that process it obtained its first ministry in a state government, Wilhelm Frick becoming minister of interior and education. There were extended negotiations on this matter, largely involving DVP objections, but in the end Thuringia had a coalition government which contained all parties except Social Democrats, Communists, and Democrats. The DVP "support of [the] National Socialist minister" then became an issue in the Saxony state election in June 1930. Another coalition government which linked the People's party and the National Socialists was formed in Brunswick in November 1930. And, at the Harzburg Front demonstration in Brunswick in September 1931, along with all the other antirepublican forces, one found General Hans von Seeckt, who at this point was a member of the Reichstag for the DVP.[32]

The party's crisis had not dissolved the right-left division. The right was still present and active in pursuit of its aims. Specifically, by the end of 1930 and throughout 1931, it called for increasing opposition to the Brüning government. Dingledey and his moderate supporters found they could work with Brüning, and, an even more decisive consideration, they recognized that no alternative was available. To counter the demands of his party's right wing, however, Dingeldey was forced to make concessions to it. When other parties sought to force dissolution of the Prussian legislature, he, yielding to this internal pressure and seeing some tactical advantage for his position within the party, had the DVP join the effort. In October 1931, a majority of the faction voted against Brüning's government. The best that Dingeldey could do in the aftermath was to protect the dissenting minority from expulsion. (It should be noted that at this time the party had only thirty representatives in the Reichstag.) The rightist members, centered in the Ruhr and Rhine area and reflecting big business sentiment, wished to clean up the DVP and get rid of its various leftist elements!

Early in 1932 an effort was made to join with various fragments that had broken away from the DNVP. Dingeldey at first moved slowly on this matter, but, after the Prussian state election, a major disaster that made all the party's previous problems seem trivial, negotiations proceeded rather quickly. By June of 1932 it was clear that this effort too had failed. The sources of failure were not entirely external to the party. The vice-chairman, Otto Hugo, leader of the party's right wing objected because, as he and his associates saw matters, such moves would have meant a shift to the left whereas they favored a shift to the right, specifically a fusion with or at least an approach to the DNVP. Worried about the possibility that the party could fall below the minimum level for Reichstag faction status in the forthcoming election, joint lists were arranged with the Conservatives. The immediate consequence was the exodus of liberal members of the party along with representatives of the white-collar trade union (DHV). The party gained only 1.2 percent of the vote in the July Reichstag election, enough to give it seven seats in the Reichstag, six of those coming as a result of the joint listing with the DNVP.

The party supported Papen's government, for what that may have been worth. Joint lists were again established with the DNVP for the November Reichstag election. The DVP achieved a minuscule gain, taking 1.9 percent of the total vote to bring eleven members into the Reichstag.

From January through April in 1933, Dingeldey was ill and not able to lead the party. From the fifteenth of March, in fact, he was in a sanatorium in Switzerland. That put the leadership of the party during this crucial period in the hands of the conservative Hugo. With the National Socialists in power, many civil servants changed party membership, dropping the DVP for the NSDAP so as to gain "protective coloration." From the right wing of the party came a steady demand that the party dissolve and collectively go over to the NSDAP. Dingeldey returned, doing what he could to prevent this, but the right broke away nevertheless. Not much remained of the party; but even these remaining segments pressed for immediate liquidation. Dingeldey's dissolution statement showed more character (it was somewhat less abject) than those of most other parties.

What is striking about this dissolution is how it differs from its description in popular texts. Whereas the texts focus on the desperate and heroic struggle of a beleaguered liberalism against the demagogic right, the actual history was not that way at all. A major segment of the party worked for the abandonment of liberal principles, wishing to make common cause with the demagogic right. And from the defenders of liberalism, the moderate wing, came a tactical effort to involve the demagogic right in the government in the hope that its attractiveness would be diminished and that the time gained would allow a regrouping of the liberal or centrist forces. But that regrouping did not take place, both because of the rigidity of the various segments of the center and because of internal opposition from the party's own right wing.

Die Deutsche Demokratische Partei

The Democratic party, the favorite of liberal intellectuals then and now, had the most auspicious beginning of the republic's new parties and the most abject end. Its share of the vote for the Constituent As-

sembly, 18.6 percent of the total, was well above the vote of its predecessor, the Progressive party of the old regime, which had had only
12.3 percent in the 1912 election. But most of that vote disappeared in
the June 1920 election (the party gaining only 8.3 percent), most of the
loss going to the right liberal People's party. With a single exception,
in December of 1924, the party's history was one of decline in every
subsequent election. In November of 1932, it gained only 0.9 percent
of the vote.

The portents in 1919 seemed all the best. The collapse of the former
regime had, so it seemed, been so thorough. The involvement of both
Conservatives and National Liberals in the war had been such as to
discredit both. With the Social Democrats taking working-class voters
and the Zentrum taking Catholic voters, the way seemed open for a
broad-based new party of the remaining segment, the Protestant middle
class. And, at the beginning of the new regime, there seemed a chance
that the much-misprized German liberalism could now come into its
own, as a full-fledged partner in a democratic state.[33]

It was recognized that a party of notables was not well suited to
electoral struggles in the modern age, especially when it had to fight
against highly structured parties of organization like the Social Democrats and the Zentrum (the more highly organized Communists had not
yet made an appearance on the electoral scene). The party, accordingly,
began its career by making considerable use of new or modern organizational methods. No less a figure than Gustav Stresemann complained
of the DDP's use of "clever propaganda," its "influential press," its
"financial means suggesting American conditions," and its "advertisements that reminded one of department store merchandising." The party
organization in Württemberg, the best organized of all its units, established an advertising office in Stuttgart as early as November 1918 putting it in the hands of a man who had spent many years outside of
Germany, and had learned American advertising methods including those
used in American presidential elections.

The recommendations circulated at that time sound very much like
those used and criticized in United States elections of the sixties and
seventies. Films were produced for showing in all theaters of Germany.
Printed material, more than fifteen million pieces of it, was circulated.
Among the advertising possibilities discussed were pill boxes, enve-
lopes, and men's ties bearing the party's colors and pencils stamped with
the word "Democrat." The party did have powerful support from three
leading dailies, the *Berliner Tageblatt*, the *Vossische Zeitung*, and the
Frankfurter Zeitung.[34]

The party drew members in hitherto unknown quantities, 788,000
being reported at the time of the first party meeting in July 1919. That

would have meant that some 14 to 16 percent of the January 1919 voters were enrolled as members of the party.

But the initial success was misleading. Many people were apparently voting for the DDP for tactical reasons, for a lack of a better alternative. Many, according to one formula, took out membership in the party as a "life insurance policy against the feared St. Bartholomew's massacre."[35] Many of these intended the party to form a coalition against socialism (or Marxism) but instead found the DDP, together with the Zentrum, in coalition with the Social Democrats. And so, on the occasion of the next election, they chose the right liberal People's party or the Conservatives as providing a more adequate means for their purposes.

In one respect this reorganization of the party was incomplete; there was no tightly knit central leadership group as was the case with the SPD and the Zentrum. This failure had obvious roots, such control ran up against the well-entrenched liberal principles of free choice and autonomy for each member (including those in the parliamentary faction); for liberals, party discipline was an alien concept. On a related question, an attempt was made to limit the influence of the parliamentary group, but this too failed. And that failure in turn led one prominent member, Theodor Wolff, chief editor of the *Berliner Tageblatt* and one of the founders of the party, to quit in protest.

The transformation of the party, in short, was not successful. The party remained what it had always been, a loose association of notables. And then, in the course of the early years of the republic, the party lost many of its most renowned leaders. Friedrich Naumann, its first chairman and the intellectual father of left liberalism, had influenced nearly all the important figures in the new party; he died in 1919. Max Weber, a supporter of the party although not an active member, died in 1920; Conrad Haussmann died in 1922; Walther Rathenau, again a supporter but not in the leadership of the party, was assassinated in 1922. Hugo Preuss, the author of the Weimar constitution, died in 1925. When Theodor Wolff left the party it meant the loss of another notable. It also meant that the *Tageblatt* was not as closely aligned with the party as it might otherwise have been. Friedrich von Payer, formerly a leader of the Progressives, had retired from active politics. He quit the party in 1930.

After Naumann's death, the leadership passed to men of lesser renown and lesser ability. Carl Petersen was chairman from December 1919 to January 1924 when he left to become mayor of Hamburg. The new leader, Erich Koch-Weser, formerly mayor of Kassel, was brilliant and capable in organizational affairs; as one author puts it, his "industry and relish for party business and political negotiations made him indispensable." But, it is also said, he "lacked tact." Many found him arrogant. Some said he ran the party as a "personal dictatorship."[36]

The party did not have much in the way of party organs or party literature. Its leading journal, *Die Hilfe*, had been established by Friedrich Naumann. During most of the Weimar period this journal was edited by Gertrud Bäumer and Anton Erkelenz. Bäumer had been a member of the Naumann circle, was a leading feminist, and a hardworking activist within the party. She was also, it is said, "partially responsible for the theoretical and abstruse image of the party through her contributions to *Die Hilfe* and her campaign tracts." Erkelenz was a liberal trade unionist, one of the few union leaders in the party. He quit the party in 1930 when it shifted to the right (discussed below) and joined the Social Democrats.[37]

The Democrats, like all the other parties, were an amalgam of diverse forces. Like any other party, the DDP had its right and left wings, the former containing businessmen and industrialists and the latter intellectuals and pacifists. The right wing obviously contained persons of a more liberal persuasion than their equivalents in the People's party. The members of this right wing were much more practical than the intelligentsia who were concerned with the purity of liberal practice. Otto Gessler, one of the more prominent members of the party, was for many years the republic's minister of defense. The tactical requirements of that office (which included secret rearmament efforts combined with an official policy of fulfillment) made him anathema to the party's left. He in turn saw the left as "doctrinaire pacifists and literati with deeply rooted complexes," as "blinded doctrinal fanatics," and as "emotional radicals." As a left liberal party, that is, as one with a strong commitment to civil liberties, the Democrats also attracted many members of Germany's Jewish population. No very precise estimates are available, but the best guesses are that somewhat more than half of Germany's Jews voted for this party.[38]

The losses, which came with depressing regularity in nearly all elections, stimulated equally regular discussions of the need for new responses and the possibility of a united liberalism. The 1928 election results stimulated the discussion once again. The problem was seen as one of middle-class losses, the fear being that the Economic party, which was more aggressive in representing middle-class interests, was drawing away DDP supporters. Influenced by economist Gustav Stolper, the party attempted at its Mannheim conference in 1929 to counter this movement by presenting a program geared specifically to middle-class needs.[39] Stolper's program represented "a decisive shift to the right," and, simultaneously, was seen as providing the basis for unification with the People's party. Koch-Weser, the party's chairman, also signaled a new direction at this party conference. Defining the national political problem as one of "aging, undisciplined parties and egotistical interest groups," he advocated constitutional reforms, a strengthening of Reich unity (actually an old theme of his), abolition of proportional representation, and an increase of presidential powers. It was this last change, the "energetic presidential initiative," that would end the "sheer horse trading" associated with the present regime. Gertrud Bäumer too indicated a change in orientation with an attack on the centralizing "spirit of Preuss," which in this case meant opposition to the "radical, metropolitan and cosmopolitan spirit of Berlin." The party's industrialists blamed the 1928 defeat on the party's left wing, attacking its "socialistic reform tendencies" and "politics of charity."[40] A mouthpiece for these sentiments within the party was the periodical *Deutsche Einheit.* It had taken a rather sharp turn to the right after the 1928 elections. The cost in this case was the resignation of a prominent editor, Senator Peter Stubmann of Hamburg.

A dramatic manifestation of this new direction was the DDP's participation in a right-wing state government in Württemberg together with the DNVP, the DVP, and the Zentrum. This move led to Payer's resignation. The Württemberg coalition again stimulated discussion within the party and increased pressure for liberal unity. For some, the obvious conclusion was the need for a DDP-DVP merger and for "a sharper delimitation of the Left as primary conditions for survival." They exerted pressure on the party leadership to take initiatives toward "closing the ranks" and containing the party's left wing.[41]

These sentiments and pressures provided the background for Koch-Weser's response. Working behind the scenes, "over the dead body of the DDP" if necessary, he was arranging a "wider unity." Things went slowly at first, but the dissolution of the Reichstag on July 18, 1930, and the forthcoming election set for September 14, caused an acceleration of the pace of his negotiations. Rather than unity with the People's party, however, what was announced on July 28, was the formation of a new party, the German State party, the principal associates of the DDP in this new enterprise being the Jungdeutscher Orden (Young German Order), a rightist (and anti-Semitic) paramilitary group under the leadership of one Arthur Mahraun, and its political arm, the recently formed Volksnationale Reichsvereinigung (People's National Reich Association).

Two days later, the DDP executive committee met. Koch-Weser had to defend his high-handed procedures, which he did with all the skill available to him. He argued that this was the new, tough, and unsullied political formation now required in the changed circumstances of German politics. He asked the DDP to put its organization at the disposal of the Deutsche Staatspartei. This request was ultimately carried although not because of any widespread enthusiasm for the move. The committee members seem to have been moved more by the accomplished fact; a rejection would probably have split the party in the midst of the election campaign, forcing selection of a new chairman and so on. And so the result was a reluctant submission.

The outcome was highly predictable. Erkelenz and many of his friends in the left wing of the party quit and joined the Social Democrats. Most of the pacifists also withdrew, in this case to found their own party. The chairman of the DDP in Düsseldorf-West wrote an angry letter to Koch-Weser complaining of his undemocratic maneuvering. Given only two days' notice of the executive committee meeting, he and many others had not been able to attend. He also would not join the new organization.

Koch-Weser and his supporters welcomed the exodus; they now felt relieved of the burden posed by the party's left wing. Gertrud Bäumer saw them as rid of the "egotistical and self-righteous orthodoxy that had always been a danger to the party and [which had] isolated it from the outside world." She saw the Young German Order as a rather innocent movement, one that "in its own language, expresses the democratic idea by the word 'volksnational.' "[42]

The linkup with the People's party did not follow. The DVP viewed this new formation as a thrust against it, as a one-sided effort to force it to submit to DDP plans and refused to have anything to do with the new creation.[43]

The September election, as might well be expected, brought another disaster. Koch-Weser resigned as chairman of the new formation. Mahraun took defeat as the occasion for stronger, more arrogant demands rather than for analysis and possibly even compromise. This was rather galling for the DDP forces since they had "provided virtually all of the facilities—organization and finance—for the running of the election campaign." In the ensuing struggle, Mahraun and the other new forces withdrew from the coalition leaving the Deutsche Staatspartei as nothing more than the Democratic party stripped of its left wing and many of its more prominent leaders.[44] There was some discussion about abandoning the new formation, but, since the members of the Reichstag had been elected as representatives of the Staatspartei, the decision, in mid-November 1930, was to dissolve the Democratic party. At this point it was estimated that 80 percent of the local organizations were not functioning properly.[45]

Koch-Weser's successor as party leader was Hermann Dietrich, who was at the time also finance minister. The 1930 election had left the party with "pressing election debts" and to deal with these, Dietrich ordered a "reduction of the party bureaucracy." This further diminished the cadres available to the party. Under the circumstances there was little choice.

Even more important for the party's fate, however, was Dietrich's and the government's classical liberal behavior in the face of the depression. The cuts in government spending, particularly the reduction of civil servant salaries, no doubt took their toll in party support. One party leader said that the "fact that our party leader was at the same time the man responsible for the emergency measures had broken up entire local party organizations."[46] Dietrich himself complained that the Zentrum gave the credit for all popular measures to Chancellor Brüning. Credit for the unpopular ones went to the finance minister. In October 1931, party leaders convinced Dietrich to give up his post as head of the party. This did not mean, however, a return to the status quo ante; the damage was already done. Dietrich, incidentally, after a reshuffle, remained in the government as vice-chancellor until the end of the Brüning regime. Here, too, the party had little choice; to distance itself would have threatened the entire fragile governmental structure.

Although the party was successful in paying off the 1930 election debts, it could not obtain sufficient funds to conduct subsequent campaigns. The period of large sums from industrial circles was long past. The industrialists now saw the party as merely another splinter group; as one of them put it, money spent on it was so much "thrown out the window." Collections from members proved difficult, because there were ever fewer members and because many of them, the civil servants for example, had lost their enthusiasm. In a letter from early August 1932, a member from Zwickau reported that it was completely impossible, "without money, without a press, and without organization to continue under this electoral system. They have exaggerated our strength in Berlin, and that, unfortunately they have done continuously in recent years not knowing for just how little the party counts in the countryside."[47]

The long and the short of the matter is that the party was not in a position to hold election meetings. It had no private army to protect the meetings it did hold (leaving them open to both National Socialist and Communist disruptions). It had no money for advertisements. What it had in the way of a press now found it desirable to back off and take a noncommittal position.

The party won only four seats in the July 1932 Reichstag election. In November it gained only two. Through the use of joint lists, it gained five seats in the March 1933 election. All five votes were cast for the Enabling Law giving Hitler dictatorial powers. The party leaders adopted a resolution declaring their support for civil liberty, but then agreed it would be best not to publish it. The party was then dissolved, its dissolution coming one day after that of the Conservatives.

The Zentrum

The Conservatives, the People's party, the Democrats, and the Zentrum were the four major bourgeois (nonsocialist) parties of the Weimar regime. In the last years of that regime the Zentrum was unique in that it was the only one of the four that could be considered a genuine governing party. The Conservatives, after two episodes in government, had decided, under Hugenberg's direction, to serve only as an extraparliamentary opposition. The People's party and the Democrats, although participating in governments, were by then too small to carry much weight in political affairs. Most of the efforts of those parties, clearly, had to be expended in keeping their modest forces together and functioning. But the Zentrum, which regularly gained approximately one-eighth of the Reichstag seats, was still an intact party. True to its traditions (and interests), it was active in nearly all the governments of the fourteen-year republic. It led or participated in every one of the first seventeen governments, dropping out for the first time in the Papen regime of 1932. It held a single ministry in the brief Schleicher government. It did not participate in Hitler's coalition of late January 1933, but as we shall see, that was not because of a lack of interest.

The Zentrum, as mentioned earlier, had its own internal divisions; it attempted to accommodate agrarians, aristocrats, industrialists, middle classes, and workers within a single organization.[48] The religious tie helped to contain the internal struggle but certainly did not eliminate it. The wings of the party had formed about two of the party leaders, both of whom had been heads of the government. Joseph Wirth, the leader of the left liberal forces, was generally allied with the Catholic trade unionist Adam Stegerwald and with the Zentrum youth group. The conservative faction was led by Wilhelm Marx. As chancellor, Marx had formed a coalition with the Conservatives in 1927 to aid the passage of a law to protect church schools.[49] Both the direction of the alliance and the issue priority tell something about the basic sentiments within the Marx faction. This group also wished at the time to form a Zentrum-Conservative coalition in Prussia to replace the long-term and, for some, the embarrassing connection with "the Socialists." But the protests of the other faction were sufficient to halt this effort. It had, however, provided another clue attesting to the rightist pressure within the party.

The Marx government introduced a law to increase the salaries of civil servants. It had an innocent enough beginning. Arguing that civil service salaries had fallen behind those of other groups (it was part of the much-discussed proletarianization), the government asked for a 10 percent increase. Approximately one-third of the Reichstag members were themselves civil servants. Such was the convergence of party sentiment and individual self-interest that when all had been discussed, a sweeping majority voted raises of 21 to 25 percent for those in public employment. In addition to adding to the costs of government (in the nation, in states, and in localities), it provided another theme for National Socialist propaganda, one that was to prove especially telling as the depression became more severe.

The school reform law did not carry. In fact, the struggle over that issue broke the coalition when the People's party representatives, whose anticlerical tradition favored secular education for all, voted against it.

An agreement was reached not to call a new election until the budget was passed. A last item of business, one that, technically, was not resolved, concerned funds for construction of a pocket battleship, the famous (or infamous) Panzerkreuzer A. This, the first of four such ships, was to be Germany's first major naval construction under the Versailles restrictions. This effort, intended to placate the military, provided a major theme for the parties of the left in the course of the subsequent election.

The 1928 election, as we have seen, brought some losses to the Zentrum in working-class and mixed districts (see, for example, the Cologne evidence in Chapter 6). The losses were especially heavy in the Rhineland and in Silesia, both centers of Catholic working-class populations. The combination of the new rightist direction in the Zentrum and the Panzerkreuzer A issue appears to have been sufficient to break the increasingly tenuous loyalties that had tied these workers to the Zentrum. Not so surprisingly perhaps, the Social Democrats and Communists were the big winners in this election. The new government, that of Social Democrat Hermann Müller, was a "great," (or more precisely, a large) coalition government, extending across the spectrum to include the People's party. It also contained the Zentrum, of course, Joseph Wirth making a reappearance after his absence from the two Marx governments.

At this point some important changes took place within the Zentrum. Marx, now 65, resigned as chairman in early October. There was some struggle over the succession, but eventually Ludwig Kaas, a member of the clergy, was elected by a large majority. It was the first time in the history of the party that a clergyman had been chosen as leader. This too was widely portrayed as evidence of the move to the right within the party, of a falling back to the conservative tradition in Catholicism in which the clerical bourgeois wing was dominant. Stegerwald, initially, contributed to this view through his public statements, but the choice of Kaas actually had been intended as a compromise between the factions. Shortly thereafter Stegerwald accepted this more positive reading and in January of 1929, through Kaas's efforts, was chosen as head of the Zentrum's parliamentary group. He later accepted a post in the Müller government at which time Heinrich Brüning became head of the parliamentary group.

The Müller government fell in March of 1930. The details of that event are discussed in the next chapter when we consider the Social Democratic party history. A new Zentrum government, with a very tenuous parliamentary majority, was then formed under Brüning's leadership. In response to Brüning's initial statement of aims, the Social Democrats moved an immediate vote of no confidence. The new government was saved by the votes of the Conservatives; Hugenberg, although "fundamentally" opposed to any Weimar regime was at the same time practically in favor of whatever benefits he could obtain for his agrarian supporters. Although surviving this initial challenge, Brüning's government was destined to be a presidential, as opposed to a parliamentary, regime. That is to say, its legislation would have to be carried by presidential decree rather than by parliamentary majorities.[50]

The basic problem facing Germany at this point was the absence of an effective governing coalition. With Communists, Conservatives, and National Socialists dedicated to extraparliamentary opposition, governments had to be formed out of a narrow spectrum within the center. A part of that spectrum, approximately one-sixth of the total, consisted of a host of splinter parties, some of them (the Economic party, for example) also being generally oppositional in character. Given the mutual hostilities among the remaining potential partners, the formation of a center coalition had become well-nigh impossible. The end result of this continual destruction of center coalitions was that effective power was passed upward to the president. And many political leaders of the center parties became increasingly willing to accept exceptional arrangements, at least until such time as a stable government could be achieved. As one Zentrum leader put it after the fall of the Müller government, "If a dictator were possible for ten years—I would wish it."[51]

Matters came to a head in July of 1930 when Brüning introduced some extremely unpopular fiscal measures and declared that they would be carried by decree if not passed by the Reichstag. The Social Democrats objected as did the Conservatives and the Communists. The program was defeated on July 16, a development that would normally have required the resignation of the government. But at this point, Brüning and Hindenburg proceeded to institute the measures by decree, this being

the first time in the history of the republic that the principle of ministerial responsibility had been violated. On the eighteenth, the Reichstag
exercised its constitutional prerogative and voted to lift the decree.
Brüning then dissolved the Reichstag, setting new elections for September. Under the circumstances it did not appear to be the wisest of
moves. There was a thin—and not very realistic—hope that the shift of
one or two dozen seats would allow a bourgeois government, that is,
one in which the Zentrum would not have to rely on Social Democratic
participation.

The 1930 election differed from previous ones in that the Zentrum
conducted sharp attacks on the Social Democrats—its only viable coalition partner. This was another signal to make clear its rejection of a
left coalition, this in an effort to gain conservative support. The consequence, according to one Zentrum source, is that many of the young
supporters split away, going to right and left, to the National Socialists
and the Communists. The election, which yielded an 18.3 percent vote
for the National Socialists (and which, given the results of previous state
elections, was easily foreseeable from the outset), only worsened the
chances for any coalition of the democratic parties. Brüning then continued to govern without Social Democratic participation. Faced with
the threat from the extreme left and right, the Social Democrats undertook a policy of toleration; they either voted for the government or
abstained.

In the following year, in the period that has been referred to as one
of "semiparliamentarianism," the Zentrum came under increasing pressure to move to the right. President Hindenburg, in response to various
conservative pressures, wanted Brüning to replace two of his ministers,
one of these being Wirth. This Brüning resisted, realizing the problems
it would create within his own party. There was serious pressure from
the Vatican encouraging the party to sever its remaining connection
with the left in Prussia. The hope, in that distant center, was for a
coalition with various forces on the right. This option, however, became less likely in the course of 1931 as the Conservatives became increasingly critical of Brüning and the policies of his government.

At a meeting of the party's central committee in November, Kaas
announced his rejection of any coalition with the Conservatives or with
the parties of the center. At the same time, however, he broached the
idea of a people's assembly in which, for a specific time and for specific
limited aims, various groups of the right and left—organizations, he
said, "that previously had not yet known joint effort"—would work
together. This plan for an assembly of forces opened the possibility of
a coalition that would include the National Socialists. While not explicitly mentioned at this point, since Stegerwald and others were opposed

to that possibility, it was, according to Morsey, unquestionably intended by Kaas. The idea developed in the minds of some of the party's leaders that such a coalition could be viable. The antidemocratic character of the National Socialists, they convinced themselves, was a temporary phenomenon. They recognized the excesses of the uneducated leaders of this party but thought they could be contained. These leaders, possibly, could be tamed through official proscriptions of the SA and of the party newspapers. The notion of taming the party found special favor among the Zentrum's Reichstag faction, which had found that one could work with individual National Socialists in committees. The less skilled they were, the less they had in the way of factual or technical information, the more they relied on their colleagues in the other parties.[52]

The April 1932 state election in Prussia yielded a new and more formidable victory for the National Socialists. At this point, the recommendations for a change of coalition, that is, that the Zentrum give up its link with the Social Democrats to form a black-brown (Zentrum-National Socialist) coalition, again became frequent.

It was at this point that the blow came: Hindenburg dismissed Brüning and appointed Franz von Papen in his place. There was a twofold betrayal in this move. Hindenburg had just been reelected to office in a difficult two-round campaign, his success, in great measure, being due to Brüning's effort. And Papen, at the moment of his appointment, was a member of the Zentrum; his acceptance of the chancellorship thus undermined the position of the party's chosen leader. As one might expect, all factions of the Zentrum reacted with considerable outrage. Papen quickly resigned from the party, thus narrowly avoiding expulsion.

Papen, who now found himself without any party support, undertook negotiations with the National Socialists, who, in exchange for an easy assurance of support, received Papen's agreement to call new elections and to lift the ban on the Sturmabteilung. The Reichstag, accordingly, was dissolved on June 4 and the new election called, in order to facilitate, as the government declaration put it, the "creation of domestic political clarity." Given the results in Prussia (and in Württemberg, Hamburg, Anhalt, and Bavaria) from the state elections of April 24, there could have been little doubt as to the basic outcome. The Zentrum conducted its campaign largely against Papen ("revenge for Brüning"). Many people on the right, however, approved of his government and its announced programs. Much of the bourgeois press, as we have seen, was advocating national support (Conservative and National Socialist) for Papen.

In July, with the national campaign in full swing, the Zentrum undertook its first discussions with the National Socialists, this about the composition of the still-to-be-decided character of the Prussian government. The National Socialists broke off the negotiations abruptly when the whole question became moot; in the aftermath of some Communist–National Socialist bloodletting, Papen removed the continuing government of Otto Braun and replaced it (under the exceptional powers provided in the Weimar constitution) with his own appointees (this action is discussed in greater detail in the following chapter). The move accomplished what conservatives had sought for years. To head the Prussian government Papen chose the mayor of Essen, a former member of the right wing of the Zentrum.

The Reichstag election did clarify the political scene in that it removed two democratic parties from the stage. Hindenburg continued with his Papen experiment, but at the same time, some parties sought to create a viable replacement. Given the Zentrum's rejection of its former ally the Social Democrats, and given the sweeping hostility toward Marxists found everywhere among the bourgeois parties, it was clear that under no circumstances would the Social Democrats be forming a government. The remaining possibilities were very simple: a new government could be formed with National Socialists in alliance with parties of the right, or one could be formed with National Socialists in alliance with the Zentrum (and the Bavarian ally). Morsey describes matters as follows: "The thus changed parliamentary constellation allowed those forces in the Zentrum leadership to win the upper hand that had decided on a political reorientation and that stood on the so frequently cited basis of facts and for the so-called total solution. . . . [They] hoped, through including the NSDAP in responsibility, through its coalition with the Zentrum, to achieve its taming."[53]

The decision to undertake negotiations came two days after the election, with the Zentrum's sometime ally, the Bavarian People's party, joining it in the effort. As guidelines for the negotiations, the Zentrum insisted on "strict adherence to constitutional procedures" and "loyal cooperation with the elected representatives." This willingness to negotiate with the NSDAP involved a very dramatic shift for the Zentrum. For many years they had argued and preached against the National Socialists, denouncing them and all they stood for. Some voices were opposed to the negotiations, but such was the compelling force of circumstances that they went unheard. The negotiations, it should be noted, were being conducted while Papen was making competitive offers to gain NSDAP support.

There was a peculiar asymmetry to both discussions. The National Socialists, with most of the votes, understandably were demanding most of the offices. Papen and the Zentrum negotiators were offering far less, reserving the chancellorship and leading ministries for themselves. Both efforts ultimately failed since neither Papen nor the Zentrum was willing to grant Hitler's demands.

Negotiations were undertaken simultaneously by the Zentrum to consider the possibility of a coalition with the NSDAP in Prussia. Here the National Socialists asked for the posts of minister president, interior, education, and finance, a demand that shocked those negotiating for the much smaller Zentrum. Nothing came of these discussions either. With the failure of discussions at the national level, Papen once again dissolved the Reichstag, setting the second parliamentary election that year for November. At the suggestion of the NSDAP, discussion of the Prussian government was dropped pending the outcome of the national election.

Considerable opposition arose within the Zentrum during the period of these discussions. The party's leaders felt it necessary to respond and again stressed their aim of "securing political stability" within the framework of the constitution. They were very confident of their ability to keep their proposed coalition partner within those limits. One of the negotiators was very optimistic. As he put it: "My impression of Hitler was a much better one than I expected. His statements were consistent and clear and his conceptions, on the whole, coincide in great measure with ours."[54]

The November election brought a loss of five seats to the Zentrum (they blamed it on the lower participation). Taken with the NSDAP losses (thirty-four seats) that meant the two parties fell just short of a majority. There were further negotiations, however, but these again were overtaken by subsequent events. Papen resigned on November 17 and was replaced by Schleicher. The Zentrum leadership, on the whole, found him acceptable and gave him its support.

During the last weeks of 1932 the pronouncements of various Zentrum leaders had taken on a different tone, one that offered even less promise for the republic. They still advocated a government of "national concentration," but, for example, in the case of Kaas, there was an edging away from the "framework of the constitution" in favor of a more authoritarian option. In one discussion he declared: "We do not want to fall back again into parliamentarianism; instead we wish to create for the Reich's president a political and moral support for an authoritarian government, [one] that will be inspired and instructed by the Reich's president."[55] In his New Year's declaration, Kaas declared that the only way out would be "from the side of a leader [Führer]." A "sick people" could not vote itself health. Among other things, he declared that, "whoever leads in Germany, is actually of little consequence. What he is, is not important, only what he can do."[56] Morsey indicates it was not surprising that four weeks later many Zentrum voters felt that Hitler had been declared acceptable.

The change was even more serious as indicated by private discussions. In late October, Brüning stated his position to some rightist leaders—after the November election, he declared, "the Nazis must be engaged with responsibility in the Reich."[57] In mid-November, Kaas held it to be absolutely essential that the NSDAP be brought into a government of "national concentration." Despite the evident willingness, that possibility was not achieved, it being initially eclipsed by the Schleicher episode.

Unaware of the weakness of the Schleicher government, the Zentrum initiated a discussion of the *Osthilfe* (help for the east) in the Reichstag, a discussion that stimulated some very agitated reactions in President Hindenburg's office and set in motion the events that ultimately led to Schleicher's downfall and the naming of Hitler.[58] These events took most outsiders by surprise. Schleicher even expressed to the cabinet on the twenty-eighth of January, two days before his dismissal, his conviction that Hindenburg would not name Hitler. At the eleventh hour, while the behind-the-scenes discussions were going on, the Zentrum's executive committee met in Berlin and carried on extended debates over internal party affairs. The committee addressed such questions as the expansion of its membership and the improvement of dues collection.

Little more need be added to this brief review. The leaders of the Zentrum hoped to be taken into Hitler's government, but in the course of the 1933 election campaign, they experienced the banning of party journals, the dismissal of Zentrum members from the civil service, and attacks on them by the SA. Kaas offered some brave words—"We have no intention of pulling down our flag"—and continued to hope for an understanding with Hitler.[59] After the election, the party, still out of power, began to suffer membership losses.

At this point Hitler asked for an exceptional grant of power under the so-called Enabling Law. Since this required a two-thirds vote of the Reichstag, the Zentrum became the object of much attention. The pressures included more prohibitions of newspapers and more dismissals (Konrad Adenauer was forced out of office as Cologne's *Bürgermeister* on the thirteenth of March). Despite these attacks, the Zentrum leaders still agreed to participate in a spectacular National Socialist ceremony in Potsdam. In discussions between the leaders of the two parties, Hitler gave various assurances to the Zentrum leaders. The latter even presented a set of conditions required for their support. On the day of the vote, March 23, Hitler made a conciliatory speech that solicitously assured them of virtually everything they had asked for. In the meeting of the parliamentary group during the following intermission, the Zentrum representatives decided to give the measure their unanimous support.

The attacks on the party continued unabated in the following months. A significant division developed in Catholic ranks at this time. Drawing on Hitler's assurances of the twenty-third, the Bishops' Conference published a statement withdrawing its former general prohibitions and warnings vis-à-vis the National Socialists. The bishops expressed their loyalty to the new regime with a statement of fundamental opposition to "all illegal or subversive behavior."[60] Hitler, Papen, and Kaas undertook discussions with the Vatican for a concordat that, among other things, would resolve the long-discussed school question. (It would also prohibit political activities by the clergy.) In the course of these negotiations it was insinuated, by National Socialists and some Catholic leaders, that political activities by the Zentrum would damage these negotiations.

Then, in the midst of the continuing assault on the party, its leader disappeared. Prelate Kaas quietly left the country, for Rome as it turned out, never to return. The Zentrum was without direction for a month. Individual members and local units were pressing for some indication of the party's response, but in that crucial period none was to come. A month later, Brüning was elected leader of the party. He still hoped for some kind of cooperation with the new government; hence, as the NSDAP attacks continued, his direction did not indicate opposition or even, at minimum, some self-defense. Party newspapers even imitated National Socialist rhetoric; Brüning became "Führer Brüning" who, "unswervingly," went his way, accompanied by a "loyal following" who would submit to his decisions.[61]

On July 5, 1933, the party declared, "in consultation with Chancellor Hitler," its own dissolution. This action, it was said, gave its supporters, "the possibility of putting their power and experience under the leadership of the chancellor. . . . In his national front [they could] stand *unreservedly at his disposal* for positive cooperation in the spirit of consolidation of our national, social, economic, and cultural conditions and for work in the new development of a constitutional order."[62] Even the National Socialists were surprised. They had expected more of a struggle.

Morsey offers some clues to explain the deterioration and disappearance of the party. There was, first of all, the initial division within the party between a left and a right, or, more specifically for this purpose, between those who accepted the republic and those who favored a more traditional or conservative social order. The electoral defeat in 1928 and the election of Kaas as the new leader definitely favored the latter faction and its acceptance and approval of authoritarian solutions including even the *Führerprinzip*. The hierarchical structure of the church and the ideologies built around it were such as to allow some to see fascism as a related system, Morsey reports, rather than as the mortal enemy. As one Catholic writer put it: "In our view of the world, the belief in authority is so deeply anchored . . . that we would be acting against our own basic beliefs if in these times of internal disorder we helped to shatter the authorities." Another author spoke of the "inner affinity of the church to authoritarian regimes insofar as they are thought to have a Christian basis."[63]

A second factor that no doubt inclined many party leaders toward an accommodation was their concern to defend the interests of the church. In the short run at least, this appeared to be best accomplished through maintaining themselves in government, either at the head of a coalition, or at least as a presence so as to have an influence on their coalition partner.

A third consideration encouraging accommodation involved a historical precedent which seemed at least to justify the effort. In 1919 the Zentrum had made an unexpected alliance with the Social Democrats, that too being aimed at the defense of interests. One argument made at that time was that a role in government would bind the Social Democrats, that is, would force responsible behavior. The notion of taming the National Socialists was a blood brother to this idea. Since it had worked in 1919, it seemed plausible that similar results could be achieved in 1932 or 1933.

A fourth factor that facilitated the accommodating stance of the party involved its internal composition. Because of its continuous governing character and because of its key position within most of the Weimar coalitions, some advantage for individuals was (or was thought to be) gained by membership in the Zentrum. The party, for this reason, attracted opportunists in addition to its idealists. That may explain the sudden shift of many Zentrum civil servants to the NSDAP after the March 1933 election. Something of this may also, perhaps, be seen in that meeting of the Zentrum caucus to discuss its position on the Enabling Law. Although that vote was ultimately unanimous, the discussion was not. There was an initial majority in favor of acceptance, with Kaas as its exponent, and an opposed minority. This minority contained most of the leading notables of the party, beginning with Brüning and Wirth and including also the trade unionists Joos and Stegerwald.[64] It was, as one commentator put it, a "small . . . but select" group. But its efforts to convince the majority were obviously without success— "right reason" (to use a favorite expression of Thomas Aquinas) is not an effective weapon in discussion with opportunists.

A final consideration in this default involves a matter of *Realpolitik*.

Since much of the struggle in this period was fought in the streets, a party's chances of success depended on having some kind of armed forces to put into that struggle. But the Zentrum had no such army. There had been some loose and rather tenuous relationships with the Reichsbanner, a force that was dominated by the Social Democrats, but this involved another of the perpetually unresolved questions. It meant that in 1932 and 1933 the Zentrum was completely exposed when faced with National Socialist-Sturmabteilung attacks; the party had no forces with which to defend itself.[65]

The last years of the Weimar republic saw a remarkable shift on the part of the four bourgeois parties: all four moved to the right. These moves had somewhat different meanings for the four parties, each being the result of a different set of forces. The reactions ranged from that of the Conservatives, for whom the new direction was one of determined extraparliamentary opposition, to that of the Zentrum, for whom it meant participation in government but now without the Social Democrats.

There were, however, common features to be found in this movement. The Weimar government had taken on some important fixed obligations in the course of the republic's good years. These included the high civil servant salaries under the 1928 adjustment, the Panzerkreuzer costs, and the backing of the unemployment insurance funds. In addition of course, there were the externally imposed reparations payments. The arrangement was satisfactory as long as good times prevailed, as long as the government's obligations were below regular revenues. But with the increase in unemployment, there came an unforeseen increase in the volume of individual payments and consequently a need for massive government support to make up the rising deficits. This occurred as tax receipts were declining, thus giving rise to awesome budget deficits. The Brüning government responded in an eminently classical manner: it sought to balance the budget. To do this, it could cut the level of individual benefits. It could instead cover the costs by increasing employer and employee contributions or taxes. The left was not willing to accept a cut in benefits or increased employee contributions, and the parties of the right would not accept the other alternatives. The result was a complete impasse. This was the key domestic political problem from 1930 to the end of the regime.

The basic economic plan worked out in 1923-1924 was premised on the availability of investment funds, most of which came from the United States. These funds first stimulated the economy after the disastrous inflation. They made possible the good times and allowed payment of both the domestic and the foreign obligations. Most of the latter obligations, however, were short term, that is, they could be recalled at very little notice. This meant that underlying the basic domestic arrangement was a mechanism which, if it failed, could easily turn a bad situation into a complete disaster.

In the good years of the republic, the bourgeois parties, particularly those that were regular participants in governing coalitions, accepted the extension of welfare benefits, although frequently with the greatest reluctance. (Some benefits, the eight-hour day, for example, had been cut out in the course of earlier crises.) With the coming of the bad years, there was of course no consideration given to extensions of benefits. Rather, following classical liberal principles, the concern was to retrench. On that the bourgeois parties could agree.[66]

As we have seen, the Zentrum had been subjected to considerable pressure, both internal and external, to break its link with the Social Democrats. Hindenburg's original selection of Brüning had been premised on this new direction. The latter's ready agreement to the new election in September 1930 was based on the assumption that it would be relatively easy to gain the small number of seats needed to form a right coalition.[67] This assumption also provided the justification for the Zentrum's sharp attack on its long-time coalition partner, the Social Democrats, in that election. The move to the right in the case of the Zentrum meant a decision to break the Weimar coalition.

The moves to the right, as indicated, meant firm commitments by these four parties to classical liberal economic solutions. At a time when they could have been priming the pump, when they could have been subsidizing, say, the construction industry in which unemployment was at its worst, these parties were behaving in a way that could easily be seen or portrayed as indifferent, heartless, calculating, or even cynical by the unemployed or those facing the imminent threat of it.

The bourgeois parties, as we have seen, were peculiarly mislabeled. The most frequently used formulas portray German politics as characterized by a close alignment of class and party, as if nearly everyone in the middle class supported the so-called middle-class parties and nearly all workers supported the left. But all parties reached across class lines to gain support, and workers were a significant element in the fate of them all. It was easy to think that losses suffered by bourgeois parties must have meant losses of middle-class voters, but another option was clearly possible—they could have been abandoned by their working-class supporters. The adoption of pure classical solutions to the depression was a policy that would have hit hard at both the interests and the loyalties of these working-class supporters. The workers' attachment to any particular party must have been rather tenuous to begin with. Put differently, their loyalties were probably residues of earlier traditional political training so that if one party abandoned them, they would have been motivated to look for another, a better, alternative.

Were no other option available to these workers, the economic policies of the bourgeois parties might not have posed a problem. But as it was, there were other choices. Liberal and left writers, somewhat obtusely, see the Social Democrats and Communists as providing the clear and obvious alternatives. It would be only natural, a proper conclusion of right reason, that they should turn to one of these parties. But that conclusion overlooks the point that they were *rightist* workers, Germany's equivalent of the Tory workers; they were conservative, nationalist, or possibly even monarchist in persuasion. Their ranks would have contained many rather traditional Protestants and Catholics, neither of whom would have seen Marxist parties as positive options. Their dislike of the parties of the left, moreover, would not have been one-sided, that is, an unfounded ideologically based aversion. The parties of the left had for years condemned their outlooks in no uncertain terms, and in everyday contacts they no doubt had been less than gentle in their treatment of such backward workers. When the crisis came, therefore, these workers were not at all likely to turn to the Social Democrats or to the Communists to find solutions for *their* problems.

When the bourgeois parties shifted to the right they helped justify the claims of their new competitor, the National Socialists. This came about not so much because of their attitudes toward unemployment benefits, but because they adopted tough nationalist lines, championed the need for leadership, and imitated the manner of the National Socialists. Clearly the greatest contribution to the legitimation of Hitler and his party was made by Alfred Hugenberg when he brought Hitler into the anti–Young Plan alliance and advertised Hitler's wares in the journals of his press empire. If the National Socialists were deserving of imitation by party leaders, a next step came rather easily for many citizens—why not vote for them?

The bourgeois parties, both moderate and immoderate ones included, in no small measure contributed to the rise of the National Socialists. Through their own actions they did much to make that party, the party that then broke them in the electoral struggle and ultimately destroyed them as organizations along with the entire republic. The process it will be noted, had a peculiar dialectical character to it in that the established parties were generating their own opposite. The National Socialists could easily have borrowed Marx and Engels's words describing the bourgeoisie of their age—"they are doing our work for us."

This shift to the right involved what might be called a competition in toughness. But the new toughness of the traditional parties earned only ridicule from the NSDAP activists. The archetypical case would be that of the, in 1932, 67-year-old Alfred Hugenberg. The National Socialists could easily agree with the sense of his words; but only in the mouths of the NSDAP's young and resourceful fighters did these words sound plausible. In entering on this competition in toughness, the parties of the right had chosen a struggle they could not possibly win. What they did do was to justify and legitimate the claims of the NSDAP and therewith contribute to their own demise.

Many middle-class and upper-class voters, having seen their party lose in the last Reichstag election and seeing further losses in the intervening state elections, had good reason to reconsider their choice. They were looking for a party strong enough to protect their interests, in particular, to protect them against what they saw as a growing Marxist threat. The National Socialists, the possessors of immense electoral strength and, more important, of a giant private army, seemed to provide an appropriate choice—even though they might have reservations about the party's policies and behavior.

This is not to suggest that these perceptions were correct ones. The threat from Social Democrats and Communists was more imaginary than real. To understand their role in this dialectical process, one must also examine their contribution to the political imagery of the period. That task is undertaken in the next chapter. We then, in Chapter 12 consider the National Socialist efforts in the electoral struggle of those last years.

CHAPTER ELEVEN

The Parties of the Left

Despite the wishes of most conservatives, and despite the wishes even of some of their own leaders, the Zentrum and the Social Democrats were destined to remain partners until the advent of Papen's government in midyear 1932. Kaas and Brüning, as we have just seen, wished to dissolve the alliance, but, as things turned out, the two parties were forced into even closer mutual dependence.

The account of the SPD side of this relationship involves more than a simple repetition of the Zentrum's history. Many of the same issues do necessarily reappear, but most of them had quite different impacts on the two parties. The school question, which loomed so large for the Zentrum's leaders, was of minor significance for the leaders of the SPD. The question of military expenditures, by contrast, was a small problem for the Zentrum but a nightmare for the SPD. In the case of the SPD, an additional range of concerns and issues appeared that overwhelmed the party's leaders.

The purpose of this review of the political struggle, it will be remembered, is to provide the basis for an alternative reading of the National Socialist electoral successes. The evidence presented in the previous chapters has shown the focus on structurally induced strains that affected the lower middle class to be mistaken; it explains the wrong things, the most important of these being the presumed lower-middle-class reaction. As an alternative to this centrist argument, we are considering the possibility that the reactions were linked to the offerings and behavior of the parties themselves. Put briefly, the suggestion is that the reaction was more politically than structurally determined. This point is discussed in more detail in Chapter 13.

THE SOCIAL DEMOCRATIC PARTY

The Social Democrats found themselves in an extremely difficult position during the last years of the republic.[1] Their situation was incompatible with a long heritage of promises and expectations that had been firmly implanted in the minds of many followers. For decades prior to their taking of power, they had promised socialism as *the* solution to working-class problems. But upon gaining power, they had, for all practical purposes, socialized nothing. From 1918-1919 on, the party's leaders had recognized the difficulties of this course. They had few people trained to manage any industry. Such attempts moreover would have frightened off both foreign and domestic investors and made a serious unemployment problem even worse. The problems associated with the routine affairs of government in 1918-1919 (such as guaranteeing minimum food deliveries) were formidable enough. Major institutional changes would only have added to the difficulties.[2] The Versailles obligations, in addition, seriously restricted the government's ability to undertake any costly institutional experiments. In later years, especially after the 1920 election, the Social Democrats lacked the parliamentary numbers to carry through any socialization, their bourgeois coalition partners clearly being opposed to any such moves. It would probably be a mistake, however, to emphasize the constraints under which the SPD leaders operated. For some, in all likelihood, the will was lacking; they did not see socialization as a viable option.

This change of position meant that they were operating against their own heritage, a fact continuously thrown in their faces—by Independent Socialists, and later by Communists, and also by some mocking National Socialists. It was difficult for them to handle the problem; they were not about to declare their major commitment to have been simply a big mistake.

Their position was also complicated by the constellation of political parties in Weimar. During the war, the Independents had broken away from the Social Democrats to demand an end to the war, the institution of a republic, and the socialization of basic industry. The first two of these demands were achieved in November of 1918, but the third had been frustrated. For this, among other reasons, the Independents refused to participate in the government of 1919, thus reinforcing the SPD alliance with the bourgeois parties, the Zentrum and the Democrats.[3]

Friedrich Ebert, the leader of the SPD and of the new "revolutionary" government, made an alliance with the head of the Imperial Army, this being one of the more fateful moves undertaken by the new regime. Ebert was no revolutionary, hating it "like the plague," and, drawing some lessons from the Russian experience only one year earlier, he arranged for the creation of some reliable military units, the Freikorps, to guarantee order.

A series of leftist insurgencies did occur, the first of these coming in January 1919. These were followed, with depressing regularity, by the insertion of Freikorps units. These sweeping countermoves touched not only the insurgents; many nonparticipants were also found among the dead and wounded. For this the SPD paid a heavy price. What is sometimes forgotten in the attribution of blame, however, is that the Communists too must have paid a price as far as working–class support was concerned. It was clear and obvious, a fact needing no unveiling, that in most instances it was the Communists who had precipitated the events.

The Kapp *Putsch* gave rise to a more complicated variation on this theme. In this case, it was rightist forces, units of the Freikorps, that initiated the action. The government and the trade unions called a general strike (the only time they did so in all of German history) which in short order brought the insurgency to an end. In the process, however, the Communists had gone beyond mere strike action and in some cities had taken power. Again the military was sent in.

The position of the Independents, in the meantime, had become more and more untenable. In the fall of 1920, at a special party meeting, a majority of the delegates voted to affiliate with the Communist or Third International and to join with the German Communist party. The minority continued for a while as Independent Social Democrats but ultimately chose to reunite with the SPD. This reunification had its greatest impact in Saxony and Thuringia, thus adding a significant left component to the SPD forces there. Both developments caused serious difficulties for the SPD. The Communists, for the first time, had a mass base. And the SPD in Saxony and Thuringia now undertook initiatives that were very strongly opposed by the party's national leadership. Late in 1923, the SPD in those states formed coalition governments with the Communists (a point considered later in this chapter) and openly defied the national government at the same time as the rightist government in Bavaria was playing its independent (some read it as "treasonous") role vis-à-vis the central government.

There was some justification for the central government's removal of both the left and the right governments. But there was also a tactical problem involving the sequence of removal. In terms of both the timing and the gravity of the offense, it should have moved against Bavaria first. But in terms of the need for army support and considering, too, the likely reactions among influential conservative groups, there were some purely political reasons for moving first against the left. This was done by the Stresemann government although, to be sure, it was with the acquiescence of the Social Democratic national leadership.[4] Once again, the party found itself moving against its own supporters. Life in government was not as easy as in the carefree prewar days of uncompromising opposition.

In the last stage of the Weimar regime, a concerted effort was made by various conservatives to bring an end to the coalitions of the Zentrum with the "Marxist" Social Democrats in both national and state governments. This effort was closely tied in with the shifts to the right by the so-called middle-class parties discussed in the previous chapter.

Never friendly to the Social Democrats, those parties now mounted a formidable demagogic effort to force the left from all positions of power. In the process, as we have seen, the moderates within the bourgeois parties came under attack for their willingness to compromise with the SPD.

At about the same time, the Communist party took a turn to the left (discussed below) and also began vehement attacks on the Social Democrats. That put the Social Democrats in the middle, desperately trying to hold onto the few accomplishments for which they could claim credit. Given this extremely vulnerable position, they became rather uncompromising with respect to those accomplishments.

One of the first social accomplishments of the new regime was the eight-hour day. Attractive as it was to all beneficiaries, it was also a very tenuous achievement. Since few other European countries had followed the Weimar example, the German economy was working at a competitive disadvantage. As the economic situation worsened, aggravated by reparations payments and growing inflation, the costs of the accomplishment became ever greater, and business interests, understandably, pushed for its abandonment. This was done under the provisions of an emergency law granting exceptional decree powers to the government. The law, which required a constitutional change, needed a two-thirds majority, which was made possible by SPD votes. Under the provisions of a subsequent decree, disallowances of the eight-hour rule were permitted. With time, the eight-hour day became more the exception than the rule. For the SPD, an important and highly visible accomplishment had been lost.

Among the remaining achievements of the Weimar regime were an arrangement for compulsory arbitration of labor disputes, a system of shop councils, and a national economic council (with worker-manager parity). The last is said to have had more symbolic than real importance; some saw it as a waste of time and effort. Later, in 1927, a comprehensive unemployment insurance system was enacted. This was destined to be the focal point of political struggle in the years to come. There was also a prewar heritage to be protected, this going back to Bismarck's health insurance plan (dating from 1884) and accident insurance plan (of 1885). Then, too, there was a later arrangement (1892) for old age insurance. Since all three had been seriously affected by the 1923 inflation, there was a need for government assistance to reestablish their financial health. This was arranged during the good years of the republic with no serious difficulty.

These were the accomplishments the SPD was determined to protect at all costs. Some of them, arbitration and shop councils, interfered with traditional management prerogatives and with time, particularly in the late period of reaction, came under heavy fire. The unemployment insurance plan proved extremely costly, and its costs, in turn, created *the* problem for the SPD leadership and for all subsequent governments prior to Hitler's accession.

If those had been the only issues, life would have been comparatively simple for the SPD leaders. The task of defense, after all, was a relatively simple one. But being in government or being necessary to a government was more complicated, in that many issues arose that were not of their choosing or making. The first issue the SPD leaders faced was the eight-hour day, an issue that, given the circumstances, the SPD had to lose. Then came the effort to replenish the social insurance programs, which, as noted, was easily accomplished, there being no serious opposition. The question of an agricultural tariff came up. The benefits for the farmers (and Junkers) were simultaneously penalties for workers in the form of higher food costs. Here the SPD lost, although the overt political effects were not very serious since tariffs did not become a major public issue. In 1927, the Unemployment Insurance Office was created. Under the terms of the law, provision was made for the support of 800,000 unemployed. It was a key accomplishment.

The civil servant salary adjustment, mentioned earlier, was carried by an overwhelming vote of the Reichstag. The SPD, together with the other supporting parties, could obviously count this as a significant accomplishment. The financial burden imposed, however, became an ominous one when the depression set in. Later, when civil servant salaries were cut back, it became clear that the accomplishment merely set the stage for widespread disenchantment within SPD ranks.[5]

Army appropriations posed an ever-recurring problem for the SPD leaders. The other parties in the governing coalitions strongly favored these appropriations; SPD opposition or intransigence would have endangered the government. Were the SPD to bring the government down on such an issue, an insoluble crisis would follow since no viable democratic government was possible without SPD support. For that reason it repeatedly accepted these obligations even though serious difficulties were thus created within its own ranks. Some SPD members, leaders and followers, it should be noted, favored support for the military. The school issue, which, it will be remembered, led to the fall of the Marx government and the calling of the May 1928 election, was not of major importance for most Social Democrats.

One of the last actions of the Marx government, as pointed out earlier, was to approve, in principle, funds for the first stage of the construction of a pocket battleship, Panzerkreuzer A. The actual appropriation of those funds was left to the subsequent government. Clearly the undertaking of a first stage would entail provision of funds for all subsequent stages up to the completion of the project. Also in the offing were plans for pocket battleships B, C, and D. It was an ideal issue for parties of the left, and both Communists and Social Democrats made ample use of the theme in the following campaign. One slogan argued: "Oppose the building of battleships! For the feeding of children!" Both left parties picked up votes in the elections, it being their best overall showing since January of 1919. Social Democrat Hermann Müller, by most accounts a capable, sensible, and humane man, was called upon by President Hindenburg to form the new government. And that government, the great coalition which included the People's party, lasted for almost two years. It was destined to be the republic's last genuinely constitutional government. It was also, after all the slogans of the campaign faded away, destined to deal with the pocket battleship question.

The cabinet decided, on August 10, 1928, to begin construction of Panzerkreuzer A. This set off a heated discussion within the SPD and led, in November, to the presentation of a resolution by the SPD Reichstag faction demanding that all work on the ship be stopped. A caucus decision bound all members of the faction to vote for this resolution. The character of SPD party discipline was such that, on November 16, Chancellor Müller and three other members of the cabinet were required to vote against their own cabinet proposal.[6] The motion was lost, with all parties of the center and right voting against the Social Democrats and Communists so that the direct impact of the caucus decision was nil.

The indirect impact, however, was enormous: the decision provided considerable ammunition to the anti-Socialist efforts of the right. For the nationalists, any vote against armaments for a disarmed Germany was close to treason. The alliance of the two Marxist parties on this issue, of course, did not go unnoticed; it provided another weapon for the right. For those of traditional authoritarian persuasions, moreover, the incident demonstrated the incapacity of Social Democratic leadership. If they could not control their own party, how could they pretend to rule a nation? It allowed them, for months thereafter, to mock Social Democratic pretensions. The incident also provided an issue for the left wing of the Social Democrats, who brought it up at the national party meeting in May of the following year. The Communists, too, made considerable use of the incident for their purposes.

Another major crisis occurred at the same time, in the last months of 1928, this one involving a wage struggle in the steel industry.[7] The struggle was arbitrated, and the industry lost the decision. Then, in violation of the law, the owners continued the struggle, locking out the workers and taking the case to the courts. Their action affected unemployment levels in Germany both directly and indirectly and, in addition, posed no end of problems for the Social Democrats. The court action threatened to bring down the entire arbitration system, one of their major accomplishments. The workers in the steel industry asked for unemployment benefits. The government mulled it over, then denied aid to the workers directly involved but allowed it to those indirectly affected. Finally, in December 1928, the struggle was ended through a compromise achieved by Carl Severing, a leading Social Democrat.

Both reality components (such as the firm's ability to pay) and image components were involved in this struggle. The Severing compromise balanced as best it could the former concerns. Later assessments, however, focused on the latter. For the left (both the left wing of the SPD and the Communists), the result was seen as a bourgeois victory. Again the Social Democratic leadership, by allowing an erosion of an achievement, appeared to have let down its own supporters. For those on the right, however, the outcome was portrayed as another left victory.

A scandal broke at about this point, one with ramifications that extended over the next two years. The Sklareks, a family in the clothing business, had obtained favors from the Berlin city government in exchange for bribes. The scandal brought down the hitherto much-esteemed *Bürgermeister*, a member of the German Democratic party. Two of the Sklarek brothers were members of the Social Democratic party and had used their party connections to further their diverse enterprises. The family was also Jewish. The event, as one might well imagine, provided a rich vein of material for the ongoing antiregime campaign of the right.[8]

That campaign, conducted in party meetings and in the rightist press, stressed Marxism, the stab in the back, the involvement with the Versailles treaty, and the attempt to live up to its provisions. It stressed the reparations burden, the vote of the Marxist parties against rearmament, and the inability of the Social Democrats to manage their own house (as in the pocket battleship affair). And finally it attacked the politicization of the civil service and corruption in government, the Sklarek affair being the presentation case. To summarize all these themes, Conservatives and National Socialists focused on "the system." The Weimar system came to be portrayed as a construction that was rotten in all its elements, as one best swept away in its entirety. This attack was directed against the Weimar parties, most notably against the two leading parties of that enterprise both in the nation and in Prussia, that is, against the Social Democrats and the Zentrum. The effort directed against the Zentrum was intended to force the breakup of what the right considered an unnatural alliance. If the Zentrum were to break away from its SPD partner, a rightist coalition would become possible. The Social Democrats also faced much hostility from the right although to be sure, for quite different reasons. In addition, they faced attacks from the left, both from critics within the party and, outside it, from the Communists. The latter too, attacked *das System* although, of course, with considerable differences in emphasis.

The steadily rising unemployment levels meant that by the beginning of 1930, the payments from the unemployment insurance fund already far exceeded its income. The new budget came up for discussion, and expenses, so it was thought, had to be covered by receipts. The forces of the right (including the DVP within the coalition) argued for a reduction in the level of payments. Having been defeated on so many previous issues, the SPD made this question the ultimate issue of principle. They initially suggested an "emergency contribution" (*Notopfer*) by those who had stable employment, by the civil servants and some white-collar employees. Although some other partners in the coalition accepted the idea, this proposal was refused by the DVP. Another proposal, which called for increases in various excise taxes, was offered by Heinrich Brüning. The SPD initially accepted this alternative although with some reluctance since it laid the costs on the ordinary consumer. But this proposal also fell through because of the intransigence of some parties to the coalition (the Bavarian People's party objected to the tax on beer) and because of SPD reluctance. The trade union wing of the party argued that it was only a stopgap measure and that support levels would once again be threatened in the not too distant future. The SPD faction voted to reject the Brüning compromise. Unable to reach any other resolution to this problem, Müller handed in his resignation.[9]

The struggle over unemployment insurance was fought at the same time as the struggle over the Young Plan. The latter struggle helped to hold the coalition together, the sentiment being that the lower schedule of reparations payments under the new plan would alleviate some of the financial strain on the government. But the coaliton parties had different plans for the freed funds; the right wished to cut taxes, and the left wanted to pay for the unemployment insurance. The death of Stresemann in October of 1929 removed his key moderating influence in the DVP, thereby freeing the dominant faction to lay on its immoderate demands, ones that could only lead to the fall of the coalition. The concern that had restrained the Social Democrats—that no other republican coalition was possible—did not bother these right liberals since their feelings toward the republic, by and large, ranged from indifference to open hostility. With the Young Plan successfully adopted and approved in mid-March, the basis for coalition unity was gone, thus setting the stage for the final struggle.

The new government, under Brüning's leadership, was announced on March 30. On the first of April he presented his program, which contained numerous measures of sound finance, to the Reichstag. The Social Democrats offered an immediate motion of no confidence. The government survived this initial crisis with all the parties of Brüning's modest coalition holding firm.

The basic problems were not solved but were in fact aggravated by the change in government, and a second crisis, described in Chapter 10, arose in July. Again it was a question of balancing government finances and government outlays, the principal costs being the support for the eastern estate owners (the *Osthilfe*) and, much more important, the support for the unemployment insurance system. Brüning declared his intention to use, if necessary, the powers of presidential decree to achieve his aims. The Reichstag voted down essential parts of this program, the opposition coming from Social Democrats, Communists, National Socialists, and also at this point, from Hugenberg's Conservatives. The next day Brüning and Hindenburg passed the retrenchment measures by decree, and the Reichstag, two days later, successfully carried a motion to lift the decree, making it null and void. The case for the motion, was made, in large part, by the Social Democrats although, to be sure, the votes of their unnatural allies were necessary for the success of the move. The intent, they said, was "to preserve democracy and the parliamentary system."[10]

Brüning responded by dissolving the Reichstag and ordering new elections for September 1930. These, as we have seen, resulted in a massive increase of National Socialist strength in the Reichstag as the party went from 12 to 107 seats. This meant that no center government was possible and that Brüning had to rely even more on the use of presidential decrees. For the Social Democrats the result meant that they would now have to support these decrees (or more specifically, to refuse aid for efforts to override them). To bring the government down in this new situation would precipitate the ultimate crisis, the one for which there was no evident democratic solution. This entire episode, in short, put them into a position in which they were forced to tolerate the Brüning government.[11] This was the situation until the end of May 1932 when Hindenburg dismissed Brüning and named Papen as chancellor.

Brüning's policies of retrenchment may strike many contemporary readers as curiously inappropriate. But at that time such orthodox classical policies were recommended by the world's leading economic experts. As they saw it, the task was to "reduce the weight of public expenditure on the economy [and thus help] drive down production costs to the level at which production again was profitable."[12] The need, then, was to undertake a ruthless trimming of government expenditures so as to balance the budget and remove the tax burden on firms. The general public, or more specifically, the unemployed, were required to sacrifice until such time as price levels allowed a turnaround. The plan, in short, called for unswerving support of deflationary measures in the midst of a major deflationary crisis.

The opposite policy, that of increased government spending, of consciously planned deficits for the creation of public works programs, was viewed as inflationary, as a policy that would increase the burden on firms, adding to their costs and making it more difficult for them to resume production. The humane public works program, as economic experts saw it, would only aggravate an already very serious crisis. Understandably, this program of inaction (or of retrenchment) could gain little favor among the unemployed or among those faced with that possibility. The policy was most helpful to the Communists who could denounce its author as the Hunger Chancellor. And the National Socialists, too, of course, made use of such "facts" for their political purposes. Not helped by this seemingly necessary policy were the parties supporting it, the Zentrum, the People's party, and the Democrats. Also among the losers was the SPD whose toleration made the continuation of the Brüning government possible.

Most accounts portray this Social Democratic toleration as something forced upon them by circumstances. To do otherwise would have meant defeating the government and bringing on the insoluble crisis. Actually, however, some leading figures in the Social Democratic party were in substantial agreement with the Brüning policies. This included the party's leading financial expert, no less a figure than Rudolf Hilferding. Since 1927, he and Brüning had been the main supporters of an interparty group of financial experts who worked out differences in government proposals before they were brought to the Reichstag. Brüning, it is reported, "trusted Hilferding more than his other economic advisers because [his] views on many key economic issues coincided with his own." Brüning wrote in his memoirs that "with this Socialist I found more understanding of the principles of the capitalist banking system than with the leaders of the great banks."[13]

Hilferding was a moderate among the Social Democrats. Opposed to Germany's war aims, he had, from 1917 to 1922, joined with the Independent Socialists. In their ranks, however, he had argued for support of the "mother party's" (that is, of the SPD's) "cautious economic policy" and had sought to calm the Independent Socialists' ardent advocates of nationalization of industry. The workers, he declared in a speech before the national congress of works committees in October 1920, were "not ready to take over production from the owners and managers of private industry."[14] Upon his return to the SPD (which welcomed him with open arms), he spent much of his time convincing that party's left wing that "the republic and its capitalist economy would work for the workers' benefit."[15] He persevered in this direction, Gates reports, even during the worst months of the depression.

It was not that Hilferding had been converted to liberal orthodoxy; his position, argued at some length, was derived from and consistent with Marxism.[16] His considerable influence within the party's leadership circles effectively immobilized the party's leaders and reinforced them in their support of Brüning and his policies of restraint. One of Hilferding's close associates expressed this position as follows: "I don't believe that we can do very much, nor anything very decisive, from the point of view of economic policy, to overcome the crisis until it has run its course. . . . the crisis with all its destruction of the value of capital, with its changes and shifts of purchasing power, is a means of correction which must necessarily be accepted."[17]

From the trade union movement, from those closer to the suffering, came a demand for an active economic policy. A plan worked out by Wladimir Woytinsky, the chief economist of the Free Trade Union Federation's statistical office, called for a public works program focused on housing and road construction. Launched with much publicity, it was in clear and open opposition to both government and SPD orthodoxy. Hilferding responded by declaring such efforts to be "un-Marxist." But the trade unionists were unmoved by the demand for ideological purity; as Woytinsky put it, "today's capitalism is no longer the capitalism of Adam Smith, but it is just as little the capitalism of Karl Marx."[18] Unmoved by such revisionism, Hilferding mobilized the SPD parliamentary group against the proposal thus denying the trade unionists the leverage they needed for use against the government.

Some evidence of the hold of ideology on the minds of Marxist leaders is provided by the experience of the Socialist Workers party, a group that split from the SPD in 1931 because of the latter's toleration of the Brüning government. On the works program question, it supported the SPD leadership and attacked the trade unions for "wanting to experiment with autarky and inflation." The Communists also opposed the trade union plan for similar reasons.[19]

The only response to the trade union proposal was a very modest proposal by Brüning, a draft of which was sought from the appropriate cabinet members the day after the trade unions opened their campaign. Papen was to prove more responsive to this demand than either the Zentrum or the Social Democrats. As Gates puts it: "The tumultuous public response to unorthodox economic proposals like the trade-union plan convinced Papen that the danger of eroding the purchasing power of the mark through controlled deficit spending was negligible compared to the catastrophic political and economic consequences of sustained deflation and retrenchment."

Gates's own conclusions are also worth citing:

What lessons should be drawn from this? The last parliamentary leaders of the Weimar Republic sacrificed the life-and-death interest of the
workers in jobs to their faith in the self-healing powers of industrial
capitalism. This observation had been made before regarding Brüning's economic policy, but it appears even more important when account is taken of the SPD's real position during the depression. Brüning
and his unofficial socialist supporters did not understand that continuing with deflation was financially unnecessary, nor did they recognize that is was politically suicidal. Both of these failures must weigh
heavily in a final evaluation of the republic's defenders.[20]

There is an additional tragic and ironic fact in all of this. "In economic
policy as in several other key areas," Gates noted, "the Nazis had a
firmer grasp on political reality and were less hindered by ideology from
perceiving pressing economic needs than the political forces opposing
them." Their economic platform for the decisive July 1932 election declared that "only the planned creation of jobs [through public works]
can bring about a change of direction."[21] In this respect, the National
Socialists were the advocates of the program that should have been presented by the Social Democrats.

Brüning's efforts (and those of the SPD's leaders) were aided by the
events of February 10, 1931. At the first meeting of the Reichstag, the
government introduced some measures designed to restrict demagogic
maneuvering in the course of parliamentary debates. When it was recognized that the motion would carry, the National Socialists and the
Conservatives withdrew in protest. Although the Conservatives returned the next day, the absence of the National Socialists made it easier
for the parties of the government, together with the SPD, to carry on
routine business, or, where needed, to sustain presidential decrees.[22]

The National Socialists, of course, did not cease activity in 1931. They
merely shifted their efforts to another sphere of operations, to Prussia,
which contained approximately three-fifths of the nation's population.
That state, it will be remembered, was governed by a Social Democratic-Zentrum coalition under the leadership of the former party's Otto
Braun. This remarkably stable, decade-long alliance came under especially heavy attack from the forces of the right at this point, with the
Social Democrats being denounced as the Marxist enemy and the Zentrum being denounced for its betrayal of both the Catholic faith and its
bourgeois obligations.

In October 1930, Braun had called on another Social Democrat, Carl
Severing, to take over the Prussian Ministry of the Interior which agency,
of course, directed both state and municipal police. Severing accepted

the position and, among his other actions, named another Social Democrat, Albert Grzesinski, to head the Berlin police. It should come as no surprise that both Severing and Grzesinski became the specific objects of heavy attacks. They had the task of dealing with the violence in the streets, both that issuing from the right, notably from the NSDAP's Sturmabteilung, and that issuing from the left, from the Communists. At that point, Braun and Severing were the SPD's highest-level officeholders. Apart from Chancellor Brüning, they had the largest share of legitimate power of any democratic leaders of the republic. For the Social Democrats, the defense of that republic ultimately came to rest with these two men.

The most important activities of the National Socialists in 1931 were directed against this Prussian government. In February of that year, they collected the six million signatures required for an initiative in support of their demand for dissolution of the Prussian legislature. The stage was thus set for a referendum campaign, the vote taking place on August ninth. The campaign was organized by the forces of the national opposition, that is, by the Conservatives and National Socialists. In this effort, however, they were joined by a majority of those in the right liberal German People's party and also, in unnatural alliance, by the Communists. The referendum failed to carry, but the 37 percent vote in favor of the move suggested what was in store for the republic in subsequent elections.[23]

The referendum campaign provided the major occasion for National Socialist propaganda efforts in 1931. Once again, a NSDAP linkage with respectable allies would have helped to legitimate it in the eyes of many members of the presumably responsible upper and upper middle classes. Later, in October of that year, the Harzburg meeting (discussed in the previous chapter) and the subsequent demonstration a week later by the NSDAP would have served the same purpose. In this case, it would also have demonstrated NSDAP organizational superiority over its Conservative allies.

Elections did take place in Prussia on April 24, 1932, immediately following the two rounds of the presidential election. The Communists and National Socialists, with 56 and 132 seats, respectively, had a majority. No government of the center could be formed without the participation (or assent) of at least one of these parties. But that was not their aim. The Social Democrats and the Zentrum continued in office as a caretaker government, no alternative majority being feasible.

On May 25, the Communists introduced a motion of no confidence in the Braun government. Consideration of the motion was interrupted when Wilhelm Pieck, the Communist leader, referred to the National Socialists as a party of murderers. The latter responded with a physical assault on the Communists, thus ending the day's deliberations. A week later, still pressing their motion, the Communists, together with their enemy-ally, the National Socialists, successfully passed their motion of no confidence. The SPD-Zentrum coalition nevertheless continued in office, there being no feasible combination of parties to replace them. This move, however, undermined this last bastion of republican strength; its spell of legitimacy had been broken. The move was to have extremely important consequences.[24]

Shortly before the Prussian election, Brüning had ordered the dissolution of the National Socialist paramilitary organizations, the SA and SS, this being accomplished with a presidential decree under the terms of the constitution's Article 48. The most important consequence for those organizations was that the decree forbade the wearing of uniforms, a point that may seem rather minor to the distant observer. It did hurt those organizations, however, making their meetings and marches illegal, and, in melees, making it difficult to tell friend from foe.

On May 29, Hindenburg asked for Brüning's resignation and the following day, Brüning gave up the office, the first chancellor to have yielded to a presidential (as opposed to a parliamentary) no-confidence decision. Hindenburg was alarmed by the "bolshevism" contained in Brüning's farm resettlement program, having been convinced of this by his Junker neighbors. As a replacement, Hindenburg selected Franz von Papen.[25]

Papen, having worked out the agreement with the National Socialists described in Chapter 10, lifted the ban on the SA and declared an election for July 31. The election campaign was filled with violence, a culmination being reached on Sunday, the seventeenth of July, when NSDAP formations marched through the streets of Altona, a largely working-class community lying just to the west of Hamburg. The Communists fired on the marchers from windows and rooftops, and the NSDAP returned the fire. The police, accompanying the march and caught in between, did what they could to contain things but also, in the end, were counted among the victims. Nearly a score were killed, and many more of course were injured.

Papen used this event as the pretext to depose the Braun government. Once again using presidential decree powers, he removed the leaders of that government and replaced them with his own appointees. This was a key moment in Hitler's progress to power, in that the republican parties, most notably the SPD and the Zentrum, were being removed from their last major positions of power. In all of the what-should-have-been-done discussions that came after 1933, this event figures prominently. The republicans, specifically Braun and Severing, it is said, should have held onto their offices, even if it meant precipitating civil war. But as it happened, they acceded to their removal, the only step undertaken being a legal action challenging the constitutionality of Papen's move. The Supreme Court judgment, rendered some months later, questioned the legality of Papen's move but left the new arrangement unchanged.

Braun was exhausted by the years of struggle and, understandably, overwhelmed by the awesome thought of a civil war. He was much depressed by the vote of no confidence; that loss, with its consequent undermining of his legitimacy, made it much more difficult to oppose Papen's move. The Communists, who had initiated his defeat, now proposed the formation of a common front but, again understandably, that offer met with little enthusiasm. Severing, who has been described as a capable and intelligent leader, was also a humane and, it is said, a gentle man. The thought of civil war distressed him, and he too opted to accept the new situation, only making the challenge through the courts.

The situation was markedly different from that of the Kapp *Putsch* of March 1920. At that time, the duly elected national government had been challenged by a band of usurpers. And in that circumstance it was easy for the SPD leaders to call a general strike. At that time too, it seemed likely that, apart from the extreme right, most of the population would have sided with the authorities against the insurgents. Given that sense, it was obviously much easier for the SPD leaders of 1920 to defend their position. In 1932, the authority of the SPD leaders in Prussia had been challenged and their legitimacy denied. And a higher-level government, in a move bearing at least a semblance of legality, had removed the defeated government.[26]

For some time there had been a general feeling of hopelessness within the highest party circles. One close observer, commenting on the response of the SPD Reichstag faction to the dismissal of Brüning, reported that "there was nothing to be resolved for we had nothing more to say." The lack of direction was accentuated by the behavior of the top leaders of the party, particularly by the responses of those still in positions of power. Braun went on "sick leave" on the sixth of June, less than a week after Papen's accession; it was, as he put it, with the "firm intention, never again to return to that office." Braun kept his distance from government affairs in the following weeks and even on the twentieth of July, although now back at his home in Berlin-Zehlendorf, made "no serious attempt to intervene in the unfolding events."[27]

Thus, at this crucial point, the SPD was without active leaders. Overwhelmed by the events, the leaders of the party chose to wait and watch. There was much discussion, then and later, about the willingness of the SPD membership and of the trade unions, those at the grass roots, to undertake action in defense of the republic, the claim being that they were only awaiting word from their leaders. It is difficult, of course, to make any definitive assessment of the leadership's judgments. It should be kept in mind, however, that in all likelihood they would have had the following forces arrayed against them: the governments of the Reich, of Prussia, and of Bavaria; all influential forces of the political right and of the right center together with all of their affiliated newspapers; the police forces of most states and localities; and finally, the Reichswehr. In a pure left–right struggle, it seems likely that the Zentrum, especially under the Kaas leadership, would have also joined with the right. And that would have left the SPD with a single and rather doubtful ally, the Communist party. Under those circumstances, it is easy to understand the hopelessness felt by the SPD leaders.

July 1932 was their last opportunity for any kind of meaningful struggle, that is, for one with even a slim chance of success. After that date, deprived of all positions of power, they could only try to hold together the pieces of a rapidly disintegrating organization.[28]

Severing later gave an unqualified defense of his decision not to actively oppose Papen's move against the Prussian government. But at the last conference of the party, on June 19, 1933, only a few days before the National Socialists' dissolution order, he expressed himself differently: "It is gruesome, when I think of it today, what blood I thought had to be avoided in July 1932. . . . I could not justify what, in my opinion, would have been needlessly spent blood of our followers. Now I have to tell you, nothing was avoided thereby. Now it will be an ocean of blood and tears. From this enemy no mercy is to be expected. I cannot do much more. But you have to do what your conscience dictates. It is worth the effort."[29]

Despite some signs of willingness at the grass roots, the leadership of the party, in the months following the Prussian takeover, refused all active intervention. Each subsequent event, most of these involving defeats, led them to ever more cautious, more defensive positions. On the thirtieth of January, there were, it is said, spontaneous mass demonstrations by workers in numerous cities.[30] The SPD and trade union leaders met the following day to discuss possible reactions. Many left that discussion with the clear impression that the top leadership had decided to undertake an active coordinated intervention. The awaited signal, however, never came.

The Reichstag fire provided the occasion for a new presidential decree, this "for the protection of people and state." It set aside civil liberties and thus allowed the National Socialists an even freer hand in the last days before the March election. The SPD maintained some freedom of action in the as yet largely untouched southern states. But in the days following the election, they all fell, Hesse on the sixth, Baden and

Württemberg on the eighth. On the ninth of March, the NSDAP took over in Bavaria.

At this point, the SPD leaders, realistically enough, saw the situation as being much worse than on July 20. The chances of success in an armed uprising were smaller than ever, even though one SPD leader, Paul Löbe, reported widespread support among the party followers for a policy of active resistance. Most leaders, however, were "convinced of the uselessness of the bloodbath that would certainly follow."[31]

Their action was inhibited by the realities of power (the Prussian police was under Goering's direction, the army was likely to come down against them) and by the appearances, namely, that Hitler had come to power through "legal" means. Their action was further inhibited by their own reading of the situation as an "episode" in the history of German democracy. At worst, they anticipated a repetition of the Anti-Socialist Law experience, that being the period from 1878 to 1890 when Bismarck, largely without success, attempted to repress the party. Some SPD people even made use of a key slogan from that earlier period— "Workers! Don't let yourselves be provoked!" The workers, it was said in another guiding formula, would be neither "provoked nor intimidated." Grzesinski made much use of the analogy, his standard speech in the March election campaign declaring that "we dealt with Bismarck and Wilhelm; we will also be able to deal with today's reaction."

The practical effect of this definition of the situation was a policy of watchful waiting. One leader assured his listeners that "reaction has played out its last card." The counsel that followed, however, was merely that the workers' organizations should not lose their nerve. A key policy statement appeared under the heading, *Bereit sein ist alles!* (Readiness is everything!).[32]

The one moment of opposition, even that largely symbolic, came on March 23, when the parties of the Reichstag were called upon to support the NSDAP's Enabling Act. Otto Wels spoke against the measure on behalf of the party. Hitler, in a fury, responded by telling them: "I do not want your votes . . . Germany will be free, but not through you. Do not mistake us for bourgeois. The star of Germany is in the ascendent, yours is about to disappear, you death-knell has sounded."[33] With the Communists already a proscribed party, the SPD's votes were the only ones cast in opposition to this grant of dictatorial powers.

From that point on, the processes of internal dissolution seen among the bourgeois parties also appeared in the Social Democratic ranks. Of prime importance was a loss of leaders. Braun left the country, in a move similar to Kaas's, that is, without consulting any others in his party. A resolution of the party's executive committee recommended that others—Philipp Scheidemann, Wilhelm Dittmann, Arthur Crispien, Rudolf Breitscheid, and Hilferding—should also leave, this out of fear for their lives. A related consideration expressed at that time was to avoid the creation of "unnecessary martyrs," a development that would make difficult the reinstitution of a constitutional regime (hope, it is said, springs eternal). Grzesinski also left the country. The principal result of these losses was that it became nearly impossible for the party to carry on any coordinated activity.

The terror and threats directed against members at the base of the party led to massive defections. Many members of the party and of the republican defense organization, the Reichsbanner, left to join the rightist paramilitary organization, the Stahlhelm. Because of the then active hostilities existing between Stahlhelm and SA, they had hoped to find both protection there and some opportunity to continue the struggle. It was this evident dissolution process that faced the remaining leaders who met at the end of April. Their decision at that point was to continue the previously determined course and to make use of the "given legal possibilities."[34]

Signs of defection also appeared within the trade unions. After the March fifth election, the leading union newspaper spoke of the need for the unions, now more than ever, to work "with their own strength alone." On the tenth of March, the union's executive sent a message to Hindenburg, addressing him as "the German leader [who] in his person combined the traditions of the old and the values of the new Germany," a letter that, as Matthias puts it, amounted to de facto recognition of that new regime. On the twentieth, the executive produced a statement that, again in Matthias's words, "amounted to an assurance of loyalty." The key sentence in this declaration indicated that the social tasks of the unions must be fulfilled "no matter what the kind of state regime." The unions were "an indispensable part of the social order itself" and "in the course of their history, for natural reasons, [had become] more and more interwoven with the state itself." Despite ever more discouraging responses from the National Socialists, the union leaders continued their "policy of ingratiation." In April, for example, they referred to their "national educational work." These efforts continued up to the Day of Labor, the National Socialists' reworking of the traditional May Day festival. On the following day, the trade union offices were occupied by the SA and the leaders arrested.[35]

On the fourth of May, the newly elected SPD party executive met to consider, among other things, its response to the dissolution of the trade unions. Its decision was to send some immediately threatened members into exile. On the tenth, the National Socialists confiscated the party treasury. At that point a majority of the party's executive committee was already in exile. On the sixteenth and seventeenth the parliamentary group met, less than half of its members being present, and resolved once again to pursue its course of "silent acquiescence." There was little more it could do. On June 22, the National Socialists forbade all further party activity.

Matthias's essay ends with a discussion of the reasons for the SPD inactivity. Analyzing the SPD's approach to problems, he offers six lines of explanation.[36]

First is what he characterizes as its habit of institutionalized thinking within the terms of the traditional party apparatus and its decade-long tested forms of struggle: the party organization was no longer viewed as a means to an end but was treated as an end in itself. Those living within this self-contained community developed a distorted view of their actual situation. They exaggerated their own strength and underestimated the threat facing them. Their faith in their organizational strength led them to adopt a very conservative policy, that is, to uphold the organization at all costs. This meant that they avoided any risk-laden political initiatives. The preferred actions were the traditional ones, use of the ballot, negotiations within the shops, mass meetings, or, something to be considered in the extreme case, the passive strike, as in 1920.

The party was also characterized by institutionalized thinking within the terms of parliamentarianism and the rule of law: the Social Democrats did not fully comprehend the change that was taking place under the National Socialists. At worst they imagined some kind of return to the authoritarian state they had faced under the kaiser. The sense that somehow or other they would be able to continue operation, even if under unfavorable circumstances, was well entrenched in their thinking.

For some decades the party had been built upon clear, fixed, and accepted notions of hierarchy, producing a bias in favor of hierarchical thinking. There was, so it was argued, a need to contain or harness spontaneous moves from below, ones that might damage or threaten the entire movement. There was accordingly, a recognition of the "need" for everyone to submit to the directives coming from the party's leaders. This obligation was at the heart of the party's well-known discipline. At the key moments, on July 20, 1932, and on January 30, 1933, some followers at least were expecting a call for action. When none came, there was neither training nor practice to allow for independent initiatives from below.

What Matthias calls "evolutionary thought"—the belief in the ultimate victory of socialism—justified passivity in the face of the developing catastrophe. One's certain theoretical knowledge promised the ultimate destruction of reaction. What was happening at the moment, therefore, was at most a temporary setback. This "knowledge" was rooted in both socialist theory and socialist experience, the reference here being to the continuous growth of working-class organizations in the decades prior to World War I. With such a heritage, it was easy to sustain a belief in one's inevitability and to assume the indestructibility of the movement. These evolutionary beliefs, Matthias argues, mixed "pre-Marxian, humanitarian progressive beliefs with a pseudoscientific social Darwinism and superficially assimilated elements of the Marxian teaching and the Marxian vocabulary into a synthesis."[37] Out of this mixture came a pseudorevolutionary set of ideas, declared to be Marxism by both supporters and opponents of the party. It was a system of beliefs that left the realization of socialism to the workings of some vaguely defined "conditions."

Humanitarian thought and concern were widely disseminated throughout the Social Democratic movement. A general pacifist outlook characterized Social Democracy before the war, it being closely linked to the just-discussed evolutionary belief system. Matthias sees this as a product of the Enlightenment, the SPD organization containing and preserving the optimistic beliefs of the eighteenth century. This too led many members, leaders and followers alike, to operate with an unrealistic belief in reason and to lack understanding of the irrational appeals used by their opponents. In the midst of this struggle they continued to stress, as an argument in the conflict, their "intellectual superiority" (geistiger Überlegenheit—the phrase is from Karl Kautsky).

Finally, Matthias offers thinking by analogy: "Social Democratic thought," he says, "to which impulsive resolution and spontaneous action were foreign, is continuously in search of the historical analogy, of the orientation point in the past."[38] The warning example of the Russian revolution strongly influenced the reaction of SPD leaders in 1918-1919. On July 20, 1932, SPD and trade union leaders were obsessed by the example of the Kapp Putsch, the lesson here being that their situation was now just the opposite of 1920. And after January 30, 1933, their experience with Bismarck provided the governing analogy. This definition of the situation as being "like" another, meant that they did not see the events for what they were.

One may usefully contrast the SPD organizational style as described by Matthias with that of the NSDAP. Unhindered by ideology, by a sacred heritage, this party had hard-headed, innovative, and pragmatic leaders available at all levels. The grass roots leaders were able to choose initiatives with a degree of freedom unknown in the SPD. These characteristics are discussed at greater length in the following chapter.

In still another way ideology proved costly to the SPD (and ultimately to Germany and the entire world). The party had a revolutionary and socialist heritage. By the time of Weimar, however, it was clear to any astute observer that the party was neither revolutionary nor socialist. In practice, it was little more threatening to the established order than any conventional left liberal party. It tended to favor the workers (unlike the right liberal or laissez faire parties) and accordingly sponsored various welfare state measures. But that was the extent of its radicalism. In the end phase of the republic, as we have seen, most of its political effort was devoted to maintaining some of the elements of this welfare apparatus. It certainly was not undertaking any moves to extend that apparatus nor for that matter was it aiming to socialize any part of the economy. The leaders of the party, many of them, had given up on socialism, seeing it as too complicated, too costly, as not providing the utopia once anticipated or, for some, as patently unrealistic.

But, despite the change in orientation, the party had not changed the visible signs and still made obeisance to the time-honored goals of socialism. There was a division between the right and the left wings of the party on this issue. It was one area in which submission to the leaders was not unqualified. Here, too, the policy of the leaders was to wait, which is to say, the party appearance and the party reality were never reconciled. That contradiction had both internal and external sources. There was, on the one hand, a need to mollify the party's own left wing and, on the other, a need to maintain a determined front vis-à-vis the Communists.

That "contradiction" meant even greater problems on the right flank. It made it easy for conservative forces to continue to denounce the Social Democrats as Marxists. It made it easier for the conservatives to generate and sustain their final campaign in 1929 and 1930 against the "Marxist" enemy, simultaneously laying pressure on the Zentrum in an effort to break up what remained of the Weimar coalition. In states and local communities therefore, this heritage allowed a division of the republican forces since the SPD was easily defined as an unacceptable coalition partner. And that in turn meant that center and right parties formed coalitions with the National Socialists while the SPD was forced to go it alone.

In summary, then, the SPD paid a heavy price for its maintenance of an inappropriate—or perhaps mistaken—tradition. It made the Social Democrats vulnerable to demagogic attacks; it reduced their coalition possibilities; and various ideological elements of that tradition lessened their ability to see events correctly and thus reduced their freedom to respond.

That said, however, it must also be noted that the Social Democratic party was the only major party actively defending the republic. By mid-1932, the two liberal parties were already negligible forces on the political scene. The Zentrum, the only other intact democratic party, did not offer even a passive defense. There was no discussion within the Zentrum similar to that occurring within the SPD following Papen's over-throw of the Braun government. And as for the Communists, as we shall see, they were supremely indifferent to the fate of the republic. In fact, some Communist spokesmen welcomed the coming of the National Socialist regime—it would help to clarify the struggle.

THE COMMUNIST PARTY

One cannot appreciate the role of the Communists in the struggles of 1930-1933 without a consideration of their previous history. There was a widespread belief, as the economic crisis broke in 1930, that the Kommunistische Partei Deutschlands, the most powerful Communist party in Europe, would be the major beneficiary. This expectation was held by the Communists themselves, by the Social Democrats, and by most observers on the center and the right of the political spectrum. But, as we have noted, that expectation was not fulfilled. One reason for this failure is to be found in their previous history, much of which would still have been very much present in people's minds.

The party had its origins within the left wing of the Social Democratic party. A struggle had been developing within the party since roughly the turn of the century over questions of imperialism, party organization, and party tactics.[39] This struggle reached its climax during World War I when the party's policy of cooperation and support for the war was confronted by the demand for opposition and struggle. The result, in 1917, was the division of the party. The Majority Socialists continued with their course of cooperation while the Independent Socialists moved for fundamental opposition to the war effort and a thoroughgoing democratization of the nation. The USPD, although frequently referred to simply as "the left," actually was a rather broad coalition of forces containing most of the SPD's left wing and, at the same time, reaching across the spectrum to include members of the reformist or revisionist wing of the party, the most notable of these being Hilferding and Eduard Bernstein, the leading revisionist. One segment of the left, the Spartakus group, remained with the Independents until late in 1918 just because of this coalitional character; it allowed the group contact and influence with the larger but more moderate body.[40]

As of November 11, 1918, the position of the Independents was dramatically changed; its two major tasks, ending the war and founding the republic, had been achieved. As a result, the compelling basis of the coalition was much weakened. The breakup of the party began toward the end of December when the Spartakus group held a convention that was intended to remove it from the Independent Socialist ranks. This was the founding of the Kommunistische Partei, the convention taking place from December 30 to January 1. This move was not without its opposition. As a faction of a faction, it was clearly going to be a minuscule operation. And, some of the more capable leaders, Rosa Luxemburg among them, recognized the serious losses. The group would lose its opportunity to influence the wider group of Independents; the new party would also be less restrained in its behavior, not having to consider the reaction of the Independents. The more capable leaders also recognized that they would have less control over these exuberant revolutionaries once they became a separate and autonomous party.[41]

Those fears were quickly realized when, four days later, on Sunday the fifth of January, a majority of the party's executive committee decided in favor of a revolution, to begin the very next day. Thus began the January events of 1919, these being largely concentrated in Berlin. Some accounts, particularly those of left historians and commentators, lead one to believe that the revolutionary masses all but overwhelmed the largely defenseless government of the Majority Social Democrats; it was only the entry of the newly formed Freikorps that, ruthlessly and with much bloodshed, put down the rising. In the aftermath, two of the KPD leaders, Karl Liebknecht and Luxemburg, after having been taken prisoner, were killed by their Freikorps captors.

What in fact happened was that *two* working-class masses were present in the city on the first days of the week; the larger one, some hundreds of thousands strong, occupied the Wilhelmstrasse thus protecting the government buildings from a Spartakus-KPD attack. Liebknecht's forces were not about to open fire on workers. There was scattered fighting throughout the city, but in the end, the forces available to the government had achieved the edge, this already being evident by Wednesday of that week. The Freikorps first entered the city on Friday. The rest of the history as recounted in the previous paragraph is accurate in all details.[42]

This revolutionary attempt, it will be noted, preceded by a week the first national election of the new regime, the election of the Constituent Assembly. The uprising was intended, in part, to thwart that effort. A democratically elected body, of course, would be a very conservative one relative to the events present on the national scene at that moment. It would also have considerable legitimacy. The alternative, that favored by the KPD and other left forces, was government by Workers and Soldiers' Councils (or *Räte*, or soviets). Being smaller and more diffuse bodies, they could be more easily directed by the KPD's militants than could the entire electorate.

Firm in the belief that they were in the midst of a revolutionary period, that the Russian achievement was merely the first in a series of risings destined to sweep Europe, and also just as firmly convinced of

Germany's primacy in these revolutionary events, the KPD activists declared a general strike in March of 1919. Here the Freikorps was the decisive factor; the bloodshed was much greater (and less discriminate) than in the earlier rising.[43]

In Munich, the capital city of Bavaria and at that point the third largest city of the Reich, the November revolution brought in a coalition government consisting of Majority Socialists, Independent Socialists, and the Farmers' League (Bauern Bund, an anticlerical farmers' party). The government was headed by Kurt Eisner, leader of the Independents, a journalist by profession, and a one-time revisionist. The state elections in Bavaria, on January 12, 1919, however, dealt the Independents an overwhelming defeat. They took only 3 of 180 seats. Eisner was obligated, at least according to the new democratic rules of the game, to resign his position. He nevertheless held onto the office until well into the following month. Then on the twenty-first, while en route to the legislature to hand in his resignation, he was assassinated. After some further episodes of violence, a new coalition was formed, this made up of Majority and Independent Socialists and led by Johannes Hoffmann, a member of the left wing of the former party.

This government lasted until mid-April when a group of bohemian intellectuals led by Gustav Landauer, a writer and anarchist, and Ernst Toller, a young poet and playwright, proclaimed the Bavarian Soviet Republic. Hoffmann and his government retired from Munich and set up their government in Bamberg. The Communists were initially very hesitant about joining this effort. A counterthrust in favor of the Hoffmann government, however, led to them to intervene and to share power with the bohemians. This brought in some tough-minded Communists, Eugen Leviné and Max Levien being the most noted of them. Leviné has been described as a man "of supreme energy and courage." At the same time, "his cold-blooded indifference to human life, which he expressed in speeches, was not the way to win a wavering population over to the soviet side." His "professional revolutionaries" from Russia were completely unfamiliar with the local conditions, and his German assistants were "wholly incompetent." The Freikorps "liberated" the city on May 1, 1919, the cost in this case being 600 lives, mostly those of workers.[44]

The remaining months of 1919 were relatively quiet ones for the party. Declared illegal after the March events and having suffered two major defeats (three if Munich is included), its efforts were given over to a reconsideration of tactics and to internal reorganization. At a secret meeting in Frankfurt in August of that year, a more moderate course was laid out (one that included participation in elections). This was the work of Paul Levi and was aimed at driving the "ultraleft" forces out of the party. Franz Borkenau refers to this group simply as the "crazy fringe." The new direction was confirmed at a second secret meeting in Heidelberg in October 1919, with only the moderate majority being represented.[45] But before these internal developments could run their course, another episode of violence intervened.

On March 12, 1920, rebelling Freikorps units marched on Berlin. Informed that it could not depend on the "loyal" army units (General von Seeckt's famous line was: "The Reichswehr does not fire on the Reichswehr"), the government obviously had to abandon the city. At the same time, however, President Ebert and Defense Minister Gustav Noske, in the name of the Social Democratic party, issued a call for a general strike. It was an ironic reversal in that the conservative SPD leadership had always been less than enthusiastic about such actions. Nevertheless, as Halperin puts it, by late afternoon of March 14, 1920, "the greatest strike the world had ever seen was a reality. The economic life of the country came to a standstill."[46]

The initial KPD reaction was to oppose this effort to defend the republic. The central committee declaration of March 13 stated: "The proletariat will not lift a finger for the democratic republic." And the following day, in the party's newspaper, it was said that the working class was "not ready for action." It would take action only "when the face of the military dictatorship has revealed itself." The very next day, on the fifteenth, the party reversed its position and issued the following call: "For the general strike! Down with the military dictatorship! Down with the bourgeois democracy! All power to the workers' councils! The Communists are against the Ebert-Noske-Bauer government."[47]

Recognizing the hopelessness of his situation, Kapp resigned on the seventeenth. Things were not, however, to return to the status quo ante since a wide range of consequences flowed from the Kapp events. The trade unions had made a series of nine demands as their price for saving the republic. They succeeded in only one of these, the removal of Noske. Most workers who hoped to be paid for their time off while defending the regime were destined to be disappointed.[48]

In some respects, the forces of the right were the gainers. The purpose of the January 1919 election was to select a constitutional, not a legislative assembly. The constitution had been written and adopted, and yet that assembly continued to function; among other things, it named Ebert as president of the republic and enacted legislation. The parties of the right had argued the necessity of new elections, both for legal reasons and because the original assembly no longer reflected the current state of public opinion. In the midst of the Kapp venture, the parties of the Weimar coalition agreed to set an early date to elect a legislature.

In Bavaria, General Arnold von Möhl, commander of the armed forces in the Munich area, announced at the outset of the *Putsch* that he could not guarantee the safety of the government unless he was given full political authority. Hoffmann urged rejection of the ultimatum. He did not receive the backing of his cabinet, who instead urged far-reaching concessions. Hoffmann chose rather to resign. The Bavarian legislature then chose Gustav von Kahr, who was supported by the clerical and conservative Bavarian People's party, as Hoffman's successor. The Social Democrats, believing that Kahr was in league with Möhl, refused an invitation to participate in the new government. The Kapp *Putsch* thus led to the removal of the Social Democrats from government in Bavaria and their replacement by conservative forces.

Noske, facing opposition from the trade unions and from within his own party, submitted his resignation. The *Putsch* attempt, quite apart from other Freikorps activities, was no commendation of his management of the defense ministry. After some temporizing, Ebert reluctantly accepted the resignation. The entire Bauer Government resigned a few days later, and Hermann Müller formed the new government, again with the three parties of the Weimar coalition. At the same time, the government of Prussia was reorganized with Otto Braun coming in as premier and Carl Severing as minister of interior.

The most serious immediate consequences were those stemming from the Communist involvement in the struggle. They followed through on their announced statement of purpose and took power in several Ruhr cities, in Essen, Düsseldorf, Mühlheim, Elberfeld, and Oberhausen. In the process they also organized a Red Army. The response of the government by this time could not have occasioned much surprise. Units of the Reichswehr, now under the direction of the new defense minister, Otto Gessler, a member of the Democratic party, were sent into the Ruhr, and, once again, that meant the deaths of many workers, insurgents and innocents alike.[49]

Such results must have discredited both Communists and Social Democrats. It seems likely that most workers would have opposed the Communists' action. Most would have opposed the manifest aim, toppling the regime, and most would have recognized the nearly automatic correlate, the sending in of Reichswehr and Freikorps units. But those same workers would have been unable to stop the Communist initiatives. It also seems likely that those same workers would have opposed the ruthless activities of the army and Freikorps, much of the blame for this response falling on the Social Democrats. For most workers, for their wives and their children, it must have seemed as if there was no way out. They were faced with two left parties, both claiming to represent their interests. The policies of both parties, however, had deadly implications for them. For those whose basic loyalties were on the left, the choice of party was thus subject to considerable strain or ambiguity. It is this strain, perhaps, that accounts for the vast swings, involving some millions of voters, that appeared in the following years.

Matters were further complicated by the resolution of the *Putsch* attempt. Although it had been stated publicly that there would be no negotiations, arrangements were in fact made with the conspirators, specifically to guarantee many of them immunity from subsequent prosecution. Even after five days of the general strike, the putschists were not completely powerless. They still had the rebellious military units at their disposal, and, had they so chosen, they could have added a few thousand deaths to their other accomplishments. For the members of the government, a guarantee seemed a small price to pay for a quick resolution of the affair.

But the ultimate price was much larger. The Kapp putschists got off while the insurgents of the left received full punishment, including that dealt out by the military and the official sentences dealt out by the courts. The asymmetry of the result was very striking. This unequal justice was widely used by the left to attack Social Democratic loyalties and intentions. Reactionary prosecuting attorneys and judges were playing favorites, and the immobility of the Social Democrats in the face of such facts, their refusal to carry out a thoroughgoing reform conclusively demonstrated their complicity with the bourgeoisie and the old regime. For many persons, including those of liberal as well as those of left persuasions, it was one more reason for backing away from the parties of the Weimar coalition.[50]

It was, understandably, rather difficult for the parties of the Weimar coalition to argue their case. That would have involved going before the public to state the, in part, hypothetical case: for practical reasons (to save some thousands of lives), it had been necessary to give special favor to the rightist enemies of the republic.

Another consequence of the *Putsch*, as already noted, was the displacement of the Social Democrats in Bavaria. Kahr's new conservative government embarked on a notably independent course, refusing to follow direct orders from Berlin to dissolve Freikorps units and rightist paramilitary organizations. The refusal was justified by reference to Bavaria's previous history, specifically its experience with the revolutionary governments in Munich. It was argued that the local police forces could not deal with such risings, hence the need for maintaining these units. It was this support and protection that made Bavaria a haven for such forces in the years to come. Kahr and his associates, not too surprisingly, had close relations with Hitler and his party and were, to say

the least, very much compromised by Hitler's *Putsch* attempt in November 1923.[51]

In the June 1920 election, the first national legislative election of the
regime, the most striking development for purposes of the immediate
discussion was the sharp decline of the SPD vote. It fell from 37.9 percent in January 1919 to 21.7 percent some eighteen months later. The
move was not to the Communists; they acquired only 2.1 percent of
the total vote.[52] The push rather, was to the third leftist option, to the
one party not directly involved in the intervening episodes of bloodshed, namely, the Independent Socialists. The other major result of this
election, it will be remembered, was a resurgence of the rightist forces,
both the Conservatives and the right liberal German People's party picking
up considerable strength.

The Independent Socialists again refused to participate in government. The Social Democrats had had enough of governing, for the moment at least, and they refused to continue. The result was the first of
a series of bourgeois governments, this one under the direction of Kon-
stantin Fehrenbach, a member of the Zentrum. Although not directly
participating, the Social Democrats nevertheless gave this government
its support. Not too surprisingly, this government paid no attention to
the nine demands granted the trade unions as part of the Kapp settlement.

The Communists at this point, mid-year 1920, were a small and largely
discredited sect. But some efforts were already in motion that were
destined to make them a mass party by the end of the year.

The Independent Socialists, because of the events described above,
had come to be a sizable party. In the June 1920 election they nearly
equaled the Majority Social Democrats in popular votes. They had, as
was reported in their October 1920 party meeting, 893,923 members,
fifty-five daily newspapers, and eighty-one Reichstag delegates. They
were the dominant influence in the state governments of Saxony, Thuringia, and Brunswick. They also had considerable influence in the unions,
particularly among the metalworkers.

Because the party lacked clear direction or purpose, it became the
object of a struggle between factions anxious to move it either to the
right (to reunite it with the Majority Social Democrats) or to the left
(to join the Communist International). A decision had already been
reached at the Leipzig party meeting, late in 1919, to begin negotiations
with Moscow on the latter question, and a delegation sent there in June
1920 acceded to Lenin's "twenty-one conditions." A special party meeting was called for October that year, and by a vote of 237 to 156, it
was decided to join the Communist International. Zinoviev, the Comintern emissary, spoke for four hours at the meeting. But Flechtheim

attributes the result to prior organization and effort by the left wing of the Independents who, months earlier, had joined with members of the Communist party to work for this goal.

The end result was not a complete victory for the left; it involved instead a division of the prize. The left wing of the party joined with the KPD to form the United Communist party (VKPD) in December of 1920. But many of those in the party *Apparat*, most of the Reichstag members, and the most important newspapers remained with the minority, most of them later rejoining the SPD. Flechtheim estimates that 900,000 members divided into three more or less equal groups, one third going to the Communists, one third remaining with the USPD, and the other third becoming politically indifferent. Despite the losses, however, the Communists had become a mass party with hundreds of thousands of members, dozens of newspapers, and numerous positions in the trade unions. They were also a factor in national and state parliaments. It should be noted that the victory was gained through an organizational coup rather than through grass-roots campaigning. The vote in the Reichstag election of June indicated the party's very modest popular appeal.[53]

A leadership change took place shortly after the achievement of this broad base, a change that ultimately was to cost the party a large part of its recent gains. Under Paul Levi's direction the party had followed a moderate course, one that aimed to avoid outbreaks of "infantile leftism" (that is, senseless and unplanned uprisings). Levi had addressed an open letter to the SPD, the USPD, and the trade unions, offering a minimal program upon which they could all agree. The SPD leadership refused the offer, but, according to Flechtheim, much sentiment in favor of this plan was found in SPD local organizations. Some complicated internal struggles developed in the Communist leadership circles at this time. Levi opposed some directives of the International. The KPD's left wing in turn opposed Levi's course and denounced him as a "conciliator" (*Versöhnler*), his successes in Germany being "opportunist" and not revolutionary. Defeated in the February 1921 meeting of the party's central committee, Levi and his group withdrew. The leadership of the party was then turned over to its left or Soviet faction under Heinrich Brandler. The accession of Brandler meant a sharp deterioration in the quality of its leadership.

The party was visited by three Comintern representatives in early March 1921, who argued that the time was ripe for another revolutionary attempt. The members of the party's central committee, well aware of the inadequacy of that premise, nevertheless launched an effort that came to be known as the March action.[54] Lacking any realistic basis whatsoever and, in addition, lacking any serious planning, this revolution was an unqualified disaster. The results, once again, were highly predictable; heavy use of police and Reichswehr units and a considerable loss of life. Recognizing that the workers were not rising on their own or even at the request of the party, some leaders, including the Comintern representatives, resorted to provocative measures to stimulate the rising. These efforts gained considerable publicity in the aftermath of the struggle.[55]

The party was now banned throughout the Reich. Over half of the members gained in the last months of 1920 were lost in the first months of 1921. Not unexpectedly, there was considerable discussion of this action within the party and, ultimately, at a Comintern meeting in Moscow. And, not too surprisingly, the party's course was changed once again, to one of strict defensive tactics, that is, to Levi's original course.

These few paragraphs can hardly do justice to an event of such complexity. A key omission here (and in most such descriptions) is the view from the grass roots. Some sense of how the workers saw and experienced the events may be gained from one of Angress's footnotes. The Communists had used unemployed workers as shock troops—in Hamburg, for example, they were used to invade and shut down the shipbuilding yards. This use of the unemployed, Angress reports,

was Communist practice everywhere throughout the March risings. Factories which continued to work after a general strike had been called were frequently attacked by Communist-led mobs of unemployed and strikers, in an effort to dislodge those who were unwilling to join the walkout. The ensuing pitched battles heightened the state of confusion but did not substantially further Communist objectives. In some cases the owners closed down the plants, thereby creating more unemployed. Those who lost their jobs in this way harbored no tender feelings for the Communists who were responsible for their misfortune. More often, however, the employers refused to shut down, and with their employees defended the premises against assaults from the outside. They also used the disturbances to discharge workers who were suspected of being Communists or Communist sympathizers. In such a case the party was deprived of the opportunity to agitate from within the factory. Finally, the assault troops of unemployed were easily demoralized, after they were beaten up by the defenders of the plants, and cursed the Communists for having led them into trouble.[56]

Thrown onto the defensive (and directed to that policy by the Comintern), the Communists devoted the rest of 1921 and most of 1922 to repair work, husbanding their strength, and now, following the original

Levi tactic, working for the establishment of a united front with other working-class organizations.

The French occupation of the Ruhr, begun in January of 1923 changed all this. The government announced a policy of passive resistance, and, along with ardent nationalists, the Communists joined in the effort. To pay the striking workers, the government manufactured currency, thus turning a modest inflation into the runaway variety that figures so prominently in the history books. The resultant strains, for workers and middle classes alike, led to some radicalization. This was reflected by a modest increase in the number of KPD members and a more sizable increase of support in state elections.[57]

As a part of its united-front strategy, the KPD attempted to broaden its appeal. Karl Radek suprised many with his very favorable assessment of Albert Leo Schlageter, a Freikorps fighter who was captured and executed by the French in the course of the Ruhr struggles. Ruth Fischer made appeals to nationalist students, among other things making liberal use of anti-Semitism. It was a period of "national bolshevism."[58]

The party's position was a complicated one, not the least of the reasons being the "foreign" demands on it. Domestically, it was obliged to remain on the defensive and to achieve a united front. But it was also a revolutionary party; cooperation in a united front with the Social Democrats, that is, with the "opportunists" and "reformists," would undermine its reason for existence. Thus the policy involved moving simultaneously in two contrary directions. As Angress puts it, the party "could not afford to, and never did, conduct this [united-front] policy in good faith."[59]

Given its basic revolutionary commitment (and given the same outlook on the part of the Comintern members), it will come as no surprise that sentiment once again developed for a change of direction. Members of the Comintern saw an opportunity in the catastrophic inflation. Sensing rising unrest on the part of the workers, they again concluded that the time was ripe. They had the support of the party's left wing in this reading of the situation and managed to convince Brandler, against his better judgment, that it was a correct reading. And accordingly a general uprising was agreed upon, and plans were laid for its execution.[60]

The heart of the plan involved the state of Saxony. There, the left wing of the SPD was in power, and, to achieve its revolutionary aim, the KPD, for the first time in the Weimar regime, had joined in the government. The initial aim was to take the Ministry of the Interior (that is, the police). The Saxon government was soon in open rebellion against Berlin, and the national authorities, accordingly, deposed the Saxony regime, acting under the provisions of the Weimar constitution's Article 48. The Communists were thus forced to revise their planned uprising and with their Social Democratic allies in Saxony, called for a general strike. The Social Democrats, however, refused to participate and, as a result, the uprising in this bastion of the left was called off.

Less than forty-eight hours later, however, KPD units in Hamburg launched a revolutionary effort there, taking over several police stations. Lacking any significant working-class support, the uprising was quickly put down. This episode has provided something of a puzzle for subsequent commentators. The KPD histories offer a failure-of-communication theory, an emissary having left the central committee (*Zentrale*) meeting in Dresden prior to the decision to call it all off. A second emissary failed to overtake the first, and thus the effort, mistakenly, went ahead as planned. Angress casts doubt on the claim, noting that there were many ways in which the message could have been communicated and plenty of time to do it. He sees, rather, another attempt at manipulation, the hope being to save this revolutionary venture. Once Hamburg's revolution was in motion, presumably, workers elsewhere in the Reich would rise and come to the city's defense. But the end result was the fifth revolutionary disaster since the founding of the party.[61]

The government's moves against rebellious Saxony had caused much resentment within SPD circles and, more generally, among workers. Since Bavaria was also in open rebellion and had rebelled before Saxony, an obvious question arose as to why the government had chosen to move against the left. But when the National Socialist *Putsch* came a few days after the Saxony-Hamburg events, Berlin did move against the Bavarian government. The tension was thus somewhat relaxed, Angress argues, as the government appeared to have balanced things.

What may be said about the heritage of 1919-1923? What residues remained in the minds of those who had witnessed the Communist activities of those years?

The party, Angress concludes, had in the course of these years "degenerated into futile and irresponsible putschism." The formation of cliques, these characterized by an increasing rigidity of outlook, resulted in debilitating intraparty squabbles. "Hackneyed revolutionary phrases," he notes, "repeated over and over with tiresome persistence, became the trademark of the KPD." The party, Angress observes, was isolated from the rest of the labor movement, that condition having existed from the day it was founded. "The majority of German workers were repelled by the extremist attitude of the KPD, [and] looked with indifference, if not with contempt and derision, upon the party's inclination for irresponsible political ventures . . . on the whole [they] stood loyally behind the democratic republic which the Communists wanted to transform into a proletarian state."[62]

The party's manipulative attempts also generated hostility. Even if

initially successful (that is, in gaining support on the basis of false premises), many such efforts were exposed after the fact. Many, to be sure,
were transparent to begin with and needed no special unveiling. The
policy of the united front was also transparent (that is, patently fraud-
ulent) to many workers, especially to Social Democratic and trade union
leaders. That policy, as noted, involved an inherent contradiction, attempting to be both moderate and revolutionary at the same time. The
latter aim could never be very well hidden, and the party's aspirations
for control (as opposed to cooperation) continuously pressed to the
forefront. "Even with a more capable and resolute *Zentrale*," Angress
declares, "it is unlikely that the KPD would have done much better
than it did, as long as it insisted on alternatively wooing and insulting
other labor organizations, and calling this method a united front policy."[63]

There was another inherent strain present within the German working class at this point. It has been a source of continuous lament on the
part of the left, in Germany and elsewhere, that workers are so concerned with "narrow" bread and butter issues; they continuously fail to
take the "larger view" recommended to them by the intellectuals of the
"vanguard." This diversity of focus underlay much of the struggle of
this period. When workers struck for wages, the KPD leaders attempted
to transform those efforts into actions against the regime. Whereas the
wage strike is intended as a short-term event, one with a specific concrete and immediate goal, the aim of the party was to take workers out
for longer, indefinite periods and for goals that, at best, seemed a doubtful gamble.[64] The experience of having to fight one's way into the shops
over the opposition of Communist-led forces must have left an indelible
impression on many workers.[65]

Given this heritage, then, it is not too surprising that when the capitalist economy collapsed in 1930, the move to the Communists was not
a flood, but at best a modest trickle. And much of this trickle must have
had a negative character to it; workers chose the Communists not because of any special attraction but rather because of their dissatisfaction
(or feelings of repulsion) vis-à-vis the Social Democrats.

It is also not too surprising that the upper and upper middle classes
(and, no doubt, significant portions of the lower middle class) reacted
to Communist initiatives with considerable alarm and hostility. Recognizing the threat posed to them and their interests and recognizing
also the KPD's frequent use of extralegal, violent, and manipulative
methods, they came to sanction the use of exceptional means against
the KPD. It is also not surprising, given the limited strength of local
police forces and the Versailles-imposed limitations on the Reichswehr,
that these groups looked with particular favor on the irregular forces of

the Freikorps and, later, on various nationalist paramilitary organizations. As we have seen, this was the basis for the Bavarian government's refusal to dissolve the local Freikorps units. When the KPD in 1928 again turned to offensive action, these concerns were quickly aroused; the lessons of 1919-1923 were not easily forgotten.

The conclusions offered in the preceding paragraph suggest a direct, clear, and unambiguous reading of the events of those years. That is not likely to have been the case. Most observers would have seen those events through the perspectives provided by the local press, and much of the press imposed a very political (that is, highly tendentious) reading on those events. The right liberal and conservative press exaggerated the threats. Whereas many of the events of the period were wild and chaotic, lacking any serious plan or guidance, the pattern of press distortion put the KPD in the forefront of the action, controlling and directing its (presumed) tens of thousands of dedicated followers, with the ultimate lines of control reaching back to Moscow. Some actions were spontaneous eruptions, that being particularly the case with workers' wage demands. Some events were stimulated by anarchist groups or various other left splinter groups. But much of the rightist or conservative press made no distinctions, instead assigning all such activity to the Communists.

Another kind of distortion was occurring in the left press. While the "specter of communism" was arousing the upper and upper middle classes, stimulating their support for the right, proponents of the left world view, quite understandably, came to focus on the "specter of fascism." Two mutually dependent images thus arose. The relationship, however, was not a symmetrical one inasmuch as sharply contrasting realities underlay these images. The Communists, as will be seen, were losing strength while the NSDAP was gaining. The principal distortion in the left account (and in many liberal accounts) is the refusal to recognize the contribution of the left to this NSDAP growth.[66]

The defeats of the 1919-1923 period (and the exigencies of the Soviet Union's internal political affairs) led to a decisive shift in the orientation of Communist parties throughout the world. A new era, characterized by a "relative stabilization" of the capitalist world, had begun. A complex internal struggle occurred within the German Communist party in the aftermath of the October fiasco, the concern being to shift the blame for the defeat. This struggle was closely linked to one taking place in Moscow, as the factions of the Russian party fought for control after the death of Lenin.

The outcome in the German case was rather ironic. The party was being directed to chart a clear and unambiguous moderate course, but it was the left faction, under Ruth Fischer, that was elevated to the leadership positions. This, however, proved to be a short-lived arrangement. In this period, the bolshevization, or as some would put it, the Stalinization of the party occurred. In the process what remained of internal party democracy or autonomy disappeared, and leaders were chosen on the basis of demonstrated fealty to the Moscow leadership. The Fischer group, with one significant exception, was removed. Ernst Thälmann, the exception, was elevated to the top position within the party. Unlike most of the party leaders, he had an impeccable proletarian background. At the same time, however, his was a distinctly average talent; his leadership was characterized by tough aggressive slogans and abject subservience to Moscow's directives.[67]

In this period of relative stability, much of the KPD's effort was devoted to electoral politics and another large part to organizational matters. The first national campaign in which it participated was the Reichstag election of May 1924. At that point it took approximately one-eighth of the vote, most of that, apparently, coming from previous supporters of the Independent Socialists (see Table A.1).[68] Its electoral campaign stressed opposition to the Dawes Plan. Positively, it urged "complete socialization" and the dictatorship of the proletariat. Its newly elected members, some sixty-two of them, caused a considerable uproar at the opening of the new Reichstag, this being justified under the slogan of "revolutionary parliamentarianism." A new election was called in December of 1924, and, perhaps in reaction to the evident improvement of German domestic affairs, the KPD lost more than one million votes; over one-quarter of its May 1924 strength had disappeared. Much of the loss in this case appears to have gone to the SPD.[69] The volatility of KPD support over the years was one of its most striking features. This deserves special emphasis given the sense, shared by KPD defenders and opponents alike, that its followers possessed a unique commitment to their political enterprise. For many, that was clearly not the case.

The next major election was the presidential contest in March and April of 1925. In the first round, Thälmann gained 1.8 million votes. This must again be counted as a sharp loss, that figure being well below the 2.7 million obtained in the December Reichstag election. For the second round of the presidential election, the SPD and Democratic party candidates withdrew in favor of Wilhelm Marx (of the Zentrum), the agreed-upon candidate of the republican forces. The parties of the right withdrew their first-round candidate and ran instead the aged military hero Paul von Hindenburg. Despite the manifest hopelessness of his candidacy, the KPD maintained Thälmann in the second round. The respective votes for Hindenburg, Marx, and Thälmann were 14.6, 13.7, and 1.9 million. Had the KPD accepted the republican candidate and had only half its votes gone in that direction, the Zentrum's Wilhelm Marx would have presided over the fortunes of Germany until at least April of 1932.[70]

Toward the end of 1925, the Communists conducted an initiative and a referendum campaign. The issue involved was the expropriation, without compensation, of property of the nobility. Given the character of the issue, the SPD and the trade unions were more or less obliged to support the Communist move, and some support was also found in left liberal circles. Although the effort ultimately failed, it was a signal success in that over 12 million voters signed to hold a referendum on the issue, and, in June of 1926, some 14.4 million voted for the move. It was the Communists' only successful united-front campaign.[71]

In May of 1928, the parties of the left recovered much of their lost ground, this being the pocket battleship election. At this point, it will be noted, most of the gains went to the Social Democrats. In state and local elections of the period, the KPD was merely holding its own at roughly the level of December 1924. The condition of the party at this point, just before the depression hit, is indicated by the results of a second referendum campaign effort. The SPD government, it will be remembered, went along with the pocket battleship proposal after the election, despite its election promises. The KPD organized an appropriate popular action. But the party that had gained 3,265,000 votes in May of 1928 was able to muster only 1,277,000 signatures in October of that year in opposition to Panzerkreuzer A.[72]

The failure of the pocket battleship initiative provides a more accurate reflection of the party's internal state than did the 1928 election. The party's official membership figures, as given by Flechtheim, indicate a steady decline throughout the period of stabilization. The party reported some 380,000 members as of March 1922. Over 100,000 of those had disappeared by the end of 1923, the official figure then being 276,000. The figure declined to 180,000 in 1924, then to 150,000 in January 1927, and again to 130,000 at the end of 1928. Even in the first year of the depression, at the point of the National Socialists' September 1930 election victory, the figure reported was 120,000. All these figures have a suspicious roundness to them and should probably be taken as high estimates.[73]

The party also lost influence within the trade unions. The 1923 inflation took a heavy toll of all union memberships. The numbers affiliated with the General German Trade Union Federation (Allgemeine Deutsche Gewerkschaftsbund) fell from seven to four million in the course of that year. Those losses affected both SPD and KPD interests. The Communists were divided on the question of proper trade union policy, some preferring to work from within (the united front from below tactic) and some wanting to establish competing unions. The conflict of policy was to cause them problems, dispersing their limited strength, until the end of the regime. Their reduced influence within the trade unions appears also in the results of factory council elections.[74]

In sharp contrast to the SPD, the Communist party aimed to be a revolutionary organization, not an electoral machine. The party's activities were not organized by electoral district and around election campaigns. Organizational efforts were instead to be concentrated in the factory cells. It was official party policy that all members be simultaneously affiliated with a trade union. But that requirement, in Germany as in all other capitalist nations, proved impossible to carry out. The organization of factories was Comintern policy as of the summer of 1921. But in May of 1923, in the assessments of the March action, it was already recognized that the policy had not been carried through; it was, nevertheless, reaffirmed and the attempt continued. But the directive was not easily reconciled with the needs and requirements of working-class life, and party activity continued to drift toward the neighborhoods and away from the factories. In 1930 the number of factory cells was roughly half of what it had been five years earlier (1,411 as against 2,673). At that point the party had cells in less than 1 percent of Germany's factories.[75]

Another source of concern to the party's leaders was the composition of the membership. A Communist vanguard should be found in the large factories, at the heart of the capitalist economy. But as Flechtheim reports, the party was peculiarly weak there. Then, too, the percentage of members who were factory workers fell as the depression worsened, the figures being 63 in 1928 but only 20 to 22 in 1931. In part, of course, that was the unavoidable result of rising unemployment.

One might expect a vanguard party to have its strength in the largest and most industrial cities. The Berlin- and Hamburg-centered histories would lead one to believe that this was in fact the case. But at the annual party meetings concern was expressed over the number of members coming from the small towns and villages. In 1927, it was reported that more members came from communities of 3,000 to 4,000 inhabitants than from industrial cities of 30,000 to 50,000.[76]

The historian Arthur Rosenberg, writing in 1927 when still a member of the party, summarized the situation thus: "We are extremely weak in the large factories and therefore also in the union effort. The largest part of our following is unemployed or in the small factories. And therefore we are on the periphery and not at the heart of the working class." Sensing the forthcoming policy changes, he argued that the party should *not* concentrate its efforts exclusively on the unemployed. Were it to give in to the left direction, it would continue to remain on the periphery of the working class.[77]

Perhaps the most alarming fact facing the party leaders was the inconstancy of the membership. In 1929, they gained 143,000 but lost 95,000. These figures suggest that the sources of repulsion were almost as strong as the sources of attraction.[78] Their situation, as of 1930, was far removed from what Lenin intended when he called for revolutionaries who would dedicate the "whole of their lives" to the party.

At the end of the period of relative stabilization, then, the Communist forces were weak, poorly located for their purposes, and, judging by the high turnover, of doubtful reliability. In sharp contrast, the NSDAP had more members, was gaining strength, and, on the whole, had more loyal cadres. The National Socialists, in short, were well prepared to make use of the events of the depression for their purposes. The Communists, by comparison, were poorly prepared and, moreover, had to work against a heritage of ill feeling that they themselves had done much to create over the prior decade.

There was, clearly, a considerable disparity between the appearance and the reality of Communist strength at this point. No doubt many Germans saw a strong and growing party. In the September 1930 Reichstag election, it added more than a million votes to its May 1928 strength for a 4,590,160 total, more than one of every eight. Given the vociferous claims of the party and given also the evidence provided by its various street actions (especially as filtered through the bourgeois press), it was easy for many to conclude that the Communist threat was real. Few sources bothered to point out the KPD's membership figures—no more than 120,000 at that time. And even fewer indicated the unreliable character of even that core group. Few citizens, in short, were likely to have known the underlying reality. The conservative or nationalist bourgeois, not knowing the reality, would react to an image that was largely fantasy. Again it should be noted that the Communists themselves had done much to create that fantasy. And they continued to sustain that image in the ensuing years of struggle.[79]

It was at this point that the party undertook a shift to the left. This new direction, referred to as Third Period Communism, actually began in 1928, before the onset of the depression, and was stimulated by the internal needs of the Soviet Union. The so-called right wing was expelled and Thälmann made party chairman. A personal cult, modeled after the Hitler cult of the NSDAP, was developed, this adulation being all the more remarkable by virtue of Thälmann's undistinguished character and ability. Flechtheim refers to him as a "mediocre personality."

The most distinctive feature of the new direction was the sharp attack on the Social Democrats. They were said to be "objectively" fascist.

The specific term, to distinguish them from the National Socialists, was Social Fascist, meaning those who while not actually intending to, were "objectively" aiding "reaction." The underlying aim, clearly, was to discredit Social Democracy and to sustain the KPD aspirations for exclusive direction of working-class affairs. Given the Communists' minority position and their weak organizational strength, it involved (were one to assume the operation of right reason) a major strategic error. It reinforced the already serious division of the left forces and made cooperation impossible at a time when it had become a pressing imperative.

But the KPD was not much interested in cooperation. Its entire policy involved denunciation and attacks on other groups, democratic as well as fascist. It would be a mistake to assume any devotion to democratic forms or procedures on its part; its indifference or hostility was manifested in numerous declarations. A resolution of the central committee from May of 1931 declared that "the fascist dictatorship does not in any way represent a contrast in principle to bourgeois democracy under which the dictatorship of finance capital is also carried out . . . [it is] simply a change in the forms, an organic transition." In February 1932 the committee declared that "democracy and fascist dictatorship are not only two forms that harbor the same class content. . . . They approach each other also in their external methods . . . intertwining one with the other." Thälmann cited the following statement from a KPD publication with evident approval: "A Social Democratic coalition government faced with an incapable, divided, confused proletariat, would be a thousand times greater evil than an open fascist dictatorship, one that confronts the united masses of a class-conscious proletariat that is determined to fight." A Communist parliamentarian described the anticipated development as follows: "When the fascists come to power, then the united front of the proletariat will come into being and sweep everything away. To starve under Brüning is not any better than under Hitler. We are not afraid of the fascists. They will mismanage faster than any other government."[80]

Another feature of Third Period Communism was the change of direction with respect to the trade unions. Having failed in its efforts to gain control from within, the party now attempted to create separate or parallel organizations. By and large a failure, this effort, which also involved direct attacks on already established democratic organizations, nevertheless continued until the dissolution of the unions in 1933. Given the general level of unemployment, it is not too surprising that strike activity fell off sharply with the deepening of the depression. The Communists did sponsor some strikes to fend off wage cuts, but these were of short duration and yielded little in the way of positive results.[81]

Disregarding the objective circumstances, the party made repeated calls for general strikes in support of its political goals. According to Borkenau it issued such calls on six occasions between 1929 and 1932. In response to the first of these, in May 1929, a single factory came out in support. After that there was no response. Most decisively, the party's call for a general strike to protest Papen's overthrow of the Prussian government in July 1932 generated no response whatsoever.[82] And the same was true of its call on January 30, 1933, when Hitler was named as chancellor of the Reich. The somewhat distant, rather out-of-touch bourgeois might have been alarmed by Communist "growth," but the more astute and more in-touch National Socialists must have recognized the reality of the KPD situation. In such a situation, the KPD's repeated call for a general strike would have served little purpose other than to advertise its own weakness.

The demagogic tendencies within the party surfaced once again at this point. Following the tactic previously used by Radek and Ruth Fischer, Heinz Neumann now went to National Socialist meetings—"to curry favor with the fascists." At a Goebbels meeting in Berlin-Friedrichshain he is supposed to have said: "Young Socialists! Courageous fighters for the nation! The Communists do not want a fratricidal struggle with the National Socialists!" Before the September 1930 Reichstag election, Neumann had attempted to undercut the National Socialist effort with a Communist declaration calling for "the national and social liberation of the German people." This suggestion was in fact actually adopted by the central committee. The opening statement could easily pass for the words of any convinced German nationalist—"We will tear up the rapacious Versailles 'peace treaty' and the Young Plan which enslave Germany. We will annul all international debts and reparation payments."[83]

The most disastrous of the KPD policies were those undertaken vis-à-vis the SPD-led government of Prussia. In the summer of 1931, as noted above, the nationalist forces, the National Socialists, the German National People's party, the Stahlhelm, and others, undertook an initiative to bring down the Braun-Severing government. The KPD initially denounced the effort as a swindle but then, in a complicated series of moves, came to support the move. Heinz Neumann had argued in favor of the effort; it would accentuate the political crisis. This suggestion was overruled by Thälmann and others on the central committee. But their decision in turn was overruled, this time through a directive from the International.[84] The unnatural front of right and left successfully collected the required signatures but the referendum, on August 9, 1931, as noted, did not yield the sought-for majority.

Much more serious, of course, was the previously mentioned Communist effort of late May and early June 1932 that ultimately yielded a no-confidence vote for the Prussian government. Pieck, who introduced the KPD motion, referred to the NSDAP as a party of murderers. The National Socialist deputies who outnumbered the KPD delegates three to one, responded with a physical attack and drove them from the chamber, injuring many in the process. Undeterred, the Communists proceeded in their course and, on June 3, with the aid of National Socialist votes, carried their motion. The Braun government, as we have seen, continued in office, there being none other available, until it was deposed by Papen on July 20. Under the circumstances, it was not surprising that the SPD paid little attention to a KPD offer of a front to oppose the Papen move.

Even after the July election, the Communists' position remained unchanged. Just before the November election, they worked with the National Socialists in support of a strike by Berlin transport workers. This was seen as one more thrust against the established trade union leadership which had not recognized the strike. In the election itself, the National Socialists lost two million votes while the Communists gained some 700,000. This fitted in well with their conceptions of inevitability; the National Socialists clearly were now fading, and the Communists' moment fast approaching.[85]

Even after Hitler's accession, Third Period Communism continued. The Social Democratic mayor of Altona, Max Brauer, spoke to the chairman of the Communist Reichstag faction, Ernst Torgler, urging him to fight the National Socialists and to give up the struggle against the Social Democrats, this occurring on February 23, 1933. Torgler replied: "It doesn't enter our heads. The Nazis must take power. Then in four weeks the whole working class will be united under the leadership of the Communist Party." A few days later Brauer urged the same change of policy to the Soviet ambassador. He replied that the National Socialists "must come to power now, and then at last the old fight will come to an end. In four weeks the Communists will have the leadership of the whole working class."[86] In less time than that, the Reichstag fire occurred on February 27, the party was outlawed and most of its leaders arrested.

The infallibility of the KPD's judgment was reaffirmed once again on April 1 when the following statement was issued: "The President of the Executive Committee of the Communist International, having heard the report of Comrade Heckert on the situation in Germany, declares that the policy carried out by the Executive Committee of the Communist Party of Germany with Comrade Thälmann at its head, up to and during the time of the Hitlerite coup, was absolutely correct."[87]

Other judgments have been less flattering. Hermann Weber speaks of the Stalinized party and its "ultraleft" policies as having "made an essential contribution to the destruction of the Weimar republic."[88] Flechtheim makes a similar judgment: "The KPD, therefore, even if half reluctantly, nevertheless in no way accidentally or unknowingly, contributed to the victory of the worst enemy of all, namely that of National Socialism, and thereby also to the destruction of its own party." He speaks of this as the "logical conclusion" of a development to be traced back to the founding of the party. The KPD had always been too weak to achieve a victory over reform or reaction; it was, however, just strong enough to weaken the reform effort and simultaneously to provoke the reactionaries. It was this "continuously threatened but never accomplished revolution from the left" that gave reaction and fascism such impetus. The Communists, he notes, never achieved their united front. The KPD's activities, however, were a considerable aid to the National Socialists in *their* efforts to create a united front of the right.[89] There can be little doubt that the Communists, at the very minimum, provided important elements of the setting for the drama being played out by the National Socialists. Only a supreme faith in the inevitability of the historical outcome could justify their tactics and conclusions; Bullock refers to them as having a "childlike faith in Marxist prophecy."[90] Their contribution to the disaster was to provoke a struggle for which they were at no time prepared.

One essential component of the theoretical system guiding KPD activity was the notion that workers generally were destined to move in *its* direction, that is, once the objective realities were unveiled. But this notion itself involved a veiling self-deception. It assumed that the economic conditions were going to be so powerful as both to guarantee the move and to determine its direction. More specifically, it assumed that those conditions would be of such a compelling character as to outweigh the impact of the KPD's own past actions. It assumed, in short, that the workers who had been victims of KPD policy at one time or another in the course of the previous years would, as the crisis deepened, turn to that party as their only saving agency.

But, as we have seen, effectively the only change to occur on the left was some shift from the SPD camp. Workers in the centrist or rightist camps clearly viewed *both* Marxist parties as unacceptable alternatives. During the crisis, then, a crucial segment of the working class did change political direction; but the change was in accordance with ideological determinants rather than the "requirements" of the objective economic conditions.[91] The ideological determinants, to be sure, did not operate in a vacuum; what gave that factor such weight was the effort of the KPD itself, fourteen years of Communist praxis. That heritage was such as to effectively block off or deny what might otherwise have been the normal or natural tendency. One of the "objective conditions" that many workers would have considered in 1932 was the behavior of the party; it could hardly have been irrelevant to their calculations and assessments.[92]

In very different ways, both parties of the left contributed to Hitler's electoral victory.[93] In their different ways they both denied the possibility of a leftist solution to Germany's problems, or more specifically to the problems facing Germany's workers. The consequence of this denial is that many workers chose an unforeseen direction, one not predicted in the guiding lines of theory.

The likely motives of the various working-class segments are considered at greater length in Chapter 13. But first, in the next chapter, it is necessary to consider the activities of the National Socialists in relation to both the bourgeois and the left parties.

CHAPTER TWELVE

The National Socialists

The two previous chapters examined the internal conditions of the established parties. Most of those parties experienced a serious decline in strength and ability; in two, the SPD and Zentrum, the forces were more or less intact, but there one found a peculiar self-defeating immobility. All these parties, moreover, either had undertaken initiatives, or, as the crisis developed, chose initiatives that alienated traditional voters, that led them to search for what, to them, seemed a more positive alternative. To complement the discussions in those chapters, this chapter examines the internal condition of the NSDAP. Chapter 13 then considers the character of the political struggle as it unfolded within the major segments of German society.

The basic question being considered in these chapters is a simple one: why did so many of the disaffected voters choose the National Socialists? Many accounts have answered this question by pointing to the appeal of the National Socialist program or to the appeal of its "ideology." And many have cited the efforts of the top leaders of the party, most especially those of Hitler and Goebbels, who, before audiences of thousands, transmitted the party's message. Without necessarily denying either the importance of the program, the ideology, or the top leadership, one must make some important specifications.

The top leaders could have reached only a small portion of the 6,380,000 people who voted for the NSDAP in 1930 or the 13,746,000 who voted for it in July of 1932. Many of those who did attend the mass meetings at which the top leaders appeared must already have been among the party faithful. The party itself had only a very limited press, one that, given the small circulation, could not have reached far beyond the most devoted activists.

Some people have misread the history, putting events subsequent to the taking of power into the period prior to the takeover. Hitler and Goebbels made every use of the radio after taking power. But prior to that event they had only very limited access to the state-owned medium, which strictly regulated political broadcasts. The Hugenberg press empire did speak on the National Socialists' behalf during most of the crucial years of their growth, and, as we have seen, they did receive favorable treatment in much of the bourgeois press. That support, as has been indicated in previous chapters, was an important factor in their growth. At the same time, however, it should be noted that these news-papers were also giving favorable treatment to various bourgeois par-ties, these being, in most cases, the publishers' first choice. And yet those parties suffered serious losses, as in the case of Hugenberg's own party, the Conservatives, or complete disasters, as in the case of the German People's party.

If one asks what further differentiated the parties,the answer is very simple: it was the size and ability of their cadres. The National Socialists had large numbers of militants; the other parties, particularly those that lost, did not. Much of this chapter is devoted to showing these differ-ences, indicating the quantitative and qualitative advantages of the Na-tional Socialists in this regard. This exposition of the history in turn raises still more questions: why did the National Socialists have such a distinct advantage? How did it come about that they were able to com-mand such large numbers of devoted activists? These questions are con-sidered at some length later in this chapter.

The Importance of the Militants

It is useful to begin with a vignette. The impact of the militants is suggested in the following account, written by one of the party's activ-ists. He cites what might be counted as a natural experimental case:

I came to Korschen, a railroad center in East Prussia with about 2400 inhabitants. Here was an entirely virgin field as far as National So-cialism was concerned. Far and wide our movement was unknown. . . . [He joined with another activist] and now began systematic re-cruiting in the districts of Rastenburg and Gerdauen. From these two districts the wave of propaganda spread over the whole province, the latter at that time completely untouched territory. . . . In consequence of the national point of view which prevailed among the people who lived in this province, we seldom made a trip in vain. Our election campaigners in 1928 raised the hundred nationalist votes [Deutsch-völkische Freiheitspartei] of the Korschen district to nearly 1100. One can evaluate this success only when one takes into consideration that on the same day the city of Rastenburg with its 14,000 inhabitants gave only forty votes for Adolf Hitler. If the day before . . . the party members of Korschen had not distributed handbills and newspapers on a large scale, the city would not have furnished even this number of votes.

This account contains a major inaccuracy. The official publication of the 1928 voting results puts the NSDAP total for Korschen at 98 votes, not, as this activist puts it, as "nearly 1100." Even when one corrects this elevenfold exaggeration, however, a significant lesson remains. Those 98 votes constituted 8.4 percent of the district total in contrast to 0.8 percent for the whole of East Prussia. A corrected statement of the accomplishment would stress the role of the activists in *maintaining* nationalist voting strength at a time when the nationalists were suffering serious losses everywhere in the province.[1]

The presence of an underlying nationalist predisposition, by itself, had no payoff for the party. It will also be noted that neither the mass media nor the top leaders played any role in determining this result. The success in Korschen would appear to be attributable exclusively to the presence and efforts of these militants. Basically what the National Socialists did in subsequent elections was to multiply such efforts many times over. It is useful to examine these efforts in some detail.

A convenient starting place is the work of William Sheridan Allen. He has written the leading community study dealing with the rise of the National Socialists.[2] The town in question, called Thalburg in his account, was a rail and administrative center having a population of approximately 10,000 persons. The town was divided into two camps, a conservative nationalist middle class and a Social Democratic working class. Middle class in this case appears to be used as equivalent to the term "nonmanual." It includes lower-middle- and upper-middle-class segments as well as the town's tiny upper class. In local politics the middle class supported an organization called the Civic Association (Bürgerliche Vereinigung). This middle class was strongly anti-Marxist in outlook, that position being for all intents and purposes the central concern of its members' individual and collective consciences. In the local context, hostility to "Marxism" meant opposition to the Social Democrats.[3]

The Social Democrats had long been present on the local scene, but it was the revolution of 1918 and the changed electoral arrangements that first gave them strength in accordance with their numbers, thus giving them an important but not a majority voice in the city council. In November 1929, they gained another two mandates putting them only two seats away from a majority. They also increased their vote slightly in the national election in September of 1930. This late growth of the Social Democrats provided the background against which the National Socialists made their appearance.

In the 1929 local election, the National Socialists gained 213 votes from among the 5,133 cast. They were, as Allen puts it, "an insignificant fringe" in Thalburg. At the same time, however, they were "tireless in putting their ideas before the public."[4] In the early months of 1930, long before even the suggestion of a general election, they were holding meetings approximately every other week. Among their offerings was a speech for the workers entitled "The German Worker as Interest-Slave of Big International Capitalists" and, for the town's other camp, "Saving the Middle Class in the National Socialist State."

A significant feature of these meetings was an admission charge. For these provincial gatherings it amounted to some thirty pfennigs, which Allen says was equal to the price of two loaves of bread. Where some writings on the NSDAP have stressed the role of big business in financing the party's effort, this account, along with others discussed below, indicates that the local effort was self-financed.

In April of 1930, the Social Democrats announced a mammoth rally on the theme "Dictatorship or Democracy?" The NSDAP forthwith announced a counter rally, which was scheduled for the same day, the same place (the community's central square), and exactly the same time. It was a part of the provocative style so much appreciated by National Socialist activists. The aim, clearly, was a demonstrative challenge intended to answer the question: who controls the streets? Not too surprisingly, the local police forbade both meetings.

Undaunted, in fact challenged by the prohibition, the NSDAP announced that the meeting would go ahead as planned, but in a village about three kilometers from Thalburg. Some 2,000 people came from throughout the district to see, among other things, a parade of 800 storm troopers. Thalburg's oldest and most established newspaper reported this as "a powerfully impressive recognition of Nazi ideas." Allen summarizes the overall result as follows: the National Socialists "had not only blocked the Socialist meeting; they had dominated the press and 'powerfuly impressed' Thalburgers with their size and determination."[5]

This organizational agility, it should be noted, was the work of local activists. The meeting was not organized and directed from the top. The local militants were able to plan a relatively large operation, to shift their strategy quickly, and to coordinate the efforts of a territorially dispersed following. The only outside contribution was a guest speaker. The newspapers were used to advertise the event, and they were obliged to report it to the larger audience. The local NSDAP organization did not control the press; it did, however, make rather shrewd use of it and, in this case, clearly had a sympathetic ally.

As indicated, the National Socialist and Social Democratic efforts were very much interlinked. In reaction to this NSDAP demonstration, which took place on April 27, "May Day of 1930 was celebrated in full strength. Workers from all areas, especially the railroad workers, were present for the march through town in closed ranks. There was much drinking, many speeches, and of course the sentimental singing of the Internationale."[6]

The Social Democrats, clearly, could also mobilize and assemble their forces. The suggestion in Allen's brief comment, however, is that they were somewhat less serious than the National Socialists. It was a traditional convivial gathering, a friendly get-together, as opposed to one of determined purposefulness.

The NSDAP continued its frequent meetings thoughout May and June (its offerings included talks on unemployment, the "Protocols of the Wise Men of Zion," and youth in Germany). But these, Allen reports, had not generated much interest; the party felt the need for a more dramatic showing. Late in June, it organized a march to protest Severing's prohibition against the wearing of uniforms by political groups. Wearing white shirts instead of their usual brown, some 400 SA men marched through the main street of Thalburg accompanied by a fife-and-drum corps. There was a speech in the main square of the town and several speeches later in the afternoon at a local meeting hall. The Social Democrats responded a few days afterward with a larger meeting in another hall. The NSDAP responded the following day by distributing a leaflet attacking the SPD speaker.

The National Socialist speaker at this protest meeting had promised that "heads will roll in the sand." The local Social Democrats subsequently instituted an action against the deputy chief of police, a leader of the rightist faction in the city council, who had been present at this meeting. By failing to have the speaker arrested for inciting to violence, it was said that he had shown himself partial to the NSDAP. As a result, he was divested of his police powers by the provincial authorities (who happened to be Social Democrats) and replaced by the leader of the town council's SPD faction.

The Social Democrats sponsored and organized a Constitution Day celebration for August 8, a celebration of the republic with which they were so closely identified. And they successfully carried through some local public works measures thus putting them in a favorable position for the forthcoming Reichstag election.

The NSDAP escalated its already high level of activity during the 1930 election campaign. Its first meeting, on August 10, two days after the Constitution Day festival, saw an outside speaker lecture on "eleven years republic—eleven years mass misery." Less than a week later another outside speaker lectured on the subject "down to the last tax penny." This brought an overflow crowd to the city's second largest meeting hall. Then came a lecture by an NSDAP member of the Prussian legislature, also to an overflow crowd, and still another speaker appeared a week later. It will be remembered that admission was charged at all of these events.

Against these activities, the Social Democrats staged two large meetings (one requiring an admission fee). The efforts of the other parties, Allen says, were "far less strenuous." The conservative DNVP held only one small meeting. It used the press as its "main campaigning instrument," placing many advertisements in a sympathetic local newspaper. In the last days of the campaign this paper was "filled almost excusively with [DNVP] . . . propaganda." The right liberal DVP made use of the town's other bourgeois newspaper for its advertisements, attacking the SPD for "causing the depression" and the NSDAP for "destructive radicalism." It too held only one meeting during the campaign. The Staatspartei, the reactionary successor of the Democratic party also held only one meeting. Its speaker "called for orderly, middle class parliamentary rule, and for laws by which 'Jews would be allowed citizenship only according to their character and accomplishments.' " Attendance was limited.[7]

Several acts of violence occurred in the last days of the campaign (Communists beat up a Social Democrat; National Socialists beat up a Social Democrat), and various official prohibitions followed. The SPD and NSDAP both held final mass meetings. A Lutheran minister appeared for the National Socialists, assuring his listeners that the party was neither economically radical nor antireligious.

The NSDAP increased its vote from 123 in 1928 to 1,742 or 28 percent of the total. Since the People's party suffered only a slight loss, it meant that the National Socialist votes came from the various splinter parties, from the DNVP, from the Staatspartei, and from new voters. Since there were so few newly qualified voters, most of the gain, Allen reports, came "from those who were not especially young but had either voted for another party in 1928 or had not bothered to vote at all."[8]

It is difficult to sort out the causes of these results. At minimum one may note a strong correlation with activity, the most active of the parties, the NSDAP, being the biggest gainer and the second most active party, the SPD, doing well in holding its own. By and large, the inactive parties were all losers. The most advertised party, the DNVP, did poorly. The next most advertised, the DVP, did somewhat better. The Staatspartei, which had changed its character, which had no significant advertisement and only one meeting, which essentially had nothing going for it, was a major loser.

The dialectical struggle between the SPD and the NSDAP did not end with the election. At this point, the Thalburg SPD made a serious tactical error; it decided to enter candidates for the election of elders in the town's Lutheran church. The argument was that workers, most of whom were Lutheran, were not represented in church affairs. The ministers, moreover, were placing too much stress on nationalism in their sermons. Not too surprisingly, this new development generated a concerted effort on the part of conservatives, nationalists, and established middle-class populations generally to turn back the Marxist challenge. Many Social Democrats found their new campaign an embarrassment. For the National Socialists it provided a new occasion to "portray themselves as effective opponents of 'Marxism.' "

Just prior to the election the NSDAP held a meeting in the town's largest hall. A Lutheran pastor, who was also an NSDAP member of the Reichstag, was the featured speaker, his topic being: "Marxists as Murderers of the German *Volk* in the Pay of the Enemy." The admission charge this time, for an anticipated middle-class audience, was fifty pfennigs. The hall, which had seats for 1,500 people, had an overflow audience.

Participation in the church election was three times what it had been previously. But the SPD was able to turn out only a quarter of its usual following, and its candidates lost by an overwhelming margin. The NSDAP could claim a major contribution to this defeat, its meeting just prior to the vote being the largest it had ever held in Thalburg. Possibly the most serious consequence was the lesson learned by the town's solid citizens—that "the SPD could be beaten."

The NSDAP continued its activity in the weeks following the election of elders. Its first meeting came ten days afterward, and at the next meeting, five days later, a member of the Reichstag was brought in for a speech. There were two showings of a film "The Growth of National Socialism," each followed by a speech. And a month after the election the party's chief candidate from the area, now a member of the Reichstag, appeared for a lecture. The NSDAP held as many meetings in the month following the election as in the month preceding it. Allen refers to this as the tactic of "perpetual campaigning."[9]

The party filled out the remaining months of 1930 with "fairly ordinary meetings"—a commemoration gathering on November 9, the anniversary of the Munich *Putsch*, a discussion evening, a speech on foreign reactions to the September election, one on economics stressing the NSDAP's concern for the lower middle class, and another attacking the SPD. The political year's activities ended with a Christmas party for the town's children and an "evening of entertainment" for the adults. Altogether the NSDAP held thirty meetings in the course of the year and the SPD fifteen. The other parties combined held a total of five.[10] It was clear which party occupied center stage in Thalburg's political affairs.

The SPD-NSDAP competition continued in January and February of

1931 although now the meetings were larger, the provocations and violence more frequent. The entire atmosphere of the town was being heavily politicized. In one thirty-one-day period, twelve political events took place including parades, rallies, and meetings. Six of these were sponsored by Social Democrats and six by the National Socialists. But this was not, Allen notes, a competition of equals. "In the game of matching radicalism with the Nazis," he states, "the SPD could not hope to win, for they lacked the brutality and irrationality of their opponents. Furthermore, every move in the game simply added to the troubled spirit of Thalburg's middle classes, making them more vulnerable to extremist appeals."[11] After February, the SPD "no longer attempted to match the Nazis meeting for meeting." The one organized and active local organization defending the republic and its institutions was no longer able to keep up with its opponent.[12]

A significant parallel development was occurring at this time, namely, an imitation of NSDAP themes and tactics by other rightist groups. The Stahlhelm held a meeting in the town, its first in over a year. Its speaker attacked liberals, Marxists, Jews, and the SPD. He also had some positive words for the organization's new competitor, referring to Hitler as a "drummer of Nationalist ideas" and proclaiming Bismarck the "first National Socialist." This meeting was held in the best hotel in the town and presumably had a smaller but more select audience than the large NSDAP gatherings. The impact, presumably, would be to justify and legitimate both the NSDAP's existence and its major themes. The local Civic Association also held a meeting, and its leader too championed the "tough" line, attacking the Treaty of Versailles and prophesying "that when Germany became internally united she would once again become a world power."[13]

The major NSDAP activity of 1931, as indicated in Chapter 11, was the organization of an initiative and referendum to bring down the Prussian government. Gathering signatures took up much of the party's time and reduced somewhat the number of meetings. It still, however, was able to organize a few marches and rallies. A wide range of local parties and organizations was drawn into this NSDAP-directed effort. The SPD could do little to counter this campaign except to point out various contradictions and irrationalities. It stressed, for example, the Communist support for the campaign while the local coalition of rightist anti-republican forces did its best to ignore its embarrassing ally. The referendum eventually lost so that as far as its manifest purpose went, the effort came to naught. But for Thalburg, it was one more step in converting the middle classes, in bringing them to accept NSDAP leadership.

The remainder of the year saw a resumption of the previous high activity level, this including speeches, a theatrical presentation, and an "evening of entertainment" sponsored jointly with the Stahlhelm. The party's leading economic theorist, Gottfried Feder, came to give a view of things to come, speaking on "financial and economic policy in the National Socialist state." He promised "no nationalization of the productive free economy" and "organic economic leadership." The crowd was enormous; it was "one of the Nazis' most effective meetings."[14] The year continued with a play, the commemoration of the Munich *Putsch*, a welfare concert, and the customary Christmas party. At the party's only mass meeting, an NSDAP member of the Prussian parliament declared that the SPD was responsible for the current economic distress and indicated that when his party came to power it "would not use soft gloves."

The final tally of meetings for 1931 was: National Socialists, twenty-eight; Social Democrats, twenty-three, Conservatives (DNVP), seven; and all others, seven. The Social Democratic total, it will be noted, is not far behind that of the NSDAP. That result, however, is deceptive in that most of its meetings preceded the referendum campaign in August. After that effort, the NSDAP held nine meetings while the SPD held only two.[15]

For a small town that was not normally overflowing with entertainments or diversions, the NSDAP provided many opportunities. The speakers who appeared there were not, by and large, local figures. The party brought in five Reichstag delegates, the president of the Prussian parliament, the leader of the NSDAP Prussian parliamentary group, and, as already mentioned, Gottfried Feder, who, in the "eyes of the general public was a top Nazi leader." It was "a rich selection of speakers for a town of ten thousand."[16] For those having more nationalist (as opposed to political) interests, the party provided speeches by three former officers and also held five "paramilitary parades." In 1930 it had rented the town's largest hall only once; in 1931 it filled the hall ten times, on each occasion having an audience of over 1,000. It also held many meetings in the town's second largest hall. A very large part of its effort in 1931, clearly, was given to *mass* meetings. Given the admission charge, the financial returns (quite apart from the political impact) must have been considerable. Collections, also a regular feature of these meetings, provided between one-third and one-half of the income derived from these events.

Another organizational effort deserves more than passing mention. Late in 1931 the party opened a soup kitchen to feed the unemployed. This welfare activity was financed largely by contributions. The owner of a canning company (who went bankrupt in 1929) supplied rooms in his now unused factory building. With the help of the Stahlhelm, the

Harzburg Front now being successfully established, a collection campaign was organized. Food was donated by farmers and by some of the town's shopkeepers, by its grocers, bakers, and butchers. By mid-December, Allen tells us, they were "feeding two hundred people per day, including forty families, twenty single people, and numerous SA men."[17]

NSDAP spokesmen declared that they charged those who could pay and gave food to all regardless of party loyalty. There were some counterclaims, one man saying he was refused because he was leftist and the local SPD newspaper claiming the kitchen only fed unemployed National Socialists. In any event, the project may well have yielded some support for the party among the unemployed. It may also have stimulated further middle-class support; once again the NSDAP appeared as a dynamic force, as a party that knew how to get things done.[18] The alliance with the Stahlhelm certainly could not have hurt.

The efforts undertaken in 1932, the year of elections, require no detailed presentation. The NSDAP held thirty-seven meetings, the SPD twenty-three, and the Conservatives thirteen; the total for all the other parties was eleven.[19] In terms of size and drama, the NSDAP events far outdid those of its competitors. The biggest event of the year for the party was a speech by Hitler. This occurred in a neighboring town about fifteen kilometers away. The party arranged special trains bringing in listeners from the entire region. It was an open air meeting, with room for an audience of 100,000. Although the speeches were not scheduled to begin until eight o'clock in the evening, all seats were taken by early afternoon. Tension mounted in the hours of waiting. Just at eight Hitler's airplane flew over; from the crowd there were shouts of "Heil!" and a waving of swastika flags and handkerchiefs. The speech itself was an immense propaganda success.

This appearance, it will be noted, was Hitler's first in the area, occurring in the midst of the July 1932 Reichstag election campaign. This giant meeting came as an end product of all those previous years of local effort. This is not to say that such a meeting would be without effect on its listeners; the effects, however, would probably be ones of reinforcement, or of final conversion in a process begun long before.

The sheer volume of NSDAP effort in Thalburg suggests a large number of active followers but in point of fact, Allen reports, they had "only about forty actual members . . . prior to 1933."

They were aided, he says, "by many party members from the county, and also by many fellow-travelers, but the core was a strictly limited one. . . . not many Thalburgers suspected how few dues-paying members there were in the town. [They] believed that the Nazis were numerous and young."[20]

In part the illusion of numbers and youth was provided by the fellow travelers. "Students at the Thalburg *Gymnasium*," we are told, "were strongly attracted to Hitler." And, furthermore, most of the work "done in public was done by young people in the SA or the Hitler Youth."[21] These young people undertook much of the advance work prior to meetings, distributing leaflets and literature, and, at election times, delivering party newspapers.

Although this effort served an important instrumental purpose and had an additional effect in creating one aspect of the party's image, the principal activities of the Hitler Youth and the motives for joining lay in quite another direction. One former member said he joined because of a wish to be in a boys' club where he could strive "towards a nationalistic idea." The Hitler Youth went on hikes and camping trips and held group meetings. It made no social or class distinctions, which this member saw as a positive factor. Prior to Hitler's takeover there was "no direct or obvious political indoctrination." Discounting the political factor as the main reason for joining, Allen's respondent says: "We enjoyed ourselves and also felt important." At the end of 1932, the local unit had about seventy-five members.[22]

The real workhorses of Thalburg's NSDAP were the members of the Sturmabteilung. Although some overlap existed with the party membership, the two categories were not identical. Prior to 1933 there were "not more than fifty members" in Thalburg's SA, although once again there was a widespread illusion among the townspeople that there were "anywhere from three to eight times as many."[23] For many of its public functions, the party was able to call on SA men from the surrounding rural areas. They provided protection at party meetings and, at massed demonstrations, were used to impress the general populace. They also put up the posters announcing meetings and solicited new members, following up lists of prospective candidates. The party members "kept close track of whoever came to their meetings and afterwards worked hard to get such people to join, contribute to, or at least vote for, the NSDAP."[24] The continuous appearance of uniformed SA men in these diverse roles contributed to the exaggerated conception of their numbers.

The storm troopers, not too surprisingly, were rather tough characters. SA discipline, Allen reports, "systematically promoted nihilistic brutality." The leather shoulder straps of the uniform were intended to serve as a weapon. Easily detached, the straps were wound around the fist; the weighted buckles carried in the fist provided additional impact. Many carried blackjacks, brass knuckles, and other items of ingenious weaponry.[25]

Many SA men were unemployed. The Sturmabteilung provided a meaningful activity to fill out their days, the alternative being long and boring stretches of enforced idleness. For a number of more or less obvious reasons the SA men tended to congregate around the soup kitchen. This made it a staging area, a point for recruitment of other unemployed men, and a place where, in the course of everyday conversation, rather diffuse political loyalties could be reaffirmed and refined. The SA also recruited from among the *under*employed sons of farmers in the surrounding areas. This once again shows the party's ability to mobilize unused resources. One should not assume, however, that all SA men were unemployed or lower class. That was by no means the case.

For a party to have large numbers of troops available is one thing; the ability to move them about and to coordinate their efforts is quite another. In general, Allen's account leaves little doubt as to the capacity of the NSDAP to dispatch these forces as its needs required. The tactical mobility of these territorially dispersed forces is one of the most striking features of their local operations, both in Thalburg and elsewhere. By the end of 1932, Allen concludes, Thalburg's SA "had developed into a formidable instrument."[26]

One other point deserves some stress here. Given the enormous volume of activity, the presence of a continuous flow of literature, the regular appearance of posters, and given also the costs of meeting halls and the provision of transportation, it is easy to assume that money must have come from outside. Given too the sense that the party was made up of impoverished lower-middle-class individuals and unemployed workers, it is a plausible conclusion that money flowed down the party chain of command. That image was also reinforced by the Communist and Social Democratic emphasis on the support for the National Socialists coming from business and finance.

Allen's conclusion in this respect is just the opposite: "Like the whole of Nazi operations in Thalburg," he states, "the SA was financed exclusively from local sources; far from receiving money from the national NSDAP, it was constantly called on for contributions. Money came from dues, contributions, and from the proceeds of meetings where an admission fee was always charged."[27]

Allen's work provides little information on the backgrounds of either the party members or those in the SA. In the few cases discussed, emphasis is placed on the "lower middle class" or the "broken existences" theme. Nor is much information provided about the motivations of these actors. Other than pointing out that one faction of the NSDAP was concerned with idealism and national renewal, few clues are offered to indicate what distinguished these people from the remainder of the citizenry. Essentially what the work establishes is the immensely high level of NSDAP activity, which in turn is linked to a response by the middle-class population of the town. Information is also provided on the responses of the other parties to the NSDAP incursion into their routines. These responses are discussed in the following chapter.

A more wide-ranging portrayal of National Socialist activities appears in the work of Jeremy Noakes.[28] His study covers events in three Reichstag election districts (*Kreise*), those of Hanover-South-Brunswick, Hanover-East, and Weser-Ems. Geographically, the three districts form the northwest corner of Germany, with the Netherlands to the west and the North Sea, Hamburg, and Schleswig-Holstein to the north and northeast. Including therein were the Prussian province of Hanover, the tiny independent states of Oldenburg, Brunswick, and Schaumburg Lippe, and the city-state Bremen. Aside from the cities of Hanover and Bremen, the area was generally rural and small town in character. Except for a few Catholic pockets, it was overwhelmingly Protestant. The region was similar to Schleswig-Holstein in many ways and accordingly showed a political development closely paralleling that reported in Rudolf Heberle's study.[29] In July 1932, 51.0 percent of the vote in Schleswig-Holstein went to the NSDAP. Hanover-East was not far behind with 49.5 percent. Those were the highest figures among the thirty-five election districts of Germany.

Extremely high and sustained levels of activity by local NSDAP units are reported throughout Noakes's work. At an early point, in the span of thirteen months between February 1, 1925, and March 1, 1926, the party held 850 public meetings in *Gau* Hanover. This was the work of a small number of unusually devoted individuals, one leader alone holding 290 of that total and another holding 155. The remaining 400 meetings were the work of nineteen speakers. Eight of these speakers were from outside the *Gau*, and they only held a few meetings each.[30]

In November 1929, a local leader of the DNVP reported to his superior that "the National Socialists are making big gains in this *Kreis* because they hold meetings with good speakers in almost every village."[31] Noakes reports that

> phenomenal propaganda activity continued to be the most striking feature of the NSDAP. In the last four weeks of 1928 and the first four weeks of 1929, for example, 160 meetings were held in *Gau* Weser-Ems, excluding the routine weekly branch meetings. The other *Gaue* showed similar activity. From 3-31 May 1929, for example, two of the main speakers in Hanover-East . . . addressed forty-six meetings between them. It should be emphasized that these were normal periods—there was no election in the offing. In the autumn of 1929 *Gau* South-Hanover-Brunswick introduced a new propaganda technique, whereby all the leading speakers of the *Gau* would descend on

a single *Kreis* over the week-end and hold six meetings each. On 8-9 February 1930, for example, twenty-four meetings were held in the Göttingen area in twenty-eight hours with a total audience of 1,500. As a result four new branches and nineteen cells were founded.[32]

The party both held routine meetings and undertook special purpose campaigns, such as the anti–Young Plan campaign, that being its last major effort prior to the September 1930 Reichstag election. An Osnabrück police report, incidentally, stated that the NSDAP "concentrated more on winning party members than on the plebiscite."[33] The end result of these activities was a functioning political machine, skeletal at some points to be sure, but an apparatus that nevertheless was ready and available for a more ambitious effort. The relative positions of the NSDAP and its leading competitors in the September 1930 campaign are indicated in Noakes's summary: "The directives from *Gau* Hanover-South-Brunswick give the impression of a formidable propaganda machine and a campaign of exceptional skill. The NSDAP in fact had the advantage that it could simply increase the tempo of its already well-oiled machine, while the other bourgeois parties had to improvise a campaign specifically for the election."[34]

The ordinary political party, in Germany and elsewhere, is likely to see its task as a simple matter of carrying out the word. One makes contact with "the voters," imparts a message, and hopes for the best on election day. An important laissez faire component is indicated in that phrase "hopes for the best." But the NSDAP activists recognized (or had it pointed out to them) that the lesson learned today is forgotten tomorrow. For that reason, the wandering speakers were not only concerned with carrying out the word, they were also instrumental in founding and sustaining local units. Members were signed up at their meetings, their capacities were assessed, and one of them was designated as the local leader. Return visits by the speakers or by SA groups were scheduled to encourage the newly founded units in turn to carry the word to still others in their area.[35]

Another follow-up procedure involved the organization of discussion evenings (*Sprechabende*). At these, a less prominent speaker would review the principal themes covered by the orator at the latest rally. As Orlow puts it, these "were smaller, more intimate meetings of already committed militants who were joined by those who had been partially won over by the larger rally and wanted to know more about the party."[36]

One might expect a pattern of centralized direction and close supervision within the NSDAP. The actual relationship between top and bottom, however, appears to have been intermediate between the extremes of complete control and complete autonomy. It was recognized that organizations easily fall into warm, friendly, clublike routines. This had been noted as a problem for some of the *völkische* predecessors of the NSDAP and for the Conservatives. It is easy, a natural human tendency perhaps, for organizations to become introverted, to turn to discussion instead of outwardly directed action.[37] The selection of leaders, therefore, was based on evidence of the contender's willingness to lead a fighting campaign. As one local leader put it, he would prefer to found a branch only where there was an adequate leader; otherwise the party would face the problem of its forerunner the Schutz-und-Trutzbund, which in the end "existed everywhere and yet nowhere." Summarized another way, this leader declared that "a farmer's boy who has got complete control of his village is of more value to the movement than so-called 'leading personalities' whose activity is practically worthless."[38] Once the local unit was formed and a leader chosen, the practice was to allow it considerable autonomy. As Noakes puts it: "The NSDAP believed in granting independence to its smallest units as soon as possible on the grounds that 'a smaller group which must work independently and on its own responsibility inevitably develops much greater activity than if it is directly dependent on another branch.' The *Gau* head-quarters rewarded the efficient branches by assigning to them the most popular speakers."[39]

Once established, the local units followed a kind of social Darwinist survival-of-the-fittest principle. Since they were intended as activist fighting organizations, it was logical that the best organizer-fighter should be the local leader. That was not something to be decided by fiat or by outside direction; it was something to be demonstrated in the course of actual struggle. This principle, understandably, gave rise to a fair amount of internal conflict, and although the party did have an internal arbitration department, the tendency was to let the factions work it out, the idea being that the toughest and most capable leader would win out. One request to Munich headquarters for a decision in favor of a contender brought the following reply: "As a matter of principle Herr Hitler does not believe in 'appointing' branch leaders. Herr Hitler believes today more than ever that the most effective fighter in the NS movement is the man who wins respect for himself as leader through his own achievements."[40]

The democratic procedural rules found in most clubs were prohibited in the NSDAP. Quite early on, a local leader in the Hanover area declared that "our preparation for the coming dictatorship as well as our experience in the movement have occasioned the need for a dictatorial constitution for our regional organization. It is essential for the leaders to have absolute authority within their branches. . . . Membership meetings together with parliamentarism, that is 'voting' are absolutely forbidden as seeds of corruption."[41] The time and effort of the local units, in short, were not to be expended in motions, discussions, and votes. The capable, tested leaders would announce a line of action, and the others, trusting his ability, would follow without question. This was the meaning of the *Führerprinzip*. The autonomy of the local leaders, it should be noted however, was not total. The Hanover area directive announced an absolute right of intervention: "The leadership . . . is . . . permitted to interfere in the affairs of the branches at all times."[42]

The entire operation, moreover, was held together through a steady stream of memorandums, suggestions, and guidelines (*Richtlinien*) coming down the chain of command, and activity reports passing up. Again, however, it should be noted that the operation was not that of a fully developed bureaucracy (in Max Weber's sense), one characterized by monocratic direction from the top. From the top came guidelines, or suggestions as to how issues should be handled in a given campaign, or a review of techniques that had proved useful in recent elections elsewhere in Germany. The activity reports let people at the top know which units were performing and which ones were lagging. They also indicated which tactics had been used and with what success; such information in turn could be passed on to other units of the party for more general use. The higher echelons did, unquestionably, reserve an absolute right of intervention. But that was something of a reserve clause, something to be used for a malfunctioning or insubordinate unit. The intended relationship of top to bottom was to be one of close monitoring (as opposed to close control), of guiding, helping, encouraging. The ideal was an openhanded relationship rather than tightfisted control.[43]

To obtain a sense of the party effort as it was manifested over a larger area, it is useful to review its operations in Lower Saxony between September 1930 and July 1932. Three days after the 1930 Reichstag election, the propaganda headquarters of the Hanover-South-Brunswick *Gau* sent a directive to all branches emphasizing the need to "continue the struggle without any let-up." The principal immediate task within the region was a city council election in Bremen in November of 1930. The resources of the party, from the city itself and from the *Gau* Weser-Ems together with additional outside speakers, were concentrated there for a full-scale effort culminating in a big Hitler rally. In the twelve-week span following the Reichstag election, the NSDAP managed to double its strength, going from 25,045 to 51,324 votes.[44]

County elections followed in the state of Brunswick on the first of March 1931. In January and February, the party held 600 meetings within this small state, more than 100 of them with outside speakers. The next task was a state election in Oldenburg on May 29. This was a priority concern for the party, since it hoped to gain a majority there.

Then, throughout the summer, its activity was concentrated on the campaign for the dissolution of the Prussian Landtag. During the month of September, *Gau* Hanover-South-Brunswick "held eleven big rallies, 400 public meetings, 400 indoctrination and discussion evenings and fifty other functions (such as SA concerts and 'German Evenings')."[45]

The party militants could maintain the level of activity, but at about this time they recognized "a surfeit on the part of audiences." The party's response was to diversify the range of offerings. A Lower Saxony NS Theater Company presented plays (for example, "Poison Gas 506"), and the party obtained the services of a film library. *Gau* Hanover-South-Brunswick published a booklet, sent to all local propaganda directors, indicating the range of techniques available.[46]

This same *Gau* developed a technique for dealing with the weaker branches. A large rally would be held making use of the best speakers of the *Gau*. The proceeds were used to finance a "shock troop" consisting of a "few speakers from different occupations" who then spent two weeks in the backward district, blanketing it with meetings. One such effort stimulated the creation of several new branches and brought in 221 new members. The technique, which was duly reported to higher levels, received the approval of Goebbels who in turn passed the information on to other *Gaue* urging them to try the method.[47]

A significant change in the propaganda focus came about in the course of 1931. The Reich propaganda headquarters, recognizing that "the bourgeois parties were finished," declared that henceforth efforts should be directed against the still intact forces of the Zentrum and of Marxism. This new direction came complete with precise instructions for the conduct of the struggle—attacks "must never extend to religion or church institutions." "Continually repeat," it said, "that National Socialism is not a religious *Weltanschauung*." A basic claim to be used was that the Zentrum had "misused religion for political purposes."[48] Simultaneously, the National Socialists could stress their own support for religion (as happened in Thalburg) while conducting an attack on "atheistic socialism." For this purpose they were able to enlist the support of many Protestant clergymen.

The main target for their propaganda, Noakes declares, was Marxism. To support this effort, special indoctrination courses were organized and material prepared. Courses were given throughout the Reich; in addition, *Gau* Hanover-South-Brunswick organized its own course for the training of "special anti-Marxist agitators."[49]

These campaign efforts reached their culmination, of course, in 1932, the year of elections. The second round of the presidential elections, in the early spring, posed special tactical problems that were dealt with in a set of guidelines (Why vote at all, when it was clear Hindenburg would win? Why vote for Hitler? How were they to avoid a direct attack on Hindenburg?). In the Prussian election, the party could concentrate its attack on the SPD and the Zentrum, emphasizing the failure of that government's job-creation policies and in turn giving publicity to its own work program. One incidental lesson learned in these three months and three campaigns was a need for greater decentralization; that would avoid delay and allow campaigns to be more precisely tailored to specific population segments.

By the time of the July Reichstag election, the problem of voter ennui had once again become acute, the branch leader in Göttingen reporting "a feeling of exhaustion among audiences." Again the response was to diversify the offerings, placing more emphasis on mass rallies, entertainment evenings, and military displays. The party also paid attention to film propaganda, used loudspeaker vans, and made use of a technique developed in the presidential elections, personal letters.[50]

Delicate tactical considerations also arose in this election, and, accordingly, guidelines were sent down telling the local units how to deal with the problem of opposing Papen without ruining the possibility of future influence. To attract working-class support, the party had to stress its independence from Papen and his "cabinet of barons." For the bourgeois voters "the party was ordered to point out . . . the increased danger of civil war owing to the emergent united front of the *Reichsbanner* and the KPD. And, as an aspect of this tactic, the party press was ordered to concentrate for a whole week on the street fight in Altona as a symptom of the growing danger. In this situation, the NSDAP pointed out that the bourgeois parties were simply not strong enough to have any effect on the issue and votes for them would therefore be wasted."[51]

What this adds up to is a portrait of a propaganda machine of extraordinary capacity. Noakes's summary touches on

> its willingness to experiment with different media and techniques—for example, [Hitler's] aeroplane tour and films; its adaptability to changes in the mood of its audiences—for example, the switch from ordinary meetings to entertainment and rallies; and its efficiency in employing its resources with maximum effect and in mobilizing the membership. This flexibility and sheer administrative efficiency was the result of the excellent channels of communication between the local branches, the *Gau* head-quarters and the Reich leadership. . . . Speakers were trained and given financial incentives; the technical aspects of propaganda were explained in an easily comprehensible form

in manuals and directives; above all, the local departments were kept constantly up-to-date about the various themes and techniques which required particular emphasis. They not only felt fully involved in the party's activities and in its successes and failures, but were also able to keep the membership fully informed. Finally, the NSDAP's propaganda organization was distinguished from all its rivals . . . by its open-mindedness and freedom from the inhibitions of tradition. Local leaders were encouraged to report on their experiences and to experiment with new techniques (though not with content) which, if successful, would be recommended by the *Gau* or Reich leadership.[52]

To summarize more economically, we may borrow once again from Noakes who describes the party's propaganda effort as one showing "energy, efficiency and virtuosity."[53]

THE NSDAP CADRES

It is clear that the party had large numbers of militants and, moreover, that it had very capable ones. One must consider why that was the case. Or, put somewhat differently, one must ask how they were able to assemble this army of militants. Because the thesis of this chapter is complex, it is useful to consider it first in brief outline.

Everything begins with the war. All the individual and organizational developments, in one way or another, stem from the 1914-1918 experience. By itself, the war would provide only the necessary conditions for the later development, since other countries, England and France, for example, were also major participants in the war and yet did not see the equivalent quantitative development of fascist movements. But, as we shall see, there were some peculiar organizational developments within the German military, elements of which were carried over into the postwar period. Germany was unique too, among the combatant nations, in its widespread and fervent belief that the end result was unjust. Then, too, for Germany the war did not end in November 1918. For many, it was continued in struggles on the borders of the Reich, both east and west, and in the nation's cities. The most important organization here, of course, was the Freikorps. As a consequence, the most enthusiastic fighters were provided with continuous military experience; for some, it lasted to 1923.

At that point, with the ending of the inflation and the arrival of the American loans, neither government nor business was interested in supporting these freewheeling armies. To obtain the loans, it was necessary to provide at least the appearance of order and stability. The official Freikorps units were disbanded, not without considerable difficulty, as we have seen, and the operations of the unofficial ones were severely checked. This control was possible because a degree of centralization had occurred during the inflation. With official sources of support withdrawn, only the major industrialists were still in a position to support these free-enterprise armies. The "uncontrollables" lost out because they could simply be denied funds.

There were signs of a major strain within the ranks at this time. The devoted fighters wished to continue the relentless struggle. But the major fighting organizations available to them now restricted their activity. This was a period of search and movement as the old fighters shifted from one paramilitary organization to the next. Some authors have argued that the bases for both left and right extremism dried up during this flourishing middle period of the republic. But this is doubtful since the membership of the Stahlhelm, and later of the Sturmabteilung, showed steady and continuous growth during those years. Some Freikorps fighters felt a professional disdain for the National Socialists, seeing the Munich *Putsch* as a miserable amateurish performance. To march through a narrow street without weapons and with no cover, to march directly in the face of enemy guns was, in their expert opinion, idiotic. But in the good years of Weimar, the uncontrolled National Socialists proved to be the most relentless of the available organizations, and they, accordingly, drew the fighters into their ranks. It was the *failure* to receive major industry support that left them free to take the radical position. And that freedom was the condition that allowed them to gain the numbers and talents enabling them to move in the early 1930s.

The positive side of the argument of this book, then, is that the National Socialists' core cadres consisted of men who had followed this peculiar career, first in the war, then in the five years of intermittent postwar combat, then in various paramilitary organizations of the middle period, eventually, in ever-increasing numbers, coming over to the National Socialists, to the party, and to the Sturmabteilung. Drawn from all over Germany, these cadres were highly mobile (in the military sense of that term). Young, tough, and resourceful, they were also, because of their wide-ranging experience, adept in the tactics of small-unit struggle. They also served as heroic models for later generations of German youth, particularly for the more nationalistic segments of the middle classes. These cadres carried the National Socialist message first to the cities, and then, most importantly, to the towns and countryside. There, they were responsible for the party's decisive electoral victories. Evidence supporting these claims is provided in the following pages. There is a further implication of this argument: were it not for these cadres, the conditions alone (whether historical, social, cultural, or economic), would not have been sufficient to generate those victories.

THE WAR AND THE *Fronterlebnis*

The impact of the war and its influence on postwar developments are discussed by Ernest H. Posse, the author of a leading work on the paramilitary organizations of the Weimar period. After a brief discussion of the youth movement, Posse declares that

> for the postwar Germans, the World War was decisive. . . . for the total population, including the generation that did not see the trenches, the war itself is the catastrophe that will remain for decades as the experience. For the combatants, everything is concentrated in the *Fronterlebnis* [front, or combat, experience]. In the words of the leading men of the organizations founded after the war, the strongest theme is that the front experience had created a new man, one who has discarded the old Wilhelminian ways and who, within himself, senses entirely new and different centers of activity. The officer in the trenches, who came from a privileged stratum, fought side by side with the artisan and next to the ordinary worker. There, the subordinate turned into a comrade, a fellow soldier. In the trenches what counted was not just passing on the received orders and seeing to it that they were carried out correctly. In place of the order, which the officer was to have received from above but which in battle did not reach its destination, there came the officer's own initiative. In place of the constant supervision of the troops by the officers, there came . . . also for the ordinary soldier, an awakening of initiative. Under fire, the trench officers were affected the same as the soldiers when the meals were not able to reach either of them. Thus necessity made into comrades the men who had been estranged by the overabundance of prewar Germany.

Some of the same themes appear in a long footnote in which Posse states that "experiencing the front and experiencing the comradeship are one . . . [they] mean a cutting loose from yesterday's class situation." He cites Schultze-Pfaelzer, author of a generally acceptable account of the revolution, who says, "The fighting troops have put behind them that which was, that which happened in the peaceful days of yesteryear. For them, the bourgeois and the proletarian concepts melt into a completely new sphere of existence." Then Posse notes some important lines of distinction: "This, however, only counts for the fighting trench formations, not for higher headquarters, not for the fleet, and not for the homeland. Among the fighting troops one can also observe a growing estrangement of their officers from the mass of higher ranking officers and the general staffers who stand accused of not knowing the technique and psychology of actual battle. . . . Much of the front fighter's way of feeling and thinking remains incomprehensible to the higher ranking officers. They, then, speak of the 'frog's perspective' of the front fighters."[54]

These quotations suggest the major impact of the war to have been the following: first, the front soldiers were cut off from their prior experience, and, to use the language of the social sciences, were resocialized. Second, the content of the new socialization included a sense of egalitarianism, of *Kameradschaft*, a requirement for personal initiative, and a hostility to the older, in some ways less capable, distant and sheltered higher ranks.[55] To this list should be appended still another characteristic, this being best summarized in a single word—ruthlessness (*Rücksichtslosigkeit*). By this is meant a preference for direct immediate action in pursuit of a goal with little or no regard for side effects or concern for moral questions (for example, about the means to be used). Not only did the front soldiers act in this way, many came to consider it a fully justified, completely legitimate mode of behavior.

The above summary claims, put forth with so little qualification, make no mention whatsoever of frequency distributions (as if to suggest that *all* front soldiers reacted in the same way). The extreme formulation, however, is clearly unjustified. One can immediately think of exceptions in the popular literature, the most notable being Erich Maria Remarque's *All Quiet on the Western Front*. The frequency of the traits asserted by Posse cannot be established with any degree of certainty. Men reacted differently no doubt, some with war-trained ruthlessness, some with a heightened pacifism. The significance of these diverse reactions is considered below.

One good reason for accepting Posse's claims, aside from the large number of impressionistic sources vouching for them, is the appearance of similar traits elsewhere, for example among American soldiers in World War II, this being one of the best researched of all wars. The American soldiers also saw combat as the source of a kind of egalitarianism, as creating a *Kameradschaft*; they too reported a general disdain for the higher and more removed ranks, and also, a considerable amount of ruthlessness appeared. (See the discussion in note 87, this chapter.) It seems likely that all conditions of sustained mass combat generate these results—they are likely to have appeared in both World Wars and in the French, English, and Russian armies as well as in the German. Putting it still more generally, all conditions of sustained common danger induce *Kameradschaft*, force initiative from all, and lead to the reduction in the significance of formal rankings. In war, in coal mining, in police work, and among prison guards, the same developments occur. That leads to a further question: why did the war-created ruthlessness win out in Germany, whereas in the other countries it was more or less contained? To answer this question one has to inquire more carefully into the character of combat on the German side and into the special features of its resolution.

The war, so it is said, was greeted with widespread enthusiasm by all segments of the population, most of whom were fully confident of victory in a short, decisive campaign.[56] The expectation was that König-grätz and Sedan would be repeated, those being the single-day battles that effectively decided the Austro-Prussian and Franco-Prussian wars. But the setback in the first battle of the Marne and the resulting failure of the entire Schlieffen strategy brought a completely unexpected result, a war of position with both sides dug in along a line from the Swiss border to the English Channel and with movement virtually impossible. The remainder of the war, particularly in the west, involved attempts by both sides to achieve the breakthrough that would then allow encirclement of the enemy and a decisive victory. A wide range of military experimentation followed—planes flew over the lines machine gunning, dropping spikes and then bombs, week-long artillery barrages were used prior to attack, tanks and gas were used as weapons on the ground, and miners worked under the ground, tunneling under enemy lines, placing charges, and blowing up huge sections of the trenches. Most of this effort was without significant effect, and many soldiers, especially the more committed, were intensely frustrated.[57]

Quite early in the struggle, the Germany armies created specialized combat units to solve this basic problem. These units, initially called shock troops, were used, unsuccessfully, in 1914. They also came to be referred to as storm troops (Sturmtrupps or Sturmbataillone). The plan, in brief, was to develop "superlatively conditioned, well-trained elite troops whose task it was, literally, to 'storm' the enemy lines and force a breakthrough for the regular infantry."[58] Special equipment was designed for these troops including carbines, flame throwers, and portable machine guns. They were the first to wear the familiar steel helmet (*Stahlhelm*) of the German armies in both World Wars. Their favorite weapon, one they introduced and which was to be their trademark, was the hand grenade.

These soldiers were distinguished by many special signs. They had special uniforms and special insignia; they received the best food and equipment; they all (not just the officers) carried pistols; they had a relaxed discipline (in exchange for their special military contributions); and more than anywhere else in the army, the men were on familiar terms with their officers, frequently addressing them with the *Du* form. In these units, the comradeship and the collapse of formal rank occurring throughout the army were carried to their greatest extreme.[59]

Such work would clearly have an extraordinary effect on the outlooks of these combatants. The leading chronicler of their activities, the writer Ernst Jünger, could write on a "lovely April day" early in the war that

> Surely this day that God has given
> Was meant for better uses than to kill.[60]

But the subsequent years of combat would lead him to conclusions such as "living means killing" (*Leben heisst töten*).[61] Describing the feelings of the storm troops in combat, Jünger wrote: "The turmoil of our feelings was called forth by rage, alcohol and the thirst for blood. As we advanced heavily but irresistibly toward the enemy lines, I was boiling over with a fury which gripped me—it gripped us all—in an inexplicable way. The overpowering desire to kill gave me wings. Rage squeezed bitter tears from my eyes. . . . Only the spell of primaeval instinct remained."[62]

Jünger, too, writes of his "resocialization," describing his previous education and training as follows: "As the son of a thoroughly convinced materialist epoch, I was drawn into this war, a cold, precocious, city dweller, the brain, through a concern with natural sciences and modern literature, cut to steel crystals. I have been greatly changed because of the war and believe that the same thing probably happened to the whole generation."[63] His attitude toward the received cultural tradition is indicated in more detail in the following passages: "Most important is not what we fight for, but how we fight. Move toward the goal, until we win or die. The fighting spirit, the risking of one's life, and be it for the smallest idea, weighs more heavily than all mulling over good and evil. . . . the soldier . . . knows little about the philosophers and their values. But with him and his deed, life expresses itself far more impressively and deeper than any book could have conceived."[64] "This is the New Man," Jünger wrote, "the storm soldier, the elite of *Mitteleuropa*. A completely new race, cunning, strong, and packed with purpose." As Hermann Goering put it, here were "fighters who could not become de-brutalized."[65]

Some distinctive features of these units and their implications for postwar Germany are indicated by Waite:

> The Storm Troop system [involved] a tremendous increase in the number of young commanders. The ratio of officers, or noncommissioned officers, to enlisted men sometimes reached as high as one to four. [And] only a very special type of officer could be used. He must be unmarried, under twenty-five years of age, in excellent physical condition (former athletes were given preference), he must be mentally alert, and above all he must possess in abundance that quality which German military writers call "ruthlessness." The result was

that at the time of the Armistice Germany was flooded with hundreds of capable, arrogant young commanders who found an excellent outlet for their talents in the Free Corps movement.[66]

REVOLUTION AND THE WAR'S END

Before turning to the development of the Freikorps, it is important to consider the circumstances of the war's end. The predilections of generalizing social sciences lead one to overlook wars; they do not lend themselves to easy generalization. The effects on participant nations are rather diverse, the greatest asymmetry occurring when one side wins and the other loses. The diverse reactions to that fact might be moderated or aggravated depending on whether or nor the outcome was viewed as just or legitimate. In Germany, of course, a myth grew up, ultimately having very wide currency, of the *Dolchstoss*, the stab in the back. The argument, put very simply, was that Germany, if not winning the war, at least had not lost it. Only the revolution on the home front turned the tide, forcing not only a surrender, but requiring the acceptance of ignominious terms.

The history of the *Dolchstoss* has been repeated too often to warrant extensive review here. In a sense, "the facts" are largely irrelevant, since what people believed is what really mattered. That Ludendorff had repeatedly and with great urgency called on the government to negotiate a peace did not deter him, only a few days after the Armistice, from exclaiming, as if with a shock of recognition, "Yes, yes, that's it exactly. We were stabbed in the back."[67]

The legend was not just the product of conservative nationalist publicists. There was a "realistic" basis to the myth, one that was recognized by every German soldier at the front in November 1918. Although Germany was on the edge of collapse, on all fronts her troops were located on foreign soil. Nowhere had the Allies crossed the German borders although, to be sure, had the war lasted another few months they would most certainly have done so. The "frog's perspective," however, provided the basis for this belief that they had been cheated out of victory by treason on the home front. Another slogan, second only to the notion of the *Dolchstoss*, referred to the German army as *"im Felde unbesiegt"*—undefeated in the field. This was a phrase used by Friedrich Ebert, the SPD leader and later president of the republic, in his greeting to the returning troops as they entered Berlin in December 1918.[68]

The Armistice signed on November 11, 1918, provided for more than just a cessation of hostilities, it also required that Germany immediately turn over huge quantities of weaponry. It was an agreement, in short, that demanded a drastic reduction of the military capacity of the de-feated nation. It also required, within a matter of weeks, the removal of German troops from the front lines. The last major task of the general staff was to arrange for the return home of millions of combatants.

At this point a series of events occurred that were of decisive importance for the future of the new republic. These events received hardly a mention in most general histories of the period. They are usually not mentioned at all in left histories. But they come into sharp focus—even if only for a page or two—in the accounts of nationalists and Freikorps fighters, and, later, in those of Hitler's cadres.

In many places the troops returned to their home communities to be greeted by revolutionary mobs who treated the veterans, most notably the officers, as a species of criminal, ripping insignia off their uniforms, tearing away the signs of rank together with their medals. In many cases, this was done by women within the mob, which doubtless fore-stalled an immediate response but which also, no doubt, increased the sense of helplessness and fury. Many of Abel's respondents reported this experience. "In the streets of Harburg," one of them wrote, "the mu-tineers tore the uniform piece by piece off my back." Another says, "We sat in our bunkers and heard about the mess behind the lines, about the dry rot setting in back home. . . . We felt that Frenchmen and Tommies were no longer our worst enemy, that there was worse com-ing. . . . The march home was my most bitter experience." Another speaks of "very young boys, degenerate deserters, and prostitutes [who] tore the insignia off our best front line soldiers and spat on their field-gray uniforms. . . . That was the liberty these heroes from behind the lines were talking about. . . . For the first time a searing hatred rose in me against these subhumans who were stepping on everything pure and clean." If one assumes the revolutionary leaders had at least some influ-ence over their ranks, allowing these actions to occur must be counted as a disastrous error of judgment.[69] It would be difficult to find another instance anywhere in history in which the triumph of feeling over po-litical judgment, of personal rancor and spite over good sense, was to have more deadly consequences. Many of the veterans were probably at least open to the idea of a revolution or to a republican regime, and such experiences would have been decisive in turning them against the new government. As one of them put it, "I knew I did not want to have anything to do with those people."[70]

The impact of the Versailles treaty would have been more complex, the implications more far-reaching. By the time of its acceptance and signing, in June of 1919, many veterans would have joined the various Freikorps units and would have fought in several urban campaigns. For this group, clearly, the Versailles stipulations could not have played a causal role.[71] For them, it would have had the effect of sustaining anger rather than creating it. In addition to accepting large unspecified reparations and facing both immediate and prospective losses of border territories, Germany was required to acknowledge war guilt, that is, to accept a sweeping claim that Germany had caused the war. Details of the treaty were worked out over a period of years, first in the Dawes Plan and later in the Young Plan. The later implementations, as we have seen, provided a continuous source of difficulties for Germany's parties and governments, ultimately providing considerable ammunition for the NSDAP when the depression aggravated all problems. The treaty probably moved other segments of the German population, not just the militant nationalists; it probably moved those with mixed feelings about the war and the peace, those who, initially at least, were well-disposed toward the republic.

Another group affected by the treaty was the refugee populations. The separation of various parts of German territory brought hundreds of thousands of them into the now-reduced Reich. Many of them nursed their special grievances; some among them, of course, hoped to return. Many uprooted young people, having to begin a new career, found employment in the Freikorps.

THE FREIKORPS

Individual grievances, even those that are widespread and deeply felt, do not ordinarily affect events. Only when those holding the grievances come together, when their grievances take an organizational form, is an impact possible. In this case, the organization in question, the Freikorps, was created by the revolutionary government and, for a while at least, received support and approval not only from the government but also from some major business interests, from the landed aristocracy, from the official SPD press, and, up to the time of the Kapp *Putsch*, from the liberal press, most notably, the *Vossische Zeitung* and the *Berliner Tageblatt*.[72]

The German revolution of 1918 was a most peculiar instance of the species. As many writers point out, it did not involve the overthrowing of a government; more accurately, it was the withdrawal of a government. Prince Max of Baden, the last chancellor of the old regime, simply turned the powers of government over to the leader of the majority Social Democrats. "Herr Ebert," he said, "I commit the German Empire to your keeping."[73] Ebert, the leader of the revolutionary government, somewhat reluctant to accept this grant, asked his predecessor to stay on as an administrator, but the prince refused.

The new government found itself in a difficult position. The municipal police forces were not strong enough to deal with the assorted revolutionary forces present on the streets of Germany. The army units, many of them, dissolved as soon as they arrived in their home communities, and many of the others were of questionable reliability. There were, in short, few loyal forces available to back up the new government. Any small group of semiorganized hoodlums could, however, impose its will on the government. An instance of this sort appeared just before Christmas when a battalion of revolutionary sailors, in Berlin ostensibly to protect the government, instead at one point captured the government to back up its wage demands. Faced with such problems, the government felt it necessary to rely on more "dependable" military forces.[74]

One must consider the processes of recruitment into the Freikorps; again our discussion is based on the important work of Robert Waite. The key figures in the Korps were young officers, mostly lieutenants and captains. The organizer of one of the earliest of these groups had at first used older officers, following the principles of the old imperial army, but he soon changed his mind. "I learned," he said, "that my earlier theory was completely wrong. I have observed many very young officers in difficult situations in which they conducted themselves admirably. . . . Youth has the advantage of carelessness, or enterprising spirit, and above all, of patriotic fervor on its side—qualities that are not to be despised."[75]

The forces were exclusively volunteer units. And careful selection was made among those offering their services. There is little evidence available on the details of these processes, but it is clear that urban manual workers did not volunteer in any significant numbers and that the young ex-officers, most of whom would originally have been from nonmanual backgrounds, did respond. There are some suggestions that workers, particularly those with left orientations, were discouraged from joining.[76] Selection, it seems, followed the lines of personal contacts, the leaders of the new units seeking out members of their former companies who were proven fighters. Where the mass conscript army would contain a wide range of outlooks, extending from enthusiasts to haters of war, the highly personal volunteering and selection processes used here resulted in battalions composed almost exclusively of military enthusiasts, or, if one will, of war lovers.

Waite notes the ample material advantages to be gained by enlistment. There was the base pay of thirty to fifty marks a day (in 1919). Soldiers were guaranteed food, pension contributions, family allotments, demobilization payments when they ended their service, and uniforms. In the Baltic campaign, it was widely believed that they would receive land grants on the occasion of their ultimate success. In addition to the material perquisites, there were also the psychic benefits. The soldiers who could not fit into *bürgerliche* (civilian or bourgeois) society could in these units continue the work they had done for the last four years. As for their outlooks, the future supreme SA *Führer* for western Germany put it this way: "People told us that the War was over. That made us laugh. We ourselves are the War. Its flame burns strongly in us. It envelops our whole being and fascinates us with the enticing urge to destroy. We obeyed . . . and marched onto the battle fields of the postwar world just as we had gone into battle on the Western Front: singing, reckless and filled with the joy of adventure as we marched to the attack; silent, deadly, remorseless in battle."[77]

And the future National Socialist minister president of Saxony claimed that "the pure *Landsknechte* [freebooter, a favorite expression of the Freikorps members] didn't much care why or for whom they fought. The main thing for them was that they *were* fighting. . . . War had become their career. They had no desire to look for another. . . . War made them happy—what more can you ask?"[78]

The numbers involved in the Freikorps have been variously estimated. Ernst von Salomon, the leading chronicler of Freikorps activities, gives figures between 50,000 and 150,000. Gustav Noske, the minister of defense, estimated the numbers at 400,000, and the Independent Socialist Hugo Haase put their numbers at over a million. Part of the difficulty stems from the fact that they were irregular troops and that their numbers fluctuated considerably. Another problem stems from the variety of the units classified under the heading Freikorps. Apart from the basic units, there were also emergency volunteers (Zeitfreiwilligen), civil guards (Einwohnerwehr or citizens' defense), security police (Sicherheitspolizei), and armed student formations (in Münster there was the Akademische Wehr). The "real" Freikorps units were the highly mobile, self-sufficient fighting forces, the other units serving more specialized functions. The civil guards performed garrison duty, "maintaining order" in the community after the Freikorps' "liberation." Waite estimates the number of men directly involved in the "real" Freikorps units as "somewhere between 200,000 and 400,000."[79]

A major source of recruits, as already indicated, was the younger officers. Again Waite supplies some important details. The war had created numerous opportunities for social mobility. Roughly half of the 22,112 active officers in the army at the beginning of the war were killed. By the end of the war most of those surviving had been removed to the rear echelons so as to preserve them for further duty. The losses among the 29,230 reserve officers were also extremely high. This being a mass war, "opportunities" were also created by the enormous expansion in the size of the military operation, the army having 270,000 officers at the end of the war. The overwhelming majority of the newly promoted officers would have assumed positions of power and responsibility for the first time in their lives. Many would also have recognized that equivalent positions were not likely to be available for them in civilian life. Since the Versailles-imposed limit allowed only 4,000 officers for the 100,000-man army and since these were to be drawn almost exclusively from the surviving members of the active officer corps, this meant that over a quarter of a million young battle-trained officers faced civilian careers. For many of them, particularly for the war lovers, it was not a happy thought. As they put it, once "peace broke out," they faced a very unpleasant prospect, that being the "soul-destroying" life of a civilian. Going to work as a salesman, or as the representative of an insurance company, or even, if lucky, rising to the rank of office manager, were possibilities they viewed with little enthusiasm.

For them the Freikorps provided an outlet for their interests and talents; it gave them a second chance. A study of Bavarian officers, one of the few studies of occupational mobility available for this period, showed that 22.6 percent of the second lieutenants and 27.6 percent of the first lieutenants continued their military careers in the Freikorps. Waite notes that the percentages among the higher officers were definitely lower. Von Salomon (as quoted by Waite) says that "senior officers showed surprisingly little inclination to enter Free Corps service" and that "majors were received by the troops themselves as an unwelcome burden."[80]

Waite summarizes the usefulness of the Freikorps for these displaced officers:

> The Free Corps Movement was an almost perfect answer to the psychological and social needs of the junior officer. Indeed, life in the volunteers was even better than it had been in the Imperial Army. In those days he had commanded a platoon or at best a company; now he was the master of mixed formations of battalion or even regimental strength. In the Imperial Army men were assigned to him and he had to train them according to rigid Army regulations; now he could recruit his own men and train them as he saw fit. He no longer was rigorously supervised by military superiors; under the Free Corps system he was responsible to no one. In brief, the life of the *Freikorpsführer* was eminently satisfactory. Indeed it was so satisfactory that the young leader did everything in his power to perpetuate the system. Hence, in the days when the Free Corps were theoretically dissolved, the captains and the lieutenants turned to the various military and semimilitary organizations sponsored by National Socialism as the nearest approximation of the Free Corps system.[81]

Next to the veterans, Waite reports, students formed the largest group in the Free Corps. He described them as young idealists, brought up to believe "in the moral righteousness of Germany's cause" and at the same time as persons "stunned by the magnitude and the suddenness of the collapse." Many of them, he says, felt cheated of their right to fight for the fatherland by the Armistice; now, in the Freikorps, they were getting a second chance.[82]

There was a back and forth movement between the military and academic settings. Demobilized soldiers came into the universities. Some of them left later on to join the Freikorps. Members of the more irregular of these units would drift back into the universities again between campaigns. Thus some of the war-created outlooks were brought into the universities. These fighters provided role models for many of the younger students, particularly for those of nationalist persuasions. And here, too, the highly selective volunteering and recruitment processes were continued, thus replenishing and adding to the ranks of the older fighters.[83] This linkage allowed the units to bridge the generations, bringing in even younger cohorts. This is a point to which we will return later in this chapter.[84]

What did the Freikorps do? An answer to this question has been provided at various points throughout this work; therefore only a brief overview is required here. As official government-sponsored units, they made their first appearance in Berlin, toward the end of the week-long uprising in January of 1919. They played a decisive role in defeating the KPD's March undertaking of 1919, displaying their lethal capacities for the first time. In addition to "cleaning up" some smaller cities, Bremen, Leipzig, Halle, Gotha, and Brunswick among others, their most renowned action of this early period was the "liberation" of Munich in the first days of May.[85]

Some complex border struggles then occupied them, the most important of these being the Baltic venture of 1919. With British approval, these German units operated in the Baltic, at first fighting against the invading Red Army. Nominally under the authority of a newly created indigenous government, they proceeded to overthrow this sponsorship thus making the British position untenable. Many of these fighters wished to salvage the war through the creation of a satellite state under the leadership of the ethnic-German barons whose families had settled there in previous centuries. Having been promised land (a promise that had no justification, incidentally) they saw themselves as the vanguard of a new German settlement in the east. But their victories (including the overthrow) undid them. As one of them put it, in typically pungent prose, "Wir haben uns totgesiegt" (roughly, "We have killed ourselves with victory"). The German government ordered them home. After refusals, mutinies, and assorted acts of rebellion, they did finally return to Germany.[86]

The Baltic was the scene of unbelievably vicious combat. Von Salomon, a veteran of the campaign, gives some sense of what occurred in the hands of such select and devoted fighters:

> We made the last push. Yes, we roused ourselves one more time and stormed ahead along the entire line. Once again we pulled the last man with us, taking him from his cover, and plunged into the forest. We ran over the fields of snow and came to another forest. We fired into the surprised enemy and raged and shot and beat and chased. We drove the Latvians like rabbits over the fields and threw fire into every house and pulverized every bridge into dust and broke every telegraph pole. We threw the bodies into wells and threw hand grenades in after them. We slew whatever fell into our hands; we burned whatever could be burned. We saw red; we had nothing more of human feelings in our hearts. Where we had lived, there the earth groaned under our annihilation. Where we had attacked, there lay, where once were houses, ruins, ashes, glowing beams, like suppurating wounds in the open fields.[87]

The next major event in the Freikorps' history was an attempt to overthrow the Weimar government. Various units, the most notable of which was the Ehrhardt Brigade, marched on Berlin forcing the government to flee, this being the initial event in the Kapp *Putsch* of March 1920. The collapse of this five-day government was recounted in the previous chapter, the principal weapon of the government, it will be remembered, being the use of the general strike. In the discussions following its collapse, the Freikorps fighters placed the blame squarely on the generals and politicians. The politician Kapp was clearly incompetent. And their commanding general, Walther von Lüttwitz had also demonstrated incompetence in the organization of the *Putsch*. In the face of the general strike, moreover, he had reacted with what to the average Kämpfer (fighter) was a distressing and incomprehensible restraint. "Everything would still have been all right," one of them said, "if we had just shot more people." Another agreed; as he put it, "Blood is the cement of revolution."[88]

In addition to further discrediting politicians and higher-level officers, this failure meant, as von Salomon expressed it, "that for the first time the road was now completely open to the young men's own political thinking." Hitler's bid for power in November 1923, he says, was "not conceivable without this development in their political thinking." Hitler's movement, for them, had a very striking advantage; it was a movement of front soldiers, of fighters, not of "higher ups."[89]

The last action of the Freikorps prior to the official dissolution, was the effort against the Communists in the Ruhr. The latter, it will be remembered, had taken over cities from Düsseldorf to Dortmund as their contribution to the general strike effort. Freikorps units, including that of the putschist Hermann Ehrhardt, were ordered into the Ruhr for one last government-sponsored operation.

At this point, the government, under increasing pressure from the Allies, moved to dissolve its own creation. Understandably, the members of these organizations were very much opposed to this prospect. A hasty search for guises or fronts occurred, to provide the cover under which the formations could be maintained. Some settled on estates in Silesia and elsewhere in the east; there they continued their activity as "farm laborers." Some groups reappeared as patriotic veterans' organizations. One famous Freikorps leader, Gerhart Rossbach, organized a part of his force into a "detective bureau" and another part into a "savings society." The latter was outlawed by the Prussian minister of interior. Rossbach then changed it into a Union for Agricultural Instruction, declaring that he could "organize new outfits faster than [the authorities] can dissolve them."[90] Some joined the already existing veterans' organizations, many going into the Stahlhelm, but most Freikorps veterans found it "too stuffy and conservative." The great favorite of the ex-Freikorps fighters, Waite says, was the fiercely anti-Semitic Deutschvölkischer Schutz-und-Trutzbund.[91] Most of the men who joined these groups also had to seek some kind of civilian employment, the veterans' organizations being an after-work affair.

The various local units of the Einwohnerwehr were coordinated and brought under common leadership in the Organisation Escherich (Orgesch for short) before going underground. The Bavarian government refused to disband these units, thus providing the occasion for the 1923 test of strength with the Berlin government. Some ex-Freikorps people joined this outfit.[92]

One underground organization of considerable importance was the Organisation Consul (O.C. for short). Its task was to dispense vigilante justice. This included murdering officials in the republican government, especially those identified with the collapse in 1918 and with the fulfillment of the Versailles *Diktats*, and those said to have exposed underground military operations or to have acted in the service of the nation's enemies, as for example, the Palatinate separatists. One of the leaders of this organization later testified in court that it had killed some 200 persons in Silesia alone. Among its victims were Matthias Erzberger, a leader of the Zentrum, who, among other things, had signed the Armistice (thus saving Hindenburg the embarrassment), and Walther

Rathenau, the nation's foreign minister and architect of the policy of fulfillment.[93]

There was one last occasion on which units of the Freikorps went into battle. Continuous controversy had existed over the Polish border. In the spring of 1921, a group of Polish irregulars crossed over the frontier with the intention of capturing Upper Silesia for Poland. Ex-Freikorpsmen left their jobs and got on the trains crossing Germany, reformed their ranks, and won a decisive victory. Two days after this event, after the storming of the Annaberg, the government order came through declaring the final dissolution of all Freikorps units. Once again the old fighters saw themselves stabbed in the back. While they were giving their lives for Germany, the November criminals, their term for the republic's leaders, did them in.[94]

Without government support, without money basically, the units did decline in 1922. All the organizational ingenuity in the world could not maintain their fighting condition especially as, with the developing inflation, private funds also became more difficult to obtain. The French-Belgian invasion of the Ruhr in January, however, gave them another opportunity. Simultaneously the Poles demanded a "rectification" of their border with Germany. Shortly thereafter, Lithuania seized the city of Memel. Finding itself unable to protect Germany's borders, the government, in February 1923, agreed to a covert expansion of the army beyond the 100,000-man limit. This was the beginning of the so-called Black Reichswehr. The units of this reserve army were originally called "labor troops" and later Arbeitskommandos (labor commandos). By September of 1923, in spite of the inflation, the illegal army had between 50,000 and 80,000 men. These units, as Waite describes them, consisted of "thousands of former Free Corps fighters." In addition, they "sought recruits among the student youth of Germany."[95]

In September of that year, in the midst of all the nation's other difficulties, a unit of the Black Reichswehr undertook a mini-*Putsch*, this the so-called Kustrine *Putsch*. General von Seeckt and other Reichswehr leaders concluded that these units were a bit too irregular for their tastes, and they were officially declared dissolved. Unofficially, however, some of them continued to be supported, some again finding refuge in the great estates of rural Prussia. For many of the Freikorps fighters, however, it was merely one more betrayal, like those of March 1920 and May 1921. "Many of the leaders of the Black Reichswehr," Waite reports, "went directly to Munich and joined the ranks of the NSDAP and the SA. Those who remained behind helped to forward the cause of National Socialism in northern Germany in the years which lay ahead."[96]

The struggle in the Ruhr against the French occupation was not primarily a Freikorps operation. Many Freikorps veterans did fight there, most notably the NSDAP martyr, Albert Leo Schlageter. But the effort there was undertaken by individuals or small underground guerrilla units rather than by organized formations. The government policy, it will be remembered, was one of passive resistance, and that was the policy of both the Free and the Christian trade unions.[97]

Another struggle against the French occupation was taking place on the other side of the Rhine. There, the French were supporting a separatist movement, the idea being to create out of German territory a buffer state between the two major powers. The armed struggle in this case was carried on by local forces, not by the Freikorps. The only contribution of the Freikorps and its affiliates was made by members of the Organisation Consul. Five former Freikorps fighters crossed the Rhine and assassinated Heinz-Orbis, the president of the Autonomous Republic of the Palatinate. Men involved in this struggle later formed the first units of the NSDAP in the occupied areas.[98]

THE SHIFT TO THE NSDAP

It was these experienced fighters who, after the dissolution of their units, eventually found their way to the NSDAP and its fighting arm, the Sturmabteilung. Some made the shift early, some after first trying one or more other rightist organizations. As of 1932, the ex-Freikorps men would have formed only a small part of the total membership, as more and more younger persons joined. The argument here is not that they were at all time the numerically dominant force in the party, only that their efforts and abilities were crucial to its early formation, setting the direction for much of the later development. Without this core of Freikorps fighters, the party could not have developed as it did. They provided the local organizing talents and the high level of tactical ability. They also provided the ruthlessness that overwhelmed all opponents. In addition, they played an important role in training the younger generations who later joined their ranks.

The available data do not allow anything even approaching precise statistical support for these claims. Some sense of the flows, may, however, be gained from NSDAP memoirs, from the autobiographies generated by Theodore Abel and further analyzed by Peter Merkl, and from Robert Waite's research.

One of the heroic memoirs, typical of the many that came out of the NSDAP's central publishing house in Munich during the thirties, opens with a gathering of three men in February 1925. They were planning the reconstitution of the NSDAP group in Starnberg, a lovely resort town southwest of Munich (discussed in Chapter 9). The three are the author, described as a minor civil servant, Max, the paperhanger, and Gustl, the bricklayer. The introduction continues with a brief review of their military and organizational history—"front soldiers, all three, Freikorps fighters"—none older than 27, all three in the SA, and all three marchers on the ninth of November, 1923.[99]

These three, the author claims, for all practical purposes created the local organization and made it what it was. Others joined in, of course, and worked hard at it, but it was these three who provided the bridge between the old, the pre-1923 party, and the new one, the second try. There is a recurring theme in these recruitment efforts, which the author stresses at one point: "Behind him [the new member] lay the steep, old path: front soldier, Free Corps, Hitler."[100] At another point they pick up another old fighter, and again one hears the same stress: front fighter, Freikorpsman, SA man. The author adds that "in his veins flows purest soldier blood. Golden middle courses, weakness, flexibility, he hates like the plague."[101]

Given the character of Abel's sample of pre-1933 party members, one cannot, of course, have any assurance as to its representativeness. It is likely that the sample would be better educated and have higher class backgrounds than party members generally. Nevertheless, because it is one of the few samples of any kind bearing on the subject, it is worth closer examination.

Some 18 percent of Abel's respondents had "participated in some form of post-war military activities, such as the fights against the Spartacists, the Kapp Putsch, the guerilla warfare in Upper Silesia, or the skirmishes during the Ruhr occupation in 1923."[102] Three out of five of those engaged in the postwar struggles were young men, between 17 and 30 in 1914. In 1930, these men would have been in their thirties or early forties. Contrasting the core group with the entire sample of members (as of 1934), one finds a small segment that was older than the core group and a much larger younger segment, the latter constituting roughly half of the total. The party, then, was an amalgam containing some older members, frequently persons with some traditional military connections and old-school nationalist outlooks, the core of old fighters, and finally, the large group of younger persons attracted to the party in the republic's last years. The key to the NSDAP's later organizational success was to be found in the core group's ability to attract and mobilize this younger cohort.

Merkl handles Abel's qualitative materials somewhat differently, paying more attention to these different generations, to the patterns of flow and recruitment, and to the motivations of each segment. Where Abel indicated that just under one-fifth of his respondents were involved in the postwar struggles, Merkl shows that the war and its aftermath touched and moved a much larger portion. "The vitae of the Abel collection," he says, "largely present the war, the defeat, or the 'revolution' of 1918 as the formative experience of many respondents' lives. If we consider the central experience or influence of each autobiographical statement, we find nearly one-half under the spell of war, revolution, or foreign occupation."[103]

Merkl also reports that the respondents touched by the war mention the enthusiasms of the *Fronterlebnis*, the shattering experience of the collapse, and the hostile reactions to those groups blamed for the defeat. These sentiments he discovers to be most pronounced among the volunteers (as opposed to the professional soldiers and reservists). He also finds that "sustained war enthusiasm and performance actually seem to grow with the length of service."[104] He, too, reports the flow from the military into the Freikorps (and into related paramilitary organizations).[105] The National Socialists old enough to have participated in the early postwar organizations were divided in their choices. The veterans, particularly the volunteers, went into the paramilitary organizations. Those without military experience tended instead to join noncombatant rightist organizations, that is, the *völkische* or conservative opposition groups. They still, however, expressed strong sympathy for the Freikorps and strong hatred for the domestic insurgents.

There were, of course, two distinct periods in the party's history prior to 1933. In the first, ending with the 1923 *Putsch*, its membership obviously came from the prewar and wartime generations. The membership in this period consisted of those affected by the war, those dissatisfied with the outcome and wishing to continue the struggle after 1918. This group continued working for the party in the second period, beginning with its refounding in 1925, their ranks being enlarged, in the later upsurge, by youthful recruits. The segment of the party not directly touched by the war, Merkl says, was moved by "youthful comradeship, schooling, or unemployment."[106]

In the course of this transformation, there appears to have been a shift in the class base of the membership. Abel noted that two-thirds of those involved in the immediate postwar struggles were middle class. Merkl notes that the "economically secure and freewheeling" were first to join the very early party and that "even during the crisis of 1923, and in the following quieter years, the 'haves' continue to be more heavily represented in the brown movement." Only in 1930, he reports, "do the 'have-nots' catch up."[107]

The line of continuity between Freikorps and NSDAP is attested to in the brief biographies contained in an appendix to Waite's book. Friedrich Alpers, a member of the Maercker Freikorps appears as an SA *Sturmführer* in 1930. Willy Andreeson, a veteran of the Baltic campaign and a participant in the Kapp *Putsch*, is later active as an NSDAP *Gau* speaker and in 1929 is the director of a *Gau* leadership school. Some joined earlier, such as Karl Busch, active with the Freikorps in Berlin, the Baltic, Upper Silesia, and East Prussia; he joined the party in 1923. Kurt Daluege was a section leader of the Rossbach Freikorps. After a brief period as leader of a "gymnastic society," he joined the NSDAP in 1922, later founding and organizing the Berlin SA. Among those contained in Waite's review is Martin Bormann, who was a section leader in the Rossbach Freikorps and later active in the Organisation Consul. One also finds such leading National Socialists as Hans Frank, Rudolph Hess, Reinhard Heydrich, Erich Koch, and Ernst Röhm.[108] Still another National Socialist who followed this distinctive career was Rudolf Höss, later the commandant at Auschwitz.

The path to National Socialism, then, involved a complicated series of moves—from the war into units of the Freikorps, then into civilian life and into various patriotic, veterans', and paramilitary organizations, eventually reaching the NSDAP.[109]

The Recruitment of Younger Cohorts

A second aspect of the party's growth involved the recruitment and assimilation of younger populations into its ranks. This too appears to have been a product of interpersonal efforts by the early activists, or, if one will, of small-group dynamics. To see how this process worked, we turn once again to Noakes's account, an unfailing source for details on the organizational history. This discussion also points up a source of strain that was to cause the party difficulties right up to 1933.

The first unit of the NSDAP in Lower Saxony was formed in the city of Hanover in the summer of 1921. It had a slow and troubled beginning, but, showing characteristic energy, the founders moved ahead, even disregarding a cautionary warning from Hitler, and extended their activities into the surrounding countryside. The appearance of outside speakers, among them Hermann Esser from the party's Munich head-quarters, brought in large audiences and gave the unit both funds and members.[110]

This effort, however, was soon to be eclipsed. Despite its base in the provincial capital, which was also the province's largest city, the party did not find this setting a fertile one. Having escaped the twin plagues of leftist insurgency and Freikorps counterinsurgency (see note 11, Chapter 8), the city did not have the same heritage of fear, hate, and ideological commitment found elsewhere. After 1920, the fortunes of city and province were directed by *Oberpräsident* Gustav Noske who, Noakes reports, "suppressed extremism from whatever quarter it came."[111] There were, moreover, inadequacies within the local NSDAP leadership; hard-fought factional struggles dissipated the party's efforts for some years.

The "most effective group in Lower Saxony" eventually appeared in Göttingen, that is to say, in the famous university town, the initiative there being taken by a medical student, one Ludolf Haase. Before the war, he had been active in anti-Semitic agitation, an interest he continued after the war before joining "a volunteer battalion, part of the Free Corps." He later came to Göttingen to begin his studies and there, as an extracurricular activity, joined a *völkische* organization. With two other students, he overthrew its leadership and, shortly thereafter, was himself elected chairman. Unhappy with its rather ineffectual membership, he turned to another nationalist and anti-Semitic group. Then, still searching for the adequate vehicle, he traveled to Munich to acquaint himself with a "completely new type of organization" he had heard about, one "which was really aggressive." Finding what he wanted, he joined the NSDAP. In February 1922 he founded the Göttingen branch of the party with twelve members. Because "of a dislike of students among the workers, a caretaker was elected chairman, while Haase controlled the branch from the background." Intellectuals, moreover, were "temporarily banned from joining." And thus, apart from the medical student and a sculptress, the group had a very pronounced lower-middle-class character.[112]

The Göttingen branch soon extended its efforts into the surrounding countryside. Of the units it founded, the most successful one in fact was that of neighboring Northeim, better known to us as Thalburg in William Allen's work. The two founders of Northeim's NSDAP, both eminently lower middle class, had been members of a nationalist paramilitary organization, the Jungdeutscher Orden, when they were picked up by an NSDAP contact man who encouraged them to attend a demonstration in Göttingen that was to be addressed by Haase. Dissatisfied with the vagueness of the Jungdeutschen and moved by the passion of Haase's speech, they joined at once. They were especially impressed by the demand for fellow fighters (*Mitkämpfer*) as opposed to fellow travelers (*Mitläufer*).[113]

Haase's resourcefulness was shown in November 1922 at a point when the NSDAP had been banned. He had scheduled a mass meeting, the unit's first, for November 18, but it was forthwith banned by the local police. Undaunted, Haase raised support from the local paramilitary organizations and, together with "a large number of student associations," marched through Göttingen in a protest demonstration that lasted several hours. The branch doubled its membership as a result, going from twenty-five to fifty, even picking up a chemistry professor in the process. The professor began canvassing, with some success, among his university colleagues. They also formed an SA unit of forty-five members, "largely ex-soldiers and Free Corps."[114]

In the following month Haase organized a front organization to take the place of the banned party. At the first meeting it acquired seventy new members, "mostly students." Success in this transparent effort was aided by the police, many of whom apparently looked the other way when members were placarding the town. The unit also had the support of the leading bourgeois newspaper in the town, the *Göttinger Tageblatt*. Its proprietor, a "racialist since before the war," printed material for the branch free of charge.

In a key paragraph, Noakes makes some important observations about the membership characteristics of this pivotal branch, also telling us something about the grounds for attraction to the NSDAP. Under Haase, we are told, "the Göttingen branch was dominated by a group of student activists." Some of them, we learn, were "to reach important positions within the NSDAP at *Gau* and even at Reich levels." The category "students," it should be noted, especially at that time, meant something quite other than lower middle class.[115]

These student members, many of them obviously younger men, preferred the NSDAP to other *völkische* organizations because of its radical stance and also because the "form of organization" had great appeal. Specifically, the "*Führerprinzip* and the SA, both of which were unique to the NSDAP among the political parties, gave [it] features similar to the organizations of which they had experience and in which they had been moulded—the army and the Free Corps."[116]

In the years following Hitler's *Putsch* attempt and the refounding of the party in 1925, an issue arose that gave rise to considerable controversy within the party, this being the question of electoral activity. Given the limitations placed on the party's activities and given the possibility of a complete ban of the party, Hitler declared legality to be *the* line to be followed. Many of the party's fighters rejected such a tepid course, Ludolf Haase being one of them. The leadership in both Hanover and Göttingen refused to participate in local elections in November 1925. In 1926, however, Hanover decided to go along, accepting the justifications Hitler gave at the national meeting in Weimar that year. But Göttingen continued to reject completely any participation in elections. Early in 1927, the neighboring Brunswick unit sent a complaint to Hitler, arguing that "the failure of *Gau* Göttingen to follow the party line . . . might create difficulties . . . in the coming *Landtag* elections." The incident illustrates Hitler's leadership style. Rather than intervening immediately and giving a direct order, he "continued to humour the extreme anti-parliamentary attitudes of the Göttingen leaders for another year."[117]

It is not clear from Noakes's account what eventually transpired. A decline of activity in the area in 1926 caused some concern in the higher echelons of the party. Noakes thinks that Haase may have returned to his studies. At the end of 1926, the effective leadership of the *Gau* (Hanover-South) was exercised by an ex-agricultural student, and Haase disappears from the later pages of Noakes's work. The organization at this point was no longer dependent upon the abilities of a single individual. When it did finally take up electoral activity, in 1929, in a period when the effects of the economic crisis were already being felt, the NSDAP in Göttingen "succeeded in winning its largest representation in any Council in Germany with the exception of Coburg, where it had a majority."[118] This concentration of NSDAP strength in Coburg, a cultural center and spa, noted as a retirement place for former officers, and in Göttingen, a university city, should have given some pause to those who so uncritically advanced the lower-middle-class hypothesis. At minimum, it should have stimulated some recognition of the complexities of the new development.

Noakes summarizes the relationship of the National Socialists and university students very simply—the student population, he says, "proved peculiarly vulnerable to the appeal of Nazism." This was attested to by the results of student council elections in which the lists of the National Socialist German Students' League showed astonishing successes throughout the nation. One remarkable feature of this development is that it *preceded* the breakthrough of the party in the nation as a whole, a dozen institutions of higher learning already showing percentages of 18 or more in the academic year 1929-1930, that is, well before the NSDAP gained 18 percent of the vote in the September 1930 Reichstag election.[119]

The liberal *Vossische Zeitung* undertook an analysis of these elections in July of 1930 and, drawing on a combination of mass-society and threatened-middle-class themes concluded that it was the "free" students (those not in fraternities) who were most vulnerable. But Noakes indicates that the shift at Göttingen involved a simple exchange—the fraternities lost four seats in the 1929-1930 election and the National Socialists gained four, the free students retaining their single seat.[120]

In terms of ideology and beliefs, the linkage between the student associations and National Socialism was very close. The student associations formed what was probably the leading center of anti-Semitism in the entire nation, the *völkisch* influence there being very strong. At a national meeting of their representatives in Eisenach in 1920, a ban on Jewish members was adopted, and individual units were encouraged to educate their members to believe that "marriage with a Jewish or coloured woman is unthinkable." Demonstrations against Jewish or "politically suspect professors" were organized by these groups in the 1920s. Two hundred students at the Technical University (TH) in Hanover broke up a lecture there in 1925. The university disciplined 11 of the offenders whereupon 1,200 of the university's 1,500 students transferred to the TH in neighboring Brunswick.[121]

The attraction of students to Hitler and his movement, moreover, was not something that began only in the late twenties. A meeting was held at the University of Munich on November 12, 1923, three days after the *Putsch* attempt; attended by two rectors and some eminent professors, it was apparently aimed at conciliation. The police report says that the faculty tried to calm the radical mood, while at the same time, "recognizing the valid national goals of Hitler and his followers, and in part also condemning the government." They were, nevertheless, unable to prevent "a stormy demonstration in support of Hitler."[122]

Harold Gordon presents data on the occupations of pre-*Putsch* members of the party in Bavaria. Out of 1,126 persons for whom such information was available 20 "were professionally trained teachers at the university (technical university) and university preparatory secondary school level, with the bulk being Gymnasium professors." There were 104 university level students, a scattering of other students, and 27 grammar school teachers. One does not need comparative census figures to recognize that the students were well overrepresented in comparison to their presence in the general population. The Munich students were reported as recruiting for the party there and in their home communities in the Bavarian provinces.[123] Even the timing of Hitler's *Putsch* was affected, at least in a minor way, by the student involvement. Gordon notes that the return of the students to the university for the winter semester "had swollen the ranks of the SA noticeably." "These young men," he says, "were full of enthusiasm for the cause and anxious for action. Not only would they chafe at delay, but the pressures of the semester's work might soon reduce the political activity of many of them." Support was also noted elsewhere. In Mannheim, Gordon reports, the fraternities of the Handelshochschule "marched as a unit to join the Putschists."[124]

Those were the students of the early Weimar period, the students who were involved in or otherwise touched by the war. The motives of later student cohorts were somewhat different. Fraternity students, Noakes argues, remained insulated from National Socialism by virtue of their traditional upper-middle-class apolitical outlooks. They were nationalists; they celebrated traditional holidays, wore colorful regalia, drank a lot, and sang patriotic songs, but, he says, this was still a long way from the street marches and beer hall fights of the National Socialists. Eventually, however, especially with the onset of the depression, the party touched on some themes that moved many of these hitherto apolitical idealists: "a movement in which action had priority over thought and which played on the guilt feelings of upper middle-class youth for their social isolation and appealed to their idealism by its claim to a socialist policy and a close relationship with the workers as opposed to what increasingly appeared to be the anti-social exclusiveness of the Corporations. The Nazis offered middle class students the opportunity to indulge their social concern, while remaining true to their nationalist and *völkisch* values which the alternative idealism of the Left repudiated."[125]

Part of the NSDAP's "energy, efficiency and virtuosity" may be explained as the result of this unique selection process, one that recruited tough and capable fighters, men with strong motivating hostilities directed against the republic and its representatives. The party was, moreover, able to replenish and enlarge its ranks by drawing on nationalist student populations, among others, for new recruits among the younger generations.

THE TRAINING OF PARTY MEMBERS

The party's selection processes provided it with its cadres, with its militants, giving it persons with unique talents and rather unusual degrees of commitment. Those talents were then refined and improved through a series of special training programs, these making still another contribution to the party's efficiency and virtuosity. The people it recruited, especially those drawn from the Freikorps and its affiliates, were specialists in the organization and management of small-scale combat. But Hitler's directive made on the refounding of the party demanded the use of legal means; party activists were now required to engage in everyday routine electoral activities. Such a demand went against the first principles of many old fighters and, as we have seen, this provided a major source of internal dissent. Some old fighters, however, made the transition with ease and soon took obvious delight in defeating the enemy with his own weapons. But for some, the transition, for purely technical reasons, was not easy. They could quickly shout out appropriate orders in hand-to-hand combat, but the making of an election speech was something else; their virtuosity did not lie in that area.

But the virtuosity *of the party* is to be seen once again in its handling of this problem. It created "schools" to provide the necessary training.[126] Since public speaking was so central to its entire operation, it is useful to examine this effort in some detail. Again, it will be seen that the party's efforts stand in sharp contrast to those of its competitors.

The speakers' school, essentially a correspondence school, began as a local initiative in *Gau* Upper Bavaria. Its value was quickly recognized, and it became the official National Socialist Speakers' School in June of 1929. The aim, according to Himmler's memorandum, was to "impregnate each speaker with lasting and incontestable material so that with the certainty of his knowledge he does not from the outset suffer from stage-fright, as he knows that his material is irrefutable even for his sharpest opponent."[127] Essentially what the school did was to take untrained natural talents and, by drilling them in a basic routine, give them a level of confidence that would carry them through their public speaking efforts and, at the same time, give the audience an appearance of superb competence. The basic technique went as follows:

> After some theoretical instruction, the student in effect memorized a simple speech . . . and did some mirror-practice with it. At the same time, he wrote a speech on his own and sent it [in] for corrections. Along with the corrected version, [the school] sent questions to prepare the student for the next month's topic. (For example: "A Factory worker complains about low wages. What would you answer?") Thus the training institute had very limited objectives. It offered no political education in any broad sense, but it did provide a large number of speakers with some knowledge of the rudiments of public-speaking techniques, a store of set speeches, and some memorized answers for typical questions from the audience.[128]

At the end of four months of such training, the candidate made his first speech, this in the presence of his *Gau* leader who sent in a report to the school. If the performance was considered suitable, the remaining eight months of training involved actual practice, the student making as many as thirty public speeches before being declared an "official party speaker."[129] Orlow describes the arrangement as "primitive, single-minded, but highly effective."[130]

The *Gau* leaders were expected to nominate two candidates from each of their districts. The students were obliged to pay for their education (two marks per month) once again showing that wherever possible the operations of the party were to be self-financing. As of May 1930, 2,300 party members "had taken part in the course," and the school is said to have trained 6,000 party speakers by January 1933.[131]

To aid local organizations in planning their programs, the party circulated lists of party speakers. The speakers, obviously, varied considerably in their abilities. Some were to be used for large urban gatherings; others were destined for smaller rural audiences (where a bungled performance would have fewer ramifications). Given the limitations of many such speakers, the "party did not expect them to persuade any large number of disengaged Germans to vote for or join the NSDAP, but, hopefully, they would demonstrate the party's interest in the village audience and stir at least some of the hearers to undertake a . . . journey to a nearby town to hear a rhetorically far more effective Gau or Reich speaker."[132] The speakers also worked out a degree of specialization by subject. The Upper Bavarian *Gau*, for example, not only had speakers on standard NSDAP themes (such as Jewry, Marxism, race, the peasantry, and history), but one whose specialty was attacks on the Bavarian People's party.[133]

The above paragraphs describe what the party offered to its local units. Some sense of the operation as seen from the units themselves and from the perspective of the speakers may be gained from Noakes's account. Why, for example, would one become a speaker? Why would members of the party take the time for a year-long course and pay the required fees in addition to their regular membership dues and frequent assessments? For many, Noakes reports, a financial incentive was involved; speakers were paid seven marks per speech and received free board and lodging while away from home in addition to being reimbursed for travel costs. The sum was not enormous, but, as the employment situation worsened, it became "increasingly important since for many members their income from public speaking became their only means of support."[134]

That fact provides some explanation for the dynamism of the party; it had a strong incentive for continuing political activity after the end of an election campaign. In May 1932, for example, after the two rounds of the presidential election and the Prussian election, the party justified its continued effort because of the need "to employ those *Gau* speakers who, because of their activity for the party have lost their jobs. . . . We must keep them going so that they are ready for the next election." At that point, in *Gau* Hanover-South-Brunswick alone, there were thirty-two such speakers. It was not only for the speakers, however, that the effort was continued. "The fact that an entrance fee was charged was also an incentive for branch leaders to ensure that their meetings were organized efficiently and with adequate advance propaganda."[135]

Thus, through the simple device of an admission fee, NSDAP meetings were turned into profitable ventures. A *Gau* speaker would be paid his seven-mark fee out of the evening's receipts. He could be fed at the home of a member and, if necessary, also be housed with one of the members. Even if a speaker had to eat on the road and spend the night in a *Gasthaus*, the costs would not be exorbitant. All money then remaining was available for the organizational and propaganda efforts required for the next events. A speaker with a national reputation or a member of the Reichstag would cost more, and because of heavier demands, their services were not as easily obtained. But then, because of their greater prestige, a local group could anticipate a larger audience and a greater return.

The situation of the NSDAP's competitors at this point, especially within the bourgeois parties, was disastrous. Since they did not charge admission, their meetings were pure cost factors, bringing in no return whatsover. They did not have large cadres to plan ahead and organize meetings. They typically had no forces to defend their meetings from attacks or takeover attempts. They lacked a trained core of specialized speakers. Most of their speakers, moreover, would have had some full-time employment and hence would not have been able to give the same time for this effort as was possible for the NSDAP's speakers. And finally, the depression caused very serious damage to their position. Membership declined bringing a reduction in dues payments and voluntary contributions. Their ability to hold meetings (or to place newspaper advertising) thus declined sharply just as the NSDAP was experiencing its phenomenal takeoff.

It seems likely that these divergent experiences would have had sharply contrasting impacts on party morale. The local NSDAP activists would know that theirs was a winning effort, and that knowledge would make it easy for them to continue, to set things up for the next round. The opposite effect had already occurred at a DVP meeting in a village in Brunswick in April 1928. Despite the "distribution of 200 invitations," only twelve people turned up, and all of them were members of the NSDAP. The speaker found it "the most unedifying meeting" he had "ever experienced . . . every time I began to speak someone interrupted me. There wasn't a single person there from our lot—they are scared of the national socialist methods."[136]

The National Socialists' first major election victory, in September 1930, brought 107 members into the Reichstag. But the notion of their "coming into" the Reichstag is misleading since much of their activity was conducted elsewhere. The point was expressed by Hitler as early as 1926 when he declared that "for us the deputy's [railroad] ticket is the main thing. This makes it possible for us to send round agitators thereby serving the interests of the Party. The men who represent us in the parliaments do not travel to Berlin to cast their votes but travel around uninterrupted with their tickets in the service of our movement. It was largely through this that we were able to hold over 2,370 mass meetings in the past year."[137] Goebbels made the same point after his election to the Reichstag in 1928: "I am not a MdR [member of the Reichstag]—I am a PI and a PRP: a Possessor of Immunity and a Possessor of a Railway Pass."[138] The railway passes, in short, gave the party a core of public speakers who could make appearances in local communities at a relatively small cost. The Reichstag members were not ordinarily engaged in parliamentary work; it will be remembered that the party staged a demonstrative exodus from the Reichstag in February of 1931, leaving the delegates free for this wide-ranging propaganda effort.[139]

"Political technique" was also developed as a byproduct of the annual mass meeting. Most accounts focus on the massed formations at Nuremberg and the Hitler address, usually laying emphasis on the irrationality of the entire performance.[140] The view from the grass roots, however, was somewhat different. The assembled members lived in tent communities during their stay and had some time for informal socializing, either before the big events or in the late evening after those events. One NSDAP memoir writer says the meeting gave him a sense of the size of the movement, a sense of being part of a large and growing movement. It was an occasion too, he reports, at which one could learn and trade experience. Another of his observations focuses on the diversity of the struggle. As he puts it: "Everywhere the struggle is different. Here they squabble with senile philistines. There with fatheaded farmers. The South Germans defend themselves against the blacks [Catholics] who want to mix church and politics. The East Prussians run up against reaction. In the large cities they have the commune on their necks. The East Hanoverians have to fight with the Guelphs. Everywhere it's different, but everywhere there is struggle."[141] There is a recognition here of the need for different kinds of appeals and tactics, a recognition that is frequently absent from both popular and scholarly works on the subject.

CLASS AND MOBILITY

It is appropriate at this point to reconsider the class-base question as it applied to the NSDAP membership. Merkl concludes that the Abel sample, and "probably the whole Nazi party *at the time* were not dominated so heavily by clearly identifiable lower middle-class interests as to be characterized as part of the 'revolt of the lower middle class.' "[142] Although a precise answer to this question is impossible, especially on the basis of the Abel-Merkl sample, some suggestive qualitative observations can be considered. These touch on a point first raised in Chapter 3, namely the problem posed by the interrelations of class and age. Despite its much-commented-upon youthful character, the party membership's age distribution in Abel's sample (in 1934) was not especially striking. Only one-eighth of the members in his sample were young, that is, between 20 and 26. One-third were at least middle-aged, between 41 and 59 years. There were, to be sure, very few old persons, only 4 percent being 60 or more.[143]

But the image of youth does appear to have a real basis. Merkl indicates that one-quarter of those in the sample were what he describes as "mere members," those who undertook little activity and who might be best described as sympathizers. They were substantially older than the more active segments of the party and, moreover, tended to be late joiners. Most of them were in the war, but during the 1920s they were apolitical or members of the DNVP. That means the National Socialists that people saw, the ones continuously on the street, were younger men. And it would also mean that a sample picked at an earlier point, say in 1930 or 1928, would show a younger membership.[144] It was the younger group, obviously, that sustained the party effort and created the successful political machine. One may inquire as to the class background of these young men.

In the normal course of events in contemporary societies, whether one is looking at the bureaucratic segment or the older entrepreneurial segment, people generally begin at the bottom and work their way up. That is, to be sure, a rather commonplace observation, but it is regularly overlooked in discussions of the lower-middle-class hypothesis. At its simplest, it means that an upper-middle-class career normally begins with a modest position, one that could easily be labeled lower middle class. The bank manager did not begin in that exalted position. He may not have begun as an office manager, but, to gain experience, may have started as a bank clerk.[145]

This raises an important question: should one consider that bank clerk to be lower middle class even though, perhaps unbeknown to the observer-commentator, he is in training for a much higher position? Many people, in short, may be mistakenly classified, the analysts taking the current occupations as fixed for the rest of the person's life.

This same point has implications for the discussion of university students. We have noted the peculiar attraction that National Socialism held for students. And yet, in the general membership figures, students prove to be a rather insignificant group. A peculiar irony is involved here. The student member of, say, 1922 who continued his involvement might appear in the 1926 or 1927 records as a white-collar employee. In the case of a student, one may easily assume an upper-middle-class background. But for a white-collar employee (*Angestellter*), the easy assumption is that he (or she) is lower middle class. For the academically trained, however, that assumption would be open to question.

When dealing with National Socialist activists, one is not dealing with the normal, that is, typical or average middle-class experience. Activists who put politics ahead of careers are likely to be denied promotion. They would be given another job, one with no future, or removed from the firm entirely. After the Baltic campaign, Ernst von Salomon worked in an insurance company, presumably with good opportunities for promotion. But upon hearing of the Polish uprising in Silesia, he packed up and left to do battle. Employers do not ordinarily view such behavior with great favor.

The point here is that the traditional line of analysis may have reversed the direction of cause. Many National Socialists may not have become party members *because* they were lower middle class (or had suffered economic failure and frustrated expectations); rather they may have been National Socialists first, and, then, because of their political activity, they either were viewed as not promotable (thus remaining lower middle class) or worse, were demoted or fired, thus frustrating many expectations and causing downward mobility. Merkl cites many such instances, giving also an alternative reading of the psychology involved. Some two-fifths of those who engaged in partisan street fighting, he says, report

> having been fired or ruined, and another [three-tenths] report an unfriendly work environment. Nearly as large a share of those who participated in demonstrations, provocations, or proselytizing also report political friction on the job, though with a smaller share being fired or ruined. In the majority of these cases, it would seem unlikely that the respondents were victimized by their environment. Rather, we are dealing here with a highly politicized generation of social misfits who . . . were bent on "doing it" regardless of the consequences to themselves or anyone else. The greater their political activism, the greater their urge to polarize their immediate environment.[146]

Merkl refers to this latter type as an "economic suicide."

Carrying the argument a step further, Merkl raises a question about the timing of such losses. The standard argument couples the turn to the party with the onset of the depression, with the aggravation of the already very serious strains. But Merkl discovers that the economic suicides were "concentrated among the early joiners and [the catastrophe] took place long before the Depression." The on-the-spot commentators would be quite correct in their claim that many party members were "broken existences" (*verkrachte oder gescheiterte Existenzen*). The problem, however, lies in what the commentators could not see, that being the sequence of cause and effect.[147]

THE MILITANTS AND THE MASSES

It will be remembered that the National Socialists reached a peak in the election of July 1932. The November election of that year resulted in a loss of some two million votes. While still leaving it the largest party in Germany, the election did cause severe psychological damage; as Bracher puts it, "the myth of the irresistible advance of National Socialism had suffered a heavy blow."[148] The punishing blows continued in the weeks that followed. Local elections in Saxony and the council elections in Lübeck on the thirteenth of November yielded serious losses, Bracher citing figures of roughly 30 percent in Dresden, Lübeck, and Chemnitz. In Thuringia in the November Reischstag election the NSDAP lost 14.5 percent compared to July. In the subsequent municipal elections in Thuringia on December 4, the party declined some 20 percent as compared to November, only a month earlier, this despite its being an NSDAP stronghold and despite the National Socialists' considerable efforts to reverse the negative trend.[149]

Not too surprisingly, the NSDAP concentrated all of its efforts on the next election in the dwarf state of Lippe on the fifteenth of January 1933. "The nervous attention," says Bracher, "with which the entire public looked toward that fifteenth of January raised the vote of 100,000 Lippe electors to a decision also about the fate of the Schleicher experiment and the political future of a nation of 68 million."[150] The party did manage to stem the unfavorable tide, increasing its total some five percentage points over that of November, taking most of this from the DNVP. It was a modest enough victory; the level did not reach that of July 1932, but it was sufficient to encourage the anti-Schleicher intriguers in their work. Two weeks later Hitler was named as chancellor.[151]

This six-month episode of reversals is of no great significance for the history of the world. What had been in process for many years did finally come to be. It is, therefore, only a matter of intellectual or analytical interest to note that the well-tuned political machine was not all-powerful. Even when operating at high efficiency, it could not stem the losses of November and December. And, with all available forces concentrated in a tiny area, it was only barely able to turn things around in the Lippe election. This suggests that a significant portion of the National Socialists' July voters had seen through their arguments and tactics, had defected, and were not easily regained. It also indicates that there were some limits beyond which even this very efficient machinery could not pass.

That decline, presumably, would have continued had Hitler not been named to head the government, thereby giving him an immense range of additonal means for manipulating opinion. It must always remain one of the great "what if" questions: what would have happened if the republic had been given an additional six months? What would have happened if, as Brüning expressed it, he had not been stopped "a hundred meters short of the goal"?

In Chapters 10 and 11, histories of the major parties of the right and left were reviewed. In the last years of the republic, those parties suffered a serious decline, as with the Conservatives, or total collapse, as with the Democrats and the People's party, or a kind of paralysis, as with the Zentrum and the Social Democrats. The National Socialists, by comparison, were making substantial gains, particularly in the creation of their organizational infrastructure. They were, in other words, acquiring and training capable cadres and, with this apparatus, proceeding to mobilize millions of votes.

The key factor in the analysis, as presented thus far, is the organizational one. The traditional parties, with deteriorating organizations, were losing their ability to campaign and fight elections. The Zentrum and the Social Democrats were peculiarly bound by their traditions, making them unable to respond to the new circumstances.

Intimately linked to this focus on organization is the concern with content, with the political choices adopted and advocated by the parties. Possession of "organizational weaponry" by itself is one thing, but if the new activists had not had some *relatively* attractive political content to offer, they could not, presumably, have swayed so many voters. Here, too, the National Socialists successfully extemporized, working up and developing their winning positions. Their competitors among the traditional parties were seriously hampered in this respect. They were committed to laissez faire solutions to the economic crisis or hampered by traditions that limited their ability to respond freely. As a consequence, they were unable to reach out to new segments of the electorate. The problem of tradition was particularly acute for the parties of the left: in large part, they had to work against a heritage of their own making.

The line of argument developed to this point, which focuses on organization and political content, stands in opposition to other prominent explanations, to the argument of Germany's unique cultural heritage, for example, or the great-man theory, the argument that the top leaders, beginning with Hitler and Goebbels, made the movement what it was through their unique demagogic abilities. It also stands in opposition to that line of argument focusing on conditions, particularly on the structural strains that, supposedly affect and move the lower middle class. The present argument also has implications for the last-stage-of-capitalism theory, for the view that the National Socialists were an agency of big business. The materials presented to this point suggest that the National Socialists, by virtue of their independent organizational and financial base, were able to act with a considerable degree of autonomy. It will be noted, moreover, that much of their activity had the effect of undermining the bourgeois parties, those supported by big business.

Before turning to consideration of these larger theoretical questions, one further elaboration of the organizational and political struggles must be undertaken. The previous chapters have considered the parties separately. It is also important to see them in operation, that is, to look at their actual political struggles. The National Socialists faced different contenders in different settings and, accordingly, had to organize differently and to put forth different issues as the need required. For this reason, a general analysis of the political struggle, one supposedly applying to the nation as a whole, must necessarily be inadequate. In the conduct of this differentiated struggle, the National Socialists again demonstrated their "efficiency and virtuosity" by developing different styles of combat for each of these fields of combat. Even that "virtuosity," however, was not enough to guarantee success in every context since, as has been indicated, some areas proved remarkably immune to the efforts and appeals of the party's militants.

A recognition of this differentiated struggle is of central importance for one's understanding of the NSDAP's electoral victory. Any theory intending to explain that victory must be able to take such facts into account.

CHAPTER THIRTEEN

The Character of the Political Struggle

The political struggles in Germany during the years 1928 to 1932 varied considerably, depending on the local or regional circumstances. An all-encompassing general description, therefore, one applied to the entire nation, must necessarily be inadequate. Instead, a series of descriptions is needed, one for each of the major fields of combat since the parties and the cultural traditions facing the National Socialists varied from place to place as did also the existential problems confronting the voters. The National Socialists approached these settings with different themes, different emphases, and different styles. In some, they were eminently successful; in others, from the outset, they seemed destined to failure. This chapter describes the struggles as they developed in each of the major contexts of the society.

Broadly speaking, the fields of combat may be defined by two variables: community size and religion. In the large cities, one must add a third variable, that of class. Germany's communities, for present purposes, may be divided into three categories: small rural communities, middle-sized communities, and large cities.[1] The pattern of farm settlement in Germany is somewhat different from that of North America. The tendency, generally is for farm populations to cluster in small communities rather than, as in the United States and Canada, living scattered on isolated farms. Within those rural communities one found a high degree of homogeneity based on shared experience, common religion, and a cluster of kinship linkages.[2] "Class" does not mean very much in these settings given a rough equality in the size of farm holdings. A few families might have larger farms than most, but the differences would be matters of degree rather than of kind. Changes in farm prices, or in the price of seed or farm implements, or in mortgage interest rates would affect all alike.

The middle-sized communities, which for present purposes might vary from 2,000 up to 100,000, would show some class division and some conflict, an example of this being found in Thalburg, as described in Allen's work.[3] Speaking very generally, it was a conflict of "the workers" versus all the rest. In terms of organization, this tended to be a struggle of Social Democrats versus a range of bourgeois parties, or, in local politics, of Social Democrats versus a bourgeois bloc.

The class divisions were most pronounced in the cities. There the neighborhoods were more sharply divided and the political distinctions more finely delineated. There one was more likely to find open, violent struggle between the classes, or more precisely, between the various organized forces purporting to represent those classes. In the cities, too, the struggle was more likely to be three-cornered; there the tougher Communists tended to dominate, at least in the public consciousness, the left pole of the struggle.

German communities were also differentiated by religion. In rural Protestant communities, accordingly, the National Socialists moved against liberal and conservative parties. In Catholic regions, of course, they would be moving against the Zentrum, or, in Bavaria, against the Bavarian People's party. In the larger communities, the National Socialists faced a more complex struggle with Social Democrats and Communists on the one hand and bourgeois parties on the other. The Zentrum counted for less in the larger communities; loyalties to that party, especially among the workers, had been seriously eroded in the cities.[4]

Still another line of differentiation deserves consideration. A minor tradition in the social sciences has distinguished the "parties of notables" from the "parties of integration." The former variety, typified by classical liberal and conservative parties, was run by a handful of potentates, people of some local reputation or prominence, who in caucus selected candidates and undertook the organizing and management of their party's election campaigns. Organization in these parties was extemporized for the purposes of the election; between campaigns little or nothing was retained in the way of a permanent political apparatus.

The parties of integration, on the other hand, attempted to create a permanent political apparatus, one with full-time officials or highly committed volunteers. The aim was to integrate the clientele into the party, to embrace as much of the voter's life as possible. Typically, the Socialist parties were the first of the so-called parties of integration to appear on the European scene. The lives of their members, it was hoped, would be contained within trade unions, cooperatives, book clubs, recreational activities, youth organizations, and so forth. Because of the lesser commitment of the working-class clientele (compared to the high consciousness, power, and resources of the *haute bourgeoisie*) it was recognized that a more coherent organizational weapon was necessary to achieve any electoral success. Acceptance of the loose organizational style of traditional notables would have meant failure in the struggle for power. This alternative organizational style was adopted in a later period, in even more accentuated form, by the Communist parties and also by the various fascist parties that appeared in Europe in the 1920s and 1930s. To some extent also, the Christian Democratic parties have used this form of organization; in some areas they have been able to depend on natural communities, specifically, on the small rural communities, to provide the integration otherwise provided by formal organizations.

The reality of the so-called parties of integration has always fallen well short of the ideal. The Communists, following Lenin's prescriptions, made the most consistent efforts to integrate their members. But as we have seen, that integration proved to be short-lived. In general, the aspiration to control and politicize the life of a member runs up against and stimulates some rather natural contrary feelings. The attempt at political domination of members' lives also, typically, overlooks personal and familial concerns, and these too serve to undermine the attempt at control.[5]

This is not to say that the distinction is without meaning or value. The conceptually pure notion, however, needs to be tempered by an appreciation of social realities; integration was an ideal that was only very approximately achieved. It is important to bear in mind, too, that the extent of integration for a given party would vary with the context. The Social Democratic members, for example, were better integrated into that party's ranks in the larger communities. In the small towns, where the party tie was necessarily weaker, party support was badly eroded in the face of the National Socialist onslaught. For the Zentrum, an opposite pattern had been apparent for some decades, the integration of its members being most adequate in the smaller communities and with the erosion occurring in the cities, to the right in Catholic bourgeois circles and to the left in the ranks of Catholic workers.[6]

Probably the most decisive move undertaken by the National Socialists in the period 1928-1932 was their turn to the countryside. Most modern analysts believe that the cities provide the key to power in contemporary societies; it is there that the decisive struggle will be fought, with the capture of the metropolis, presumably, deciding things for the nation as a whole. In Germany this outlook is attested to by the Berlin-centered character of historical, social scientific, and literary works (or in France, by the Paris-centered character, or in the United States, by the New York-centered focus—Chicago counts for little, Houston for still less). But the majority of the population was not found in metropolitan Berlin, nor in the other large cities. The NSDAP's shift to the countryside therefore brought it to a largely untouched segment of the population; it also put the party in contact with a segment whose party ties were very loose. In essence, it brought the National Socialist activists into a territory, the Protestant countryside, that was dominated by very feeble parties of notables.

Because of the importance of the National Socialists' activities in the Protestant countryside—the scene of the most decisive shift in voting—

our analysis begins with the events there. The second focus of attention is the Catholic countryside, where very little shifting took place. With the main action taking place elsewhere, the concern with the stability or persistence of political orientations in Catholic villages has been given little attention by students of the period. The third context to be explored is the middle-sized communities with Protestant majorities. Allen's study of Thalburg is examined once again; it provides the best available account of the changes in this context. The equivalent Catholic communities have been largely neglected; hence little can be said about the fourth of the major contexts of the society.

In the larger cities, as has been noted repeatedly, the role of religion was sharply attenuated, and class proved more salient. Accordingly, the contexts to be discussed here are the working-class districts, the mixed districts (those containing workers and the lower middle class), and the upper- and upper-middle-class areas.

Given the relationship of NSDAP voting with Protestantism and given the inverse relationship with city size, it is clear that the largest segment of its electoral support came from the Protestant villages with the next largest coming from the middle-sized Protestant communities.[7] The decision of the NSDAP leaders to go to the country, therefore, was of crucial importance for the 1932 successes. Some discussion of the reasons for this choice is clearly in order.

RURAL COMMUNITIES

The Protestant Countryside. Dietrich Orlow has linked the shift to the countryside to the 1928 election result. Apart from the overall loss, the distribution of the NSDAP vote was not at all impressive "for a party whose organizational strength . . . lay in the urban areas." The party had made some significant gains, but these bore "no relation to the major organizational efforts of the party in the last two years." The NSDAP was, he observes, "the unanticipated beneficiary of economic fear and frustration among parts of Germany's rural population."[8] The party's top leaders met at the end of May to assess the election, and, so Orlow reports, they accepted the implications of those results. The lessons, as stated in the *Völkischer Beobachter* at this time, read as follows: "The election results of the rural areas have proved that with a smaller expenditure of energy, money and time, better results can be achieved than in the big cities. In small towns and villages mass meetings with good speakers are events and are often talked about for weeks, while in the big cities the effects of meetings even with 3 or 4,000 people soon disappear. Surprisingly, local successes are almost invariably the result of the activity of the branch leader, or of a few energetic members."[9]

At a subsequent meeting in August of that year, this one including also the regional leaders, Hitler, again according to Orlow, demanded "a complete abandonment of the urban plan" (with its strong anticapitalist emphases). He reaffirmed the party's use of electoral means and called for "a far greater organizational penetration of the rural areas."[10] The obvious prerequisite to such a penetration was the development of "propaganda lines that appealed to the rural population."

Gau boundaries had to be redrawn, which was accomplished with relative ease. Some strain was engendered by the renewed commitment to electoralism and also, presumably, by the party's abandonment of its "socialism." The most serious obstacle facing the NSDAP, however, was its lack of rural specialists. Although Orlow speaks of this change as decisive, suggesting immediate implementation, the reality seems to have been much more complex. Whereas Orlow says flatly that "all vestiges of a strong anti-capitalist line in the NSDAP propaganda had to be eliminated," the subsequent research of Max Kele has shown that that line continued to be propagated until the end of the republic.[11]

Noakes provides some of the background to this "accidental benefit" for the party. A movement of agrarian protest, the Landvolk movement, began in Schleswig-Holstein in October of 1927 and quickly spread to neighboring areas, most notably to Lower Saxony. A series of poor harvests had caused distress, this being aggravated by an outbreak of foot and mouth disease. Although the farmers had generally profited from the inflation, paying off their indebtedness in the inflated currency, they were caught short by the sudden termination of that crisis. Many had to dump their produce in order to buy seed for the 1924 crop while others had to borrow once again. For some years the farmers had faced serious competition from foreign imports. In addition, there was the problem of new and heavy taxes stemming from the republic's social concern. The massive increase in civil servant salaries, passed in December 1927 (see the discussion in Chapter 11), led to a renewed demand for cuts in public expenditures. The farmer's situation, in brief, was one of high indebtedness and high interest rates combined with poor harvests and a general decline in land prices. Not too surprisingly, the farm populations demanded relief, and, when their traditional parties did not respond, they turned to other ones. Some Landvolk activists turned to violence, for example, blowing up tax offices. The NSDAP decision, clearly, brought its cadres into a context in which political loyalties were, to say the least, rather volatile. This was especially the case in the Protestant countryside.[12]

Given the early recognition of the opportunity, it is surprising that the NSDAP was slow to implement the decision; its agricultural program was not published until March 1930. The preamble saw the farm problem as stemming from the Weimar tax policies, from the competition of foreign agriculture, from the high profits of middlemen, and from the "usurious" prices farmers had to pay for fertilizer and electricity. Except for the competition of foreign agriculture, these problems were said to have Jewish origins. On the positive side, the first point of the "immediate program" called for a halt "to the increasing indebtedness of agriculture by a legislated reduction of the interest rate for lending capital to the prewar level and by a severe action against usury." Not too surprisingly the program called for import duties and government regulation of imports. The speculative influences of the produce exchanges were to be ended; the exploitation of farmers by wholesale distributors was to be "made impossible." In conclusion, it stated that "the crisis of the agricultural population is one part of the crisis which involves the whole population, and the National Socialist movement is fighting to free the whole country."[13]

One should not lay too much emphasis on this program. Other parties, notably the DNVP, had programs that were very similar. Noakes feels it was primarily a means for undercutting opposition arguments that the NSDAP was neglecting agriculture. It was necessary for the National Socialists to make some concrete offerings to the farm population, but by itself that was not sufficient to explain their success. In their actual speeches, he reports, they spent much of their time on questions of Weltanschauung, principally in attacks on Jews and on liberalism. The latter attack was directed against the traditional parties of the farmers in both Lower Saxony and Schleswig-Holstein. Liberalism "seemed to have let them down," and the NSDAP speakers wished to emphasize and reinforce that sense.

The NSDAP speakers, Noakes reports, "accused Liberalism of producing the 'divisive' party system which had undermined national unity, of exalting the profit motive at the expense of integrative national values, and finally of putting international obligations before national ones. In contrast, they put forward the concept of the *Volksgemeinschaft* which envisaged a society in which the old communal relationships, disrupted by the process of modernization and its liberal ideology, would be restored. It was the combination of these ideological generalities with the activist style of the Nazi party which convinced audiences that the NSDAP was offering something new."[14]

The focus on Jews and liberals stands in sharp contrast to the experience in the larger communities, where the thrust was very pronouncedly against Marxism. Even these rural themes, as we shall see, could be varied according to circumstance. Anti-Semitism, was used where it worked, where it could count on a tradition of hostility. In settings where no such hostility existed, it was played down or abandoned.

Noakes stresses the Weltanschauung as key to the NSDAP success in the rural areas. One might, however, with more justification, place the emphasis on another factor, namely the organizational one. The NSDAP had a means for carrying its message out to its potential voters. The DNVP would have been limited in this respect, having only traditional means, newspapers and speeches by party notables. Its ability to organize meetings and carry out the message diminished in the last years of the republic, and its credibility, moreover, was somewhat eroded. It would not be too much of an exaggeration to say that the NSDAP was able to insert activists in the farm villages and that the other parties were not. Some sense of the National Socialist distinctiveness may be gained from the comment of a one-time member who, after the war, reported that the NSDAP "was the *only* political party that had even held a recruiting meeting in our village as far back as anyone could remember."[15]

There is very little literature on the NSDAP activities in the villages or on its reception there. Essentially what we have are a few lines or at best a paragraph or two appearing in studies focused on a larger community or a region, plus the evidence of the voting tendency in those communities. One can, therefore, only offer speculations about the likely character of the rural political struggles.

The small towns and villages of Germany (and most other countries) generally tend to be rather placid politically. Such communities are usually dominated by local notables, by the best-off family of the locality, or perhaps by the best-off politically oriented family. The dominant party, typically, would be a party of notables headed by this local family, or, more specifically, by the patriarch of this family. Small-town or village politics is ordinarily a one-party affair since no serious opposition is present.

Political leadership is passed along within the family in such villages, the patriarch of one generation passing the task on to a son who in turn would train one of his sons for the ultimate succession. No serious political struggle exists in such an arrangement so that politics comes to be little more than a ritual practiced at election times against an opponent who, typically, is not represented in the local community. The general population in such communities tends to be apolitical; the setting is one that trains political illiterates. Marx had only praise for the advance of capitalism on this score; it would rescue people from "the idiocy of rural life."[16]

There is some reason to believe that the war interrupted this normal routine of small-town politics. Wartime mortality varied directly with

rank up through the level of lieutenant. Given the recruitment of officers (including those of the reserve) from the upper and upper middle
classes, this would mean that the children of those classes were found
disproportionately among the fallen.[17] And that, in turn, would have
meant that in many instances local notables would not have had a successor to take over their political role. This problem would be especially
acute in the smaller communities where politics was so distinctively
personal; in the larger communities, even within the liberal parties, a
larger pool of leaders and some minimum organization would help sur-
mount the difficulty.

The break in the continuity of leadership would mean, in many cases,
that the local political leaders were, to put it politely, rather superan-
nuated. In the *normal* state of affairs, local notables would have had a
high average age. The war would have accentuated the tendency. Another likelihood is that when the ruling notables died (or were forced
by failing health to withdraw from politics), a period would follow in
which no serious leadership was present, or else, some new and less
experienced notable would attempt to pick up the reins.

In the Protestant countryside, the traditional notables would be identified with the German People's party, with the Democrats, or with the
Conservatives. Adherents of these parties would face a considerable difficulty—unavoidable identification with the republic and its policies. From
the spring of 1930 to the end of the republic, the Ministry of Agriculture
(*Ernährung*) was headed by a one-time Conservative. The weight of
such burdens increased considerably as the depression worsened.

The political struggle, then, especially in places ruled by the liberal
parties, probably had something of the following character: on the one
side were the traditional elites, the town and party notables, who had
run their communities more or less unchallenged for their entire adult
lives. They were considerably older than the challengers; they were not
veterans and hence could not claim the legitimacy that is claimed by
and granted nearly everywhere to combat soldiers. They were, moreover, identified with the policies of fulfillment in international affairs,
with the institutions and accomplishments and failures of the republic,
and, of special relevance in this context, with the government's persistent immobility in the face of the farm crisis.

On the other side one found the new men, the fresh and enthusiastic
NSDAP activists, men who were young, resourceful, and resolute, and
who had a near-monopoly of tactical political expertise. Nearly every
advantage lay with the insurgents. Where they did not have the immediate advantage, clearly time was on their side. They came armed with
a farm program and a hard-hitting, dramatic style, and given the seem-

ing logic of their arguments and the force or dynamism of their presentation, they must have overwhelmed the general public.

If one were to guess about the dominant considerations leading the voters of the Protestant countryside to support the NSDAP, it would seem likely that they were moved by the apparent ability of the National Socialists to solve the farm problem. It was clear that the traditional parties had not been able to deal with it, and in the voters' immediate milieu the only serious new contender offering a plausible alternative was the NSDAP.[18] In the struggle between the forceful and dynamic newcomer and the traditional or established party, one could, in 1930 or 1932, hardly speak of a contest at all; given the character of the economic disaster at that time and place and the relative strengths and weaknesses of the contenders, "pushover" might seem a more appropriate term.

One should note some other facilitating factors. Among the elites or notables having influence in the Protestant villages would be the clergy. The NSDAP was able to mobilize some members of the clergy to attest to its virtue. If the local pastor was not committed one way or another, preferring to leave such matters to Caesar, the testimonials provided by outside clergymen would no doubt have helped political conversion.

There was also a tendency for the provincial press in Protestant regions to view the National Socialists with some favor, if not to give outright endorsement (see Noakes's remarks about small-town newspapers in the section on Hanover in Chapter 8). The factors working for the party, then, would be the farm crisis as basic motivator, the presence of NSDAP activists as the effective agents of political change, and the supportive words of some clergymen and of the provincial press aiding and abetting the change, justifying or legitimating it.

Some suggestions appear here and there in the literature about the political dynamics operating within farm families. Pridham, describing conditions in Protestant Franconia, indicates that younger farmers there were drawn to the National Socialists "because they were less conservative and found the radical message of the party attractive." Moreover, they "felt less attachment to traditional peasant organizations." Another point he mentions is that younger sons "felt aggrieved for they were less likely than ever before to inherit anything from their fathers, who were most reluctant during the Depression to hand over or parcel out their land."[19] This same point is made by Noakes, speaking of developments in north Germany. As he puts it, "The agricultural crisis had interfered with the process of transition within the peasantry from one generation to the next. . . . The older peasants were unwilling to give up their farms and face penury, while there was not enough cash to pay off the younger sons. Increased competition for employment in the towns meant that surplus youth from the land could no longer be absorbed."[20]

Noakes sees the resulting strain leading to militant activity within the party: "Agricultural youth . . . thus discontented sought satisfaction and compensation in SA activities." The depression, in short, slowed down or halted the normal coming of age in the rural areas. As in the cities, here, too, the depression created unused human resources (unemployed rural youths), and once again it was the National Socialists who found an outlet for their talents. Among other things, these farm youths would have appeared in the parades and demonstrations in the Thalburgs of the region, impressing and converting others in the area. It also seems likely that they would have been active political agents within their own families, playing an important role in converting their own fathers.

One might also consider a negative factor, namely the absence of other contenders. No Communists or Social Democrats were on the scene. A Communist option for the farmers might well have been completely beyond all credibility, but that was not so with the Social Democrats, as is attested by their successes in the Scandinavian countryside. What was involved in this case was an ideological refusal on the part of the SPD, that and a closely related organizational immobility. The SPD *choice* denied the countryside a third option, thus simplifying the struggle and, in effect, giving the NSDAP an easy victory there.[21]

A final matter deserving consideration in a discussion of the Protestant countryside is also a negative one, this being the question of the issues that were *not* central to the struggle there. The claim that the struggle had its origins in the farm problem, in the indebtedness and falling farm prices, means that the heart and core of the farmer's concern was with the price of his product, be that potatoes, rye, or milk. The Treaty of Versailles would probably have been of secondary importance; National Socialist speakers would include it in their basic speeches (along with other standard themes), but it would receive less emphasis than elsewhere. The same would be true, probably, of the attack on "the system." It would be present in routine speeches in the countryside, but not as the central focus. The concern with Marxism and with the political Catholicism of the Zentrum would also, no doubt, have been included in the basic antiregime package, but again peripherally. Anti-Semitism appears to have had a prominent role in rural propaganda. It was linked with NSDAP arguments about the sources of the farm problems, especially when Jewish middlemen could be used as a convenient target. Matters of culture and of threatened German traditions were no doubt also mentioned, but it does not seem likely that potato farmers would be especially moved by such themes. The theater productions of Ernst Toller and Bertolt Brecht in some distant metropolis would not figure prominently on their list of priorities in contrast to the prosaic but urgent concerns of the family enterprise.[22]

The press of economic concerns and the importance of the National Socialist focus on solutions to those problems are indicated in a summary paragraph by Pridham:

> The authorities in Upper Bavaria were uneasy about the promises of Nazi speakers of freedom from taxation for two years, new protective tariffs, cheaper manures and the exclusion of Jews from the cattle-trading business, which were turning the heads of the peasants. Some peasants had been aroused to a pitch of intoxication at the prospect of the Nazis coming to power soon, and were withholding the payment of their taxes. Many peasants voted for Hitler in the Presidential Election of March 1932 in several districts of Middle Franconia, because speakers at Nazi meetings had continuously emphasized that the party would cancel all debts to Jewish cattle-traders.[23]

The Catholic Countryside. The voting tendency in the Catholic countryside stood in sharp contrast to that of the Protestant farm areas. Since the Catholic farmers and the Catholic shopkeepers and tradesmen in the villages presumably faced the same problems as their Protestant equivalents, the arguments about economic stress, those focused on the circumstances of *the* petty bourgeoisie, are not sufficient to explain these very diverse results.[24] The transformation of the Protestant countryside has been explained in terms of two factors: the activity of National Socialist militants there and the weakness of (or conversion of) local political leaders. Some shift in the direction of the local press also, presumably, had an impact. The lack of change in the Catholic farm areas may be explained in terms of these same factors. There appear to have been fewer National Socialist militants in the Catholic areas, and, because of the solid commitment of local notables to the Zentrum (or to the Bavarian People's party), they had much less success. This united front of opposition to the NSDAP was supported by the church hierarchy, of course, as well as by the local and regional press. Unlike the situation in Protestant communities, where some elites or notables, if not actively supporting the National Socialists, at least vouched for them as worthy allies in the national struggle, in Catholic communities, the leaders, both lay and clerical, were overwhelmingly opposed to their aspirations.[25]

Some of this opposition went back to the early years of the movement. Julius Streicher, the NSDAP leader in Franconia, although most noted for his virulent anti-Semitism, also made vehement attacks on Catholicism.[26] Ludendorff's diatribes against the church made during the trial of the Munich putschists in March 1924 gained considerable attention. He and his wife later wrote anti-Catholic pamphlets, one of his being devoted to the "might of the Jesuits." Matilde Ludendorff's *Salvation from Jesus Christ* sold over 400,000 copies.[27] These beginnings were sufficient to ensure a solid anti-NSDAP orientation on the part of the Catholic leaders. In the middle years of the republic, however, following the apparent decline of the party, the church paid it little attention. On the occasion of its subsequent reappearance, in 1929 and 1930, the hierarchy was forced to recognize its presence and this time expressed sharp condemnation.[28]

The opposition of the church hierarchy undercut the NSDAP effort to portray itself as a protector of religion. This tactic, so successful in Protestant areas, was not possible when the party was only able to gain support from the clergy in a few isolated instances. Catholic priests, Pridham says, were an "extreme rarity in the party." One such "rebel priest" gave a sermon at an NSDAP Christmas festival in Augsburg. The bishop of Augsburg responded with a public statement forbidding the priest from speaking at any future NSDAP meetings.[29] Thus the support of one key group of notables was denied to the party. Moreover, there was little possibility of fakery here, of trying to convince the public otherwise, because of the relative ease with which hierarchy and local clergy could issue definitive statements to the contrary.[30] The clergy in the Ingolstadt area (in Upper Bavaria), for example, challenged NSDAP claims with the statement that "we hereby declare finally and emphatically that a Catholic priest, no matter what his position, can never go along with a movement like that represented by National Socialism."[31]

Where the Protestant towns and the surrounding villages typically had two competing bourgeois newspapers available to them, a point discussed later in this chapter, the Catholic towns typically had only one, and it was firmly committed to the interests of the Zentrum (or, in Bavaria, to the BVP). This would mean that the average Catholic farmer or village dweller would find all of the local notables along with the local press reaffirming his traditional political commitments. There would, in short, be no influential persons or opinion leaders within his milieu to argue for, champion, or otherwise attest to the merits of the NSDAP. And, it will be remembered, at least until his dismissal in May of 1932, Chancellor Brüning, of the Zentrum party, was in a position to give a regular defense of his policies over the state-owned radio network.

Although National Socialist activists did appear in such communities to advertise their political wares, it is clear that they did not make as much headway as in equivalent Protestant localities. The suggestion, then, is that in any given community, what sustained the traditional direction and prevented a shift to the NSDAP, was the unbroken consensus on the part of local notables, both clerical and lay, which in turn was supported and reinforced by the local or regional press.[32]

The stability of the voting patterns in the Catholic countryside might conceivably have another explanation; it might result from especially militant efforts by party cadres of the Zentrum or the Bavarian People's party. Evidence on the subject is very scarce. The sense one gets from the literature, however, is that the dominant parties in rural Catholic areas functioned very much like the parties in rural Protestant areas. A coterie of local notables offered the traditional line in a few ritual speeches. The time-honored voting pattern in such areas then followed through sheer inertia. But that routine was interrupted in the Protestant areas when the spell of the traditional notables was broken through the efforts of the new and dynamic political insurgents. In the Catholic countryside, no such conversion of the notables occurred; the hold on the rural Catholic electors then appears to have resulted from the still functioning spell (or the unbroken sense of legitimacy) of the traditional elites rather than from organized party efforts. Pridham, in a casual aside, says the Bavarian People's party "was not in the habit of holding regular meetings in the country areas."[33]

MIDDLE-SIZED COMMUNITIES

The Protestant Towns. The third context to be considered is the middle-sized Protestant communities, a wide and diverse range of towns and cities including those from 2,000 to 99,999 persons. These communities provided a large block of National Socialist votes, being second in importance only to the rural Protestant sector. Some of the communities within this range would have been provincial administrative centers. There would also have been commercial centers or market towns, manufacturing towns, rail centers, mining communities, and, of course, many towns that combined these functions. As compared to the farm communities, the most distinctive feature of these towns would be the presence of workers, of a proletariat and, the ever-present correlate in the Weimar years, support for one or another of the Marxist parties. This fact gave a distinctive stamp to the political struggles in those communities.

Allen's work, already discussed at some length in the previous chapter, is extremely important because it provides a detailed analysis of events as they unfolded in one of these middle-sized Protestant communities. It is, moreover, one of the few works that provides any information at all on the motives of those who voted for Hitler and his party.

Allen's conclusion on this subject is contained in a single sentence: "It was hatred for the SPD that drove Thalburgers into the arms of the Nazis."[34] That is the dominating consideration in his entire discussion. This dialectical struggle of SPD and NSDAP came into ever sharper focus in the course of the years of struggle as the other parties fell by the wayside.

But the National Socialists would not have been chosen by the middle class, Allen notes, were the party not acceptable on other dimensions as well. In this respect, the NSDAP played its game well, its "intense nationalism [and] manipulation of religion" doing much to make it "respectable." It might be easy to assume, particularly from the vantage point of some distance, that the NSDAP consisted only of déclassés, of vulgar interlopers who faced a skeptical and rather disdainful middle-class audience. Such a reading is inaccurate and, moreover, seriously misleading. Throughout "the entire pre-Hitler era" in Thalburg, Allen writes, the NSDAP was in alliance with the DNVP. They shared political outlooks, agreeing on such "principles" as "hyper-nationalism, fanatical anti-Socialism, and commitment to the destruction of the Weimar Republic." As a consequence of that alliance, the town's DNVP notables did not view the party with skepticism or disdain; just the opposite, they showed it great favor and offered much approval. Allen describes the relationship as follows:

> In Thalburg, leading Nationalists were pleased by Nazi successes despite the frequent and clear signs of contempt which the Nazis showed them. [Their newspaper] gave them editorial support, reported frequently and favorably on Nazi doings, and apparently provided cut-rate or free advertising space. In the early years of the Nazi growth [the paper's printing press] was available for Nazi pamphlets and posters and its columns were the only way the Nazis could reach a mass audience. . . .
>
> In Thalburg most of the members of the DNVP were either high-ranking civil servants, entrepreneurs, or noblemen. . . . the "best" people [were] members. . . . By giving enthusiastic support to the Nazis and by limiting its opposition (in the periods when the parties were at odds) to Nazi social goals, the DNVP helped pave the way for Hitler. To Thalburgers it was clear that the best people were for the Nazis except where it might affect their moneybags.[35]

The local National Socialist organization, according to one of Allen's respondents, contained two groups, "the decent ones and the gutter type." The latter type, one of whom is described as "cold, cynical, crude, ruthless, and brutal," eventually "won out."[36] But in the period of struggle, apparently, many people in the middle class had their eyes on the other type. The proprietor of a local bookstore was one of the "decent ones." He is described as a "spare, lively man . . . gentle and kindly, friendly to everyone yet thoughtful and reserved enough to hold people's respect." His bookstore, moreover, "was the intellectual center of the town, for he was acquainted with many of the writers and poets the town admired." He was chairman of the Lecture Society and a prominent member of the Lutheran church. As one Thalburger put it, he "bears a heavy burden, for it was mainly his example that led many people to join the NSDAP. . . . People said, 'If he's in it, it must be all right.' "[37]

This was not an isolated case for, as Allen reports, "many respectable Thalburgers were Nazis: the owner of one of the town's hotels, the director of the *Lyzeum*, about three teachers, both judges at the County Court, and several high officials of the railroad directory. And of course a leading Nazi who lived in Thalburg County was the Baron von Barten, a man of impeccable credentials—nobleman, landowner, and Major in World War I. When he quit the Nationalists to join the Nazis, it was page one news."[38]

There were two bourgeois newspapers in the town. One was tied to the DNVP and was favorable to the NSDAP. The other was closer to the DVP and was generally more moderate or neutral in tone. But neutrality means neither favor nor disdain; hence its bourgeois readers would find no serious criticism of the NSDAP there. Allen's summary comment on the performance of the town's press holds that "unless Thalburgers believed the Socialist press, which was probably the case only for those townspeople who were already Socialists, they had little chance to hear unfavorable opinions of the NSDAP."[39]

The National Socialists, in short, did not operate alone in Thalburg. They could count on the aid and sympathy of significant numbers of established or influential upper- and upper-middle-class notables. Most significantly, perhaps, they were actively supported by one of the local bourgeois newspapers and had no serious opposition from the other. One could hardly ask for conditions more favorable to growth.

The comparison of Allen's account with the conventional picture of NSDAP offerings and public responses reveals some striking disparities. Where that conventional picture is focused on the lower middle class with its strains and anxieties, Allen speaks more generally of the middle class, a category that comes to include many persons who would ordinarily be considered upper middles and some who would even be counted among the town's most prestigious segment, its upper class.

What is even more striking is what he has to say about the impact of the economic crisis. This begins with an unexpected observation about the events of 1930. In that year the economic effects of the depression, he says, were "scarcely noticed in Thalburg. The number of motor vehicles in the town increased by about 15 per cent between the summer of 1929 and the summer of 1930. Savings deposits in the City Savings Bank rose by almost a half-million marks in 1930, and the number of accounts was increased by about five hundred. In that bank alone there were close to 3,600 savings accounts with an average of 537 marks per account."[40]

In another significant statement, still describing events of 1930, Allen declares that

> it was the depression, or more accurately, the fear of its continued effects, that contributed most heavily to the radicalization of Thalburg's people. This was not because the town was deeply hurt by the depression. The only group directly affected were the workers; they were the ones who lost their jobs, stood idle on the corners, and existed on the dole. Yet paradoxically the workers remained steadfast in support of the status quo while the middle class, only marginally hurt by the economic constriction, turned to revolution.
>
> The economic structure of Thalburg kept the middle classes from being hard pressed. Merchants lost only a small portion of their trade. Artisans, apart from those in the building trades, found plenty of work. Civil servants had their wages reduced, but none of them lost their jobs, and if their pay was less, prices also dropped so that their relative position was not weakened. Total savings increased slightly during the years of the depression . . . and the number of savings accounts also rose.[41]

The point appears again and again in Allen's pages, the principal stress being that it was fear, not the objective facts of their condition that moved them. The fears did have real consequences since "the more Thalburgers became concerned about the depression, the more they curtailed their consumption in favor of savings. The depression thus affected their emotions more than their pocketbooks, and if spending in Thalburg fell it was not because the middle classes were hurt; it was because they were hoarding their cash."[42] Their hoarding, in turn, did affect others, notably the artisans and workers engaged in construction trades. The presence of these men, unemployed and on the streets, then reinforced the initial anxieties.

But what of the bankruptcies? What of those who were forced into the proletariat? Very few enterprises in the town suffered that fate. "There were only seventeen bankruptcies," Allen tells us, "in the entire depression era." Eleven of those involved small, marginal shopkeepers, the rest occurred "for causes dissociated from the depression" (for example, mismanagement).[43] De facto losses of middle-class standing, in short, were not very frequent in this community. The reactions of the middle classes, then, were not caused by the "fact" of widespread or even imminent proletarianization. Most were employed in still functioning enterprises, and most apparently, had adequate, or even somewhat increased, savings. Allen describes their condition in another of his terse summary statements: "The middle classes were hardly touched by the depression in Thalburg, except psychologically."[44] If this state of affairs was general throughout Germany, it would clearly present a serious challenge to the entire heritage of theorizing based on the assumption of a vulnerable and declining middle class.[45]

While on the subject of rejected hypotheses, it is worthwhile noting what Allen says with respect to another of the National Socialist appeals, namely anti-Semitism. There were incidents to show that such orientations were present within the local NSDAP, but a rather striking feature of its activities in this community was the relative absence of anti-Semitism. This neglect in turn has a simple explanation:

> Social discrimination against Jews was practically non-existent in the town. Jews were integrated along class lines; the two wealthiest Jewish families belonged to upper class circles and clubs, Jews of middling income belonged to the middle class social organizations [and so on.] . . . If Nazi anti-semitism held any appeal for the townspeople, it was in a highly abstract form, as a remote theory unconnected with daily encounters with real Jews in Thalburg. Thalburg's NSDAP leaders sensed this, and in consequence anti-semitism was not pushed in propaganda except in a ritualistic way. . . . Thalburgers were drawn to anti-semitism because they were drawn to Nazism, not the other way around. Many who voted Nazi simply ignored or rationalized the anti-semitism of the party, just as they ignored other unpleasant aspects of the Nazi movement.[46]

Why did Thalburg's middle classes come to support the NSDAP? Allen's conclusions go as follows: "Thalburg's Nazis had established themselves as both respectable and radical. They were seen as patriotic, anti-socialist, and religious. They enjoyed the apparent blessings of the conservatives. But at the same time the Nazis appeared to be vigorous, determined, and, above all, ready to use radical means to deal with the crucial problem—the depression."[47] The support was not without some reservation: "Enough of the character of the Nazis was apparent in their words and actions to make even those who voted for them dubious, but the fact remains that few Thalburgers had any real conception of what the Nazis would do if they ever came to power. Thalburgers were mainly aware that conditions were currently very bad and that the Nazis were a young, energetic group pledged to rectify the situation."[48]

The National Socialist effort did not take place in a vacuum; they were not the only agency seeking the favor of the voters. It is important, therefore, to see what the other parties in this community were doing. How did they respond to the National Socialist threat? Once again Allen provides us with some valuable portraits.

By 1932 the situation of the other parties in Thalburg had become desperate. In the course of the Prussian state election that year the foundering Staatspartei held a meeting, but, says Allen, "about the only people present were a strong contingent of Reichsbanner men who turned the meeting into an anti-Nazi demonstration."[49] This experience shows again the difficulties facing the so-called center parties because they lacked loyal defense forces of their own. It became more and more difficult for them to gain an audience, and with the diminution of their numbers and the drying up of contributions, they were also unable to buy advertising space in the newspapers.

As was pointed out in Chapter 10, the Democratic party undertook a fatal change of direction just prior to the 1930 election, becoming the "tough" Staatspartei. In Thalburg it showed itself as "authoritarian, hyper-nationalist, anti-Socialist, and anti-semitic—a poor imitation of Hitler's movement." The consequence, since Thalburgers "preferred the real thing," was that its vote total dropped from 505 in 1928 to 246 in 1930. In the Prussian state election it was down to 105 votes, and in the July Reichstag election it fell again, this time to 66 votes.

As of 1928, Thalburg's second largest party, after the SPD, was the People's party, the DVP. It withstood the onslaught of 1930 better than other middle-class parties, losing only 46 votes (falling from 834 to a 788 total). But it too was crushed in the Prussian state election when its total fell to 154, and it lost again in the subsequent Reichstag election when its total fell to 69. Allen refers to the local unit of the party as having strong support among the civil servants. But being "unequivocally capitalistic and nationalistic," it also had, as "leading personalities," some of the community's most substantial citizens, such as the director of the grain mill and the publisher of one of the two bourgeois newspapers.

Allen sees this party's major problem to have been its ambivalence in the choices it faced in this period. Enthusiasm for democracy did not run high in the party whereas hostility to "the Socialists" did. As a result, the party did not prove to be a consistent defender of the republican regime. More important, it could not find its way to an alliance with the SPD to defend that regime. In key specifics it vacillated, for example, openly combatting the NSDAP in September of 1930, then joining with it to bring down the Prussian government in the following spring, and still later, in the spring of 1932, coming back to effective alliance with the SPD in support of Hindenburg's candidacy. There was, Allen reports, a lack of any clear positive line. One speaker, in April 1932, attacked the Communists, opposed "emotion in politics," and "excoriated Brüning for not admitting Hitler to the government!" "It was not wholly clear," Allen says, "what he favored." Later in the year the party did develop a clearer positive alternative. What it wanted "was an authoritarian state based on the power of the president, which would 'destroy the awful party politics of the Reichstag.' "[50]

Thalburg's DVP had a daily newspaper at its disposal. It was the community's largest daily, having a circulation of nearly 4,000. For several reasons, however, it proved to be a very ineffectual agency for the party's purposes. Founded "primarily as a business venture," it strove for maximum circulation by trying "to remain as moderate as possible." To its credit, this journal was "first with the news, generally accurate, and gave the most complete coverage." In this respect it stood in marked contrast to the other bourgeois journal, the much smaller DNVP newspaper in which, Allen reports, "bias found its way into every article."[51]

The DVP daily did oppose the NSDAP, but this opposition was mainly to its "radicalism"; it was a problem of NSDAP "excesses." Allen refers to the paper's general tone as one of "prissy moderation," which served to "relax its readers after supper." Because of its approach, it "could not combat Nazism effectively." "Had the DVP and its organ pushed for a reasoned and progressive democracy," Allen concludes, "the NSDAP might have found it a more dangerous opponent than the SPD. But by its fuzzy opportunism and blind 'anti-Marxism' the DVP in Thalburg not only proved incapable of dealing with the Nazi threat but also probably denied Thalburg's middle class [its] only feasible alternative to the NSDAP."[52]

The weakness of the provincial press, its susceptibility to National Socialism, extended well beyond Thalburg. Noakes's discussion of the dynamics involved is reported in Chapter 8, in his account of the *Hannoverscher Kurier*. Caught in a competitive squeeze, bourgeois newspapers began to court NSDAP favor.[53]

Possibly the most striking and most unexpected development in Thalburg was the decline in the fortunes of the SPD. Prior to the NSDAP breakthrough, and even as of September 1930, the SPD was the largest single party in the town.

The SPD had a daily newspaper with an audience of about 2,000. Like many Socialist newspapers, in Germany and elsewhere, this was not strictly a local organ, being published in a neighboring town but having enough local news to allow it to compete with other Thalburg newspapers. Given its close SPD ties, this journal was not likely to have had a general appeal especially since it "made no pretense of neutrality." After the National Socialists' local offering, it was the worst publication among the community's none too rich sources of information—"a scandal sheet, full of scathing attacks and red ink."[54] It conducted steady attacks on the claims, credibility, capacities and honesty of the community's leaders. Some of these attacks were fully justified although in any given instance it was not always possible to tell which claims were factual and which merely scurrilous. In any event, under the circumstances this delegitimizing effort could have done little more than reinforce the convictions of the already convinced. The middle classes, after all, were not likely to join the SPD ranks as a result of their newly acquired wisdom.

The SPD, unlike most of the threatened middle-class parties, had a fighting force at its disposal. This force, the Reichsbanner, had considerably greater numerical strength than did the NSDAP's Sturmabteilung. Allen reports them as having 400 trained members at the beginning of 1932 as compared to the local SA force which had "not more than fifty" members prior to 1933. The Reichsbanner, like the SA, undertook covert military maneuvers. It too could quickly mobilize its forces. Repeated test alarms had showed it could assemble its entire force within a half-hour without recourse to telephones, automobiles, or bicycles.[55]

The events of the period generated a sense of despair within SPD ranks, despite the Reichsbanner's strength and apparent readiness. By the summer of 1932 a "feeling of resignation" spread through the SPD, which ultimately helped to ensure a "frictionless" seizure of power in Thalburg. Papen's takeover in Prussia certainly stimulated that feeling. And, on the local scene, an NSDAP victory in the Works Council election among the railroad workers together with the failure of an SPD boycott of NSDAP storeowners gave rise to the feeling that nothing the SPD did seemed to have the desired effect. The SPD suffered a loss of over 200 votes in the April 1932 Prussian state election (falling from 2,246 in September 1930 to 2,024). The results of a school election in June showed the SPD suffering a serious defeat in a working-class district, that is, on its own ground. In the July 1932 election the losses were even more serious, the party now being down to 1,639 votes. It suffered still another loss in the November election.

In the face of these blows, it should cause little wonder that the SPD came to be "gripped by a peculiar fatalism" in the months prior to Hitler's taking of power. The townspeople generally were "convinced of the inevitability of a Nazi victory."[56] Although the Reichsbanner "continued its preparations for a fight," a less visible process of dissolution was occurring, such as the precautionary destruction of membership lists.

Some sense of the reasons for the SPD disillusionment, despite its superiority in numbers of members and fighting forces, appears in Allen's pages. Where the NSDAP efforts were expansive and aggressive, the "mood of SPD, Reichsbanner, or union meetings was wholly defensive."[57] Some of the reasons for that incapacity were indicated in Chapter 11, the most notable of these being its acceptance of Brüning's deflationary economic program and the refusal of a general public works plan. Another source of SPD concern, a continuous problem for the party, was that when it "strove to match the Nazis in determination [it merely] drove the middle class into the Nazi embrace."[58]

Allen's final comment on the SPD reinforces one of the conclusions offered in Chapter 11 with respect to the penalty paid by the SPD for maintaining an inappropriate "heritage." As he puts it, "the nature of the SPD had something to do with the burghers' attitudes. Thalburg's Socialists maintained slogans and methods which had little correspondence with reality. They maintained the facade of a revolutionary party when they were no longer prepared to lead a revolution. They never seriously attempted to mend fences with the middle class and frequently offended bourgeois sensibilities by their shortsightedness and shallow aggressiveness."[59]

As noted earlier, the later erosion of SPD strength was associated with a growth on the part of the Communists. Some growth of KPD strength occurred also in Thalburg, but it was by no means proportionate to the SPD losses. Between September 1930 and November 1932, the KPD there gained 223 votes, going from 115 to a 338 total. But in the same period the SPD had lost over 600 votes. Many of these, Allen notes, "must have gone to the Nazis." SPD losses appear to have been even more serious in the surrounding countryside, where isolated supporters were much more exposed to NSDAP pressure and persuasion than was the case with the massed followers of the town.[60]

The Communists, although never a serious force in Thalburg, were a force in the minds of many townspeople who believed them to be serious revolutionaries unlike the SPD. Despite tough talk and much bravura, the local Communists, Allen reports, "were not prepared to fight. When Prussian police searched the homes of all leading Communist functionaries in Thalburg County in August, 1932, the total of weapons from sixteen houses consisted of one pair of brass knuckles, two 'daggers,' four 'clubs,' and a revolver. But the possibility of Communist growth in Thalburg continued to provide the Nazis with a whipping boy, the middle class with new reasons for concern, and the Socialists with another cause for a siege atmosphere."[61]

The Catholic Towns. There is little one can say about the situation in the middle-sized Catholic communities; like the Catholic villages, they are an unstudied field. Accordingly, the comments made here must be both brief and, in great measure, speculative.

These communities were similar to their Protestant equivalents in two important respects: they contained an industrial working class, and they had some considerable Social Democratic or Communist voting. Although the workers in such communities were of Catholic origin, many having come from the surrounding farm area, the disaffection from traditional political outlooks occurring in their new work places took place with remarkable speed and consistency.

The responses of the middle-class populations in Catholic communities, typically, were very different from those of their Protestant peers. Specifically, this means that they maintained their loyalties to the Zentrum. Since the Zentrum was in power, in one way or another, throughout the last years of the republic, in local governments, in coalition in Prussia, and, under Brüning, as the governing party of the nation, it remained the best available party for the defense of both the religious and the class interests of the Catholic middle class.

It seems likely that here, too, as in the Catholic villages, one would have found a general consensus among the local elites; the town's notables, clerical and lay figures alike, would have been in substantial agreement about the merits of the Zentrum. They would not have provided supportive cues that would have allowed or encouraged voters to shift to the NSDAP. The local middle-class newspaper did not face the competitive pressure found in the Protestant communities, and it too would have supported the Zentrum.

The patterns of influence within these communities, in short, were such as to contain the political affections of the various segments of the electorate; Communists and Social Democrats stayed within their camp (with possibly some drift to the former occurring), and the Zentrum followers stayed loyally within theirs. There would have been fewer NSDAP activists present within this setting than in equivalent Protestant areas, and their opportunities for gaining entry in the face of these entrenched forces were severely limited. For the NSDAP, in short, the going was not as easy as in the Protestant communities where they fought against loosely organized parties of notables, parties that were divided on matters of principle and tactics and that, to one degree or another, were seriously discredited. Those parties, to fall back on metaphor, contained the seeds of their own destruction.

The above comments should not be taken as saying that the NSDAP made *no* gains in Catholic areas. In six middle-sized communities of Upper Bavaria, the NSDAP's share of the vote in the July 1932 election ranged from 16.5 to 35.8 percent. The former figure came from Freising, once the seat of a bishopric and in the early thirties, the setting of a Catholic university specializing in philosophy and theology. The high figure was for Bad Reichenhall, a resort town at the foot of the Alps (discussed in Chapter 9). A rather detailed account of one of these six communities, Ingolstadt, appears in the work of Geoffrey Pridham. After Munich, it was the second largest city of Upper Bavaria, having a population of some 27,000, the overwhelming majority of whom (87 percent) were Catholic. In the July 1932 Reichstag election, 31.1 percent of the valid votes cast there went to the National Socialists. Just over a third of the votes went to the Bavarian People's party and just under 30 percent went to the left, to the Social Democrats and Communists. A brief review of Pridham's account will prove useful.[62]

Ingolstadt, located some seventy kilometers north of Munich, had been one of the largest garrison towns in Bavaria and had also been a center of military production. The postwar economic difficulties facing this community, obviously, were directly dependent on the stipulations of the Treaty of Versailles. The ex-soldiers, officers and men, did not conveniently disappear with the dissolution of the imperial army. Rather, following the pattern described in the previous chapter, many of the "demobbed soldiers remained there . . . and joined the Free Corps and later the SA."[63] A key figure in the rise of the National Socialists was the commandant of the city fortress, Colonel Hans Georg Hofmann. He was a close friend of Franz Ritter von Epp, the leader of the Freikorps unit that "liberated" Munich. Because of his official position, Hofmann at first maintained only informal links with the town's National Socialists. He retired from the army in 1926 and, for a while, headed the United Patriotic Associations of Ingolstadt. Finally, in 1931, he joined the NSDAP, soon becoming a regional SA leader.

Another key figure in the party, Dr. Ludwig Liebl, had a flourishing medical practice, was a member of the local Board of Health, and a "patron of various cultural associations." Born of a Catholic family in 1874, the son of a country-court judge, he studied in Munich and later, in 1909, migrated to Ingolstadt where he became active in town politics as a member of the liberal bourgeois Democratic party. During the war he served as an army doctor, afterward continuing his medical career along with his local political efforts. A close friend of Colonel Hofmann, he was popular in both military and artistic circles. Pridham describes him as "a classic example of the much-respected local personality who lent his prestige to the Nazi movement."[64]

Liebl visited Hitler in Landsberg prison in 1924 and, on the refounding of the party, served as its local leader for four years. His preference, however, was for behind the scenes work rather than for the everyday tasks of organization, administration, and propaganda. He provided the money for a local NSDAP newspaper, a daily, a rather unusual accomplishment for the party at that point. This paper was in competition with the *Ingolstädter Zeitung*, linked to the BVP, and the *Ingolstädter Anzeiger* of the SPD. His money also made it possible for the local NSDAP group to invite some of the party's leading figures. On those occasions Liebl, who is described by Pridham as something of a social climber, chaired the meetings and shared the limelight with Gregor Strasser, Heinrich Himmler, and Hitler. When Hitler visited Ingolstadt, which he did on several occasions, he was usually entertained at the Liebls. The doctor's efforts no doubt went a long way to legitimate the party for many of the town's voters.

Because of his liberal background, Liebl might ordinarily have had little opportunity for a political career in a Catholic community. But the BVP in Ingolstadt was divided and poorly organized, and the National Socialists exploited those divisions. With his personal charisma, Liebl was able to draw support from the military and from liberal elements of the town, thus making him a significant figure in the community's affairs.

For reasons of health, Liebl was forced to withdraw from active participation in politics. In 1929 he resigned as local group leader and was replaced by Johann Bergler, an official employed by the German railways. Bergler was of "more radical bent" than Liebl. A Streicher sympathizer and founder of the National Socialist trade union in the town, he supported the "social revolutionary aspects of National Socialism." He made appeals to the town's unemployed workers, at one point cooperating with the Communists, but otherwise his aim was to take support from their potential followers.

The party, in summary, benefited by having at least some notables in this community. Some, like Liebl, had a rather general appeal; others had special links to key segments of the electorate—Colonel Hofmann with his ties to the military, and Bergler, who although a public official, made systematic attempts to reach the town's workers. As Pridham puts it, the NSDAP "became 'respectable' through its associations with such prestige figures as Ludwig Liebl, Hans Hofmann and Franz Ritter von Epp."[65]

For those trained to expect lower-middle-class dominance in the National Socialists, for those expecting local leaders to be nearly bankrupt shopkeepers or lowly clerks, the presence of such respectable figures may come as something of a surprise. The Ingolstadt case, moreover, does not appear to be exceptional. Of another middle-sized Bavarian community Pridham reports the following:

> If the lower middle classes provided the backbone of the activist element in general, the professional middle classes were more prominent at the leadership level. Doctors and lawyers were often found as branch or district leaders . . . to an extent out of proportion to their share of the total membership. A prominent example of a lawyer as local party leader was Wilhelm Schwarz, branch leader and from 1927 district leader in Memmingen. Schwarz was born in Memmingen in 1902, joined the NSDAP in 1926 and set up legal practice in the town in April 1930. He was a gifted public speaker and was the leading light in the local party, as Dr. Liebl was in Ingolstadt.[66]

In Lindau, a summer resort community on Lake Constance, the NSDAP gained 37.3 percent in July 1932. The party's leading notable was the mayor of the community. Since 1919, he had served in that capacity for the Bavarian People's party. In January 1931, he changed loyalties and joined the NSDAP. In the same month, he gave his first speech on behalf of his new party. The police declared it to have been the largest crowd ever assembled for a political meeting in the town. This man, Ludwig Siebert, later became prime minister of Bavaria when the National Socialists took power.[67]

The National Socialist vote-getting effort in the Catholic communities shows some similarities to the processes found in the Protestant towns. The key role of upper- or upper-middle-class notables who vouched for them (and paid some of the costs) is similar in both cases. The basic difference appears in the extent of this behavior. In the Catholic communities the National Socialists ran up against a bloc of notables who, together with much of the ordinary middle-class citizenry, did not defect, who did not abandon its former political faith. It was this persistent hold of political Catholicism that limited the National Socialists to a 25 to 35 percent share of the vote in these communities as against, for example, the 62 percent gained in Protestant Thalburg. The relative successes of the NSDAP in Catholic cities were linked to the presence of significant numbers of Protestant outsiders (as in the case of Bad Reichenhall) or to the presence of liberal notables, of defectors from Catholicism (as in the case of Ludwig Liebl). A linkage to the army and the Freikorps, as in Ingolstadt, provided another path to success within the Catholic context.

LARGE CITIES

Germany's large cities, those of 100,000 or more, form still another arena for political struggle. In this context it proves useful to discount the religious factor and instead consider the political struggles as they developed within three class settings: in the working-class, in the mixed, and in the upper- and upper-middle-class areas.

The Urban Working Class. The working-class milieu, like that of farmers and villagers, is by and large an unknown setting in any modern society. Workers themselves do not write much; they do not typically keep diaries or notebooks, leave a rich and extensive correspondence, engage in autobiography, recording for posterity the "fullness of their days." Those people who do write about workers tend to be leftist intellectuals and activists. Their reports are generally rather selective; they pick up the heroic periods of working-class struggles, neglecting both the demise of those struggles and, more important, the everyday routines of working-class life. This rather selective literature typically imputes motives (like "rising class consciousness") rather than discovering them. A characteristic feature of this literature is an evident distance from its subjects, this being made manifest by the lack of attention to individuals. The highly reified claims focus on "the workers" or on "the masses." Missing from such accounts are the faces and voices of individual human beings.[68]

The present account must necessarily suffer from this same lack of first-hand materials. Like much of the discussion of the previous contexts, it, too, must be based largely on surmise and speculation.[69] This speculation, however, does not come out of the blue, but rather begins with some of the evidence on voting presented in Chapters 4-9. It was shown, for example, that in Berlin and Hamburg, approximately one-quarter of the voters in working-class districts supported the NSDAP in July 1932 (see Chapters 4 and 5).

An unresolvable element of ambiguity appears in this connection: is this a working-class vote or the vote of the middle-class minority living in those districts? Rather than making an a priori stipulation that the vote was neatly divided along class lines (with workers supporting the left and the depressed middle class supporting the National Socialists), an alternative line of argument was suggested. The alternative has a purely logical component, but is also consonant with at least a fragment of evidence.

The "logical" argument holds that outlooks will reflect origins or, more specifically, the socialization associated with those origins.[70] As noted, many of the middle-class people living in the working-class neighborhoods would have been born and raised in working-class families. They would have gone to school with working-class children, and, still living in the same communities, would have continued to maintain regular contacts with people who, after all, were their friends and kinsmen. Although currently employed as small shopkeepers, or as minor clerks (many of them in or around the factories and shops, in cooperatives, in trade unions, or within the vast Social Democratic party bureaucracy), it seems unlikely that they would have developed a sharply differentiated class consciousness that in turn would have led them to adopt a different life style and different politics. The evidence on white-collar trade union membership would tend to support this view since, particularly in the larger cities, many white-collar workers joined a trade union with close ties to the Social Democratic party. The fragmentary evidence from Berlin indicates that these middle-class Socialists tended to be located in working-class districts.[71]

For these reasons, it seems likely that the political differences between the working-class and middle-class populations in urban working-class districts were rather limited. The assumption, then, is that approximately one-quarter of both segments would have been supporting the National Socialists; the other three-quarters, again of both segments, would have been voting for one or the other of the parties of the left.

The next step in the argument can be made with somewhat greater confidence, namely that those who shifted to the NSDAP were not previous supporters of the SPD or KPD. The shifts within the urban working-class districts probably had much the same character as those found in other contexts; they were shifts away from one of the so-called middle-class parties.[72] The National Socialist support in those districts, in short, appears to have come from Germany's equivalent of the Tory workers.

Germany's Tory workers would be those with some lingering affection for the monarchy, for the German nation, and for the lost Reich. They would also, presumably, have a considerable respect for authority, being psychologically attached to the hierarchy and forms of the old regime and to the people, noblemen, officials, and military leaders alike, who had ruled in that era. The Protestants among them would also, in all likelihood, have maintained connections with the Lutheran church, unlike the rest of the largely unchurched working class. An important correlate of this world view would be strong opposition to the initiatives and directions proposed by the parties of the left.[73]

The outlooks of these Tory workers may be explained in much the same way as those of the Socialist middle class. Their views, in short, probably derived from early political training and subsequent reinforcement. The Tory workers would have received their political training from conservative and nationalist parents. Many of them, probably, would have first learned those lessons in smaller towns or in the villages of the German countryside, only later moving to the large cities. In those original settings, the nationalist lessons would have been reinforced within the schools, possibly in the churches, and also in a rich array of public display and pageantry. In such settings the forces of the left would have provided only a weak challenge to the dominant ideology and symbolism.

Those conservative and nationalist lessons would probably have been reinforced through experience with the military, most especially through the experience at the front during the war years. While many enlisted men would have come away from the war with strong pacifist outlooks, especially given the efforts of the left in support of that position, the Tory workers might well have reacted in an opposite way. They might have been attracted by the new-found egalitarianism, by the *Kameradschaft* of the trenches. The discussion of the *Fronterlebnis* in the previous chapter focused on the officers, but there must have been many ordinary soldiers who also made the same discovery. The Tory workers, who identified with the nation, the cause, and the military organization, would probably have reacted to the ending of the war, to the revolution, to the *Dolchstoss*, and to the defeat, in much the same way as did the officers and noncoms. Although their feelings might have been similar, their reactions, it seems, were somewhat different. Where the young officers moved into the Freikorps and continued their military careers, the workers returned home and picked up their careers in the shops and factories.

Within the factories, the Tory workers would probably have found themselves in a rather beleaguered position. Possibly three out of every four coworkers in one way or another supported the Marxist parties. Those leftist workers would probably have been organized in many ways, both within and outside of the shops; the rightist or Tory workers, by comparison, would have found themselves largely without organizational weapons. In those circumstances, it seems likely that they would have taken a considerable amount of psychic or even physical punishment from left activists, especially from the tougher and more ruthless Communists.[74]

It seems most unlikely that the workers who maintained their national loyalties through to 1928 and 1929 would abandon those views in 1930 with the onset of the economic crisis. More important, when they abandoned their previous *party* choices in the midst of the crisis, it seems unlikely that they would turn to the Social Democrats or to the Communists as their next best alternative. The previous years of antagonism and hostility would most certainly have closed off that possibility.[75]

The so-called middle-class parties, it will be remembered, undertook a shift to the right at this time, effectively abandoning the interests of their working-class clientele. They had, to be sure, taken fiscally conservative positions in previous economic crises; by itself, that was nothing new. What was different about this occasion was, first, the seriousness of the crisis, and second, the presence of an alternative party, one that was both social and national, to which this clientele could move.

Presumably then, for this segment of workers there was a very special sense in which their traditional parties were discredited. The abandonment of their interests must have seemed a bitter recompense for the years of hard-fought loyalty. When this better option appeared, a party that aggressively championed their world view, that had the fighting forces to make an effective defense of those views, and that simultaneously offered a job-creation program, the shift was relatively easy.[76]

One other consideration requires attention in this connection, that being the question of the party's socialism. One line of argument appearing in much of the relevant literature holds that there was a left faction within the party, the key figures in the group being Gregor and Otto Strasser, and, until his defection, Joseph Goebbels. This line of argument holds that through a combination of manipulation and demagogy, Hitler broke this faction, this happening at a famous meeting in Bamberg in 1926. But the recent work of Max Kele, based on a detailed examination of National Socialist publications indicates that the leftist themes, those appeals intended for the workers, continued to be made through 1932. Given the wealth of supporting quotations from various party publications, this aspect of Kele's argument is very compelling.[77]

The argument that the NSDAP broke its left faction has been an attractive one, especially for writers on the left. For them, it resolves the nationalism or socialism question by demonstrating Hitler's "real" ideological direction.[78] It proves the party's socialism to have been merely demagogic, something that was quickly sacrificed when it threatened Hitler's attempts to gain favor with the bourgeoisie. This early move by Hitler also sets the stage for another key claim in the leftist version of the drama; it makes plausible the argument of early, continuous, and substantial financial contributions to the party by the bourgeoisie. But Kele shows the first of these claims to be mistaken; the left direction continued to be a significant theme in NSDAP propaganda throughout the Weimar period. Goebbels did not change but continued his aggressive anticapitalist attacks, even authorizing support for the Berlin transport workers' strike in November of 1932. And Gregor Strasser continued his activities within the party, Hitler having put him in charge of party organization, a position he continued to hold until December 1932. At that point, in the aftermath of a controversy over participation in the Schleicher government, Strasser gave up his offices within the party.

There is a peculiar irony in all of this. The so-called leftist themes, those aimed at attracting workers, probably did not play much of a role at all. Few convinced Marxists would have been moved by this ersatz product. And those workers who did move to the party were not likely to have done so because of leftist themes. This would mean that the NSDAP continued a demagogic line that had little payoff among workers and that simultaneously caused serious problems with the bourgeoisie. It is a point to bear in mind when one is told about NSDAP shrewdness, cunning, and mastery of demagogic appeals. From its point of view, this particular line of propaganda appears to have been a serious error.

The National Socialists did provide one offering that would appeal to workers, a comprehensive economic program calling for deficit financing and direct job-creation efforts. This was first put forward by Gregor Strasser in a Reichstag speech in May of 1932. Although meeting with some opposition in bourgeois circles, it was one of the party's major themes in the July 1932 election campaign. The program, it will be noted, was a close parallel to that put forward by the German trade union leaders at approximately the same time, the one rejected by SPD leaders and the parliamentary faction. It seems likely that this NSDAP message was heard, and heeded, by Germany's Tory workers and also, possibly, by some apolitical workers and by those putting bread and butter concerns ahead of ideology.[79]

The Mixed Districts. As indicated in previous chapters, the lower middle class did not have a distinctive base within the large cities; that is, it did not have its own separate communities. Instead one found districts containing a mix of populations, roughly half being middle class and the other half better-off workers. Lacking any adequate surveys or public opinion polls from the period, it is virtually impossible to establish the voting tendencies of these segments. What follows, therefore, is largely speculative or hypothetical.

The most likely hypothesis one can offer with respect to the urban lower-middle class (including here both independent and salaried subgroups) is that politically it was very divided. This assumption, of course, stands in opposition to the received claim that the lower middle class gave very heavy support to the NSDAP (see the arguments and limited evidence presented in Chapter 3).

The absence of pure lower-middle-class districts makes an unambiguous test of the received hypothesis impossible. Since urban districts, at least in the cities analyzed here, had strong middle-class majorities (most of these being *upper* middle-class districts), strong working-class majorities, or roughly equal middle- and working-class populations, there were no settings in 1930 or 1932 that could have provided the voting evidence needed to support the original claim.

The best test of the received hypothesis, it was argued earlier, would be found in the results for the mixed districts. It seems likely that these districts would have contained that part of the middle class with strong middle-class identifications, those who would have feared proletarianization. It is conceivable too that the mixed districts would contain "bourgeoisified" workers, those who emulated the life style of the middle class and who adopted its politics. But in these districts the argument is faced with another difficulty. In those cities for which we have the best data, Berlin, Hamburg, and Cologne, the three largest cities of the nation, *none of the mixed districts gave majority support to the National Socialists.* In the four mixed districts of Berlin, the average support in the July 1932 election ran at 29.9 percent, a figure that was not significantly different from that for the city as a whole.[80] The vote for the left in these districts ran at approximately twice the level of the National Socialist vote, the former dividing almost equally between Social Democrats and Communists. There is, in short, a good prima facie case for arguing that the urban lower middle class (as represented by the vote in these districts) voted for the left. The only saving alternative would be to assume that it was the workers in these districts who voted for the left and that the middle class voted heavily for the NSDAP. This, too, it should be noted, is an untestable hypothesis.

Another possible result (also untestable) would be that both classes within these mixed districts had similar voting patterns. There may have been slightly less support for the left within the middle class and somewhat less support for the right within the working class. But the assumption in this case is that there was a fair-sized Socialist middle class and a fair-sized Tory working class within these districts, as in the working-class subareas.[81]

The overall pattern of vote shifting found in these mixed districts was much the same as that noted elsewhere: it too involved movement from the Democrats, from the People's party, and, to a lesser extent, from the Conservatives, to the National Socialists. If the assumption about the original voting patterns were correct, it would mean that the National Socialist support there came from moderate or conservative middle-class populations and also from moderate or conservative working-class populations.

What can one say about possible motives for the NSDAP support? Among the workers in these districts the motives may well have been the same as those of the previously discussed Tory workers. They were loyal (to a previous regime), nationalist, and anti-Marxist. They were not likely to have been attracted to a left party at any time. They may have abandoned their previous party because of a feeling that that party had abandoned them and their interests. They may have been attracted to the NSDAP because of the party's evident ability to fight it out with both the KPD and the SPD. It might also, to be sure, have been a question of economic stress or anxiety that led them to make the change. Another possibility is that the conservative and right liberal press played a facilitating role by legitimating the NSDAP, as in the smaller communities, thus aiding the change.

As for the middle-class populations in those districts, they may well have suffered the strains and anxieties so frequently reported in the literature on the subject; they may have faced imminent proletarianization and have reacted to that threat. One should, however, consider some alternative possibilities.

This middle class, one must note, was not homogeneous, there being some very important differences in the economic conditions and likely prospects of the various segments. Most white-collar workers were employed although, to be sure, a significant minority, approximately one-quarter of those in the private sector, were not. All civil servants, of course, were employed. And those employed groups, as we have seen, experienced some improvement in their real incomes, their experience being just the opposite of proletarianization. They would certainly have recognized that fact. Many of them, of course, could have been employed but fearful of layoffs. But many others must have known their positions were relatively secure. It seems likely, again judging from other times and places, that the insecure employees would have been young and, with greater likelihood, of leftist persuasion. One gains job security with age, and, moreover, employers would be inclined to reward those with reliable political outlooks. This would mean that it was young urban white-collar workers who faced immediate economic strains or threats thereof. But they, nevertheless, seem likely to have supported the left. The older employees, possibly, were not directly touched by the crisis (or, in terms of real incomes, actually benefited). But they, for different reasons, appear to have shifted to the NSDAP. One likely reason is that reported by Allen for Thalburg, that is, a fear of Marxism. In urban areas, of course, such fears would probably have been focused on the KPD. These voters, moreover, would have been conservative, part of the nationalist middle class. Unlike the Tory workers, these voters would never have seriously considered the possibility of turning to the left.

These lower-middle-class voters may have been attracted by the tougher and seemingly more effective NSDAP, sensing it to be the better means for achieving their nationalistic political and cultural goals than the now-discredited middle-class parties. Then too, there were various legitimating agents, the respected individuals and the press vouching for the party and attesting to its merits. This segment of the middle class would have read the conservative press or the right liberal DVP-linked press, and, as we have seen, much of that press gave Hitler's party warm and sympathetic treatment, presenting the NSDAP as a member in good standing of the broad nationalist coalition. Those readers would also have seen accounts of the National Socialists doing battle in working-class areas. Reading also of the threat of communism, it was easy for them to draw the conclusion that the NSDAP had the necessary defense forces to ward off that threat. Thus, despite some possible lingering qualms, they felt the NSDAP to be deserving of their support. The NSDAP also held meetings in all urban districts. Unlike the provocative meetings planned for the working-class districts, those held in the mixed districts would probably have been rather routine. There, the interested or curious citizen could have picked up the NSDAP arguments, possibly passing on the lesson to others within his milieu.

The Bourgeoisie and the Upper Middle Class. The upper and the upper middle classes are considered together, first, because it is difficult to separate them in the electoral data, and second, because it seems likely that similar motivations would have prevailed in both groups. One might also assume relatively close contacts between these two segments, the former being owners of the major means of production and many of the latter being their top-level employees, the managers of their firms, the administrators and professionals. Others, the middle-level managers, would have been aspirants to these top positions and may well have adopted the behavior and outlooks of their superiors. Even if they were not in daily contact, the social distance between the upper and upper middle classes would have been relatively small and the opportunities for the bourgeoisie to communicate a political line or direction relatively large. The members of the upper middle class, presumably, would be eager and anxious to follow the directions offered by their superiors. Given the easy assumption of both formal and informal chains of command, it is appropriate to begin this discussion with a consideration of the bourgeoisie, of the capitalists.

Geiger's estimate, based on the 1925 census, has "the capitalists" of Germany (including all family members) constituting 0.9 percent of the population. That meant, again using his figures, some 574,752 persons. Even if one focused only on the adult males, on the politically active, the more directive members of the class, one would still have a rather large population. Making very restrictive assumptions it would amount to more than 100,000 persons. Given their territorial dispersion, it is difficult to see how a consensus, a common class position could be worked out with respect to any newly emerging concerns or issues. Even allowing for a wide range of shared experience in upper-class communities, in schools, in the universities, and in the *Korporationen* (fraternities), it is still difficult to see how a broad consensus could be established, especially on new issues. In addition, one must also consider the problem of transmission, of communicating an approved position to others within the class or to those in the upper-middle-class ranks. There would also be a problem of "enforcement," of overcoming the opposition of dissenters or mavericks within their ranks.

One alternative possibility, of course, is that *the* bourgeoisie did not work things out collectively. Political affairs, in this alternative reading of the situation, would be delegated to, or assumed by, an "executive committee." There is some basis for this notion in that German big business, over the years, did organize such smaller groups, some with general responsibilities, some with appropriate functional and regional specializations. And these "committees" did make systematic efforts to work out and implement policy. The rather extended review that follows addresses the following questions: what were the political directions chosen by the bourgeoisie (or by its executive committees) in the Weimar period? What means did it have at its disposal for the realization of its goals? And, how successful was it in the realization of its aims?

For a symptomatic case from the immediate prewar period, consider Albert Ballin, the prewar managing director of the Hamburg-America Line (HAPAG), at that point "the largest steamship company in the world."[82] Ballin was self-made, a man of enormous organizational ability, a charmer and a diplomat. He was also an arch reactionary, this orientation being most obvious in his attitude toward organized labor. He broke two strikes by HAPAG workers, in both cases using imported (English) strike breakers; his threats to the unionized ship's officers of the firm led 305 of the 309 members to resign quickly. His biographer tells us that he "took a conspiratorial view of organized labor and believed that the peril it represented could be met only if management presented a united and obdurate front." But much to his regret, he found that "German employers did not seem disposed to act in unison, nor did they receive much support from Berlin in dealing with this menacing problem."[83]

The war brought substantial changes in the relationship between business and government. The imposition of various controls allowed the government to direct and plan the economy. Not indifferent to the trend, big business organized to work for the earliest possible dismantling of the state agencies.[84] Even more important, as the military collapse approached, business organized to save what it could of its property and privilege. This effort resulted in the Stinnes-Legien Agreement of November 15, 1918. Hugo Stinnes, possibly *the* dominant figure in German heavy industry, was the leader of a giant coal, iron, and steel combination, and Carl Legien was the leader of the Free Trade Unions (those linked to the Social Democrats). Among other things, the agreement provided for recognition of trade unions, collective bargaining, and industry-wide contracts. It also created the Zentralarbeitsgemeinschaft (the Central Work Community), an organization in which business and union leaders would work out their differences. It was a dramatic shift in direction for most German businessmen, a far cry from their previous *Herr-im-Hause* (master of one's house) attitude.

Another change instituted in the same period involved a transformation in the character of the "executive committee" itself. Its prewar association, organized on a regional basis, was replaced by the Reichsverband der Deutschen Industrie (RDI), which was organized by industry (*Fach*) as was appropriate given the new industry-wide bargaining and contracts. The subsidiary organizations in this federation represented the major industries. This step, too, was carried through with efficiency and dispatch. It would be no exaggeration to say that big business *imposed* this overall solution, forcing it on smaller manufacturers over their objections.[85]

This might sound like the smooth workings of an elite group, with all leading participants aware of their class interests and knowing full well what was necessary to protect them. The reality, however, was quite different. Some of the complexities of the situation are portrayed by Gerald Feldman, a leading expert on German business:

> By the First World War this business community was highly differentiated and complex. Such diverse types as Upper Silesian magnates, Rhenish-Westphalian entrepreneurs, Hamburg merchants and shippers, Berlin bankers, Saxon textile industrialists, inventive entrepreneurs of the machine building, electro-technical and chemical industries, managers and syndicate directors are not easily lumped together. This heterogeneity was not simply a matter of typology but also of economic antagonism and political conflict. Difficulties between raw materials producers and finished product manufacturers over prices and tariffs, tensions between big business and medium sized business, and rivalries within big business between the dominant older sectors of coal, iron and steel production and the newer sectors of chemical and electro-technical production were sources of organizational division. These divisions were often closely, although by no means uniformly, paralleled by conflicts over political and social issues. The leaders of heavy industry in the Ruhr and Silesia sought alliance with the large East Elbian landowners and opposed the recognition of organized labor, while some of the leaders of the newer industrial sectors and important segments of middle sized and small

business took a more reformist position concerning both politics and social relations. Needless to say, businessmen were most concerned with economics, not politics, and their political involvement was usually severely limited because of preoccupation with their own enterprises and an unpolitical attitude which identified the general welfare with the prosperity and autonomy of the business community."[86]

One specific example of such internal division involves Ballin. His business, as might well be expected, was paralyzed by the war (although he did receive compensation). He "did not appreciate" the wartime boom in heavy industry and disliked its use of wartime profits, specifically the buying of newspapers, which allowed it to rule "not only the people but also the government." To counter this he joined with a Stuttgart industrialist, Robert Bosch, to plan some competition. Ballin and Bosch thought heavy industry was "digging its own grave" by its "rigid adherence to immoderate war aims and its opposition to internal reform." In a statement from September 1917, Ballin complained that these industrialists were "tying themselves down to a definite program and placing themselves in radical opposition to the majority in Germany. Sooner or later, however, this majority will have the power in its hand and then it will be easy for it to take revenge, for nothing would be simpler than crippling heavy industry through a few laws. The gentlemen do not think of this because they are driven on by blind vanity and unspeakable ignorance concerning the actual situation."[87]

But the leaders of heavy industry were not entirely blind. Stinnes, although a 1917 supporter of Ludendorff, was the creator of the new Arbeitsgemeinschaft. Another instance of flexibility is provided by Carl Duisberg, the founder of the chemical combine I. G. Farben. He was a staunch supporter of Ludendorff as late as September 1918. But in mid-October that year, just before the collapse, he wrote that "from that day when I saw that the cabinet system was bankrupt, I greeted the change to a parliamentary system with joy, and I stand today, when what is at stake is what I consider to be the highest value, namely the Fatherland, behind the democratic government and, where it is possible, I work hand in hand with the unions and seek in this way to save what can be saved. You see, I am an opportunist and adjust to things as they are." By November, Feldman reports, Duisberg was convinced that the "red republic" was characterized by a "more commercial-technical spirit [which] would replace the largely formalistic, even if strictly logical way of thinking and doing things brought into our administration by the jurists." He would shed no tears for the "holy bureaucratism" of the past.[88]

Various big business figures also "actively participated in the discussions of socialization in 1918-1920." They contributed, Feldman notes, "not as ardent supporters of free enterprise but as experts helping with the job at hand. As Paul Silverberg, a leader of the lignite industry, later noted, big business killed socialization by constantly presenting new ideas." In a minor peripheral effort, Bosch and a much more conservative figure, Paul Reusch, corresponded over the question of providing financial support for a noted right-wing Socialist journal, the *Sozialistische Monatshefte*. The journal ultimately "received substantial financial assistance."[89]

The portrait presented thus far is one of a business elite which, although divided in many ways, did nevertheless have affairs rather well in hand. Although sharing or participating in power on many fronts with groups who are frequently seen as the business community's primordial enemies, these businessmen were able to cooperate and, more important, managed to preserve much of their position and autonomy. Ultimately, they even made some gains, with business leaders serving as chancellor and foreign minister, something that never happened under the kaiser. Those who might expect an unyielding ideological intransigence, an uncompromising commitment to reaction, are clearly mistaken. There were some, like Ballin, who could not make the transition, but others, like Stinnes and Duisberg, proved very adaptable.

Some elaboration of this portrait may be gained through a consideration of the events surrounding the Kapp *Putsch*. Although many commentators have written of the Kapp affair as an unsuccessful effort by business to recapture its lost position, some key figures in the business world were very much opposed to the venture.

The nucleus or base of the *Putsch* was a right-wing organization called the Nationale Vereinigung. That association had received support from big business, but, Feldman argues, it was "meant as a contribution to the fight against Bolshevism and as support for the propaganda of 'nationally minded' organizations seeking to move public opinion to the right in the anticipated elections." Duisberg had made contributions to the organization, but says Feldman, he "never imagined that its leaders were going to launch a putsch, and he was infuriated by the foolishness, untimeliness, and inconvenience of their action." His own words are worth quoting at some length:

> Who would have thought that the military party would seize power and drive out the government at just the most unfavorable moment there could be for our poor downtrodden Fatherland. . . . Just at the moment when we are again beginning to work more than before, at least in the coal mines—and coal is the chief thing at the moment—, when in London the perception is maturing that an act of fearful

economic stupidity had been committed by imposing the Treaty of Versailles and accordingly the exchange rate was beginning to improve, the military party again throws everything overboard, and this under the leadership of a man who is deplored as a reactionary, and compels our workers to general strikes and demonstrations, which are also not necessary because nothing will be achieved by them. . . . One holds one's head and asks whether men with brains and understanding or fools and lunatics have taken over the new leadership. As a businessman, therefore, I condemn what has happened thoroughly and completely, and I hope that the military hotheads in Berlin will soon come to their senses.[90]

The *Putsch* attempt was also thoroughly condemned by Fritz Semer, the Berlin lobbyist for the Thyssen interests. Unlike liberal and left complaint, however, his objection also was not focused on principle, but on the manifold ways in which it interfered with the larger plans of business. As he put it,

The act of Kapp and Lüttwitz was, in the manner in which these people undertook it, a crime. The drive to the right was powerfully underway, and we actually would have had good elections if this miserable Kapp had not come along with his putsch. These people from East Prussia believed they could conquer Germany, but they did not think that is was necessary first to negotiate with industry and to have the West on their side. The matter had already leaked out and I had personally given Noske a warning signal, but there was no stopping it. . . . To be sure, the putsch from the radical [that is, left] side undoubtedly would also have come . . . but [it] would have been easier to beat back if the Kapp Putsch had not preceded it."[91]

Far from being on top of things, the Reichsverband was ill prepared to deal with the events and ultimately suffered considerable losses. The first of the difficulties involved the simple matter of getting its presidium together to work out some kind of a response. A meeting did take place on Saturday, March 13, the first day of the *Putsch*, and although the members present did not constitute a majority, they continued to meet daily until the following Thursday. Among those missing from this "executive committee" were such potentates as Duisberg, Siemens, and Stinnes.[92]

Two policy considerations faced the presidium, the need for a statement about the *Putsch* itself, and the need for some statement addressed to the trade unions. The unions, it will be remembered, were joining in a general strike. After some discussion, the Reichsverband leaders settled for an "uninspiring" one-sentence statement declaring continued support for the principles that led to the formation of the Stinnes-Legien creation, the Zentralarbeitsgemeinschaft. This was the case, they added, "however the political situation of Germany might be structured." Such an extraordinarily equivocal statement, by failing to condemn the *Putsch*, allowed the easy conclusion that big business was in fact behind it and backing it. The more politically sensitive members of the presidium felt some kind of statement about the strike was necessary, but they were overruled by the others, and here too their final decision was "to do nothing."[93]

Not too surprisingly, relations with Legien were severely strained by this equivocal declaration. He faced considerable pressure from various forces on the left because of his involvement in the Gemeinschaft. When the German Metalworkers' Union was taken over by Independent Socialists in June 1919, for example, it promptly withdrew from the arrangement. Now, with the general strike developing spontaneously, Legien had little choice but to declare it an official union action. Some of the employers, rather obtusely, complained that by acting unilaterally he was violating "the principles of parity and mutual consultation" agreed upon as the basis for their Gemeinschaft.[94]

While the presidium members present at these meetings were struggling with such questions, Stinnes, on his own, tried to obtain a separate agreement on behalf of the mining industry with its unions in the Arbeitsgemeinschaft. His plan aimed to deny coal supplies to Kapp and other insurgents (that is, separatists). But since this proposal rejected the ongoing strike, and moreover, since it took no position with regard to the *Putsch*, the unions, not too surprisingly, turned it down. The absence of industry unity was further demonstrated by the decision of the Arbeitsgemeinschaft for the Berlin chemical industry "to support the general strike and to act in solidarity with the workers." This decision stirred much opposition; the local employers' association in Hanover, for example, was so filled with "bewilderment and outrage" that it quit the Gemeinschaft.[95]

In the aftermath of the *Putsch*, the question of compensation arose: should workers be paid for their efforts in defense of the republic? This question also caused serious strains within the Reichsverband and again threatened the Arbeitsgemeinschaft.

Employers generally opposed the demand, but some, those in the chemical industry again, some Saxon textile firms, and some employers in Düsseldorf, established a contrary precedent that had implications for all. Various compromise arrangements were eventually worked out, but their very diversity caused difficulties. The accusations and recriminations that followed seriously undermined the Reichsverband. Although the Arbeitsgemeinschaft survived, that was more an appearance than a reality. The employers agreed to bury it at some other time when they could shift the blame onto the unions.[96]

The understanding of business attitudes toward the Kapp venture is seriously hindered by a narrow reading of the possibilities, one that classifies people as either for or against the republic and, implicitly, counts those not expressly for as evidently being against, or in this case for Kapp. But businessmen were not for or against, at least not in this principled sense, and they therefore are not easily fitted into either category. As Feldman puts it, "Most businessmen did not want the putsch, and they did not support it, but they often condemned it for the wrong reasons and in a manner that did little to strengthen the Weimar Republic. . . . The putsch was a 'crime' because it disrupted the economy and threatened to 'politicize' business organizations and relations with labor. . . . Neutrality toward Kapp reflected a general feeling that his actions, morally speaking, were not on a much different level than those of the workers in November 1918."[97]

The attitudes of big business toward the republic have been summarized somewhat more generally by Henry A. Turner, Jr., another leading historian of German business. Most big businessmen, he says,

> were not, as is often assumed, unreconstructed monarchists; they displayed, on the whole, a surprising indifference to governmental forms. What offended them about the new state was its adoption of costly welfare measures, its introduction of compulsory arbitration in disputes between labor and management, and, most particularly, the influence it accorded to the prolabor Social Democratic party, which was most pronounced in the government of the largest federal state, Prussia. Despite abundant objective evidence that the republic, at least during its years of prosperity, provided generally favorable conditions for business enterprise, Germany's business leaders continued to eye it with misgiving. . . . [they] refused to commit themselves to the new state, regarding it as a potentially transitory phenomenon, while viewing themselves as the guardians of something of more permanent value to the nation—in their case, *die Wirtschaft*, the industrial sector of the economy."[98]

Their self-conceptions, as already suggested, are not easily placed within the frameworks of most conventional analyses. Turner notes that the most frequent terms used by these men to describe their political outlooks were "national" and "liberal." The latter generally had free enterprise connotations, but some complicated overtones are indicated by the letter of one businessman who wrote to an acquaintance saying that "as you well know, I have always been liberal, in the sense of Kant and Frederick the Great."[99]

Turner's findings with regard to the politics of big business are based on a detailed review of documents and correspondence from the files of major firms. He also has had access to the records of some key business organizations, records that provide information about their preferences and the financial support given by them to the various parties of Germany. His basic conclusion is that

> most of the political money of big business went, throughout the last years of the republic, to the conservative opponents of the Nazis. In the presidential campaign of 1932 most of the business community backed Paul von Hindenburg against Hitler, despite the Nazi leader's blatant appeal for support in his *Industrie-Klub* speech. In the two Reichstag elections of 1932, big business was overwhelmingly behind the bloc of parties that supported the cabinet of Franz von Papen, the first government since the Revolution of 1918 to arouse enthusiasm in business circles. If money could have purchased political power, the republic would have been succeeded by Papen's *Neuer Staat*, not by Hitler's *Drittes Reich*. But the effort to transform marks into votes proved a crushing failure.[100]

At another point, Turner summarizes the matter in one sentence: "On balance, big business money went overwhelmingly against the Nazis."[101]

That conclusion obviously does not mean that *no* big businessmen supported the NSDAP. The prime contrary case is that of Fritz Thyssen, the chairman of the board (Aufsichtsrat) of the Vereinigte Stahlwerke, Germany's largest steel company. Thyssen had a falling out with the Hitler government in the late thirties and, in 1939, went into exile. In the fall of 1941, a book appeared under his name entitled *I Paid Hitler*. The book was actually ghostwritten on the basis of stenographic notes of a series of conversations. The key passages in the book, those attesting to his financial support for the party, however, do not appear in the stenographic record. There can, nevertheless, be no doubt about Thyssen's orientation toward the party in the last years of the republic. He did give money, and he did use his influence to support the NSDAP within business circles. The only questions at issue are: how much money did he give? Over what period? And, what effect did his support have on fellow industrialists? The answer to the last question appears to be very little. Until after the November 1932 election, they, as noted, gave their support to other parties.[102]

Another stellar figure from the world of German business, a man who unquestionably provided financial support to Hitler, was Emil Kirdorf. He had been managing director of a major coal, coke, iron, and steel combine and was a key figure in the cartelization of the bituminous coal industry. More than just a businessman, he had been active in numerous rightist organizations. He was friendly to Hitler from an early point and, among other things, introduced him to other Ruhr magnates. Kirdorf joined the NSDAP on August 1, 1927. Numerous claims about his substantial financial contributions have appeared in the scholarly and not-so-scholarly literature.

Most of those claims, however, have been undermined by subsequent evidence. Possibly the most decisive fact in this regard was Kirdorf's demonstrative resignation from the party in August 1928, the basic reason being "his alarm about the leftist elements" in the party's ranks. The specific cause was a "scathing attack" on his bituminous coal cartel which appeared in *Die neue Front*, a National Socialist publication in the Ruhr. Later, with the election of Hugenberg as chairman of the DNVP, he rejoined that party and, in a public statement, gave its new direction his full endorsement. He remained a friend of Hitler, however, and rejoined the NSDAP after it took power. For propaganda purposes the party was more than happy to drop all references to his 1928 defection.[103]

Another business figure frequently referred to as a spokesman for big business and, more plausibly, as the man providing the link between it and Hitler, was Alfred Hugenberg. The available evidence makes it more than clear that Hugenberg was *not* a spokesman for big business. Even the industrial backers of the DNVP opposed his leadership candidacy, seeing him as "too inflexible, too provocative, and too highhanded for their tastes." When that party split, many of the industrial leaders abandoned Hugenberg so that in the last years of the republic he was forced "to rely increasingly upon the backing of agricultural interests." Hugenberg did direct some funds to the NSDAP in the course of the 1929 campaign against the Young Plan. But Turner states that for the subsequent period "there was not a trace of documentary evidence . . . that any of Hugenberg's resources were thereafter diverted to the Nazis."[104]

In some instances individual businessmen or firms gave money to the party, but these donations, Turner states, represented "insurance premiums" rather than outright or committed support. The proof is that the support was not exclusive; in these cases money was given to a wide range of bourgeois parties, to all those who were thought to have some chance of gaining power.[105] In some other instances, money was given to favorite members of the party, to those who were thought to be more moderate, persons who would somehow check the influence of the radicals."[106]

The key formal organization of big business, the Reichsverband, proved cumbersome and unwieldy for the purposes of the leading men of German industry. Immediately after the war, a small group of Ruhr industrialists had arranged to meet once a month "to consider matters of common interest." This group, the Montagsgesellschaft, was formed through the efforts of Paul Reusch, the general director of the Gutehoffnungshütte, a coal, steel, and manufacturing combine with operations extending far beyond the Ruhr, most importantly, into Bavaria. But the Montagsgesellschaft also proved unwieldy. It was "too large a body for the conduct of confidential affairs," and so, after the interruption caused by the Ruhr occupation, Reusch and some other leaders decided against reviving it.

Sensing the need for some kind of informal coordination, however, Reusch made a new effort in the fall of 1927. The new organization, called the Ruhrlade, had its first meeting in January 1928. Its founding members were Reusch, Gustav Krupp von Bohlen and Halbach, chairman of the board of the Krupp firm, and Fritz Thyssen, who, as we have seen, was chairman of the board of Germany's largest steel corporation. The Ruhrlade, in contrast to the Montagsgesellschaft, was to be a small organization; its twelve charter members were to represent the traditional core components of the region's heavy industry, that is, coal and iron. As Turner puts it, the Ruhrlade became in many ways "the unofficial cabinet of the leading circles of German heavy industry."[107] Because of the importance of this organization, it is useful to trace its activities from 1928 to the end of the republic.

Although not formed for this purpose, the group quickly became the central coordinating agency for dispensing funds to Germany's political parties. This task had been handled previously by the Reichsverband der Deutschen Industrie, but to circumvent Hugenberg's designs on the leadership of the DNVP, an informal arrangement was worked out by Reusch and Fritz Springorum (also a member of the Ruhrlade) to assess firms and dispense money independently of the Reichsverband. At the March 1928 meeting of the Ruhrlade, the members decided to "institutionalize the new arrangements" with their group handling matters for the Eisenseite (for the iron side, that is, for the iron and steel manufacturers) while the Bergbau-Verein dealt with assessments and payments for the coal side of the industry.

The Ruhrlade gave money to a variety of parties, reflecting the diverse personal commitments of its members. Most of the money, not too surprisingly, went to the DVP, the DNVP, and the Zentrum. In addition, it supported candidates within these parties, backing those it saw as helpful to its interests. One of its first efforts in this area proved a nearly complete failure. The group preferred Count Westarp, the chairman of the DNVP, to Hugenberg, who was actively seeking the chairmanship. It also wished four nominees placed in a favorable position on the electoral lists of that party. But despite its efforts, two of its candidates were displaced by Hugenberg's nominees, and then, despite its financial and personal support of Westarp, Hugenberg emerged victorious in the leadership struggle.

After the dissolution of the Reichstag and the calling of the September 1930 election, the members of the Ruhrlade decided to push one of their favorite projects, the reduction of political fragmentation. A bürgerliche Einheitspartei, a unified party of the right, had long been desired by German business leaders. At this point they made it clear to the parties that they "could expect financial support from heavy industry only if they worked together." But this project, too, was hindered by Hugenberg's activities in the DNVP. By this time, he had provoked many defections. The Ruhrlade efforts to encourage some of the splinter parties to write a joint campaign declaration came to naught when the executive committee of the Wirtschaftspartei disavowed the entire project. The executives of the Ruhrlade ultimately were forced to abandon their unification plans and to dispense funds as they always had. "In a test of will," as Turner puts it, "the politicians had triumphed, obtaining the money of the *Ruhrlade* without surrendering their freedom of action.[108]

The members of the Ruhrlade were initially enthusiastic about the Brüning government. They approved his use of emergency powers in the absence of a parliamentary majority and hoped for a "strong and unequivocally *bürgerlich*" direction of national affairs. They also anticipated the abrogation of some of the earlier republican legislation, particularly that providing for "compulsory and binding state arbitration of wage disputes." Brüning listened to their representations but did nothing, which was not surprising given his dependence on the Social Democrats in the Reichstag. The Ruhrlade members gradually lost their initial enthusiasm, ultimately becoming strong opponents of the Brüning government.

Some strain arose within the Ruhrlade over its subsidies for two daily newspapers. The deficits incurred by these journals mounted as the depression worsened, and, as the funds from the iron and steel companies diminished, the problem became a pressing one. When Hugenberg offered to buy one of the papers, some members of the Ruhrlade saw it as the solution to their problem. Others, including Reusch, strongly opposed the sale, which would have enlarged Hugenberg's already formidable empire. That problem disappeared, however, when Hugenberg, by then having ascertained the extent of the paper's difficulties, chose to drop the matter.[109]

Hugenberg caused the organization still other internal difficulties. Two of the members, Krupp and Reusch, held him to be a "liability to the *bürgerlich* cause" and refused to contribute any funds to the DNVP.

This disrupted the Ruhrlade's normal procedures so that in the Prussian state election of 1932 it was able to intervene only at the last minute. This late move was with restricted funds and only for a minimum goal, "to maintain its political contacts," the contributions having come too late to allow any influence on the campaign. The Ruhrlade had no role in the fund raising to support Hindenburg in the prior presidential election; this was left to Duisberg. One significant factor that helped to immobilize the Ruhrlade was Fritz Thyssen's open advocacy of the National Socialists in 1932. Since this ran up against opposite sentiments among the other members, it prevented them from reaching a consensus.[110]

Aside from Thyssen, the members of the Ruhrlade generally opposed the National Socialists. Their opposition was not principled, but practical or pragmatic. In the course of the 1930 election, for example, one of the conditions ultimately set for Ruhrlade contributions to the DNVP was that Hugenberg sever his ties to the National Socialists. After the election, however, the group had some hope of enlisting the National Socialists as part of its bourgeois bloc in support of Brüning. But that hope, it soon became apparent, was illusory. In December of that year, Reusch expressed his judgment about the party: its presence might be useful for Germany's foreign relations (it would aid in the demand for concessions with respect to the Versailles obligations) but its domestic effects, he thought, would be highly undesirable.

The Ruhrlade also undertook some efforts to moderate the party. This involved giving a "small sum" to Walther Funk, the former editor of the Berlin Börsen-Zeitung, a conservative financial newspaper. He had joined the NSDAP and served as an economic adviser to Hitler. But the Ruhrlade people soon developed doubts about Funk's economic policies, and apparently gave him no further subsidies.[111]

Despite the lack of direct involvement in the spring elections of 1932, the members of the Ruhrlade, especially Reusch and Springorum, its "most active political spokesmen," were very much concerned with the NSDAP. The major line of policy considered at this point was one of "saddling the Nazis with a share of the responsibility" by getting them to participate in governments, first in the states and then nationally. Springorum hoped that the National Socialists could be included in the Prussian government, but that did not occur even after Papen's removal of the SPD–Zentrum government in July of that year. Reusch hoped for their inclusion in the Bavarian government and met twice with Hitler to convince him of the advantages of such an arrangement. Hitler encouraged Reusch's hopes, using the occasion to exact concessions to his own advantage. But this plan for NSDAP involvement also failed.[112]

One might expect a concerted effort from such an executive committee on the occasion of the July 1932 Reichstag election, but at that point the Ruhrlade was in disarray. In mid-June it had been disclosed that the Reich government had purchased a majority of the stock of the Gelsenkirchener Bergwerks-AG. The interlocking connections were such that this purchase gave the government a controlling interest in the Stahlverein (the Vereinigte Stahlwerke), Germany's largest steel producer. This gave rise to a bitter dispute within the Ruhrlade, with Reusch and others attacking those members connected with the Stahlverein, notably Thyssen, Vögler, and Poensgen, for "acquiescing in the establishment of a massive state beachhead in heavy industry." They saw the move as one that "imperiled the whole private enterprise system" and demanded, without success, that the Stahlverein directors reverse the decision. An effort was made, in early August, to effect a reconciliation, but this failed with the result that no further meetings of the group took place in 1932.[113]

Despite the internal difficulties, individual members of the Ruhrlade did cooperate to raise funds for the July election. They could agree on this matter because of their "enthusiastic approval of the new cabinet of Franz von Papen. Although they had previously subsidized Papen's political activities, they appear to have played no part in his appointment as chancellor or in the ouster of Brüning. But once Papen was in office, they quickly acclaimed his probusiness policies and applauded his deposition of the SPD dominated Prussian government." The money collected from the iron side of the industry at this time, some 360,000 marks, was placed at the disposal of the Reichswehr minister, General Kurt von Schleicher, with the understanding that it was to be used "to support the parties backing the Papen cabinet."[114]

After the election, one member of the Ruhrlade, Paul Silverberg, set out on his own to moderate the NSDAP, but this resulted only in some rather indecisive meetings between his representatives and Hitler. The other principle line of Ruhrlade effort involved the continued support of Gregor Strasser, but this effort came to an abrupt end with Strasser's abject resignation of his offices in December of that year.[115]

For the November Reichstag election, Springorum again made the approaches and collected the funds, once again to support the Papen government. One significant change in the procedure on this occasion was the circumvention of Schleicher, who at this point was viewed by the leaders of heavy industry as a rather questionable figure. In the aftermath of that election, Papen, the Ruhrlade favorite, resigned, and Schleicher, the object of the group's doubts, was named his successor. In addition to suspecting that Schleicher had misused the election funds entrusted to him in July, the business leaders "were alarmed by [his] publicly professed indifference toward economic doctrines, by his seeming readiness to abandon the probusiness policies of the Papen cabinet, and by his cultivation of trade-union spokesmen."[116] One consequence of this alarm, apparently, was the resumption of regular meetings of the Ruhrlade, the first of these taking place on January 2, 1933.

A series of meetings between the National Socialist leaders and Papen took place in January of 1933, the end result of which was Hitler's accession to power on the thirtieth. The first of these meetings, originally intended as secret but instantly covered in the national press, occurred on January 4, at the home of Baron Kurt von Schröder in Cologne. Three days later Papen conferred with Reusch, Springorum, Vögler, and Krupp at a meeting in Dortmund. It would be easy to assume that this meeting was part of the same chain of causation that brought Hitler to power, but letters recently made available indicate a different scenario. As Turner summarizes the discussion, Papen "gave the industrialists to understand that his goal was to bring Hitler to accept the status of a *Juniorpartner* in a coalition government consisting preponderantly of *bürgerlich* elements. Papen also clearly implied that he regarded himself as the appropriate chancellor in such a government. . . . In order to facilitate his efforts to unite the *bürgerlich* forces behind him as a counterweight to the strength of the NSDAP, Papen asked the industrialists at the Dortmund meeting for funds to finance an office and staff of aides for his use."[117] This request was turned down. They had no hope for such "a one-man undertaking" and suggested instead that he "secure for himself a power base by capturing an already existing political organization, the DNVP." For some time, Turner continues, these industrialists "had been looking for a suitable replacement for Hugenberg; now they concluded they had at last found such a man in Papen. That the men of the *Ruhrlade* could in January 1933 have seen a remedy for Germany's crisis in a takeover of the DNVP by Franz von Papen is the most eloquent possible testimony to their lack of political acumen and their remoteness from the realities of that month."[118]

Turner concludes that the Ruhrlade members had no direct role in the naming of Hitler to the chancellorship. Far from being in on or on top of events, far from directing every move, they were very much out of things. It is useful, because of the importance of the subject, to quote Turner's summary conclusions.

There is no evidence that [the men of the Ruhrlade] played any direct role. Even those members of the group who were most active politically apparently had no knowledge of, much less part in, the machinations that were to result in the installation of Hitler as chancellor at the end of the month. Krupp von Bohlen, for example, departed in mid-January for a rest cure in Switzerland where he received highly misleading information about the political situation in Berlin from the office of the *Reichsverband der Deutschen Industrie*. Springorum left, as planned, for his trip in the last week of January, after having been assured by one of his political agents in Berlin that no fundamental political changes were to be expected prior to his planned return on February 7. Reusch and Vögler, as well as Springorum before his departure, continued during January 1933 to look for a way to replace Hugenberg at the head of the DNVP with Papen. All indications are that the members of the *Ruhrlade*, like most business leaders, were taken totally by surprise by the news that Hitler had been named to head the government.[119]

This conclusion, it will be noted, goes very much against the claims of various authors on the left who see a united bourgeoisie supporting and managing the National Socialist effort from an early (usually unspecified) point. The conclusion of various liberal commentators, that business support was the work of some individuals rather than of the collectivity and that much of this effort was aimed at taming the NSDAP, seems much more in accord with this latest evidence.[120]

Some of this evidence, in addition, goes very much against an assumption shared by liberal and left commentators alike along with, possibly, nearly the entirety of humankind, this being the assumption of business power. Since the conclusion in this instance goes so very much against common sense, it is important to consider this more general point at greater length. The relationship of big business and political power in the late Weimar period is discussed by Turner as follows:

In the political sphere the *Ruhrlade*'s efforts were characterized, almost without exception, by ineffectuality. Its members commanded financial resources unrivaled by any comparable pressure group and enjoyed ready access to the leading political figures of the Republic. But although they were in general agreement among themselves with regard to political aims, their efforts to realize those aims were sometimes paralyzed at decisive junctures, as in the spring of 1932, by internal dissension. Even when they were fully united, they repeatedly discovered that there were severe constraints on their political effectiveness, despite their prestige and their financial resources. This was revealed by their ill-fated efforts to strengthen what they saw as "moderate" elements in the Nazi Party. It was made even more evident by the response of the *bürgerlich* politicians of the Republic to their political efforts. Repeatedly, the politicians listened to their demands, took their money, and then acted with scant regard for their wishes, despite vehement threats that such disregard would result in the termination of subsidies. The politicians were able to act in this manner because they knew from experience that the *Ruhrlade* had no real political alternative. They knew that it would, in the end, after delays and admonitions, support the *bürgerlich* parties as usual, fearing that failure to do so would only strengthen the enemies of capitalism at the polls. The politicians were also aware that the *Ruhrlade*, unlike many far less wealthy organizations which also spoke for special interests, was unable to deliver the prime commodity of electoral politics: sizeable blocks of votes. From the politicians' point of view, the *Ruhrlade* was only one among many clamorous pressure groups, and by no means the most important. The result was a long succession of painful frustrations for its members and a record of failure that should give pause to those who subscribe to the proposition that economic power is readily convertible into political influence.[121]

In another context, Turner summarizes the business elite's situation with a simple phrase when he speaks of "the political impotence of money."[122]

Turner emphasizes the business leaders' lack of control over politicians. They found their power limited in other areas as well. One might note that business could, potentially at least, "control" public opinion through its direction of the mass media. In Weimar Germany this would, in effect, be a question of a single medium, specifically the newspapers.

An effort had been made to achieve such direction of public affairs through support of Hugenberg's press activities. The original attempt involved channeling advertising money to dependable newspapers. But later, in the period of inflation, Hugenberg was able to gain direct control of some journals, and, because of his wire service and regular syndicated features, his editorial content appeared in many others. The press empire also had an important motion picture affiliate. Over the years, Hugenberg, too, escaped the control of big business, or, put more precisely, he chose his own direction, one that increasingly gained him the intense hostility of most business leaders. Their later efforts were oriented toward containing and circumventing his influence.[123]

Some newspapers were either directly or indirectly controlled by members of the Ruhrlade. But here too one finds some unexpected developments. Some members of the Ruhrlade, as was noted earlier, directed the affairs of the Berlin *Deutsche Allgemeine Zeitung* (*DAZ*). Disenchanted with Brüning, the Ruhrlade people wished to exert pressure on his government and sought to use the *DAZ* for this purpose. In the summer and autumn of 1931, they pressed the editor, Fritz Klein, "for an all-out editorial campaign against the economic policies of the cabinet." But, Turner reports, they were "disappointed" with Klein's response and increased their pressure. Still they did not find the editorials having the "desired degree of sharpness." Klein's private papers now reveal his "covert defiance" of the newspaper's industrial backers. Klein was aware of their wishes and agreed with their policies but thought the tactics wrong. He preferred to cultivate Brüning rather than conducting a "frontal assault." Klein therefore "placed restraints on the DAZ's public criticism of the cabinet while privately working closely with Brüning, seeking to win his gratitude by strengthening the cabinet's position. On at least one occasion, Klein brought Brüning to conspire with him to appease the industrial backers of the DAZ by complaining to them, at the editor's request, that the paper's editorials were excessively harsh on him."[124]

After the September 1930 election, a typically pragmatic acceptance of the new situation was made, Klein and others on the DAZ looking to the "worthwhile elements" (wertvollen Elemente) of the NSDAP, to those who could be directed for the good of the whole. One account, in the issue of October 6, portrayed the NSDAP as a strong counter to communism, the importance of which was being underestimated in Germany. Brüning's use of emergency decrees to secure the economy were praised under the heading "Abdication of a System." This denigration of the republic was very much in accord with the disenchantment found in top business circles at this time.

In its issue of December 12, 1930, the DAZ published an excerpt from Mein Kampf under the heading "Propaganda." An editorial three days later celebrated Hitler as the "only politician of the right who has understood how to bring the masses to him." The "problematic socialism" of the party was mentioned, but the party was complimented at the same time for its rejection of class struggle. And "naturally," the editorial went on, concessions had been necessary with respect to the use of crude anticapitalist propaganda ("antikapitalistische Vulgärpropaganda").[125]

Another unexpected development involved a newspaper in the possession of the firm Reusch headed, the Gutehoffnungshütte. The firm had extended operations into southern Germany, acquiring there some finished goods manufacturing companies. It also bought into a publishing house, Knorr und Hirth, the owner of the important Munich newspaper, the Münchner Neueste Nachrichten (MNN). The MNN had the largest daily circulation in Bavaria and the fifth largest in Germany. The firm also acquired important newspapers in Nuremberg and Stuttgart, in part to keep them out of Hugenberg's hands, in part because they were seen as profitable enterprises. The MNN had, for a decade, been left to manage its own editorial affairs, but given the pressure of events in the early thirties, Reusch decided to make use of the newspapers for his political purposes. But here too unexpected opposition appeared.

Despite repeated efforts, the newspaper refused to take the proper line demanded by Reusch with regard to the Brüning government.[126]

It will be remembered that Reusch had thought to moderate the NSDAP by bringing the party into coalitions, starting in state governments. He met with Hitler on February 23 and again on March 19, 1932, to discuss the matter. Hitler, as noted, was very encouraging and made use of the occasion to obtain an agreement to his own advantage. Reusch's newspapers would refrain from all personal attacks on the NSDAP leaders during the presidential elections, and the NSDAP press would do the same in its treatment of the BVP leaders. It was not, on the whole, the most intelligent arrangement since there were vast differences in the size and, presumably, in the influence of their respective media. Moreover, since the BVP was not directly involved in the presidential election, most of the advantage in the arrangement came to Hitler. Reusch set severe restrictions on the freedom of the *MNN*'s editors during the presidential campaign, and they complained bitterly about the implications readers were drawing. The NSDAP, for its part, proceeded as if no agreement existed, its attacks being as frequent and vitriolic as ever.[127]

Reusch had numerous occasions for dissatisfaction with subsequent *MNN* editorial policy despite all his efforts to achieve control. Although, as noted in Chapter 6, he did succeed in depoliticizing the newspaper to some extent in the April Landtag and more completely in the July Reichstag election, Reusch still had serious objection to various specifics of the newspaper's content. In early June, the newspaper carried a polemic against the new Papen government and, as Reusch put it, opposing the demand of all "reasonable thinking people," had argued against an increase in the powers of the Reich's president.[128] One might anticipate that someone would be fired for such insubordination, but in the end it was Reusch who withdrew. Unable to accomplish his aims, he quit the board of directors in protest. For a while, nevertheless, he continued his work of editorial supervision at the request of Karl Haniel, an owner of the Gutehoffnungshütte and a fellow member of the Ruhrlade. But his frustration continued, and he cancelled his *MNN* subscription in February 1933.[129]

One additional instance of big business "control" over media is of interest here. In September 1932 an anonymous two-part article "The Social Reconsolidation of Capitalism" appeared in the magazine *Deutsche Führerbriefe*. This publication was known to be supported by big business interests and was clearly a vehicle for the expression of their views. This article advocated support for the NSDAP as a means for capturing the workers, that is, for taking them away from the Marxist parties. Not too surprisingly, the article has been repeatedly cited as proof of the intentions of big business. Nearly four decades later, however, the author of the article revealed himself and provided some illuminating details. In 1932, he was a young, occasional employee with the magazine and had written the article on his own, that is, not at someone else's behest. He was also, so he reports, a secret Communist, and his intention was to provide a convenient target for KPD propaganda. In this he was eminently successful since the KPD press immediately picked the article up, frequently republishing its contents.[130]

The principal lesson of this review is that the ability of big business to reach out and influence the masses was rather seriously limited. The leaders of heavy industry had few journals at their immediate disposal since a large part of the bourgeois press was in the hands of their enemy Hugenberg. And some of the journals that were in their hands showed at least some signs of independence.[131]

One other newspaper under the general supervision of Ruhrlade members was the *Rheinisch-Westfälische Zeitung* of Essen. As was indicated in Chapter 7, this newspaper was among the most openly pro-Hitler of any major dailies reviewed in this work. Its owner, Theodor Reismann-Grone, had close connections with the National Socialists and was clearly a committed supporter. In this case, big business (specifically the Bergbau-Verein) bought out his remaining minority shares and replaced him.[132]

The leaders of big business lacked one very important political means; they did not have large numbers of militants at their disposal. The *parties* had the militants, and the bourgeois parties, as we have seen, were rapidly losing all supporters. In some key respects, the party leaders were not mere agents of their business supporters. As we have seen, they refused to follow the directions called for by the business leaders, specifically their demand for bourgeois unity. So with respect to the control of parties, here, too, money proved unexpectedly impotent.

Closer to home, in its own milieu, German big business lacked what might have been a possible channel of influence. Social clubs, so numerous and, it is said, so important in Anglo-Saxon countries, are absent from German society. And that meant that big business leaders did not have the extended interpersonal networks that might have allowed them wider influence among their class peers, that is, among those outside of the board rooms and the immediate circle of the Ruhrlade or the Reichsverband der Deutschen Industrie. Their ability to reach into the upper-middle-class ranks therefore would have been severely limited. For that reason, many people in the upper class itself and millions in the upper middle class were free to make their own political choices. Their choices, it would appear, were *not* the product of directives, recommendations, or suggestions issuing from the executive committee of *the* bourgeoisie. This means, in short, that the proximity of upper and upper middle classes did not have the effect anticipated. The conclusion that influence (or a command) would be easily transmitted and just as easily accepted seems unwarranted, at least in this case. While undoubtedly logically plausible, the influence in this instance did not flow as that logic predicted.

What can one say about the motivations and behavior of the other members of Germany's upper and upper middle classes, that is, of those not directly involved in the affairs of these so-called control centers? Here we have something of a paradox. With only a few exceptions, the leaders of heavy industry supported the various bourgeois parties in all elections of 1932. Yet, within their own circles and in the not-too-distant upper middle class, one found substantial support for Hitler and his party. How can one account for this disparity?

Some part of that vote, no doubt, came from true believers, from those who made positive committed choices. The early support for the party, in May of 1924, that found in the upper- and upper-middle-class districts of Berlin and Hamburg would reflect that kind of motivation. It would appear to be the choice of the very committed nationalists, of those who found all the other parties, including the Conservatives, too weak or too ineffectual. Some of the true believers, obviously, made other choices in December of 1924 and again in 1928. But for them it would have been easy to return to the NSDAP once again in September 1930 and remain loyal to it in the elections of 1932.

That kind of outlook was held by some of the most highly placed individuals in Germany's status structure—that is, by members of the kaiser's family. Prince August Wilhelm was an early party member and a very public supporter of Hitler. His appearance on the speakers' platform seated next to ordinary workers and artisans was visible testimony to the party's concern with the promised *Volksgemeinschaft* (people's community, the nationalists' equivalent of the "classless society"). In a public meeting in Brunswick, August Wilhelm confessed that "there, where a Hitler leads, a Hohenzollern may with confidence join the ranks." Hitler, he said, is "sent by God to the German people." Crown Prince Wilhelm offered his public support for the party only after the 1932 presidential election at which time "he clearly went all out for the NSDAP."[133]

It seems likely that such testimonials would have carried much weight in the decisions of a second category of upper- and upper-middle-class NSDAP voters, the politically uncommitted but deferential members of those ranks. It seems likely that these deference voters would have been moved by appeals to nationalism, by anti-Marxist and by antiregime declarations.[134] Some, too, may have been influenced by the positive side of National Socialist arguments, by the party's stress on "national renewal." It is also likely that the *völkische* arguments, in particular, those involving anti-Semitism would have moved the deferential voters (along with many true believers). The hostilities fostered within the university milieu, especially within the fraternities, would have appeared later on within these ranks of the society. And also, the orientations generated by some of the less attractive products of German culture would have been found among these educated upper- and upper-middle-class populations.[135]

A third category of upper- and upper-middle-class NSDAP voters might best be described as tactical supporters. These voters had seen their favored parties reduced to a point where they could no longer be viewed as adequate means for their political purposes. Many of these voters, it would appear, turned to the National Socialists as their next best option.[136] The likely dynamics of this process deserve more detailed attention.

When their preferred party declined to the point of disappearance, such voters would have chosen from among the remaining parties one that, in one way or another, met their requirements. While much uncertainty was generated by the word "Socialist" in the name of Hitler's party, it would, nevertheless, have been clear to the readers of most bourgeois newspapers that the NSDAP was an anti-Marxist party. Its opposition to the SPD and KPD, moreover, was not just ideological but was backed up by a private army, the Sturmabteilung. For those who were worried about the threat of a Communist (or Marxist) uprising, the NSDAP probably appeared, despite its many questionable features, as their best choice. This is to suggest that the major concern moving these tactical voters was the "specter of communism."[137] Having lost the means to control or direct the affairs of their nation, they then chose the National Socialists as a kind of stopgap, as the organization that, as they saw it, shared some important elements of their political perspective and, more significantly, had the weaponry needed to defend their threatened position.

This sense of threat was created and dramatized in the pages of the bourgeois press, its content communicating to the ordinary reader a sense that Germany stood on the edge of revolution. This lesson appeared in accounts of KPD actions throughout the nation, of attacks on police, on officials, and, during political election campaigns, of attacks on the bourgeois parties. These stories were embellished with bold declarations of revolutionary purpose, these being generously supplied by Communist writers and speakers. In the rightist press, these attacks had a very unidirectional character, the violence of the streets and meeting halls always being attributed to KPD, SPD, or with indifference, to

Marxist protagonists. Mixed in with this stream of alarmist reports one also found accounts of the NSDAP and its Sturmabteilung, which told of their valiant struggle against the Marxist onslaught.

Many of Germany's bourgeois newspapers, as has been repeatedly noted, took an avuncular attitude toward the National Socialists. A principal emphasis in their commentary was that the NSDAP was a party of young, dedicated, and enthusiastic nationalists. The only failings to be reported involved the National Socialists' impetuousness, their ready resort to violence, and the ever-troublesome signs of radicalism within their ranks. As for the violence, these newspapers provided an easy excuse: it was a justified response to the provocations or attacks that had come first from the other side.

This suggests that the tactical voter's decision was made within a context of high hysteria. The rightist press communicated an extreme sense of urgency in the face of which the bourgeois voter had to consider whether to remain with a weak traditional party, one that was manifestly helpless in the face of the events confronting Germany at that moment, or whether to support this new contender, the NSDAP, a party that was generally acceptable and that possessed obviously effective combat forces. Even where a newspaper recommended specific bourgeois parties, such as the DVP or the DNVP, many readers apparently considered instead the *implications* of the news stories and made different assessments of the priorities. Some newspapers, it was noted, made rather open-ended recommendations, defining the choices in such a way as to include the National Socialists.

Much of the content of the press in that period could have done little but erode the legitimacy of the republic. The constant attacks on the institutions and personnel of "the system" would also have provided justification for the shift to the openly antiregime party. The loyalties to the short-lived republic were weak and tentative to begin with. Many were, as Stresemann described himself, *Vernunftrepublikaner*, republicans of reason, practical supporters of the regime, as opposed to heartfelt or principled supporters. When it was no longer reasonable to continue that support, when the experiment was shown to have failed, they were ready to try another arrangement. The occasional flattering reports of circumstances in Mussolini's Italy would no doubt have worked to ease any lingering qualms.

Another common notion, which also made it easier to choose the National Socialists, was the idea that the party could be tamed through the exercise of power. This notion appeared in many rightist newspapers and was also a principal direction of Zentrum policy in the period. Even one left liberal journal, the *Kölnische Zeitung*, otherwise solid in its opposition to National Socialist aspirations, in mid-1932 accepted the

belief that the party would be tamed by power. The political arrangement considered in most newspapers, especially in the July 1932 election, was that the NSDAP could provide support to Papen and Hindenburg; it could become part of the coalition backing those leaders.
There was no advocacy of Hitler being made chancellor. Within the
terms of that framework, a vote for the NSDAP might have appeared
to be relatively costless.

One theme from the National Socialist repertory deserves attention
here, that being its antibourgeois line. In general these arguments have
not been taken seriously by writers on the subject, being viewed as little
more than a confidence game, a tactic used to win the support of workers. In line with the standard misreading of Gregor Strasser's activities,
many have assumed that this emphasis disappeared along with, presumably, the disappearance of the Socialist theme. But if anything the antibourgeois arguments became even more insistent, especially after the
July 1932 election when Papen and Hugenberg became the party's most
prominent targets. Much of the loss suffered by the National Socialists
in November of that year probably stemmed from their attacks on "the
plutocrats."

How would the average bourgeois have viewed these antibourgeois
attacks? Again, of course, one can only speculate about the perceptions
and reactions. Here too one finds the usual tactical shifts in emphasis,
depending on the audience. The antibourgeois theme did unquestionably appear in National Socialist publications, for example, in Goebbels's
Der Angriff. But it does not seem likely that such sources would have
been favored reading for Germany's bourgeois citizenry. The "best"
newspapers did not dwell on these themes; they appear instead to have
screened out such content. The press could not, of course, overlook all
such hostility, but when it was recognized, it was accompanied by a
justifying excuse.[138]

Systematic evidence bearing on the media behavior of Germany's up-
per- and upper-middle-class populations is virtually nonexistent, and
the same is true, obviously, of studies dealing with personal contacts
and influences. The fragmentary insights available to us suggest that the
behavior of these urban populations was highly individualized, at least
as far as their political choices were concerned. The major link to the
world outside their immediate milieu was the newspaper. Outside of
Berlin, the good bourgeois had only a limited choice. For a Protestant
bourgeois, the options in most cities would be a DNVP newspaper, or
one linked to the DVP, or the general mass circulation paper. Depending on his political preference, he would ordinarily have chosen either
the DNVP or DVP newspaper, rarely both. The mass circulation general newspaper would ordinarily be avoided, as being too far below the

level of an educated person. Some of the better newspapers had a more than regional circulation, but their followings outside their home communities would have been small. In some instances these newspapers were read for their special features rather than for their accounts of national and international news. This means that most educated bourgeois citizens were linked to the larger world through a single news source. And that source, in most of the cities reviewed here, had the characteristics just indicated: anti-Marxist alarmism, antiregime attacks, occasional favor shown for the Italian Fascist model, an avuncular attitude toward the National Socialists, and a belief that the party could be tamed.[139]

One might also speculate about the possible role of personal influence. Political conversations, it seems, were relatively infrequent in Germany. Politics was viewed with some distaste; it was not a subject for polite conversation.[140] A social gathering that extended beyond one's immediate circle of friends, moreover, was likely to contain persons with differing political loyalties, and a serious political discussion in that context could easily offend someone. A remark about the Zentrum's political clergy could mean the loss of a Catholic customer. The admission of DNVP loyalties, let alone advocacy, might lose a Jewish customer. So informally, by general agreement, people tended to avoid discussion of politics.

Another possibility for personal influence was political meetings. Many tens of thousands among the urban bourgeoisie would, no doubt, have attended such meetings, including those of the NSDAP. In the last years of the republic, the number of meetings held by the bourgeois parties declined considerably, while the number of meetings held by the National Socialists showed a dramatic increase. It seems likely that many concerned upper- and upper-middle-class citizens would have been drawn to NSDAP meetings. It should be remembered that the National Socialists held meetings on a year-round basis, not just during elections. It would seem a mistake to focus only on the mass rallies, on those addressed by the party's national leaders. There were local groups in all neighborhoods, and they, presumably, would have provided content designed to appeal to their educated listeners. One may assume this political effort would have had at least *some* effect, especially given some initial nationalist feelings in such an audience and given also the legitimation provided by many bourgeois newspapers.[141]

Applying the findings of contemporary audience research to the situation of Germany in the early thirties, one would assume that those attending meetings would be more interested and more involved in politics than the average citizen. They would probably be the informal opinion leaders among their close associates.[142] If converted to the new faith (or sensing the tactical need), they could have stimulated conversations among their relatives, friends, and trusted associates. Even if not themselves converted, but only maintaining a friendly disposition toward the party, they still might have had further influence. By vouching for the NSDAP, by declaring that the National Socialists were all right, that their hearts were in the right place, and so on, such opinion leaders might have made possible the conversion of others.

A change in party choice might occur without the direct personal intervention of a local opinion leader. Some less-politicized voters might reach out for a more distant surrogate influence. Many deferential voters, presumably, would not review the news in all its available detail; they might only scan the headlines and look at the pictures. But if, in those headlines or pictures, it was discovered that the crown prince had vouched for the National Socialists, that might have been enough to move them. That kind of change would probably be more frequent among older persons, particularly older women. Many of them would never have been trained to make their own political judgments. Many would have been widowed and thus without the guidance once provided by their husbands. In the upper and upper middle classes, such women would ordinarily have been nationalist, conservative, and probably monarchist in tendency; they would also, in all likelihood, have been extremely deferential. It seems likely that such persons would have sought direction from some authority figures, from someone known to share their basic sentiments. That direction could have been provided by the crown prince, or by Prince August Wilhelm. It could have been provided by a respected army officer, or by a headline or the rather diffuse recommendation of a trusted conservative newspaper.[143]

In the urban context, the NSDAP's message was very similar to that communicated in the middle-sized communities, as for example in Thalburg. The number-one theme again appears to have been anti-Marxism.[144] But the *process* of communication in the cities appears to have been somewhat different. In Thalburg, as in the farm communities, direct personal influence probably was a key factor contributing to the conversions. But in the cities, notables and activists probably played less of a role, and the newspapers, with their peculiarly equivocal content, probably counted for more. It is a point of some irony that the educated upper- and upper-middle-class populations, those who react so enthusiastically to the claims of mass-society theories, should themselves have been the victims of a process that they, with such evident disdain, assume to be moving other people. In this case, it would appear that the demagogues, with some aid from the media, had considerable success in moving the upper- and upper-middle-class masses.

The anti-Marxist hysteria generated by the rightist press was based on a very selective reading of the evidence, one that stressed appearances more than reality. The overall support for the left as evidenced by Reichstag election results, the most visible evidence of its strength, declined after the May 1928 election, this being the case in both the September 1930 election and that of July 1932. There was a shift within the left, with the KPD making some gains, but that amounted to only 2.5 percent of the total in 1930 and another 1.2 percent in July 1932. In July 1932 the KPD was supported by one-seventh of Germany's voters, not an overwhelming share of the total and, by itself, hardly enough to justify the alarm manifested in news columns and editorials.[145]

The internal condition of the KPD, the decay and general disarray found within the leadership and cadre ranks (see the discussion in Chapter 11), was not reported in these journals. It is hard to believe that editors and publishers would not have known of those difficulties. The police monitored the internal affairs of the NSDAP with great thoroughness, and they, no doubt, gave at least equal attention to the affairs of the KPD. Information about NSDAP affairs seems to have been made available to persons outside of official ranks, and one might expect a similar discreet use of information concerning the Communists. The newspapers, moreover, had their own means for gathering information; their journalists obviously could have looked into the question. And the findings published in one newspaper could obviously have been picked up and reprinted by another. The rightist press could certainly have drawn on the resources of the Social Democratic press, including both its newspapers and its magazines, the SPD being especially concerned with the problems, capacities, and chicanery of the KPD.

But for the most part, the rightist press chose to ignore these possibilities. Rather than presenting balanced reporting, rather than setting the electoral returns in perspective, indicating the membership turnover and the steady loss of capable KPD leaders, they made a very selective presentation of the news, focusing on the various signs of alarm, on the revolutionary phrases of the party's spokesmen, on their provocative actions, magnifying these words and deeds into what for many readers must have been a convincing and threatening picture. The rightist press, in short, played a significant role in generating the anxieties that then, contrary to most publishers' intentions, helped to undermine the strength of their own preferred parties.

CHAPTER FOURTEEN

The Weimar Catastrophe

The beginning point for this work is the claim that the lower middle class (or petty bourgeoisie) provided the decisive support for Hitler and his party, the support that gave him his electoral victories in 1930-1932. As noted in Chapter 1, the basic conclusion, from a very early point, was that Hitler's support came from the petty bourgeoisie, from the economically depressed lower middle class. An initial review of some of the more prominent statements of the position revealed a lack of precision in the definitions of the term itself and, even more surprising, a remarkable absence of appropriate evidence.[1]

The most easily accessible evidence relevant to the thesis comes from the German countryside, but this rural evidence poses a very serious problem for the accepted theory in that the farm experience is sharply divided according to the religious composition of the area. Protestant farm areas voted very heavily for the National Socialists, but the Catholic areas voted very heavily against them. At the very least, then, any statement about lower-middle-class support among the farm population would require a specification to indicate that the theory applied in one context but not in the other. But, most expositions of the received theory, even when recognizing the importance of the religious cleavage, simply pass over the problem.

One would anticipate a surfeit of evidence from German cities attesting to the validity of the claim. But in this case, the literature is remarkable for the nearly complete absence of supporting data. A review of some of the available studies of National Socialist electoral support (in Chapter 3) provided grounds for doubting this easy assignment of blame to the lower middle class. The absence of direct supportive evidence, together with initial evidence supporting an alternative reading of the electoral history, stimulated the present research on urban voting patterns. This investigation yielded the following results.

First, it was impossible to discover any relatively pure lower-middle-class urban areas that would allow one, through ecological analysis, to establish a lower-middle-class voting tendency.[2] Thus the original claim about lower-middle-class propensities could not have been supported with the data available in the early 1930s. To establish that point would have required survey evidence. Although some surveys were conducted in that period, none of them asked a question on party choice. The problem of the early 1930s, then, remains with us to the present day. Strictly speaking, it is impossible either to establish or to reject the lower-middle-class hypothesis in urban areas.

Although the specific data required for that test seem unavailable, an alternative line of exploration was possible. One could rank urban districts by class, on the basis of census data in the larger cities and less reliable personal judgments elsewhere. The resultant array extends from the upper- and upper-middle-class districts at the top of the class hierarchy to lumpenproletarian districts at the opposite extreme. Many districts were working class in their majority, these being most frequent in the industrial cities. The remaining districts were not lower middle class but mixed, containing some combination of manual and nonmanual populations, with the actual proportions coming close to fifty-fifty. While it was not possible to separate the voting tendencies of the various populations within these mixed districts, the overall voting tendencies could be examined to determine the support for the National Socialists in all districts, from the best off to the very poorest.

This line of investigation yielded the crucial finding that support for the National Socialists in most cities varied directly with the class level of the district. The "best districts" gave Hitler and his party the strongest support. In the few cities where this was not the case, in Cologne and Munich or in Frankfurt, the deceptive case, the pattern still did not yield evidence consonant with the received claim. Instead the tendency was either one of no difference among the nonmanual districts, or, in the case of Cologne, of a below average level of support in the best-off district of the city, with the other well-off districts being generally above the city average.[3] In *no* city did the results show the expected pattern of a pronounced and distinctive National Socialist tendency in the mixed districts, those with large lower-middle-class populations.

This new finding required consideration of the explanatory question: how did it happen that the results, both rural and urban, followed the patterns indicated? The answer suggested here has focused on various agents or agencies carrying out the National Socialist message, and—the other side of the relationship—it has examined the circumstances of the party's various audiences, considering the factors that led some groups to respond while others rejected its message. A key component of these interactions, of course, was the message itself; as we have seen, the content of the party's communication varied from context to context.

The explanation of the new findings has focused on the role of three agents or agencies: (1) the National Socialist party activists, who, in number and ability appear to have outdone all of their competitors in carrying their party's lessons to the general populace; (2) the press, much of which was certainly very friendly to the party, defining it as acceptable for a role in a conservative nationalist coalition; and (3) many elite figures or notables who, in one way or another, vouched for and helped make the party widely acceptable. The combination of these efforts was such as to allow a sweeping impact. This was most clearly the case when all three agencies were working in the party's favor. Where the press was opposed, or where there was widespread opposition from the local notables, as in Catholic or working-class communities, the party made little headway.

The agents or agencies provided only the means or the channels for contacting voters. The substance of the communication, as noted, varied with the context. Basically the party workers appear to have fed in whatever content they thought would work with a given segment of the electorate. The message was then changed or adjusted in the light of reports received from the field. In the rural areas, the principal emphasis appears to have been on the economic disaster and on the various means the party would undertake to relieve the problem, the most important of which was the promise of debt relief. In the middle-sized and larger cities, the principal emphasis was on the Marxist threat and on the National Socialists' ability to check or counter that allegedly imminent danger. Other elements unquestionably appeared in their presentations. There was the revolution, the stab in the back, and the work of the "November criminals." There was the whole Versailles question, including the war-guilt clause and the reparations, the last being a key contributing factor in the financial disaster. And, of course, there was a persistent focus on the Jews with their supposedly deleterious effect on German culture and institutions. But these other elements were peripheral, ancillary contributions to the larger or central themes of the message, debt relief in the countryside and anti-Marxism in the cities.

The National Socialist activists carried the party's message into the various fields of combat, most notably into the Protestant countryside. They provided the first serious opposition that had appeared there in the entire modern period. Outside challengers would not normally have a high chance for success in a struggle against local notables. But in this case, several factors were working in favor of the protagonists. The notables were attached to and defending the positions of seriously discredited parties. They were, in effect, defending laissez faire strategies in the face of the most serious economic disaster in living memory. Normally that would not lead to a change of party, because no other viable or plausible alternatives would be available. But here was a party, personified by these young and dynamic activists, that seemed to have a plausible alternative. In any event, the National Socialists spoke the key words "debt relief" when no one else was doing so. As the depression worsened, the parties of the local notables shifted to the right, rejecting any suggestion of relief. But for the first time, a plausible alternative was present and actively appealing to the rural voters.

Although the same general factors, discredited traditional parties and a plausible opposition, were present in the cities, the content of the struggle there was different; the prime consideration for the converts was the "specter of communism." That was a factor, presumably, for some urban workers and for some segments of the lower middle class, but it seems to have been especially important for the upper and upper middle classes. It is likely, however, that each of these groups saw the threat somewhat differently and interpreted the National Socialist solution in somewhat different ways.

The changing fates of the contenders, of the National Socialists and the so-called middle-class parties, are also traceable to the efforts of the agents or agencies discussed above. The NSDAP activists, particularly those organized in the Sturmabteilung, were able to close down the meetings of the middle-class parties. As a consequence, it became ever more difficult for those parties to get any message through to their traditional followers. In addition, as funds dwindled, those parties were unable to buy newspaper advertising to attract new voters or simply to retain the loyalties of their previous followers. Many newspapers hedged their election recommendations, as we have seen, giving rather diffuse support to parties supporting the regime, while at the same time indicating that the National Socialists had at least something to recommend them. Many local notables also played a similar role in this process of transferring legitimacy from the traditional parties to the new contender.

THEORIES OF THE CATASTROPHE

It is useful to consider these findings in relation to some of the larger theoretical explanations of National Socialism. The principal theory dealt with in this work is the centrist argument, which focuses on the lower middle class, on its social and economic difficulties, and on its presumed reactions (see Chapters 1 and 2 and the beginning of Chapter 10 for statements of this position). A closely related theory, one that assumes all of the first principles of the lower-middle-class argument, is the Marxist idea that fascism is the last stage of capitalism. This argument sees a more or less unified bourgeoisie supporting the fascist party financially, putting it on its feet, and giving it the means to campaign. This view sees fascism, in this specific instance the National Socialists, as an agency of the bourgeoisie, as the means used in its last-ditch effort to maintain its position and prerogatives. (This position is reviewed in Chapter 2 and also, with relevant evidence, in Chapter 13.)

A third theory that attempts to explain the rise of fascism, a theory that has been given only passing attention in this work, is the mass-society argument. The vast majority of contemporary populations, it is claimed, have been uprooted and deprived of their traditional or communal bases of support. This malady is said to stem from urbanization and industrialization, and from the competition inherent in capitalist societies. The isolated and powerless individuals of modern industrial society are thought to be highly anxious and extremely susceptible to demagogues who promise to remedy their condition.[4]

This list of explanations is not intended to be all-encompassing. Other less prominent theories could be added. Some works of history do not easily fit into any category. Many of them, following the evidence found in various archives, have arrived at their own unique conclusions about the origins and development of National Socialism. More often than not, such works have bypassed the general frameworks, developing instead more complex, multicausal explanations, ones that characteristically give considerable weight to political factors. The criticism offered throughout the present work is directed at the leading general theories, principally the centrist theory. Those detailed historical monographs have provided abundant evidence to support elements of the present critique.

The Centrist Theory. The centrist argument holds that the transformations of advanced capitalist societies are such as to damage the interests of lower-middle-class populations. They are either driven to the wall, as in the case of independents put out of business by the competition of giant firms, or, in the case of the salaried white-collar employees, reduced to the level of workers (proletarianized). Because of their very strong attachments to their middle-class status, these individuals desperately seek to restore their lost social position. They react by supporting the movements or parties that promise to return the middle class to its former position of social, economic, and political eminence.

The theory, it will be noted, makes two very sweeping claims, one about major structural changes in modern society, the other about lower-middle-class psychology. The losses are experienced by all (or a vast majority) of the persons in the class, and all (or a vast majority) of the persons in the class possess a distinctive psychological syndrome and react within the terms of that framework.[5] There is also an exclusiveness to the claims in that no countering or cross-cutting factors are offered that would limit or restrain, let alone outweigh, the impact of these determinants. The only other factors contained in the typical presentation of this view are accentuating factors, those that would add to or

otherwise enhance the effects of the initial factors. These other considerations include the loss of the monarchy, the uprooting of rural populations, the attacks on tradition found in modern art forms, the role or
activity of Jews, and certainly the impact of the depression.

It might be expected that fundamental questions would be raised about
such formulations, especially given the a priori character of the conclusions. The structural argument has the greater initial plausibility. Census materials do show dramatic changes in occupational structures. It
was evident, too, that there had been a phenomenal growth of big business and also a growth of big labor; both of these institutional developments, plausibly, might lead to a reduction of the power, income,
and status of the lower middle class. And income data could be cited
showing the relative loss of position by various middle-class groups vis-
à-vis the blue-collar workers.

Initially, at least, those structural facts seem so well established as to
make the conclusions unassailable. But it is not at all certain that those
structural facts brought with them the implications so often assumed.
The census data do unquestionably show a long-term decline of independent status.[6] But it is not clear that the persons involved would have
experienced that change as a loss, as meaning a decline in their income,
power, or status. Most of the loss of independence stemmed from a
decline of the farm sector. In this instance we do have some systematic
evidence on preferences; people wanted to leave the farms for urban
employment.[7] Put differently, they wanted to give up their independent
status for the advantages of dependent urban employment. Blue-collar
work (or a poorly paid white-collar job) provided clear advantages over
the uncertainties and marginal existence offered on the small farms they
left behind. The evident enthusiasm with which these people left the
land (and their independence) sharply challenges the evaluations im-
puted by "critical" intellectuals.

It is not clear that the vast majority of white-collar workers would
have seen the development of big business and big labor as threatening,
as something reducing their status. Those coming from working-class
backgrounds would not have brought with them a memory of former
middle-class grandeur. It seems more likely that they would have made
comparisons with their former condition, with the circumstances of their
families when they were growing up. It is not at all clear, or even
plausible, that they would have rejected their family backgrounds (along
with their friends, schoolmates, and neighbors) to adopt a new and
different life style when making the move to a middle-class position.
Nor is it evident that the occupational move, from blue-collar to white-
collar position, entailed a corresponding move from a blue-collar neighborhood. There is another possibility with at least equal a priori plau-

sibility, that they continued their previous existence, maintaining family connections, social ties, and life style.

It is not at all clear either that white-collar employees of middle-class backgrounds would have felt a sense of loss because of the recent institutional developments. Big business, with all its added layers of hierarchy, would provide a range of new and better-paying jobs, and these employees, not the more poorly trained children of blue-collar workers or of farmers, would be the likely candidates for those newly created positions. The entry of women (many of working-class background) into office employment would also provide new opportunities for these middle-class males. They would now move up one or two steps in the hierarchy, as supervisors or office managers.[8]

Even the income dynamics, as we have seen, have been misrepresented in some crucial respects. The real incomes of many white-collar workers were increasing as the economic crisis worsened. At minimum, these alternative possibilities call for a more hypothetical treatment of the initial centrist conclusions. They also indicate the need for a more differentiated treatment of "the" lower middle class.[9]

The second part of the centrist argument, the social psychological aspect, presents even more serious problems. How would one know that lower-middle-class people generally felt the loss of their former status and that they reacted with feelings of anxiety and desperation? The lower middle class of Germany, it should be remembered, including its men, women, and children and both the farm and the nonfarm segments, would have numbered in the tens of millions. Without serious representative cross-sectional studies, it is clear that those conclusions are no more than hypotheses, plausible ones perhaps, but nevertheless untested.[10] The research establishing the existence of those structurally based anxieties was never undertaken. The conclusion was merely assumed.

Some fifty years after the event, it is hardly possible to reconstruct the psychological outlooks of millions of persons. Investigations of the structural changes are possible, and the objective consequences of those changes can be studied as, for example, in the case of real income levels. But the character of individual reactions to those structural changes would seem lost forever.

One line of inquiry is, however, open to us. As has been done in this work, it is possible to examine the political consequence that is supposed to follow from these psychological changes. If the predicted result is not systematically present among those presumed to be affected psychologically by the structural changes, then the entire explanatory effort is misdirected. Theorists would have been explaining a nonfact, or pseudofact, a not uncommon occurrence in the social sciences.

Most formulations of the centrist theory predict a massive and distinctive shift of lower-middle-class voters to the National Socialists. The evidence presented in this research indicates that any statement of results for the relevant elections must indicate the sharply *differentiated* reactions of the various segments of that class. Lower-middle-class Protestant farmers were, overwhelmingly, moved by the National Socialist appeals. Lower-middle-class Catholic farmers were, overwhelmingly, left unmoved by those same appeals.[11] And the reaction of the urban lower-middle-class population, as far as can be discovered, was not exceptional. Its voting did not differ significantly from the overall vote in those cities. There certainly was no clear and unambiguous evidence showing massive majorities for the National Socialists in the most likely districts. In fact, in most of the larger cities, those districts provided more votes for the Social Democrats and Communists than they did for the National Socialists.

The preceding paragraph addresses only one side of the lower-middle-class question. Most formulations of the position claim a lower-middle-class distinctiveness in this regard. No other segments of the population, supposedly, were providing that kind of support. But here, too, the theory falls down. In the Protestant countryside, in the area in which the claim is best supported, the lower middle class was not distinctive. In some villages, as we have seen, *all* voters—whether farm laborers or small, middle, or large farmers—were supporting the NSDAP. Where some division of the vote occurred, where the NSDAP, for example, took "only" 80 percent of the vote, most of the minority went to the Social Democrats. Apart from some blue-collar workers, who were either farm laborers or commuters to nearby cities, almost all rural voters supported the National Socialists.[12] For the Protestant countryside, then, the theory has focused on and explained the wrong thing. Rather than being concerned with a specific *class* tendency, it is necessary to explain the tendency of entire communities, or, for that matter, of entire regions.

The results from the cities also contradict the centrist views. While the theory argues a clear and distinctive lower-middle-class tendency, the results for most of the cities reviewed here indicates instead a pattern of upper- and upper-middle-class distinctiveness. The claims of the centrist theory, in short, do not begin to describe the actual distribution of the vote in most of those cities. Even in those cities where the support for the NSDAP did not vary directly with class level, the results still do not conform to the expectations. Instead, NSDAP support tended to be high in all nonmanual districts, that is, in both mixed areas and the upper-middle-class ones. The exceptions, in other words, showed a lack of differentiation within the nonmanual ranks. Once again the centrist theory has provided miscues.

The remarkable thing about the widely accepted centrist argument is its imposition of an interpretive framework that does not accord with the most rudimentary facts of the late Weimar election results, facts, moreover, that are readily available. Some of the possible reasons for this misreading are considered later in this chapter.

The Marxist Theory. As noted, the Marxist argument that fascism represents the last stage of capitalism accepts the first principle of the centrist theory, that the lower middle class provided the NSDAP's mass base. The key contribution of this argument, however, is that the effort was both paid for and directed by the bourgeoisie. Where this argument depends on the lower-middle-class claim, it obviously suffers from the same disabilities as the pure exposition of that position.[13] In addition, the Marxist argument is inadequate in the area of its specific contribution, in its assumptions about the intentions and actions of the bourgeoisie.

Hitler's party, as we have seen, had already achieved a breakthrough in late 1929, in the period of the anti–Young Plan campaign, as evidenced in state elections of the period, most notably those of Baden and Thuringia. Then, in September 1930, the party gained 18 percent of the votes (and of the seats) in the Reichstag election. If Hitler were the agent of big business, one would expect a significant effort to give him power, or, at minimum, to bring the party into coalition with other conservative forces. But the initial response of most business leaders was renewed support for the Brüning government.

Business leaders could have demanded National Socialist participation in the government throughout 1931 had that been their preference. But a documented case to that effect has yet to be made. In 1932, the year of elections, there were many occasions for an expression of a preference and for a demand to change governments. The two rounds of presidential elections offered opportunities to campaign for Hitler had business leaders thought it to be in their interests. For the bourgeoisie, the effective choice in both rounds was between Hitler and Hindenburg. Most men in the top echelons of Ruhr industry, with the obvious exception of Fritz Thyssen, preferred Hindenburg, and their money was given to secure his reelection. If there were any doubts about that conclusion, which is based on the private documentary record, they should have been dispelled by the editorial recommendations of the leading bourgeois newspapers, the overwhelming majority having declared for Hindenburg.[14]

The first of the Reichstag elections of 1932 provided another occasion for a clear declaration of NSDAP support, should the bourgeoisie have wished it. But the first choice of most business leaders was Franz von Papen. This assertion is based, once again, on the evidence of both private documents and newspaper editorial declarations. At best, they saw Hitler and the National Socialists as playing the role of support troops in a broad conservative nationalist alliance behind Hindenburg and Papen. It was eminently clear, incidentally, from the state elections three months earlier that the National Socialists were destined to win big in this election.

If the National Socialists had been the agency of big business, one should have found its leaders engaged in a concerted effort immediately following this election to have Hitler named as chancellor. He had, after all, gained three-eighths of the votes, by far the largest share of any of the parties. Given normal democratic conventions, he was the most legitimate of the candidates for that position. Moreover, in a coalition with the Zentrum, Hitler and his party would have had a majority in the Reichstag, thus solving the standing governmental crisis. Negotiations were undertaken by the leaders of the two parties to explore the possibility of a coalition. But if serious business pressures existed to have Hindenburg name Hitler, that has yet to be discovered in the archival records. The negotiations failed, and Papen continued as chancellor. Most business leaders remained loyal to him.

There was a resurgence of the NSDAP's leftism in the November Reichstag election, and that, not too surprisingly, reduced business enthusiasm for Hitler and his party. An election appeal by the Deutscher Ausschuss "Mit Hindenburg für Volk und Reich" (German Committee "With Hindenburg for People and Reich") called for support of the parties backing Papen. This bore 339 signatures including those of many prominent business leaders. Shortly after the election, a petition asking for Hitler's appointment was sent to Hindenburg, this bearing the signatures of many eminent figures in the nation. Although the petition is said to have been the work of, among others, "finance magnates [and] monopolists," the only leading business figure to sign it was Thyssen. Hjalmar Schacht also signed, but he was neither in the ranks of big business nor in its good graces at that point. Turner feels Schacht is best classified as a "political adventurer." Then, too, the actual list of signators has been compared with the list the sponsors wished to obtain. The great majority of the businessmen on this second list of potential signers, apparently, declined the opportunity.[15]

The naming of Hitler to the chancellorship on January 30, 1933, came as the result of a series of meetings, the first of these occurring in the home of a Cologne banker, Baron Kurt von Schröder, just after the new year. Bracher refers to this meeting as the "hour of birth of the

Third Reich." The direct participants in this and the subsequent meetings never numbered more than a score. The most important figure making this new direction possible was Papen. He is generally seen as wishing to bring down Schleicher, his one-time friend and coworker, who the previous November had undermined and replaced Papen's government. Also present, of course, were the top leaders of the NSDAP, Hitler and Goering being those most continuously involved. Since the new government was to be a coalition of forces, Hugenberg and other Conservative leaders were also involved in the discussions.

A pivotal figure in the process was Hindenburg, who, as president of the republic, possessed the constitutional power to name the chancellor. Playing important roles in convincing the reluctant president were his advisers, including his son Oskar, who was also a strong advocate of the change. Most of those advisers were aristocrats, not businessmen. Playing what was largely a facilitating role were the members of the so-called Keppler circle, an agency of the NSDAP, consisting largely of lesser figures from the German business world.[16]

Those negotiations were conducted largely without the guidance or counsel of big business leaders. Papen, who was in touch with those leaders, did report on the negotiations, in the process supplying some misleading information, to wit, that he would be the chancellor in the coalition. The striking characteristic of the role played by these big business leaders, at least those in the Ruhrlade, was their distance from and ignorance of the events then being planned.

Twenty-seven leading industrialists were summoned to a meeting on February 20, 1933, shortly after Hitler had been named, to "discuss" the next Reichstag election. The meeting took place at the palace of the Reichstag president, Hermann Goering, with Schacht presiding. Hitler spoke first, offering a long monologue. He was followed by Goering, who ended his "request" for funds with the comment that "industry would find the asked-for sacrifice easier if it knew that the elections of March 5 were bound to be the last in ten years, and presumably in a hundred." Schacht then made the briefest speech of the evening: "*Und nun, meine Herren, an die Kasse*" (roughly, "and now, gentlemen, time to pay up"). A fund of some three million marks was forthwith planned, to be divided between the National Socialists, who would get 75 percent, and the DNVP and the People's party, who would get the rest. It was the first systematic, direct financial contribution by German industry to the NSDAP.[17]

Many of the accounts of the business role stop at this point, that is, with the National Socialists safely in power and the big winner of the last Reichstag election. With the left either banned, in the case of the Communists, or seriously weakened and fully isolated, in the case of the Social Democrats, it was no problem for Hitler to secure dictatorial powers under the Enabling Act passed on March 23. Armed with those powers, it was also no problem to break what remained of the left, to destroy the trade unions and the Social Democrats, the only significant sources of potential opposition to the new government. It is this systematic destruction of the left that gives such plausibility to the agency theory of National Socialism.

But one very significant aspect of the coordination effort, of the *Gleichschaltung*, is omitted from many such accounts. Among the parties and associations that were coordinated were those of big business. All of the bourgeois parties were dissolved, including the Conservatives of Hitler's coalition "partner," Alfred Hugenberg. The rightist paramilitary organizations, most notably the Stahlhelm, were coordinated. In this case it meant they were brought into the Sturmabteilung, thus losing all independent existence and autonomy. But perhaps most significant of all for the NSDAP-as-agent theory was the dissolution of the central organization of German business, the Reichsverband der Deutschen Industrie, and its integration into a party-dominated front.[18] The words of Paul Reusch, possibly the most important of the political leaders of German business, do not indicate the optimism or confidence one would expect were business in control. As he put it, "Influence on legislation or government administration seems to me, at this time, to be impossible. What then remains to be done?"[19]

Business fared little better in the years from 1933 to 1939. In a general review of the experience of business in the Third Reich, David Schoenbaum refers to an "economic policy in which business paid the piper and the State called the tune." As he puts it, "Public domination of the economy was the tune the economy danced to, and Nazi fiscal policy alone is a revealing indication of the price business paid for it. This included maintenance of Brüning's high deflationary tax rates, prohibitions on the issues of new securities, blocked dividends, 'organic'— which is to say discriminatory—interest policy, foreign currency controls, variable exchange rates restricting imports."[20]

There is, of course, no question about the increase in military expenditure; Schoenbaum estimates the increase at about 2,000 percent (from a low initial base, it will be remembered). Expenditure for transportation, including the autobahns, also showed a significant increase, over 170 percent. Public expenditure in 1938, as a portion of national income, was above that of France, well above that of the United Kingdom, and more than three times that of the United States.

But, Schoenbaum reports, business was obliged "to pay and sacrifice for the war economy from which it hoped to profit." "Profits came under control," he reports, "virtually from the date of their reappearance." Dividends were restricted to 6 percent with anything above that having to be invested in nonnegotiable Reich bonds. In 1935, a sweeping conversion of interest rates was declared, with rates on mortgages and municipal and Reich bonds being reduced from 6 to 4½ percent.[21] Perhaps the most telling of the National Socialist economic measures involved corporation taxes. These were "increased from 20 per cent in 1934 to 25 per cent in 1936, 30 per cent in 1937, 35 per cent in 1938, and 40 per cent in 1939-40."[22] One might try to imagine the reaction had such "confiscatory" measures been imposed by the parties to the Weimar coalition.

A conflict developed between business and government over the question of autarchy. Business leaders in general were internationalists; that is, they conducted business wherever it appeared profitable. Hitler's political aims, however, required a considerable degree of national autonomy, of independence from foreign markets and supplies. The government sought to achieve this autonomy in steel manufacturing by developing the Reichswerke-Hermann Göring. This involved substantial public investment in a relatively low-grade, and hence unprofitable, domestic ore. The steel industry opposed the plan but met defeat and was forced to buy shares in the venture, which had a relatively low fixed dividend. The owners were forced to retain the shares for at least five years. Not too surprisingly, given the basis of the enterprise, when the owners were free to sell their shares, they could do so only at some loss.[23]

There is no indication that business had control over other areas of government. In the all-important sphere of foreign policy, business had no role. One historian summarized this matter as follows: "All the important foreign policy decisions in 1938 and 1939 were taken by Hitler personally. It is not yet possible to state with any degree of certainty how far he may have taken economic factors into consideration in these decisions. As yet there are hardly any positive proofs that he did."[24]

This history hardly supports the party-as-agent theory of National Socialism. Rather, it indicates the independence or autonomy of the party and the dependence of business. Rather than directing affairs, business was being ordered about by the party. Since business had no instruments of power—no police, no army, and no paramilitary units at its disposal—things could hardly have been otherwise. The party, by contrast, had all of those forces. In short, the available evidence challenges the Marxian assumption concerning the power and autonomy of the bourgeoisie, as well as the notion held by most Marxists that economic power *means* political power. Instead, these observations are consonant with a more classical image, that of Caesarism, the notion that an armed force can take power and that it can do so independently of the will of an established ruling class.

The Mass-Society Theory. The third theory to be assessed is that of the mass society. The ever-recurring phrases here are: uprooted populations, atomization of society, competitive conditions, urbanization and consequent anomie, isolation and loneliness. The end result in such life circumstances, presumably, is desperation-level anxieties. The prime consideration in all variants of the theory is the notion of vulnerable masses; people are willing to do almost anything to alleviate their condition. There are, so it is said, no lack of people proffering solutions of one kind or another. In the typical presentation, these solutions are said to be "facile" or "easy," the point being that they are spurious. The "real" solutions to their problems are said to be much more complicated. This disparity of means poses serious problems for any statesman in competition with the demagogues. The latter, having no scruples whatsoever, are willing to pander to those mass needs.

This line of theorizing has two principal variants. One, associated with the political right, sees the demagogues arising from among the masses and manipulating them for their own ends. The other, associated with the political left, sees the demagogues as sponsored by established elites; in this view, the demagogues manipulate the anxious and vulnerable masses so as to serve the aims of those elites. Especially in the latter view, one finds much attention paid to the role of the mass media. With their money and influence, the established elites are able to use the media to sway the masses. The latter, typically, are portrayed as rather helpless, as unable to withstand the clever appeals transmitted to them. Although elements of both mass-society variants have been touched on at various points thoughout this work, a more comprehensive assessment of those claims may prove useful.

The theory runs up against several difficulties. The first of these is an obvious question about the location of *the* masses. The theory focuses on uprooted and anomic *urban* masses. But, as we have seen, the greatest attraction to the NSDAP appeared in the Protestant countryside, that is, among a segment of the population that was very much rooted. For Germany's Protestant populations, the direct opposite of the mass-society claim could be argued, that support for National Socialism *increased* with the rootedness of the population. But even that statement appears to involve a spurious causal argument since Catholic and Protestant rootedness, as exemplified in their respective small towns and villages, was associated with sharply opposed political responses.[25]

Some parallel problems appear for the mass-society theory within the urban context. The least rooted population of the cities, presumably,

would be the lumpenproletariat, and, as has been noted, many commentators have assumed a considerable vulnerability on their part. But
lumpenproletarian districts generally gave the lowest support of all urban areas to the National Socialists. A problem is also posed by the
working-class masses since they too generally gave below average support to that party. And by contrast, it was the well-off upper and upper
middle classes, with their at least relatively intact social structures, that
provided the National Socialists with their strongest support. It is not
necessary to pursue this matter further. It is clear that this line of theorizing, like the centrist view, was developed and disseminated without
undertaking the requisite investigation of the actual voting patterns among
Germany's masses.

There is one strand of the mass society argument that does have
something to be said for it. Some bits of evidence have appeared
throughout this work to suggest some media role in the determination
of mass political choices. The Hugenberg press empire, for example,
was instrumental in the revival of Hitler's party in the late 1920s in the
course of the anti–Young Plan campaign. The party's inclusion in the
broad national coalition at that time and the dissemination of that fact
in the Hugenberg press and its affiliated journals helped to legitimate
the NSDAP in the eyes of many good conservatives.

The likely media effects, however, were clearly of a more varied character than is suggested in most mass-society arguments.[26] Although *the*
media are typically viewed as possessions or instruments of *the* elites,
the evidence reviewed here yields a more differentiated picture. Many
owners did make use of their newspapers for political purposes although, at least in a few cases, that effort ran up against some internal
resistance.[27] There was also a strain present in many newspapers between their political and economic concerns. Publishers are not always
free to maximize their political interests, or, putting it differently, to
have done so would have meant serious economic losses, ones that in
some instances threatened the entire enterprise.[28] Possibly the most important emendation required of the standard version of the mass-society
theory involves the role of outside players. The National Socialists, quite
simply, were very adept at gaining the headlines, at using someone
else's means for their own ends. The lesson, then, is that the mass media
were not narrowly or unambiguously controlled by an established elite.

It is evident, too, that the newspaper publishers of Germany at this
point were not acting in concert. Some of the bourgeois press, it is
clear, were very favorable to the National Socialists (as in Essen and
Wuppertal). Some of that press had a moderately favorable avuncular
attitude, seeing the party as supplying useful support for their first choice
(that being Brüning, then Papen). And some of the bourgeois press

were above party, making no clear recommendation whatsoever in the election campaigns of the period.[29] At minimum, these observations would require a more differentiated analysis of *the* elite.

Another modification required of the mass-society theory involves the assumption of elite rationality. Some allowance must be made for inadvertent or unintended effects. It is unlikely that Hugenberg, as leader of the German National People's party, intended that his press be instrumental in converting *his* followers to the NSDAP. And yet that seems to have been the case. It is unlikely that most of the other bourgeois publishers wished to undermine their preferred parties, and yet it seems likely that they too, inadvertently, did just that.

If Germany's publishers had had a concerted plan to convert their readers to the NSDAP, they could, presumably, have best accomplished that aim by direct advocacy, by an open and forthright recommendation of National Socialist voting. But while some journals seemed to edge in that direction, most made other specific recommendations or, alternatively, rather diffuse, open-ended ones. The argument offered here, which of course can only be speculative, is that many readers drew another conclusion from the content of those newspapers. Sensing the imminence of a Communist rising, the supposed facts of the matter being amply demonstrated in the rightist press, many readers concluded that an active anti-Communist fighting force was the prime need of the moment. They saw the urgent message contained in their local newspaper and responded to the logic of that message rather than to the publisher's preelection recommendation.

If this reading of the matter is accurate, it would mean that it was upper- and upper-middle-class masses who were vulnerable to the demagogic appeals; their lives were characterized by high levels of anxiety. But that anxiety did not stem from "a highly atomized society," nor from society's "competitive structure," nor from a "concomitant loneliness." The problem was not something that had been prepared "by historical circumstances," at least not as that expression is conventionally understood.[30] The anxiety would have had its origin in the content of the daily newspapers, the specific source of the fear being neither structural nor, broadly speaking, social psychological. Its roots would have been very distinctly political, or, at least, that is the way it would have appeared to most readers.

The mass-society view, in summary, makes two fundamental misreadings of the situation. First, by failing to pay attention to the detailed voting results, it seriously misrepresents what actually happened; it focuses on the wrong masses. And second, as a consequence, like the theories that assume lower-middle-class vulnerability, it too explains the wrong things. Had these authors focused on the vulnerable upper- and upper-middle-class masses, on those who, within the urban context, actually supplied Hitler with his greatest percentage support, they might have been led to examine *their* social circumstances, and perhaps also, their media behavior. And that might have led those authors to somewhat different conclusions.

The conclusion of a media influence, as noted, goes against the view that the media cannot change fundamental values, such as a party preference. But that position is based largely on the American experience, and one should be cautious about extending that conclusion to other times and places. The party struggle in the United States has been characterized by a remarkable simplicity and an equally remarkable continuity. Apart from a few third-party episodes, the United States has seen only two major parties, the struggle between these contenders extending back over more than a hundred years. Given those circumstances, it is perhaps not too surprising to find high levels of party identification and considerably greater party loyalty from one election to the next than was evidently the case in Weimar Germany.

The German situation was markedly different. In 1912, Germany had even more parties than in the early years of the republic. There was, however, little continuity. The events of 1918-1919 caused the breakup of most, with only the Zentrum and the SPD surviving more or less intact, bearing the same name, and having continuity with a prewar organization. Although one could recognize similarities in the tendencies of the new parties—that the People's party, for example, was a continuation of the National Liberals—the changes of the period might have done much to break the spell of tradition. Except for the SPD and the Zentrum voters, no one's party affiliation could have been in existence for more than fourteen years as of 1932. Given the volatility of the vote in the republic's history, many party loyalties would have been of brief duration.

The events impinging on the new regime (and on the most directly involved parties) would have tested even the strongest loyalties. These include the various challenges to the legitimacy of the regime, the attempts at insurgency, both from the left and the right, and the ruthless counterthrusts. There was the Ruhr occupation, the passive and not-so-passive resistance to that occupation, and the resulting runaway inflation. There was an endless series of seemingly hopeless political struggles, ones fought with heavy ideological commitment, over the schools, the welfare measures, the building of battleships, and the color of the marine flag. And, in the final period of the republic, there was the problem of growing violence on the streets and in the meeting halls. The economic crisis provided still another bludgeoning. Under those circumstances, it would not be surprising that newspapers played a greater role than in the rather stable, almost placid, American circumstances. Given the newness of most party loyalties, given the many disrupting changes, and given the complexity of options facing voters, it seems likely that the counsel of a trusted source would have had a weight that was missing in other, more stable, times and places.[31]

This discussion should not be read as saying that a media influence was the only factor, or even that it was the key factor accounting for social change in the period. It says merely that the media played some role, its precise importance being difficult to measure at any time, let alone some decades after the event. The argument offered here differs substantially from some of the sweeping claims found in mass-society formulations. It argues a media impact within a rather specific set of circumstances, that is, where party loyalties were weak to begin with and where many unsettling political events led people to consider a change of party. It argues further that the media impact was not that intended by the publishers and owners. It argues that the National Socialists were able to put themselves into the news and thus could command attention in the press.

AN ALTERNATIVE THEORY

To this point, three major lines of theorizing have been reviewed and assessed.[32] As explanations for the development of National Socialist electoral support, they have been shown to be seriously deficient. What better explanation is there for the development of that electoral support? One line of theorizing that proves useful has been called the "social bases" or "group bases" position. The principal exposition of this position is derived from American experience. In fact, it forms a key part of the tradition discussed in the immediately preceding paragraphs.

The group-bases position, briefly described, contains the following major elements. Party loyalties and party choices are largely the result of interpersonal influences. The initial influence, for most people the decisive one, occurs within the family. Political outlooks are learned from one's parents—in most cases, especially in times past, from the father. The family also plays some role in placing children, in terms of both occupation and residence. The children themselves, obviously, make the major contributions to these choices, but, outfitted with the family's traditional values, they tend to locate themselves in a like-minded milieu. In most cases they will locate within the same class and within the same ethnic and religious communities. That placement then puts people within a context that, again in the most frequent case, would reinforce and support the original family values. These two processes, the original training plus the subsequent reinforcement, provide the continuity of mass politics extending over generations. They explain or account for the political traditions of regions or of ethnic groups. They also explain much "false consciousness," a given tradition being passed on over generations regardless of changes in a group's real condition. The two processes, obviously, would have immense conservative implications; they provide the key elements in the static aspect of this theoretical tradition. Indeed, were no other factors operating, party choices (apart from specific issue orientations) would continue unchanged over three, four, or even more generations.[33]

The original formulation of this position did provide some elements that would allow one to account for change. The principal dynamic factor could be termed "misplacement." Not all children, after all, end up in a social milieu identical to that of their parents. Upward mobility could, in the United States, transfer Democrats into a Republican milieu, and downward mobility could have the opposite effect. Regional mobility might also lead to a break with tradition. Migrants to the large cities do not have an entirely free choice in housing and, in a socially mixed area, might acquire new and different values and outlooks. Even if not leading to outright conversions, the diverse milieu could mean some cross-pressures (that is, conflicting influences), and these could in turn lead to a moderation in the intensity of one's views or, possibly, to either a postponement or an avoidance of choices.

Even making generous allowance for the quantities involved, these processes of change would normally affect a smaller portion of the population than the forces of stability or continuity. Many of these changes in milieu, moreover, would not lead to changes in political outlook. Farm-to-city migrants can in some cases locate in self-selected areas within the metropolis, in subcommunities where most persons would share their values and outlooks. In those cases the migration would probably involve a transplantation rather than a change of values.[34]

The distinctive feature of these dynamic elements is that they would ordinarily lead to relatively small changes, or, more precisely, to relatively slow and continuous ones. In any given year, the farm-to-city or working-class to middle-class moves would provide only small accretions to the benefit or detriment of a party. Even the dynamic elements of this theoretical position, then, would not normally account for a sudden or massive shift, for a dramatic change. Since it is obvious that such changes do occur, as for example, with the rise of the NSDAP, it is necessary to provide some additional terms of explanation.

The principal explanation that had been offered for large and sudden shifts is one that steps outside of the group-bases or personal-influence framework and, in a rather ad hoc way, argues the role of rationality or issue-oriented voting. A major catastrophe, such as a war or depression, or alternatively, some decisive issue, could force people to rethink their group traditions and, either with or without benefit of group pressures, could generate a shift in political direction.

In the United States, this kind of realignment occurred in the 1896 election. William Jennings Bryan's great issue, the evils of the gold standard, together with his plans to inflate the currency, presumably caused many Democrats to abandon their traditional loyalties and become Republicans. Many of those changing to the Republicans were urban workers, the Bryan proposal being seen by them, quite accurately, as a threat to real incomes. This new tradition would, at a later point, be condemned as false consciousness, but as of 1896, at the point of its inception, it was a very rational choice.

An instance of an issue-based realignment occurred in the first years of the newly unified Germany. Many Catholics at that time supported liberal parties. But Bismarck's assault on Catholicism, in the course of his *Kulturkampf*, caused a dramatic shift to the newly formed Zentrum, thus beginning a tradition that was to last down into the Weimar period.

Discussions of realigning elections, understandably perhaps, tend to be somewhat global in character. One can easily point to the big causal event, and, just as easily, to the consequent change. What is missing is consideration of the intervening processes. Few commentators are in a position to demonstrate or establish the details of any process of mass opinion change, whether, for example, it stemmed from a series of individual decisions, all moving in the same direction, from a media impact, or from some coordinated campaign.[35] In some cases the details of the process may be a matter of complete indifference, but if one wishes to explain or account for the historical change, one must examine the details of the causal process. Otherwise there is a possibility of *post hoc–propter hoc* errors. One may wish, for example, to explain event B. An analyst of a structural persuasion might search among the prior events for the plausible structural cause. And, addressed to an audience attuned to the appropriateness of such explanations, the claim might be easily accepted. But if the outcome were determined by a series of individual decisions or by a planned, a concerted interpersonal effort, those possibilities would escape that audience's attention entirely. Again what one would have is an unjustified (not empirically established) read-in.

This question of process takes on greater significance when one recognizes that the responses to the economic catastrophe of the 1930s were not "determined" by general structural factors or by a closely correlated social psychology. Some sense of the range of possible reaction may be seen by consideration of some relevant cases. In the United States, in 1932 voters turned to the laissez faire Democrats (it was not clear at the time of the election that major welfare legislation would be forthcoming). Voters in the Scandinavian countries turned to the Social Democrats who, at that time, were declared socialists. In the United Kingdom one saw a major shift to the Conservatives in 1931 after a rather indecisive experiment with a Labour government under Ramsay MacDonald. Canada voted in the Conservatives in 1930 and then turned to the laissez faire Liberals in 1935. One farm province, Saskatchewan, saw the development of a significant socialist movement. And in Germany, of course, it was the National Socialists who made the most dramatic gains and who, in coalition with the Conservatives, were named to the government. It is evident that one must go beyond consideration of the structural facts (and the concomitant strains) to account for such diversity.

The sharp disparities between the German result and those of the Scandinavian countries have been the object of some interest and study. The petty bourgeois populations of Norway, particularly the small farmers, suffered the same economic strains as the German farmers. And yet, in the period of massive National Socialist increase, the big winner in Norway was the Labor party, a party with an unambiguous socialist program. In the 1933 election, it won 40 percent of the votes, a significant increase over the 31 percent obtained in 1930. Much of that gain, of course, came from among the manual workers, but another large part came from small farmers. The National Socialist party of Vidkun Quisling at this time gained only about 2 percent of the votes.[36]

One brief comparative study has attempted to explain the disparity between the Geest region of Schleswig-Holstein and similar farm regions of Norway. That study focused on the role of party activists, on the personal-influence factor as the key to the difference in results.[37] Germany's Social Democrats had few activists in the rural areas. Their attitudes toward farmers had traditionally been rather negative (the term "petty bourgeois" was as much one of opprobrium as of analysis). The result, effectively, was that they had abandoned the farm populations. By comparison, as we have seen, the National Socialists were very solicitous of the farm vote. They extemporized a farm program and sent activists into farm areas to carry out the message.

The situation was just the reverse in the equivalent areas of Norway. Quisling had few activists and was in no position to carry any program out to the masses. And in sharp contrast to Germany, here is was Labor party activists who, unhindered by a Marxist heritage, extemporized and delivered an attractive farm program. Many of these activists were first-generation blue-collar workers. Having grown up on farms, they could understand the farmers' problems and discuss them with ease.

Unlike the German Social Democrats, the terms of analysis used were neither insulting nor denunciatory but positive and appealing.

The lesson, it would seem, is that many so-called petty bourgeois voters could as easily have turned to socialism as others did to National Socialism. The key factor determining the outcome in this two-country comparison was the organizational one, the ability of a party to generate a plausible program and to mobilize cadres to sell it. The growth of the socialist Cooperative Commonwealth Federation (CCF) in Saskatchewan in the 1930s appears to have stemmed from the same kinds of effort, from the CCF's ability to make use of personal influence in the form of new and capable political cadres.[38]

The key focus in the present explanation of National Socialism involves the role of the party's cadres, of its militants, or, to use a social science expression, of its "opinion leaders." What they do, when seen in terms of the group-bases position, is to provide a new set of political influences, a new source of informal social pressures.

A new influence, by itself, would not guarantee a change; not any pressure would work. To be effective, there must be some net balance of attraction. The activists must be seen as attractive figures; the program must appear to be plausible; there must be some incentive to shift, some dissatisfaction with the previous political choice. Certainly, any such change would be aided if the option were approved by other authoritative opinion leaders. Both the Communists and the Social Democrats had opinion leaders at work in at least some sectors of German society. But there were few settings in which all of these facilitating conditions were working in their favor.

The possibilities can be summarized more systematically as follows. First of all, there is what might be called the normal election. Most voters are rooted in their social networks and have no special incentive to change parties. They make their traditional choices in the election so that the outcome is very similar to the results obtained in previous contests. This would be the case for the overall result and for the patterns among all major subgroups.

Second, there is the normal turnover election. Again most voters are rooted within their social networks, but in this case there is some incentive to change. A serious depression, let us assume, has disrupted the economy. No serious new political option has appeared on the scene. In this circumstance, some voters temporarily abandon their traditional party and vote for the major opposition party regardless of its platform or its basic ideology. In such circumstances the choice appears to be motivated by a simple concern—to punish the party thought to be responsible for (or not doing enough about) the economic catastrophe.

This would appear to be what was happening in Great Britain, Canada, and the United States during the 1930s.

A third possibility involves the creation of a new political option. This would be the case with the National Socialists in Germany, with the Social Democrats in the Scandinavian countries, and with the CCF in Saskatchewan. These cases involved the injection of new cadres to argue and make plausible the new political option. Their successes, it would seem, were dependent on an extended effort to educate the voters as to the merits of their respective options.

Some observers, for good theoretical reasons, anticipate a nearly automatic shift to the left in periods of serious economic decline. But that was clearly not the case in Great Britain, Canada, or the United States during the 1930s. The tiny left parties in those countries remained minuscule throughout the decade, the principal protest being the more limited one of voting the rascals out, as in the second of the possibilities elaborated here. A political option does not speak for itself, that being true even of the left options that, for many, seem so logical in the midst of a major economic disaster. Without organized and intelligent effort, all that happens, in the ordinary case, is a simple turnover with one traditional party replacing another. But the situation is not so narrowly determined; in the other cases mentioned above we saw a range of options developed by new political movements that were seen to be plausible by many voters.

The standard (or static) version of the group-bases position, that accounting for the first of these possibilities, is premised on what one might call the routine processes of everyday life. The explicit political influences exercised by party and the media count for very little since most people's political directions are so completely embedded within their interpersonal networks.[39]

One may assume that these basic routine processes were found also in Germany. Most people would have gained their initial political training within the family; similar processes of adult placement would also have occurred there. But the original political loyalties of many persons were forcibly broken with the end of the monarchy and the reorganization of the parties in 1918-1919. The new attachments formed at that time, obviously, would have been tentative. That is clearly indicated by the vast swings of the period, first to the Weimar coalition, then to the Conservatives and to a range of splinter parties, and ultimately to the National Socialists. Many voters, clearly, were open to new options from the beginning of the republic.

The conservative reaction that appeared in the 1924 elections would appear to be an instance of the second kind of election, that involving a vote against an incumbent and for an established opposition party, in this case the DNVP. The rise of the NSDAP later in the decade was, as indicated, an instance of the third kind of election. The new party's cadres provided a new set of influences, a new set of social pressures that, taken in connection with the other factors aiding them, led to the generation of a mass following.

If this explanation is accepted, two major implications follow. First, one must shift the focus of explanation and ask why Germany had such unique insurgent cadres. For this purpose, the historical sources of an *organizational* development must be examined rather than, as in the centrist position, the transformations of the class structure and the strains thought to accompany that development. Those transformations, after all, were occuring in all economically advanced nations. As was seen in Chapter 12, the German development was linked to features of combat in the World War, to the circumstances of the war's outcome, and to the continuing struggles of the postwar period.

The second major implication is that widely varying developments may occur within the same structural frameworks. Put somewhat differently, the variety of results indicates the *openness* of the historical possibilities; it definitely challenges any argument of historical necessity, particularly any claim of a necessary connection between structures and political responses. As will be seen below, there were indications of such structural indeterminacy even within Germany during this period. And in those instances too, the deciding factor was that of personal influence. It is important to consider both of these implications at greater length.

First, there is the matter of the new or insurgent cadres. The argument offered in Chapter 12 held that the National Socialist cadres were created through a series of rather exceptional socialization experiences. Trained first in *the* war, many of these insurgents continued their military careers with the Freikorps, refining both talents and outlooks in the process. Ultimately they came to the NSDAP or its fighting arm, the Sturmabteilung.

It is instructive to note how the conventional structural analysis deals with such facts. First, because of its focus on the more "basic" structures, those of class, it generally ignores the military. To the extent that the military is recognized at all, it is seen as an agency of the ruling class, of the aristocracy, or later, of the bourgeoisie. The possibility of its independence, relative or absolute, is rarely considered, and even on those infrequent occasions it is a hypothesis that is usually discarded. For the most part, the army, despite its massive size and manifest power, is an institution that is regularly omitted from discussions of macro theory. This failure follows from the logic of the initial argument; if that institution is a mere means, someone else's agency, there is little point to studying it since the important determinants of its behavior are to be found elsewhere. The behavior of the army (in all its parts) is assimilated to the larger analysis of class and its dynamics.

Another feature of the so-called structural argument is, as noted, the persistent avoidance of specific political issues, that tendency also following from the same logic, namely the a priori assumption about what is basic or causal and what "must be" either an effect or of peripheral importance. But in the Weimar case, one political determinant had a very great structural impact. One provision of the Versailles treaty, it will be remembered, drastically reduced the size of the Germany military establishment and, in so doing, shifted the structural location of hundreds of thousands of young men (plus having similar implications for younger aspirants). The Versailles *Diktat* forcibly transferred those people into civilian careers, this political determinant, in other words, rather decisively interrupting the normal or routine processes of social placement for large numbers of German men. Many of the persons thus transferred experienced the change as a loss of position, as downward mobility, and among those thus forced into civilian life one found strong feelings of resentment (not anxiety as predicted in the centrist and mass-society arguments).

Given that resentment, given the widespread sense of unjustly terminated careers, it is not especially surprising that these displaced men, when given the opportunity, attempted to reconstruct their military careers within the context of a demilitarized nation. The explosion of paramilitary organizations in Germany in the twenties appears to be closely connected to this special impetus provided by the Versailles treaty stipulation. Had the peacemakers arranged things differently, had they left the military institutions more or less intact, providing instead for gradual, stepwise reductions in their numbers, the resulting veterans' organizations might have been smaller and less offensive (or virulent), attending instead to the routine ceremonial functions undertaken by such organizations everywhere. The war lovers might well have continued in their chosen occupations, remaining in their segregated communities, with no substantial incentive to challenge and bring down the regime. As it was, the arrangement provided these men with one very substantial additional grievance and then injected them directly into civilian life. They were, when seen from the perspective of the mass-society theory, the most uprooted and déclassé population to be found anywhere in the nation. The source of their rootlessness, however, and hence the target for their resentment, was markedly different from that predicted in this theory.[40]

The line of explanation being offered here may seem to verge on historicism, on the tendency to see history as no more than a series of unique events. But that would be a false opposite; to abandon one line

of historical generalization does not mean abandonment of all such effort. The obvious alternative line of generalization in this case focuses
on insurgent organizations stemming from the same kind of cause, from
stubbornly fought wars, particularly those in which one side rejected
the legitimacy of the outcome.

One of the peculiarities of nineteenth-century European history is its
lack of stubbornly fought wars. After Waterloo, the last venture of
Napoleonic warfare, no such intense campaigns were fought in central
or western Europe until 1914. That sweeping claim does not lose sight
of the Austro-Prussian and Franco-Prussian wars; in both instances, those
were "campaigns of a season," with the decisive battles, Königgrätz
and Sedan, being fought on a single day. In the nineteenth century one
must look elsewhere for that type of campaign, the most likely instance
being the American Civil War, a four-year struggle in which one-quarter
of the participants died. The Confederacy was defeated and a peace imposed that had revolutionary implications; the disenfranchisement of
Confederate leaders and officers meant the displacement of the established elites of the Old South. The North's Reconstruction policies
brought in new leaders, among them, newly rich upstarts, carpetbag-
gers, and the recently enfranchised blacks, all of these backed up by a
military occupation.

The dispossessed elites in this case formed paramilitary units, essentially roving bands of cavalry (nightriders), whose aims were very simple: they sought to undo Reconstruction and to reestablish their former
power. The most widely known of these organizations was the Ku Klux
Klan, but many others were working toward the same goals. The Klan
was broken under the so-called Force Acts of the early 1870s, but the
organized violence continued under different auspices. Like the National
Socialists with their slogans of national renewal (stressing their idealism), these paramilitary forces also had a positive, an idealist stress; they
called themselves the Redeemers or the Redemptorists. They too were
going to reestablish the ancient virtues. These organizations of battle-
trained veterans, also, like the Freikorps, behaved with extraordinary
ruthlessness in the conduct of this postwar campaign. Their aim was
accomplished in the Compromise of 1877, in the tradeoff whereby the
Republicans retained the presidency (with the stolen electoral votes of
the southern states) in exchange for an end to the military occupation.[41]

Another parallel to the National Socialist development appeared in
France in the last years of the Fourth Republic. The French military had
suffered a series of humiliating defeats, the first of these at the hands of
Germany in 1940. A second came in the Indochina struggle which lasted
from 1945-1946 to the fall of Dien Bien Phu in 1954. The embittered
veterans of that campaign saw the loss as having its origins at the home

front, in a lack of consistent political support. They could also point to a betrayal by significant segments of the civilian population. Only a few years later many of the same troops were fighting in Algeria. That struggle proved even more brutal than the war in Indochina. And there, too, the army saw its effort undermined by the governments in Paris. In this case, however, the army brought down that regime and inaugurated a new one, the Fifth, or de Gaulle, Republic. Shortly thereafter, President de Gaulle undermined the army's effort and agreed to an independent Algeria. Once again there was a *Putsch* attempt, although in this case the effort failed.

There were other respects in which this extended struggle showed similarities to the NSDAP development. A strong sense of *Kamerad-schaft* developed among officers and men at the front in both Indochina and Algeria. And a considerable amount of hostility was directed toward the higher-level officers, toward those who did not understand or who, for political reasons, opposed their effort. A novel dealing with Indochinese (and later Algerian) veterans contains the following account: "In 1950 . . . a train full of Far East wounded had been stopped by the Communists who had insulted and struck the men lying on the stretchers. A Paris hospital advertising for blood donors had specified that their contributions would not be used for the wounded from Indo-China. At Marseilles . . . they had refused to disembark the coffins of the dead." This writer says that on their return to France, in a reaction very similar to that of German soldiers returning from the front in 1918, "even the morning air smelled alien to them."[42]

A parallel case may be found in the recent history of Portugal. The army in this instance was involved in a long, and ultimately futile, colonial struggle. Recognizing the imminence of defeat and having experienced a lack of support by the government, it turned against that government and overthrew it. In this instance, it was not a democratic government that was brought down but rather a conservative authoritarian one, that of Salazar and his successor Caetano.[43]

The Portugese case is of special interest because it indicates that the process has no inherent political coloration. The disaffection and antagonism is directed against "the state" (or "the system"), the one that happens to be in power. It indicates that the army is not inherently rightist in orientation, not automatically an instrument of the ruling powers.[44] In defense of its perceived interests, the army can as readily condemn a rightist regime as one of the center or left. This option is not easily recognized if one is hampered by a rigid or dogmatic assumption that the army is automatically an agency of the bourgeoisie. If the Caesarist option is recognized, however, one is prepared theoretically for this otherwise unexpected possibility. The Caesarist option recognizes the possibility of the army operating as a class in its own right (as a class *für sich*). Its members may have a conception of their interests that is opposed to those of the presumably dominant or controlling bourgeoisie. In the extreme case, those interests are sharply opposed, the bourgeoisie generally wishing to keep down taxes and the army wishing to have the latest and best weapons money can buy. One might refer to this as one of the fundamental contradictions of advanced capitalism except that it is probably found more generally, for example, between the political and military sectors of the Soviet Union's leadership.

Another feature of the position being put forth here that makes it more credible than the centrist argument involves what might be called its technical aspect. The centrist position makes a rather implausible assumption. The petty bourgeoisie is portrayed as completely overwhelmed by the events facing it; its members are scarcely able to handle the foundering affairs of their own shops. And yet, one is supposed to believe that in their spare time they are able to put together a large and capable fighting organization, one that, ultimately, overcomes all opposition; they presumably, develop the appropriate programmatic themes, organize the specialized agencies such as, for example, the speakers' school, generate immense funds from the grass roots to support a large permanent staff, coordinate and move their fighting forces when and where needed, and, in local combat, show an extremely high level of tactical competence. Such characteristics are more plausibly attributed to former members of the military than to what is supposed to be a generally incompetent assemblage of clerks and shopkeepers. The best one could argue, at least on an a priori basis, is that the petty bourgeoisie might have supplied mass voting support; but the organizational talents, it would seem from the outset, would have had to come from elsewhere. In other words, one would have to argue the coalitional character of the movement; the necessary organizational arm of that coalition "must have" depended on those with considerably greater organizational and fighting experience.[45]

The second of the major implications delineated above, the claim of *in*determinacy, holds that a given structure allows a wide range of political possibilities. We have already seen this in the comparative evidence, the supposedly powerful and ineluctable conditions giving rise to a diversity of political responses depending on the presence and character of the political activists. This claim of openness, the argument that conditions do not, by themselves, force a single unambiguous development, is also confirmed by some experience within Germany. This evidence also shows the variation to be a function of the personal-influence factor. None of the cases to be reviewed here had more than a modest impact since so few persons went against the major tendencies of the period. They do allow, however, some test of the indeterminacy assumption. They also provide some crucial natural experimental evidence allowing at least some answer to the "what if" questions of history.

One such instance appeared at the time of the NSDAP's first electoral effort. In the May 1924 Reichstag election, one found the familiar clustering of National Socialist strength in Bavaria, Protestant Franconia standing very high on the list of the nation's thirty-five election districts with 20.7 percent (as against the national figure of 6.5 percent). Then came Upper Bavaria-Swabia (17.0 percent) and Lower Bavaria (10.2 percent). There is nothing especially surprising in that result since that party was based in Bavaria and its activities up to that point had been centered there. But the highest NSDAP percentage, 20.8 percent, did not appear in or even near Bavaria. It appeared far to the north in the Mecklenburg district. That area's distinctiveness was even more pronounced in the December election of that year, when the support for the party in Bavaria plummeted. Mecklenburg was again out in front, this time with 11.9 percent, well ahead of the Franconia figure of 7.5 percent. In the 1928 election, Mecklenburg once again was exceptional, but this time in an opposite way, now being below the NSDAP figure for the nation. In the September 1930 election, the district was again in the above average category, although this time only by a small margin (at 20.1 percent versus the national figure of 18.3 percent).

How can one account for these peculiarities? Structural arguments would seem to be of little help. Mecklenburg, located on the Baltic, is a farming area similar in many respects to Schleswig-Holstein and East Hanover just to the west and to Pomerania immediately to the east. The religious factor can also be excluded since all of those areas are heavily Protestant. Mecklenburg was different in that it was an independent state within Germany (the others mentioned being part of Prussia), but that was not likely to have been a factor (at least no one has argued that case). With no significant urban centers, it was, on the whole, little more than a rural backwater, something that could also be said of Pomerania. The structural and religious factors, moreover, were constants; they could not account for the significant fluctuations in the NSDAP support found within the area.

The only viable explanation provided anywhere in the literature is an organizational one. Mecklenburg had been a center of *völkische* activity. The actual electoral list in May 1924, it will be remembered, involved a coalition of the National Socialists and the Deutsch-völkische group (a split-off from the Conservatives). In Mecklenburg, it was the *völkische* group that carried the electoral effort in both May and December.

With the reorganization of the NSDAP, in the spring of 1925, a struggle took place within this coalition, and, in most areas, the National Socialists were the victors. But in Mecklenburg, because of its initial advantage, is was the *völkische* group that won out, holding both the party apparatus and the voters. The NSDAP had to operate with only minimal resources, and that, presumably, is what accounted for its poor showing there in the 1928 election.[46]

In Schleswig-Holstein also, the organizational factor provides an explanation for much of the electoral history. The variability of political sentiment within this region of small and middle-sized farmers may be seen in voting results over much of the previous century. Schleswig-Holstein had a long liberal history, already being described in 1848 as an "overwhelmingly liberal state [Land]." Much of that liberalism had disappeared by the turn of the century, the vote going, rather unexpectedly, to the SPD. In the 1903 Reichstag election, 44.3 percent of the province's vote went to the Social Democrats, that obviously including "a certain part" of the small farmers. In 1919, the province voted overwhelmingly for the SPD and for the left liberal DDP, giving very heavy support, in other words, to two parties of the Weimar coalition. But then, the pathologies of the republic's brief history made their appearance. An immense shift to the conservative DNVP occurred in 1924, the extent of that shift being greater in Schleswig-Holstein than in any other area of the nation. Ultimately, as noted, the province provided strong support for the NSDAP, giving that party the highest percentage of all thirty-five election districts, 51.0 percent.

Between the period of Conservatism and that of National Socialism there appeared a very active, and violent, movement of farm protest, called the Landvolk movement. The farm difficulties were acute even before the general economic collapse, and to prevent foreclosures and sales of farm properties, the Landvolk arranged mass protest meetings. In addition, some members of the movement proceeded to blow up various public buildings, most notably the tax offices. A number of the movement's leaders were brought to trial, convicted, and sent to prison for these actions.

The NSDAP was the Landvolk's principal competitor. After the jailing of the movement's leaders, the National Socialists easily replaced it as the principal agency of farm protest. One Landvolk leader later reported that during his imprisonment the NSDAP took over, almost intact, the twenty or so local groups he had formed in one area of the province.

The NSDAP used the same provocative tactics we have seen used elsewhere. In one struggle with local Communists, they gained a martyr, and Hitler made a personal appearance at the funeral. Before some

6,000 SA and Stahlhelm members, Hitler and *Gauleiter* Lohse roused the local populace with demagogic attacks on both Communists and representatives of the state. The party experienced a considerable growth in members at this point, in the spring of 1929, even before the creation of the anti–Young Plan coalition. Thanks to Hugenberg and other conservatives, Hitler's movement gained acceptability just at the point when the NSDAP was ready for a broad expansion of its efforts. The secession of the People's Conservatives (together with the Christian Social groups and some farm supporters) from the DNVP in December 1929, seriously weakened Hugenberg's party, leaving the field even more open to the NSDAP. National Socialist attacks on the other bourgeois parties went largely unanswered since, outside the cities, the DVP and DDP had "no organization worthy of mention."[47]

Heberle provides more detail on the channeling of NSDAP influence. In some cases, he indicates, its influence was largely indirect. It converted influential members of the local population, who, in turn, converted the rest of the community. In one village where the upper class went over to the National Socialists at an early point, almost the entire population voted for the National Socialists in July 1932. In a neighboring town, the influence of a Catholic landowner, he says, hindered the NSDAP effort, although even there it achieved a majority.[48]

The growth of the party in Schleswig-Holstein in this period then, may be seen as the result of several organizational facts. The prior effort of the Landvolk appears to have provided an important bridge for the NSDAP, making antiregime propaganda and tough tactics acceptable. The leadership loss suffered by the Landvolk then made it easy for the NSDAP to replace this forerunner. And the absence of a serious bourgeois or left opposition in the rural areas to counter or challenge the NSDAP insurgency also facilitated its efforts. The absence of the middle-class and left parties from the rural areas was not in any way structurally determined. It depended on previous choices, on those parties' rather impolitic indifference to the farmers and their concerns.[49]

An instructive quasi-experimental instance of *leftist* activism occurred in rural Schleswig-Holstein in the early thirties. In mid-year 1930, some moves were undertaken by Otto Strasser, Gregor's brother, to reemphasize the left tendency within the party. After the failure of that effort he quit the party, taking with him a number of sympathizers. In Schleswig-Holstein, the NSDAP lost some 800 members from a total of roughly 11,000. This group attempted to set up its own local organization and even undertook some campaigning (in favor of abstention). But SA units broke up its meetings and, on the whole, this effort had no significant result.

Two of these left activists, Bodo Uhse and Bruno von Salomon, toward the end of 1930, joined the Communist-oriented Reichsbauern-bund (Reich Farmers' League) and, shortly thereafter, joined the KPD. With rather limited forces, they campaigned in the Steinburg area, on the edge of the Geest, an area where the small farmers faced especially difficult conditions. In one village of this area they managed to generate unexpectedly high support, 33.8 percent for the KPD in the July 1932 Reichstag election.[50]

Another instructive instance of the personal influence-organizational factor comes from the small state of Brunswick. In the first months of the new republic's existence, this state was led by a Spartacist, Sepp Oerter, otherwise known as the state's "red dictator." Oerter was by-passed in an internal struggle within the Independent Socialists. His successor, Otto Grotewohl, went so far as to arrange for his expulsion from the party, and for a while he was politically homeless. But then, early in 1925, he appeared as the lead candidate on the National Socialist list in the Brunswick municipal elections. To this new political home he brought some 8,000 persons who had once supported him in the USPD.[51]

Two kinds of evidence have been reviewed here, international comparisons and those internal to Germany. Both indicate that the linkages between social structures and political responses are extremely loose, so loose, in fact, that one is led to wonder about the sources of the original assumption that they would be highly correlated. One can, of course, speak of variability within limits, but even that saving argument would not do much for the original line of theorizing. It would be difficult, pointless one might argue, to establish those limits through some logical deductive process. Apart from the obvious extreme case—would the bourgeoisie vote to abolish property?—little else can be established through the exercise of "pure reason."[52] For most population groups the objective conditions do not speak so clearly, so unequivocally; those conditions, by themselves, do not provide an unambiguous definition of their true interests.

Interests are not objective entities (like shoes, the potato crop, coking ovens, or a labor ministry). Interests are *definitions* of appropriate policy. And definitions are intellectual creations, constructs, something generated by human beings. A statement beginning with the declaration that "the objective interest of the workers is" provides no more than a definition, a logical construct that in this formulation attempts to mask its subjective character. Put properly, that statement would read: "I think, for the following reasons, that it is in the interest of workers that they. . . ." That formulation clearly indicates the subjective, judgmental basis for the claim. It also indicates the need for some justification of the position taken. The argument of "objective" interests is one that aims to bypass the requirement of justifying reasons. It aims to solve such normative questions by a simple process of declaration. But that, at least for intellectual purposes, is no solution at all since for any given declaration one can always find any number of competing alternatives.

Since interests are matters of definition (and assessment), it is appropriate that researchers, commentators, and analysts explore the processes whereby those orientations come to be defined. One has to consider such questions as: who defines the interests? Why do they define them in those specific ways? When competing definitions exist, one must ask why one definition is accepted and the others rejected. There is, in short, an important voluntarist component to the process that has to be recognized and researched. The structural argument bypasses these questions entirely.

It would be easy, once again, to leap to a false opposite. If interests are not firmly based in social structures, one might conclude that definitions of interest have no clear or obvious basis. But to reject the argument of structural determination does not mean the acceptance of indeterminacy. The focus on *social* or *group* bases indicates an emphasis on another set of determinants, on the interpersonal influence provided by the routines of everyday life (as in the static Berelson, Lazarsfeld, and McPhee formulation) or on the influences provided by an insurgent group of activists (as in the case developed here). Those social or group bases, the orientations contained within a given group, are not uncaused, and they do appear, on investigation, to have a kind of logic or rationality to them. The orientations of the National Socialist activists, we have argued, had their origins in the experiences of the war and in the disrupting influence of the Versailles *Diktat*. The orientations of the Protestant farm populations had their roots in the efforts of these same activists. The message they communicated provided what seemed to the Protestant farmers to be the best of the available options. The rationality of that judgment depended in turn on some *denied* options. The liberal parties and those of the left had failed to provide, or more precisely, because of various commitments, had *refused* to provide attractive alternatives for those populations.

It is obvious that the tracing of these social or group determinants is a much more complicated process than the simple declaration of class interest. It involves study of the major parties' definitions of issues. It requires examination of their campaign efforts, of their actual communication of those definitions. And it requires a consideration of audience reactions, of how people came to assess the various offerings. In many instances, especially in the study of historical cases, such explanation would require use of much fugitive source material for there are very few records of the social processes or political influences operating within rural communities, small towns, or, for that matter, within urban working-class communities.

The discussion thus far has assumed a basic rationality about the political process. Activists have their goals and choose appropriate means to achieve them. Voters have their goals and choose from among the rather limited means offered to them. That model of rationality, which is useful for describing much of human behavior, also provides a base line for assessing some other, less than rational efforts. The failure of a party to generate positive appeals for a segment of voters who, if given the chance, might support them would be an instance of such irrational political behavior. Such deviations from the rational model would also require explanation. In this example, it might stem from the party's ideological commitments (which in turn, presumably, would have some group or social base).

There are, of course, many varieties of irrationality that require explanation. Political activists vary in their effectiveness. Some succeed in their intended task; some squander their time in meaningless or inappropriate activity; some, through their use of insulting political argument, turn their audiences against them. The Social Democratic, and later, the Communist hostility toward the petty bourgeoisie and toward the so-called bourgeois workers probably turned many away from them. What their "activity" did in such cases was to build an important heritage that in many contexts worked decisively against them. In other instances, the efforts of some activists have been so patently manipulative that they too succeeded only in alienating potential followers.[53] Some activists, despite the name, are rather lazy. These kinds of behavior, too, presumably have discernible social roots; they are not to be explained away as merely random or erratic behavior.

The Other Fascisms

The comparisons between Germany and the United States, the United Kingdom, Canada, and the Scandinavian countries are not intended to provide a systematic or comprehensive review. The purpose, rather, is to consider some crucial test cases, those allowing assessment of the assumption of *necessity* in the centrist argument. They also, by virtue of the diverse political responses actually observed, allow further exploration of one explanatory argument made in this work, namely that organized activists made the difference, that they determined the result. One might make international comparisons in another obvious direction, with the openly fascist regimes, particularly those of Italy and Spain. There were, in addition, fascist movements of one kind or another in all countries of Europe, and in some cases they too managed to acquire significant strength.

The striking thing about the German, Italian, and Spanish cases is that they involve three very different kinds of political takeover. In Germany, the NSDAP, organized for electoral politics, came to power legally by gaining a significant share of the vote. In Italy, Mussolini took power in the first of the successful fascist takeovers (in some ways providing the model for all the other fascisms), through a coup or *Putsch*, through the so-called march on Rome. And in Spain, of course, the takeover was the product of a military coup and a subsequent civil war. Furthermore, in Spain the fascist movement itself, the *Falange*, was not the leading or the moving force; it actually played a rather ancillary role.[54] Given the differences in process, it is obviously rather difficult to apply the general claims of the centrist position, especially those involving the lower middle class.

A brief review of the Italian case proves useful. Although Italy is counted among the victors in World War I, many Italians, it is reported, "felt cheated of the fruits of victory."[55] Although gaining the Alto Adige (Süd Tirol) region in the peace settlement, they were denied Fiume and Dalmatia, areas promised to them in the secret Treaty of London that had secured Italian participation in the war on the Allied side. In support of these expansionist aims, Mussolini's Fasci di Combattimento joined with the *arditi* (described as shock troops, special formations created during the war for assaults on enemy positions). They conducted attacks on their domestic enemies as early as April 1919 when they broke up a Socialist mass meeting and wrecked the offices and printing presses of *Avanti*, the leading Socialist daily. On another front, a group of ex-military men, led by the poet D'Annunzio, occupied Fiume in September 1919 in a move very much reminiscent of the freebooting activities of the Freikorps units.

A deteriorating economic situation in the summer of that year had led to riots in protest against rising prices. The crowds, demanding price reductions, had invaded stores and freely appropriated the goods they found there. Mussolini and the *fasci* sided with the rioters and attacked the profiteers, their slogan being "Squeeze the rich!" His program bore some resemblance to the leftist themes of National Socialist propaganda. It advocated an 85 percent tax on war profits, demanded nationalization of war industries, workers' participation in management, and a minimum wage. There was somewhat greater plausibility to such demands in Mussolini's case since he had been prominent in the Socialist party. He had, in fact, been editor of *Avanti*.

A dramatic upsurge of leftist activities occurred in this period. Demobilized farmers had returned home and occupied the large estates, carving out farms for themselves. In municipal elections the Socialists' hold on many communities was considerably strengthened compared to their prewar position. At the Socialist party congress in October 1919, the majority overwhelmed the party's moderate right wing and voted for affiliation with the Communist International. In the general elections of November, campaigning under the slogan "all power to the proletariat united in the councils!" the Socialists took one-third of the vote; in Milan they gained a majority. Some factories were occupied in the fall of 1919, and the persistent inflation stimulated a continuation of the tactic. A widespread campaign occurred in August 1920 with hundreds of factories occupied in Milan and Turin and elsewhere. The municipal elections in November of that year indicated further gains for the Socialists. The party at that time had more than 200,000 members, ten times its prewar figure, and the Socialist trade union, the General Confederation of Labor, had over two million members. One can imagine the alarm these events generated in middle-class circles.

The Italian case differs substantially from the German in that the evidence of bourgeois support for Mussolini's *fasci* is clear and unambiguous. Landowners and industrialists, to fight the seizures of estates and factories, were especially generous. His movement also received official support. In many cases, the Fascists received weapons and ammunition directly from army depots. Ex-military men joined the Fascist cadres in large numbers, in this case there being both unofficial and official inducements to do so. In some communities officers had been "publicly insulted, spat upon or beaten up by the mob," actions that went a long way to determine their sentiments with respect to the revolutionary developments. A decisive contribution was made by the minister of war who, in October 1920, announced that "officers who were being demobilized and joined the *Fasci di Combattimento*, to control and lead them, were to receive four-fifths of their former pay."[56] Carsten's description of these units and their outlooks is worth quoting at some length:

Many ex-servicemen, especially from the ranks of the *arditi*, joined the Fascist squads. They were proud of the military victory they had won, but felt humiliated by not receiving what they considered their "due" from the government. They thought themselves entitled to substantial rewards for their war services, but none were forthcoming. They were uprooted and no longer fitted into bourgeois society. Large numbers of students and youths, eager for adventure and action, embittered about the rising wages of the workers, and their own misery, detesting the boring routine of their daily lives, also joined the *squadre d'azione* of the Fascists. Finally, there were the toughs, never-do-wells and semi-criminal elements of Milan and other towns.[57]

These squads engaged in "countless deeds of violence," most of them directed against the institutions of the Socialist party and its trade union allies. The police rarely intervened, indicating another element of official complicity. In the countryside, landowners frequently provided the trucks needed to transport the Fascist squads to distant fields of combat. In the first half of 1921, the Fascists "destroyed eighty-five agrarian cooperatives, fifty-nine chambers of labor, forty-three unions of agricultural workers, twenty-five people's centers, and many left-wing printing presses and newspapers." They did not stop at private voluntary associations but also, under threats of violence, forced left-wing mayors and councilors to resign their offices. One Fascist leader boasted of having forced sixty-four local councils to dissolve themselves within the span of a few days. On a more "positive" note, they forced farmers to sell their products at low prices; in Naples they imposed a 50 percent reduction in restaurant prices.[58]

Giolitti, the Liberal prime minister, formed a National Bloc for the May 1921 general election. This coalition included the Fascists, the purpose being to make them "more respectable [and] to assimilate them" as well as to weaken Giolitti's main enemies on the left.[59] This effort, too, foreshadows a development seen later in Germany.

There was a pause in the struggle in the fall of 1921 at which time Mussolini sought to achieve a rapprochement with the Socialists. But rebellion within his own ranks led him to abandon this policy and continue the assault. This time, it was to be a fight to the finish.

In late October 1922, under threat of a march on Rome, the king of Italy named Mussolini as prime minister. The march on Rome itself involved no bloodshed; there was no armed resistance at all. Carsten sums up as follows: "The march on Rome succeeded largely because there was no one to oppose it. All the forces of the state—the army, the police, the civil service, the judiciary—supported it in one form or the other, exactly as they had condoned Fascist violence and lawlessness during the previous years. Without this collusion the enterprise could never have succeeded."[60]

One additional aspect of the history deserves attention: what were the Socialists doing by way of response? Carsten summarizes their effort succinctly: "The Socialists were incapable of countering these tactics of military concentration and assault."[61] In August 1922, shortly before the march on Rome, the Socialists attempted a last major defensive effort, the declaration of a general strike. The Fascists moved in and, with regular police cooperation, broke the strike. They thus demonstrated the impotence of the Socialists and simultaneously showed themselves to be "defenders of law and order."[62] In this respect, too, there is a parallel to the later developments in Germany. Despite its threatening appearance, the left actually was a sheep in wolf's clothing.

It would be a mistake to assume that the left uprising was all of a piece, that it was something planned and organized from one center (that is, by the maximalist—as opposed to the reformist—leaders of the Socialist party). Most authorities see the phenomenon as more diverse, as an uncoordinated series of autonomous or spontaneous events, much of it stimulated by inflation rather than by party directives. The factory takeovers, apparently, caught both party and trade union leaders by surprise. The men who for decades had talked revolution were at a loss when the first signs appeared. In the end, they even cooperated with the owners to help clear the factories.[63]

Carsten's account includes a declaration that the revolutionary developments in Italy had "aroused the fears and the hatred of the middle and lower middle classes."[64] But those classes do not figure elsewhere in his review. As far as the class basis of Fascism is concerned, his account has the decisive contribution being made by those higher up in the social structure, by those in the Italian upper and upper middle classes. His account indicates widespread complicity by government leaders and officials, by the established upper classes, and, in general, by well-off segments of the population. As for the party activists, the *squadristi*, Carsten states that, as in Germany, they came from the armed forces, from the demobilized troops, and, secondarily, from among the university students. In Italy, as in Germany at this time, students would, almost exclusively, have been upper- and upper-middle-class children.

Were one to summarize the Italian case in a few phrases, one would have to include the following: the leftist insurgency; the flow from the military to the *fasci*; and the support and complicity of the better-off classes. Except for the extensive business support and for the specific process of the takeover, a mock *Putsch* instead of the electoral route, the history proves to be very similar to the German case. In both instances there was a dialectical struggle between "Marxist" and "Fascist" forces. And in both, the combat arm of the latter was recruited from the ranks of the military. In neither case does the lower middle class appear to have played a clear and unambiguous, let alone a decisive, role.[65]

In a brilliant review of fascist movements in Europe during the twenties and thirties, Juan Linz lays the principal emphasis on the common features of recent historical development rather than on the more general factor of class transformations and attendant strains. He delineates four factors: first, the impact of the World War on society and on the participant generation, this factor being especially important for the defeated nations or for those in which many felt cheated of the fruits of victory; second, the appearance of revolutionary attempts either by

Communists or by maximalist Socialists; third, the heightened sense of nationalism, this being stimulated first by the war, then by a peace settlement in which the locations of nationalities did not coincide with the boundaries of states, all of this accentuating the closely related problem of the proper place of nations in international hierarchies of power and prestige; and fourth, unresolved cultural conflicts within states, particularly those involving ethnic minorities.

There are impressive correlations between the strength of fascist movements and the first two of these factors, being on the losing side in the war and experiencing a serious revolutionary attempt. These are the factors central to the present explanation of the German case and, in previous paragraphs, of the Italian one. In some instances, Linz shows the revolutionary attempt led to the establishment of a conservative authoritarian regime headed by traditional elites. Such regimes discouraged the development of any new political movements, whether of the right or the left, thus limiting the impact of any subsequent events. But for the countries in which political movements were free to develop, that is, those with liberal democratic regimes, those factors go a long way toward explaining the degree of success of the fascist movements across Europe prior to the outbreak of World War II.[66]

It is important to speculate on the relationship of "ruling classes" and "fascist movements" more generally, in an attempt to account for the wide variations in the observed patterns. The following discussion is intended as a hypothetical account, as a set of guesses about the relationships between the two groups. The quotation marks here are intended as a caution against reification. In all cases one would expect diversity both within a "ruling class" and within a "fascist movement." The relationship will be considered first from the perspective of a ruling class.

The situation of such a class, for this purpose, may be seen in terms of two dimensions: first, the extent to which its members feel their position to be threatened, and second, if they sense a threat, the extent to which they are able to organize to counter that threat.[67] The ruling classes of many European nations probably felt some kind of threat in the twenties and thirties. Not only had the Soviet Union come into existence, but many nations had experienced internal risings by the left, or later, in the years of the depression, felt that such a rising was imminent. Such perceptions did not always have a realistic basis since, as seen in the German case, some circumstances can magnify the appearances even when there is little substantial basis for alarm.

It is frequently assumed, given the ultimate interests involved, that a threatened ruling class, whether an aristocracy or a bourgeoisie, would use its money, contacts, and all its ability to organize for the defense of its interests; that conclusion seems to follow like the night the day. But the review of the German case (in Chapter 13) indicates a markedly different reality. German business leaders (and the aristocracy) were overwhelmed by the November 1918 revolution and, effectively, offered no defense whatsoever. The first serious business reaction, that organized by Hugo Stinnes, accepted the given facts and made arrangements for living with the new situation. Although it is frequently claimed that the bourgeoisie later regained control, business leaders felt otherwise, continually indicating their dissatisfaction with the policies adopted by national, state, and local governments. They were also dissatisfied with those agencies that, presumably at least, were under their direct control, the so-called bourgeois parties. Despite the demands of business leaders for a unification of the various fragments, for the creation of a Bourgeois Bloc, those parties also showed unexpected independence and failed to comply. Rather than acting with careful plans and high cohesion, the key directive organization of German heavy industry, the Ruhrlade, ceased functioning in the crucial months of 1932, so divided was it on policy matters.

This experience suggests the need for an alternative hypothesis or general orientation, one that emphasizes the serious problems facing business leaders in organizing for the defense of their perceived interests. This alternative focus, actually, should not come as a complete surprise. Businessmen, after all, run firms, and the management of a large enterprise requires almost all of one's time and energies. They have limited experience or skill in the political area, there being little time available in their lives for such efforts. Politics is something ordinarily delegated to political leaders. And if those leaders fail, or disappear, business leaders have few resources at hand with which to begin anew. This is speaking of ordinary or routine political efforts. When a situation called for paramilitary forces, for extraordinary, for exceptional efforts, they would be even more helpless.

This is to suggest that political responses to real or imagined threats typically come to be organized and led by others, by persons or groups outside of business circles.[68] It is to suggest that "business," in the usual case, must support someone else's plan. Business leaders might not find any of the plans offered them entirely to their liking, but because of their lack of political skills, they would not have a completely free choice. When one of those plans was successful, that is, where someone else took power, business, with typical opportunism would attempt to achieve a working relationship.[69] The image of business insisting on domination, demanding control or the right to call the shots, may be mistaken. An uncompromising attitude, any rigid, unyielding, or intransigent position would have serious consequences for a firm; apart from endangering profits, in a revolutionary period it would provide an incentive for immediate punitive socialization of the enterprise. Although business spokesmen frequently make use of the language of command, that hides an underlying reality, that their basic orientation is to go along with existing arrangements.

What possibilities existed, then, for a threatened bourgeoisie? Again, still by way of hypothesis one might speculate that its first preference would have been for a conservative authoritarian regime like Horthy's in Hungary or Salazar's in Portugal. A conservative regime of that variety would be headed by persons known to the members of the bourgeoisie, by persons either in or close to their own circles. They could have trust in such leaders, and also, should the need for specific policy changes arise, they would have ready access to them for presentation of their views. A conservative authoritarian regime, moreover, would not ordinarily be interested in radical transformation of existing institutional arrangements, its basic concern being to reestablish order. Such a regime would not ordinarily have any far-reaching plans, say for national renewal or for readjustment of national boundaries. Its basic task would be to remove the source of the difficulty, and that would be achieved through prohibition of the threatening left party and its related trade unions. In addition, there would be some control over the press, some additional censorship, some restrictions on freedom of assembly, and so forth. Otherwise, no significant changes in the existing institutional arrangements would be envisaged, and business could be conducted as usual.

A second option, that promised by a Mussolini or a Hitler, would probably, from the outset, be viewed with less favor by businessmen (or by aristocrats). Business leaders felt they did not know Hitler. They were always unsure about his program and, accordingly, were uncertain about the extent of the changes his new order would bring. There were disquieting signs, too, with respect to the problem of access. National Socialists were clearly different from businessmen. They thought differently; they spoke a different language, one that left much to be desired by way of clarity. Some of those with access to Hitler had reason to doubt his ready assurances of sympathy and good faith.[70]

The evidence from Germany does indicate that the basic preference of most business leaders was for the conservative authoritarian option. If the National Socialists were to be in government at all, it was preferable that they occupy a subordinate role in one headed by conservatives that is, by Hindenburg and Papen. Business leaders also wished to see a change toward a presidential regime, with powers taken away from the parties and the parliament. Although not designed by business leaders, the original Hitler government, as worked out by Papen and accepted by Hindenburg, followed this basic model. Hitler was to be surrounded and contained by the conservative authoritarian majority in the cabinet.

Later, when Hitler dissolved that arrangement, when he dismantled the parties and voluntary associations of the business and aristocratic authoritarians, they were powerless to do anything about it; Caesar had conquered. From then on, it was the business leaders who sought the working arrangements. They adjusted to the demands of the new regime, not vice versa.

In most other countries of Europe, the fascist offerings were very diverse and, with few exceptions, almost completely unsuccessful. That diversity has posed something of a challenge to subsequent scholars. Given what one might call a bias in favor of generalization, many commentators have attempted to find across-the-board patterns, arguing the existence of a generic fascism. But the diversity has defeated every such attempt.[71]

There are some basic reasons for that diversity. Those movements did have one thing in common; they were all strongly nationalistic. And that meant, of necessity, that they were diverse in their orientations and programs, each reflecting a unique national reality. Allardyce mentions in this connection that the slogan "nationalists of the world unite" involves a logical impossibility.

The various fascist movements were also, in most cases, strongly oppositional in character. They were fighting *against* things, against the established authorities, against "the system" on the one hand, and against leftist or Marxist threats on the other. In many cases those authorities were identified with liberal parties; "the system" referred to a heritage of liberal politics. Both liberalism and Marxism, it will be noted, are internationalist in character. They both operate with a general world view; and they both, in their original formulations at least, assumed nationality to be something of minor and diminishing importance. Nations, in both views, were seen as impediments to human improvement.

In dialectical reaction, the various fascisms almost compulsively stressed their unique national plans and aspirations. Mussolini organized a meeting of fascist parties at Montreux in 1934. It was to be a kind of international of the fascist parties, but for his purposes it was a dismal failure. There was serious division on "the Jewish question." Most areas of agreement were so general as to be almost meaningless. The strongest support, for example, came for the proposition "that each nation must solve its problems in its own way." José Antonio Primo de Rivera refused Mussolini's invitation to attend. His movement, the Falange Española, he said, was not fascist; it was Spanish.[72]

Still another important source of diversity within the fascist camp, Linz points out, stems from their being latecomers on the political scene. They came after the Conservatives, the Liberals, the Socialists, and the Communists. And, in some cases, too, they also followed farmers' parties, religious parties, and regional particularists. This meant that they had to fit themselves into the political space that, in a sense, was left over. Where a conservative authoritarian regime was in power, little space was open on the right. But, given the prohibition of the Communists, there was room for growth on the left. In these cases one saw the development of a left fascism. In authoritarian Romania, for example, one did not find anti-Marxism given the same emphasis it received from fascist groups elsewhere. The voting support for this kind of fascism, however, as far as we can tell, had a different character, coming disproportionately from the working class.[73]

What this means is that the leaders of a national-renewal group would put together a unique package for each nation, one reflecting their country's specific conditions. Where the electorate had been mobilized, where all important groups had formed attachments to a party, there was little room available for the new movement. If, unlike Hitler and Mussolini, they did not have adequate cadres, they would have been unable to break into someone else's political space. In some nations the conditions favoring the formation of such militant cadres were missing. In others, the leaders of the movement lacked charisma; that is, for one reason or another, they were unable to generate support from any large group of the population. Unlike Hitler and Mussolini, most of these other leaders came from upper- and upper-middle-class backgrounds and, so it is said, lacked the popular touch.

There was little reason for business (or an aristocracy or established elites) to support any of these other fascisms. Businessmen had little incentive to give up the governing arrangement they had in favor of a minuscule and possibly, rather exotic, sectarian organization. In the authoritarian regimes, where they already had what for them was a viable arrangement, they were certainly not likely to abandon it in favor of a left fascism.[74]

INTELLECTUALS AND THE WEIMAR EXPERIENCE

Because the massive literature on National Socialism developed over the last fifty years has misrepresented the extent of voting support within key segments of the population, it has led commentators to explain the wrong things. The admonition of sociologist Robert K. Merton seems most relevant here. He points out that "before social facts can be 'explained' it is advisable to ensure that they actually are facts. Yet, in science as in everyday life, explanations are sometimes provided for things that never were."[75] The lower-middle-class propensity, as far as we can tell, is one of those "things that never were."

This conclusion, in its turn, raises another question: how did it come about that scholars and commentators so thoroughly misread the evidence and, throughout the course of five decades, sustained a consensus based on a pseudofact? This leads us to a consideration of the social psychology of the scholarly intelligentsia and to a consideration of the sociology of knowledge. Both are concerned with the social, as opposed to the scientific and intellectual, roots of knowledge.

One finds the conventional explanation of National Socialism accepted without question from the moment of the party's reappearance in the late twenties. The liberal *Vossische Zeitung*, in July 1929, made use of the sloganlike summary phrase; the National Socialists, it said, represented the "petty bourgeois gone mad." In February 1931, a lead article in the *Frankfurter Zeitung*, the most intellectual of Germany's liberal newspapers, offered the same basic line: "National Socialism is the revolutionary eruption of the despair of the proletarianized middle classes."[76] In Germany's political and scholarly sources, too, as we have seen, there was a ready acceptance of the position. And with Harold Lasswell's famous article "The Psychology of Nazism," published in 1933, the argument appeared in English and has been cited, with unquestioning approval, many times since.

It does not take much effort to recognize that all the key elements of this position appear as part of the Marxian heritage. The explanation imposed on the events of the late Weimar period had been available for some four-score years, the basic position having already appeared in Marx and Engels's 1848 work, *The Communist Manifesto*, possibly the most frequently read of all their writings.

Marx and Engels speak there of "the lower strata of the middle class— the small tradespeople, shopkeepers, and retired tradesmen generally, the handicraftsmen and peasants—all these sink gradually into the proletariat." A few paragraphs later, they pick up this theme again, this time making a specific political prediction: "The lower middle class, the small manufacturer, the shopkeeper, the artisan, the peasant, all these fight against the bourgeoisie, to save from extinction their existence as fractions of the middle class. They are therefore not revolutionary, but conservative. Nay more, they are reactionary, for they try to roll back the wheel of history."

One other element of the explanation of the Weimar catastrophe is prefigured here. Marx and Engels speak of "the 'dangerous class,' the social scum [lumpenproletariat], that passively rotting mass thrown off by the lowest layers of old society [which] may, here and there, be swept into the movement by a proletarian revolution; its conditions of life, however, prepare it far more for the part of a bribed tool of reactionary intrigue.[77]

Although the *Manifesto* might best be viewed as a brief sketch or outline, as a set of guiding hypotheses, the claims contained there have generally been treated as final conclusions rather than as beginning points for research.

Marx and Engels do, in passing, make mention of a more positive development, or possibility, within the ranks of the bourgeoisie. Some part, a "small section of the ruling class," they write, cuts itself off and "joins the revolutionary class." This refers to that "portion" of the bourgeois ideologists who "have raised themselves to the level of comprehending theoretically the historical movement as a whole." They "supply the proletariat with fresh elements of enlightment and progress." This "progressive" possibility, significantly, applies only to the "ruling class"; it is not said to be a possibility for the petty bourgeoisie, who continue to be described in a not particularly inventive variety of condemnatory terms.[78]

This means that long before the appearance of National Socialism, there existed a ready-made explanation for the forthcoming event. Built into the consciousness of many members of Germany's intelligentsia, this viewpoint (or "paradigm" as it would be called by many intellectuals today), constituted a set of blinders that excluded other possibilities from consideration. There was another equally plausible paradigm that could have been read into the events, that of a Caesarist takeover (one that, to be sure, made use of democratic procedures). Given the links of NSDAP cadres to the military and to later paramilitary organizations, given their continuous reference to military models, given their military language, there was at least *something* to be said for the Caesarist argument. But, with remarkable uniformity, those biographical links were overlooked in favor of the stress on the presumed origins within a given class.[79]

The consensus on the lower-middle-class role extended beyond the ranks of Germany's Marxists. The focus on, or blaming of, the lower middle class was a staple also with many of Germany's liberal intellectuals, making, as noted, an early appearance in leading liberal newspapers. One important fact about German liberalism at that time was its susceptibility to and adoption of a large part of Marxian class analysis, a development distinctive to Germany. Elsewhere, in England, France, and the United States, liberal thinkers generally retained their more individualistic explanations at least until after World War II.[80]

It would take a separate study of German intellectual history to account for this "paradigmatic shift." One may nevertheless speculate about the different processes that were operating. German liberals, from a very early point, faced a serious intellectual challenge from the left, from the Marxist Social Democratic Party. That party, because of its bureaucratic character, provided full-time employment to hundreds of intellectuals who staffed its newspapers and journals, generating serious analyses of economic and social developments. Many of these intellectuals were academically trained, which is to say, there was some intersection of the radical and academic ranks, and some intellectual exchange resulted. Germany's scientific socialism betrayed something of its academic origins, the terms of analysis and intellectual methods being superior to the productions of the left in other countries. By virtue of that intellectual superiority, liberal and conservative commentators were forced to pay attention to these analyses (that is, in addition to the attention they gave to the growing power of the party and of the related trade unions). In the process, it would appear, Social Democracy taught its opponents to think in terms of class.[81]

Conceivably, were one able to tap the underlying reasons for the shift, another element, a tactical one, would be discovered. The class analysis allows enormous simplification of complex historical processes. With a stroke of the pen, all of that complexity is categorized, ordered, and seen to be flowing on a recognizable course. For the liberal, on the other hand, history involves a complex clutter of unique events, the liberal world view providing no such helpful simplification. For those knowing the history, a given episode might involve a group of specific individuals, and the role of personal whim or fancy could easily prove decisive. That is not the kind of stuff out of which to generate sweeping world-historical claims. It does not provide one with the key to history; there are no levers allowing easy appeal even to the intellectual masses. Either in written or oral form, its very complexity, its detail, its historicism would mean defeat in any competition with the simplifying formula (or, as some would put it, with the powerful generalization). Conceivably, Germany's liberals, either unable or unwilling to discuss the historical development in those complex or historicist terms, fell back on the more commanding terms of analysis. It was one way of meeting the Marxist challenge.[82]

Eventually all important political movements of the nation came to talk in class terms, accepting the Marxian delineation of the classes. Many could accept that nomenclature while, at the same time, rejecting the Marxian claims about the exclusivity of class interests and expressing doubts about the "inevitable" outcome of modern history.[83] When National Socialism gained its election victories, the ground was prepared in the sense that a preformed "explanation" was there and ready for use. In the years following Hitler's takeover, the centrist theory was destined to gain an even larger following. Many of Hitler's opponents, the more fortunate ones, went into exile and from there disseminated this world view to even larger audiences. This process is considered in more detail below.

One would expect that at some point the major claims of the position would have been put to the test; some research should have been done. Certainly in the period from September 1930 to late 1932, one should have seen some comprehensive analyses of the election results to establish definitively the claims about the social origins of the National Socialist infection. If it were in fact the lower middle class, that should have been established, clearly and unambiguously, with results from Berlin, Hamburg, Cologne, Munich, and so forth. That research would have established or thrown into question the validity of the principal claim. And in the latter case, it would have forced immediate consideration of alternative lines of explanation. But, except for a handful of very sketchy and ambiguous analyses, that research task was neglected by the scholarly community, by the leading newspapers, and by the more serious publications of the political parties.

Several factors may be suggested to explain this neglect. There was, first of all, a simple technical factor. Even the best of the newspapers presented the results in a way that did not allow easy assessment of the lower-middle-class claim. The better newspapers would give the results for the nation and the city, giving both the number of votes and percentages, in most cases also providing contrasting results from the previous election. Those newspapers would also give figures and percentages for the thirty-five major election districts of the nation. They might also give the results for other major cities. But, at best, those results would enable one to make only a rather global assessment of the sources of NSDAP support.

Within the cities, it will be remembered, votes were cast and counted by precinct (*Stimmbezirk*). In many cities, usually a day or two after the election, the better newspapers would provide these very detailed precinct results. Such presentation did not appear in the largest cities of the nation; in Berlin, for example, that kind of presentation would have required eight or ten large pages. But elsewhere, the reader would be presented with an immense quantity of raw data. One Munich newspaper, in early August 1932, reported the votes for nearly 800 precincts. For the same election, the *Düsseldorfer Nachrichten* produced seven columns of figures for each of 326 precincts. The *Frankfurter Zeitung* reported results for 301 precincts and the city's hospitals. It gave eleven columns of figures for each precinct and, for comparative purposes, also provided nine columns of figures for the Landtag election a few months earlier. In the smallest of the cities covered here, in Mannheim, a local newspaper gave fifteen columns of figures for each of 155 precincts. Since no percentages were supplied in any of these presentations, the data, as they stood, were not particularly informative. Moreover, little information was given describing the precincts; typically all that appeared was a precinct number and a place, for example: 234. Pestalozzi School, Room 1; 235. Pestalozzi School, Room 2. To draw a lesson out of those results, the diligent reader would have had to sort out the precincts by class level (which would require an unusual personal knowledge of the city or the collection of an additional range of information on those districts). Then it would have been necessary to calculate a large number of percentages, or alternatively, to combine a lot of figures and then calculate percentages.

A second and closely related factor accounting for the neglect of this needed research involves an absence of technical expertise. The German universities did not train people to do election studies. The first major study of this kind was undertaken in the years 1932-1934 by Rudolf Heberle, who was then a *Privatdozent* at the University of Kiel. The stimulus for his work, he reports, came from elsewhere, the possibility first having occurred to him during a stay in the United States. He was also moved by the work of the French scholar André Siegfried, who in 1913 had published a path-breaking study showing the support for the parties in the west of France. But even in 1932, Heberle notes, that kind of study had gained little attention; "sociographic" treatments of political parties and movements, he says, were only in their early beginnings in Germany at that time. The basic point, then, is that the German universities, in history, in sociology, and in what there was of political science, trained people in other kinds of specialties. Formal training to do analyses of elections came first in the years following World War II. As a consequence, few studies of this kind were done in the universities. It follows, too, that the students who later found employment in newspapers or who worked for the parties were poorly trained for the task of analyzing election results.[84]

Strangely enough, this complex task of reorganizing and recalculating the massive quantities of urban election data was in fact undertaken in a few cases by people who possessed considerable expert knowledge. Those results were published and were available to any interested person in the early 1930s. Results for Hamburg, for example, were available in great detail. Some publication of Cologne results had occurred. Some analysis of the Essen results had been published, the lessons reported here coming through with great clarity.

But in these instances, a social obstacle intervened, this third source of neglect involving a problem of compartmentalization. These results were developed in municipal statistical offices and appeared in the publications of those offices. Except for a small coterie of cognoscenti (many of whom, no doubt, were to be found in other statistical offices), those results were to remain unknown. With rare exceptions those publications did not come to the attention of concerned scholars, political commentators, or the educated public.

There are, it should be noted, two sides to every nonrelationship. If the informed commentators paid no attention to the publications of the statistical offices, the analysts in those offices paid little attention to the favored hypotheses of the concerned commentators, much of their work consisting of dry-as-dust tabulation. Had they focused on those hypotheses, they might have come up with some unexpected findings which, if publicized at all, could have forced some rethinking of the entire lower-middle-class question.[85]

It is evident that most scholars, intellectuals, and commentators in Weimar Germany accepted the lower-middle-class hypothesis regardless of its lack of supporting evidence. For all their high technical qualifications in many areas, Germany's intelligentsia do not appear to have been oriented toward, nor trained for, the kinds of studies required to answer the key questions about the mass support for National Socialism, that is, election studies. More than a mere technical problem was involved; some were openly hostile to empirical investigation.[86] For them, the concern with Hegel and the World Spirit was more important than the pedestrian demands of any research. The need to refine one's understanding of the concept of alienation outweighed any interest in learning the methods required for studying that (possible) alienation. Germany had a renowned Institute for Social Research, but the proprietors of that enterprise, although very much concerned with the rise of Hitler, undertook no voting studies.[87]

While from one perspective it is surprising that the empirical efforts in this area should have been so limited, from another it is no problem at all. If the members of a group are sure of something, if it is seen as obvious or defined as nonproblematic, then there is no need to undertake that research. Indeed, to do so would seem foolish, a waste of one's time. What is being suggested here as a fourth possible explanation for the neglect, is that there was (and is) a considerable amount of conformity operating within intellectual circles. This is to say that the conclusion depends on and is supported by processes of group dynamics, the same processes made familiar to us from studies in social psychology. This is to suggest that the group-based processes of thought, of reinforcement or change, those processes observed in work groups, in neighborhoods, in the classroom, and among back-yard gossips, are also to be found among intellectuals.[88]

Where such processes were operating it would mean that the original attitudes and outlooks of a group (or school) would come to persist over intellectual (as opposed to biological) generations. The process would occur in much the same way as the transmission of a Conservative or a Zentrum political tradition. The key difference would be in the opinion leaders. In lieu of fathers providing the basic political socialization, prominent professors, writers, artists, eminent journalists, and so on, would provide the training in these circles. As in the society generally, that initial training would be undertaken within primary groups, in classes or seminars in the universities, or, in the political parties, among small groups of activist intellectuals. Those opinion leaders would also recommend or approve various printed materials, thus arranging for "media" reinforcement of the group's original views. If there were no solid empirical base to the knowledge passed along within those circles, if there was no feeling of obligation to reckon with evidence, then the decisive determinants of outlooks would be the words and judgments of influential or charismatic professors, or, in another context, those of the equivalent political leaders.

The centrist argument was destined to be transmitted to a sizable audience beyond Germany's borders. Many scholars, writers, and intellectuals, along with many political leaders, particularly those of liberal or left persuasions, were forced into exile and had to reestablish themselves elsewhere. The elements of their analysis of National Socialism thus came to be implanted in the new, host countries.[89] With considerable frequency, the elements of that line of analysis were then generalized and applied to other countries. Possibly the most significant instance of this process in the United States involved the work of the German exile Hans Gerth and his American collaborator, C. Wright Mills. In Mills's influential book, *White Collar*, one finds all of the principal elements of the centrist position applied to the United States.[90] Once again, however, the basic claims, those concerning the political orientations of the American lower middle classes, were largely unresearched.

A later review of relevant survey evidence (evidence that had long been available, it should be noted) did not support the centrist claims as applied to the United States. The lower middle classes there, allowing for some differences by ethnicity and religion, proved to be generally liberal, that is, favorable to the welfare state, approving aid to the poor and needy. They did not appear to be desperate or anxious. Nor did they appear to be hostile either to business or labor or to racial or ethnic minorities. They did not show any unique propensities to vote for rightist candidates, either for Barry Goldwater or for George Wallace. A very large portion identified themselves as working class. This means that in the United States, too, the centrist claims have been sustained through processes of group dynamics rather than through the presentation of appropriate evidence.[91] As in the case of the German original, here, too, one finds a consensus on the part of mapmakers who had failed to undertake the obvious prior task, exploration.

The views found within any self-segregated community will, over time, come to diverge from those present within the general population. Those differences would, from the outset, be even greater where the members of a community planned their own segregation to protect their unique views from erosion, from the secularizing influences of the larger society (as, for example in the case of the American Pilgrims, of the Hutterite communities, or among the Doukhobors). A similar development arises, understandably, within self-segregated intellectual communities. One sees there the appearance of a distinctive language, much of which cannot be understood without years of training and initiation. One frequently finds distinctive speech patterns and styles of dress. The intellectual orientations found within such a community in the course of time come to be ever more exotic, that is, in relation to the understandings and outlooks found elsewhere in the society.

A very serious problem is associated with this kind of arrangement: those intellectuals whose lives are contained within such communities become increasingly unable to deal with the facts of everyday life. Their distance from everyday routines unfits them for dealing with ordinary or prosaic matters. In the midst of a major depression, farm prices would be a central focus in the lives of most farmers. And a central fact for unemployed (or underemployed) workers would be the price of bread. But one must look far and wide in most sources to find any serious attention given to the prosaic facts of farm prices or of the price of bread. The outlooks of other ordinary people are also systematically overlooked, the views of butchers, grocers, haberdashers, real estate salesmen, and government clerks, of their wives and children, all being subsumed under a few sloganlike phrases purporting to describe *the* lower middle class. There were, as we have seen, important differentiations to be found within all of these broad categories, those being dependent on, as far as one can tell, some other prosaic facts, those of subgroup traditions and interpersonal influences. Because of their other-worldliness, the self-segregated intellectuals can hardly see, let alone deal with, the implicatons of the price of bread.[92] Given their distance from the events of everyday life, and given their disdain for research (which could tell them something about that life), it will come as little surprise that their basic method comes to involve a considerable amount of crude stereotyping and of projection (in the psychological meaning of the term).

If one's conceptions are not based on a direct observation of external events, then they must have internal sources. One possibility, that elaborated to this point in the discussion is that the orientations are internal to a group, part of its received tradition or heritage. One may also, however, consider possible psychological roots. If one were projecting or assigning a framework onto some distant event, that framework could, in some way, be an extension of personal psychological needs, this being a fifth possible reason for the persistence of the intellectual focus.

There is an element in many formulations that suggests the psychological process of scapegoating. Although difficult to establish empirically, an element of anger or wrath appears in some accounts, this having little to do with analysis but instead involving highly charged declarations of moral condemnation. An example will prove useful.

In an unusually prescient novel first published in 1923, *Das Spinnennetz* (The Spider Web), Joseph Roth describes a Lieutenant Lohse who, on returning from the war, finds disorder and disappointment in the new Germany. He joins several rightist underground organizations (among them, one with links to Ludendorff and Hitler) and works to overthrow the republic. In a recent reissue of this novel, the author of a postscript neglects this military background, making Lohse into the prototypical lower-middle-class individual. He is, so the reader is told, one who has "broken out of the bounds of the social order. [He is] the petty bourgeois gone mad, who lives from resentment, is consumed by his frustration, who is cowardly and out of cowardice, is dangerous, because he must furnish himself with bloody countering evidence; he is just intelligent enough to recognize his own incapacity in life, but not intelligent enough to accommodate himself to this reality, this, so to speak, as a positive narrow-mindedness, which narrow-mindedness must turn into aggression, aggression against everything which, with his available intelligence is ascertained to be superior."[93]

Given what we have seen of the actual political behavior of the lower middle class, given the manifest political diversity within that rather broad stratum, one would have to count those judgments as simply mistaken, or at minimum, as much too sweeping. While the processes of personal influence can easily give rise to simple mistakes, the intensity of feeling indicated in this quotation, the evident stereotyping, the extreme hostility directed toward its subject, the concern to degrade every motive, suggests something more, that is, scapegoating. The lower middle class is being used as a convenient target for the projection of hostility. The same might also be said of some treatments of the so-called lumpenproletariat.

One author has provided us with some suggestive hypotheses for understanding such behavior. In the ordinary course of everyday life, he indicates, it is difficult to express feelings of hostility. Most people do not appreciate being made the targets of hostility, most especially of

gratuitous hostility. But a political movement (like the religious movements, or those concerned with spiritual renewal, or social uplift) provides an answer for that kind of need; such movements give moral
justification for the expression of hostility.[94]

To the extent that such motives are operating within a movement or
party, they would clearly interfere with normal cognitive processes, both
those of the affected individuals and the collective understanding of the
group. Given the need for a scapegoat, such persons would resist the
presentation of evidence tending to exonerate their chosen target; that
would interfere with their (largely unconscious) purpose. At the same
time, where a party did come to serve essentially psychological purposes, that effort would interfere with its manifest political purpose. It
would alienate those persons made the targets of such hostility. Worse
still, it would provide an incentive for them to affiliate with an opposed
political direction. Conceivably, some of the anti-Marxism found within
Germany (and elsewhere) is a dialectical response to this kind of "politics."

A sociology of knowledge may be said to have two principal focuses.
There are processes through which the knowledge is first produced, and
there are processes through which that knowledge comes to be accepted
or rejected by some larger audience. The striking feature of the history
of the centrist position is the ease with which that view gained a very
wide acceptance, there being scarcely a shadow of doubt indicated about
the validity of the principal claims. In the normal case, one would expect scholars to have posed a basic methodological question: how do
you know that? And one would have expected a serious review of the
research procedures used to establish the position. But in this case, for
all practical purposes, the argument was accepted on faith alone. The
success of the position has rested largely on ad hominem arguments.
Professor Schmidt, the "noted authority," author of the "profound"
analysis, etc., has said that . . . But the positive ad hominem argument
is just as inadequate as its negative counterpart in that it too avoids
confronting the principal claims with relevant evidence.

There were, from the outset, some features that should have caused
at least some doubt. The views being presented, after all, were those of
the losers in the political struggle. In the course of everyday life, one
does not ordinarily accept one-sided accounts of struggle and contention. When an employer, for example, presents his views on a labor
dispute, one asks to hear the employee's side. In everyday life people
make ready use of phrases expressing this fundamental relativism, as in
the statement that there are two sides to every question.[95]

But in this case, the exiles' account has been taken at face value and
accepted as providing a full and adequate explanation of the causes of

National Socialism. One might consider some parallels. Would one give the same easy assent to White Russian émigré accounts of the bolshevik revolution? Or to the accounts of émigré aristocrats explaining the French Revolution? What of a conference of generals and field marshals, those defeated by Napoleon, meeting sometime prior to the latter's Russian campaign, this to provide the definitive analysis of his military successes? One may surmise that any such attempt would be rejected out-of-hand, as so patently biased and one-sided as not being worthy of attention.

Systems of thought and belief in the Marxian view are seen as partial, as determined, as functions of class position, as having specific social roots, or as serving a group's interests. The assumption of a distinctive lower-middle-class reaction is itself based on such relativistic assumptions. Given the ready reduction of thought—of other people's thought—to its social or economic roots, it comes as something of a surprise that the thought of intellectuals has escaped such critical analysis. Would there be no social determinants in their case? Would there be no partiality? Is one to assume that their's was the only unbiased, the only disinterested analysis available? Why should everyone else be moved by interests and scholars alone be disinterested? Defeated generals can scarcely hide their involvement; they can only attempt to excuse or shift the blame for their failures. The scholars and intellectuals were certainly not, like the generals, at the center of things. But is one to believe, as their analyses would suggest, that they were not somehow or other involved in the events they describe? Would they not have an interest in covering up unpresentable involvements? And would they not, like the generals, have an interest in excusing their failures or in shifting the blame?

In the continuous stream of mutual praise and self-congratulation issued by the scholars themselves and by their devoted followers, such questions are steadfastly avoided. It is a rare occasion when one hears words of criticism such as those offered by Henry Pachter, himself an intellectual and an exile from Hitler's Germany, who declared that "we were a generation of first-class mediocrities. It probably is no exaggeration to say that the myth of the Weimar intellectuals was created by us refugees who needed so much to identify with one element, one memory or assumption of the paradise which had so suddenly been turned into hell."[96]

The history of Weimar Germany, as is well known, was a history of intense and continuous struggle. It was more a struggle of parties than of classes, more a conflict of ideologues than of ordinary citizens. In many instances even, the ordinary citizens, those so summarily categorized and analyzed by party leaders and intellectuals alike, appear to have been seeking to avoid conflict, trying to avoid the damage being done them by those supposedly acting in their interests.

There were some signs in the later history indicating a recognition of this possibility. In the early 1930s, political leaders across the entire spectrum had fought the issues of the day with a high sense of intellectual certainly and an equally high sense of rectitude, the result being the intransigence that contributed so much to the breakdown of normal political processes. In the late forties, many of the same men undertook the construction of a new republic, this time appearing on the scene with remarkably changed outlooks. They were now willing to listen to conflicting viewpoints; they were now anxious to find the workable compromise. It was as if they recognized that they shared some part of the responsibility for the catastrophe. No longer was the government to be brought down over the question of the colors in the flag; the black, red, and gold of Germany's previous democratic effort were accepted with scarcely a word of objection. Major constitutional questions were discussed, arrangements were worked out and accepted, all with remarkable ease as the survivors of Weimar's left, center, and right showed this new-found appreciation of the virtues of compromise.

Once again, Henry Pachter has drawn the lesson. "The great discovery . . ." he said, "was that the dividing line is not between Left and Right but between decent people and political gangsters, between tolerant people and totalitarians."[97] It was a lesson that was prominent in almost everyone's consciousness in the years following World War II. Unfortunately, as the immediate experience with and knowledge of Hitler's Third Reich recede into the past, so too does the significance of that lesson. And regrettably, one again sees the emergence of political gangsterism and the surfacing of totalitarian aspirations in many places throughout the world, this time, to be sure, with changed symbols, with different words and slogans, with a new face.[98] It is as if human beings were condemned to experience such things as a phase in an ever-recurring cycle. There is a task for the genuinely critical intellectual—to break that cycle, to assure a more human course for human affairs.

A. The Reichstag Elections: 1919-1933

For those not familiar with the Weimar history, a brief overview may be helpful. What follows is a very simple sketch of that history, taking it from election to election, with some indication of the principal intervening events. There is nothing new or original in this account; almost everything contained in the following pages is drawn from three of the leading histories of the period.[1] The text of the present work analyzes electoral developments in some of Germany's largest cities. To see where these cities stand in relation to the national trends, some reference point is necessary. The national election results presented in this Appendix provide the basis for such a comparison.

It should be noted that virtually all of the assertions about the general populace contained in this brief sketch constitute unsupported hypotheses. One can establish what happened in a given election (Party A increased its vote, Party B lost some) with relative ease. One can indicate a range of antecedents (the Freikorps "liberated" cities, inflation became serious, a government fell over a given issue), again with relative ease. One can link such events with a given result and claim a causal relationship. Although easily done, it is, in most cases, no more than a plausible assertion. Most narrative histories, for reasons of time and space, list only a handful of prior events. The causal connections are established by assertion rather than by investigation and proof. Lacking the possibility of direct interviewing, there is sometimes little else one can do. It would, nevertheless, be useful to have monographic studies of each of these elections to tie down and establish as much as one can. At minimum, some possibilities could be excluded, and the more probable options could be distinguished from the doubtful ones.

There were nine national legislative elections in the Weimar period. The first of these, on January 19, 1919, actually involved the election of a constitutional assembly. The arrogation of legislative powers by this assembly provided a source of complaint, one of many, for various groups on the right. That election, nevertheless, provided an auspicious beginning for the republic. Coming as it did in very troubled times, after the military collapse, in a period of serious food shortages and unemployment, and less than a fortnight after an uprising of leftist forces,

TABLE A.1. REICHSTAG ELECTION RESULTS, 1919-1933
(in percent)

Party	January 19, 1919	June 6, 1920	May 4, 1924	December 7, 1924	May 20, 1928	September 14, 1930	July 31, 1932	November 6, 1932	March 5, 1933
SPD	37.9	21.7	20.5	26.0	29.8	24.5	21.6	20.4	18.3
USPD	7.6	17.9	0.8	—	—	—	—	—	—
KPD	—	2.1	12.6	9.0	10.6	13.1	14.3	16.9	12.3
Zentrum	19.7	13.6	13.4	13.6	12.1	11.8	12.5	11.9	11.3
DDP	18.6	8.3	5.7	6.3	4.9	3.8	1.0	0.9	0.8
DVP	4.4	13.9	9.2	10.1	8.7	4.5	1.2	1.9	1.1
DNVP	10.3	15.1	19.5	20.5	14.2	7.0	5.9	8.3	8.0
NSDAP	—	—	6.5	3.0	2.6	18.3	37.3	33.1	43.9
Others	1.6	7.4	11.8	11.5	17.1	17.0	6.2	6.5	4.3
Total	100.1	100.0	100.0	100.0	100.0	100.0	100.0	99.9	100.0
Participation	82.7	79.2	77.4	78.8	75.5	82.0	84.0	80.6	88.7

SOURCE: Based on results as given in *Statistisches Jahrbuch für das Deutsche Reich*.

one might have expected a disaster. But as it turned out, the three parties most strongly committed to the new republic, the three that came to be known collectively as the Weimar coalition (Social Democrats, Zentrum, and Democrats) took a very substantial majority of the vote, over three-quarters of the total (see Table A.1). Under the new system of proportional representation that vote very precisely determined party strength in the assembly.

It is not easy to summarize the subsequent ebbs and flows in a party system that contained seven major and a host of minor parties. On first view, there seems to be no pattern whatsoever. On closer inspection, however, one can detect a pattern of waves or shifts. These developments may be summarized as follows:

1920:	bifurcation, shifts to right and left
1924:	conservative reaction, a flow to the right
1928:	a flow to the left
1930 and after:	the flow to the radical right accompanied by a modest shift within the left.

A cautionary note is in order when attempting to interpret these shifts. It is customary to view elections as involving positive choices; people choose parties they like and trust, with the outcome constituting a mandate for the victor, a declaration of approval for its policies. It is useful to bear in mind, especially in the German case, that many voters might view all of the parties negatively, or, at best, with some disdain. Rather than choosing among positive options, they might have been looking for the best available option, or as it is sometimes put, the lesser evil.

It seems likely that many conservative voters shifted to the left in 1919 for just such tactical reasons. Given the discredit in which the traditional right momentarily found itself and given also a widespread fear of communism, many people apparently voted for a best available option. Much of the vote for the left liberal Democrats has been explained in those terms; it was an insurance policy against worse options.[2] Another consideration pressing in the same direction involved the pending settlement of the peace. Were Germany an unambiguous democracy, some thought, the possibility for favorable terms would be enhanced.

The Democrats at that moment provided the best available bourgeois option. There was also, to be sure, the possibility that for some voters this represented a genuine, that is, a positive choice; with the monarchy discredited, by reason of both the collapse and the hasty exile, some voters were indicating a willingness to try the new republic. For most, however, the republic was probably seen as having only a tactical value. With the monarchy gone, the choice, as they saw it, was either the republic or bolshevism. And since, as the adage goes, one cannot fight something with nothing, it was necessary, for the moment at least, to accept the republic as a stopgap arrangement.

Two events appear to have led to the early decimation of the Weimar coalition in the 1920 election. The first of these involved the coalition itself. For many conservative voters, the Social Democratic party was the enemy incarnate. Their 1919 vote for the Democrats had been intended to provide a strong opposition to the Socialists, not a supportive partner in coalition with them. And so, at this point, the tactical Democrats withdrew their support and shifted to the right, turning to the successors of the National Liberal party (now called the German People's party) and the German Conservatives (now called the German National People's party). The former offered a little rhyme, "Von roten Ketten macht Euch frei / Allein die Deutsche Volkspartei" (From red chains make yourself free / Only with the German People's party). The hope for easier peace terms had been dashed; hence the second tactical reason for support of the Democrats had also disappeared.

The Zentrum, a Catholic party formed at the time of Bismarck's *Kulturkampf*, also suffered a considerable loss. Some of this may have been linked to the decline in turnout, the Zentrum traditionally having a reservoir of support that was only mobilized in times of crisis.[3] But another part of the decline was linked to a breakaway having sources very similar to those leading to the Democratic losses. The Zentrum was made up of a broad coalition of forces. It included aristocrats and farmers, businessmen both big and small, white-collar employees, and working-class populations. Holding them together was their concern with the church, almost all of the Zentrum's voters being practicing Catholics.

The party's leadership, prior to the war, had come largely from big business and aristocratic circles. Because of the malapportioned districts, most of its Reichstag members came from the Catholic countryside. Under the new proportional representation system, however, its electoral base was now located in the urban industrial districts, and the Catholic trade unions accordingly demanded a much larger share of party offices. Then, too, for various tactical reasons, the party had joined the Weimar coalition. Conservative Catholics found the company of the Socialists and the resulting policies uncongenial. In Bavaria this led to a defection; the conservative aristocracy, business, and farm populations removed themselves from the Zentrum to form an independent party, the Bavarian People's party. It was this defection, largely, that accounted for the Zentrum losses. If the defection had not occurred, and if all the BVP voters had remained with the Zentrum, it would have had 17.8 percent of the total vote. As it was, however, 4.2 percent of the voters supported the BVP, and in Table A.1 they are counted among the "others."

Much had transpired in the year and a half since the first of the elections. The Versailles treaty had been signed with Germany forced to accept war guilt, enormous reparations, the occupation of large parts of its territory, and the loss of other territories.[4] Unemployment still ran high, and inflation was steadily growing. The most serious event of all was the Kapp *Putsch* in March of 1920, an attempt on the part of some rightists to topple the new regime. A general strike was called and within a few days the entire attempt collapsed.

During this time, however, the Communists had made use of the events for their ends, taking over several Ruhr cities to establish their own rule. The Reichswehr was sent in, and, with considerable bloodshed, the hegemony of the government was reestablished. This appears to have generated a left reaction, the main beneficiary at this point being the Independent Social Democratic party. The Independents were a loose coalition of left forces which at this moment had the advantage of being a third party, that is, the one party of the left having no responsibility for either the Communist insurgency or the counter to that attempt. Many working-class voters, it would seem, chose the USPD as their best available option on the left.

One other observation is worth emphasizing at this point. The combined left vote in 1919, some of which was probably tactical, amounted to 45.5 percent of the total. Tactical voting had probably diminished by 1920 at which time the total left vote was 41.7 percent. That level was *never* surpassed in any of the subsequent elections, not in the left wave of 1928 or in the elections of the 1930s. Many of the left voters of 1919 and 1920, in short, never returned to those parties.[5] For all the talk about the role of conditions found in Marxist literature, none of the later conditions was sufficient to make good the losses, let alone to allow gains.

The end result of these left and right shifts was that the share of the vote given to the three parties of the Weimar coalition fell from 76.2 percent to 43.6 percent.

The four governments that existed in this brief span had all been headed by Social Democrats. Hermann Müller, who headed the last of these governments, was asked to form a new one, but at this point the balance of advantage appeared to have changed. The Social Democrats saw their losses as stemming from the responsibilities of office and drew the lesson that the Independent Socialists, the second largest party in the Reichstag, must also participate in this government; otherwise the SPD would continue to decline. But the Independents, confirmed oppositionalists, refused the offer. As a consequence, the next government was formed by the Zentrum and included the right liberal German People's party. It was, of course, a minority government with its success dependent on toleration by the Social Democrats. With the exception of the second Müller government of June 1928, all subsequent governments prior to 1932 were coalitions headed by center or right leaders. In some of these the right parties were out and the Social Democrats in, as with the Stresemann government. Otherwise the SPD was out, either tolerating or opposing, and the Conservatives were in.

The Social Democratic governments, despite the longstanding promises, had socialized nothing. This was a source of disappointment for many workers who found their lives only little different from conditions in the old regime.[6] Some writers have viewed the social or welfare accomplishments of the Weimar coalition as essentially nonexistent. The Social Democratic governments had, however, established the eight-hour day (which was later abandoned). They had introduced the system of shop councils (Betriebsräte) and later in 1927 had adopted an expanded system of unemployment insurance.

The Social Democrats were in a very difficult position in the later years of the republic. Suffering some embarrassment over the failure to socialize (and regularly attacked by their left competitors on this score), they were forced to defend these other accomplishments with almost fetishistic intensity. When the crisis came in 1930 and with both the center and the right intent on reducing the costs of the unemployment insurance system, the Social Democratic position was one of uncompromising refusal.

It is difficult to summarize the tumultuous events of 1920 and 1924. The period saw two Communist uprisings. There was a plebiscite in Silesia to determine national boundaries. There was armed struggle there between Poles and the Freikorps. The leader of the Zentrum, Matthias Erzberger, was murdered by rightists. Germany surprised the world by signing a mutual aid treaty with the Soviet Union. A few months later the foreign minister, Walther Rathenau, was assassinated. In January of 1923 the French and Belgians occupied the Ruhr. The German government declared "passive resistance" while paramilitary forces undertook more active efforts. The most immediate consequence was that the moderate inflation of the previous years became the runaway inflation so well documented in the history books. Recognizing the inevitable, Stresemann ended the passive resistance in September of that year.

There were complicated struggles involving Socialist-Communist coalition governments in Saxony and Thuringia and the rightist government of Bavaria. Hitler's Putsch attempt came on the ninth of November in 1923. The new currency was introduced on the fifteenth of that month. On the twenty-second, the Social Democrats brought down the

Stresemann government over the Saxony and Thuringia questions. In March of 1924 the Reichstag was dissolved. This time the problem was the Social Democratic refusal to support use of a presidential decree that threatened the eight-hour law. In the course of the following election campaign, the Dawes Committee issued its report on reparations, and the German government accepted its terms. The Conservatives objected strongly.

Again the election showed a very clear lesson. Those parties in the government or even near it, as in the case of the Social Democrats, suffered losses. The parties of the original Weimar coalition were now down to 39.6 percent of the total. Stresemann's party also suffered a considerable loss. The big gains were made by the Conservatives and by the National Socialist-Völkische (anti-Semitic) coalition. Together they had over one-quarter of all the votes.

Two changes occurred on the left. There was, as mentioned earlier, a considerable decline in overall left support, its vote falling from 41.7 to 34.9 percent. And within the left a shift in strength had occurred. The Independents had dissolved (leaving only a splinter behind) with some supporters going over to the Communists (KPD) and some returning to the SPD. Most of the followers clearly chose to go with the Communists although some of this support, as we shall see, was short-lived, suggesting again the lack of a better alternative.

The most significant political development in the immediately following months was the implementation of the Dawes recommendations. This required constitutional changes and hence a two-thirds vote in the Reichstag. Had the Conservatives been true to their words, they (together with the Communists) could have blocked the entire proposal. But on the day of the vote, the party divided with the ideological wing remaining true to principle and the practical wing voting for what seemed the only viable course for the nation at that moment. An effort was undertaken to broaden the basis of the government in the month that followed, this to provide the support needed for Stresemann's foreign policy initiatives. The effort failed, and new elections were set for early December.

One might have anticipated a loss for the DNVP after this rather dramatic exposure. It nevertheless showed a slight gain, reaching its highest point in the fourteen years of the republic. On the whole, however, the December 1924 election indicated a relaxation of tensions. The parties of the Weimar coalition together with Stresemann's party showed slight gains. The National Socialist-Völkische coalition lost more than half its strength. And on the left, the Communists lost over a quarter of their May 1924 strength, most of this apparently going to the Social Democrats. A period of relative tranquillity had begun in Germany.[7]

Friedrich Ebert died in February 1925, and the first presidential election of the Weimar Republic followed with former Field Marshal Paul von Hindenburg, the idol of conservatives and nationalists, becoming his successor. The political situation was relatively calm for four or five years, first under the governments of Hans Luther (no party) and then under those of Wilhelm Marx (Zentrum). Stresemann was foreign minister throughout, negotiating first the Locarno treaty and then, in a related move, bringing Germany into the League of Nations. The domestic issues of the period seem rather insignificant when compared to those fought earlier; they were, nevertheless, carried on with much the same intensity, as for example in the question of the colors to be used in the merchant marine flag (whether the black-white-red of the kaiser's empire or black-red-gold of the republic). This issue brought down the Luther government. An issue of confessional schools was sufficient to cause the fall of the Marx government in the spring of 1928. A related matter, one that figured prominently in the May election campaign involved the question of funds for a pocket battleship.[8]

The May 1928 election brought gains for both parties of the left and losses for all other major parties. The splinter parties appeared on the scene at this point with 17.1 percent of the total, much of this being the vote for a rightist free enterprise party which in English has been referred to as the Economic party and the Business party. The most serious losses were suffered by the Democrats and by the Conservatives. Both parties, accordingly, undertook intense discussions of the problem, and both made fatal decisions with respect to party reform (see Chapter 10 for details).

The next government was formed by Social Democrat Hermann Müller. It was a "great" (that is, large) coalition government, containing Social Democrats and People's party ministers. The Conservatives, now in opposition, demagogically labeled it a left government and made it the object of serious attack.

The terms of the reparations payments were revised, this time by the Young Plan, with Stresemann again conducting Germany's negotiations. This plan was the object of an immense campaign which brought together the forces of the Conservatives, a large veterans' organization (the Stahlhelm), and the National Socialists. It was during the period of this campaign that the NSDAP experienced its electoral takeoff (again see Chapter 10 for the details).

The depression came at about this point, unemployment reaching crisis levels in the spring and summer of 1930. The National Socialists (and their Conservative allies) attacked both the republic and the governing parties with the following themes: the stab in the back, the treason that ended the war and brought down the Kaiserreich; the Versailles settlement that accepted German war guilt and imposed the monumental reparations payments; government by Marxists in combination with weak and incompetent bourgeois parties; Marxist violence in the streets threatening the entire German society and culture; the instablility and bickering by the governing parties; corruption in government, scandals, and party preferment; Jewish involvement in all of the above; and finally, the incapacity of the government to deal with the economic crisis. To summarize these problems, they referred to "the system," to the entire package, which they intended to destroy and replace.

The Müller government fell in March of 1930, the specific issue involving the deficit in the unemployment insurance fund. Business groups wished to reduce the level of payments. The Social Democrats sought to increase employer contributions. The great coalition government fell, and the first of the Brüning governments took its place.[9]

Lacking a wide base of support, Brüning had to rely more than his predecessors on government by presidential decree. In the wake of a discussion of his government's economic measures, Brüning was defeated by a vote of 256 to 193, with Social Democrats, Conservatives, Communists, and National Socialists forming the antigovernment majority. That evening, his proposals were instituted by presidential decree under the constitution's Article 48. It was the first time, as Halperin puts it, that "the principle of ministerial responsibility had been violated."[10] Two days later, the Social Democrats introduced a motion, which also carried, calling for the abrogation of these decrees, this to preserve democracy and the parliamentary system, and to prevent presidential rule. Brüning, in what was perhaps the most questionable government decision of the entire period, dissolved the Reichstag and set new elections for September 1930. Given the results of recent state elections, it was clear that the National Socialists would make considerable gains.

The outcome was a disaster for the center parties. The National Socialists took 18.3 percent of the vote, most of that coming from the so-called middle-class parties. The Social Democrats lost some votes to the Communists. The splinter parties remained at a high 17.0 percent. The end result was that Brüning had to make even greater use of presidential decrees over the next months. The economic crisis continued to worsen—in no small part because of Brüning's deflationary policies. National Socialist growth continued, as indicated in state and local elections.

In 1932 five major elections occurred, beginning with two rounds of the presidential contest. Hindenburg won a slight majority in the second round against the strong Hitler candidacy. A state election in Prussia followed, one that allowed a reading of public sentiment as of April.

The National Socialists came in very strong at this point. In May, Hindenburg dismissed Brüning and brought in the nonparty government of Franz von Papen. The latter called new elections, these being set for July 31. In this election the National Socialists gained the highest percentage they ever took prior to Hitler's coming to power, 37.3, approximately three-eighths of the total. The parties of the Weimar coalition, which had gained three-quarters of the vote in January of 1919, had only 35.1 percent. The right and left liberal parties were the major losers, each with only 1 percent of the total. The Communists and National Socialists together had over half of the seats in the Reichstag. The Conservatives could also be counted on for support in any antirepublican maneuvers.

Just before this election, the Communists and National Socialists in Prussia had cooperated in a successful vote of no confidence against the Braun government. Since these two parties were not able to form an alternative government, Braun's Social Democratic-Zentrum government continued in office until mid-July when, following an incident of Communist-National Socialist street violence, Papen dissolved that government, making use of exceptional powers and naming his supporters to all key positions there.

Still lacking a parliamentary basis for his rule, Papen again dissolved the Reichstag and set elections for November. At this point, the Conservatives and National Socialists had a falling out. The National Socialists stressed, for the moment, their left direction and were sharper than usual in their hostility to the plutocrats. Hitler's party suffered some loss in this election, the gains on the right being made by the Conservatives and, to a trivial degree, by the People's party. On the left some shift from Social Democrats to Communists was again in evidence.

Hindenburg dropped Papen and replaced him with a rather notorious intriguer, Kurt von Schleicher. His government was short-lived, and on January 30, 1933, it was replaced by Hitler's government, initially in a coalition with the Conservatives.

New elections were again called. Just before the election the Reichstag building was set afire. The National Socialists declared the Communists responsible and proceeded to arrest leaders of that party as well as some Social Democrats. With the National Socialists in control of the police throughout the Reich and now using the SA (Sturmabteilung) as police auxiliaries, the March 1933 election was not exactly a free contest. Even then, however, they fell short of the majority they had so long sought.

In the months that followed, the dictatorship was consolidated, the remaining parties dissolved, and the institutions of the republic dismantled.

B. Germany's Largest Cities: Population (1933), Religion (1933), and National Socialist Percentage (July 1932)

City	Population	Protestant	Catholic	Jewish	Without Affiliation	NSDAP Percentage
1. Berlin[a]	4,242,501	71.1%	10.4%	3.8%	14.2%	29
2. Hamburg[a]	1,129,307	77.4	5.3	1.5	15.6	33
3. Cologne[a]	756,605	19.6	75.3	2.0	2.9	24
4. Munich[a]	735,388	15.2	81.1	1.2	1.3	29
5. Leipzig	713,470	77.9	3.6	1.6	14.3	32
6. Essen[a]	654,461	40.9	54.0	0.7	4.2	24
7. Dresden	642,143	83.7	5.9	0.7	8.7	38
8. Breslau	625,198	59.6	31.5	3.2	4.8	43
9. Frankfurt a.M.[a]	555,857	57.2	33.1	4.7	4.4	39
10. Dortmund[a]	540,875	53.6	40.0	0.8	5.3	20
11. Düsseldorf[a]	498,600	31.5	61.2	1.0	6.1	29
12. Hanover[a]	443,920	80.9	10.6	1.1	6.3	40
13. Duisburg[a]	440,419	42.7	51.7	0.6	4.8	27
14. Stuttgart[a]	415,028	74.6	20.2	1.1	3.9	27
15. Nuremberg[a]	410,438	62.7	32.1	1.8	1.6	38
16. Wuppertal[a]	408,602	70.1	20.3	0.6	8.8	43
17. Chemnitz	350,734	86.0	3.7	0.7	9.1	42
18. Gelsenkirchen	332,545	47.6	47.9	0.5	3.9	23
19. Bremen	323,331	84.7	6.6	0.4	7.3	30
20. Königsberg in Pr.	315,794	91.3	5.2	1.0	2.3	44
21. Bochum	314,546	55.5	40.1	0.4	3.7	29
22. Magdeburg	306,894	83.3	4.9	0.6	9.5	38
23. Mannheim[a]	275,162	50.2	41.2	2.3	4.5	29
24. Stettin	270,747	89.9	3.8	0.9	4.5	42
25. Altona	241,970	83.4	4.8	0.8	10.9	38
26. Kiel	218,335	87.0	4.8	0.2	7.8	46
27. Halle a.S.	209,169	88.8	4.6	0.5	6.0	41
28. Oberhausen	192,345	37.1	60.0	0.3	2.5	25
29. Augsburg	176,575	18.9	79.0	0.6	1.3	23
30. Kassel	175,179	87.7	8.5	1.3	2.4	43

Source: *Statistik des Deutschen Reichs*, vol. 451, pt. 1. The NSDAP percentages are from Samuel A. Pratt, "The Social Basis of Nazism and Communism in Urban Germany," M.A. thesis, Michigan State College, 1948, pp. 270-275.
[a] Indicates the cities studied in some detail in this work.

C. Occupational Structures of the Cities Studied in Chapters 4–8

(in percent)

Occupations of Economically Active Persons	Berlin	Hamburg	Cologne	Munich	Essen
Males					
Independents	14.2	15.9	14.8	18.1	8.4
Civil servants	8.3	6.4	8.2	13.9	5.1
White-collar employees	21.9	23.8	20.9	18.7	15.8
Workers	55.0	53.6	55.3	49.2	70.0
Domestic servants	0.1	a	a	0.1	0.1
Helper (in family firm)	0.5	0.3	0.8	0.1	0.6
Females					
Independents	7.4	8.4	7.5	9.2	7.5
Civil servants	1.9	1.9	2.6	2.3	2.2
White-collar employees	27.9	30.3	29.1	27.1	30.3
Workers	38.5	29.7	28.7	30.8	25.1
Domestic servants	18.9	22.9	25.3	25.6	27.4
Helper (in family firm)	5.4	6.8	6.8	5.0	7.5

	Dortmund	Düsseldorf	Duisberg	Wuppertal	Frankfurt
Males					
Independents	9.0	13.5	7.8	15.3	16.6
Civil servants	5.7	6.8	5.5	6.5	8.5
White-collar employees	14.0	21.4	14.3	16.9	23.9
Workers	70.6	57.5	71.9	60.4	50.2
Domestic servants	a	a	a	a	0.1
Helper (in family firms)	0.7	0.8	0.6	0.8	0.8
Females					
Independents	7.9	6.9	7.2	6.7	6.6
Civil servants	2.2	1.9	2.3	1.5	2.3
White-collar employees	27.9	31.8	26.7	23.9	29.2
Workers	22.1	24.2	21.4	41.0	28.2
Domestic servants	30.0	27.4	33.6	19.6	26.6
Helper (in family firms)	9.8	7.8	8.7	7.4	7.1

	Hanover	Stuttgart	Nuremberg	Mannheim
Males				
Independents	14.4	16.5	15.6	14.0
Civil servants	10.1	11.0	10.8	8.0
White-collar employees	21.7	21.7	18.3	22.7
Workers	53.1	49.8	54.7	54.4
Domestic servants	a	a	a	a
Helper (in family firm)	0.6	1.0	0.5	0.8
Females				
Independents	7.4	6.9	7.4	7.2
Civil servants	1.9	2.5	2.6	2.1
White-collar employees	26.3	24.7	22.5	29.6
Workers	33.3	29.1	41.6	31.4
Domestic servants	24.0	29.5	19.8	22.3
Helper (in family firm)	7.1	7.4	6.2	7.4

Source: *Statistik des Deutschen Reichs*, vol. 457, "Volks-, Berufs-, und Betriebszählung vom 16. Juni 1933," "Berufszählung: Die berufliche und soziale Gliederung der Bevölkerung in den grossstädten," Berlin, 1936.

Note: Because of rounding, percentages do not necessarily add to 100.

a Less than 0.05 percent.

ONE. THE PROBLEM

1. The best account of the second step, the work of the coterie of intriguers, is to be found in Karl Dietrich Bracher, *Die Auflösung der Weimarer Republik*, Villingen/Schwarzwald: Ring-Verlag, 1964, pp. 707 ff.

2. Theodor Geiger, "Panik im Mittelstand," *Die Arbeit*, 7 (1930): 637-654.

3. See Seymour Martin Lipset, *Political Man; The Social Bases of Politics*, Garden City: Doubleday, 1960, especially ch. 5 entitled " 'Fascism'—Left, Right, and Center." See also Richard F. Hamilton, *Restraining Myths; Critical Studies of U.S. Social Structure and Politics*, New York: Sage-Halsted-Wiley, 1975, chs. 2 and 3.

TWO. A REVIEW OF THE LITERATURE

1. The full name of the party was Nationalsozialistische Deutsche Arbeiterpartei (National Socialist German Workers' party). Throughout this work this will be abbreviated to National Socialists or more simply to NSDAP.

2. "The Psychology of Hitlerism," *Political Quarterly*, 4 (1933): 373-384.

3. Lasswell did have access to some studies when writing this article. In a letter to this author (January 16, 1976), he states: "The best data . . . I saw in Germany was in the hands of the Police Institute in Charlottenburg. Very competent social scientists (usually sociologists and social psychologists) made studies of the Nazis from the earliest years of the movement to 1932, which was the last year that I saw the files and summaries." His notes on these studies were destroyed in an accident.

The focus of these studies—whether on leaders, members, audiences at meetings, or voters—is not clear, nor is it clear how the evidence was gathered. Representative sample surveys seem highly unlikely, very few of them having been done by any researchers in the period; none of them, to my knowledge, contained a question on party choice. If the Police Institute researches were done through participation or observational approaches, the standard problem of ascertaining frequencies would arise. One must consider the case of the observer at a National Socialist meeting where some thousand persons were present. How does he (or she) establish the occupational backgrounds of the audience? And, more important, moving to a central claim in the Lasswell quotation, how is it established that "psychologically speaking . . . the lower middle class was increasingly overshadowed" or that "emotional insecurities" were precipitated in their personalities?

4. Alan Bullock, *Hitler: A Study in Tyranny*, rev. ed., New York: Harper & Row, 1964, p. 45.

5. Ibid., p. 37.

6. Ibid., p. 68.

7. Ibid., pp. 152, 153.

8. Ibid., p. 159.

9. Ibid., pp. 171-175.

10. The quotations appear on pp. 366-367 of his chapter "Germany: Changing Patterns and Lasting Problems," pp. 354-392 of Sigmund Neumann, ed., *Modern Political Parties: Approaches to Comparative Politics*, Chicago: University of Chicago Press, 1956. The second account referred to is his chapter on Germany, pp. 323-451 of Taylor Cole, ed., *European Political Systems*, New York: Alfred A. Knopf, 1961. Both works, incidentally, contain general bibliographies. The problem is the lack of specific supporting references.

11. For a more limited sampling, see Barrington Moore, *Social Origins of Dictatorship and Democracy*, Boston: Beacon Press, 1966, p. 448; Ernst Nolte, *Three Faces of Fascism*, New York: Holt, Rinehart and Winston, 1966, pp. 298, 313-314, and 322; S. William Halperin, *Germany Tried Democracy: A Political History of the Reich from 1918 to 1933*, New York: Norton, 1965, pp. 405-406; Kurt Sontheimer, *The Government and Politics of West Germany*, London: Hutchinson University Library, 1972, p. 12; Hajo Holborn, *A History of Modern Germany: 1840-1945*, New York: Alfred A. Knopf, 1969, pp. 722-723.

12. Kornhauser, *The Politics of Mass Society*, Glencoe: The Free Press, 1959, p. 162. In the text, the reference is to Pratt, 1936. In the bibliography the reference is to Pratt, 1938. In fact, it is Pratt, 1948. See note 38, this chapter, for the complete reference and note 42 for comment on the point about unemployed white-collar workers.

13. Kornhauser, *The Politics of Mass Society*, p. 162. And, Evelyn Anderson, *Hammer or Anvil: The Story of the German Working-Class Movement*, London: Victor Gollancz, 1945, p. 137.

14. Kornhauser, *The Politics of Mass Society*, p. 162.

15. "The Nazification of the Lower Middle Class and Peasants," pp. 576-594 of International Council for Philosophy and Humanistic Studies (no editor named), *The Third Reich*, London: Weidenfeld and Nicolson, 1955. An American edition of this work was brought out by Praeger in the same year.

16. The articles cited by Schweitzer appeared as chapters 3 and 4 of Rudolf Heberle's *From Democracy to Nazism*, Baton Rouge: Louisiana State University Press, 1945. This volume is a very much shortened version of a manuscript Heberle completed in the fall of 1934. The full version was not published until nearly thirty years later; this is his *Landbevölkerung und Nationalsozialismus: Eine soziologische Untersuchung der politischen Willensbildung in Schleswig-Holstein 1918 bis 1932*, Stuttgart: Deutsche Verlags-Anstalt, 1963.

In the light of Kornhauser's stress on uprootedness and anomie, on the "mass society" as providing the conditions for extremist social movements, it is of some interest to note Heberle's description of an area of small farming. There, he reports, "class distinctions are scarcely noticeable, and a spirit of neighborliness and true community prevails. . . . It was here on the *Geest* that the Nazi party . . . scored its greatest successes." *From Democracy to Nazism*, p. 39.

17. Kornhauser, *The Politics of Mass Society*, p. 203.

18. Ibid., p. 204.

19. The sources discussed in the above paragraphs are: Peter Gay, *The Di-*

lemma of Democratic Socialism, New York: Columbia University Press, 1952, pp. 210-211; and Rudolf Küstermeier, *Die Mittelschichten und ihr politischer Weg*, Potsdam: Alfred Protte, 1933, p. 45.

Kornhauser cites Franz Neumann with respect to the membership trends (i.e. his *European Trade Unionism and Politics*, New York: League for Industrial Democracy, 1936, p. 20). Neumann is accurately cited in that he provides a couple of brief paragraphs indicating the decline of the Social Democratic union and the growth of the conservative nationalist one.

A more comprehensive presentation by Heinz Hamm yields a rather different picture. All three organizations registered membership gains in the period from 1926 to 1930. The conservative union gained 39 percent, the democratic centrist union, 21 percent, and the Social Democratic one, 15 percent. But most of that difference had been achieved in the period 1926-1928. Between 1928 and 1930, the growth of all three, understandably, tapered off. In that period, moreover, the pattern of growth reversed, the respective percentages for the three unions being 5, 9, and 12.

Another difficulty with the Kornhauser-Gay position arises from the easy assumption that the political motive determined the choice of organization. There is, however, another easy possibility, one noted in passing by Hamm (p. 40) who suggests some of the growth of the conservative organization resulted from its good health insurance program. See Heinz Hamm, *Die wirtschaftlichen und sozialen Berufsmerkmale der kaufmännischen Angestellten (im Vergleich mit denjenigen der Arbeiter)*, Borna-Leipzig; Universitätsverlag von Robert Noske, 1931 (originally a doctoral dissertation, University of Jena). The percentages are calculated from the membership figures given on p. 41. Another very useful account is that provided by Fritz Fischer, *Die Angestellten, ihre Bewegung und ihre Ideologien*, Wertheim a.M.; E. Bechstein, 1932 (originally a doctoral dissertation, University of Heidelberg). Also of considerable importance for its discussion of the nonideological advantages of the largest organization in the conservative national federation is the work by Iris Hamel, *Völkischer Verband und nationale Gewerkschaft: Der Deutschnationale Handlungsgehilfen-Verband, 1893-1933*, Frankfurt: Europäische Verlagsanstalt, 1967.

20. Kornhauser, *The Politics of Mass Society*, pp. 198, 201, and 210-211.

21. Karl Dietrich Bracher, *The German Dictatorship: The Origins, Structure, and Effects of National Socialism*, New York: Praeger, 1970, pp. 152-155. The original is entitled *Die deutsche Diktatur: Entstehung, Struktur, Folgen des Nationalsozialismus*, Cologne-Berlin: Kiepenheuer & Witsch, 1969.

22. The DHV was the largest of the white-collar unions in the conservative nationalist federation mentioned in the Kornhauser discussion. It provided a majority of the federation's members.

The point about middle-class distress seems so obvious as to scarcely need any support; it is, however, one of those claims that has gained acceptance through a steady recital rather than through presentation of evidence. One leading source on the subject has calculated the trends in real incomes with 1929 as the base point (equal to 100). By 1932, the real incomes of workers had fallen to 93. The real income of employees, on the other hand, had increased to 113.

The real income of civil servants, who had suffered some cuts, was 102. The explanation is rather simple: price levels fell more rapidly than salaries; hence, those who were still employed experienced absolute increases in their living standards. See J. Heinz Müller, *Nivellierung und Differenzierung der Arbeitseinkommen in Deutschland seit 1925*, Berlin: Duncker und Humblot, 1954, p. 140.

23. The memoir referred to is Albert Krebs, *Tendenzen und Gestalten der NSDAP: Erinnerungen an die Frühzeit der Partei*, Stuttgart: Deutsche Verlags-Anstalt, 1959. Unlike Bracher, Krebs stresses the limited influence of the DHV, saying it dealt with only a "small part" of the population (p. 20). On the links between the party and the union and for a discussion of some of the complexities of the relationship, see p. 25. For the National Socialists' suspicions of Krebs as working for DHV interests, see p. 91. Another useful account, one also showing the complexities of the relationship between the DVH and the NSDAP, is that of Larry Eugene Jones, "Between the Fronts: The German National Union of Commercial Employees from 1928 to 1933," *Journal of Modern History*, 48 (1976): 462–482.

The NSDAP attempted to take over the DHV in 1929, but this effort was successfully fought off. The DHV leaders were able to maintain the organization's integrity until after the takeover, this being indicated by their support of Brüning in 1930 and, more important, of Hindenburg in 1932. Expulsions followed in the course of the rivalry between the two, many NSDAP members being forced out during the presidential election. See Krebs, *Tendenzen und Gestalten*, ch. 2.

The DHV was the largest of the white-collar unions; it was not, however, a "typical case." Some white-collar workers, as noted above, were organized into the democratic union of salaried employees, the Gewerkschaftsbund der Angestellten, which in 1931 had 327,000 members. Another 203,000 were members of the Allgemeiner Freie Angestellten-Bund, which was allied with the Socialists. In addition, 125,000 foremen and 62,000 technicians were organized in Socialist unions. These figures come from Franz Neumann, *European Trade Unionism*, p. 20. Neumann gives a 1931 membership figure for the DHV of 409,000. It is difficult to see how the DHV case comes to be "typical."

24. The National Socialists did in fact attempt to take over farm organizations (and other trade and professional associations). Some evidence on the Schleswig-Holstein experience may be found in Gerhard Stoltenberg, *Politische Strömungen im schleswig-holsteinischen Landvolk 1918-1933*, Düsseldorf: Droste Verlag, 1962, pp. 138 ff.; and in Timothy Alan Tilton, *Nazism, Neo-Nazism, and the Peasantry*, Bloomington: Indiana University Press, 1975, pp. 68-69.

The causal linkages, it will be noted, are not established by the fact of a takeover. The latter may be easily accomplished through superior organization (especially against rather inept incumbents; see Stoltenberg, *Politische Strömungen*, pp. 138-139 on this point). That could then indicate a coup rather than an election based on a groundswell of support. If a coup, it does not necessarily follow that the use of the "organizational weapon" would yield the desired result, influence and votes. One must ask about the extent of coverage (how many farmers were members?) and about the closeness of contact between organization and members. The same result, a substantial increase in votes for the party, might be obtained through other channels, such as direct campaigning in farm communities. The linkage of organization takeover and subsequent voting change, in other words, might involve a *post hoc–propter hoc* error.

One glides easily from discussion of "farm organizations" to consideration of "the farmers." It seems likely, following the tendencies discovered elsewhere, that membership would vary with income. In depressed times, membership would probably fall off, especially among the poorer farmers, thus reducing the range of the organization's influence. It would also mean that to the extent that the organization's behavior "reflected" member sentiment, it would reflect the sentiment of the better-off farmers. There is, finally, no need to think in either/ or terms since both organizational domination and grass roots campaigning may have been operating, both processes possibly contributing to the National Socialists' electoral success. For further discussion of the farm regions see Chapters 3 and 13.

25. Bracher, *The German Dictatorship*, pp. 155-156. Evidence on working-class membership in the party is discussed later in the present chapter. The voting in working-class districts is considered in Chapters 4-8.

26. Ibid., p. 157.

27. Theodor Geiger, *Die soziale Schichtung des deutschen Volkes: Soziographischer Versuch auf statistischer Grundlage*, Stuttgart: Ferdinand Enke Verlag, 1932. The discussion of National Socialism and the middle class appears on pp. 109-122. The discussion of the mentalities contains a rich array of observations about the classes of German society. The richness and detail suggest that Geiger was in fact a very conscientious observer of the German scene. But, by themselves, those observations may be taken as no more than suggestive hypotheses.

28. Villingen/Schwarzwald: Ring-Verlag, 1964. My remarks refer to the following discussions: (1) pp. 106-127 where he first discusses the NSDAP at length, (2) pp. 150-173 where the crisis of the middle class is discussed, and (3) pp. 648-656 where the electoral developments from 1928 to November 1932 are reviewed. The last proves of little value. He presents the election results in what must be described as an "odd lot" collection of localities and sets those results next to figures showing the industrial and occupational composition in these settings. There is no compelling evidence about the voting patterns of the lower middle class to be found in these pages.

29. In addition to sources presenting no evidence at all (see note 11, this chapter), many sources offer references to works that in turn contain no evidence, again offering only assertion. In, for example, the work of Svend Ranulf, *Moral Indignation and Middle Class Psychology: A Sociological Study*, New York: Schocken Books, 1964, (1st ed., 1938), we learn that "Nazism is the psychological reaction of [the] lower middle class to the recent economic depression which in Germany also brought about a recrudescence of the bitter memories of the last war" (p. 9). This conclusion depends on quotations from Geiger's *Die soziale Schichtung*; Frederick L. Schuman's *The Nazi Dictatorship: A Study in Social Pathology and the Politics of Fascism*, New York: Alfred A. Knopf, 1935; and Lasswell's "The Psychology of Hitlerism." See also Erich Fromm's much

discussed work, *Escape from Freedom*, New York: Rinehart, 1941. The standard allegations about the lower middle class appear on pp. 184-185, 219-220, and elsewhere. One such statement (on p. 211) does have supporting references—to Harold Lasswell once again and to Frederick L. Schuman. Elsewhere Fromm cites Ranulf. Of some interest is a footnote reference to a larger study (p. 212). This reads: "The view presented here is based on the results of an unpublished study of the 'Character of German Workers and Employees in 1929/1930.' . . . Analysis of the responses of six hundred persons to a detailed questionnaire showed that *a minority* of the respondents exhibited the authoritarian character, that *with about the same number* the quest for freedom and independence was prevalent, while the great majority exhibited a less clear-cut mixture of different traits" (emphasis added). No other information or results from this study is presented in Fromm's work.

30. The quotations cited to this point appear in Lipset, *Political Man: The Social Bases of Politics*, Garden City: Doubleday, 1960, pp. 133 and 140.

31. The shift from Prussian to German conservatism is covered in Hans Booms, *Die Deutschkonservative Partei*, Düsseldorf: Droste Verlag, 1954, pp. 5-13. He shows that the latter never successfully transcended the boundaries of east elbian Prussia. For the early history of the Deutschnationale Volkspartei, see Werner Liebe, *Die Deutschnationale Volkspartei, 1918-1924*, Düsseldorf: Droste Verlag, 1956; and Lewis Hertzman, *DNVP: Right-Wing Opposition in the Weimar Republic, 1918-1924*, Lincoln: University of Nebraska Press, 1963.

For a comprehensive overview of the parties in both Reich and republic, see Ludwig Bergstrasser, *Geschichte der politischen Parteien in Deutschland*, 10th ed., Munich: Gunter Olzog Verlag, 1960. And also for Weimar, see Sigmund Neumann, *Die deutschen Parteien: Wesen und Wandel nach dem Kriege*, 2d. ed., Berlin: Junker und Dünnhaupt, 1932.

32. These figures are taken from Alfred Milatz, "Das Ende der Parteien im Spiegel der Wahlen 1930 bis 1933," pp. 743-793 of Erich Matthias and Rudolf Morsey, eds., *Das Ende der Parteien 1933*, Düsseldorf: Droste Verlag, 1960, p. 772.

33. Heberle, *From Democracy to Nazism*, pp. 1 and 4. As it stands, Heberle's judgment is also unsupported assertion (as are the Vogel and Haungs and the Mellen citations in the following text and in note 35, this chapter). But their conclusions, unlike Lipset's, are generally supported by the evidence drawn from German cities in the Weimar period (reported in Chapters 4-8).

34. Reinhard Behrens, "Die Deutschnationalen in Hamburg, 1918-1933," doctoral dissertation, University of Hamburg, 1973.

35. Berhard Vogel and Peter Haungs, *Wahlkampf und Wählertradition: Eine Studie zur Bundestagswahl von 1961*, Cologne/Opladen: Westdeutscher Verlag, 1965, pp. 101, 135. Another source refers to the prewar Conservatives as "primarily a Prussian Junker party" and the National Liberals as "the party of the wealthy middle class . . . their members included many of the leading industrialists." Speaking of the postwar period, this source declares that the German National People's party "continued as the representative of the great landowners (together with the conservative Protestant peasantry)." It did have an urban

following, this source indicating that "some wealthy urban groups and nationalistic intellectuals and civil servants" also supported that party. It was the People's party (DVP), however, that "became the party of big industry and finance; it, of course, had numerous supporters among the lower middle classes but the party's policies were largely determined by its industrialist leaders." From Sydney L.W. Mellen, "The German People and the Postwar World," *American Political Science Review*, 37 (1943): 604, 609.

On the Deutsche Volkspartei, see the article by Hans Booms, "Die Deutsche Volkspartei," pp. 523-539 of Matthias and Morsey, *Ende der Parteien*. An extremely important source is Henry Ashby Turner, Jr., *Stresemann and the Politics of the Weimar Republic*, Princeton: Princeton University Press, 1963. See also Wolfgang Hartenstein, *Die Anfänge der Deutschen Volkspartei 1918-1920*, Düsseldorf: Droste Verlag, 1962; and Lothar Döhn, *Politik und Interesse: Die Interessenstruktur der Deutschen Volkspartei*, Meisenheim am Glan: Verlag Anton Hain, 1970. See also the discussion in Chapter 10.

36. Henry Ashby Turner, Jr., "Big Business and the Rise of Hitler," *American Historical Review*, 75 (1969-1970): 56-70. The quotation appears on p. 60. On the transformations of the DNVP, see Friedrich Hiller von Gaertringen, "Die Deutschnationale Volkspartei," pp. 543-652 of Matthias and Morsey, *Ende der Parteien*. Also Manfred Dörr, "Die Deutschnationale Volkspartei, 1925 bis 1928," doctoral dissertation, University of Marburg, 1964. The Conservative People's party is covered in Erasmus Jonas, *Die Volkskonservativen, 1928-1933*, Düsseldorf: Droste Verlag, 1965. The divisions within the DNVP are discussed in greater detail in Chapter 10.

37. See the treatment of the NSDAP in the Conservative press of Berlin, Essen, and Wuppertal in Chapters 4 and 7.

38. Samuel Alexander Pratt, "The Social Basis of Nazism and Communism in Urban Germany: A Correlational Study of the July 31, 1932, Reichstag Elections in Germany," M.A. thesis, Michigan State College, 1948, ch. 6.

39. The percentages in the previous paragraph are taken from *Statistik des Deutschen Reichs*, vol. 453, pt. 2, "Volks-, Berufs- und Betriebszählung vom 16. Juni 1933," Berlin, 1936, p. 34. These catagories would have different meanings in different contexts. In some farm areas, a high percentage of independents might mean marginal middle-class proprietors. In others, it might mean middle and large proprietors. In some cities, particularly those specializing in heavy industry, the categories would be disproportionately lower middle class. In administrative and cultural centers, the tendency would be toward the upper middle classes. The same problem would arise within cities. In some city areas, those in these categories would be disproportionately lower middle class. In the "best" areas of the cities, the same categories would contain an urban industrial upper class of owners, managers, and officials.

In addition to the problems already discussed, there is a serious problem posed by the possibility of what has been called the "ecological fallacy." This is discussed in note 6, Chapter 3. Still another difficulty to keep in mind involves the age question. The independents are an older segment relative to the civil servants and the white-collar workers in private employment. Pratt recognized this fact but was not able to control for its influence.

40. The problem would have been solved if the census had included one question on income or if it had sorted the middle-class occupations into those of low, middling, and high rank. An examination of some of the original manuscript census forms indicated that this latter sorting was not possible with the limited information received at the time. Many respondents listed themselves simply as "*Kaufmann*" (businessman, merchant, or salesman) with no further information given. They could have been clerks in small shops; or they could have been major dealers in real estate, stocks and bonds, or wholesale commodities. In the subsequent chapters, the "better" middle-class areas will be sorted out through the use of this occupational data in combination with data on the size of housing units and on the presence of domestic servants. The judgments of informed citizens were also used where such data were not available.

41. Pratt, "The Social Basis," p. 118. The original correlations (*r*s) of National Socialist vote and percentage of voters who were (in Pratt's terms) upper middle or lower middle class are shown in the table.

City Size (in thousands)	Upper (Independent Business)	Lower (White Collar)
25-50	.23	.25
50-100	.58	.57
Over 100	.33	.27

A correlation coefficient expresses the extent of relationship between two variables. A perfect correlation is one in which a change in the value of one variable is associated with a precisely specifiable change in the value of the other, yielding a correlation of 1.00. If there were no relationship at all between the two variables, the correlation would be zero. Correlations may be either positive (increases in the values of one are associated with increases in the values of the other) or negative (increases in the values of one are associated with decreases in the values of the other).

In his subsequent analysis based on region (using the post–World War II occupation zones) Pratt found for the upper and lower groups in the British zone correlations of .61 and .57 respectively (p. 120). In the Soviet zone the figures were .33 and .14. In the combined United States and French zones, they were .28 and .01. As indicated, some additional controls reduced even these differences.

42. Lipset, *Political Man*, pp. 147-148. Even if one accepted Lipset's conclusion, it would be necessary, given Pratt's data in the previous footnote, to make some specification of the claim by region.

Kornhauser, it will be remembered, also made use of the Pratt thesis, this to support a claim about unemployed white-collar workers voting for the NSDAP. Pratt's figures do indicate that, "The Social Basis," p. 178. Again there is a question as to how much trust one ought to put in this result. The number of unemployed white-collar workers must have been a tiny fraction of the total NSDAP vote being predicted. And not all of those unemployed, of course, would have been voting National Socialist. This suggests that the correlations in fact are reflecting some other factor or factors associated with those communities. One obvious possibility is that they reflect the overall percentage of white-collar workers in those cities.

43. Quoted by Lipset, *Political Man*, on p. 147. The Heberle quotation appears on p. 112 of his *From Democracy to Nazism*. Heberle does not provide any supporting evidence for the cities. He does offer a footnote that contains the standard claims about the resentments against big business and labor. The relationship, he notes, has been "treated frequently." The most thorough analysis, he says, is to be found in Geiger. But Geiger, as we have seen, presents no evidence on the subject. Similar linkages of the petty bourgeoisie to the NSDAP are to be found in Heberle on pp. 58 and 124, although again these are no more than casual asides.

44. Lipset, *Political Man*, p. 147n. Günther Franz, *Die politischen Wahlen in Niedersachsen, 1867 bis 1949*, Bremen-Horn: Walter Dorn Verlag, 1957, p. 62.

45. The Lipset quotation is from *Political Man*, p. 142. The Heberle figures are from *From Democracy to Nazism*, p. 99. The point about the generational split in the upper strata is suggested by Heberle who says (with no supporting evidence) that "even in the nobility the younger generation often joined the NSDAP" (p. 87).

46. Lipset, *Political Man*, p. 143; Heberle, *From Democracy to Nazism*, p. 113.

47. Lipset also devotes a paragraph to the voting patterns of the sexes (*Political Man*, p. 143) noting that the Center party and the Conservatives had disproportionate support from women, while the NSDAP had disproportionate support from men. This is intended to show that "the Nazis did not appeal to the same sources as the traditional German right." At this point, a consideration of the sex patterns would constitute something of a digression from the main theme, the class bases of the National Socialist support; hence the subject, an important one to be sure, is deferred to Chapter 3.

48. Hans Gerth, "The Nazi Party: Its Leadership and Composition," *American Journal of Sociology*, 45 (1940): 517–541. Gerth too argues many of the themes reviewed in the text. See especially pp. 526–528. As is indicated immediately in the text, his *evidence* does not support his specific claim that "the common element in the situations of all these different strata was their despair and lack of social and economic security."

49. Lipset, *Political Man*, p. 148.

50. It would make sense to compare membership figures with the male population since other sources have shown that the membership was overwhelmingly male. Michael Kater, for example, found 95.6 percent of his 1923 list of members to be male. "Zur Soziographie der frühen NSDAP," *Vierteljahrshefte für Zeitgeschichte*, 19 (1971): 124–158; the percentage appears on p. 151. Harold J. Gordon found only 32 women in a file of 1,672 party members dating from 1923. See his *Hitler and the Beer Hall Putsch*, Princeton: Princeton University Press, 1972, p. 82. The comprehensive *Partei-Statistik* put out by the party's

Reichsorganisationsleiter, Munich, 1935, indicated that 94.1 percent of the members who joined before September 14, 1930, were male. Of those joining from September 15 that year through January 30, 1933, 92.2 percent were male. From vol. 1, p. 16.

In assessing the level of working-class membership in the party one must keep in mind factors that might discourage joining, such as cost. Gordon cites both Social Democratic and NSDAP sources as reporting that "strong labor discipline," meaning "expulsion from work and physical punishment," was a factor keeping workers from the party. He does show, nevertheless, significant working-class involvement in the NSDAP as of 1923. *Hitler,* pp. 74–81.

Still another factor to bear in mind is the possibility of membership in the parallel organization, in the party's private army, the SA or Sturmabteilung. The available indications are that this organization had proportionately more working-class members than the party and that the working-class membership increased as the depression worsened. Gordon states (ibid., p. 77) that workers "filled the ranks of the SA in Erding. A former Freikorps officer found to his surprise that the local SA was led by the same men he had disarmed when they led the local Red Guard." The best available statistical evidence on the working-class membership of the SA is to be found in Eric G. Reiche, "The Development of the SA in Nuremberg, 1922 to 1934," Ph.D. dissertation, University of Delaware, 1972, pp. 143, 257.

51. Lipset, *Political Man,* pp. 148–149. See also p. 139 where he notes that Hitler, "a centrist extremist, won backing from conservatives who hoped to use the Nazis against the Marxist left."

52. Some evidence from the earliest years of the party, 1919 and 1920, appears in Georg Franz-Willing, *Die Hitlerbewegung: Der Ursprung, 1919-1922,* Hamburg und Berlin: Decker's Verlag–G. Schenck, 1962, pp. 126 and 130. Some analysis based on 1920 and 1922 lists for selected communities appears in Werner Maser, *Der Sturm auf die Republik; Frühgeschichte der NSDAP,* Stuttgart: Deutsche Verlags-Anstalt, 1973, p. 255. The analysis based on the fragmentary list of 1923 is that of Kater, "Zur Soziographie." For a more detailed analysis, one showing the membership trends from 1925 onward, see Kater's "Sozialer Wandel in der NSDAP im Zuge der nationalsozialistischen Machtergreifung," pp. 25-67 of Wolfgang Schieder, ed., *Fascismus als soziale Bewegung,* Hamburg: Hoffmann und Campe, 1976. See also Gordon, *Hitler,* pp. 80–82. The working-class figure given in the text includes both skilled and unskilled workers. Kater classifies the former with his lower middle class, thus increasing the size of that category and strengthening his claim that it was a lower-middle-class party.

53. This point is easily overlooked in the very much abridged presentation in *From Democracy to Nazism,* pp. 116, 118. For a more detailed and somewhat different presentation see *Landbevölkerung und Nationalsozialismus,* pp. 110-111.

54. R. Palme Dutt, *Fascism and Social Revolution: A Study of the Economics and Politics of the Extreme Stages of Capitalism in Decay,* New York: International Publishers, 1935, p. 97. See also p. 38 where he speaks of the "new middle class" as "one of the breeding-grounds of Fascism."

55. Ibid., pp. 98-99.

56. Ibid., pp. 100, 102. See also p. 139.

57. Another author making the same stress is the political scientist Frederick L. Schuman, author of an early and detailed book on the subject, *The Nazi Dictatorship*. He devotes a dozen pages to "Neuroses of the Kleinbürgertum," touching on all the standard themes in that repertory and ending up with the conclusion that "fundamentally the disorder was a disease of the *Kleinbürgertum*" (of the petty bourgeoisie). At a much later point, Schuman introduces another note: "Fascism is the social philosophy and the State-form of the bourgeoisie in the monopolistic epoch of late capitalism." In support of this point he refers to R. Palme Dutt and John Strachey. The fascist takeover in his view was unquestionably aided by this "disease" of the petty bourgeoisie. It was, nevertheless, the work of business and banking that made a government by the NSDAP possible: "Without this alliance the Fascist State would never have come into being." The section on the *Kleinbürgertum* appears on pp. 95-109. The summary discussion of the role of the bourgeoisie appears in the final pages of the book, on pp. 480 and 482. Strachey's position is the same as Dutt's. See *The Coming Struggle for Power*, New York: Covici-Friede, 1933. His discussion of fascism (in chapter 14) contains no supporting references.

Trotsky's analyses of the German developments also made unsupported claims about the role of the petty bourgeoisie. See *The Struggle against Fascism in Germany*, ed. Ernest Mandel, New York: Pathfinder Press, 1971, pp. 58-59, 73. Mandel's introduction is even richer in unsupported assertions of this claim; see pp. 14, 19, 20, 22, and 35-36. The most recent contribution in this tradition is that of Albert Szymanski, *The Capitalist State and the Politics of Class*, Cambridge, Mass.: Winthrop Publishers, 1978, pp. 280-286.

58. "National Socialism: Totalitarianism or Fascism?" *American Historical Review*, 73 (1967-1968): 410. See also Henry Ashby Turner, Jr., who states: "It has long been widely recognized that the German lower middle class proved especially susceptible to the appeals of Nazism and provided disproportionate popular support for Hitler's rise to power." *Central European History*, 8 (1974): 84. Or Heinrich August Winkler who, in discussing the "attraction of the Nazis for the lower middle classes," declares that "it was these groups that provided the Nazis' strength in the elections." See his "From Social Protectionism to National Socialism: The German Small-Business Movement in Comparative Perspective," *Journal of Modern History*, 48 (1976): 10.

Not all works have this emphasis. One recent book that denies the validity of the lower-middle-class claim, at least for an early period in NSDAP history, is that of Harold J. Gordon, Jr.; see *Hitler*, pp. 6 and 68 ff. Another work that discounts the emphasis is the Konrad Heiden biography, *Der Fuehrer: Hitler's Rise to Power*, Boston: Houghton Mifflin, 1944. Without presenting any supporting data, he lays the stress on "young people" (pp. 351-352). Still another author, Koppel S. Pinson, argues that the dictatorship "rested on the following and support of millions of people who represented a true cross section of the German population." One of the least likely hypotheses for any time or place, in the German context, as will be seen in the next chapter, it is seriously in error. See his *Modern Germany: Its History and Civilization*, 2d. ed., New York: Macmillan, 1966, p. 492.

59. One tends to assume that clear thinking and rationality prevail in the top levels of society, that is, among governing elites, big businessmen, and most especially intellectuals. It is in the other ranks of the society, supposedly, that one finds irrationality, perceptual distortions, and false consciousness. For a series of case studies showing such processes in operation among the "best and the brightest," see Irving L. Janis, *Victims of Groupthink: A Psychological Study of Foreign-Policy Decisions and Fiascoes*, Boston: Houghton Mifflin, 1972.

60. This conclusion is based on the illustrative listings of lower-middle-class occupations that sometimes appear. Pratt, for example, describes the lower middle class of the nineteenth century as containing "small property owners . . . craftsmen, shopkeepers, small businessmen, professionals, rentiers, and pensioners." I am assuming that his word "craftsmen" refers to *Handwerker*, that is, to independent artisans. The tendency in German writings is to count them as part of the middle class. At a later point he adds government employees and white-collar workers to the list. See his "The Social Basis," pp. 98 and 117. See also Fromm, *Escape from Freedom*, p. 211.

61. For examples of this shift in usage see Gordon, *Hitler*, pp. 72-73; and Kater, "Zur Soziographie." An opposite procedure appears in the work of Max Kele. He argues a working-class attraction to the National Socialists and for his purpose includes a segment of white-collar employees (*Angestellte*) among his workers. See his *Nazis and Workers: National Socialist Appeals to German Labor, 1919-1933*, Chapel Hill: University of North Carolina Press, 1972, pp. 166-167. For a recent statement of the traditional position, one that emphasizes the gap between blue-collar and white-collar workers, see Geoffrey Barraclough, "The Social Dimensions of Crisis," *Social Research*, 39 (Summer 1972): 351; see also his earlier book *The Origins of Modern Germany*, 2d. rev. ed., Oxford: Basil Blackwell, 1947, pp. 449-450.

Another work that might be mentioned in this review is that of Heinrich August Winkler, *Mittelstand, Demokratie und Nationalsozialismus: Die politische Entwicklung von Handwerk und Kleinhandel in der Weimarer Republik*, Cologne: Kiepenheuer & Witsch, 1972. Most of the argument of his work depends on a review and analysis of statements made by various trade and professional organizations. How accurately they reflected member sentiment is not clear, nor is it clear that the organizations voiced the complaints and sentiments of non-member artisans and small businessmen. The brief analysis of electoral figures (on pp. 134-139) provides no compelling evidence as to the voting tendencies of these groups. This is not to say that Winkler's conclusion, that these groups supported the NSDAP, is wrong, only that it lacks precise proof of the decisive claim. The questions of how many voted for the Zentrum and how many for the SPD remain unanswered. In some regions it is possible that the overwhelming majority of these occupations voted for the NSDAP. But, given the tendency of all segments in those regions (except possibly the workers), the *Handwerker* and small businessmen would not be at all distinctive. And that in turn would raise questions about the sources of the development. The causes of the

NSDAP growth in such regions would appear to extend well beyond the occupations he has studied.

THREE. A RECONSIDERATION OF PREVIOUS EVIDENCE

1. This is speaking of the 1932 elections. The same was generally the case in 1930. Prior to that time, National Socialism was largely an urban phenomenon. It began in cities and was carried out, with great success, to the small towns and the countryside. For details on the "decision" to go to the country, see Dietrich Orlow, *The History of the Nazi Party: 1919-1933*, Pittsburgh: University of Pittsburgh Press, 1969, pp. 131-133, 137, and 304; and Jeremy Noakes, *The Nazi Party in Lower Saxony 1921-1933*, London: Oxford University Press, 1971, pp. 121-127. For further discussion of the National Socialist campaign in the countryside, see Chapters 12 and 13.

The number of *publications* dealing with the Weimar elections is, of course, much larger than the roughly three dozen serious empirical studies. Official reports of election results were put out by national, state, and local authorities. There were journalistic commentaries on the elections. And, as indicated in Chapter 2, numerous scholarly commentaries exist that do not make adequate use of the available evidence. For a comprehensive bibliography, see Martin Schumacher, *Wahlen und Abstimmungen, 1918-1933: Eine Bibliographie zur Statistik und Analyse der politischen Wahlen in der Weimarer Republik*, Düsseldorf: Droste Verlag, 1976. It reviews nearly 2,000 titles. For a summary of still more recent materials, see Jürgen W. Falter, "Wer verhalf der NSDAP zum Sieg?" *Aus Politik und Zeitgeschichte*, B 28-29 (July 14, 1979): 3-21.

2. Samuel A. Pratt, "The Social Basis of Nazism and Communism in Urban Germany. A Correlational Study of the July 31, 1932, Reichstag Election in Germany," M.A. thesis, Michigan State College, 1948, p. 61; and, *Statistik des Deutschen Reichs*, vol. 434, "Die Wahlen zum Reichstag am 31. Juli und 6. November 1932 und am 5. März 1933," Berlin, 1935.

Pratt's study includes all cities in the two largest size categories, plus most of those in the third. The official figures (in vol. 434) did not contain results for twenty-nine of the cities in the 25,000–50,000 category; hence the results given in the third line of the table cover only 76 percent of those communities. Pratt's figures have been subtracted from the official total to give the result for the smaller communities. It should be remembered, however, that the results for the twenty-nine cities (which of necessity were omitted from Pratt's study) are included in the fourth line. The number of voters in these communities is not likely to have exceeded 25,000 in any given case. Even if one took that as a maximum figure, the twenty-nine cities would have provided only 725,000 of the 21,397,000 votes in this last category.

3. See Appendix B for the National Socialist percentages in the largest cities. For the fifteen largest cities the percentage was 30.8.

4. Pratt, "The Social Basis," pp. 85-86. The subsequent sentence reads: "The evidence is thorough enough to indicate that in urban Germany, very few Catholic voters cast ballots for Hitler." That judgment, as we shall see in later chapters, is mistaken. See also Günther Franz, *Die Politischen Wahlen in Niedersachsen*

1867 bis 1949, Bremen: Walter Dorn Verlag, 1957, pp. 43-44, 59-61. Virtually every empirical analysis of the voting patterns makes some observation about the Catholic-Protestant split. It would be pointless to mention them all, but some diverse examples include: Charles P. Loomis and J. Allan Beegle, "The Spread of German Nazism in Rural Areas," *American Sociological Review*, 11 (1946): 724-734; Dee Richard Wernette, "Political Violence and German Elections: 1930 and July, 1932," Ph.D. dissertation, University of Michigan, 1974, ch. 2; Heinz Herz, *Über Wesen und Aufgaben der politischen Statistik*, Waldenburg/Sachsen; E. Kästner, 1932 (originally a doctoral dissertation, University of Leipzig); and Jerzy Holzer, *Parteien und Massen: Die politische Krise in Deutschland, 1928-1930*, Wiesbaden: Franz Steiner, 1975, pp. 44-46, 93-98.

5. Loomis and Beegle, "Spread of Nazism," p. 732.

6. Throughout this work we will be undertaking what has been called "ecological analysis. What that means is that we will be inferring individual behavior from data for an *aggregate* of individuals. The subject under consideration in the text provides a simple case in point. Districts known to have large percentages of Catholics provide very little support for the National Socialists. The inference is that Catholics did not support the National Socialists. In such cases we have no information about the behavior of individual voters. We have two statements about the entire aggregate of individuals in the districts, one about their religion and one about their politics. A conclusion linking these factors seems most reasonable.

One problem in such analyses is that "slippage" can give rise to an erroneous conclusion. In such instances the linkage suggested by the aggregate result is not present among the involved individuals. The most frequently cited case concerns a correlation between the percentage of blacks in southern United States counties and the percentage of illiterates. Since the two factors are closely related, the conclusion, that blacks had higher rates of illiteracy, seemed a plausible one. But observations of individuals showed no differences in literacy levels by race. In counties with high percentages of blacks the schools provided poor quality education for both races. But that fact was lost in aggregate analysis.

The basic problem in ecological analysis stems from the fact that the aggregates are rarely pure. Few districts, for example, have a 100 percent Catholic population. If a district were 70 percent Catholic and the Zentrum received 70 percent of the votes, it would be easy to conclude that it was the Catholics who had voted for the Zentrum. But strictly speaking, if one assumed 100 percent participation, all one can be sure of is that at least four out of seven Catholics voted for the Zentrum. While in this case there would be little justification for such a conservative reading of the data, in other settings the question might be completely open. The most difficult case involves the near fifty-fifty division of the aggregate. If half the population of a district were Catholics and the other half Protestants, and if half of the population voted for Party X, one could not say anything with certainty about the source of that party's support. The key desideratum is to find homogeneous districts, those where a sizable majority of the population shares the presumed causal trait or traits. But then there is an additional difficulty; the factors operating in the homogeneous context may not operate (or may be countered) in the heterogeneous context. For that reason it is hazardous to infer individual behavior in a mixed district from the experience of the known (i.e. pure) districts.

It would be a mistake to assume that all ecological analysis automatically entailed a fallacy. The concern is with the *possibility* of one. Some of the measures one can take to guard against that possibility are considered in Chapters 4-8. Much of the effort in Chapter 9 is intended as an additional safeguard against the possibility of this kind of error. One must also note that in historical analysis of the kind being undertaken here, ecological analysis is effectively the *only* kind of empirical study open to the contemporary researcher. If one rejects this option, the remaining possibilities are purely judgmental, that is, the opinions and guesses of various experts.

The literature on the subject is large and growing. For the interested reader, the following may be helpful: W. S. Robinson, "Ecological Correlations and the Behavior of Individuals," *American Sociological Review*, 15 (1950): 351-357; Herbert Menzel, "Comment on Robinson's 'Ecological Correlations,' " *American Sociological Review*, 15 (1960): 674; Leo A. Goodman, "Ecological Regression and Behavior of Individuals," *American Sociological Review*, 18 (1953): 663-664; Leo A. Goodman, "Some Alternatives to Ecological Correlation," *American Journal of Sociology*, 64 (1959): 610-625; Otis D. Duncan and Beverly Davis, "An Alternative to Ecological Correlations," *American Sociological Review*, 18 (1953): 665-666; Gerald T. Slatin, "Ecological Analysis of Delinquency Aggregation Effects," *American Sociological Review*, 34 (1969): 894-907; Gerald T. Slatin, "A Factor Analytic Comparison of Ecological and Individual Correlations: Some Methodological Implications," *Sociological Quarterly*, 15 (1974): 507-520; W. Phillips Shively, "Ecological Inference: The Use of Aggregate Data to Study Individuals," *American Political Science Review*, 63 (1969): 1183-1196; Donald E. Stokes, "Cross-Level Inference as a Game against Nature," pp. 62-83 of Joseph L. Bernd, ed., *Mathematical Applications in Political Science*, vol. 4, Charlottesville: University of Virginia Press, 1969; Desmond Cartwright, "Ecological Variables," pp. 155-218 of Edgar Borgatta, ed., *Sociological Methodology*, San Francisco: Jossey-Bass, 1969; E. Terrence Jones, "Ecological Inference and Electoral Analysis," *Journal of Interdisciplinary History*, 2 (1972): 249-262; J. Morgan Kousser, "Ecological Regression and the Analysis of Past Politics," *Journal of Interdisciplinary History*, 4 (1973): 237-262; and L. H. Hammond, "Two Sources of Error in Ecological Correlations," *American Sociological Review*, 38 (1973): 764-777. A compendious work on the subject is that of Mattei Dogan and Stein Rokkan, eds., *Quantitative Ecological Analysis in the Social Sciences*, Cambridge, Mass.: MIT Press, 1969.

7. For a picture of the nefarious role played by the Bavarian government, see Erich Eyck, *Geschichte der Weimarer Republik*, Erlenbach-Zurich: Eugen Rentsch Verlag, 1956, vol. 1, pp. 239-240, 243, 257, 294-295, 307, 333, 349, and 357. See also Karl Schwend, *Bayern zwischen Monarchie und Dikatur; Beiträge zur Bayerischen Frage in der Zeit von 1918 bis 1933*, Munich: Richard Pflaum, 1954, chs. 6, 7, 9, 10, 15. For a brief English-language account of the Bavarian scene,

see Carl Landauer, "The Bavarian Problem in the Weimar Republic, 1918-1923," *Journal of Modern History*, 16 (1944): 93-115 and 205-223. For more detail see Harold J. Gordon, Jr., *Hitler and the Beer Hall Putsch*, Princeton: Princeton University Press, 1972, chs. 5 and 7; and Dietrich Thränhardt, *Wahlen und politische Strukturen in Bayern 1848-1953*, Düsseldorf: Droste Verlag, 1973.

The sharp differentiation by religion was characteristic of the later elections of the Weimar period. In earlier elections, in 1924 and 1928, this was not the case. Thomas Childers, "The Social Bases of the National Socialist Vote," *Journal of Contemporary History*, 11 (1976): 17-42, especially p. 19. See also Walter Dean Burnham, "Political Immunization and Political Confessionalism: The United States and Weimar Germany," *Journal of Interdisciplinary History*, 3 (1972-1973): 1-30.

8. *Statistik des Deutschen Reichs*, vol. 434, p. 8.

9. Meinrad Hagmann, *Der Weg ins Verhängnis: Reichstags-wahlergebnisse 1919 bis 1933 besonders aus Bayern*, Munich: Michael Beckstein Verlag, 1946, p. 18. All figures are for the rural districts. Urban districts gave less support to the NSDAP, but even here it was substantial. Ansbach (*Land*), as noted, gave that party 76.3; the city of Ansbach gave it 53.2 percent. Some of the same ground is covered in Loomis and Beegle, "Spread of Nazism," p. 727. See also Franz, *Die Politischen Wahlen*, p. 61.

10. Rudolf Heberle, *Landbevölkerung und Nationalsozialismus: Eine soziologische Untersuchung der politischen Willensbildung in Schleswig-Holstein 1918 bis 1932*, Stuttgart: Deutsche Verlags-Anstalt, 1963, pp. 38, 58.

11. These data come from *Die Ergebnisse der Landtagswahl am 19. Juni 1932 und der Reichstagswahl am 31. Juli 1932 im Volksstaat Hessen*, a publication put out by the Landesstatistisches Amt, Darmstadt; Hessischer Staatsverlag, 1932. Although no indication of who wrote this outstanding work appears in the publication, the author was in fact Erwin Lind, the head of the statistical office. For comparison, there is a similar analysis of the earlier Reichstag election, *Die Ergebnisse der Reichstagswahl im Volksstaat Hessen vom 14. September 1930*, Darmstadt: Hessischer Staatsverlag, 1930. A popular version of the latter appeared in two articles by Lind, "Die Wähler der NSDAP," in the *Frankfurter Zeitung*, December 2 and 3, 1930.

The state in question, the Freistaat Hessen (or the Volksstaat Hessen, or Hessen-Darmstadt as it was sometimes called) consisted of areas immediately surrounding Darmstadt (just to the south of Frankfurt and the Main River), areas to the west of the Rhine, and an area to the north and northeast of Frankfurt. It formed *Wahlkreis* 33, Hesse-Darmstadt.

12. As, for example, in the following quotation from Carl Friedrich: "The rural population constitutes the compact mass which stands behind the uncompromising emotional nationalism. That is perhaps the most important reason why movements like National Socialism and fascism are first of all supported by the peasants." See "The Agricultural Bases of Emotional Nationalism," *Public Opinion Quarterly*, 1 (April 1937): 60-61. This passage is also cited, with evident approval, in William Kornhauser, *The Politics of Mass Society*, Glencoe: The Free Press, 1959, p. 210.

13. The results indicated here do appear to be typical of the experience of other areas. Rural Protestant areas everywhere (in East Prussia, in Schleswig-Holstein, in Lower Saxony, in Franconia, and in the Palatinate) gave overwhelming percentages to the NSDAP. And rural Catholic areas gave equally overwhelming support to the Zentrum.

An examination of national results did yield a general confirmation of the point made here. A correlation of community size (based on the 1925 census) with National Socialist percentages (in the July 1932 election) for 1,037 districts (including all cities and rural areas) yielded a modest negative correlation of .11, meaning that there was a slight tendency for the smaller communities to give stronger support to the NSDAP. Half of these districts (N = 519) were overwhelmingly Protestant (that is, 80 percent or more). In those districts the correlation was somewhat stronger, −.20. Roughly a quarter of the districts were overwhelmingly Catholic with the correlation in this case being close to zero (actually, it was very slightly positive, +.02).

These correlations were generated through the courtesy of the Inter-University Consortium for Political and Social Research at the University of Michigan from their Weimar elections data. I wish to thank especially Michael Traugott and Janet Vavra for making these results available.

14. Some lines of argument do exist that would be consonant with at least the rural location of the National Socialist sentiment. Talcott Parsons speaks of the unsettling effects of rapid social change and of the consequent free-floating aggression that results. The compulsive debunking efforts of emancipated intellectuals moreover stimulates a fundamentalist reaction on the part of traditionalists. Something of this sort might have been occurring in Weimar; the "advanced" intellectuals may have provoked a reaction. Or it may have been that various rightist publications were more than happy to purvey examples of such "free" expression to an audience they knew would react with outrage and fury. The Parsons variation of the cultural argument, however, does not explain the differentiated reaction of the Protestant and Catholic countryside. See his chapters, "Democracy and Social Structure in Pre-Nazi Germany" (especially pp. 117-120) and "Some Sociological Aspects of the Fascist Movements" (especially pp. 135 ff.) from his *Essays in Sociological Theory*, rev. ed., Glencoe: The Free Press, 1954.

15. Lind, "Die Wähler der NSDAP," December 2, 1932. See also "Die Ergebnisse 1932," pp. 10-11. Although the percentages declined, the absolute number of votes cast for the two left parties increased slightly.

16. This may be seen in the Heberle figures for the July 1932 election cited above. In the rural area, the NSDAP received 63.8 percent of the July 1932 total. The left (SPD and KPD combined) received 24.4 percent against 9.2 percent for the Conservatives and 5.8 for all other parties. Lind's study ("Die Ergebnisse 1932," pp. 22-23) provides numerous examples of the same kind of polarization.

17. As indicated, the speculations in this paragraph can only be rather tenuous. On the other hand, the assumption of a lower-middle-class propensity

for the NSDAP is also based on guesswork—largely unacknowledged guesswork.

18. Heberle, *Landbevölkerung und Nationalsozialismus*, pp. 78-79.

19. This is obviously a very simplified account, which leaves some important points unspecified. With possibly a few exceptions, the notion of worker (*Arbeiter*) is clear: it refers to the blue-collar or manual workers. The best and easiest denotation would involve reference to the census category.

As was indicated in the previous chapter, there is no census category equivalent to the concept "lower middle class." Moreover, there is no easy and obvious line that may be drawn across the middle-class or nonmanual ranks to separate the lower and upper segments. All such divisions, like the distinction between small and large farmers, are ultimately arbitrary. One simply has to stipulate where the division will be made.

A similar problem occurs with the distinction between upper middle and upper classes. One may say that the latter consists of the owners of the means of production and that the former refers to their, the owners', highest paid salaried workers, the managers and highly trained professionals. But this too, in many cases, does not provide a clear and unambiguous line of division. Corporate ownership, depending as it does on shareholdings, may involve a controlling interest, or it may involve only tiny fractional shares. Both classes in short, could be "owners" of the means of production, but the significance of their holdings would vary considerably. Then, too, there was nothing to stop an owner (or the son of an owner) from taking a full-time managerial position.

The terms as defined here obviously can provide little more than rule-of-thumb guidelines to the Weimar social structure. The terms of analysis are largely economic, thus omitting all other considerations such as those of education, prestige, political power, and the like. The situation of the university professors, who, according to Ralf Dahrendorf, still rank among the very top within the social hierarchy of Germany, even though not so highly placed with respect to income or power, must be neglected along with questions about the location of déclassé aristocrats. Such cases, while of possible interest for an hour of classroom discussion, are not likely to affect the present discussion in any significant way since in the Weimar period both groups accounted for, at best, a few thousand persons in a labor force of more than twenty million.

It will be noted that I am using the terms "petty bourgeois" and "lower middle class" as equivalents. Although "bourgeois" originally referred to independent proprietors, in the language of this period "petty bourgeois" came to include also economically marginal, salaried white-collar employees. For a more detailed discussion of the problems of delineating upper and lower middle classes, see Richard F. Hamilton, *Class and Politics in the United States*, New York: John Wiley & Sons, 1972, chs. 4, 9, and 10.

20. See Hans Zeisel, *Say It with Figures*, 5th ed., rev., New York: Harper & Row, 1968, ch. 3.

21. The original study is entitled "Die soziale Zusammensetzung der sozialdemokratischen Wählerschaft Deutschlands," and appears in the *Archiv für Sozialwissenschaft und Sozialpolitik*, 20 (1905): 507-550. This is not an obscure or

out-of-the-way journal. It was the most important social science publication in Germany at the time. This particular volume contained Max Weber's "Die protestantische Ethik und der 'Geist' des Kapitalismus." Weber was one of the editors of the publication. Speier's commentary appears in his *Social Order and the Risks of War*, Cambridge, Mass.: MIT Press, 1952, p. 55. The original version appeared in the *Magazin der Wirtschaft*, March 27 and April 3, 1931. I have referred to these secondary sources to show that the extensive lower-middle-class support for the Social Democrats has not been lost from view; it was a fact available to both German- and English-speaking scholars. This research is also discussed in Richard N. Hunt, *German Social Democracy, 1918-1933*, New Haven: Yale University Press, 1964, pp. 129-130, 140.

In his analysis of the 1903 election, Blank takes the most extreme minimal estimates. He derived first an estimate of the number of blue-collar workers eligible to vote in the election. There was a 76 percent overall rate of participation in that election, and Blank recognized that for several reasons workers were more likely to abstain than others (the election falling on a weekday, i.e. a work day, and the hours of the election corresponding closely with the hours of work). He again, nevertheless, assumed equivalent working-class participation which would lead to an *under*estimate of middle-class SPD support. There were several additional steps in his procedure, the end result of which was an estimate that 19 percent of the SPD vote came from middle-class ranks. Given the restrained character of his initial assumption, it would seem that the one-quarter figure given for the previous elections would also be more realistic for this one. At a later point, applying his estimation procedure to the larger cities he declares that in most of them the middle class must have accounted for one-third of the SPD total and in some "perhaps even for half" (p. 527). The consequence, he noted, was that the SPD was becoming less and less a purely class party (see especially p. 528).

Another contribution on this same theme, focused on the Social Democratic party's membership, was made by Robert Michels, "Die deutsche Sozialdemokratie. I. Parteimitgliedschaft und soziale Zusammensetzung," *Archiv für Sozialwissenschaft und Sozialpolitik*, 23 (1906): 471-556.

22. Speier, *Social Order*, p. 55.

23. Blank, "Die soziale Zusammensetzung," p. 521.

24. "Germany: Changing Patterns and Lasting Problems," p. 366 in Sigmund Neumann, ed., *Modern Political Parties: Approaches to Comparative Politics*, Chicago: University of Chicago Press, 1956. The 40 percent figure is a compositional one, that part of the SPD vote coming from the nonmanual ranks. Neumann does not address the related questions: what part of the middle class vote went to the SPD? And, what part was "available" for the NSDAP?

25. *Political Man: The Social Bases of Politics*, Garden City: Doubleday, 1960, p. 149. Both Lipset and Neumann provide very accurate summaries of Neisser's article. See Hans Neisser, "Sozialstatistische Analyse des Wahlergebnisses," *Die Arbeit*, 7, (1930): 654-659. His estimates of the SPD vote in the various middle-class segments are based on the union affiliation of persons in those categories.

A summary analysis by Alexander Weber has reviewed a wide range of empirical studies dealing with National Socialist electoral support. On the subject of the class bases of the party he was able to cite only a single study, one that contrasts the voting in Berlin Steglitz with "upper-class" Berlin-Zehlendorf (discussed in Chapter 4). This study also presents similar data for Bremen. From there Weber proceeds to a review of the previously discussed works of Heberle and Pratt. See his "Soziale Merkmale der NSDAP Wähler," doctoral dissertation, Freiburg University, 1969. The one study cited is that of Werner Stephan, "Zur Soziologie der Nationalsozialistischen Deutschen Arbeiterpartei," *Zeitschrift für Politik*, 20 (1931): 793-800. That evidence is discussed in greater detail in note 15, Chapter 4. Once again, it will be noted, only a very limited basis exists for the original conclusion about the lower middle class. See also Stephan's "Grenzen des nationalsozialistischen Vormarsches," *Zeitschrift für Politik*, 21 (1932): 570-578. Also of some interest, bringing some data to bear on the question, is the work of S. Erkner, "NSDAP und die Klassen," *Die Internationale*, 14 (1931): 323-333.

26. The 1933 census reported that 62.7 percent of the population was Protestant and 32.5 percent was Roman Catholic. The Catholic representation was slightly lower in the largest cities, those of 100,000 or more, running at 28.5 percent. In the cities of 50,000 to 99,999, the percentage was 35.2. Not all Catholic voters supported the Zentrum (as we shall see in Chapters 6 and 7), but most of the urban defection appears to have been on the part of Catholic workers. For middle-class populations, the estimate given here might well err in underrepresenting Zentrum strength. See *Statistik des Deutschen Reichs*, vol. 451, "Volkszählung: Die Bevölkerung des Deutschen Reichs nach den Ergebnissen der Volkszählung 1933," pt. 3, "Die Bevölkerung des Deutschen Reichs nach der Religionszugehörigkeit," Berlin, 1936, p. 8.

27. In the following chapters an attempt is made to supply actual figures for the estimates made here. As will be seen, the task is not as easy as might first appear. It should also be kept in mind that the cities vary widely in their Catholic-Protestant proportions. That variation is usually associated with an equivalent variation in the relative strength of the Zentrum and, to a lesser extent, of the left. The discussion in the text averages the cities of a given size.

28. Between 1928 and July 1932, the two parties of the left lost 4.5 percent of the total vote. In many of the rural areas the loss was greater, e.g. in the election districts Frankfurt an der Oder (6.0); Mecklenburg (6.6); Schleswig-Holstein (6.3); and the Palatinate (7.8). This compares with losses in Berlin of 2.9 and in Hamburg of 4.2. Within Schleswig-Holstein the urban districts showed a loss of 5.3 percent in the share of votes for the left. In the rural districts (those of 2,000 or less), the loss was 7.0 (Heberle, *Landbevölkerung und Nationalsozialismus*, p. 38). Some rural districts showed a less than average decline for the left (e.g. East Prussia, 3.7 and Franconia, 3.4). A limited investigation of Franconia, comparing the 1930 and first 1932 elections, did, however, show the same pattern of disproportionate losses in the rural districts. In Nuremberg, for example, the largest city of Franconia, the loss was 0.5 percent; in the cities generally it was 3.2, and in the rural communities (*Bezirksämter*) the loss was 4.6. Recalculated from Hagmann, *Der Weg ins Verhängnis*, pp. 17-19. The initial

figures in this note are taken from Alfred Milatz, "Das Ende der Parteien im Spiegel der Wahlen 1930 bis 1933," pp. 743-793 of Erich Matthias and Rudolf Morsey, eds., *Das Ende der Parteien 1933*, Düsseldorf: Droste Verlag, 1960.

29. From Speier, *Social Order*, p. 65. The chapter in question is entitled "The Worker Turning Bourgeois." The GDA's study is entitled *Die wirtschaftliche und soziale Lage der Angestellten*, Berlin: Gewerkschaftsbund der Angestellten, 1930. Regrettably, it contains no information on the political orientation of the respondents.

30. Speier, *Social Order*, pp. 72 and 77. It would be incorrect to assume that the remainder of the white-collar workers are of white-collar or middle-class origin. A small portion of them came from farm families. Speier's chapter containing this discussion of working-class origins is entitled "The Salaried Employee in Modern Society." The leading works on the subject from the Weimar period are cited in Speier. The most useful are Heinz Hamm, *Die wirtschaftlichen und sozialen Berufsmerkmale der kaufmännischen Angestellten (im Vergleich mit denjenigen der Arbeiter)*, Borna-Leipzig: Universitätsverlag von Robert Noske, 1931 (originally a doctoral dissertation, University of Jena); and Fritz Fischer, *Die Angestellten, ihre Bewegung und ihre Ideologien*, Wertheim a.M.: E. Bechstein, 1932 (originally a doctoral dissertation, University of Heidelberg).

31. There are many claims on the subject but precious little evidence. Geoffrey Barraclough, for example, declares (in an ad hominem argument incidentally) that "no one who did not live there can realize the cleft in Weimar Germany, not simply between rich and poor . . . but between the white-collar and the blue-collar workers; they were two societies at arm's length from each other." Some sense of the *evidence* underlying such assertions comes from Hamm, *Die wirtschaftlichen Berufsmerkmale*, p. 64. He states that female white-collar workers fear the possibility of marriage to a worker. In support of that claim he supplies a footnote; Götz Briefs, a noted professor, had reported at one point in a lecture that he had been observing a group of department store saleswomen and heard them express their decided dislike of the idea of such a working-class marriage. This was the case even though most of them came from working-class families. The Barraclough quotation is from "The Social Dimensions of Crisis," *Social Research*, 39 (1972): 351.

32. Individuals do not create the structure of the labor force. When seeking out jobs, they must choose from among those available. Given the gradual long-term shift in the direction of white-collar jobs (on the male side of the labor force) or the rapid change in that direction (on the female side), some people will "happen to have" white-collar jobs whether they initially desired them or not.

There is a steadfast tendency to assume that the choice of a white-collar job is the result of positive motivation. A scatter of evidence is available that suggests the opposite. Some middle-class parents in a French study recommended working-class occupations for their children, that is to say, they recommended downward mobility or, put in other words, they recommended "falling into the proletariat." One American study indicated very high levels of satisfaction among skilled workers, higher than was found among most middle-class segments. And one American study reported that a slum settlement house systematically undermined the relationship of its "clients" with their immediate environment in order to *force* upward mobility.

The recommendation of downward mobility is to be found in Alain Girard and Henri Bastide, "Niveau de vie et répartition professionnelle: Enquête sur l'information et les attitudes du public," *Population*, 12 (1957): 60-63. See also my *Affluence and the French Worker*, Princeton: Princeton University Press, 1967, pp. 76-80. The satisfaction of the skilled workers is reported in Gerald Gurin et al., *Americans View Their Mental Health: A Nationwide Interview Survey*, New York: Basic Books, 1960, p. 225. The activities of the settlement house are reported in William F. Whyte, *Street Corner Society*, 2d. ed., Chicago: University of Chicago Press, 1955, pp. 98-104.

33. There is little evidence available dealing with such questions. An initial inquiry which touches on the matter may be found in my *Class and Politics*, pp. 211-212.

34. For evidence on this point in another context, contemporary United States, see again my *Class and Politics*, pp. 159 ff.

35. The comments in this paragraph constitute little more than speculations and guesses about the outlooks that would have been found among this segment of the middle class. There is, to be sure, an alternative reading of the matter, that being the one under criticism here, namely that the proximity to the working class might increase status anxiety and that the crisis and unemployment would accentuate those concerns. That too is little more than speculation and guesswork.

This raises the question of how one should decide between two contrary sets of speculation; one guess, presumably, is as good as another. In this case, one has to make some assessment as to what is probable. Is it likely that people who come from working-class families, who have gone to school with and associated with workers and working-class children (among these, their own brothers, sisters, cousins) would develop a separate and opposite consciousness? Is it likely that they would develop or yearn for a different style of life, especially when they earn the same or less than the workers and cannot, therefore, afford a distinctive and more costly living standard? Would they really attempt to maintain such a pretense, the impossibility of which would be demonstrated every day of their lives? Would they attempt to maintain such elusive goals even though such actions must give offense to their relatives, friends, and neighbors? It seems to me that such assumptions are extremely unrealistic and therefore highly improbable. This is not to say that there are no instances of such behavior; rather it is unlikely for the generality of this particular segment. Few people in any population willingly cut themselves off from all their known, tried, and trusted sources of friendship and affection. The more plausible alternative is that they were well integrated in the milieu, shared the values of their friends, relatives, and associates there, and did not fear proletarianization—because working-class life was not something separate from and alien to them. If hit by unemployment, moreover, one's continued survival and well-being would depend on the help and assistance that came from friends and relatives; maintaining distance in such circumstances would be a disaster course.

For these reasons, the first set of guesses seems the more probable. If one is going to argue the received alternative, the status anxiety and social distance hypothesis, one must provide a lot of additional explanation before the case becomes plausible. One has to explain how people born and raised in a working-class milieu come to set themselves in opposition to that milieu. One must explain how and why they persist with such illusions even though they lack the necessary income. One must explain how they manage the interpersonal stresses that would ordinarily result from such behavior. And, especially in this case, one must explain their willingness to support the National Socialists—to protect them from falling in among their "Marxist" friends and relatives! The casual (and unsupported) declarations of this position, clearly, will not suffice. The hypothesis, to be sure, would have greater plausibility in another context, in the case of those who have made the break, that is, of those who have moved away from their communities of origin.

These questions are explored in considerably greater detail in my *Class and Politics*, chs. 4 and 9; and in my *Restraining Myths: Critical Studies of U.S. Social Structure and Politics*, New York: Sage-Halsted-Wiley, 1975, chs. 2 and 3. These chapters deal with independent businessmen and lower white-collar workers in the United States.

36. This entire formulation, clearly, is put in terms of the conventional hypotheses about the motivations of these groups. That constitutes only one reading of (or perhaps better, one projection onto) a largely unresearched field. It is possible that entirely different motivational structures were present, e.g. a concern simply with making ends meet, or a concern with bettering oneself in absolute terms, that is, without any reference to one's position relative to other groups. It is possible that openness and generosity were combined here with sympathy for the less privileged; many of these people, after all, would have known what it was to be poor. In other words, the argument of competition, strain, status anxiety, desperation, and reaction is without any solid basis in fact. One can just as well assume decent motives, certainly prior to the necessary investigation, as dishonorable ones.

37. Speier, *Social Order*, p. 79. This chapter, entitled "The Salaried Employee in Modern Society," originally appeared in *Social Research* in February 1934. See also his book, "The Salaried Employee in Modern Germany," New York: Columbia University, mimeograph, 1939.

38. Some important suggestions to this effect are contained in Iris Hamel, *Völkischer Verband und nationale Gewerkschaft: Der deutschnationale Handlungsgehilfen-Verband, 1893-1933*, Frankfurt: Europäische Verlagsanstalt, 1967, pp. 206 ff. She also reports some differences in the abilities of the early organizers, the DHV, at that point at least, appearing to have some edge in competence. It provides an interesting comment on biases of intellectuals that ideology is regularly put forth as *the* reason for membership in an organization. The simple and obvious bread and butter fringe benefits offered to members in a given organization are systematically overlooked.

39. Hamm, *Die wirtschaftlichen Berufsmerkmale*, p. 48. The unions also provided an employment service. Again there may have been differences in the adequacy of these bread and butter services.

40. Ibid., p. 45. The ZdA was disproportionately urban. And, of course, the work-force participation of women is more frequent in urban locations.

41. Based on figures in ibid., p. 43. The bourgeois districts were Wilmersdorf, Charlottenburg, Schöneberg, and Steglitz. The proletarian ones were Wedding, Friedrichshain, and Spandau. Hamm gives the percentage of DHV voters from the bourgeois, the proletarian, and (implicitly, by subtracting the previous two figures from 100%) the remaining districts of the city. To see how the vote was distributed in the districts (that is, what percentage of those in the bourgeois districts supported the DHV, what percentage supported the GDA, etc.) it was necessary to make some assumptions and to recalculate his results.

42. There are, of course, no end to the complexities that enter into such an estimate. It should be borne in mind that this judgment is based on the experience of only three of the nine working-class districts of the city. See Chapter 4 for further detail. Küstermeier's claim about the GDA tendencies was quoted in Chapter 2.

43. The task of the following chapters is to provide a range of new evidence so as to make possible a more precise test of the traditional claim.

Another indirect approach to the question may be made by taking survey results from the Federal Republic of Germany and projecting those findings back in time. This procedure obviously does not provide compelling proof that similar findings would have appeared in the Weimar period. The results can only be viewed as suggestive, as something to provoke thought, as another reason for giving serious consideration to the alternative hypothesis.

A large and comprehensive survey of West Germany undertaken in 1953, before the considerable growth of the SPD that came in the late fifties and in the sixties, found 25 percent of the salaried middle class supporting the Social Democrats. Among the more conservative independent business segment, 15 percent supported that party. In both cases the level of support by males was somewhat higher, being 30 and 18 percent, respectively. SPD support among lower white-collar employees in private employment (men and women) was 29 percent. The figure for civil servants (men and women, upper and lower) was 25 percent.

Another breakdown showed that salaried lower-middle-class men from working-class backgrounds had a much higher level of SPD support, 43 percent. Those of working-class background, incidentally, formed the majority of the lower-middle-class segment. This study also found the SPD preferences of salaried white-collar workers increasing with both size of work place and size of community. All of these findings, it will be noted, are consonant with the speculative assumptions offered in the text.

These findings stem from the study undertaken by Erich Reigrotzki and published in his *Soziale Verflechtungen in der Bundesrepublik. Elemente der sozialen Teilnehme in Kirche, Politik, Organization und Freizeit*, Tübingen: J.C.B. Mohr–

Paul Siebeck, 1956. The study was also used in the dissertation of Juan Linz which is the major study of West German politics of the early postwar period. See "The Social Bases of West German Politics," Columbia University, 1959; see pp. 509, 512, 535, 539-546 for the figures cited. Another postwar study, based on a survey undertaken in the Federal Republic of Germany in 1961, allows us some additional insight into the orientations of white-collar workers. Nearly three-tenths (actually 29 percent, N = 1,211) of the male white-collar workers in this study came from working-class backgrounds. A fair-sized minority, 22 percent, had been employed as workers in their first job after completing their formal education. Asked which stratum (*Schicht*) they belonged to, 54 percent said "middle class," and another 24 percent said "upper middle class." The 15 percent who said "working class" stood in sharp contrast to the 76 percent among the male workers in the sample who so identified themselves. Asked if there were differences between workers and white-collar employees, 62 percent of the latter agreed there were. That might, on first glance, sound like an evaluation, a judgment of the "justice" of class differences, a judgment that would accord with the received line of theorizing. A subsequent question, however, asked if there were differences between white-collar employees and civil servants. In this case 83 percent of the employees affirmed that here too there were differences. This suggests that they are referring simply to actual differences in job characteristics and circumstances. Fortunately, the study went a step further; rather than assuming the obvious answers to the evaluative questions, it asked how the respondents evaluated these differences. The first of these questions read: "Do you consider it necessary that there be differences between white-collar employees and workers?" Sixty-four percent said such differences were not necessary as opposed to a 29 percent minority who approved of them. A subsequent question was even more pointed: "The workers demand complete equality with the white-collar workers. What do you think of this?" Fifty-five percent approved of that equality, 31 percent disapproved, and 14 percent had no response. Another question presented a statement: "Many say that white-collar workers would not be so well off if not for the workers' demands." Fifty-one percent agreed with that statement, 36 percent disagreed, and 13 percent had no response. Asked whether workers and white-collar employees had more common or more opposed interests, 52 percent stressed the common ties, 34 percent stressed the opposed concerns, and again, the rest had no opinion.

The study provided breakdowns by social standing, that is, by whether the white-collar workers were of low, middling, or high rank. In general, the relationship between rank and opinion on these questions was very clear. It was the lower-middle-class white-collar workers who were most egalitarian in orientation, that is to say, who were indifferent to the need to maintain differences, who had favorable attitudes toward the workers, and so on.

Again it is a matter for personal judgment; the result is at best suggestive. It suggests that many lower-middle-class white-collar workers in the earlier period were not status strivers, they were not anxious to maintain their distinctive positions, and so on. It *suggests* that they were more egalitarian in outlook, that they stressed the common qualities of their condition rather than their distance from the workers. The findings of this study, in short, are consonant with the *implication* of ZdA memberships and the *implication* of the middle-class vote for the SPD reported by Blank and later by Neisser.

If one did not accept this interpretation, it would be necessary to explain both the SPD voting and the ZdA membership in 1930 and before. It would also be necessary to recognize and account for an extremely important shift in attitude in the intervening years. One would have to answer the question of why the lower-middle-class salaried white-collar workers had become so egalitarian by the early sixties.

These results appear in a study entitled *Angestellte und Gewerkschaft*, done by the Ifas Institute for the Deutsche Gewerkschaftsbund in the summer of 1961. The report is dated July 1964.

44. The best available evidence on the subject is to be found in Hans Beyer, *Die Frau in der politischen Entscheidung: Eine Untersuchung über das Frauenwahlrecht in Deutschland*, Stuttgart: Ferdinand Enke Verlag, 1933; and in Gabriele Bremme, *Die Politische Rolle der Frau in Deutschland*, Göttingen: Vandenhoeck & Ruprecht, 1956. See also Herz, *Über Wesen und Aufgaben*, pp. 70-73; and W. Phillips Shively, "Party Identification, Party Choice, and Voting Stability: The Weimar Case," *American Political Science Review*, 66 (1972): 1203-1225.

45. The point about the know-nothings joining the electorate to vote for Hitler appears in Lipset, *Political Man*, pp. 149-152 and also pp. 216-219. See also Karl O'Lessker, "Who Voted for Hitler? A New Look at the Class Basis of Nazism?" *American Journal of Sociology*, 74 (1968): 63-69; and Allan Schnaiberg, "A Critique of Karl O'Lessker's 'Who Voted for Hitler?' " *American Journal of Sociology*, 74 (1969): 732-735. The Shively article, "Party Identification," is also of some relevance here. See also the discussion and estimates contained in Theodore W. Meckstroth, "Conditions of Partisan Realignments: A Study of Electoral Change," Ph.D. dissertation, University of Minnesota, 1971, pp. 132-143; and in Loren K. Waldman, "Models of Mass Movements—The Case of the Nazis," Ph.D. dissertation, University of Chicago, 1973, p. 252. The arguments are reviewed in Falter, "Wer verhalf," pp. 10-11.

46. See Bremme, *Die Politische Rolle*, p. 41; and Herz, *Über Wesen und Aufgaben*, p. 42. Both cite data from a study of the May 1924 Reichstag election, data drawn from four selected districts. "Die Wahlbeteiligung bei den Reichstagswahlen am 4. Mai 1924 nach Altersstufen und Geschlecht der Wähler," *Wirtschaft und Statistik*, (1926): 235 ff. Some 15.5 percent of the eligible voters in those districts did not vote in that election. The figures were 12.1 and 18.4 for males and females respectively.

Among the 40-45-year-old women, nonvoting amounted to 14.3 percent of the total. The percentages increased steadily in each of the older age categories, reaching 41.6 among those over 70. A similar, though not as pronounced, pattern appears among the men, that rate rising to 21.0 percent in the oldest category. The levels of nonvoting among the younger citizens (17.1 and 19.2 for the males and females) were only slightly above the respective overall figures given above. This result stands in sharp contrast to the pattern one finds in the United States. The difference between the high (75-80 percent) participation in the Weimar elections and the low (50-55 percent) levels in the United States at present is largely the result of this early participation by young Germans. The mobilization of the previous nonvoters in Weimar, therefore, in great measure, must have meant the mobilization of elderly populations. A careful distinction must be made, however, between the votes of previous nonvoters and the votes of first-time voters, the latter obviously being a very young segment.

Religion was also linked to nonvoting, the Catholics having lower average participation levels than Protestants. The origins and significance of this difference are discussed in note 11, Chapter 6.

47. See Pratt, "The Social Basis," ch. 10, especially pp. 206 ff. For Childers's finding on the age relationship, see "The Social Bases," p. 38, n. 55. His finding with respect to the retired appears in his "National Socialism and the New Middle Class," in Reinhard Mann, ed., *Die Nationalsozialisten: Analysen faschistischer Bewegungen*, Stuttgart: Klett-Cotta, 1980, p. 25.

The discrepancy indicated here has a very simple explanation. The members of the party and of the Sturmabteilung were young; all membership studies agree on that point. The commentators based their conclusion about the youthfulness of the party on that highly visible fact. The behavior of electors, on the other hand, was less easily ascertained.

48. Some authors have stressed the role of independent business or "old-middle-class" support in both rural and urban areas while some have placed special emphasis on the "new middle class" (the salaried white-collar workers). Many, to be sure, have taken both groups together, as the component parts of the lower middle class, both presumably being moved by National Socialist appeals. Most of that discussion appears without any serious supporting evidence.

Pratt's original finding, with city size controlled, was of no difference between the two (see the discussion in Chapter 2). But, in a subsequent examination by region, he found a stronger link with the old middle class in some areas. Childers ("The Social Bases," p. 40) provides findings from the 1924 elections through to 1932. During most of that period, the old middle class gave more pronounced support to the NSDAP. In 1932, however, the difference between the two disappeared, a result that is consonant with Pratt's result (based on the July 1932 election). In a later analysis, Childers examined the relationship in predominantly Protestant communities (also controlling for religious composition). In this analysis he found a very pronounced old-middle-class tendency, the respective regression coefficients for old and new middle classes being .672 and .188 for the July 1932 election. See his "National Socialism," p. 25.

The findings of Heinrich August Winkler's study of artisans and shopkeepers are in accord with Childers's findings although, strictly speaking, his study is concerned primarily with old-middle-class organizations and deals only in passing with electoral behavior. See his *Mittelstand, Demokratie und Nationalsozialismus: Die politische Enwicklung von Handwerk und Kleinhandel in der Weimarer Republik*, Cologne: Kiepenheuer & Witsch, 1972.

For the most part, the following chapters focus on the middle-class contribution. The key specification to be explored is that between upper and lower. The old–new distinction is taken up only peripherally.

FOUR. BERLIN

1. An outstanding work on the city's social and cultural history is that of Walter Kiaulehn, *Berlin: Schiksal einer Weltstadt*, Munich: Biederstein Verlag, 1958. Also very useful is the work of Otto Friedrich, *Before the Deluge: A Portrait of Berlin in the 1920's*, New York: Harper & Row, 1972. Of less value is the work of Gerhard Masur, *Imperial Berlin*, New York: Basic Books, 1970. Also of some use, for descriptions of the different city areas, is the famous Baedeker.

2. Some of those living in the new metropolitan area were still engaged in rural occupations, the 1933 census reporting that 1.3 percent of the economically active population was engaged in agriculture and forestry. *Mitteilungen des Statistischen Amts der Stadt Berlin*, no. 18, pt. 10, p. 7. Some of the complications involved in descriptions of the urban scene may be noted here. The 1.3 percent means 29,225 persons. That figure is *up* 47 percent over 1925. Some 12,800 or 43.8 percent of those in agriculture and forestry were unemployed at the time of the 1933 census. It is likely that, lacking other opportunities, they had migrated to the city. Some 8,000 of them were living in the center of the city, far from any agricultural possibilities. The economically active population in this case included those currently at work and those who were unemployed, the latter being classified according to their previous employment.

3. For statistics showing the distribution of the city's economically active males and females, see Appendix C.

The unemployment figures given earlier in the text are overall figures for the male and female segments of the labor force. The unemployment levels in the most seriously affected categories ran as follows: white-collar employees, male and female, 27.7 percent and 25.8 percent; workers, male and female, 47.7 percent and 37.1 percent. For a discussion of the differences in male and female patterns of employment, see Richard F. Hamilton, *Class and Politics in the United States*, New York: John Wiley & Sons, 1972, ch. 4.

A key census category, as noted in Chapter 2, combined all independent businessmen with top-level salaried workers (managers) and top civil servants. The last two segments formed minuscule fractions of the total. That was the overall result for the Reich, but in Berlin the percentages must have been considerably higher, and in the city's affluent districts they must have been higher still. In the affluent districts, moreover, the number of small businessmen would decline proportionately.

In Chapter 3, some hypothetical figures were offered to describe the composition of the nonfarm labor force. The working class, it was suggested, formed 60 percent of the total. For business and administrative centers, the percentage is somewhat lower, as here in the Berlin case. Elsewhere it would be higher. Taking the figures for economically active males, one finds very high percentages in the Ruhr cities, for example, 71.9 in Duisburg, 70.6 in Dortmund, 70.0 in Essen, and 78.6 in Gelsenkirchen. Even in Düsseldorf, a provincial administrative center, the figure is 57.5. From *Statistik des Deutschen Reichs*, vol. 451, pt. 1. See also J. Michael Hemphill, "The Occupational and Class Structures of Germany in the Twentieth Century," M.S. thesis, Department of Sociology, University of Wisconsin, 1968. He finds (p. 11) that overall, 60.8 percent of the nonfarm male labor force were manual workers (*Arbeiter*) as were 56.1 percent of the equivalent females. The latter would include domestic servants. These results support the working-class estimate given in the previous chapter. The upper-class estimate matches that of Theodor Geiger. The division between upper and lower middle class, as noted, is an arbitrary one.

4. A study of participation in a Danzig Volkstag election in 1927 found that 17.3 percent of eligible women voters had not voted. The equivalent figure for domestic servants (women) was 35.6 percent. Widows, incidentally, were also above average with 23.4 percent. See Dr. Hartwig, "Das Frauenwahlrecht in der Statistik," *Allgemeines statistisches Archiv*, 21: 2 (1931): 167-182. A study of voting for city councilors in Mainz found only 56.6 percent of the electorate participating. Among women the figure was lower, at 50.4 percent. And for domestic servants (women only), the figure was lowest of all, 38.5 percent. See "Die Wahlbeteiligung bei der Stadtverordnetenwahl in Mainz am 15. November 1925 nach Geschlecht und Berufen der Wähler," in the publication of the Reich's statistical office, *Wirtschaft und Statistik*, 6 (1926): 896. Although domestic servants form a relatively large percentage of the employed population in upper-class districts, it should be remembered that many of them were not eligible to vote, being below the legal age.

5. Karl Baedeker, *Berlin: Handbook for Travellers*, Freiburg: Karl Baedeker, 1971, p. 60.

6. Nearly 10 percent (actually 9.6) of the housing units in Berlin in 1927 had six or more rooms (exclusive of kitchens and bathrooms). The range, however, was considerable with Zehlendorf (43.1 percent) and Wilmersdorf (35.2 percent) at one extreme and Wedding (1.3 percent) at the other. From the *Statistisches Jahrbuch der Stadt Berlin*, 1929, Berlin: Verlag Gebrüder Grunert, 1929, p. 37. Those figures in turn are derived from the Reich's census of housing of May 16, 1927.

To the contemporary upper-middle-class sensibility, six rooms plus a kitchen might not sound like a luxurious dwelling place. It must be remembered that standards have escalated somewhat since the twenties. Much of the housing that was upper middle class at that time might well be considered only middle middle at present. Zehlendorf was building up in this period as is evidenced by the supply of dwelling units with seven or more rooms. In May of 1925 that amounted to 2,910 units. In May of 1927, it was 3,623 units. And in January 1934, there were 4,669 such units.

7. Except for some cities with heavy industry (e.g. Gelsenkirchen), all German cities had rather imbalanced sex ratios with women far outnumbering the men. Berlin, for example, had 1,169 women per 1,000 men. An imbalanced sex ratio, because of the presence of female domestics, provides another index of upper- or upper-middle-class status of the city districts. The first six districts in terms of women per 1,000 men were: Wilmersdorf, 1,414; Zehlendorf, 1,343;

Schöneberg, 1,313; Steglitz, 1,247; Charlottenburg, 1,246; and Tiergarten, 1,234. The data are from *Mitteilungen*, no. 18, pt. 11, p. 7.

The three measures of the status or well-being of the districts are strongly intercorrelated. The Pearsonian r between the percentage in nonmanual occupations and the percentage in domestic service was .79. The correlation between percentage in nonmanual occupations and the percentage of dwelling units with six or more rooms was .87. Those correlations, based on percentages, do not reflect the rankings as given in Table 4.1. The respective Spearman correlations between the districts as ranked in that table and the two other variables are .72 and .82.

8. See Annemarie Lange, *Das Wilhelminische Deutschland, Zwischen Jahrhundertwende und Novemberrevolution*, Berlin (East): Dietz Verlag, 1967, p. 177. Like the claims in the sources reviewed in Chapter 2, those dealing with the orientations of the well-off or bourgeois workers are presented without any supporting evidence or reference to such evidence.

9. Friedrich, *Before the Deluge*, p. 202.

10. See Appendix A for the comparable national figures. And see Chapter 10 for further discussion of the shifts to the right within the middle-class parties.

Percentage figures based on valid votes reflect *relative* gains and losses. In some cases those results may not accurately reflect absolute gains and losses. The 1928 election saw a slight increase of participation in Berlin, and, in part because of that change, there was an increase in the number of valid votes (by 181,000). The slight relative loss of the DVP in this case did not mean a loss of votes. The party gained some 10,000 votes, but that was not enough to hold its previous relative position. The difference between these possibilities is an important one: in the one case the problem is to account for a failure to hold voters; in the other the problem is a failure to attract at least a proportional number of new voters. If the researcher-analyst-commentator does not recognize the different possibilities, it can lead to explanations of nonfacts (that is, explaining the supposed loss of *voters* when the party had actually gained some).

11. It is difficult to do justice to the complexity of the electoral development in a few sentences. The movement from middle-class parties to the NSDAP is clearest in the case of the DDP and the DVP. Much of the DNVP loss, it would appear, went to three splinter parties that broke away from the Conservatives when Alfred Hugenberg took over the leadership. The Conservatives lost about 90,000 votes. These three splinter parties took 58,000 votes. Although the overall percentages for the splinter parties were roughly the same in the 1928 and 1930 elections, those votes were cast for different parties, some disappearing and others replacing them. A Völkisch-Nationaler Block appeared in the 1928 election and took 21,698 votes. This party appears to have taken votes from the Conservative total of December 1924. Those Völkische votes probably went to the National Socialists in 1930.

The increase in valid votes over 1928 might reflect a mobilization of previous nonvoters, or it might stem from the participation of first-time voters, those born in 1908-1910. It is difficult to make any assessment of those changes because there exists still another possibility: it might also reflect the participation of people who had moved into the district. There was an increase of over 5,000 votes in Zehlendorf since the May 1928 election (when 29,242 votes were cast), and the NSDAP increase was also just over 5,000. But Zehlendorf was adding housing units at a rate of approximately 500 per year. If one assumes an average of two voters per unit, it would mean that roughly 2,000 of the 5,000 new voters were people who had just moved into the district. There is, however, no reason for assuming that these new voters would differ sharply from the previous residents in their party choices. These estimates are based on figures taken from the *Statistisches Jahrbuch der Stadt Berlin*, 1927, p. 27; 1929, p. 37. The housing constructed in this period included units of all sizes; it was not merely a result of the Onkel Toms Hütte development. Housing construction continued in the outlying districts at relatively high levels well into the depression period.

12. The Communist vote in working-class districts was somewhat more stable than its vote elsewhere. In Wedding, the Thälmann vote fell to 86.0 percent of the March level; in Friedrichshain it fell to 86.4; in Kreuzberg, to 84.4. In Zehlendorf support for Thälmann fell to 78.6 percent of the former level; in Wilmersdorf to 77.8; in Steglitz to 78.5; and in Charlottenburg to 81.0.

13. The effects of vacationing on the election result were not lost on contemporaries. A report in a Berlin local newspaper the day after the election commented at length on the phenomenon. It reported that a fifth of the registered voters in the western districts of Berlin had obtained *Stimmscheine*. *Lichterfelder Lokal-Anzeiger*, no. 178, August 1, 1932.

Joseph Goebbels evidently studied these results in some detail, noted the losses vis-à-vis the April result, and also saw the losses as linked to the votes of the vacationers. See his *Vom Kaiserhof zur Reichskanzlei*, Munich: Zentralverlag der NSDAP, 1937, pp. 135-136. The original edition appeared in 1934.

14. From issue no. 32, August 7, 1932. This issue contained precinct (*Stimmbezirk*) data for these communities.

15. From the *Lichterfelder Lokal-Anzeiger*, no. 178, August 1, 1932. One early study picked up the Steglitz peculiarity, this being the work of Werner Stephan, "Zur Soziologie der Nationalsozialistischen Deutschen Arbeiterpartei," *Zeitschrift für Politik*, 20 (1931): 793-800. He contrasts the "worker district Wedding, the middle-class district Steglitz, and the villa district Zehlendorf" using results from the 1930 election. In the case of Steglitz, he omitted Lichterfelde because, with its big business (*grossbürgerlichen*) population, it did not match the rest of the district. Steglitz without Lichterfelde gave the National Socialists 25.8 percent, the highest for any area of Berlin. Stephan found an even more pronounced NSDAP tendency in a middle-class district of Bremen, again contrasting it with a working-class and a villa district there. Fragmentary as it is, the evidence in this article is, to the best of my knowledge, the only *evidence* from the period supporting the claim of middle-class support for the National Socialists.

16. The basic work on the Zentrum's electorate is that of Johannes Schauff, *Die Deutschen Katholiken und die Zentrumspartei: Eine politisch-statistische Untersuchung der Reichstagswahlen seit 1871*, Cologne: Verlag J.P. Bachem, 1928. While

there is a general *agreement* that the Zentrum's voters were almost exclusively Catholic, there were some late changes in that pattern. As the so-called middle-class parties disappeared, some voters looked for a next best alternative, and some chose the Zentrum. Some sense of this development may be gained by examining two institutions in Schmargendorf (in the Wilmersdorf district), one an old people's home run by the Berlin Jewish community, the other a Protestant institution, the Martin Luther Hospital. People cast their votes in such institutions, and these would be reported as if they were independent precincts.

There were 175 votes cast in the old people's home in the July 1932 election and 173 cast in November, most (115 and 108 respectively) going to the SPD. The Zentrum gained 12 votes in July and 27 in November. The Economic party gained 38 votes in July, and the German State party took none. In November, the State party took 36 and the Economic party took none. One senses a desperate search for a viable alternative in this shifting.

In the Martin Luther Hospital, 249 votes were cast in July, 274 in November. Most went to the DNVP and the NSDAP. In July, the respective figures were 43 and 165; in November, 105 and 107. From the *Grunewald-Echo*, no. 32, August 7, 1932, and no. 46, November 13, 1932.

While not entirely accurate, the assumptions in the text are close enough to serve as the basis for rough estimates. In the old people's home, for example, the Zentrum percentage was 6.8, and in the hospital it was 1.6 as of July. Three votes were cast for the NSDAP in the old people's home. Senility with its resultant confusion is one obvious explanation. See also the following note.

17. In Wilmersdorf, 13.5 percent of the (1933) population was Jewish (taken from a figure based on the census report). The figure of 15,413 given above in the text is 13.5 percent of the number of valid votes cast in the district. This probably underestimates the Jewish vote because of the demographic structure of the Jewish community (lower fertility) and because of likely higher turnout. Many Jews had converted in the previous decades, a problem that alarmed· religious leaders of the Jewish community. If one assumed that they would follow the voting patterns of their previous coreligionists, this too would mean some underestimation.

The Zentrum vote figure is taken directly from the election results. The working-class left vote figure is two-thirds of the combined SPD-KPD vote which is again taken directly from the election results. This two-thirds estimate is derived from the Neisser figure reported in Chapter 3. Since his conclusion was that 40 percent of the SPD voters were not manual workers and since he made no allowance at all for middle-class Communist votes, this judgment is a high figure; that is, it reduces the amount of left support coming from the middle class and thus provides a conservative base for the present estimates. The figure for segments A and B is derived by subtracting that subtotal from the total number of valid votes.

The assumption of a random distribution of the Catholic population is made on the basis of census figures for Berlin, which show roughly equal proportions of Catholics in all city districts. This pattern contrasts sharply with the experience elsewhere, for example, in Cologne (see Chapter 6) and Essen (Chapter 7).

18. Seymour Martin Lipset, *Political Man: The Social Bases of Politics*, Garden City: Doubleday, 1960, pp. 141-142.

19. One is so accustomed to thinking of working-class districts, especially those of Berlin, as bastions of the left, that it is worth reviewing some election statistics. In Kreuzberg, the largest of the working-class districts, in December 1924, 23.6 percent of the voters chose the conservative DNVP. Another 10.1 percent favored the left liberal Democrats, and 6.0 chose the right liberal People's party. Only about half of the districts' voters chose the left parties at that point. Even in Wedding the middle-class parties were not without support. There, in December 1924, the DNVP took 16.8 percent of the total. The DDP took 7.3 percent, and the DVP took 3.0. One-quarter of the district's votes went to the Conservatives or to the liberal parties.

20. The best study of this transformation, a retrospective one, is that of David Butler and Donald Stokes, *Political Change in Britain*, New York: St. Martin's Press, 1971, ch. 7. Some suggestive evidence is contained in Juan J. Linz, "The Social Bases of West German Politics," Ph.D. dissertation, Columbia University, 1959, chs. 10 and 27. See also the discussion of this question in the previous chapter. Some indication of the age relationship in the British context, particularly among the older working-class women, may be seen in Robert T. McKenzie and Allan Silver, *Angels in Marble*, Chicago: University of Chicago Press, 1968, pp. 88 ff. and 223 ff. The assumptions of this line of argument would be consonant with the findings of Pratt and Childers (reported in the previous chapter) who found NSDAP support and age to be positively related.

21. The table shows the vote in July 1932 as a percentage of the votes the party received in December 1924. In Berlin, the DNVP consistently outdrew the right liberal DVP. This was generally the case in all districts, even in the best-off ones, Wilmersdorf and Zehlendorf. This finding goes against the point made in previous chapters, that the DVP was *the* party of Germany's upper and upper middle classes. This pattern, however, reflects the city's geographic location, it being the major city in the center of traditional Prussia. The city's upper and upper middle classes would have migrated from the surrounding provinces and would have brought their politics with them. The situation is different in the cities of western Germany, especially those in the Ruhr, the center of heavy industry.

Area	DNVP	DDP	DVP
Middle class	45.5	18.3	15.3
Mixed	54.2	29.0	16.9
Working class	32.7	6.2	4.3

One tends to forget the left liberal German Democrats in these discussions. That party also drew disproportionately in the best districts. In 1928, for example, its best showings were: 15.3 percent in Wilmersdorf, 12.6 percent in Charlottenburg, 11.9 percent in Schöneberg, and 10.4 percent in Zehlendorf. Its poorest showing was in Wedding—4.5 percent.

22. Zehlendorf produced 14,715 National Socialist votes in April and 12,395 in November, a fall to 84 percent of the former level. The latter figure still left

29.4 percent of the district's voters favoring that party. Similar findings appear in Wilmersdorf. See Paul Kluke, "Der Fall Potempa," *Vierteljahrshefte für Zeitgeschichte*, 5 (1957): 279-297. Many groups objected to the death sentences. Most of them were rightist, but even the liberal *Frankfurter Zeitung*, which for years had opposed the death penalty, felt the killers should not be executed. Kluke, "Der Fall Potempa," p. 284.

One consideration that appears to have entered in some people's thinking was another act of political violence. On July 10 of that year, some members of the Reichsbanner (a republican paramilitary organization closely linked to the Social Democrats) had disrupted a National Socialist meeting, killing two men and wounding many others. Their sentencing occurred on the same day as that of the Potempa murderers, but in this case the maximum penalty was four years' imprisonment. The difference was that their crime was committed before the presidential decree of August 9 providing the death penalty for planned political murders. The Potempa killing came one and a half hours after the decree came into effect, the murderers, supposedly, not knowing of its existence. Hitler and others, of course, made much of the disparity.

23. The evidence presented in this chapter is based on figures for the twenty administrative districts of Greater Berlin plus some more detailed breakdowns for Wilmersdorf, a part of Zehlendorf, and the major subareas of Steglitz. Results for the precincts (*Stimmbezirke*) would have been most helpful for further analysis but, unfortunately, a review of the holdings of the most likely Berlin libraries and archives failed to turn up any results for those units other than the *Grunewald-Echo* report. In addition to those institutions listed in the Preface, an assistant has checked out the holdings of the following organizations: in West Berlin: Verwaltungsarchiv Schöneberg; Heimatmuseum Schöneberg; Verwaltungsarchiv Steglitz; Bibliothek des Abgeordnetenhauses; Bibliothek und Archiv des Otto-Suhr-Institut (Freie Universität); Bibliothek und Archiv des Instituts für Publizistik (Freie Universität); Einwohnermeldeamt Schöneberg; Bücherei des Statistischen Landesamts; Amerika-Gedenk-Bibliothek; Landesarchiv. And in East Berlin: Stadtbibliothek; Deutsche Staatsbibliothek. Local newspapers were examined only in the districts indicated. There might well be some more detailed breakdowns for other districts in their local press.

24. The quotations are from Alan Bullock, *Hitler: A Study in Tyranny*, New York: Harper & Row, 1962, p. 115.

25. The quotations come from the *Vossische Zeitung* of April 1, 1924 (evening edition), April 12 (evening), April 13 (Sunday), and April 26 (evening). The text here reports only a small portion of their coverage of Hitler and of Deutschvölkische party affairs.

The national meeting of the Conservative party (DNVP) was in progress when the verdict of the Munich trial was handed down. Because the Conservatives are sometimes portrayed as different from the National Socialists, as moderate and responsible, it is useful to present the report of their meeting on that day from the *Vossische Zeitung*, April 2, 1924 (morning edition): "The verdict in the Hitler trial was made known at the German National party meeting in Hamburg shortly after the conclusion of a speech by Hergt. The acquittal of

Ludendorff was received with tumultuous applause and loud calls of 'Heil' by those present."

26. The "hard" sentence was, as Bracher puts it, "the lowest possible sentence for high treason: five years' imprisonment, with the expressed probability of an early pardon." See *The German Dictatorship: The Origins, Structure, and Effects of National Socialism*, New York: Praeger, 1970, p. 121.

27. The quotations from the *Neue Preussische Zeitung* appeared in the issues of April 1, 2, and 3. The anti-Semitic references appeared in the discussion of the election result, in the issue of May 6. Here, too, presentation of only a small part of the paper's coverage is possible. One additional item, however, appears in the issue of April 4. Hitler and the rest are referred to as "men who are moved by pure love of the fatherland."

28. The *Börsen-Zeitung* was quoted in the *Vossische Zeitung* of April 2, 1924 (morning edition).

29. Goebbels's diary entry reads: "The 'Berliner Börsenzeitung' behaves very decently toward us." See his *Vom Kaiserhof*, p. 83. Funk's activities are described in Bullock, *Hitler*, p. 172.

30. The following accounts are taken from Eva Pfeifer, *Das Hitlerbild im Spiegel einiger konservativen Zeitungen in den Jahren 1929-1933*, Munich: UNI-Druck, 1966 (originally a doctoral dissertation, University of Heidelberg, 1965).

31. Pfeifer, *Das Hitlerbild*, pp. 10 ff.

32. Ibid., pp. 56-99.

33. Ibid., pp. 100-142.

34. Ibid., pp. 143 ff.

35. *Grunewald-Echo*, no. 31, July 31, 1932. The *Lichterfelder Lokal-Anzeiger* (which also put out a journal in Lankwitz) recommended a right coalition after the July election, one that was to include the Zentrum, the Bavarian People's party, the DNVP, and the NSDAP. These local Steglitz papers contained only NSDAP advertisements. They seldom made comments or recommendations of their own; the recommendations they did carry stemmed either from the government or from the parties of the right.

36. The quotation is from Joseph Goebbels, *Kampf um Berlin: Der Anfang*, 18th ed., Munich: Zentralverlag der NSDAP, 1940, p. 50. For the National Socialist operations in and around Berlin see also his *Vom Kaiserhof*, and J. K. von Engelbrechten, *Eine braune Armee Entsteht: Die Geschichte der Berlin-Brandenburger SA*, Munich: Zentralverlag der NSDAP, 1940. Speaking of events in March 1926, this author states (p. 39) that "the SA-Group Spandau with its eighty men remains for a long time the strongest. Mainly formed out of workers and front soldiers, it bears a hard proletarian-military character." See also Martin Broszat, "Die Anfänge der Berliner NSDAP 1926/27" *Vierteljahrshefte für Zeitgeschichte*, 8 (1960): 85-118.

37. This February 1927 event, known as the Pharus Hall battle, is frequently referred to in the National Socialist literature; it was *the* exemplary heroic struggle against overwhelming odds. Goebbels, incidentally, did not invent the tactic; it had been used frequently in earlier years. The episode is also referred to in scholarly and, more frequently, in popular literature where it adds an element

of drama and helps to explain how the party reached a larger audience through the newspapers. Friedrich, for example, gives three pages (*Before the Deluge*, pp. 201-203) to the battle: "Glasses, bottles and table legs flew through the air. There was a deafening uproar." "The next day," he adds, Goebbels had "all the headlines he wanted."

That statement exaggerates. A review of three rightist newspapers found only very brief notice given to the event. The *Kreuzzeitung* gave it approximately three column inches. A smaller report appeared in the *Deutsche Allgemeine Zeitung. Der Tag* provided no report. These were all brief and factual, on the same level as these newspapers' reports of automobile accidents or robberies. The liberal *Vossische Zeitung* did not report the event.

The Pharus Hall battle, in short, appears to have received its major attention in National Socialist mythology. From there it has been picked up and passed on in works of popular history. Also accepting the claim of a massive press response to the event are: Ernest K. Bramsted, *Goebbels and National Socialist Propaganda, 1925-1945*, East Lansing: Michigan State University Press, 1965, pp. 21-22; Viktor Reimann, *Dr. Joseph Goebbels*, Vienna: Verlag Fritz Molden, 1971, pp. 89-90; and John Toland, *Adolf Hitler*, Garden City: Doubleday, 1976, p. 224.

Five. Hamburg

1. There are no equivalents to the rich city histories available for Berlin. A useful brief history is that of Bernhard Studt and Hans Olsen, *Hamburg: Eine kurzgefasste Geschichte der Stadt*, Hamburg: Hans Köhler Verlag, 1964. A very useful account covering the period just prior to the rise of the National Socialists is that of Richard A. Comfort, *Revolutionary Hamburg: Labor Politics in the Early Weimar Republic*, Stanford: Stanford University Press, 1966.

2. The basic source is: Statistisches Landesamt, *Statistik des Hamburgischen Staates*, p. 33, "Die Volks-, Berufs- und Betreibszählung vom 16. Juni 1925," Hamburg: Otto Meissners Verlag, 1928.

The percentages of unemployed in 1933, for the males and females in the principal categories were: white-collar employees, 28.4 and 24.4; workers, 48.4 and 37.3. (See note 3, Chapter 4, for comparable Berlin figures.) Except for the smaller civil servant category, the occupational composition of the city very closely matches that of Berlin; see Appendix C. In contrast to those of Berlin, the city districts to be discussed here are small ones; only three had more than 100,000 persons, and some had less than 10,000.

Some of the place names are now spelled differently. The Finkenwärder of 1930 is now Finkenwerder. The same vowel change occurred with Steinwärder and Billwärder. Barmbeck is now Barmbek; Eilbeck is Eilbek. The 1930's spelling has been retained in all cases.

3. In Hamburg in the mid-twenties, 4.5 percent of the housing had seven or more rooms. In the three best areas of the city, Harvestehude, Rotherbaum, and Hohenfelde, the respective figures were 31.9, 22.4, and 17.0. In working-class Barmbeck, by contrast, the equivalent figure was 0.8 percent. From Sta-

tistisches Landesamt, *Statistisches Jahrbuch für die Freie und Hansestadt Hamburg: 1925*, Hamburg: Lüteke & Wulff, 1926, p. 121.

4. A dissertation by Reinhard Behrens presents data from 1892-1897 on per capita income for the city districts. At that time the distribution was as follows: Harvestehude: 2,855 Reichsmark (RM); Hohenfelde, 1,220; St. Georg Nord, 822; Barmbeck, 331; Billwärder Ausschlag, 278. See his "Die Deutschnationalen in Hamburg, 1918-1933," doctoral dissertation, University of Hamburg, 1973, p. 313.

5. The contrasting demography of the upper-class and working-class districts, already noted in Berlin, is found again in Hamburg. Harvestehude has nearly twice as many single women as men. Barmbeck, St. Pauli, and the Neustadt, by comparison, have a modest surplus of single men. The numbers of married men and women in all districts, of course, are more or less equal. All districts show a surplus of widows and divorced women. The single persons in the working-class districts must be, overwhelmingly, children of the families in those areas. In the upper-class districts the single persons include domestic servants as well as children. Some of the former probably come from the city's working-class areas. Some children in the upper-class districts, sons mostly, could of course be away at a university, in Göttingen for example. This would normally be a very small percentage of the total. See *Statistik des Hamburgischen Staates*, pt. 33, p. 71.

6. If, for example, some of the Barmbeck women engaged in lower-middle-class occupations were the wives or daughters of men employed in working-class occupations, then, because of the convention that defines the class of family members in terms of the occupation of the head or the main earner, the working-class percentages would actually be somewhat higher than is indicated in Table 5.1.

It is easy today to overlook the prominent role of household servants in previous periods. In 1882, Hamburg had 25,752 female household servants (*Dienstboten*) out of a total population of 466,516. Male servants can be overlooked because of their small number, 699. In subsequent decades the number of male servants fell; the number of female servants increased to the peak recorded in the 1907 census. In 1882, 40.1 percent of the employed women in the city were household servants. That percentage fell dramatically in later years; in 1925, the equivalent figure was 13.3 percent. The decline, however, resulted from an increase in the number of alternative opportunities for women, not from a shift out of domestic service: the *number* of household servants in 1925 was greater than the number in 1882. One other point: the 1925 census reported 30.8 percent of the women household servants as under age 20, that is, below voting age. Another 35.4 percent were between 20 and 24, an age group that usually had relatively low levels of political participation. From Statistisches Landesamt *Hamburger statistische Monatsberichte*, 1926, special suppl. 1, pp. 223-225.

7. *Statistisches Jahrbuch, 1925*, pp. 360-362. Also of some interest is Helga Krohn's "Die Juden in Hamburg: Die politische, soziale und kurturelle Entwicklung einer jüdischen Grossstadtgemeinde nach der Emanzipation: 1848-1918," doctoral dissertation, University of Hamburg, 1970. There must have

been considerable occupational mobility on the part of the Hamburg Jewish population. In 1885, 55 percent of the city's Jews lived in the Altstadt or the Neustadt. By 1925, that percentage had fallen to 7.3 percent (ibid., p. 71).

8. The voting results were published in *Statistische Mitteilungen über den hamburgischen Staat*, no. 14, "Die Reichstagswahl am 4. Mai 1924," Hamburg: Otto Meissners Verlag, 1924. In addition we have: no. 20 (1924) for the December 1924 election; no. 23 (1928) for the 1928 election; no. 25 (1930) for the 1930 election; no. 29 (1932) for the July 1932 election; and no. 30 (1932) for the November 1932 election. The last two numbers (29 and 30) were printed by Lüteke & Wulff, Hamburg, 1932.

9. For reasons indicated earlier (see note 10 of the previous chapter), statements about relative shifts that are based on percentage tables such as Table 5.2 may not accurately reflect absolute changes in the voting patterns. All of the statements made in the text, however, do describe both relative and absolute changes. The KPD vote in 1930, for example, was larger, both relatively and absolutely, than in 1928. The slight percentage decline in July 1932 meant an absolute decline of 2,280 votes from the 131,148 total of 1930.

10. This was an urban parallel to the much larger reaction occurring in Schleswig-Holstein which surrounds Hamburg. For history and documentation of that development see Rudolf Heberle, *Landbevölkerung und Nationalsozialismus: Eine soziologische Untersuchung der politischen Willensbildung in Schleswig-Holstein 1918 bis 1932*, Stuttgart: Deutsche Verlags-Anstalt, 1963, pp. 29 ff. For figures on the DNVP vote in earlier elections, see Comfort, *Revolutionary Hamburg*, p. 180.

The dominance of the liberal parties over the Conservatives in the "best" districts of Hamburg may be seen in the table which presents figures from the 1928 election.

District	DVP	DDP	DNVP
Harvestehude	27.9%	21.1%	20.8%
Rotherbaum	22.2	20.0	18.0
Hohenfelde	24.7	11.5	23.6

Behrens sees the city's DNVP as a lower-middle-class party, one that to some extent at least, provided opposition to the dominant or established National Liberals (and later DVP). "Die Deutschnationalen," pp. 8-14 and 50-56. Another point of some interest is a quotation to the effect that in Hamburg "the 'new middle class,' the white-collar workers, were already [prior to World War I] decisively influenced by the SPD" (p. 28).

11. On the history of the National Socialists in Hamburg see the following: Werner Jochmann, *Nationalsozialismus und Revolution: Ursprung und Geschichte der NSDAP in Hamburg, 1922-1933–Dokumente*, Frankfurt: Europäische Verlagsanstalt, 1963; Helga Anschütz, "Die Nationalsozialistische Deutsche Arbeiterpartei in Hamburg: Ihre Anfänge bis zur Reichstagswahl vom 14. September, 1930," doctoral dissertation, University of Hamburg, 1956; Albert Krebs, *Tendenzen und Gestalten der NSDAP: Erinnerungen an die Frühzeit der Partei*, Stuttgart: Deutsche Verlags-Anstalt, 1959. Also of considerable interest is Werner Joch-

mann's *Im Kampf um die Macht: Hitlers Rede vor dem Hamburger Nationalklub von 1919*, Frankfurt: Europäische Verlagsanstalt, 1960. Albert Krebs was for a while the Hamburg *Gauleiter*. His memoir provides one of the best available accounts of the internal dynamics of the party. See also the references in note 21.

12. In the 1930 election, the highest percentages gained by the National Socialists were in Hohenfelde (29.7); Rotherbaum (25.5); Eilbeck (25.4); and the Altstadt (25.2). Anschütz, in her analysis of this election ("Die Arbeiterpartei") says that the NSDAP achieved its largest number of votes in Eppendorf, "Hofenfelde" (*sic*), Borgfelde, and Eilbeck. I am assuming that her expression (*grösste Stimmenzahl*) is intended to mean highest percentage. It would make little sense if absolute numbers were intended since they obviously depend so much on the size of the district. In that case her list would be even more inaccurate since only Eppendorf would come among the top four. The four districts she lists, incidentally, in keeping with her stress on the middle-class character of the National Socialist support, are described as "the residential areas of Hamburg's white-collar employees." Eppendorf, it will be noted, had a combined figure for civil servants and white-collar employees of only 38.7 percent, a level that is roughly equal to that of the workers in the area. If one knew the Hamburg circumstances only through Anschütz's dissertation, one would take it as providing evidence for the lower middle class–National Socialism link. The actual pattern in Hamburg, as we have seen, is very different.

13. These figures were obtained through the generous assistance of Herr Bocklitz of the Hamburg Staatsarchiv. The figures for Blankenese, Gross and Klein Flottbek, and Wellingsbüttel appeared in the *Hamburger Echo* of August 1, 1932. Those for Poppenbüttel and Wellingsbüttel appeared in the *Hamburger Nachrichten* of the same date. And those for Reinbek were found in the *Bergedorfer Zeitung* of that date.

14. These precinct results are contained in the *Statistische Mitteilungen über den hamburgischen Staat*, no. 29 (1932).

15. Hamburg was once a free port. After German unification Bismarck pressed to change the city's status. The compromise achieved in 1888 reduced the duty-free area to a few parts of the harbor, the most important of which was Steinwärder-Waltershof. Goods could be unloaded, manufactured, and processed there. They would be taxed when moved outside the free port area. The population living there would have been largely engaged in lower-middle-class occupations—clerks attending to the billing and lading, tax officials, guards and watchmen, and police.

16. From *Statistik des Hamburgischen Staates*, pt. 32, p. 92.

17. The occupations of Jewish males in 1925 were as follows: independents, managers, etc., 57.4 percent; white-collar employees and civil servants, 36.1 percent; workers, 6.3 percent; and helping family members, 0.2 percent. In Harvestehude and Rotherbaum, the assumption of the argument is probably a close approximation to the actual situation. See "Die katholische und die jüdische Bevölkerung in Hamburg," *Aus Hamburgs Verwaltung und Wirtschaft* (Monatsschrift des Statistischen Landesamts) 6:5 (1929): 129-136.

18. The figures in the table show the July 1932 vote as percentages of the

Area	DNVP	DDP	DVP
Middle class	29.2	55.6	17.8
Mixed	30.6	61.4	19.2
Working class	21.7	55.7	15.6

votes the parties received in December 1924. The equivalent figures for Berlin appear in the previous chapter, note 21.

19. The "losses" are obtained by subtracting the figures in note 18 from 100.0 percent. In the first instance, for example, the suggestion is that the DNVP lost 70.8 percent of its 1924 voters in Hamburg's middle-class districts. As indicated previously in the text, this is a crude way of assessing losses. Given the increased size of the electorate and the somewhat higher levels of participation, this procedure underestimates actual losses. The procedure, moreover suggests a fixed stock of electors, and that clearly was not the case, some having died and some having retired from active participation. Others would have entered the electorate for the first time.

20. From *Aus Hamburgs Verwaltung und Wirtschaft*, 8:6 (1931): 177.

21. See Krebs, *Tendenzen und Gestalten*, p. 42. A brief memoir dealing with the Rotherbaum group contains little of intellectual value, this being the work of Alfred Bordihn, *10 Jahre Kreis Rotherbaum der NSDAP*, Hamburg: Paul Meyer Druckerei und Verlag, 1935. An NSDAP history of the party's struggle in this city is that of Hermann Okrass, *Das Ende einer Parole—"Hamburg bleibt rot,"* Hamburg: Hanseatische Verlagsanstalt, 1934. See also Wilhelm Recken and Julius W. Krafft, *Hamburg unterm Hakenkreuz: Eine Chronik der nationalen Erhebung in der Nordmark, 1919-33*, Hamburg: Paul Hartung Verlag, 1933.

22. *Hamburger Nachrichten*, issues of September 1-15, 1930. Specific reference has been made to issues of September 1, 5, 6, 7, 11, 12, and 13. For the July 1932 election, I have covered the issues from July 23 to August 1. Specific reference has been made to issues of July 23, 24, 26, 28, and 31.

23. *Hamburgischer Correspondent*, issues of September 2-15, 1930; April 10, 1932; and July 30-31, 1932.

24. *Hamburger Fremdenblatt*, issues of September 6-13, 1930.

25. *Hamburger Anzeiger*, issues of September 2-13, 1930; April 9 and 23, 1932; July 30, 1932; and November 5, 1932.

SIX. COLOGNE AND MUNICH

1. The statistics on city size and religious composition are taken from the 1933 census, *Statistik des Deutschen Reichs*, vol. 451, pt. 3, "Die Bevölkerung des Deutschen Reichs nach der Religionszugehörigkeit," Berlin, 1936, pp. 32-33.

2. *Statistisches Jahrbuch der Stadt Köln*, 1932, vol. 22, Cologne, 1933, p. 1.

3. *Kölner Verwaltung und Statistik*, vol. 7, pt. 2, Cologne: Oskar Müller, 1929, p. 62.

4. The only report I was able to find that gave occupations in the various subareas of the city was a post–World War II publication. This gave percentage

distributions for 1939 and 1946. The city districts given there did not match the districts in the election reports, in most cases combining subareas and in some instances cutting across the election districts. *Statistische Mitteilungen der Stadt Köln,* 4:2/3 (1949): 41.

5. For a brief overview of the postwar events in Cologne see Paul Weymar, *Konrad Adenauer: Die authorisierte Biographie,* Munich: Kindler Verlag, 1955, pp. 60-77; or Terence Prittie, *Konrad Adenauer, 1876-1967,* Chicago: Cowles, 1971, pp. 36-65. For more detail, see Karl Dietrich Erdmann, *Adenauer in der Rheinlandpolitik nach dem Ersten Weltkrieg,* Stuttgart: Ernst Klett Verlag, 1966.

6. The Cologne figures are from Lorenz Huber, "Die politischen Wahlen in Köln in den Jahren 1919 bis 1926," *Kölner Verwaltung und Statistik,* 6:1/2: 14. The Berlin figures are from the *Statistisches Jahrbuch der Stadt Berlin,* vol. 34, Berlin: P. Stankiewicz Buchdruckerei, 1920, p. 884, and are, of course, for the old Berlin, prior to the 1920 consolidation. And the Hamburg figures are taken from Richard A. Comfort, *Revolutionary Hamburg: Labor Politics in the Early Weimar Republic,* Stanford: Stanford University Press, 1966, p. 180.

7. Much of the work in the field of electoral studies in the United States has emphasized the general population's lack of awareness of political issues and, consequently, has stressed early training ("political socialization"), fixed party identifications, and irrationality when describing mass political behavior. This problem, presumably, should be much more acute in a country with a multiparty system than in one with a mere two parties. There does, nevertheless, appear to have been considerable awareness of this right shift on the part of the Zentrum's leaders. With participation being similar in the elections of December 1924 and May 1928, the Zentrum lost 10,000 votes or roughly 10 percent of its 1924 total. In the best-off communities, however, in Marienburg, Bayenthal, and Lindenthal, the party increased its votes. In Marienburg the new level was 62.8 percent above 1924. With one minor exception, the Zentrum lost votes in all other subareas.

8. Because of the changes in turnout, the voting trends and the percentage trends can sometimes diverge. The SPD lost more than 5 percent of its share of the vote between 1928 and 1930. At the same time, however, it increased the absolute number of its votes by nearly 2,000. The participation, it will be noted, had gone from 60.4 to 74.0 percent. The statements in the text are to be taken literally: vote means vote, and percentage means percentage.

9. Several commentators have noted the tendency for Catholic workers, when defecting from the Zentrum, to turn to the Communists rather than to the Social Democrats. See, for the best discussion of this point, Johannes Schauff, *Die Deutschen Katholiken und die Zentrumspartei: Eine politisch-statistische Untersuchung der Reichstagwahlen seit 1871,* Cologne: Verlag J. P. Bachem, 1928, p. 113.

10. It is regrettable that English-language work on German history and politics has paid so little attention to the character and role of the Zentrum. For nearly the entire prewar period, it was the largest party in the Reichstag. In the postwar period (under proportional representation) it was smaller but nevertheless still occupied a pivotal role, being a key party in liberal left or Weimar coalitions. It was this link of Zentrum and SPD that disturbed Catholic busi-

nessmen, aristocrats, and small farm populations. The outstanding brief work
on the electoral position of the party is that of Schauff, *Die Deutschen Katholiken*.
A very useful work on the strains within the party is that of Helga Grebing,
"Zentrum und Katholische Arbeiterschaft 1918-1933: Ein Beitrag zur Geschichte des Zentrums in der Weimarer Republik," doctoral dissertation, Free
University of Berlin, 1952. A useful account of the Zentrum in some rural
communities to the west of Cologne, communities that over the years had pro-
vided many migrants to that city, is that of Günter Plum, *Gesellschaftsstruktur
und politisches Bewusstsein in einer katholischen Region 1928-1933; Untersuchung am
Beispiel des Regierungsbezirks Aachen*, Stuttgart: Deutsche Verlags-Anstalt, 1972.
On the more political aspects of the Zentrum's history see Rudolf Morsey, *Die
Deutsche Zentrumspartei 1917-1923*, Düsseldorf: Droste Verlag, 1966 and his work
"Die Deutsche Zentrumspartei," pp. 281-453 of Erich Matthias and Morsey,
eds., *Das Ende der Parteien 1933*, Düsseldorf: Droste Verlag, 1960. Also useful
on the rightward shift is Ellen L. Evans, "The Center Wages *Kulturpolitik*: Con-
flict in the Marx-Keudell Cabinet of 1927," *Central European History*, 2 (1969):
139-158. See also the works cited with respect to Düsseldorf and Essen in
Chapter 7 and the discussion in Chapter 10. The definitive history of the party
is Karl Bachem's *Vorgeschichte, Geschichte und Politik der Deutschen Zentrumspartei*,
Galen: Scientia-Verlag, 1927-1932.

    11. The Zentrum had an almost exclusively Catholic clientele. And the Cath-
olic population of Germany was clustered in areas that were overwhelmingly
Catholic, only a small portion being found as a minority in what were called
"diaspora" areas. Under the single-member district plurality vote arrangement
of the Kaiserreich, this meant that turnout was not very important since the
election of Zentrum candidates in Catholic areas was generally a sure thing.
And since a vote for the Zentrum in the diaspora areas was a lost vote (an
equally sure thing) most Catholics there had an incentive to support some other
party. In many such instances the Zentrum would not even present candidates.
The low-turnout tradition that developed made sense under the old electoral
arrangement; it was very problematic, however, under the proportional representation system of Weimar in which every vote counted. The Catholics in the
diaspora regions could, with reason, now vote for the Zentrum for the first
time. But in the areas of Catholic concentration, the party continued to be
plagued by low turnout. Only on occasions of great alarm or concern, as in
1919 or later in 1932, would these electors participate. It meant that normally
the Zentrum operated with less than its "real" strength. It also meant, however,
that it had a reservoir of voters on whom it could draw in times of need. The
rate of participation in Cologne was one of the lowest among Germany's large
cities. See Schauff, *Die Deutschen Katholiken*, for further details.

    The best analysis of this matter making use of national data is that of Allan
Schnaiberg, "A Critique of Karl O'Lessker's 'Who Voted for Hitler?' " *American Journal of Sociology*, 74 (1969): 732-735. An analysis of the results in four
large cities (including Cologne) showed that "only in the last election—March,
1933—could the Nazis have drawn disproportionate support from among previous non-voters." See W. Phillips Shively, "Party Identification, Party Choice,

and Voting Stability: The Weimar Case," *American Political Science Review*, 66 (1972): 1203-1225. The quotation is from p. 1215.

12. This result parallels the experience of Berlin (see note 11, Chapter 4) and also of Hamburg. It is a point worth noting because it means that the bulk of the Conservative losses at this point went to the splinter parties, not to the NSDAP. Among the beneficiaries were two Protestant splinter groups.

13. In Weymar, *Konrad Adenauer*, p. 146; see also p. 148. For further discussion of the supposed immunity of Catholic cities to the NSDAP infection, see Chapter 7. Cologne did not suffer in any exceptional way in the economic crisis. The 1933 census reported 48.4 percent of the male workers to be unemployed, certainly a grim figure. But exactly the same figure is reported for Hamburg. For Berlin the equivalent figure was 47.7 percent.

14. The Cologne election results reported to this point are taken from the *Kölner Statistisches Handbuch*, 13:1 (1958): 272-273.

	Berlin	Cologne
Left	57.5%	39.2%
Zentrum	3.3	29.1
Center right parties	32.0	21.7

The "Catholic presence" does have some meaning for the electoral result. Whereas 3.3 percent of the Berlin voters favored the Center party in May of 1928, the equivalent figure for Cologne was 29.1. A somewhat simplified version of the contrast between the two cities in the 1928 election is shown in the table.

15. The inner-city districts have been ordered in terms of their support for the trio of center right parties. The vote in the December 1924 election, expressed in percentages, is shown in the table. The same rank order appeared in the 1928 election.

Marienburg was a very small community, its 1933 population being only 2,999. Bayenthal was somewhat larger with 7,062 and Lindenthal still larger with 22,626 persons. Neustadt-North was larger still with 41,853, and Neu-

Inner city	DVP	DNVP	DDP	Combined
Neustadt-North	20.1	11.5	8.0	39.6
Neustadt-Center	17.5	9.5	11.0	38.0
Neustadt-South	15.5	8.9	6.4	30.8
Altstadt-North	12.9	7.8	4.1	24.8
Altstadt-Center	12.2	6.8	5.0	24.0
Altstadt-South	8.7	5.9	3.2	17.8
Outer city				
Marienburg	34.2	19.3	12.9	66.4
Lindenthal	18.3	11.9	6.9	37.1
Bayenthal etc.	12.2	7.2	4.8	24.2
Nippes etc.	11.8	7.9	4.2	23.9
Cologne	11.9	7.2	4.8	23.9

stadt-Center had 40,314 persons. Although the last two areas were obviously more heterogeneous than the smaller and more exclusive communities, most local authorities still report that they had generally well off populations. Neustadt-North contained the courts and the head offices of insurance companies, as well as the zoological gardens. Many high-level civil servants are said to have lived there. Neustadt-Center is also described as a "good bourgeois area" (*gutes Bürgerviertel*). At one time there were substantial villas located on the Ring (the broad avenue separating the Altstadt and Neustadt).

16. The election statistics were taken from the following sources: Huber, "Die politischen Wahlen"; Huber, "Die Reichstags und die Landtagswahl in Köln am 20. Mai 1928," *Kölner Verwaltung und Statistik*, 6:3; "Die Ergebnisse der 5. Reichstagswahl am 14. September 1930 in Köln nach Stimmbezirken," *Beilage zum Monatsbericht des Statistischen und Wahlamts der Stadt Köln für August 1930*; "Die 6. Reichstagswahl am 31. Juli 1932 in Köln," *Beilage . . . für Juli 1932*; "Die 7. Reichstagswahl am 6. November 1932 in Köln," *Beilage . . . für November 1932*; and, "Die Wahlen vom 5. und 12 März 1933 in Köln," *Beilage . . . für März 1933*.

The above sources, from 1930 onward, contain detailed breakdowns, the results being given for males and females by precinct (*Stimmbezirk*). This means that for someone with a knowledge of local areas, a much finer analysis is possible than that presented here.

The dissertation of Gunnar von Schuckmann has also been consulted; see "Die politische Willensbildung in der Grossstadt Köln der Reichsgründung im Jahre 1871," doctoral dissertation, University of Cologne, 1965. Although the available statistics for Cologne are not as rich as those for Berlin and Hamburg, I do not feel that Schuckmann's judgment is warranted when he says (pp. 174-175): "From which classes of the population the votes of the NSDAP were recruited in the Cologne elections up to 1933 cannot be answered with . . . the available statistical materials." Most of the approximately 23,000 volumes in the library of the city's statistical office were destroyed in an air raid on June 29, 1943.

17. A comparison of the July Reichstag election result with the election for the Prussian legislature in April 1932 indicates a percentage decline for the National Socialists in Marienburg. Given the decline in valid votes, that also meant an absolute loss of votes, the respective figures for April and July being 482 and 438. At least a part of the explanation appears to involve the vacationers. Some 288 ballots were given out to Marienburg citizens prior to the election, a figure that amounts to 12.0 percent of those on the electoral list.

18. For an account of this newspaper and its history, see Kurt Weinhold, *Die Geschichte eines Zeitungshauses, 1620-1945*, Cologne: Verlag M. DuMont Schauberg, 1969. The report given in the text is based on the issues of the *Kölnische Zeitung* for September 1-16, 1930. After the election, the reactions of various political figures were reported. Otto Wels, the leader of the SPD, was quoted as follows: "Even the sudden rise of National Socialism does not disturb me. This party, without any kind of program and without any kind of principle, should fade away again just as fast as it appeared." Of somewhat greater interest

is the reaction of the stock markets. The immediate response was a fall in stock prices. This reaction, it will be noted, does not accord with the Marxist view of the movement. If anything, businessmen should have felt greater confidence because of the NSDAP success and prices should have increased.

19. The newspaper issues from July 20 through August 11 were covered. For evidence on the unreality of the fear that the left parties would form a coalition, see Chapter 11. On the whole, one may rate the reporting of political events in the *Kölnische Zeitung* very highly. It provided the best, the richest, the most detailed, and the most accurate portrait of political events of any newspaper in any of the cities studied here. The paper's editorial judgment, however, did not show the same high level of intelligence as its news columns.

Again it is useful to examine the reaction of the stock markets to the election since this provides some indication of the collective sentiments of the nation's bourgeoisie. If investors saw the NSDAP victory as an opportunity to stabilize political and economic affairs in their interest, this was not reflected in any sudden surge in stock prices. The initial reaction according to the business section (*Handelsblatt*) of the *Kölnische Zeitung* was one of "enormous restraint and lifelessness." For ten days following the election there were negotiations with respect to the formation of a new government with Hitler's party being an obvious contender for some major role. During this period the markets continued "dull and weak." On August 11, it was reported that Hindenburg had "doubts" about Hitler's participation. The market responded with its best performance of the week. The Sunday newspaper announced Hindenburg's "refusal to Hitler." On the following day a report from Berlin was entitled "Confident Exchange." The Cologne markets, however, continued to be "lifeless."

20. Issues of August 23-28, 1932.

21. Issues of November 1-8, 1932. After the election the paper again raised the question of whether the National Socialists could be called on for responsible "collaboration in the government." Nothing could be served, it said, by still another election. It called on the National Socialists for "practical collaboration" and hoped that the party would abandon its "all or nothing" stand.

22. *Kölnische Volkszeitung*, issues of September 1-15, 1930; July 21-August 1, 1932. This newspaper, incidentally, was more than just a religious or political journal. It carried the subtitle *und Handelsblatt* (and Business Paper).

23. *Stadt-Anzeiger*, issues of September 12-15, 1930; July 20-August 1, 1932.

24. *Kölner Tageblatt*, issues of September 1-15, 1930; July 25-August 1, 1932.

25. It is difficult, however, to establish with any precision the influence of the National Socialist cadres, to say where they were active or where they found the greatest resonance. There is one local party history, Peter Schmidt, *Zwanzig Jahre Soldat Adolf Hitlers: Zehn Jahre Gauleiter: Ein Buch von Kampf und Treue*, Cologne: Verlag Westdeutscher Beobachter, 1941. It did not prove particularly useful.

26. For the history of the Bavarian events see the following: Karl Schwend, *Bayern zwischen Monarchie und Diktatur; Beiträge zur Bayerischen Frage in der Zeit von 1918 bis 1933*, Munich: Richard Pflaum, 1954; Harold J. Gordon, Jr., *Hitler and the Beer Hall Putsch*, Princeton: Princeton University Press, 1972; Carl Lan-

dauer, "The Bavarian Problem in the Weimar Republic, 1918-1923," *Journal of Modern History*, 16 (1944): 93-115 and 205-223; Erich Eyck, *Geschichte der Weimarer Republik*, Erlenbach–Zurich: Eugen Rentsch Verlag, 1956, vol. 1, pp. 291 ff., 347 ff., 363 ff.; Dietrich Thränhardt, *Wahlen und politische Strukturen in Bayern 1848-1953*, Düsseldorf: Droste Verlag, 1973; Klaus Schönhoven, *Die Bayerische Volkspartei, 1924-1932*, Düsseldorf: Droste Verlag, 1972; Falk Wiesemann, *Die Vorgeschichte der nationalsozialistischen Machtübernahme in Bayern 1932/33*, Berlin: Duncker und Humblot, 1975; Geoffrey Pridham, *Hitler's Rise to Power: The Nazi Movement in Bavaria, 1923-1933*, New York: Harper & Row, 1973.

27. The distribution of the economically active population in Munich appears in Appendix C. In Munich there was a smaller percentage of workers than in Berlin or Hamburg and a larger percentage of independent businessmen. Neither difference was very large, both amounting to roughly 5 percent of the male total.

28. It will be noted that different patterns appear in the different cities and also that the relationship between Communist growth and decline and economic well-being or distress is more complex than the simple economism formula would indicate. Put somewhat differently, other factors prove to be of greater significance than the simple fact of well- or ill-being. For a more detailed analysis from a completely different context, post–World War II France, see my *Affluence and the French Worker*, Princeton: Princeton University Press, 1967.

29. The Democrats took 7.8 percent of the vote in the 1920 election. In the first election of 1924, the National Socialists (campaigning in the Völkischer Block) did very well, while a liberal coalition, the Deutscher Block in Bayern, took only 2.7 percent.

30. See Pridham, *Hitler's Rise to Power*, pp. 15 ff.

31. One might also note the significance of another comparison. Munich gave greater support to the NSDAP than did Berlin in every election up to July 1932, at that point the percentages being roughly the same. The November falloff was somewhat greater in Munich, and that put Berlin ahead for the first time. This indicates once again the minimal importance of the religious factor in the urban context as far as NSDAP chances were concerned. It also once again suggests that Goebbels's accomplishment in Berlin was not particularly distinguished. These results are taken from: *Statistisches Handbuch der Stadt München*, Munich: Carl Gerber Verlag, 1928, p. 302; and *Statistisches Handbuch der Stadt München*, Munich: R. Oldenbourg, 1954, p. 243.

32. These results are to be found in the Munich Stadtarchiv, in the following files: Wahlamt 86, 54, and 108.

33. Pridham, *Hitler's Rise to Power*, pp. 21-22; Landauer, "The Bavarian Problem," p. 101.

34. The November 1932 election saw a four-percentage-point falloff in the Munich NSDAP total as compared to July. In the Bogenhausen districts the falloff was somewhat greater, their support going from 29.7 percent to 23.0. The support for the BVP was remarkably constant. The biggest correlated change involved the DNVP, which more than doubled its vote. Some of those sup-

porters, no doubt, were convinced Conservatives. But others, it seems likely, were turning again to the DNVP as their best available current option.

Some indication of the voting patterns of various subgroups within the city may be gained by examining the votes cast in the city's hospitals. The Catholic institutions, not too surprisingly, all provided extremely strong support for the BVP. The most extreme instance of this pattern appears in the case of the Cloister of the Ladies of the Good Shepherd, where 181 of the 182 votes cast went for that party. One voter there supported the German People's party. In November 1932, the vote in the Cloister was unanimous. In the Hospital of the Third Order, the BVP gained 78.9 percent of the total as opposed to the National Socialists' 7.9 percent. In the St. Martin's Old People's Home, the respective figures were 80.8 and 5.0. Similar results were found elsewhere. These results closely parallel those noted in Cologne. It is reasonable to assume that the population found in these institutions would tend to be older, to be disproportionately female, and to be rather devout.

In the course of research of this kind, one discovers much more information than can possibly be presented, let alone investigated and explained. The results for the May 1924 election, for example, were on two separate typewritten lists, one giving the men's, the other the women's vote. The latter list reported one precinct (no. 53) that had given 66.7 percent of its vote to the Völksicher Block. Since that was more than three times the city average, further inquiry seemed warranted. The precinct turned out to be the Max II Kaserne, the voting taking place in the Officers' Casino of the former Seventh Medical Field Regiment. In addition to the Kaserne, those living in the Lazarettstrasse 3-13 and in the Albrechtsstrasse 8 also voted in this precinct. Since men, as we have seen, typically gave Hitler's party more support than women, results for the males were examined. But there, it turned out, "only" 32.6 percent had voted for the Block. There were also, it turned out, many more male voters (408) than female (69) in the precinct. At that point this line of research had to end. Were the women voters there the wives of officers? Was the male pattern obscured? Were officers voting as heavily for the Block as the women? And were the enlisted men voting for the left or for the BVP? One would have had to search out some elderly informants from the locality to obtain further information.

35. See Gordon, *Hitler*, p. 47, for both direct quotes; and Kurt A. Holz, "Münchner Neueste Nachrichten (1848-1945)," pp. 191-207 of Heinz-Dietrich Fischer, ed., *Deutsche Zeitungen des 17. bis 20. Jahrhunderts*, Pullach: Verlag Dokumentation, 1972.

36. For the history of this internal struggle, see Chapter 13. The issues of the *Münchner Neueste Nachrichten* for the following dates were reviewed: September 1-15, 1930; March 2-April 25, 1932; and July 20-August 1, 1932.

Seven. Cities of the Ruhr

1. The religious settlement following the Thirty Years' War provided that the people adopt the religion of their rulers, the governing phrase being *Cujus regio, ejus religio* (whose land, his religion). Each king, duke, count, baron, or free state made a decision that was then binding for the underlying population.

Nearly three hundred years later the patterns imposed then were still to be seen. In some cases, in Duisburg for example, the city of 1933 embraced parts of three or four such tiny states. The historic imprint remained despite the impact of later urbanization.

For a useful overview, see Norman J. G. Pounds, *The Ruhr: A Study in Historical and Economic Geography*, London: Faber and Faber, 1952. Wuppertal, to be sure, does not lie in the Ruhr valley. Located immediately to the south of the Ruhr, it was more involved in textile manufacture than in iron and steel.

2. These struggles are considered in some detail in Chapter 11. See also Wilfried Böhnke, *Die NSDAP im Ruhrgebiet, 1920-1933*, Bonn-Bad Godesberg: Verlag Neue Gesellschaft, 1974, p. 22.

3. It is easy to forget just how recent Essen's urban development is. In 1803, it was a tiny village with 3,480 inhabitants. In 1895, with 96,128 inhabitants living within the same territorial boundaries, it was no more than what in today's terms would be counted as a small city. A decade later, largely as a result of annexations, it had 321,360 inhabitants. And just before the Great War, again partly because of annexations, it had grown to 337,439 inhabitants. Substantial annexation in 1929 brought it close to the 1933 figure in the text. The years of explosive growth, those in which most of its 1933 numbers were gained, occurred in the first three decades of the twentieth century.

The image of uprooted masses conventionally associated with the process of urbanization can apply, at best, to only a part of that population since, as noted, some of the development was the result of annexations. What uprooting did in fact occur would, presumably, have been at its peak in those decades. For those thinking in such terms (and in terms of the consequent anomie and social disorganization) it would be useful to note that as of 1880, 44.5 percent of the city's population was born within the city limits. In 1905, the percentage was 45.6. Many of the rest had not come very far from their roots. In the latter year, one-fifth of those born elsewhere came from somewhere in Westphalia (that is, from the region immediately surrounding Essen) and another slightly larger portion came from the Prussian Rhine Province (from the west side of the Rhine, only a short distance away). It is unlikely that the moves were made in isolation. Most of them were probably aided by friends, neighbors, and kinsmen. See Hans Hudde, "Die Wirtschafts- und Bevölkerungsentwicklung der Stadt Essen in den Jahren 1800-1914: Ein Beitrag zur Geschichte der Entwicklung einer ausgesprochenen Industriestadt," doctoral dissertation, University of Freiburg, 1922.

Essen is unusual among German cities in that its political development in the Weimar years has been the object of a scholarly study, Herbert Kühr's *Parteien und Wahlen im Stadt- und Landkreis Essen in der Zeit der Weimarer Republik*, Düsseldorf: Droste Verlag, 1973. Unfortunately, Kühr's work does not contain the detail needed for the crucial 1932 election: he presents maps showing the voting patterns in terms of *ranges* of support for the various parties (rather than giving exact percentages). It is also not clear from his presentation which are the "better" and which the "worse" among the middle-class districts. Hence, it is necessary to proceed independently, depending on Kühr's work only for additional supporting information.

4. "Die Stadtverordnetenwahl vom 17. November 1929: Tatsachen, Vergleiche und Grundsätzliches," *Beilage zum Vierteljahresbericht des Statistischen Amtes der Stadt Essen*, December 1929.

5. "Die Reichstagswahl am 31. Juli 1932 in Essen," *Beilage zum Vierteljahresbericht des Statistischen Amtes der Stadt Essen*, n.d. This publication provides seventeen large pages of rich detail on the election, giving both participation figures with percentages and vote figures with percentages. It compares the results with

City	Percent Catholic	Vote in July 1932	
		Zentrum	NSDAP
Essen	54.0	30.7%	24.0%
Dortmund	40.0	18.6	19.6
Düsseldorf	61.2	22.7	29.0
Duisburg	51.7	22.5	27.5
Wuppertal	20.3	9.9	42.7

those of earlier elections and contrasts the Essen results with those of other cities. Some basic figures for the five cities being considered in this chapter are given in the table. It will be noted, once again, that unlike the development in the countryside, the relationship between Catholicism and National Socialism in the cities is an erratic one. Düsseldorf, with the highest Catholic percentage of this group, had the second highest NSDAP vote.

6. The formulations in this and the following paragraphs do not accord in all respects with the limited presentation of census data for 1939 given by Kühr. His map (*Parteien und Wahlen*, p. 47) shows only three of the city's forty districts as possessing a middle-class majority, those being Bredeney, Rüttenscheid, and Fulerum. Four others appear to have divided close to fifty-fifty between middle class and working class, these being Huttrop and Heide and two areas not on our list, Rellinghausen and Bergerhausen. Kühr's data show the Stadkern, together with the Südviertel, Südostviertel, and Holsterhausen, to have had substantial (60-70 percent) working-class majorities among the employed populations. The differences between the judgments of my informants and Kühr's 1939 data are not likely to indicate fundamental contradictions but rather suggest some mixture of the populations in these districts. The better-off populations of the Südviertel, for example, lived in the neighborhood of the Stadtgarten while the workers lived elsewhere. The first coal mining in Essen was in the south of the city, some of it in the midst of what were later to become very elegant communities. And some workers from these older mining communities were still located there in the early thirties, for example, in Heide and Bredeney. Another possibility would be that the districts changed during the 1930s. The construction of a substantial block of housing, particularly in a thinly populated district, could have led to a significant change in its character by 1939. A precinct by precinct analysis would be useful were one able to find the detailed voting results and to obtain some adequate information on the social character of those subareas.

7. In Bredeney 11.7 percent of the vote went to the Social Democrats and another 8.0 percent went to the Communists. If we make some of the assumptions of the previous chapters, specifically, that two-thirds of the left vote was from workers and that the Zentrum vote came exclusively from Catholic voters, the level of NSDAP support among the remaining largely Protestant and largely nonmanual population would be just under 60 percent.

8. Kühr makes unambiguous statements stressing the middle-class character of the NSDAP but fails to consider the voting tendencies in the better districts. "The electoral development," he states, "shows that it was especially the middle classes and the petty bourgeoisie that tended toward radical rightism in the ups and downs of crisis periods . . . from 1928 on [they were] caught up in the NSDAP." *Parteien und Wahlen*, p. 99. See also note 17, this chapter. When he discusses Bredeney and Rüttenscheid (for example on p. 156), it is in terms of the disproportionate number of white-collar employees, civil servants, and independent businessmen living there. Such a description *sounds like* one is dealing with an ordinary middle-class population. The same problem occurs at another point (p. 49) where he describes this southern part of the city as "predominantly the residential and business area of the middle class with its center of gravity in Rüttenscheid and Bredeney."

9. For a brief description of the city's newspapers, see Kühr, *Parteien und Wahlen*, pp. 165-176. See also Kurt Koszyk, *Deutsche Presse 1914-1945*, Berlin: Colloquium Verlag, 1972, especially, pp. 118-126 and 170-174.

10. Kühr, *Parteien und Wahlen*, p. 91.

11. It need scarcely be noted that the intent here is merely to give some sense of the "world view" being presented to the newspaper's regular readers. The *validity* of these claims is another question. The NSDAP experiment in Thuringia was by no means the success Frick claimed it to be. The Zentrum would have presented no serious problems because in largely Protestant Thuringia it was not a significant force.

12. During the election campaign itself, the domestic scandals, mismanagement, and Versailles obligations were distinctly secondary in importance. They constituted a set of background facts against which the current struggle was played.

13. Kühr's statement with regard to the political direction of the newspaper is, for the last years of the republic at least, seriously misleading. He states that the newspaper supported "the bourgeois parties of the right: the German National People's party and the German People's party, in cases of doubt favoring the former more than the latter," *Parteien und Wahlen*, p. 168.

Reismann-Grone's connections with the National Socialists were much closer than is indicated in this paragraph. For further details on his involvement, see note 132, Chapter 13.

14. The *Rheinisch-Westfälische Zeitung* appeared twice a day during the week with a morning and an evening edition and once on Sundays. The accounts in the previous pages are based on the issues from September 1-15, 1930; April 16-25, 1932; July 24-August 1, 1930; and October 31-November 7, 1932. The first of the articles on Mussolini's Italy appeared in the issue of August 10, 1930

(no. 405). In addition to the preelection report on Italy in July 1932 there was a long and very approving story prior to the November election (no. 558, November 1, 1930) entitled "Mussolini's Significance." The *New York Times* account of July 23, 1921, incidentally, portrays the "bloody Sunday" in Sarzana as being initiated by Nationalists. See also the London *Times* account, July 23, 1921.

15. Kühr, *Parteien und Wahlen*, pp. 96-97. See also Eugene C. McCreary, "Social Welfare and Business: The Krupp Welfare Program, 1860-1914," *Business History Review*, 42 (Spring 1968): 24-49.

16. The sources are given in notes 4 and 5, this chapter. Borbeck was unusual among the working-class districts in that it had higher support for the rightist parties and less for the leftist parties and for the Zentrum than other working-class districts. The same pattern of 1929-1932 shifting, however, occurs in those other districts.

17. Kühr, *Parteien und Wahlen*, pp. 112-139. Kühr's summary is worth noting. "The NSDAP electorate is, therefore, to be found first in the middle class and then among those workers who either were Protestant and formerly had voted for the DNVP or other bourgeois parties—other than the Zentrum—or were only nominally Catholic, had no connection with the church, but at the same time had no traditional connection with the socialist parties" (p. 146). Again one may note the failure to make a differentiation within the middle class. It should be noted, though, that Kühr is one of the few writers on the subject who has accurately specified the character of the working-class support for the National Socialists. Most commentators, it will be remembered (from Chapter 2), stress the unemployed workers. Moreover, if those conservative workers were older than other workers, the working-class NSDAP vote would *not* have been a vote of the youth.

18. The annexations of 1928 made it Germany's second largest city (in area), edging out Cologne. Like Essen, Dortmund was the subject of a monographic study that focused on the city's politics, this being the work of Hans Graf, *Die Entwicklung der Wahlen und politischen Parteien in Gross-Dortmund*, Hanover and Frankfurt: Norddeutsche Verlagsanstalt, 1958. Essen and Dortmund are the only cities, of the fourteen studied here, to have been researched in such detail.

19. The 1933 census gave a lower figure, 53.6 percent. Catholics made up 40.0 percent of the population and Jews 0.8 percent. Most of the remainder, some 5.3 percent, were classed as "without confession" (*Gemeinschaftslose*). It seems likely that most of these were ex-Protestants who had adopted a left-wing political faith. For the occupational structure of this city, and of the others discussed in this chapter, see Appendix C.

20. Graf, "Die Entwicklung der Wahlen," pp. 15-16 and 21-22.

21. Ibid., p. 24. The discussion here is of the Reichstag elections. The first SPD member from the Ruhr area was elected in Dortmund. In the state and local elections the situation was different because of the more restrictive suffrage. The Weimar constitution reformed this requiring proportional representation in all elections.

22. Ibid., p. 33. Some sense of the original dispositions in this city can be

seen in the results of the June 1920 Reichstag election, the first in which the DVP and DNVP presented separate lists. The respective percentages were 20.3 and 1.9. The difference was narrowed in December 1924 (14.5 and 7.0), but still, as late as the Prussian state election of November 1929, the DVP dominance remained, the respective figures then being 15.6 and 3.6.

23. Ibid., p. 35.

24. Ibid., pp. 35-36.

25. *Dortmunder Statistik. Mitteilungen des Statistischen Amtes der Stadt Dortmund.* "Die Reichstagswahl vom 14. September 1930 in Dortmund," no. 3, November 1930. Two other city districts came in with above average percentages for the NSDAP: Asseln and Wickede, with 9.5; and Aplerbeck, Schüren, Sölde, also with 9.5. I have no information on these areas.

26. Some details are worth noting. Contrasting the percentages in the 1929 city council election with the 1930 Reichstag election, one finds a substantial loss for the DVP. Its share of the total fell from 13.6 to 8.6 percent. In other words it fell to 63.2 percent of its previous total. The losses in the better-off districts were much more serious. In the Süden, Südosten, and Osten the equivalent figures were, respectively, 51.5, 48.4, and 54.2. Elsewhere, in Mengede for example, the party did much better, there the falloff being to only 88.9 percent of the former total. In Mengede the Zentrum and the Wirtschaftspartei were the biggest losers.

27. The results presented here are based on the figures in the *Dortmunder Zeitung*, August 1, 1932, pp. 7-8. A suggestive (or provocative) result, one touching on the age question, appears in the figures for a Protestant old people's home (precinct 120a). There, 76.1 percent of the votes cast for the nine parties (N = 264) went to the National Socialists.

28. This brief description of the *Dortmunder Zeitung*'s political content is drawn from the issues of September 1-15, 1930; April 19-25, 1932; July 26-August 1, 1932; and November 3-7, 1932. See also Koszyk, *Deutsche Presse*, pp. 359-360.

29. This newspaper, moreover, was created in the late 1890s when a group bought the *Rheinische Zeitung* of Duisburg and the *Westfälische Zeitung* of Dortmund and merged them, basing the combination in Essen.

30. A National Socialist history (cited by Böhnke, *Die NSDAP*, p. 99n) blamed the *Dortmunder General-Anzeiger* for the party's lack of success there. Also mentioned was the city's especially diligent police president (the party's history actually refers to him as "subhuman [moved by] animal instinct"). It should also be noted that the *Dortmunder Zeitung* and the *General-Anzeiger*, so different in their political orientations, were in fact owned by the same family; see Koszyk, *Deutsche Presse*, p. 396. They were obviously allowed a considerable degree of editorial autonomy.

31. For a brief history, see Kurt Koszyk, "Jakob Stöcker und der Dortmunder 'General-Anzeiger' 1929-1933," *Publizistik*, 8 (1963): 282-295.

32. Böhnke, *Die NSDAP*, pp. 22, 148-149; Graf, *Die Entwicklung der Wahlen*, p. 38.

33. Walter Först, *Robert Lehr als Oberbürgermeister: Ein Kapitel Deutscher Kommunalpolitik*, Düsseldorf-Vienna: Econ Verlag, 1962, pp. 83-84.

34. Gisbert Jörg Gemein, "Die DNVP in Düsseldorf, 1918-1933," doctoral dissertation, University of Cologne, 1969; see also Wolfgang Stump, *Geschichte und Organisation der Zentrumspartei in Düsseldorf, 1917-1933*, Düsseldorf: Droste Verlag, 1971; and Hans-Peter Görgen, *Düsseldorf und der Nationalsozialismus*, Düsseldorf: L. Schwann Verlag, 1969. For Görgen's references and supporting documentation one must turn to his original doctoral dissertation, University of Cologne, 1967.

It may be that the relative dominance of the Conservatives was not an accident of organization. As the provincial capital, Düsseldorf, alone among the Ruhr cities, would have had a small but steady inflow of civil servants from old Prussia, that is from Berlin and its surrounding territories. And, bringing their Prussian Conservative politics with them, they would, of course, have made Düsseldorf different. At the same time, it would be a mistake to exaggerate the extent of the differences vis-à-vis other western cities. In the 1928 Reichstag election, more votes were cast for the DNVP in Düsseldorf than for the right liberal (free enterprise) DVP (25,537 versus 23,457). In the two "best" areas, however, in the Zoo-Viertel and the Hofgartenviertel, more votes were cast for the DVP. In the 1930 election, the DVP held on reasonably well, but the DNVP suffered heavy losses, partly to the defecting Volkskonservative, partly to the NSDAP.

35. Alan Bullock, *Hitler: A Study in Tyranny*, rev. ed., New York: Harper & Row, 1964, pp. 196-199. Bullock introduces the subject of the Park Hotel meeting with some quotes from a rather dubious source, Goebbels's diaries. He provides an entry from January 5, stating that "money is wanting everywhere" and then gives a citation from February 8, not quite two weeks after the famous speech, saying that "money affairs improve daily." One of the reasons for the change of tone, Bullock reports, was Hitler's visit to Düsseldorf. The words just before the "money wanting" quotation, however, refer rather clearly to grass-roots collections and the fact that these efforts were so inadequate: "Called together local leaders. Gave them hell because our collection of contributions has been progressing so badly." The second statement has no precise referent. It could be business contributions. It could be collections taken at party propaganda meetings, such as the one on the previous evening, a Sunday, when the Sportpalast was "overflowing." From Joseph Goebbels, *Vom Kaiserhof zur Reichskanzlei*, Munich: Zentralverlag der NSDAP, 1937, pp. 18, 42.

The Dietrich quotation is from a book published in 1934. Dietrich published another account after the war in which he described the same events rather differently. There he speaks of "insignificant contributions" following the address. See his *Zwölf Jahre mit Hitler*, Munich: Isar Verlag, 1955, pp. 185 ff. For Lehr's comment, see Först, *Robert Lehr*, pp. 235-236. Most sources, incidentally, have the Park Hotel speech occurring on January 27. See Henry A. Turner, Jr., "Fritz Thyssen und 'I Paid Hitler,'" *Vierteljahrshefte für Zeitgeschichte*, 19 (1971): 231-232, for the correction and details.

36. See also Gemein, "Die DNVP," p. 113: "However it was generally acknowledged that Düsseldorf's industry and banking world was closely aligned with the DVP."

37. From figures given in the *Jahresbericht des Statistischen Amts der Stadt Düsseldorf für das Jahr 1932*, Düsseldorf: Druck Hoch, 1932, p. 71. The Landtag election results are used for this purpose because they are aggregated for the city's twenty-two subareas. The *Nachrichten*'s results for the July Reichstag election are for 326 precincts without either percentages or aggregation.

38. The detailed results are taken from the *Düsseldorfer Nachrichten*, no. 209, April 25, 1932 (morning edition); and no. 386, August 1, 1932 (morning edition).

39. In the April Landtag election, the Diakonie "precinct," with its sisters and patients, gave the National Socialists, as noted, 70.2 percent of its votes (N = 794). In the July Reichstag election, the altered district, now reporting only the votes of the patients, gave "only" 39.6 percent (N = 144) to the National Socialists, most of the rest going to the DNVP. This suggests that it was the sisters who voted so heavily for Hitler's party.

In the institution's centennial publication, Pastor Disselhoff describes the year 1933 as follows: "The great experience. The German people awake. Under Adolf Hitler's leadership they start on the road to freedom. 'Service for the People,' the old watchword of the Diakonie, becomes the watchword of the entire people. 'We declare ourselves entirely, and with joy, for the Third Reich,' says the 96th Kaiserswerth Yearly Report."

40. Little is to be gained from a detailed presentation of the voting in the city's hospitals, the results there being similar to those found in other cities. In the city's General Hospital the NSDAP took 26.8 percent in the 1932 Landtag election (versus a city-wide 29.7). It achieved significant victories in the Protestant hospitals (39.6 and 53.6 percent). In the five Catholic hospitals it had very little success, the percentages going from 2.6 to 18.1. The Zentrum took 19.6 percent in the General Hospital, 1.4 and 3.9 percent in the Protestant hospitals, and ranged from 62.9 to 90.9 in the Catholic hospitals. Those results cannot be taken as providing cross-sections of the religious communities. It must be remembered that the hospitalized population has an unusual age structure.

41. Issues of the *Düsseldorfer Nachrichten* for April 21-25, 1932, and for July 26-August 1, 1932, were examined. The city also had a Zentrum newspaper, the *Düsseldorf Tageblatt*. The SPD, KPD, and NSDAP all had newspapers in the city. A DVP-linked newspaper, the *Düsseldorfer Zeitung*, existed up to 1926. It was not a viable enterprise and, as a result, was transformed into the apolitical *Stadt-Anzeiger*. This journal had even less political content than the *Nachrichten*.

42. The 1907 census indicated that 48.7 percent of the city's population had been born there and that another 25.8 percent had been born in the neighboring Rhineland. A study from 1926 indicated that the percentage of those born in the city had risen to 52.3. These figures, taken together with the persistence of the religious traditions, indicate that again one must be wary of the tendency to read in a picture of uprootedness and consequent anomie. The earlier figure appears in Manfred Schultz, "Die Entwicklung des Grossraums Duisburg: eine Analyse kulturlandschaftlicher Gestaltelemente seit Beginn der Industrialisierung," doctoral dissertation, University of Giessen, 1968, Table 6 of the Ap-

pendix. The later figure comes from the *Sonderbeilage zur Duisburger Monats-statistik*, November 1926.

43. "Ergebnis der Reichstagswahl vom 20. Mai 1928," *Sonderbeilage 15 zur Duisburger Monatsstatistik*, May 1928. The DVP also did relatively well (14.9 percent) in Ruhrort and in Wanheim-Angerhausen (14.8 percent). The former area, a village directly at the confluence of the Rhine and Ruhr had an above average Protestant percentage and the latter subarea, as we have seen, had a Protestant majority.

44. Calculated from the figures appearing in the *Duisburger General-Anzeiger*, September 15, 1930, no. 432, p. 6.

45. Günter von Roden, *Geschichte der Stadt Duisburg*, Duisburg: Walter Braun Verlag, 1973, vol. 2, p. 373.

46. Ibid., pp. 368-375; and Hans-Peter Becker, "Untersuchung zur Frühge-schichte der NSDAP in Duisburg," Duisburg, Staatsexamenarbeit, 1971, located in the Archiv der Stadt Duisburg. For the Pharus Hall battle, see note 37, Chapter 4.

47. There also existed a *Niederrheinische Volksstimme* (SPD) and a *Niederrhein-ische Arbeiter-Zeitung* (KPD). The back copies of both papers, I was told, were destroyed early in the National Socialist regime. The NSDAP had its own newspaper, the *Nationale Zeitung*. A local paper of lesser import was the *Hamborner Volkszeitung*. Some people may have been reading outside newspapers, but it is next to impossible to establish such matters with any precision or certainty.

48. The issues reviewed here are those of September 10-15, 1930; April 10-11, 1932; April 24-25, 1932; July 28-August 1, 1932; and November 5-6, 1932.

49. The issues of the *General-Anzeiger* reviewed were: September 12-15, 1930; April 22-25, 1932; July 25-August 1, 1932; and November 4-7, 1932.

50. See Gemein, "Die DNVP," p. 102. On Stöcker and his successors, see Paul Massing, *Rehearsal for Destruction: A Study of Political Anti-Semitism in Imperial Germany*, New York: Harper Brothers, 1949.

51. See *Wupperthaler Statistik*, no. 1, April-September 1930 for the 1930 result when the NSDAP took 23.0 percent, edging out the KPD with its 22.6 percent. For the later elections, see *Wupperthaler Statistik*, no. 8, April-June, 1932; and no. 9, July-September, 1932. For comparison with the other Ruhr cities see note 5, this chapter.

52. The amalgamation took place in 1929, and initially the city was called Elberfeld-Barmen. Shortly thereafter, the name Wuppertal was adopted.

53. The *Freie Presse*, an SPD newspaper, had precinct data in its issue of August 1, 1932, no. 178. I was only able to locate one of the three *Villenvierteln* reported by local informants. This was the Elberfeld area, Am Zoo. Its National Socialist vote in the July 1932 election was exactly equal to the party's average in the city, 42.7 percent. One of the difficulties stems from the shape of the city, the precincts in some cases extending from the top to the bottom of the valley and therefore mixing rather diverse populations. Wuppertal is the small-est city considered thus far. An upper class living in three locations would not form the identifiable mass that one would find in larger cities.

54. According to Gemein ("Die DNVP," p. 110), the *Bergisch-Märkische Zeitung* was part of the Hugenberg press empire. This does not, however, appear to have been the case. Through 1930 it was a locally owned enterprise; on the first of January 1931, it became a property of Reismann-Grone's firm in Essen.

55. This, of course, was largely true. The *Bergisch-Märkische Zeitung* cultivated the myth as long as it was useful. When it was no longer useful, the paper was suddenly afflicted with a concern for honesty and justice.

56. This combination appears a bit gratuitous, inasmuch as the paper's next headline showed that the DNVP had *lost* 40 of its former 71 seats. The victory was exclusively on the NSDAP side of the Harzburger Front; it went from 6 to 162 seats.

57. The issues reviewed were those of: September 1-15, 1930; April 10-11, 1932; April 19-25, 1932; and July 30-August 1, 1932.

58. Both the *Täglicher Anzeiger* and the *Barmer Zeitung* had smaller circulations than the *Bergisch-Märkische Zeitung*. Information on these newspapers was provided by Dr. Sander of the Wuppertal Stadtarchiv (letter of February 27, 1979).

In Wuppertal, as elsewhere, many citizens were away during the July Reichstag election. The *Barmer Zeitung* (no. 177, July 30, 1932) discussed this point under the following headline: "17,000 Wuppertalers Vote Elsewhere: Reichstag Election and Vacation Time."

59. Some investigation was made in still another Ruhr city, Gelsenkirchen, the region's sixth largest city and the eighteenth largest of the nation. Unfortunately, the lack of differentiation within the city and the inadequacies of the available election statistics made detailed study impossible. Gelsenkirchen was one of the least attractive cities of the nation at that point, and very few upper- or upper-middle-class persons, it seems, chose to live there. It was the most proletarian of all the nation's large cities. The NSDAP percentage in July 1932, accordingly, was also rather low, 23 percent. Among the thirty largest cities, only Dortmund had a lower figure. Gelsenkirchen had an official newspaper, the *Gelsenkirchener Zeitung*, which was similar to Wuppertal's *Täglicher Anzeiger*. Its official status did not prevent it from publishing an anti-NSDAP editorial prior to the decisive election, this under the heading: "National Socialism Fosters Bolshevism!"

EIGHT. FIVE OTHER CITIES

1. The overall election results appear in the *Statistisches Handbuch der Stadt Frankfurt a.M.*, 2d. ed., Frankfurt: Osterreith Verlag, 1928; for the later elections, see the *Statistische Jahresübersichten der Stadt Frankfurt am Main*, a yearly publication of the city's statistical office.

As might well be expected, in this city the two liberal parties, the DVP and DDP, generally outpolled the Prussian DNVP. In the 1920 Reichstag election, the respective figures for the three parties were 15.2, 14.9, and 10.2 percent. The DNVP increased its strength here (as elsewhere) in 1924, but it fell off thereafter, the drop from December 1924 to May 1928 being from 14.0 to 8.6 percent. In September 1930 it fell again, this time to 2.2 percent. An indication of the voting tendencies of the city's upper class is given by the vote in the western outer-city district, the "best" area of the city. There, the DNVP received 10.3 percent in 1928, while the DVP received 21.5 percent and the DDP 26.6 percent.

Frankfurt differs from most other cities in one minor respect. Elsewhere, there was a tendency for the vote in the November 1932 election to converge on the DNVP. The DNVP showed a slight increase in Frankfurt at this time, but the bourgeois resurgence in this city, for the most part, benefited the DVP. This did not result in much overall change; the DVP went from 2.3 to 5.3 percent, but the NSDAP was still at 34.2 percent. It does suggest, however, something of the differing tendencies of the upper classes in the cities of Germany.

The picture on the left also deserves some attention. The SPD showed a steady decline in every election from December 1924 on, the falloff being from 36.3 percent at that time to 23.0 percent in November 1932. That did not mean a steady rise for the Communists. They did increase from 12.5 percent in 1928 to 15.0 percent in 1930 but then fell back again to 13.6 percent in July 1932. The big jump again came in November when they reached 18.0 percent. The combined share of the vote for the left declined from 46.4 percent in May 1928, prior to the crisis, to 42.1 percent in 1930 and again to 39.5 percent in July 1932. Again the assumption that an economic depression will automatically lead to a mobilization in favor of the left is shown to be inadequate.

2. A report based on the 1939 census gave the breakdown by occupational category for the two key districts shown in the table.

	West End	Outer Sachsenhausen	Frankfurt
Independent businessmen	22.1%	16.2%	11.8%
Family helpers	1.9	1.3	3.3
Civil servants	9.5	13.7	7.4
White-collar employees	38.7	50.2	27.3
Workers	27.8	18.7	50.2

Approximately two-fifths of the West End's workers were domestic servants compared to the city's 5.2 percent. From a typewritten report by Professor Dr. Flaskämper, of the city's statistical office, January 1942, Frankfurt a.M., Stadtskanzlei, file no. 1410, vol. 1. See also Appendix C for Frankfurt and the other cities of this chapter.

The 1925 census of housing indicated that 5.8 percent of the city's housing units had six or more rooms (exclusive of kitchen and bathrooms). The western third of the Neustadt was slightly above this figure, the two administrative subareas there having figures of 9.2 and 7.5 percent. The West End, as noted, consisted of two districts: the western outer city, which contained two subareas with percentages of 30.2 and 50.0, and the adjacent northwestern outer-city district which had three subareas, the percentages there being 31.0, 30.4, and 23.9. The equivalent percentages in the five subareas of Outer Sachsenhausen were: 4.9, 26.1, 1.0, 0.4, and 7.5. Percentages calculated from figures contained in the *Statistisches Handbuch*, pp. 34–35.

3. *Statistische Jahresübersichten der Stadt Frankfurt*, 1st suppl., 1929, pp. 162-163.

4. Based on data contained in the *Statistisches Handbuch*, pp. 58, 69.

5. *Frankfurter Zeitung*, no. 571, August 2, 1932, Stadtblatt, pp. 3-4. The results for the major parties are given here both for the Reichstag election and for the previous Landtag election. The results for the city's thirty-seven districts are broken down by precinct, with 301 listed in all.

6. In contrast, Outer Sachsenhausen had only a tiny Jewish population (2.1 percent). Anti-Semites might have chosen this housing area in preference to the West End.

7. The *Frankfurter Zeitung* is so well known as to need no further comment. For information on the political tendencies of the newspaper in the Weimar years, see M. Krejci, "Die Frankfurter Zeitung und der Nationalsozialismus, 1923-1933," doctoral dissertation, University of Würzburg, 1967. He portrays that newspaper as being consistently against the NSDAP. See also Kurt Koszyk, *Deutsche Presse 1914-1945*, Berlin: Colloquium Verlag, 1972, pp. 216-219. For the later period, see Friedrich Hepp, "Der geistige Widerstand im Kulturteil der Frankfurter Zeitung gegen die Diktatur des totalen Staates," doctoral dissertation, University of Munich, 1950.

The *Nachrichten* (actually the *Frankfurter Nachrichten und Intelligenz-Blatt–Handels-Zeitung*) was quite different from many of the other right liberal newspapers reviewed in this work. It gave clear, unambiguous support to the DVP in all elections of the period. Nor did it shy away from political discussion and commentary. It gave considerable attention to the violence present in Germany, and much of this portrays the National Socialists as the instigators. Hitler appeared in Frankfurt just before the July 1932 election. Under the main heading "Adolf Hitler in Frankfurt," it had a quotation: "My life's aim is to demolish the parties" (from the issue of July 30, 1932).

8. See Paul Massing, *Rehearsal for Destruction: A Study of Political Anti-Semitism in Imperial Germany*, New York: Harper Brothers, 1949, ch. 6; P.G.J. Pulzer, *The Rise of Political Anti-Semitism in Germany and Austria*, New York: John Wiley & Sons, 1964, ch. 12; and, a sympathetic account, Eugen Schmahl, *Entwicklung der völkischen Bewegung*, Giessen: Emil Roth Verlag, 1933. See also Eberhart Schön, *Die Entstehung des Nationalsozialismus in Hessen*, Meisenheim am Glan: Verlag Anton Hain, 1972, pp. 8 ff., 156, 174-175, 179; and note 51, Chapter 14.

9. The few sentences presented here can offer little more than a hypothetical outline of a possibility. It is difficult, also, to account for the high overall level of NSDAP support in Frankfurt. Some initial predispositions found in this region may have been operating. They could have made it easy to generate a high level of organizational activity, and that organizational activity could in turn have been instrumental in transforming the initial predispositions into NSDAP votes. There is, obviously, very little evidence that can be offered with respect to this predisposition hypothesis beyond the already discussed regional anti-Semitism. One may also note that the smaller Protestant cities of the region also had high levels of NSDAP support, for example, Darmstadt, 47 percent; Giessen, 49 percent; Kassel, 43 percent; and Marburg, 53 percent.

Frankfurt's high level of NSDAP support existed *despite* newspaper opposition. One possibility is that the *Frankfurter Zeitung* did not have all that wide a circulation within Frankfurt and that within the city it was read by groups already solidly opposed to the NSDAP. Krejci ("Die Frankfurter Zeitung," p. 4) gives its circulation as roughly 100,000. Of its subscriptions 36.9 percent went to businessmen and firms (*Geschäftsinhaber und Firmen*), 14.5 percent to persons in "finance," 9.5 percent to clubs, hotels, and travel bureaus, and 9.3 percent to public agencies and higher civil servants. It seems likely that this newspaper, more than any other, had a national circulation and that much of this 100,000 went outside the city. A large part of the remainder would have gone to the Jewish families in the city. If this were the case, it might have had only a very limited deterring impact on the rest of the city's voters. Some people report that the paper was read by many for its business and financial reports, suggesting that some readers would have skipped over its general news and editorial comment.

10. In this case, the important industries included vehicle assembly; machine tool manufacture; rubber, chemical, and dyestuff manufacture; food; textiles; and cigarettes. The city was also an important rail center.

11. The election results for the entire Weimar period are summarized in Friedrich Feldmann, *Geschichte des Ortsvereins Hannover der Sozialdemokratischen Partei Deutschlands*, Hanover: Verlag Buchdruckwerksstätten, 1952, pp. 50-51.

Some side issues are deserving of attention here. Because of the forced incorporation of Hanover into Prussia, the Prussian Conservatives never had any great popularity. The National Liberals were the dominant bourgeois party as was, after the war, the Deutsche Volkspartei. There was also an autonomist party, the Deutsch-Hannoveraner that in some ways was the region's equivalent to the DNVP. But, in the course of the Weimar period, its tendency was to ally with the Zentrum. See Jeremy Noakes, *The Nazi Party in Lower Saxony 1921-1933*, London: Oxford University Press, 1971, pp. 5-6 and 18.

The Communists were never very strong in this city, their high being 12.9 percent in the November 1932 election. In the 1930 Reichstag election, the respective KPD and SPD percentages were 6.3 and 45.2. The SPD in the city had always been firmly in the hands of the moderates. When the revolution broke out, they formed the Workers and Soldiers' Council, dominated the city, and even executed one of the revolutionaries, an outsider from the north, for plundering. There was never any uprising in opposition to the Weimar coalition, and for that reason the city never had any direct experience with the Freikorps.

12. "Die Reichstagswahl am 14. September 1930: Ergebnisse nach Stadtteilen," *Statistischer Vierteljahresbericht der Hauptstadt Hannover*, 36 (1930): 3d quarter, Appendix.

13. From the *Hannoverscher Kurier*, August 1, 1932. The paper gave results for 244 precincts.

14. The issues of the *Anzeiger* covered were those of: August 31-September 15, 1930; April 22-24, 1932; and July 27-August 1, 1932.

15. The issues of the *Kurier* covered were those of: March 13-14, 1932; April 10, 24, and 25, 1932; July 31 and August 1, 1932; and November 4-7, 1932.

16. Noakes, *The Nazi Party*, p. 205.

17. The question of the direction of cause invariably arises in this connection. Did the newspaper message cause the attitude or behavior? Or was it the awareness of audience attitudes that led the newspaper to respond to a public demand?

18. From *Stuttgarter Wirtschaftsberichte: Mitteilungen des Statistischen Amts der Stadt Stuttgart*, vol. 9, pt. 1, April 1933. All the figures for the July 1932 election come from this source.

Stuttgart provides another instance of a city in which the Communist party did not grow in the first years of the depression. The KPD took 19.5 percent of the vote in the May 1924 election and fell off to 16.1 percent in December of that year. It fell off again in 1928, to 14.9 percent, and came back to 16.6 percent in September 1930. In April of 1932, more than two years into the crisis, it actually lost position, falling to 15.3 percent. In July 1932, it received 16.5 percent, less than it had had (relatively and absolutely) in 1930. At that point it was only a fraction ahead of where it had been in December 1924. The breakthrough came in the November 1932 election, a pattern that is similar to that noted in Berlin, Hamburg, and Frankfurt.

The big advance of the KPD was outside of the capital city. Its percentage in Stuttgart went from 14.9 to 16.5 between September 1928 and July 1932. The respective percentages elsewhere in Württemberg were 5.6 and 10.0.

19. Similar patterns appeared in the 1930 Reichstag election, in both rounds of the presidential election of 1932, and in the Landtag election of that year. See the *Stuttgarter Wirtschaftsberichte* of October 6, 1930, and May 8, 1932.

20. The issues reviewed were those of September 7-15, 1930 and April 1932.

21. Rainer Gömmel and Günther Haertel, "Arbeitslosigkeit und Wählerentscheidungen in Nürnberg von 1928 bis 1933," seminar paper, 1968, under Ernst Deuerlein, photo copy in the Nuremberg Stadtarchiv.

22. Klaus Krieger, "Arbeitslosigkeit und Wählerentscheidungen in Nürnberg von 1928 bis 1933," seminar paper, 1967-1968, under Ernst Deuerlein, photocopy in the Nuremberg Stadtarchiv.

23. The *Statistische Jahrbuch der Stadt Nürnberg: 1930*, Nuremberg: Fränkische Verlagsanstalt, contained the votes cast in the 1930 election for 219 precincts. The city as a whole gave 24.0 percent of its votes to the NSDAP. The figure at that time for Luitpoldshain was 33.5 percent and for Erlenstegen was 30.0 percent. A third *Villenviertel*, St. Jobst, untouched in these two seminar papers, had a 32.4 percent figure.

24. The *Fränkischer Kurier* was originally a local family enterprise. In 1923, in the course of the inflation, the MAN firm bought a minority holding with the understanding that the newspaper would continue to be edited in a "national" direction. The MAN firm in turn was owned by the Gutehoffnungshütte, the Ruhr steel firm, whose managing director was Paul Reusch. Under the same management and general supervision were the *Münchner Neueste Nachrichten* and the *Schwäbischer Merkur* of Stuttgart. Hugenberg made some efforts to gain control of the *Kurier* in the mid-twenties and Stresemann, using secret government funds, also attempted to gain some influence over the newspaper. Eventually, however, it came into the hands of MAN and thus was

under Reusch's direction. In addition to catering to its many masters during this period, the newspaper also had to pay some attention to local consumers and local pressures.

The newspaper was generally rightist and was close to the DNVP throughout most of this period. At one point in 1928, one of the competing owners described the newspaper as being on the same level as the National Socialists' *Völkischer Beobachter*. In the last years of the republic, the editor, Rudolf Kötter, followed closely the guidelines provided by Reusch. The relationship of this newspaper to Reusch, accordingly, was much closer than was that of the stubbornly resisting *Münchner Neueste Nachrichten*. It is of some interest to note that although owned by the same firm and guided by the same managing director, these papers had different political directions. The Munich paper was generally favorable to the BVP, was strongly opposed to the NSDAP, and had a serious liberal tendency. The *Kurier*, by contrast, favored the DNVP, was sympathetic to the NSDAP, and was ardently reactionary. The *Schwäbische Merkur*, as noted, was a middle-of-the-road liberal paper, at one point even supporting the left liberal Theodor Heuss. The owners clearly let the newspapers follow their traditional political directions. What influence they chose to exert was through various inserts or through additions to the routine content. They did not insist on total control of the content, which would have endangered a rather expensive piece of property.

Some of the difficulties facing bourgeois press lords appear in this connection. The *Fränkischer Kurier* experienced serious financial difficulties as the depression worsened. Circulation fell off, and much advertising disappeared. Its regional circulation, that is, its circulation outside Nuremberg proper, faced serious competition from the *Münchner Neueste Nachrichten*. There was no easy solution to this problem.

All of these details are taken from Koszyk, *Deutsche Presse*, pp. 201 ff. Another source reports that "of the city's newspapers only the *Fränkischer Kurier* failed to criticize the militant anti-semitism of Streicher. The *Fränkischer Kurier*, which was the paper most read by the middle classes there, usually reported sympathetically on the NSDAP, gave its activities generous coverage and even urged its readers to hoist swastika flags on their houses during the party rally there in 1929." See Geoffrey Pridham, *Hitler's Rise to Power: The Nazi Movement in Bavaria, 1923-1933*, New York: Harper & Row, 1973, p. 243.

25. The 1939 census figures are contained in the following: Karl Hook, *Mannheim in Wart, Zahl und Bild: Seine Entwicklung seit 1900*, Mannheim: Mannheimer Grossdruckerei, 1954, p. 102. The figures on the housing characteristics come from Sigmund Schott, "Ergebnisse der Wohnzählung vom 12. Mai 1925," *Beiträge zur Statistik der Stadt Mannheim*, no. 36, Mannheim: Mannheimer Vereinsdruckerei, n.d.

26. The figures given here are recalculated from the results published in the *Neue Badische Landeszeitung*, no. 643 of September 15, 1930, and from the *Neue Mannheimer Zeitung* of the same date. The figures in these two sources are given by precinct (*Wahllokale*). It is not clear which precincts constituted the Oberstadt. Examination of the most likely precincts in the neighborhood of the pal-

ace showed them all to be well above the city average, that is, generally at the same level as in the Oststadt.

27. The figures for the Reichstag elections of 1928 and after are taken from local newspaper reports (see note 26, this chapter). The early Weimar figures are based on Sigmund Schott, "Statistische Bemerkungen zum Ergebnis der Nationalwahlen in Mannheim," *Beiträge zur Statistik der Stadt Mannheim*, special issue no. 6, n.d., n.p. For the 1929 Landtag vote see Emil Hofmann, *Die Ergebnisse der badischen Landtagswahlen in Mannheim in den Jahren 1913-1929*, Mannheim: Gegenbach & Hahn, 1930. For the municipal election of 1930 see Hoffmann's *Die Gemeindewahlen in Mannheim in den Jahren 1911-1930*, Mannheim: Gegenbach & Hahn, 1932.

28. The figures for this election are based on the precinct results given in the *Mannheimer Tageblatt*, no. 207, August 1, 1932. Precinct figures were also given in the *Neue Mannheimer Zeitung*, no. 351, of the same date, but these are generally lower than those of the *Tageblatt*. I have taken the *Tageblatt*'s figures on the assumption that they are final counts.

As far as I was able to discover, no official description of the precincts survived the war. Initially all that seemed to be available for the period was a listing of the results by precinct, these given by number (1 through 155) and place (e.g. Pestalozzi School, Room 1, Pestalozzi School, Room 2, Moll School, Room 5, etc.). The *Tageblatt* fortunately, had a brief description of the streets served by the Pestalozzi School and the others.

NINE. THE SUMMER ELECTION

1. *Statistische Mitteilungen über den hamburgischen Staat*, no. 29, Hamburg: Kommissionsverlag von Lüteke und Wolff, 1932. Some additional suggestion as to the character of the travelers is provided by an examination of the other votes cast in the station. The second largest party, after the NSDAP, was the conservative DNVP with 208 or 17.6 percent. Only 13.8 percent of the travelers were SPD voters, well below the 31.5 percent in the city. And the Communist party received only thirteen votes in the station. Some workers, to be sure, operating railroad employees, for example, may have been found among the travelers. These railroad stations would also serve the area with local trains. A good deal of family visiting and local tourism goes on in Germany on Sundays, at least in normal times. Those using the station to go on a local outing would presumably cast their votes at home before they left or after they returned.

For a brief account of the background to the new electoral law, see Ferdinand A. Hermens, *Democracy or Anarchy? A Study of Proportional Representation*, Notre Dame: University of Notre Dame, 1941, especially pp. 214-218.

2. From the *Beilage zum Monatsbericht des Statistischen und Wahlamts der Stadt Köln*, July 1932, p. 3. The election district (*Wahlkreis*) Cologne-Aachen, which contained those two cities and the surrounding countryside, gave the National Socialists 20.2 percent in the July election. It was the lowest percentage of all the nation's thirty-five districts.

In the Cologne railroad station, the vote for the Zentrum, not too surprisingly, was considerably higher (25.4 percent) than in Protestant Hamburg (8.3

percent). The vote for the left in Cologne was well below the city-wide figures with 17.4 percent for the SPD and only 5.0 percent for the KPD.

3. From the *Völkischer Beobachter*, August 1/2, 1932.

4. The Hanover figure came from the *Anhänge zum Statistischen Vierteljahresbericht*, no. 6, "Die Reichstagswahl am 14. September 1930: Ergebnisse nach Stadtteilen." The Augsburg and Lauingen results were found in the files of the Munich Stadtarchiv, in Wahlamt files 155 and 177.

5. The voting on shipboard is given in *Statistische Mitteilungen über den hamburgischen Staat*. For information on the ships and their usual voyages, I am indebted to Walter Kresse of the Museum für Hamburgische Geschichte.

6. In general, the remaining nonleft votes went to the DNVP and the Zentrum. There are, however, substantial variations from ship to ship. On the *Tacoma*, for example, where sixty-one votes were cast, no one chose those parties. These "samples" are not likely to have contained random cross-sections of Germany's well-off populations. Advertising in a given city or area could have attracted an unrepresentative collection. A private travel club or a travel agency could have generated a rather atypical selection of passengers, especially on the smaller ships.

Not all seamen, of course, would have voted for the left. As in the cities, some, no doubt, would have supported one or another of the center or right parties. The problem of class-specific linkages (i.e. of stipulations) is not likely to be as serious on the ships at sea. For all practical purposes, these ships would contain only two classes, the well-off passengers (and the ships' officers) and the ordinary seamen. Few members of the lower middle class would be present in these contexts (the wireless operator seems one lonely possibility). The assignment of the left vote, accordingly, becomes much simpler; and since few passengers would be voting SPD or KPD, nearly all of that vote can be assigned to the seamen. Even if one adopts the previous estimating procedure and assumes that one-third of the seamen voted for parties other than those of the left (an assumption that seems unusually generous here), the passenger support for the National Socialists would still be remarkable.

7. Not all seagoing workers had the benefit of this on-board vote. To participate, some were required to cast their votes (before, after, or on the day of the election) in one of the precincts of the Altstadt, this being done with an absentee ballot. Some 547 votes there (of a 1,595 total) were absentee.

8. Meinrad Hagmann, *Der Weg ins Verhängnis: Reichstagswahlergebnisse 1919 bis 1933 besonders aus Bayern*, Munich: Michael Beckstein Verlag, 1946, p. 23. Also used for the following discussion was "Die Reichstagswahl vom 31. Juli 1932 in Bayern," *Zeitschrift des Bayerischen Statistischen Landesamts*, (1932): 425-472.

The significance of the vacation vote has been noted by other authors as well. Pridham has a one-page discussion that links this vote with NSDAP losses in the better-off districts of Berlin. He also touches on a similar development in the Baltic Sea resorts and on the island of Helgoland. Only "a handful" of voters were found there in normal times, but suddenly, in July 1932, the island had some 1,300. This was based on a report from the file of the NSDAP Propaganda Department analyzing the election. See Geoffrey Pridham, *Hitler's Rise to Power: The Nazi Movement in Bavaria, 1923-1933*, New York: Harper & Row, 1973, pp. 284-285. Karl Dietrich Bracher, drawing on Hagmann, also recognized the existence of this affiliation of National Socialism voting with the resort areas; see his *Die Auflösung der Weimarer Republik*, Villingen/Schwarzwald: Ring-Verlag, 1964, p. 650n. And, in an otherwise highly questionable source, there is a recognition that the NSDAP's absolute loss of votes in Berlin was linked to the absentee ballots cast elsewhere. Joseph Goebbels, *Vom Kaiserhof zur Reichskanzlei*, Munich: Zentralverlag der NSDAP, 1937, p. 136. Although the fact has gained at least modest recognition, few other authors have picked it up, let alone seen its significance.

9. Hagmann, *Der Weg ins Verhängnis*, p. 12.

10. "Der Fremdenverkehr im September und im Sommerhalbjahr 1932," *Wirtschaft und Statistik*, 12 (1932): 687. See also Johannes Müller, "Der Fremdenverkehr der Kur- und Badeorte nach seiner personellen Zusammensetzung," *Allgemeines statistisches Archiv*, 23 (1933-1934): 538-545.

11. The 1933 census gave the following Protestant percentages: Bad Reichenhall, 11.0; Berchtesgaden, 5.3; Garmisch, 8.7; Starnberg, 12.0. The overall figure for the rural areas (*Bezirksämter*) of Upper Bavaria was 3.8 percent. From Hagmann, *Der Weg ins Verhängnis*, p. 22. Traunstein, a frequent exception to the generalizations in the text, had a very small Protestant percentage, the figure there being only 1.6.

12. The presence and importance of this tourist trade is indicated in the figures for the July 1932 election. From Hagmann, *Der Weg ins Verhängnis*, p. 25.

Administrative District	Registered Voters	Absentee Ballots	Percent Absentee
Bad Reichenhall, city	4,330	2,964	40.6
Berchtesgaden	9,240	8,355	47.5
Garmisch	13,298	13,160	49.7
Miesbach	21,536	9,285	30.1
Tölz	10,980	4,366	28.5

13. The DNVP votes cast in September 1930, July 1932, and November 1932 in Berchtesgaden were, respectively, 800, 2,100, and 600. In Garmisch the figures were 1,200, 3,100, and 1,000. This is especially striking since the DNVP was increasing its share of the vote throughout Germany in November of 1932.

14. Nördlingen, unique in the area, was the northernmost district of Swabia, bordering on Protestant Middle Franconia. Four other administrative districts of Swabia had Protestant percentages of between ten and twenty.

15. Some of these results were made available through the assistance of the Füssen city authorities, in particular, Herr Wanner, the first *Bürgermeister*, to whom I wish to express my appreciation.

16. The authorities of the border community Pfronten (also in the administrative district Füssen) found a newspaper report showing the results for all of the precincts of the area. This report also contained a detailed breakdown of results (for three elections) within the city of Füssen.

Among the arrangements made to facilitate voting in the Reichstag election was the provision for half-price fares on the Austrian railroad. Germans in Austria could travel to a German border community, vote there, and return to their vacation spot. A memorandum went out from Munich on July 12, 1932, to Füssen, "Reichstagswahl 1932, hier Stimmabgabe im Reiseverkehr," explaining in detail the provisions of this arrangement.

Some twelve kilometers west of Füssen were the border communities Pfronten and Pfronten-Steinach. These border communities would have received the ballots of Germans coming over from Austria. Judging from the distribution and development of the vote over the three elections, it would appear that Pfronten-Berg I received only the vote of local populations. There were 479 votes cast there in the April Landtag election and 471 in the July Reichstag election. And, respectively, 165 and 164 votes were cast in those elections for the NSDAP. In Pfronten-Berg II, the number of votes cast increased from 530 to 896, and the NSDAP votes jumped from 270 to 379. There were also increases for the DNVP and the BVP. In Pfronten-Steinach, the votes cast increased from 639 to 896, and the NSDAP votes went from 319 to 369. Again there were increases in the votes of the DNVP and BVP. Not all of the added votes are those of well-off tourists. The high season also attracted many service workers from outside the local area. Their presence is reflected in the increased votes for the SPD and KPD, particularly in Pfronten-Berg II and Pfronten-Steinach.

Detailed results for the border districts of Laufen and Traunstein, made available by Herr Kastner of the Landratsamt in Laufen, were also examined. They confirm the point being made here.

17. In Hesse's Bad Nauheim, just to the north of Frankfurt, there was a state election on June 19, 1932, with the NSDAP taking 51.3 percent of the votes. In the July Reichstag election, six weeks later, when the number of absentee ballots jumped from 195 to 1,993 (out of a 7,678 total), the National Socialist percentage fell to 46.6. In Bad Salzhaufen, a much smaller resort town, the equivalent figures were 71.4 and 47.4. See *Die Ergebnisse der Landtagswahl am 19. Juni 1932 und der Reichstagswahl am 31. July 1932 im Volksstaat Hessen nach einzelnen Gemeinden*, Darmstadt: Hessischer Staatsverlag, 1932.

18. One other observation ought to be made here. The previous studies that have focused on the 1932 election have not made adjustments for the votes of the vacationers. These ecological studies have correlated data on the occupations and religious composition of the indigenous populations with the votes of the indigenous-plus-vacation populations. The overall effects would probably not be very great. Their direction would be clear: they would reduce National Socialist strength in the cities, increase it in Catholic resort areas, and decrease it in Protestant resort areas.

Ten. The Parties of the Right and Center

1. See Erich Fromm, *Escape from Freedom*, New York: Rinehart, 1941; Seymour Martin Lipset, *Political Man: The Social Bases of Politics*, Garden City:

Doubleday, 1960, ch. 5; and William Kornhauser, *The Politics of Mass Society*, Glencoe: The Free Press, 1959.

2. For a recent instance of this procedure, see Jürgen Kocka, "Zur Problematik der deutschen Angestellten, 1914-1933," pp. 792-811 of Hans Mommsen, Dietmar Petzina, and Bernd Weisbrod, eds., *Industrielles System und politische Entwicklung in der Weimarer Republik*, Düsseldorf: Droste Verlag, 1974. Some of the researchable points of the argument also tend to be overlooked. Kocka, for example, presents the leveling argument, but, although Allen's work is cited in this connection, he does not comment on one of Allen's major observations— that the middle class was *not* hurt by the depression. See William Sheridan Allen, *The Nazi Seizure of Power: The Experience of a Single German Town, 1930-1935*, Chicago: Quadrangle Books, 1965, pp. 24, 69, 102, 132. A local bank did collapse in Thalburg, but that was due to mismanagement rather than the general economic situation (pp. 56-57). There is some relevant evidence in J. Heinz Müller's work which also goes against the conventional claim. Again Kocka cites the work but neglects the lesson. See Müller, *Nivellierung und Differenzierung der Arbeitseinkommen in Deutschland seit 1925*, Berlin: Duncker und Humblot, 1954, p. 140. Thalburg, incidentally, was not at all exceptional; see Chapter 13 for further consideration of this point.

3. These objections refer specifically to the familiar abstract and general centrist analyses of the rise of National Socialism. They are not intended to apply to the specialized historical monograph that considers at length the impact of political determinants. Nor is the present argument to be taken as opposed to *all* abstract and general analysis. Some kind of abstraction is always present. The question is one of the usefulness of the various alternatives.

4. The problem with such general analysis is that without consideration of the specifically political tasks, one cannot assess the adequacy of the model. The problems facing anyone in the governments of Germany at that time were extraordinarily complex; for the democratic parties, they became ever more complex as time went on and the range of options narrowed. The failure to consider the political question means that one overlooks other possibilities, that is, other than the requirements of good will, hard work, and time. The possibility of doing nothing or of doing the *wrong* thing is also hidden if one merely assumes the center parties were hard at work arguing for, instituting, and managing "complex solutions."

5. Two major traditions in voting studies, those of the Columbia and Michigan schools, have discounted the role of such voter rationality. But those traditions are based on experience that is inappropriate for analysis of the Weimar case. See Bernard R. Berelson, Paul F. Lazarsfeld, and William N. McPhee, *Voting: A Study of Opinion Formation in a Presidential Campaign*, Chicago: University of Chicago Press, 1954; and Angus Campbell, Philip E. Converse, Warren E. Miller, and Donald E. Stokes, *The American Voter*, New York: John Wiley & Sons, 1960. For a summary discussion see Peter H. Rossi, "Four Landmarks in Voting Research," pp. 5-54 of Eugene Burdick and Arthur J. Broadbeck, eds., *American Voting Behavior*, Glencoe: The Free Press, 1959. For a criticism of the Columbia school, see Richard F. Hamilton, *Class and Politics in the*

United States, New York: John Wiley & Sons, 1972, pp. 49-63. These works do not ignore issue voting entirely. The Campbell, et al. volume, for example, has a brief chapter entitled "Public Policy and Political Preference," spelling out the conditions of "issue-oriented political behavior." The point is one of relative emphasis. In recent years there has been a rediscovery of issue voting. One significant work pointing in this new direction is that of V. O. Key, Jr., *The Responsible Electorate: Rationality in Presidential Voting, 1936-1960*, Cambridge, Mass.: Harvard University Press, 1966. The most important recent work is that of Norman H. Nie, Sidney Verba, and John R. Petrocik, *The Changing American Voter*, Cambridge, Mass.: Harvard University Press, 1976.

6. The principal sources for this account are those of: Friedrich Hiller von Gaertringen, "Die Deutschnationale Volkspartei," pp. 543-652 of Erich Matthias and Rudolf Morsey, eds., *Das Ende der Parteien 1933*, Düsseldorf: Droste Verlag, 1960; and Karl Dietrich Bracher, *Die Auflösung der Weimarer Republik*, Villingen/Schwarzwald: Ring-Verlag, 1964, pp. 83-86, 309-322, 347-355. For the antecedents and early history of the DNVP see Hans Booms, *Die Deutschkonservative Partei*, Düsseldorf: Droste Verlag, 1954; Werner Liebe, *Die Deutschnationale Volkspartei, 1918-1924*, Düsseldorf: Droste Verlag, 1956; and Lewis Hertzman, *DNVP: Right-Wing Opposition in the Weimar Republic, 1918-1924*, Lincoln: University of Nebraska Press, 1963.

The activities of the DNVP have been explored in some unpublished Ph.D. dissertations, the most notable of these being: Manfred Dörr, "Die Deutschnationale Volkspartei, 1925 bis 1928," University of Marburg, 1964; Gisbert Jörg Gemein, "Die DNVP in Düsseldorf, 1918-1933," University of Cologne, 1969; Reinhard Behrens, "Die Deutschnationalen in Hamburg, 1918-1933," University of Hamburg, 1973. See also the *Staatsarbeit* by Johann Gildemeister, "Die Politik der Deutschnationalen Volkspartei vom Oktober 1929 bis Mai 1932 mit besonderer Berücksichtigung der Abspaltung der Volkskonservativen," Hamburg, 1951. See also Sigmund Neumann, *Die deutschen Parteien: Wesen und Wandel nach dem Kriege*, 2d ed., Berlin: Junker und Dünnhaupt, 1932, pp. 60-72.

On the later history of the party see: Erasmus Jonas, *Die Volkskonservativen, 1928-1933*, Düsseldorf: Droste Verlag, 1965; John A. Leopold, "The Election of Alfred Hugenberg as Chairman of the German National People's Party," *Canadian Journal of History*, 7 (1972): 149-171; Attila Chanady, "The Disintegration of the German National People's Party, 1924-1930," *Journal of Modern History*, 39 (1967): 65-91; and D. P. Walker, "The German Nationalist People's Party: The Conservative Dilemma in the Weimar Republic," *Journal of Contemporary History*, 14 (1979): 627-649.

On the Wirtschaftspartei, see Martin Schumacher, *Mittelstandsfront und Republik: Die Wirtschaftspartei—Reichspartei des deutschen Mittelstandes, 1919-1933*, Düsseldorf: Droste Verlag, 1972. And for the Christian Social movement see Günter Opitz, *Der Christlich-soziale Volksdienst: Versuch einer protestantischen Partei in der Weimarer Republik*, Düsseldorf: Droste Verlag, 1969.

7. One of the best accounts of this shift—from the democratic parties of the center, to the German Nationals, and then to the National Socialists—is to be found in Rudolf Heberle, *Landbevölkerung und Nationalsozialismus: Eine soziolo-*

gische Untersuchung der politischen Willensbildung in Schleswig-Holstein 1918 bis 1932, Stuttgart: Deutsche Verlags-Anstalt, 1963, pp. 29-40.

8. The strains are summarized in the following quotations: "The agrarians in the DNVP pressed for tariffs, the Christian Socialists for workers' benefits, civil servants wanted security, industrialists opposed socialization. Whether this program was coherent and practicable was another question. There was hardly any need to think over its details or practical implications as long as it managed to catch the fancy of the voters—and as long as the DNVP remained in opposition." And, indicating the strains arising from participation in government, one commentator said: "If one enters a republican coalition with four ministers and allows them to take the oath on the constitution, and signs the republican statutes, then one cannot at the same time wave the black-white-red flag in the press and in meetings, blow into the monarchic horn, and thoroughly abuse the foreign policy of the government." From Chanady, "The Disintegration," pp. 70 and 81n. Fifty-two DNVP representatives voted against the Dawes Plan, forty-eight voted for it, and six were absent.

9. See Chanady, "The Disintegration," p. 77; and Kurt Koszyk, *Deutsche Presse 1914-1945*, Berlin: Colloquium Verlag, 1972, pp. 223, 226. One leading industrialist wrote, in July 1928, that "Hugenberg's activity had caused enormous damage to western [i.e. Ruhr] industry." He complained that Hugenberg's appearance in connection with any business organization led to the impression that he was *the* representative of western industry whereas in fact these appearances were destructive of their interests. In 1924, Hugenberg had already gone against the "overwhelming majority of his colleagues in the Reich Federation of German Industry" by opposing the Dawes Plan. Leopold, "The Election of Hugenberg," p. 153. See also Henry Ashby Turner, Jr., "Big Business and the Rise of Hitler," *American Historical Review*, 75 (1969-1970): 59-60; and Lothar Döhn, *Politik und Interesse: Die Interessenstrucktur der Deutschen Volkspartei*, Meisenheim am Glan: Verlag Anton Hain, 1972, p. 292n. Among the general works on Hugenberg and his activities are: Ludwig Bernhard, *Der 'Hugenberg-Konzern.' Psychologie und Technik einer Grossorganisation der Presse*, Berlin: Verlag von Julius Springer, 1928; Otto Kriegk, *Hugenberg*, Leipzig: R. Kittler, 1932; Lothar Steuer, ed., *Hugenbergs Ringen in deutschen Schicksalstunden*, Detmold: Maximilian Verlag, 1951; Valeska Dietrich, "Alfred Hugenberg: ein Manager in der Publizistik," doctoral dissertation, Free University of Berlin, 1960; Dr. Wahrmund (pseud.), *Gericht über Hugenberg*, Dillingen: Verlagsanstalt Vorm G. J. Manz, 1932; and, covering an earlier period, Dankwart Guratzsch, *Macht durch Organisation: Die Grundlegung des Hugenbergschen Presseimperiums*, Düsseldorf: Bertelsmann Universitätsverlag, 1974. See also Klaus-Peter Hoepke, "Alfred Hugenberg als Vermittler zwischen grossindustriellen Interessen und Deutschnationaler Volkspartei," pp. 907-919 of Mommsen, et al., eds., *Industrielles System*; and John A. Leopold, *Alfred Hugenberg: The Radical Nationalist Campaign against the Weimar Republic*, New Haven: Yale University Press, 1977. For the Pan German connection see Alfred Kruck, *Geschichte des Alldeutschen Verbandes, 1890-1939*, Wiesbaden: Franz Steiner Verlag, 1954.

10. Hiller von Gaertringen, "Die Deutschnationale Volkspartei," p. 546. One

argument that was widespread in Weimar political circles held that participation in government eroded popular support. One was forced to make compromises, which damaged one's ideological purity, causing voters to defect to one's unsullied competitors. This was the Hugenberg argument. It was also the argument of many who came to favor a coalition government with Hitler. The same process, it was thought, would work against him and his party. It would, moreover, serve to tame him. In an argument similar to the standard pluralism of the 1950s, it was said that by participating, he would discover the complexities of policy making. He would then see that his easy slogans would not work; they were simply not applicable.

The dynamics of the party struggle are worthy of some note. A key agency was the Pan German Association, an organization Hugenberg had helped found in 1890-1891 and which was directed by his close friend Heinrich Class. This organization undertook much of the grass-roots effort to influence local selection of candidates. Hugenberg could conduct public opposition to the party's leaders through his press. Through his control and dispensation of financial contributions, he was also in a position to exert pressure on the party to accept his candidates, which may also have affected the 1928 outcome. The more pragmatic wing of the party, including the Reichstag group, had no access to the general public to present or defend its views. This struggle, it should also be noted, was in part a generational one. Hugenberg, Class, and others were directing their attack against the "young conservative" movement within the party. The later exodus of the young conservatives must have also dimmed the party's electoral chances, especially in the competition with the young and "dynamic" NSDAP. See Leopold, "The Election of Hugenberg," pp. 160-161. On the young conservatives see Klemens von Klemperer, *Germany's New Conservatism: Its History and Dilemma in the Twentieth Century*, Princeton: Princeton University Press, 1957, pp. 120-129.

11. Hiller von Gaertringen, "Die Deutschnationale Volkspartei," pp. 547 ff. Hugenberg's statement of his leadership principle goes as follows: "I believe in a government by the elect few, not by the elected. . . . I believe in leaders, not in speakers. Words are enemies of action. I believe in government by strong men who have the will power and the strength to carry out rational decisions." Chanady, "The Disintegration," p. 82.

12. The government had some difficulty gaining a hearing in the provincial press during this campaign; see Martin Vogt, ed., *Das Kabinett Müller II*, vol. 2, Boppard: Harald Boldt Verlag, 1970, pp. 1045, 1054.

13. See Jonas, *Die Volkskonservativen*, pp. 71-79.

14. Alan Bullock, *Hitler: A Study in Tyranny*, rev. ed., New York: Harper & Row, 1964, p. 149. See also Jeremy Noakes, *The Nazi Party in Lower Saxony 1921-1933*, London: Oxford University Press, 1971. The basic work on the subject is Elisabeth Freidenthal, "Volksbegehren und Volksentscheid über den Young-Plan und die deutschnationale Sezession," doctoral dissertation, University of Tübingen, 1957. Municipal elections were held on November 17, 1929, a convenient time for the National Socialist party, which was "already in the public eye as the most active participant in the campaign against the Young

Plan . . . its association with the conservative organizations involved in the campaign helped to confirm its recent attempt to acquire a more respectable image." The *Göttinger Tageblatt* said of the anti–Young Plan campaign, that "the most active in this opposition front are the National Socialists who are increasingly taking over the leadership of the great national opposition." Both quotations are from Noakes, *The Nazi Party*, p. 132. Noakes also indicates that the September 1930 election, following the guidelines sent out from Munich NSDAP headquarters, "began where the anti–Young Plan plebiscite had left off." Local units were instructed to see that "the acceptance of the Young Plan and the resulting economic collapse is continually emphasized." Ibid., p. 148. For some additional detail on the advantage the NSDAP reaped from this alliance, see Dietrich Orlow, *The History of the Nazi Party: 1919-1933*, Pittsburgh: University of Pittsburgh Press, 1969, pp. 173-174. At one of the anti–Young Plan rallies, Hitler stood next to Admiral Tirpitz, another demonstration of his "arrival." Pridham sees the NSDAP takeoff in Bavaria as closely tied to the anti–Young Plan campaign. Through a very concentrated organizational effort, the NSDAP had scored a significant victory in a special election in heavily Protestant Coburg in June of 1929. The party gained an absolute majority, thirteen of the twenty-five seats—and this even before the announcement of the initiative and referendum campaign. It then achieved a modest vote increase on December 8 in the Bavarian municipal elections, its first increase since 1924. Pridham attributes this to the National Socialists' efforts in the referendum campaign, to "their association with the traditional conservative Right," and to the financial resources provided by the Nationalist party. The anti–Young Plan plebiscite campaign in Bavaria was run simultaneously with the municipal elections, the plebiscite coming two weeks after the election, December 22; hence any given meeting could accomplish two purposes. Pridham notes that the NSDAP "carried the burden of propaganda in the referendum against the Plan. In Upper Bavaria alone, the NSDAP held twenty-three meetings in the last weeks before the plebiscite while the Nationalists held only one. The Nazis were freer to conduct radical propaganda as they were not involved in government, unlike their main allies." *Hitler's Rise to Power: The Nazi Movement in Bavaria, 1923-1933*, New York: Harper & Row, 1973, p. 88. The NSDAP made considerable gains in the cities in these elections, and, not too surprisingly perhaps, its gains came "mainly at the expense of the Nationalist Party." Pridham, incidentally, explicitly discounts unemployment as a factor in this result (p. 85).

Leopold (in *Alfred Hugenberg*, pp. 59-60) discounts the Bullock claim, saying that others in the coalition received either the same or greater attention. But that conclusion appears to be based on the reports in three Hugenberg newspapers for the two issues of July 10 and 11, 1929, that is, for those days immediately following the announcement of the committee's formation. This discounting is contradicted by Leopold's later statement (p. 83) that Hugenberg's syndicate "had blurred the distinction between the two parties, encouraging support for radical nationalism. . . . The radical seed sown by the Reich Committee against the Young Plan was reaped by the Nazis in these September elections." The *Göttinger Tageblatt*, cited above, is listed by Leopold (p. 180, n.

73) as one of those directly owned by the Hugenberg chain. See also the discussion of the Hugenberg newspaper *Der Tag* in Chapter 4.

15. See, for example, Werner Kaltefleiter, *Wirtschaft und Politik in Deutschland: Konjunktur als Bestimmunsgfaktor des Parteiensystems,* Cologne and Opladen: Westdeutscher Verlag, 1966. Kaltefleiter (pp. 35 ff.) fails to see this divided result of 1928 and links the NSDAP takeoff only to the economic crisis. See also Peter D. Stachura, "Der kritische Wendepunkt? Die NSDAP und die Reichstagswahlen vom 20. Mai 1928," *Vierteljahrshefte für Zeitgeschichte,* 26 (1978): 66-99.

16. A more detailed discussion of the Baden election appears in Ellsworth Faris, "Takeoff Point for the National Socialist Party: The Landtag Election in Baden, 1929," *Central European History,* 8 (1975): 140-171. For Thuringia, see Donald R. Tracey, "The Development of the National Socialist Party in Thuringia, 1924-30," *Central European History,* 8 (1975): 23-50.

17. Orlow, *The History of the Nazi Party.* The election campaign in Saxony is discussed on p. 162. The NSDAP held some 1,300 rallies: "no locality in the Erzgebirge" had been missed. Orlow also reports (p. 163) that a change in the orientation of the local press throughout Germany was already occurring in late 1928 and 1929: "the 'neutral' provincial press took note of party activities and reported 'objectively' (that is, favorably) on them." His discussion of the sharp rise in membership appears on p. 175. It should be noted that Orlow links this development to the onset of the depression rather than to the campaign against the Young Plan (which he discusses on the two preceding pages).

One source has made much of the fact that the NSDAP had only a very limited press, as compared to the massive coverage available for the Conservatives and the liberal parties. That is true, but it overlooks the fact that Hugenberg was performing this service for the National Socialists. See Emil Dovifat, "Die Publizistik der Weimarer Zeit," pp. 119-136 of Leonhard Reinisch, ed., *Die Zeit ohne Eigenschaften,* Stuttgart: W. Kohlhammer Verlag, 1961. I regret to report that I once took this claim at face value and passed it on in my *Class and Politics,* p. 80.

18. This position derives from evidence presented by Berelson, Lazarsfeld, and McPhee, *Voting.* A compendious review, the basic text of this position, is that of Joseph T. Klapper, *The Effects of Mass Communication,* Glencoe: The Free Press, 1960. Some relevant contrary evidence is to be found in Richard F. Hamilton, *Restraining Myths: Critical Studies of U.S. Social Structure and Politics,* New York: Sage-Halsted-Wiley, 1975, ch. 5; and John P. Robinson, "Perceived Media Bias and the 1968 Vote: Can the Media Affect Behavior after All?" *Journalism Quarterly,* 49 (1972): 239-246.

19. The focus on stable party identification derives from Campbell et al., *The American Voter.* The assumption, there and in much of the political socialization literature, it that these identifications were instilled within the family as part of one's basic or primary learning experiences. From then on, the identifications would be stable except for some major shock, such as a war or a depression, which might be followed by a realigning election. The classic articles on the subject are those of V. O. Key, Jr., "A Theory of Critical Elections," *Journal of Politics,* 17 (1955): 3-18, and "Secular Realignment and the Party System,"

Journal of Politics, 21 (1959): 198-220. In Germany there had been little chance for the voters to form stable party identifications, except with Social Democrats and the Zentrum, since almost the entire Weimar history, all fourteen years of it, had been so turbulent. For an attempt to apply this framework to the Weimar experience see W. Phillips Shively, "Party Identification, Party Choice, and Voting Stability: The Weimar Case," *American Political Science Review*, 66 (1972): 1203-1225. Also of some interest in this connection is Walter Dean Burnham, "Political Immunization and Political Confessionalism: The United States and Weimar Germany," *Journal of Interdisciplinary History*, 3 (1972-1973): 1-30. The unique features of the American scene in the 1950s, during which time these orientations were first developed, are indicated by some recent publications, notably those of Nie, Verba, and Petrocik, *The Changing American Voter*, chs. 5 and 11; and James D. Wright, *The Dissent of the Governed: Alienation and Democracy in America*, New York: Academic Press, 1976, ch. 7.

20. The shifting on the right is indicated in the Baden election results shown in the table. Participation was approximately the same in the two elections, 61.7 percent and 61.4 percent respectively. Faris, "Takeoff Point," p. 144. The Konservative Volkspartei was not yet formed; its first appearance was in the 1930 Reichstag election.

	Reichstag May 20, 1928	*Landtag* Oct. 27, 1929
NSDAP	2.9%	7.0%
DNVP ⎫	8.1 ⎫	3.7 ⎫
DVP ⎬ traditional right	9.5 ⎬ 17.6%	8.0 ⎬ 11.7%
EVD ⎫	—	3.8 ⎫
BBP ⎬ rightist splinters	1.5 ⎫	3.0 ⎬ 10.6
WP ⎭	3.4 ⎬ 4.9	3.8 ⎭

EVD = Evangelischer Volksdienst, the Baden branch of the Christlich-sozialer Volksdienst; BBP = Badische Bauernpartei, Baden Farmers' party.

In Berlin, where the number of voters increased by more than 228,000 in 1930 over the previous Reichstag election, the DNVP lost 88,853 voters and the DVP, 60,744. The most significant new splinter parties in 1930 were the Konservative Volkspartei (formed by those who had withdrawn from the DNVP) with 22,442 votes, and the Christlich-sozialer Volksdienst (Christian Social People's Service, another one-time partner in the DNVP coalition) with 27,522 votes. The former was relatively strong in the better-off districts of the city (Charlottenburg, Wilmersdorf, Zehlendorf, Schöneberg, and Steglitz). The latter did better in working-class districts, in Neukölln, Lichtenberg, Wedding, Kreuzberg, and the like. Over two-thirds of the latter party's voters were women.

A similar pattern appears in Hamburg. The DNVP loss there in 1930 was devastating; its support fell from 82,061 to 27,930 votes. The Konservative Volkspartei took 19,646, disproportionately from better-off districts. The Christian Social movement took 11,395. See also Chapter 6 for the Cologne results.

Gemein ("Die DNVP," p. 64) reports immense membership losses in Düsseldorf. Almost all of the working-class members seem to have left, either for the People's Conservatives or for the Christian Social group. While the loss of the ordinary members (*einfacher Mitglieder*) seems to have been enormous, only a few of the more prominent members quit the party.

It is worth noting that the Hugenberg influence (in the anti–Young Plan campaign) affected his own party and the right liberal DVP. The left liberal Democrats were already at a very low point in May of 1928 with only 4.9 percent of the votes. In 1930, they lost approximately one-fifth of their 1928 strength. The DNVP and the DVP both lost roughly half of their 1928 strength. This too would be consonant with the media effect hypothesis since the DDP (later Staatspartei) voters would probably have been reading different newspapers, the *Frankfurter Zeitung* or the *Berliner Tageblatt*, papers that would have been untouched by the Hugenberg infection. There are some reports that other bourgeois newspapers, particularly some in Thuringia that were close to the DVP, joined in support of the anti–Young Plan campaign. See Vogt, *Das Kabinett Müller II*, vol. 2, pp. 1039–1040.

21. Bracher, *Die Auflösung*, p. 317.

22. See Ernst-August Roloff, *Bürgertum und Nationalsozialismus 1930-1933: Braunschweigs Weg ins Dritte Reich*, Hanover: Verlag für Literatur und Zeitgeschehen, 1961, pp. 65-78; and Bullock, *Hitler*, p. 189.

23. Hiller von Gaertringen, "Die Deutschnationale Volkspartei," p. 576n.

24. The principal sources used in this review of the party's history are: Hans Booms, "Die Deutsche Volkspartei," pp. 523-539 of Matthias and Morsey, *Ende der Parteien*; Wolfgang Hartenstein, *Die Anfänge der Deutschen Volkspartei 1918-1920*, Düsseldorf: Droste Verlag, 1962; Lothar Albertin, *Liberalismus und Demokratie am Anfang der Weimarer Republik: Eine vergleichende Analyse der Deutschen Demokratischen Partei und der Deutschen Volkspartei*, Düsseldorf: Droste Verlag, 1972; Döhn, *Politik und Interesse*; Henry Ashby Turner, Jr., *Stresemann. and the Politics of the Weimar Republic*, Princeton: Princeton University Press, 1963; and Larry Eugene Jones, " 'The Dying Middle': Weimar Germany and the Fragmentation of Bourgeois Politics," *Central European History*, 5 (1972): 23-54 and "Gustav Stresemann and the Crisis of German Liberalism," *European Studies Review*, 4 (1974): 141-163. See also Bracher, *Die Auflösung*, pp. 86 ff., 291-303, and 407-410; and Neumann, *Die deutschen Parteien*, pp. 53-59.

25. Jones, " 'The Dying Middle,' " p. 33.

26. Ibid., pp. 38-40. See also Jones's "Sammlung oder Zersplitterung? Die Bestrebungen zur Bildung einer neuen Mittelpartei in der Endphase der Weimarer Republik, 1930-1933," *Vierteljahrshefte für Zeitgeschichte*, 25 (1977): 265-304.

27. See especially Turner, *Stresemann*, pp. 46, 192, and 265. See also Lewis Hertzman, "Gustav Stresemann: The Problem of Political Leadership in the Weimar Republic," *International Review of Social History*, 5 (1960): 361-377. Stresemann was not opposed to the right coalition in principle; it was, rather, a practical matter involving the long-term development of the parties and of voter loyalties. He favored the Conservatives' entry into the Luther government; it would lessen their opposition to his Locarno plans, and he hoped they would

"learn the lesson of moderation through responsibility." Hertzman, "Strese-mann," p. 373.

The burden carried by the People's party in the face of nationalist attacks was enormous. Stresemann was the leading architect of the policy of "fulfillment" (of the Versailles terms). The object of that policy was to make an "honest effort" and thus to demonstrate that the terms could *not* be fulfilled. Ideological nationalists considered any step in that direction to be treason. Stresemann's accomplishments in this connection included both the Dawes and the Young plans and the Locarno treaty. For the nationalists, this last was again treasonous in that it "sacrificed" Alsace and Lorraine. For some of the complexities of Stresemann's policy making, see Hans W. Gatzke, *Stresemann and the Rearmament of Germany*, Baltimore: Johns Hopkins Press, 1954. While supposedly fulfilling provisions for the disarmament of Germany, Stresemann was quietly attending to its rearmament. See also Robert Grathwol, "Gustav Stresemann: Reflections on His Foreign Policy," *Journal of Modern History*, 45 (1973): 52-70.

28. Jones, " 'The Dying Middle,' " p. 39.

29. See the references in note 16 of this chapter for discussions of two of these elections.

30. See Booms, "Die Deutsche Volkspartei," p. 526 and Jones, " 'The Dying Middle,' " p. 44. For some evidence on the subject, see Chapters 4 and 5.

31. Booms, "Die Deutsche Volkspartei," pp. 528-529. Jones, "Sammlung," p. 287.

32. See Tracey, "The National Socialist Party," pp. 42-43; Jones, " 'The Dying Middle,' " p. 47; Roloff, *Bürgertum*, pp. 19-49, 71, and 75; and Bracher, *Die Auflösung*, p. 409.

33. The principal sources used here are Erich Matthias and Rudolf Morsey, "Die Deutsche Staatspartei," pp. 31-97 of Matthias and Morsey, *Ende der Parteien*; Bruce B. Frye, "The German Democratic Party, 1918-1930," *Western Political Quarterly*, 15 (1963): 167-179; Jones, " 'The Dying Middle,' " and "Sammlung"; Attila Chanady, "The Dissolution of the German Democratic Party in 1930," *American Historical Review*, 73 (1967-1968): 1433-1453. For the beginning period, see also Hartenstein, *Die Anfänge*; Albertin, *Liberalismus*; and Sigmund Neumann, *Die deutschen Parteien*, pp. 46-52.

Also of some interest are the works of Modris Eksteins, *Theodor Heuss und die Weimarer Republik*, Stuttgart: Ernst Klett Verlag, 1969, and *The Limits of Reason: The German Democratic Press and the Collapse of Weimar Democracy*, London: Oxford University Press, 1975. See also the work of Reinhard Opitz, *Der deutsche Sozialliberalismus, 1917-1933*, Cologne: Pahl-Rugenstein, 1973; Werner Stephan, *Aufstieg und Verfall des Linksliberalismus: 1918-1933: Geschichte der Deutschen Demokratischen Partei*, Göttingen: Vandenhoeck & Ruprecht, 1973; Hartmut Schustereit, *Linksliberalismus und Sozialdemokratie in der Weimarer Republik: Eine Vergleichende Betrachtung der Politik von DDP und SPD, 1919-1930*, Düsseldorf: Pädagogischer Verlag Schwann, 1975.

34. These aspects of the party's first years are reported in Ernst Portner, "Der Ansatz zur demokratischen Massenpartei im Deutschen Linksliberalismus," *Vierteljahrshefte für Zeitgeschichte*, 11 (1965): 150-161. Discussions of such meth-

ods are typically couched in terms of "clever manipulators" on one side of the relationship and "vulnerable" (or "gullible") masses on the other, with the former, of course, always winning out. The instances that do not fit into that simplistic framework, such as the present case, are simply dropped from view. For a discussion of this persistent distortion see "Myth of the Electoral Technocrats," ch. 6 of my *Restraining Myths*.

35. Heinrich August Winkler, "Extremismus der Mitte? Sozialgeschichtliche Aspekte der nationalsozialistischen Machtergreifung," *Vierteljahrshefte für Zeitgeschichte*, 20 (1972): 175-191. The quote appears on p. 176. The early losses of DDP supporters, many of whom switched to the DVP, are discussed in Hartenstein, *Die Anfänge*, pp. 200-202.

36. For the assessments of Koch-Weser see Chanady, "The Dissolution," p. 1446; Frye, "The German Democratic Party," p. 171 (the source of the quotations). See also Attila Chanady, "Erich Koch-Weser and the Weimar Republic," *Canadian Journal of History*, 8 (1972): 51-63.

37. Frye, "The German Democratic Party," p. 172.

38. Jews made up 0.9 percent of Germany's population in 1933. That would appear to be an insignificant portion of the electorate. From the perspective of the DDP, however, that support had much greater significance. In 1928, when the party received 4.9 percent of the vote, the contribution of the Jews could conceivably have amounted to one-tenth of the DDP's total vote. The best account is by Jacob Toury, *Die politischen Orientierungen der Juden in Deutschland*, Tübingen: J.C.B. Mohr–Paul Siebeck, 1966.

Gessler's comments on the left wing of the party appear in Chanady, "The Dissolution," p. 1438. The left, incidentally, is frequently seen as having founded the new party. A group of intellectuals had approached and discussed the matter with Theodor Wolff. And he had drafted the manifesto addressed to the "men and women of the new Germany" and published it in the *Tageblatt* on November 16, 1918, over the signatures of sixty persons including professors Albert Einstein, Hugo Preuss, and Alfred Weber (the brother of Max). This group then came together with former Progressives to chart the new course. At a key meeting, which was attended also by representatives from the National Liberals (including Stresemann), the discussion began with Weber making an extremely sharp attack on both liberal parties, calling them "bankrupt and unworthy of the public's trust." His comments were especially pointed with respect to the National Liberal group, Weber making it unmistakably clear that they were not wanted. Wolff suggested a break in what had come to be a very heated discussion, in the expectation that the National Liberals would take advantage of the opportunity and leave the meeting, an expectation that was quickly fulfilled. Thus, this first occasion for liberal unity in the Weimar period was blocked by liberal intellectuals. And then, within a relatively short period, they removed themselves from the party (as, for example, in the case of Wolff) thus leaving the new organization in the hands of the notables who, from the start, were destined to deal with the routines of party management and policy making. The aim of the intellectual group was a small but pure party. They even viewed

Naumann with some suspicion; their concern, as one of his supporters put it, was with "a delousing of Naumann."

Stresemann, for his part, appears to have had no intention of making common cause with these intellectuals. He certainly had no intention of playing a subordinate role. Hartenstein, incidentally, notes that nearly half of the signators of the Wolff statement possessed a doctorate. Another interesting contrast he reports is that few leaders of the People's party wrote memoirs or works of general political interest. One can, however, fill libraries with the political literature from the Progressive/Democratic side, *Die Anfänge*, pp. 57-58.

39. Jones, " 'The Dying Middle,' " pp. 31 ff.

40. Chanady, "The Dissolution," p. 1443.

41. Ibid., p. 1442.

42. Ibid., pp. 1448-1449.

43. Jones, " 'The Dying Middle,' " pp. 51-52.

44. Chanady, "The Dissolution," pp. 1450-1451.

45. Ibid., p. 1452.

46. Matthias and Morsey, "Die Deutsche Staatspartei," in Matthias and Morsey, *Ende Der Parteien*, p. 50.

47. Ibid., p. 58.

48. The principal sources used here are: Rudolf Morsey, "Die Deutsche Zentrumspartei," pp. 281-453 of Matthias and Morsey, *Ende der Parteien*; Johannes Schauff, *Die Deutschen Katholiken und die Zentrumspartei; Eine politisch-statistische Untersuchung der Reichstagswahlen seit 1871*, Cologne: Verlag J. P. Bachem, 1928; Helga Grebing, "Zentrum und Katholische Arbeiterschaft 1918-1933: Ein Beitrag zur Geschichte des Zentrums in der Weimarer Republik," doctoral dissertation, Free University of Berlin, 1952; Wolfgang Stump, *Geschichte und Organisation der Zentrumspartei in Düsseldorf, 1917-1933*, Düsseldorf: Droste Verlag, 1971; and Günter Plum, *Gesellschaftsstruktur und politisches Bewusstsein in einer katholischen Region 1928-1933; Untersuchung am Beispiel des Regierungsbezirks Aachen*, Stuttgart: Deutsche Verlags-Anstalt, 1972; Bracher, *Die Auflösung*, especially pp. 287-330, 335-347, and chs. 3–6; and Neumann, *Die deutschen Parteien*, pp. 38-46. For the earlier Weimar period see Rudolf Morsey, *Die Deutsche Zentrumspartei 1917–1923*, Düsseldorf: Droste Verlag, 1966. See also Detlef Junker, *Die Deutsche Zentrumspartei und Hitler, 1932-1933*, Stuttgart: Ernst Klett Verlag, 1969.

49. See Ellen L. Evans, "The Center Wages *Kulturpolitik*: Conflict in the Marx-Keudell Cabinet of 1927," *Central European History*, 2 (1969): 139-158.

50. Article 48, paragraph 2 of the constitution stated that "if the public safety and order in the German Reich are seriously disturbed or endangered, the national president may take measures necessary for the restoration of public safety and order." To guard against presidential excess, the following paragraph declared that "the measures are to be revoked upon the demand of the Reichstag." Use of this article by the Brüning government was not new; it had been invoked continuously throughout the previous decade. But as we shall see, Brüning and Hindenburg made a very important variation in the basic practice in July of 1930. See Frederick F. Blachly and Miriam E. Oatman, *The Government and Administration of Germany*, Baltimore: Johns Hopkins Press, 1928, p. 652.

The breakdown of the parliamentary regime, before Hitler came to power, is indicated in the table. From M. Rainer Lepsius, "From Fragmented Party Democracy to Government by Emergency Decree and National Socialist Take-over: Germany," pp. 34-79 of Juan J. Linz and Alfred Stepan, eds., *The Breakdown of Democratic Regimes: Europe*, Baltimore: Johns Hopkins Press, 1978. The table appears on p. 49.

	1930	1931	1932
Laws passed by the Reichstag	98	34	5
Emergency decrees by the president	5	44	66
Days in parliamentary session	94	41	13

51. Morsey, "Die Deutsche Zentrumspartei," in Matthias and Morsey, *Ende der Parteien*, p. 292.

52. Ibid., p. 303.

53. Ibid., p. 315. The reference to the "basis of facts" requires some explanation. The party, following the teachings of Pope Leo XIII, had no principled commitment to the republic or to democracy. It was obliged to uphold established state authority, so long as its policies were generally consonant with Christian teachings. This obligation provided the justification for the Zentrum's acceptance of the established "fact" of the 1918 revolution and for its work within the framework of the new republic. But Hitler's growing strength, through use of legal means (a point continually stressed), led the party to accept the established fact of his power too. Closely related to this emphasis was a concern to work within the constitution. While some supporters of the regime speculated about the possibility of constitutional violation, to keep the NSDAP out of power, the Zentrum's leaders worked diligently to bring Hitler into power, both because that solution was constitutional and because of their belief that he would be tamed by the experience. When Hitler did achieve power, the moral basis for their opposition, initially at least, disappeared; this was now the established "basis of facts," and many Zentrum people felt obligated to uphold this new state authority. As Prelate Kaas put it, "the revolution has already taken place." See Junker, *Die Deutsche Zentrumspartei*, pp. 131-140, 145 ff., and 179.

54. Junker, *Die Deutsche Zentrumspartei*, p. 320.

55. Ibid., p. 330.

56. Ibid., p. 334.

57. Ibid., p. 327n.

58. The *Osthilfe* was a program of financial aid for threatened agricultural properties (estates mostly) in the eastern regions of Germany. Although the plan did save many threatened estates, part of it involved a resettlement program, which transferred industrial workers to rural areas, there to take up cultivation of lands on bankrupt estates. Such was the lucidity of thought in agrarian upper-class circles that they denounced this move as bolshevism. It was their alarm and intrigue that had turned Hindenburg against Brüning in May 1932, and now, in late January 1933, it worked against Schleicher.

59. Morsey, "Die Deutsche Zentrumspartei," pp. 351, 355.

60. Ibid., p. 369.

61. Ibid., p. 386.
62. Ibid., p. 439.
63. Ibid., p. 415.
64. Ibid., pp. 364-365.
65. See Roger Philip Chickering, "The Reichsbanner and the Weimar Republic, 1924-26," *Journal of Modern History*, 40 (1968): 524-534. Defense, of course, assumes a will, an interest in or choice of that policy. A leading Zentrum newspaper, the *Kölnische Volkszeitung*, wrote on March 24, 1933, the day after the party had voted to give Hitler dictatorial powers, that "no true friend of the fatherland can wish that this government runs aground. Whoever loves his people must wish that this government be supported." With Kaas absent, three weeks followed without any clear guidance from the Zentrum's leaders. On April 14, there appeared in the party's press a very conciliatory statement embellished with elegant phrases (the "inheritance of our fathers," "the fresh winds of a new age," and the "high ideal of unity"). It closed with the statement that "we work together . . . with all state-conservative and national constructive forces on the renewal and strengthening of our fatherland." On the twentieth of April, Prelate Kaas sent Hitler a birthday telegram, assuring him of continued cooperation in the "great work" of creating "an internally unified, a socially peaceful, and, versus other nations, a free Germany." This too was published in the party press. From Junker, *Die Deutsche Zentrumspartei*, pp. 178, 219. See also pp. 227-228 for the party's florid prose outpouring just before its dissolution.
66. An exception to this statement must be made in the case of a few individuals in the left wing of the German Democrats.
67. See Erich Eyck, *Geschichte der Weimarer Republik*, Erlenbach-Zurich: Eugen Rentsch Verlag, 1956, vol. 2, pp. 341 ff., for discussion of Brüning's calculations.

ELEVEN. THE PARTIES OF THE LEFT

1. The principal sources used here are: Erich Matthias, "Die Sozialdemokratische Partei Deutschlands," pp. 101-278 of Erich Matthias and Rudolf Morsey, eds., *Das Ende der Parteien 1933*, Düsseldorf: Droste Verlag, 1960; Karl Dietrich Bracher, *Die Auflösung der Weimarer Republik*, Villingen/Schwarzwald: Ring-Verlag, 1964, pp. 70-77, 296-303, 333-335, and 370-371; Carl Landauer, *European Socialism: A History of Ideas and Movements from the Industrial Revolution to Hitler's Seizure of Power*, Berkeley: University of California Press, 1959; Richard N. Hunt, *German Social Democracy, 1918-1933*, New Haven: Yale University Press, 1964; Sigmund Neumann, *Die deutschen Parteien; Wesen und Wandel nach dem Kriege*, 2d. ed., Berlin: Junker und Dünnhaupt, 1932; Helga Timm, *Die deutsche Sozialpolitik und der Bruch der grossen Koalition im März 1930*, Düsseldorf: Droste Verlag, 1952; and Robert A. Gates, "German Socialism and the Crisis of 1929-33," *Central European History*, 7 (1974): 332-359.
2. A discussion of this point, complete with statements from the leading Social Democrats, is to be found in F. L. Carsten, *Revolution in Central Europe, 1918-1919*, London: Temple Smith, 1972, pp. 46 ff. For discussion of the same

points as they appeared in Germany's second largest city, see Richard A. Comfort, *Revolutionary Hamburg: Labor Politics in the Early Weimar Republic*, Stanford: Stanford University Press, 1966, pp. 41-50. See also, Hans Schieck, "Die Behandlung der Sozialisierungsfrage in den Monaten nach dem Staatsumsturz," pp. 138-164 of Eberhard Kolb, ed., *Vom Kaiserreich zur Weimarer Republik*, Cologne: Kiepenheuer & Witsch, 1972.

3. For the basics of this history see Erich Eyck, *Geschichte der Weimarer Republik*, Erlenbach-Zurich: Eugen Rentsch Verlag, 1956, vol. 1, chs. 3-4; Arthur Rosenberg, *Geschichte der Weimarer Republik*, Frankfurt: Europäische Verlagsanstalt, 1961, ch. 4; and S. William Halperin, *Germany Tried Democracy: A Political History of the Reich from 1918 to 1933*, New York: Norton, 1965, ch. 9.

4. See Henry Ashby Turner, Jr., *Stresemann and the Politics of the Weimar Republic*, Princeton: Princeton University Press, 1963, pp. 124 ff.

5. There is an appearance-reality problem here. One source presents evidence showing a rough constancy in the real incomes of civil servants. See J. Heinz Müller, *Nivellierung und Differenzierung der Arbeitseinkommen in Deutschland seit 1925*, Berlin: Duncker und Humblot, 1954, p. 140.

6. Eyck, *Geschichte der Weimarer Republik*, vol. 2, pp. 212 ff.

7. Ibid., pp. 248 ff.

8. Ibid., pp. 315 ff.; and Christian Engoli, *Gustav Böss: Oberbürgermeister von Berlin, 1921-1930*, Stuttgart: Kohlhammer Verlag, 1971.

9. Timm, *Die deutsche Sozialpolitik*, pp. 170 ff. See also Ludwig Preller, *Sozialpolitik in der Weimarer Republik*, Stuttgart: Franz Mittelbach Verlag, 1949.

10. Halperin, *Germany Tried Democracy*, p. 432; Eyck, *Geschichte der Weimarer Republik*, vol. 2, pp. 339 ff. For Brüning's version of the events, see his *Memoiren: 1918-1934*, Stuttgart: Deutsche Verlags-Anstalt, 1970, pp. 179-182.

11. In important qualification to this point about forced toleration is considered below.

12. Gates, "German Socialism," p. 333.

13. Ibid., p. 343. Gates also noted Brüning's frequent consultations with Hermann Müller and Otto Wels of the SPD Reichstag faction and Otto Braun, the SPD minister president of Prussia. Brüning, according to Gates, found Hilferding to be his "strongest supporter and closest confidant" in matters of economic policy.

14. Ibid., p. 344.

15. Ibid., p. 345.

16. Ibid., pp. 345 ff.

17. Ibid., p. 351.

18. Ibid. For additional information on the trade union public works program, see Michael Schneider, "Konjunkturpolitische Vorstellungen der Gewerkschaften in den letzten Jahren der Weimarer Republik. Zur Entwicklung des Arbeitsbeschaffungsplans des ADGB," pp. 227-237 of Hans Mommsen, Dietmar Petzina, and Bernd Weisbrod, eds., *Industrielles System und politische Entwicklung in der Weimarer Republik*, Düsseldorf: Droste Verlag, 1974; and Sidney Pollard, "The Trade Unions and the Depression of 1929-1933," pp. 237-248 of the same volume. For more detail see Schneider's book, *Das*

Arbeitsbeschaffungsprogramm des ADGB: Zur gewerkschaftlichen Politik in der End-phase der Weimarer Republik, Bonn–Bad Godesberg: Verlag Neue Gesellschaft, 1975. The public works program was a long shot in any case. The Communists and National Socialists might, for demagogic purposes, have supported or even expanded the plan, but none of the other parties would have backed it.

19. Gates, "German Socialism," p. 353.

20. Ibid., pp. 355, 357.

21. Ibid., p. 356.

22. Halperin, *Germany Tried Democracy*, p. 459; and Eyck, *Geschichte der Weimarer Republik*, vol. 2, p. 371. The latter mistakenly reports that the Communists also walked out. The details of the day's events are reported in *Schulthess' Europäischer Geschichtskalender, 1931*, Munich: C. H. Beck'sche Verlag, 1932, vol. 72, pp. 39-40.

23. Bracher, *Die Auflösung*, pp. 385-386.

24. Otto Braun, *Von Weimar zu Hitler*, Hamburg: Hammonia Norddeutsche Verlagsanstalt, 1949, p. 232; Bracher, *Die Auflösung*, pp. 502-503; Eyck, *Geschichte der Weimarer Republik*, vol. 2, pp. 503 ff. See also the important work by Hagen Schulze, *Otto Braun oder Preussens demokratische Sendung: Eine Biographie*, Frankfurt: Propyläen Verlag, 1977, pp. 725 ff.

25. This account must necessarily be very abbreviated. Behind each of the events, described here with a sentence or two, lay days of intrigue and negotiation. Those around Hindenburg were providing him with information to undermine his trust in Brüning and to prepare the way for others to take his place. Possibly the most nefarious role of all was played by Kurt von Schleicher who appeared in the new government as minister of defense.

26. Eyck, *Geschichte der Weimarer Republik*, vol. 2, pp. 508 ff. The most detailed account of SPD reactions to the Papen move are to be found in Matthias, "Die Sozialdemokratische Partei Deutschlands," pp. 127-145. Another detailed account of the event is that by Werner E. Braatz, "Franz von Papen and the *Preussenschlag*, 20 July 1932: A Move by the 'New State' toward Reichsreform," *European Studies Review*, 3 (1973): 157-180.

27. Matthias, "Die Sozialdemokratische Partei Deutschlands," p. 129. An alternative government was required before a government could be removed. In this case, therefore, Braun was forced to remain in office until a successor could be found. In ill health, he was tired, dejected over his recent defeat, and most anxious to leave office. When he went on sick leave, it was with an ultimatum; the parties that had voted him down should find a successor within the fortnight. Papen's move thus forced him to uphold his right to the office that he desperately wished to leave. For his account of the events see Braun, *Von Weimar zu Hitler*, pp. 245 ff.; and Schulze, *Otto Braun*, pp. 745-762. Albert Grzesinski's discussion of the question appears in his *Inside Germany*, New York: E. P. Dutton, 1939, pp. 153 ff.

28. For reactions, conclusions, and the like, see Matthias, "Die Sozialdemokratische Partei Deutschlands," p. 128. Some sense of the balance of forces may be gained by consideration of the voting results of the period. At that time, the Social Democrats were taking only a little more than one-fifth of the vote and

the Communists only about one-seventh. The left, therefore, even if one includes the remnants of the DDP, made up less than two-fifths of the total population. Given past experience, an alliance of the SPD with the KPD seemed at best a perilous undertaking. For Braun's comments, see *Von Weimar zu Hitler*, pp. 256-257.

29. Matthias, "Die Sozialdemokratische Partei Deutschlands," pp. 144-145.

30. Ibid., p. 151.

31. Ibid., p. 158.

32. Ibid., pp. 160-162. The argument for the cautious defensive struggle was spelled out and justified by no less a figure than Friedrich Engels, then drawing the lessons from Bismarck's attempted repression of the party. See his introduction to Marx's *The Class Struggles in France: 1848 to 1850*, in Karl Marx and Frederick Engels, *Selected Works*, Moscow: Foreign Languages Publishing House, 1951, vol. 1, especially pp. 124-125.

33. Alan Bullock, *Hitler: A Study in Tyranny*, New York: Harper & Row, 1964, rev. ed., p. 270. The text of Wels's statement appears in Wilhelm Mommsen, ed., *Deutsche Parteiprogramme*, Munich: Olzog Verlag, 1960, pp. 564-567. See also Rudolf Morsey, *Das "Ermächtigungsgesetzt" vom 24. März 1933*, Göttingen: Vandenhoeck & Ruprecht, 1968; and Karl Dietrich Bracher, Wolfgang Sauer, and Gerhard Schulz, *Die nationalsozialistische Machtergreifung: Studien zur Errichtung des totalitären Herrschaftssystems in Deutschland 1933/34*, 2d ed., Cologne: Westdeutscher Verlag, 1962, pp. 152-168.

34. Matthias, "Die Sozialdemokratische Partei Deutschlands," p. 173.

35. The quotations appear in ibid., pp. 177-178. The same process is described also in Hunt, *German Social Democracy*, pp. 188-189. He quotes the *Gewerkschafts-Zeitung* (April 22, 1933) as follows: "We certainly need not strike our colors in order to recognize that the victory of National Socialism is our victory as well, even though won in a struggle against a party which we used to consider the embodiment of the idea of socialism (the SPD); because today the socialist task is put to the whole nation."

36. The discussion of the six points paraphrases Matthias, "Die Sozialdemokratische Partei Deutschlands," pp. 196-199.

37. Ibid., p. 198.

38. Ibid.

39. See Carl E. Schorske, *German Social Democracy, 1905-1917: The Development of the Great Schism*, New York: John Wiley & Sons, 1965.

40. Karl Liebknecht explained matters as follows: "We belonged to the USPD so as to drive it ahead, to have it within the reach of our whip, to extract the best elements from it." Cited in Ossip K. Flechtheim, *Die KPD in der Weimarer Republik*, Frankfurt: Europäische Verlagsanstalt, 1969, p. 103. As might be expected, the Independents were less than enthusiastic about this relationship.

41. Flechtheim's *Die KPD* has been the standard work on the subject; see especially the 1969 edition which contains an extended introduction by Hermann Weber (hereafter, "Einleitung") reviewing the work done subsequent to its first appearance in 1948. Flechtheim's work has been eclipsed, at least for the 1924-1929 period, by Hermann Weber's two-volume study, *Die Wandlung des*

deutschen Kommunismus: Die Stalinisierung der KPD in der Weimarer Republik, Frankfurt: Europäische Verlagsanstalt, 1969. In addition to the general histories of Bracher, *Die Auflösung*; Eyck, *Geschichte der Weimarer Republik*; Rosenberg, *Geschichte der Weimarer Republik*; and Halperin, *Germany Tried Democracy*; see also Landauer, *European Socialism*; Ruth Fischer, *Stalin and German Communism: A Study in the Origins of the State Party*, Cambridge, Mass.: Harvard University Press, 1948; and Siegfried Bahne, "Die Kommunistische Partei Deutschlands," pp. 655-739 of Matthias and Morsey, *Ende der Parteien*.

42. Flechtheim reports that the failure of the action was already apparent on the evening of the sixth. *Die KPD*, p. 130. See also Landauer, *European Socialism*, vol. 1, p. 818; Halperin, *Germany Tried Democracy*, p. 121; and especially Rosenberg, *Geschichte der Weimarer Republik*, p. 60. Rosenberg reports that "the military task was not difficult, since the masses of the Berlin workers did not join in the fight, and one only had a few thousand insurgents to contend with. These were badly led and were distributed among a number of buildings. If one follows the individual actions of the Berlin week of revolt, one sees that the main work was performed by the troops of the democratic government. Without a doubt they could have handled the revolt by themselves, without the help of the Freikorps led by the old officers."

One can speculate about the reactions to those events. In both left and liberal histories, Liebknecht and Luxemberg have been evaluated very positively. Flechtheim, for example, says that the KPD thus lost its "best heads." *Die KPD*, p. 131; see also Rosenberg, *Geschichte der Weimarer Republik*, p. 62. Some commentators have seen the "erratic" character of the KPD in later years stemming from the loss of its most capable leaders in January and March of 1919. Be that as it may, Eyck probably catches general sentiment in Germany with his use of the biblical phrase, "He who lives by the sword shall die by the sword," *Geschichte der Weimarer Republik*, vol. 1, p. 78.

43. Flechtheim, *Die KPD*, pp. 134-135; Landauer, *European Socialism*, vol. 1, pp. 824-825; Rosenberg, *Geschichte der Weimarer Republik*, pp. 63-65. See also Richard M. Watt, *The Kings Depart: The Tragedy of Germany: Versailles and the German Revolution*, New York: Simon and Schuster, 1968, pp. 302-309.

There has been much discussion about the role of the Workers and Soldiers' Councils (see, for example, Carsten, *Revolution in Central Europe*, chs. 5-7). The principal question is whether the councils were moderate (and supportive of the republic) or radical (and aiming to overthrow it). Carsten argues, with some evidence, that they were, on the whole, rather moderate ventures. Where left forces were clustered, however, they could, with their greater coordination, exercise considerable influence within a given council, as was the case, for example, in Berlin. It was the experience with the Berlin council presumably, plus a series of street conflicts, that alarmed Ebert and the other SPD leaders and led to their increasing dependence on the "reliable" forces of the military. It should be remembered that the overthrow of the Kerensky regime had occured only a little more than a year previously.

44. The quotations are from Landauer, *European Socialism*, vol. 1, p. 829. For the entire episode see his vol. 1, pp. 826-831; Halperin, *Germany Tried Democ-*

racy, pp. 122-125; Rosenberg, *Geschichte der Weimarer Republik*, pp. 66-71; Eyck, *Geschichte der Weimarer Republik*, vol. 1, pp. 108-111.

45. Flechtheim, *Die KPD*, pp. 143 ff.; Franz Borkenau, *World Communism: A History of the Communist International*, Ann Arbor: University of Michigan Press, 1962, p. 144.

46. Halperin, *Germany Tried Democracy*, p. 179; Landauer, *European Socialism*, vol. 1, pp. 854-862; Rosenberg, *Geschichte der Weimarer Republik*, pp. 95-99; Eyck, *Geschichte der Weimarer Republik*, vol. 1, pp. 203-215. The most important study of the *Putsch* is that by Johannes Erger, *Der Kapp-Lüttwitz-Putsch. Ein Beitrag zur deutschen Innenpolitik 1919/20*, Düsseldorf: Droste Verlag, 1967. See also Gerald D. Feldman, "Big Business and the Kapp Putsch," *Central European History*, 4 (1971): 99-130.

47. Flechtheim, *Die KPD*, p. 148.

48. For the details, see Feldman, "Big Business," pp. 121 ff. It was a complicated question. By tradition, one of the rules governing a general strike was that workers would *not accept pay for such time off.* That may have suited intellectuals and some trade union leaders, but workers saw things differently. Some firms did pay, some immediately, some with only a little reluctance.

49. It should be noted that the Red Army rule had involved violence and terror, not merely against the forces of reaction but against defenders of the republic. Units of the Essen police who opposed the Communist insurgents were, as Severing put it, "murdered in the most downright beastly manner." Quoted in Eyck, *Geschichte der Weimarer Republik*, vol. 1, p. 212. See also the important works by Robert G. L. Waite, *Vanguard of Nazism: The Free Corps Movement in Postwar Germany 1918-1923*, New York: Norton, 1969, chs. 6 and 7; Hagen Schulze, *Freikorps und Republik 1918-1920*, Boppard: Harald Boldt Verlag, 1969, pp. 304-318; and George Eliasberg, *Der Ruhrkrieg von 1920*, Bonn-Bad Godesberg: Verlag Neue Gesellschaft, 1974.

50. For an account of these negotiations, see Turner, *Stresemann*, pp. 56 ff. These negotiations were hastily extemporized and unofficial. They were also publicly repudiated. The further course of justice involved an amnesty law passed on August 4, 1920. For this history, see Eyck, *Geschichte der Weimarer Republik*, vol. 1, pp. 218 ff. The judicial asymmetry is discussed in many sources. See Waite, *Vanguard of Nazism*, pp. 162-163; and also Franz Neumann, *Behemoth: The Structure and Practice of National Socialism, 1933-1944*, New York: Oxford University Press, 1944, pp. 20-23.

51. See Harold J. Gordon, Jr., *Hitler and the Beer Hall Putsch*, Princeton: Princeton University Press, 1972, pp. 212 ff.

52. See Table A.1 for the overall results. There was a slight decline in turnout in the June election, 79.2 percent as compared with the previous 82.7 percent. It should also be noted that a part of the 1919 left vote disappeared, the overall decline amounting to 5.9 percent. The Communists, incidentally, made no appreciable showing even in their later strongholds. In Berlin, for example, they took only 1.2 percent of the total vote, a figure that was *below* the national average. Even in working-class Wedding, they took only 2.3 percent, the bulk

of the vote (57.3 percent) there going to the Independent Socialists. *Statistisches Jahrbuch der Stadt Berlin*, Berlin: P. Stankiewicz Buchdruckerei, 1920, p. 885.

53. Flechtheim, *Die KPD*, pp. 155-157; Landauer, *European Socialism*, vol. 1, pp. 913-914; Comfort, *Revolutionary Hamburg*, pp. 114 ff.

54. The trio, consisting of two Hungarians and a Pole, lacked intimate knowledge of German conditions. The most renowned of the three, Béla Kun, was the leader of a bizarre (and bloody) Communist government in Hungary that lasted for some hundred days in the spring of 1919. For that history see Borkenau, *World Communism*, ch. 6. The second member of the trio was one Joseph Pogany. A year later, as John Pepper, he appeared as the Comintern's representative to the United States where he was responsible for another but much smaller disaster. For this history see Theodore Draper, *American Communism and Soviet Russia*, New York: Viking Press, 1960, pp. 43 ff.

The best account of the extraordinarily complicated March action is that of Werner T. Angress, *Stillborn Revolution: The Communist Bid for Power in Germany, 1921-1923*, Princeton: Princeton University Press, 1963, chs. 4-7. On the recognition by Central Committee members of the unrevolutionary spirit prevailing among the noncommunist workers, see p. 115.

55. On the provocations, see Angress, *Stillborn Revolution*, pp. 143-144, 146, and 159.

56. Ibid., p. 156n.

57. Flechtheim, *Die KPD*, pp. 179-180; Angress, *Stillborn Revolution*, pp. 359-360.

58. Flechtheim, *Die KPD*, p. 178. He cites Ruth Fischer as follows: "The German Reich can only be saved, if you, gentlemen from the German *völkischen* side, recognize that you must fight with the masses that are organized in the KPD." And: "He who cries out against Jewish capital is already fighting the class struggle even if he does not know it. . . . Kick down the Jewish capitalists, hang them from the lampposts, trample them!" See Angress, *Stillborn Revolution*, pp. 332-333, for Radek's comments on Schlageter. Shortly before his involvement in the Ruhr struggles, Schlageter had joined the NSDAP and, of course, was counted among the many martyrs to the National Socialist cause.

Another Communist leader, Hermann Remmele, made use of the same themes before an audience of Communists and National Socialists in Stuttgart. " 'How such anti-Semitism arises I can easily understand,' " he said. " 'One merely needs to go down to the Stuttgart cattle market in order to see how the cattle dealers, most of whom belong to Jewry, buy up cattle at any price, while the Stuttgart butchers have to go home again, empty-handed, because they just don't have enough money to buy cattle. ("Quite right!" from the Fascists).' " Later in the same speech Remmele declared that " 'You, the Fascists, now say [that you want] to fight the Jewish finance capital. All right. Go ahead! Agreed! (Stormy applause from the Fascists.) But you must not forget one thing, industrial capital! (Interjections from the Fascists: "We fight that too!") For finance capital is really nothing else but industrial capital.' " Angress, *Stillborn Revolution*, p. 341. The words in brackets were added by Angress.

In the late twenties and early thirties, Joseph Goebbels, then *Gauleiter* of Berlin, mocked the deputy police president of Berlin, Bernard Weiss, in the process referring to him as "Isidor." This same Dr. Weiss had appeared as a prosecution witness against some Communists in a Munich trial in 1923. At that point, the Communist newspaper, *Die Rote Fahne* (no. 152, July 5, 1923), anticipated Goebbels by some years, naming him "Isidor" and also adding a mocking anti-Semitic ditty. Angress, *Stillborn Revolution*, p. 340n.

59. Angress, *Stillborn Revolution*, p. 376.

60. Ibid., pp. 392-399. The Moscow discussions even included such details as choosing the day. Trotsky, over the opposition of the German leaders, pushed for November 9, the anniversary of the German revolution of 1918. It was finally decided, however, that that date was "for orientation" only. Had the KPD remained with the original decision, it will be noted, it would have attacked on the day of Hitler's Munich *Putsch*.

61. Flechtheim, *Die KPD*, pp. 183-190; Angress, *Stillborn Revolution*, ch. 13; Comfort, *Revolutionary Hamburg*, pp. 123-127; and, for a view from the top, that is, for Stresemann's reactions, see Turner, *Stresemann*, pp. 124-150.

62. Angress, *Stillborn Revolution*, p. 476; Weber, *Die Wandlung*, pp. 23-52.

63. Angress, *Stillborn Revolution*, p. 375 and also pp. 376-377 for further discussion of the same theme.

64. Ibid., p. 350 ff.

65. See, for example, the experience reported by Kühr in Essen, recounted in Chapter 7.

66. The effects of this distortion may be seen more than a half-century after the events described. The rightist distortions, understandably, have for the most part disappeared from the scene. But much of contemporary analysis is based on the leftist critique of Weimar. In brief, such analyses continuously stress the threat from the right. They attack the Social Democratic and centrist Weimar governments for failing to deal with that threat; and they either exonerate or overlook the contributions of the left, particularly of the KPD, to the emerging disaster. This problem is most clearly indicated by the absence of works that present (let alone defend) the position and viewpoint of the various Weimar governments. Two eminent works that do make this case have never been translated into English. They are: Eduard Bernstein, *Die deutsche Revolution*, Berlin: Verlag für Gesellschaft und Erziehung, 1921; and Hermann Müller, *Die November Revolution: Erinnerungen*, Berlin: Der Bücherkreis, 1928. Erich Eyck's history of Weimar and Turner's Stresemann biography are probably the leading exceptions to this rule. One recent instance of this exoneration of the left is to be found in Reinhard Rürup, "Problems of the German Revolution 1918-1919," *Journal of Contemporary History*, 3 (1968): 109-135.

67. Flechtheim, *Die KPD*, pp. 194-196, 204, 215-216, 228-231; Weber, *Die Wandlung*, pp. 120 ff; Fischer, *Stalin*.

68. It should be noted too that a considerable part of the 1920 left vote had vanished. Whereas the three parties gained 41.7 percent in June of 1920, their May 1924 share was only 33.9. Participation fell only 1.8 percent so much of the loss must have gone to bourgeois parties.

69. Flechtheim, *Die KPD*, pp. 211-212.

70. Eyck, *Geschichte der Weimarer Republik*, vol. 1, pp. 443-446. Again the many complicated details cannot be adequately covered in a brief paragraph. Many bourgeois Protestants, it is said, could not bring themselves to vote for the Catholic Wilhelm Marx and thus shifted to Hindenburg. If *they* had voted republican the outcome would have been different, without the need for Communist votes. The "what if" suggestion in the text is obviously only for purposes of speculation. It would be unrealistic to expect that the KPD, a party showing such uncompromising opposition to the regime, would suddenly come to its defense, asking its followers to vote responsibly. For many Social Democrats the suggestion that they vote for a man from the Zentrum must have severely tested party loyalties. The *increase* of Thälmann votes in the second round might have resulted from shifts by SPD voters who could not bring themselves to vote for a bourgeois and a Catholic.

71. Flechtheim, *Die KPD*, pp. 235-236; Eyck, *Geschichte der Weimarer Republik*, vol. 2, pp. 87-93.

72. Flechtheim, *Die KPD*, p. 247; Eyck, *Geschichte der Weimarer Republik*, vol. 2, p. 212. The party gained less than half the number of signatures required to put the motion to a referendum.

73. Flechtheim, *Die KPD*, p. 347. He has taken these figures from Walter Rist, "Der Weg der KPD. Die Innere Krise der KPD," *Neue Blätter für den Sozialismus*, 2 (1931): 79-91. They are drawn from official Communist sources. See also Bahne, "Die Kommunistische Partei Deutschlands," pp. 660-668; and Weber, *Die Wandlung*, pp. 280-293.

74. Flechtheim, *Die KPD*, pp. 205-207, 233.

75. Ibid., p. 239; Bahne, "Die Kommunistische Partei Deutschlands," p. 662; Weber, *Die Wandlung*, p. 240n. The pressures against activism in the factory are enormous. One could easily be singled out for punishment or firing because of political activity; workers supporting families obviously cannot be indifferent to such considerations. Ordinarily, there is little time for organizational work while on the job. Cell meetings and propaganda activity have to take place either before or after the shift. In either case this poses a problem for commuting workers. Time spent in and around the factory, moreover, is time spent away from home. For those with wives and children, therefore, the party's directive posed a very serious problem. Assenting to the party's order meant neglecting the family. For a discussion of the same problem as it appeared in the French context, see my *Affluence and the French Worker*, Princeton: Princeton University Press, 1967, pp. 24-31.

Flechtheim notes, as an area of weakness, that the party had few female members. He doubts that the percentage ever went above 10. *Die KPD*, p. 240. The word "weakness" may well understate the problem; "opposition" is probably more appropriate. Religious commitments were another source of strain for the party. Bahne reports that 22 percent of the KPD's Ruhr membership were still church members. "Die Kommunistische Partei Deutschlands," p. 660.

76. Flechtheim, *Die KPD*, pp. 239-240. Still another measure of KPD capacity and strength is to be found in its performance in combat (that is, in street fighting). For an interesting contrast between KPD and NSDAP relations with

the police, see Hsi-huey Liang, *The Berlin Police Force in the Weimar Republic*, Berkeley: University of California Press, 1970, pp. 95-96. Basically the Communists aimed to provoke the police, whereas the National Socialists tried to make them, at least the ordinary police officers, into allies. The KPD undertook an offensive on May Day in 1929 that lasted some three days. Since the Communists possessed only improvised weapons, it is not too surprising that among the twenty-five dead one found only insurgents and innocent bystanders. Liang, *The Berlin Police Force*, pp. 106-107.

77. Flechtheim, *Die KPD*, p. 241.

78. They also indicate a fundamental difficulty with Communist membership figures. Those reported by Flechtheim indicate a continued decline in the 1929-1930 period. *Die KPD*, p. 347. The turnover figures cited here are taken from the party's report of its annual meeting (*11. Parteitagsbericht*, p. 94, cited by Flechtheim, *Die KPD*, p. 240) and indicate some net growth.

Hermann Weber points to the resulting lack of continuity even among the party functionaries. Of 970 Berlin delegates to a party meeting in 1932, 700 had been members less than three years. See Weber, "Einleitung," p. 67; as well as Bahne, "Die Kommunistische Partei Deutschlands," pp. 663-667. The party's fighting organization, the Rote Frontkämpferbund suffered heavy turnover and after being banned in 1929 experienced serious losses. By the summer of 1931 it had lost half of its former members. Bahne, "Die Kommunistische Partei Deutschlands," p. 668. See also Kurt Schuster, *Der Rote Frontkämpferbund 1924-1929*, Düsseldorf: Droste Verlag, 1975; and James M. Diehl, *Paramilitary Politics in Weimar Germany*, Bloomington: Indiana University Press, 1977, especially p. 253.

79. There was an obvious two-step flow of communication at work. Communist activists made inflammatory statements, and these were duly reported, not only in the KPD press, but in the much larger circulation bourgeois journals. Just before the September 1930 Reichstag election, for example, the following report appeared on the front page of the *Münchner Neueste Nachrichten*. A Communist, Max Hölz, is reported to have called for the killing of, in this instance, their SPD opponents. "We say," he declared, "that there will be too few shot. We will see to it that in Germany too, a GPU can soon take up its work and that Severing, Zögiebel, and Company will be shot." From no. 242, Septemper 6, 1930.

80. Flechtheim, *Die KPD*, pp. 266-267; Alan Bullock, "The German Communists and the Rise of Hitler," pp. 504-521 of International Council for Philosophy and Humanistic Studies (no editor named), *The Third Reich*, London: Weidenfeld and Nicolson, 1955, especially p. 509; Bahne, "Die Kommunistische Partei Deutschlands," pp. 669-671, 674, 685; Weber, *Die Wandlung*, pp. 239-241.

81. Flechtheim, *Die KPD*, pp. 272-273. Some of the results were deceptive. In 1929, when the KPD first put up its independent lists in the shop elections, it did unexpectedly well. But as Borkenau puts it, that "did not imply any responsibility, and things were different when it came to action. After the shop-steward elections of 1929 the employers simply dismissed certain communist

shop-stewards, and the workers who had voted for them now flatly refused to strike in order to obtain their reinstatement." *World Communism*, p. 345.

82. Borkenau, *World Communism*. Bahne reports that KPD had prior knowledge of the Papen move but still did nothing; it was awaiting instructions from Moscow. "Die Kommunistische Partei Deutschlands," pp. 671-672.

83. Flechtheim, *Die KPD*, p. 275. This effort, incidentally, did win a small circle of idealistic officers and national bolshevist intellectuals. Simultaneously, for its own followers, the KPD found it necessary to distort the NSDAP position on this issue. In *Die Rote Fahne* it declared that "Hitler is for the Young Plan and the Weimar Constitution." The quotation appears in David Edward Barclay, "The Communist Response to the Rise of National Socialism in Germany, September 1930 to November 1932," M.A. thesis, University of Florida, 1970, p. 27.

84. See Flechtheim, *Die KPD*, p. 278, and, for a correction based on subsequent evidence, Weber, "Einleitung," p. 57. The key decision makers in this case were Stalin and Molotov.

85. Bullock, "The Germany Communists," p. 514.

86. Konrad Heiden, *Der Fuehrer: Hitler's Rise to Power*, Boston: Houghton Mifflin, 1944, pp. 551-552. See also Bahne, "Die Kommunistische Partei Deutschlands," pp. 685-690.

87. Bullock, "The German Communists," p. 516.

88. "Einleitung," p. 52 and *Die Wandlung*, pp 319 ff.

89. Flechtheim, *Die KPD*, p. 336.

90. Bullock, "The German Communists," p. 517.

91. The key intervening role of organization in determining the outcome is shown by comparison with the Scandinavian countries. There the Social Democrats were increasing their share of the vote in the midst of the economic crisis. For a discussion of the Norwegian case and a comparison with Schleswig-Holstein in the same period, see Sten S. Nilson, "Wahlsoziologische Probleme des Nationalsozialismus," *Zeitschift für die gesamte Staatswissenschaft*, 110 (1954): 295-311. For a brief account of conditions in Sweden and Denmark see Landauer, *European Socialism*, vol. 2, pp. 1546-1551 and 1556-1559.

92. An explanatory question deserves at least some passing attention—how is one to explain this behavior on the part of the KPD leadership? One frequently discussed factor was a negative selection process; there was a steady deterioration in the abilities of the leaders, from the beginnings with Rosa Luxemburg to the end with Ernst Thälmann. Weber, *Die Wandlung*, p. 346. The direction of the party from the distant Moscow center certainly contributed to the erratic character of the decision making (and also to the deterioration in leadership quality). Some of the factors mentioned in the discussion of the SPD failure could also be added here, notably the constraints of ideology which limited their understanding and restricted their ability to respond to events.

There appears to have been an extrarational factor present in KPD affairs that moved things in such unusual channels, namely the role of hostility. For many members, it seems, the party was a vehicle that allowed a legitimate expression of hostility. This would mean that the party served psychological (as opposed to political) functions. This hypothesis, to the best of my knowledge, has never been explored with respect to the German party. For an exploration within the American context, see Herbert E. Krugman, "The Role of Hostility in the Appeal of Communism in the United States," *Psychiatry*, 16 (1953): 253-261. See also Gabriel A. Almond, *The Appeals of Communism*, Princeton: Princeton University Press, 1954. This tendency was present in the work of Marx, a fact that is evident in his writings and in all biographical studies of the man. The best recent account is that of Fritz J. Raddatz, *Karl Marx: Eine politische Biographie*, Hamburg: Hoffmann und Campe, 1975. See also Bertram D. Wolfe, *Marxism: One Hundred Years in the Life of a Doctrine*, New York: Dial Press, 1965. Wolfe reprints a letter to Marx from Proudhon which cautions against the sectarian disease: "Let us not, because we are at the head of a movement, make ourselves the leaders of a new intolerance, let us not pose as the apostles of a new religion . . . let us condemn all exclusiveness . . . let us never regard a question as exhausted" (p. 260).

93. For an account of the KPD under the Hitler regime, see Peter C. Hoffmann, *Wiederstand, Staatsstreich, Attentat: Der Kampf der Opposition gegen Hitler*, 2d ed., Munich: Piper Verlag, 1970, pp. 36-40. There is also an English-language edition, *The History of the German Resistance, 1933-1945*, Cambridge, Mass.: MIT Press, 1977.

Twelve. The National Socialists

1. The quotation is from Theodore Abel, *The Nazi Movement: Why Hitler Came to Power*, New York: Prentice-Hall, 1938, pp. 282-283. Overall, the party suffered an immense loss in East Prussia in the 1928 election, its percentage falling from 6.2 in December 1924 to 0.8. The corrected vote total appears in *Statistik des Deutschen Reichs*, vol. 372, pt. 2, p. 7. In Richard F. Hamilton and James Wright, *New Directions in Political Sociology*, Indianapolis: Bobbs-Merrill, 1975, p. 40, I accepted this quotation at face value.

2. William Sheridan Allen, *The Nazi Seizure of Power: The Experience of a Single German Town, 1930-1935*, Chicago: Quadrangle Books, 1965.

3. Ibid., pp. 26, 38, 47-48, and passim.

4. Ibid., pp. 24-25.

5. Ibid., p. 28.

6. Ibid.

7. Ibid., pp. 32-33.

8. Ibid., p. 34.

9. Ibid., pp. 39-40.

10. Ibid., p. 294.

11. Ibid., p. 46.

12. Ibid., p. 51.

13. Ibid., p. 52.

14. Ibid., p. 70.

15. Ibid., p. 294.

16. Ibid., p. 72.

17. Ibid., p. 71.

18. In great measure, what the party did was to mobilize unused resources, those coming at little or no cost. This was most clearly the case with the unused factory rooms. To the extent that farm produce was not being harvested or brought to market, the prevailing prices being too low to justify the effort, the party was again picking up a costless resource. It might sound easy, but few groups or parties showed the ability to mobilize such obvious resources.

19. Allen, *The Nazi Seizure*, pp. 294-295.

20. Ibid., p. 72.

21. Ibid. Gymnasium students, in almost any German community at that time, would have been overwhelmingly from upper- or upper-middle-class backgrounds. The political orientations of students are considered at greater length later in the chapter.

22. Ibid., p. 73.

23. Ibid.

24. Ibid., p. 74.

25. Ibid.

26. Ibid., p. 75. The party also had an organization for women, most of them wives of members, and one for girls. Women do not figure prominently in any NSDAP accounts of the fighting years. Given the party's principal line of activity in those years, there was little place for women. They were used as service troops, nursing the wounded and attending the soup kitchens.

27. Ibid.

28. *The Nazi Party in Lower Saxony 1921-1933*, London: Oxford University Press, 1971.

29. Rudolf Heberle's work, *Landbevölkerung und Nationalsozialismus: Eine soziologische Untersuchung der politischen Willensbildung in Schleswig-Holstein 1918 bis 1932*, Stuttgart: Deutsche Verlags-Anstalt, 1963, is the outstanding analysis of electoral developments of the period. Allen's is the outstanding community study, more than any other giving some sense of how people in general saw and reacted to National Socialist campaigning. Noakes's work is based on internal records of the party and is the outstanding work on the organizational dynamics of the NSDAP at the local and regional levels.

The region covered in Noakes's account is one of the best-studied areas of Germany. Among the works dealing with the area, or with segments thereof, are: Günther Franz, *Die politischen Wahlen in Niedersachsen, 1867 bis 1949*, Bremen-Horn: Walter Dorn Verlag, 1957; Ernst-August Roloff, *Bürgertum und Nationalsozialismus 1930-1933: Braunschweigs Weg ins Dritte Reich*, Hanover: Verlag für Literatur und Zeitgeschehen, 1961; Roloff, *Braunschweig und der Staat von Weimar: Politik, Wirtschaft und Gesellschaft 1918-1933*, Brunswick: Waisenhaus Buchdruckerei und Verlag, 1964; Sigurd Plesse, *Die nationalsozialistische Machtergreifung im Oberharz: Clausthal-Zellerfeld 1929-1933*, Clausthal-Zellerfeld: Piepersche Verlagsanstalt, 1970. Allen's Thalburg, which is actually Northeim, is also located in Lower Saxony.

30. Noakes, *The Nazi Party*, p. 99. A *Gau* in the NSDAP's arrangements was a territorial subdivision of the national party organization. For the most

part they followed the lines of the thirty-five electoral subdivisions of the nation.

31. Ibid., pp. 141-142. The word *Kreis* in this sentence and in the following quotation is roughly equivalent to the English or American county, as opposed to the thirty-five larger electoral subdivisions of the nation.

32. Ibid., p. 142.

33. Ibid., p. 147.

34. Ibid., p. 151. Other indications of the high activity levels appear throughout the work, e.g., "From 15 Aug. to 14 Sept., the NSDAP in *Gau* Hanover-South-Brunswick held between 300 and 400 meetings a week, in all approximately 1,500, including two torchlight parades through the city of Hanover" (p. 151n). Some other summary statements are covered later in the text.

35. Ibid., pp. 97-100.

36. Dietrich Orlow, *The History of the Nazi Party: 1919-1933*, Pittsburgh: University of Pittsburgh Press, 1969, pp. 162-163.

37. Noakes, *The Nazi Party*, pp. 16-17.

38. Ibid., p. 36.

39. Ibid., p. 140.

40. Ibid., pp. 96-97.

41. Ibid., p. 36.

42. Ibid.

43. This is not to suggest that headquarters only provided guidance or that it never intervened. Some instances of binding orders to local units are considered later.

44. Noakes, *The Nazi Party*, p. 202.

45. Ibid., p. 203. The facts of geography and the mobility of its forces were of considerable aid to the party in this period. When the party was campaigning in Bremen or Oldenburg, party workers in nearby areas of Prussian Hanover could be enlisted in the effort. When it was campaigning in Prussia, the militants of Bremen and Oldenburg would cross the borders in the opposite direction. Because elections did not all fall on a given day, the party was able to concentrate its militants on a sequence of targets, thus using its resources to maximum advantage. Then too, from time to time the party and its affiliates would be banned (e.g. throughout Prussia). In this region, however, it could operate freely within the small states, such as Oldenburg and Brunswick. The large rallies, such as Harzburg, were held there, thus mocking the ban and gaining attention in the press throughout Prussia.

46. Ibid., p. 203.

47. Ibid., p. 206.

48. Ibid.

49. Ibid., p. 209.

50. Ibid., p. 216.

51. Ibid., p. 218. There is, of course, a considerable element of chicanery in all of this. There was, as we have seen, no "emergent united front" of Reichsbanner and KPD. And the street fighting and bloodletting in Altona stemmed from an NSDAP provocation.

Unfortunately, Noakes's work provides little information on public reactions to these NSDAP claims. This is the principal difference between it and Allen's work. In some instances we cannot even be sure the public heard the things the party ordered. For example, Noakes quotes a directive that "all discussion about von Papen's cabinet by the party in this election is forbidden" (p. 217). But whether local speakers followed the order to the letter is not made clear. There are obvious difficulties involved in establishing such a point.

52. Ibid., p. 219. The last ellipsis makes an exception for the Communists. Noakes does not offer any evidence on this point. My sense, based on the sources covered in the previous chapter, is that the KPD was very much inhibited by tradition; it was simply a different tradition from that binding the bourgeois parties. Far from being "open-minded," the party was very closed to suggestions from local militants; it was the model of the bureaucratic party with control and direction centered in the very top leadership.

53. Ibid., p. 211. One additional instance of this virtuosity is worth citing: "The party was careful to counteract propaganda from their opponents [in the Prussian election] that they were opposed to social insurance and were in favour of euthanasia for old people and cripples. Those in homes for old people and cripples were sent personal letters, while the blind even received pamphlets in Braille." Ibid., p. 215.

Sigurd Plesse's account of developments in Clausthal-Zellerfeld, only a few kilometers from Thalburg, is remarkable for its similarities to Allen's account. The town was dominated by the same hostile relations between the bourgeoisie and the SPD with its working-class supporters. *Die nationalsozialistische Machtergreifung*, pp. 6, 9. The National Socialists' takeoff came there between May 1928 and the communal elections of November 1929 (they went from 3.9 percent to 15.7 percent), this being the period of the anti–Young Plan campaign. They had the support of the leading newspaper in the town, the *Oberharzer Bürgerzeitung* (pp. 13, 44). The same extraordinary number and variety of meetings were held by the party (pp. 44, 46, 59). Student support was also indicated (p. 48). And the party collected food for the unemployed, as in Thalburg (p. 47). One also found the same low level of activity by the other parties. Some of them, notably the DVP, found some good things to say about the NSDAP; it especially liked the NSDAP's nationalist outlook.

The only significant point of difference was in a tactical innovation. The NSDAP's contributions at meetings of the bourgeois parties were reasoned and inoffensive, the party's appearance there being described as "orderly and well-behaved." At SPD meetings it was just the opposite; the party was out to disrupt and break up the meetings. Given the disparity between what the good bourgeois citizen had seen and what was reported in the Social Democratic press, it was easy to assume that the latter was a completely untrustworthy source (p. 18).

The same high activity levels were found elsewhere. For an account of the development in Bavaria see Geoffrey Pridham, *Hitler's Rise to Power: The Nazi Movement in Bavaria, 1923-1933*, New York: Harper & Row, 1973. For information on the number of meetings, see pp. 87, 105, 138, 162, and 266.

Many of the same observations appear in National Socialist memoirs published in the thirties that tell of the years of struggle. See, for example, Franz Buchner, *Kamerad! Halt aus! Aus der Geschichte des Kreises Starnberg der NSDAP*, Munich: Zentralverlag der NSDAP, 1938.

54. Ernst H. Posse, *Die politischen Kampfbünde Deutschlands*, Berlin: Junker und Dünnhaupt, 1931, pp. 24–25; the footnote is on p. 98. The work he cites of Gerhard Schultze-Pfaelzer is *Von Spa nach Weimar: Die Geschichte der deutschen Zeitwende*, Leipzig: Grethlein, 1929.

Posse, like many others, begins with the prewar Youth Movement (Jugendbewegung), with the so-called Wandervogel. That movement has not been included in the present argument for one very simple reason: there is no compelling, or even very suggestive, evidence linking the prewar Jugendbewegung with the subsequent developments. The biographical accounts and personal memoirs of NSDAP activists focus on the war as the beginning of all things. The psychological connections, moreover, do not seem appropriate. There were some similarities between the Wandervogel and the postwar paramilitary units, most notably their general antibourgeois outlook and concern with uplift or renewal. Otherwise it is the differences that are most striking. The Wandervogel were rather dreamy, one might even say ethereal, in their outlooks, seeing national renewal as somehow to be achieved through long hikes in the German countryside and the singing of folksongs by the evening campfire. The postwar paramilitary activists were very worldly by comparison; they were given to a violence and a destructiveness that stand in very sharp contrast to the gentleness of the Wandervogel. See Walter Z. Laqueur, *Young Germany, A History of the German Youth Movement*, London: Routledge & Kegan Paul, 1962. Unlike the men discussed in the text, the Wandervogel members reacted to the experience of the front with feelings of repulsion. They found it ugly; after the first flush of enthusiasm there was not much left of the comradeship *they* had expected. One of them wrote: "One was alone among the many. The uneducated hated every cultured soldier. Every conversation began and ended with obscenities." Another was distressed by his "sad days and heavy nights among vulgar and mean people." Ibid., p. 89. Laqueur's conclusion is that the youth movement "had too little political influence to have decisively affected the course of events . . . while some of its leading members had been intellectual pace-makers for National Socialism, and a small number actively resisted it, the majority did very little one way or the other" (p. 198).

Confirmation of the Youth Movement's irrelevance appears in the work of Theodore Abel, *The Nazi Movement*, and in that of Peter H. Merkl, *Political Violence under the Swastika*, Princeton: Princeton University Press, 1975. Abel's remarkable study is based on an "essay contest" launched early in June of 1934. Securing the cooperation of the National Socialists for this effort, Abel offered small cash prizes for "the best personal life history of an adherent of the Hitler movement." It was specified that they had to be members prior to 1933. They were asked to describe their personal lives, particularly "after the World War." This stipulation could have discouraged mention of the Youth Movement although the instructions did cast a wide net with respect to formative experiences, asking about family life, education, economic conditions, and membership in associations. Announced as being "organized under the tutelage of the sociology department of Columbia University," the contest was advertised in NSDAP offices and in the party press. Abel received 683 autobiographical accounts, varying in length from one to eighty pages. Omitting the one- and two-page accounts and those few accounts written by women activists, his study then was based on reports from 600 pre-1933 male activists (pp. 3-4). It should be noted that the "contest" was announced just before the Röhm purge of June 30, and the entries were to be submitted "on or before September 1934." What effect that event had on the resulting biographies is hard to say. Some "contestants" may have been eliminated that night. Many of the rest no doubt removed damaging information from their accounts. Although by no means a cross-sectional sample, it probably is the most detailed qualitative set of materials on the NSDAP activists to be found anywhere.

Merkl's work consists of a reanalysis of 581 of those accounts, some 100 or so of the originals having been confiscated by the Federal Bureau of Investigation in 1951 and never returned. In Merkl's 716 pages of text, only a few passing references are made to the Wandervogel. On p. 220, for example, that movement is mentioned in conjunction wih the youth organizations affiliated with three of the postwar parties. On p. 238, in a tabulation entitled "First Youth Group Membership," the Wandervogel is listed with the postwar *Bündische* youth groups—4.4 percent report these as their first membership. The younger respondents, those of the wartime or postwar generations, could not of course have been in the prewar movement. There is a suggestion (p. 240) that most of the older respondents were in no youth organization.

A convenient summary of the experiences of the various "Nazi generations" appears on pp. 152-153 of Merkl's work. For two of the three groups discussed, professional soldiers and wartime volunteers, his conclusions are very much in line with the position being presented here including the emphasis on the *Fronterlebnis* and the shock experienced over the outcome. For the impact of the war see also pp. 52-53. The third group, the postwar generation, obviously would have had a different history. This group is discussed later in this chapter.

Another important discussion of the experience of the front (here called the "war experience") is that of Kurt Sontheimer, *Antidemokratisches Denken in der Weimarer Republik: Die politischen Ideen des deutschen Nationalismus zwischen 1918 und 1933*, Munich: Nymphenburger Verlag, 1962, ch. 5. He reviews several other authors on the subject, including those having pacifist reactions (discussed below). Still another account of the *Fronterlebnis*, here discussed as the Front Ideology, appears in James M. Diehl, *Paramilitary Politics in Weimar Germany*, Bloomington: Indiana University Press, pp. 211 ff.

55. It would be easy to psychologize these differences in outlook, that is, to suggest they have purely idiosyncratic, internal, psychological bases. But like most outlooks, even wildly distorted ones, this one too has a realistic basis. Franz Seldte, the leader of the Stahlhelm and later a DNVP member in Hitler's first cabinet, was also the author of a dull, pompous three-volume work of fiction describing his experience in the war. At one point a general, someone

from the rear echelon, comes to tell the front soldiers how to organize for an enemy attack. They should leave their machine gun in place during the preliminary artillery bombardment and take shelter in their bunkers. As soon as the shelling ends, they must take up position and begin firing on the advancing infantry. Seldte's Lieutenant Stahl forthwith contradicts the general; these guidelines go against his procedure. The *Frontkämpfer* knew that a barrage of that sort would bury everything. At the end of the shelling they would first have to dig out (which would take some time); clogged with mud, no weapon would be ready to fire. They *knew* that during a shelling they had to take the weapon into the bunker with them. The "frog's perspective" in this case was the correct one; the general's comments provided one more reason for questioning the judgment of headquarters. At the same time, however, the basis of the headquarter's complaint should also be recognized. The men on the front only saw a small part of the whole picture, and they tended to judge things on the basis of their very limited understanding of a very large and complex picture. The Seldte novel is entitled *Dauerfeuer*, Leipzig: Verlag von K. F. Koehler, 1930. The incident appears on pp. 283-284. The collective title for the three volumes is *Der Vater aller Dinge* (The Father of All Things). In this case too, the reference is to *the* war.

56. Some sense of the initial reactions may be gained from Barbara Tuchman, *The Guns of August*, New York: Macmillan, 1962, ch. 6. Her unit of analysis is "Germans" or "the Germans." German workers are not excepted because, so one is told, the socialism that "most of Berlin's workers professed, did not run so deep as their instinctive [sic] fear and hatred of the Slavic hordes." When mobilization was finally announced, one learns, they were "instantly converted from Marx to Mars" (p. 74). While this view, which is widespread in the literature, receives some plausible support in the SPD vote for the war credits three days later, it is useful to consider the comment of another writer, Albert Grzesinski, in 1914 an official of the metalworkers' union and later the police president in Berlin. He says that despite "official reports and the usual press stories, little war enthusiasm was evident among the lower classes. Only Berlin showed any war fervor, and even there the workers were little affected by war hysteria. A visit of several days to Berlin a few weeks [before the mobilization] had given me the opportunity to see alarming war demonstrations among students, middle-class groups and those people who are always in evidence when something happens. Organized labor realized the gravity of the situation and was much concerned." From his *Inside Germany*, New York: E.P. Dutton, 1939, p. 32.

A similar pattern of support for war, middle classes generally approving and working classes reluctant or disapproving, has been found elsewhere. See Richard Price, *An Imperial War and the British Working Class: Working-Class Attitudes and Reactions to the Boer War, 1899-1902*, London: Routledge & Kegan Paul, 1972, and by the present writer and James Wright, "The Support for 'Hard Line' Foreign Policy," ch. 5 of my *Restraining Myths: Critical Studies of U.S. Social Structure and Politics*, New York: Sage-Halsted-Wiley, 1975.

It is easy to lose perspective on things. In a period in which all good liberals are self-righteously antiwar (except possibly for wars of national liberation and, of course, for World War II), it is sometimes hard to realize that Germany's liberals were so very much in favor of the war, their attitudes bordering on the euphoric. Max Weber wrote to Ferdinand Tönnies on October 15, 1914, that "this war, with all its ghastliness is nevertheless grand and wonderful. It is worth experiencing." A group of "the most distinguished German intellectuals, men of science, and artists" issued a statement denying all charges of German atrocities and violations of international law in the Belgian invasion. The list reads like a Who's Who of German liberalism. See Koppel S. Pinson, *Modern Germany: Its History and Civilization*, 2d ed., New York: Macmillan, 1966, pp. 313-316.

The composer Richard Strauss, not otherwise known for his astuteness in social or political affairs, saw the problem with remarkable clarity. He wrote: "It is nauseating to read in the papers about . . . how the youth of Germany will return from this 'noble war' purified and strengthened, when in fact we can be glad if the poor wretches, having been cleansed from lice and bugs, and cured of all their diseases, can ever again become accustomed to a life free from slaughter." From Ernst Krause, *Richard Strauss: The Man and His Work*, London: Collet's, 1964, p. 62.

57. Between October 1914 and March 1918, "no attack or series of attacks was able to move the front line ten miles in either direction." Lord Kitchener, in his frustration, exclaimed: "I don't know what is to be done—this isn't war!" From J.F.C. Fuller, *The Conduct of War*, London: Eyre & Spottiswoode, 1961, p. 160. For a discussion of the technical problems posed by this new and different kind of war, see his ch. 9. Other useful works on this subject are: Theodore Ropp, *War in the Modern World*, Durham, N.C.: Duke University Press, 1960; Cyril Falls, *The Art of War: From the Age of Napoleon to the Present Day*, New York: Oxford University Press, 1961; and Arthur Marwick, *War and Social Change in the Twentieth Century: A Comparative Study of Britain, France, Germany, Russia and the United States*, London: Macmillan, 1974. Ropp refers to World War I as "a war of attrition, one of the longest and the bloodiest in history." *War in the Modern World*, p. 243. Also of interest, for its description of the battle of the Somme, is John Keegan's *The Face of Battle*, New York: Viking Press, 1976.

58. From Robert G. L. Waite, *Vanguard of Nazism: The Free Corps Movement in Postwar Germany, 1918-1923*, New York: Norton, 1969, pp. 23-24. The account in the following pages of the text, as will be seen, makes heavy use of this extremely important work. See also Hellmuth Gruss, "Aufbau und Verwendung der deutschen Sturmbattaillone im Weltkrieg," doctoral dissertation, University of Berlin, 1939.

59. Waite, *Vanguard of Nazism*, pp. 24 ff.

60. Ibid., p. 23.

61. That is a section heading in Jünger's *Der Kampf als inneres Erlebnis*, Berlin: E. S. Mittler & Sohn, 1928. The basic view of this extraordinary work, whose title may be translated as Combat as Inner Experience, holds that man is bound by his society, by its forms, rules, laws, and so forth. As a consequence he loses

awareness of other dimensions of his being, of what he is and of what he can do. War creates this awareness. One section is entitled "Eros"—the object of this love is war.

62. Waite, *Vanguard of Nazism*, p. 23. He is quoting from Jünger's *In Stahl-gewittern: Ein Kriegstagebuch*, Berlin: E. S. Mittler & Sohn, 1926. That was the sixteenth edition of the book, bringing the number of copies printed to 125,000.

63. Jünger, *Der Kampf*, p. 83.

64. Ibid., pp. 78, 109-110. It will be noted that Jünger is indicating a direc-tionless wrath. This is a point that Waite also stresses, that the shock troops and the later Freikorps did not have much in the way of an ideology or political direction (see below for further discussion). It will also be noted that in these passages Jünger is discounting the influence of his class background and of cultural values on his later behavior.

65. Waite, *Vanguard of Nazism*, pp. 28-29.

66. Ibid., p. 27.

67. See Richard M. Watt, *The Kings Depart: The Tragedy of Germany: Ver-sailles and the German Revolution*, New York: Simon and Schuster, 1968, p. 464 for Ludendorff's reaction. A Reichstag investigating committee published a twelve-volume report on the causes of the collapse, carefully discussing and rejecting the stab in the back thesis. Waite calls the report "a monument to German industry and objectivity." It was, nevertheless, he continues, "a pathetically ineffective answer to the cheaply inaccurate but highly successful propaganda of the opposition", *Vanguard of Nazism*, p. 32.

68. For Ebert's greeting, see Watt, *The Kings Depart*, p. 464. In this connec-tion too, it should be noted, it is easy to psychologize, to attribute the view to mere irrational fancies, or, making use of the mass-society theory, to attribute the result to the machinations of clever demogogues. Both lines of analysis fail to consider the reality underlying that belief and thus cannot understand either the strength of the belief or the anger associated with it. That this belief was mistaken is quite beside the point; many of those holding it were acting on the basis of their immediate understanding of things they had directly experienced.

69. See Waite, *Vanguard of Nazism*, p. 32. The quotations in this paragraph are taken from Merkl, *Political Violence*, pp. 205, 55, and 208. See also pp. 54, 207, 214, 259, 355, and 389.

One source has no less a figure than Hermann Goering, the commander of the Richthofen Squadron, dressed in full uniform and wearing his *pour le mérite*, challenging "a government spokesman" before an audience of officers gathered in the Berlin Philharmonic Hall. Reviewing the experience of the homecoming troops, he ends with the following statement: "And therefore I implore you to cherish hatred—a profound, abiding hatred of those animals who have outraged the German people. . . . But the day will come when we will drive them out of our Germany. Prepare for that day. Arm yourselves for that day. Work for that day." The quotation appears in Otto Friedrich, *Before the Deluge: A Portrait of Berlin in the 1920's*, Harper & Row, 1972, p. 39. He in turn cites a biography by Roger Manvell and Heinrich Fraenkel as his source (*Goering*, New York: Simon and Schuster, 1962). They indicate the original source to be a work by one Erich Gritzbach, *Hermann Goering: Werk und Mensch*. It was published in Munich in 1938 by the NSDAP's Zentralverlag. Manvell and Fraenkel also point out that the work was edited by Goering. Leonard Mosley also recounts the incident in his biography, *The Reich Marshal*, Garden City: Doubleday, 1974. His report, he says, is based on "contemporary accounts and on Gritzbach." It is obviously difficult to know whether this story can be credited.

70. Merkl, *Political Violence*, p. 208. One account of such attacks appeared in a novel by Erich Maria Remarque, *Der Weg zürück*, Cologne: Kiepenheuer & Witsch, 1971, pp. 55-60. This work (in translation, *The Road Back*) first appeared in 1931. It was a sequel to *All Quiet on the Western Front*.

71. Within Germany the Versailles treaty was regularly referred to as the Versailles *Diktat*. Unlike most previous settlements, this one allowed the German delegation and government no role in the negotiations. They were told simply to accept the terms or suffer the penalty, that being the occupation of the nation. Given the hopeless military situation, the government accepted. But few Germans were to consider it a treaty, which usually entails some negotiation by the involved partners. For details see Richard Watt, *The Kings Depart*; and Erich Eyck, *Geschichte der Weimarer Republik*, Erlenbach-Zurich: Eugen Rentsch Verlag, 1956, vol. 1, ch. 4.

72. See Waite, *Vanguard of Nazism*, p. 74n.

73. Watt, *The Kings Depart*, p. 199; Eyck, *Geschichte der Weimarer Republik*, vol. 1, p. 68.

74. It is easy to blame the SPD leaders for this dependence on the military. But, as Erich Eyck asks, who is to blame for this if not the left? See his discussion in *Geschichte der Weimarer Republik*, vol. 1, pp. 75-76. Posse, in discussing Austria, says little Communist opposition existed there. As a result, there was no fight against the left and no need to depend on the right. *Die politischen Kampfbünde*, p. 66. For a more detailed discussion of the various forces and their reliability, see the important work by Hagen Schulze, *Freikorps und Republik 1918-1920*, Boppard: Harald Boldt Verlag, 1969, pp. 14-21. These questions are also discussed in Diehl, *Paramilitary Politics*; and Hannsjoachim W. Koch, *Der deutsche Bürgerkrieg: Eine Geschichte der deutschen und österreichschen Freikorps*, Berlin: Ullstein Verlag, 1978.

75. Waite, *Vanguard of Nazism*, p. 35.

76. Posse, *Die politischen Kampfbünde*, p. 9; Waite, *Vanguard of Nazism*, pp. 53-54; Schulze, *Freikorps*, pp. 53-54. People on the left, Spartacists or Independent Socialists, would not, of course, ordinarily be among the volunteers for a counterrevolutionary fighting organization. Even workers from the left wing of the majority SPD would probably have felt uncomfortable in that company. It is said that the SPD did encourage workers to join, reference being made to advertisements appearing in *Vorwärts*. Waite, *Vanguard of Nazism*, p. 54; Posse, *Die politische Kampfbünde*, p. 60. Both references, however, involve calls for worker entry into the civil defense (the Einwohnerwehr). Moreover, the dates are very late, long after the initial formation of the Freikorps. Waite gives September 11, 1919, and Posse November 30, 1919. See also, Diehl, *Paramilitary Politics*, pp. 56 ff.

Another frequent question asks, Why didn't the government form a worker's army? Most workers would have been enlisted men in the old army, at best noncommissioned officers. Few of them would have had the necessary leadership experience. Given the pressing immediate needs facing the government both on the home front and in the border areas, they chose immediate effectiveness over loyalty.

77. Waite, *Vanguard of Nazism*, p. 42.

78. Ibid.

79. Ibid., pp. 39–40.

80. Ibid., pp. 45–49.

81. Ibid., pp. 48–49.

82. Ibid., pp. 42–43.

83. Ibid., pp. 208, 242; Schulze, *Freikorps*, pp. 50–51.

84. Waite has little to say about the composition of the lower ranks of the Freikorps. Schulze says that officers and noncommissioned officers frequently served as enlisted men, in some cases entire companies being made up of ex-officers. Noncoms also enlisted in large numbers. The students, obviously, would have begun their Freikorps careers as privates. *Freikorps*, pp. 48–49.

85. Waite, *Vanguard of Nazism*, ch. 4; Schulze, *Freikorps*, pp. 69–100.

86. Waite, *Vanguard of Nazism*, ch. 5; Schulze, *Freikorps*, pp. 101–125.

87. Von Salomon, *Die Geächteten*, Reinbek bei Hamburg: Rowohlt Verlag, 1962, pp. 103–104. The work was originally published in 1930. See also Schulze, *Freikorps*, pp. 125–201.

Those familiar with the four-volume work of Samuel A. Stouffer and his associates, *The American Soldier*, (Princeton: Princeton University Press, 1949) will remember that the prime considerations in the minds of U.S. World War II combat veterans, those things that "kept them going in combat," were the thought of "getting it over with" and returning home, and second, the thought that one could not "let one's buddies down." The last notion sounds very much like the idea of *Kameradschaft*. For more on that theme, see vol. 2, pp. 96–104.

Those were the dominant motivations, but a closer examination gives a more differentiated picture. Veteran infantrymen in the Pacific were interviewed in March and April 1944. The researchers classified them according to their self-described physical condition and their degree of conviction about the war. The responses to another set of questions provided the basis for a classification of their readiness for combat. Within each of the three divisions studied, widely varying degrees of readiness were found. Among those reporting good physical condition and high conviction, 82 percent were ready versus only 26 percent of those giving the opposite (poor condition, low conviction) reports (vol. 2, p. 155).

One finds in these pages a quotation that, except for the target, could easily have come from one of von Salomon's Baltic fighters: "You don't fight a Kraut by Marquis of Queensbury rules: You shoot him in the back, you blow him apart with mines, you kill or maim him the quickest and most effective way you can with the least danger to yourself. He does the same to you. He tricks you and cheats you, and if you don't beat him at his own game you don't live to appreciate your own nobleness." The words in this case are those of the noted cartoonist Bill Mauldin (vol. 2, p. 156).

At one point the authors constructed a vindictiveness index (vol. 2, p. 163). The highly vindictive soldiers were those who felt the United States should "wipe out the whole Japanese nation," and who, on seeing Japanese prisoners, indicated they "felt all the more like killing them," and who, when the going was tough said that thoughts of hatred for the enemy "helped a lot." This group would appear to have much in common with Jünger's shock troops. Among the privates and privates first-class in the two divisions studied, the highly vindictive soldiers constituted 15 and 14 percent of those interviewed (recalculated from vol. 2, p. 165). There was a modest positive relationship between vindictiveness and combat readiness, a somewhat stronger one with thinking the war worthwhile (specifically, *never* saying it was "not worth fighting"), and a strong relationship with hostility toward a conciliatory peace with the Japanese, preferring instead to fight until the latter "give up completely."

In another context, 6,280 men from two divisions were asked how they felt about getting into an actual battle zone. Eight percent said, "I want very much to get into it just as soon as possible," and another 31 percent said "I'm ready to go any time." Asked about their feelings with respect to "combat against the Germans," more than one in eight said, "I'd like to get into the fight as soon as I can." Although all of these responses represent minority positions, one could conceivably have recruited a battle-ready Freikorps battalion from among the two divisions (vol. 2, p. 45).

Also of interest in this connection is an analysis in which the soldiers were classified into below average, average, and above average "combat performance groups" (vol. 2, p. 34). The classifications were related to brutality as indicated by the responses to the question: "How do you think you would feel about killing a Japanese soldier?" Thirty-eight, 44, and 48 percent respectively chose the response, "I would really like to kill a Japanese soldier." These were troops fighting in Europe; the comparable percentages saying "I would really like to kill a German soldier" were 5, 6, and 9.

This analysis also gives some indications of the social backgrounds of the various "combat performance groups." The authors' summary reads: "If we consider only men with high school education, relatively high AGCT score [a crude intelligence test] . . . relatively high mechanical aptitude . . . and over 24 years of age at the time of the aptitude survey . . . we find that 58 per cent are in the above average group on combat performance and 6 per cent are in the below average group. At the other extreme, if we take men with grade school education only, mechanical aptitude scores below 120, and under 24 years of age . . . we find only 22 per cent rated above average in combat performance but 40 per cent rated below average" (vol. 2, p. 37). This ties in with a more general finding indicated above, that soldiers from higher status backgrounds proved consistently more combat ready than their opposite numbers. The percentage wishing an overseas combat assignment, for example, was 37 among those with college education but only 15 among those with a grade school education. The best educated (in this case, meaning high school completion) were more favorably disposed than were others in the overwhelming number of comparisons where personal esprit and commitment were involved (vol. 1, p. 100). The well educated also expressed more criticism of the army and its ways than other groups, the greatest complaint being about officers. Like the German army complaints in World War I, much of this was focused on the rear echelons.

The highly educated were the least likely to report anxiety symptoms, the number doing so roughly doubling as one turns from the high school graduates to the grade school group. Markedly different from the rest were the young educated group, those under 20 having a high school education, among whom only 18 percent reported anxiety symptoms. Among those 25 and over with grade school educations, the figure was 51 percent (vol. 2, pp. 420-424). It should be remembered that these findings from *The American Soldier* describe American enlisted men, privates and privates first-class. The first and second lieutenants presumably would be more highly educated, more likely to be from middle-class backgrounds, and, if one were to extend the pattern indicated here, more battle-ready than the enlisted men. In rough translation, this would mean that combat readiness was much more frequent among those of middle-class backgrounds than among those from the manual ranks. It seems likely that similar results would have been found in Germany during World War I and in most other times and places as well.

If, in the postwar period, paramilitary organizations were recruited more or less along these class lines, it would mean a postwar struggle in which a technically qualified and enthusiastic army was pitted against a poorly qualified and poorly motivated one. Such was generally the case with the SA on the one hand and the republican (generally, Social Democratic) Reichsbanner on the other. There was, as we have seen, much cross-class recruitment; many workers, that is, were found in the SA where they would be commanded by leaders with much experience. It is doubtful that the Reichsbanner gained equivalent numbers, or equivalent talents, from the middle class. For a comment on the differences, see Posse, *Die politischen Kampfbünde*, who notes that the Reichsbanner was a late formation (dating from February 1924), formed in reaction to the manifest rightist threat, and that it, from the beginning, lacked the "determined ruthless fighting spirit" of the rightist paramilitary organizations (p. 63). It seems likely that there would have been a marked asymmetry between the Sturmabteilung and the Reichsbanner. The former would have contained combat-ready war lovers; the members of the latter would have contributed their services only with some reluctance. The former would have had a surfeit of leadership talents, those provided by the battle-trained ex-lieutenants; the latter would have been recruited, disproportionately, from among the followers, from among the ordinary soldiers. The former would prefer provocative or offensive tactics; the latter would tend more toward the defensive, toward fending off the other's thrust rather than initiating actions. The National Socialist style of combat was a highly mobile one, allowing for quick movement and concentration of scattered forces; the Reichsbanner style tended more toward the defensive, toward the protection of previously held positions. All of this, of course, would have had a significant effect on the outcome.

Contrasting the Freikorps units with the units of the left insurgent forces, Schulze says that they "simply lacked leaders who were capable of forming an equally competent military instrument." *Freikorps*, p. 71. See also Karl Rohe, *Das Reichsbanner Schwarz Rot Gold. Ein Beitrag zur Geschichte und Struktur der politischen Kampfverbände zur Zeit der Weimarer Republik*, Düsseldorf: Droste Verlag, 1966. The defensive character of this republican organization is indicated on pp. 35 and 114. There was some selection on the left, the tougher fighters going to the KPD, one Reichsbanner leader seeing this process as a cause of the failure of the SPD's fighting ability (p. 270). Officers, it is said, were "a rarity" in the Reichsbanner. And again, it is said that "trained and capable officers were hardly to be found in the Reichsbanner." More and more, those without military experience came into leadership positions (pp. 275-276).

It is unlikely that the distribution of combat-related attitudes in the German Army of World War I would have been identical with the distribution in the U.S. Army of World War II. All that is intended here is to emphasize that one is dealing with relative frequencies, something that tends to be lost in the impressionistic sources and in those making use of economical generalizations. If anything, because of the duration and the sustained character of the war, particularly in the west, and because of the type of combat organizations developed there, the German army would probably have had a larger percentage of war lovers.

88. Waite, *Vanguard of Nazism*, chs. 6 and 7. The quotations are from p. 161.

89. Ibid., p. 167. See also Merkl, *Political Violence*, pp. 313 ff. and 344 ff., who also reports a process of militarization followed by politicization.

90. Waite, *Vanguard of Nazism*, p. 193.

91. Ibid., p. 206. Merkl, on the other hand, does not find many of the 1934 members reporting membership in that organization, it being at best a few percent of the entire sample. *Political Violence*, pp. 359-360.

92. Waite, *Vanguard of Nazism*, pp. 198 ff. To hide its military character, the terms for areas, units, and rank were changed, "the country was divided into military areas called *Gaue* and *Kreise*; the formations were called *Hundertschaften* and *Gruppen* and the commanders addressed as *Gauleiter*, *Gruppenführer*, and so forth" (p. 199). Many of these terms were later taken over by the National Socialists.

93. Ibid., pp. 212 ff. See also the curious article by Howard Stern, "The Organisation Consul," *Journal of Modern History*, 35 (1963): 20-32. He finds it a relatively innocuous organization, the more spectacular murders being the work of individuals, rather than a result of its official policy. He fails to deal with material contained in Waite's book.

94. Waite, *Vanguard of Nazism*, pp. 227 ff.

95. Ibid., pp. 239 ff.

96. Ibid., pp. 253, 254. For another account of the military events of this period, including the Black Reichswehr activities, see Gordon A. Craig, *The*

Politics of the Prussian Army, 1640-1945, New York: Oxford University Press, 1964, ch. 10.

97. Waite, *Vanguard of Nazism*, pp. 233 ff.

98. Ibid., pp. 234-235; Merkl, *Political Violence*, pp. 201-206.

99. Buchner, *Kamerad! Halt aus!*

100. Ibid., p. 237.

101. Ibid., p. 319.

102. Abel, *The Nazi Movement*, p. 44. See note 54, this chapter, for a description of his research procedure.

103. Merkl, *Political Violence*, p. 139.

104. Ibid., p. 145.

105. Ibid., pp. 146-147, 333.

106. Ibid., pp. 139 and 410 ff.

107. Abel, *The Nazi Movement*, p. 44; and Merkl, *Political Violence*, p. 293.

108. Waite, *Vanguard of Nazism*, pp. 285 ff. A more extended list appears in his Ph.D. dissertation, "The German Free Corps Movement, 1918-1923," Harvard University, 1949, pp. 458 ff. Not too surprisingly perhaps, the irregular or freebooter character of these units also posed problems for Hitler's regime. But Hitler, not as tolerant as the republic's leaders, "solved" the problem by having many of them killed in the purge of June 30, 1934. See Waite, *Vanguard of Nazism*, p. 279; and Schulze, *Freikorps*, pp. 333-334.

109. Merkl (*Political Violence*, p. 317) reports one such complicated case: "Immediately after his discharge from the army he joined the *Einwohnerwehr* vigilantes and participated in the Kapp putsch. Following this, he had to leave town and was a *Zeitfreiwilliger* for six or eight weeks. He returned and joined the DSP of Kunze, then the Black *Reichswehr* of Major Buchrucker, and soon the *Frontbann*, which turned into the NSDAP and SA of his area. He became a stormtrooper in 1926 and eventually an SS officer." See also Diehl, *Paramilitary Politics*, ch. 8.

A study of the Sturmabteilung reports that as of 1927, "The upper leadership levels of the SA . . . [were] almost exclusively dominated by ex-military and Freikorps people." From Andreas Werner, "SA und NSDAP. SA: Wehrverband, Parteitruppe oder Revolutionsarmee," doctoral dissertation, University of Erlangen-Nuremberg, 1964, p. 381 (cited in Michael Kater, "Ansätze zu einer Soziologie der SA bis zur Röhm-Krise," in Ulrich Engelhardt, Volker Sellin, and Horst Stuke, eds., *Industrielle Welt: Soziale Bewegung und politische Verfassung*, Stuttgart: Klott Verlag, 1976, p. 816n).

110. Noakes, *The Nazi Party*, pp. 16-20.

111. Ibid., p. 18.

112. Ibid., pp. 22-23.

113. Ibid., p. 23n.

114. Ibid., p. 34.

115. One might think that with the coming of the depression university enrollments would decrease, both because of declining family incomes and because of the supposedly hopeless employment situation facing graduates. And yet, between 1927 and the summer semester of 1931, there was an increase of 44

percent in university enrollments, from 72,139 to 103,912. For the most part this was little more than a reflection of the increasing size of the prewar birth cohorts. It also tells something about the circumstances of the majority of the students; their education was unaffected by the coming of the depression. And that, in turn, would mean that the majority of them were *not* lower middle class. If anything, the depression would have removed the economically marginal lower-middle-class students (and the few students of working-class backgrounds) from the universities, making them even more exclusively upper and upper-middle-class than before. Some evidence is available on this point.

Most of the available data on the social backgrounds of students make use of those all-embracing census categories, civil servants, white-collar employees, and independent business. In some cases the top-level (*leitende*) segments are presented separately, making it easy to assume that the remaining segments are marginal or lower middle class. Again one must be grateful for the rich statistical resources of the Free City of Hamburg, which provide detailed figures on the backgrounds of students at that city's university. In assessing these results, one must keep in mind that this was a new and urban university. Unlike students at traditional institutions, such as Tübingen, Heidelberg, Jena, or Göttingen, many of the Hamburg University students could cut costs by living at home. It would, in short, have been less exclusive than the more prestigious traditional institutions. This point is indicated by the relatively large numbers of working-class children enrolled there in the winter semester of 1930-1931, 6.8 percent, a figure that was approximately three times that for the Reich. That percentage showed a small but steady decline in the following semesters, to 6.2, then to 6.1, and finally, in the summer of 1932, to 5.6. A majority of the working-class students in the first of those years, incidentally, were enrolled in *Philosophie und Pädagogik*. Most of them were probably enrolled in the latter area, that is, in teacher training.

The figures for the summer semesters of 1931 and 1932 indicate that approximately two-fifths of the students were children of civil servants (which includes those with fathers in the teaching professions). The distributions of these public servants in terms of higher, middle, and lower levels are given in the table. Approximately 8 percent of the students were children of self-employed professionals with the overwhelming majority of these fathers having an academic education, strongly suggesting upper-middle-class backgrounds. One-quarter of the students had fathers who were engaged in business and commerce (*Handel- und Gewerbetreibende*). That might, on first view, suggest a lower-middle-class tendency, but the actual picture is more complicated. One-fifth of these students were children of owners or directors of factories. Forty-four percent may have been genuinely lower middle class, their fathers being independent master

Father's level	Summer 1931	Summer 1932
Higher	10.1%	12.1%
Middle	26.6%	27.4%
Lower	3.1%	2.2%
Total	39.8%	41.7%

craftsmen or proprietors of small firms. Even here it is not at all clear that those were marginal enterprises; the presence of a child at the university would suggest the opposite. The remaining third had fathers who were employed somewhere in between these extremes, presumably in middle-sized firms either as owners or as middle-level managers. Approximately one-sixth of the students were children of white-collar workers in private employment. A majority of them had fathers in managerial positions.

There is some ambiguity about the classification of the civil servants. Michael H. Kater argues that the lower-level *Beamte* were really workers, that they were blue-collar employees in government-owned enterprises, the most familiar cases being the railroad trainmen. And that, he says, means that the middle-level civil servants are really lower middle class. *Studentenschaft und Rechtsradikalismus in Deutschland, 1918-1933*, Hamburg: Hoffman und Campe, 1975, p. 60. Even if the initial assumption were correct (it actually remains to be established), that would involve an unrealistic simplification of middle-class life—one is either upper or lower; there is no middle. If one were to grant his claim, a more precise formulation would define this middle level as consisting of those white-collar civil servants who were *not* in high-level positions; it would include therefore, both lower and middle ranks. It is reasonable to expect these students to be children of *middle*-level civil servants, for a very simple reason—the costs involved. This argument gains at least suggestive support in the figures for the early thirties. The working-class children, as we have seen, were disappearing from the university, and the same was true of the lower-level civil-servant children.

Approximately 30 percent of the students came from the upper strata and roughly 10 percent from the lower, the remaining category, some 60 percent of the total being this broad middle group. Kater, *Studentenschaft und Rechtsradikalismus*, p. 208. While no precise frequency distribution can be established with the data at hand, my feeling is that for the reasons indicated, they would tend to be skewed upward rather than toward the lower middles. Kater, however, assigns the entire group, in his tabulation of national data, to the lower middle class (*unterer Mittelstand*).

One clue to the support provided the NSDAP is provided by consideration of finances. Noakes and others have indicated the link between NSDAP support and the fraternities. Membership in these organizations involved rather substantial sums, a requirement that would effectively bar all economically marginal groups of the population. The same may be said of the National Socialist Students' League. At the University of Munich its members paid twelve marks a month in addition to their party membership fee of three marks a month. Pridham, *Hitler's Rise to Power*, p. 211. This is at a time when, as Allen notes, thirty pfennigs was equivalent to two loaves of bread. A mark would mean more than six loaves. A poor student, making his way through the university on bread, cold cuts, and cheese, would find fifteen marks well beyond his means.

The political divisions within the university reflected those found within the general, or more specifically, within the middle-class population of Germany. This means that there was a basic division along religious lines, this being built into university life in the form of Catholic and non-Catholic fraternities. On the whole, a strong Catholic presence worked against the National Socialists in the student elections. In the winter semester 1930-1931, the extreme cases were the largely Catholic Bonn University, where the NSDAP received 19.0 percent, and heavily Protestant Erlangen, where it received 76.0 percent. Jews, although a small minority, were overrepresented among the students (one of the principal issues of the *völkische* groups and the National Socialist Students' League was a quota on Jewish enrollment). There was also a very small left within the universities. If we assume that Catholics tended to vote for Catholic lists, that Jews definitely did not support National Socialists, and that the left vote tended to come from working-class and lower-middle-class students, this would mean that the remaining middle-class students, both lower and upper segments, were giving the party extremely high levels of support. It seems unlikely that there would have been enough lower-middle-class students to supply all the votes. Given the evident support, especially by Protestant fraternity students, the suggestion is that upper-middle-class support was very strong.

The Hamburg figures are taken from the publication *Aus Hamburgs Verwaltung und Wirtschaft* 8:1 (1931): 6; 8:7 (1931): 210; 9:1 (1932): 2-4; 9:8 (1932): 159-162. Figures for overall enrollment in the relevant years were taken from the *Statistisches Jahrbuch für das Deutsche Reich, 1933*, pp. 522-523. See also Kater, *Studentenschaft und Rechtsradikalismus*. For detailed studies of two German universities, see Wolfgang Kreutzberger, *Studenten und Politik 1918-1933: Der Fall Freiburg im Breisgau*, Göttingen: Vandenhoeck & Ruprecht, 1972; and Manfred Franze, *Die Erlanger Studentenschaft, 1918-1945*, Würzburg: Ferdinand Schöningh, 1972. The university elections, incidentally, were by proportional representation. The participation at these two universities in the key years ran at approximately 70 percent.

Kater treats virtually the entire student body as impoverished, losing status, and facing unemployment on completion of its studies. He does recognize a frequency distribution but generally describes only the impoverished end of that distribution and then attributes that poverty to all students. He also takes the pronouncements of student organizations and spokesmen at face value; it is a rare pressure group that admits things are just fine or even all right. At a time when approximately two-thirds of the students were in fraternities (*Studentenschaft und Rechtsradikalismus*, pp. 24, 80), it is hard to agree with his point about general student impoverishment. It cost something to be in a fraternity. There were the original dues and regular assessments. There was a drinking requirement (*Trinkzwang*) that had to be met, and that too, no doubt, cost something. Those in the dueling fraternities had also to pay for their armament. The catalog of Solingen weapons showed some thirty varieties of sabers ranging in price from six to thirty-six marks. Ibid., p. 83.

A more recent work on the subject is that of Michael Steinberg, *Sabers and Brown Shirts: The German Students' Path to National Socialism, 1918-1935*, Chicago: University of Chicago Press, 1977. His data show only very small changes in the social backgrounds of the students over time; that is, the students generally come from high-status families at all times (see his tables, pp. 24 ff.).

Steinberg does, nevertheless, give credence to the decisive-change hypothesis, pointing to the number of students who in 1922 were already "forced to seek employment both during vacations and in the semester." It is not established that the employment of students was *new*; it may well have existed earlier, that is, prior to the war. Unfortunately, the only evidence available on the point appears to be for the Weimar period.

Steinberg exaggerates somewhat when he says that in 1922 "close to half of the enrolled students reported employment either during the summer semester or the summer vacation." A footnote states that 26,803 students reported working during the summer vacation of 1922. Using his figure (p. 34), that would amount to only one-fifth of the students. If the economic need were so pressing, one would anticipate a much higher figure. His conclusion that "the numerical balance [in the universities] . . . turned in favor of the lower middle class" and that "these" students were seriously impoverished, is challenged by another set of figures; membership in fraternities increased between 1929 and 1933, going from 46 to 66 percent. Student numbers, of course, dwindled considerably after 1931, the total being off by one-quarter as of 1933. Those losses, no doubt, would involve the minority of economically marginal lower-middle- and working-class students. And, obviously, those remaining in the universities to provide the support for National Socialist slates in student elections would have come from well-off families, from those families, for example, that were vacationing at the time of the summer election in 1932. Some of the votes cast in the resort areas, in such cases, would have been those of students accompanying their families.

Another relevant work is that of Anselm Faust, *Der Nationalsozialistische Deutsche Studentenbund: Studenten und Nationalsozialismus in der Weimarer Republik*, Düsseldorf: Pädagogischer Verlag Schwann, 1973. For Faust's discussion of the social backgrounds of the students, see pp. 112-121.

116. Noakes, *The Nazi Party*, p. 35.

117. Ibid., p. 93. On Hitler's refusal to intervene in party struggles, leaving such matters to be settled through a social Darwinist survival of the fittest, see Michael H. Kater, "Der NS-Studentenbund von 1926 bis 1928: Randgruppe zwischen Hitler und Strasser," *Vierteljahrshefte für Zeitgeschichte*, 22 (1974); 186. See also Reinhard Bollmus, *Das Amt Rosenberg und seine Gegner: Studien zum Machtkampf im nationalsozialistischen Herrschaftssystem*, Stuttgart: Deutsche Verlags-Anstalt, 1970, pp. 243-246.

118. Noakes, *The Nazi Party*, p. 131. The party was "already in the public eye as the most active participant in the campaign against the Young Plan" (p. 132). For an account of the situation in Coburg, see Pridham, *Hitler's Rise to Power*, pp. 84-86.

119. Noakes, *The Nazi Party*, p. 196. Results for eighteen institutions of higher learning appear in Karl Dietrich Bracher, *Die Auflösung der Weimarer Republik*, Villingen/Schwarzwald: Ring-Verlag, 1964, p. 148. See also Wolfgang Zorn, "Student Politics in the Weimar Republic," *Journal of Contemporary History*, 5 (1970): 128-143.

120. Noakes, *The Nazi Party*, pp. 196-197. It will be noted that the informed

liberal citizen in Berlin would be left with the analysis of the *Vossische*; the actual facts of the situation would have escaped him or her. And with those mistaken facts, there would be no stimulus to consider alternative, and more appropriate, explanations.

121. Ibid., p. 197. In the winter semester of 1930-1931, 45 percent of the students voting in the Brunswick student council election supported the National Socialists. Bracher, *Die Auflösung*, p. 148. The developments in Brunswick are described in Roloff, *Bürgertum und Nationalsozialismus*.

122. Karl Dietrich Bracher, *The German Dictatorship: The Origins, Structure, and Effects of National Socialism*, New York: Praeger, 1970, p. 118. See also Harold J. Gordon, Jr., *Hitler and the Beer Hall Putsch*, Princeton: Princeton University Press, 1972, p. 443.

123. Gordon, *Hitler*; see p. 80 for the student membership, p. 69 for the activities of Munich students, and, for additional information on student involvement, pp. 190, 344, 348, 420, 441-444, and 562.

124. Ibid., pp. 392, 384.

125. Noakes, *The Nazi Party*, pp. 197-198; Faust, *Der Studentenbund*, pp. 25-29.

The bases of support among the Protestant clergy were similar to those indicated for many of the students. They felt an initial sympathy for the NSDAP because of its nationalism and antibolshevism. But some also aligned themselves and gave their services "out of a sense of guilt at the social isolation of the church. The church had been frequently criticized for its failure to emerge from its upper and middle class social background and culture and for its inability to establish contact with the people. With the emergence of the NSDAP as a mass movement, some were prepared to overlook its anti-Christian aspects in return for a sense of participating in what they saw as a *Volksbewegung* engaged in a national revival." Noakes, *The Nazi Party*, p. 208.

126. The need for schooling had been recognized earlier by the Freikorps leaders. Young people enrolled in their labor camps did work some five or six hours a day, but the rest of the time "was spent in military drill, target practice, 'defensive exercise,' and listening to 'cultural lectures' delivered by battle-tough *Freikorpskämpfer*." From Waite, *Vanguard of Nazism*, p. 211. Ex-police officials conducted school for members of the paramilitary organizations, giving lessons in unobtrusive behavior for activists working in occupied territories, in tailing and street observation procedures, in the photographing of documents, in appropriate conduct when arrested, and the like. See Friedrich Glombowski, *Organisation Heinz (O.H.) Das Schicksal der Komeraden Schlageters*, Berlin: Reimar Hobbing, 1934, p. 41.

127. See Pridham, *Hitler's Rise to Power*, p. 100.

128. Orlow, *History of the Nazi Party*, p. 159. The school also made periodic mailings to its "graduates," these containing guidelines, suggestions, propaganda material, etc.

129. Pridham, *Hitler's Rise to Power*, pp. 100-101.

130. Orlow, *History of the Nazi Party*, p. 159. Limited purpose training was also undertaken, as for example in *Gau* Hanover-North where a one-shot course

was organized for the Easter weekend of 1927. It was intended to train "workers as speakers to enable them to lead the opposition in the meetings of left-wing parties." Noakes, *The Nazi Party*, p. 101. Noakes indicates (p. 142) that some students, rather than taking the correspondence course, attended the party school in Herrsching am Ammersee.

131. Pridham, *Hitler's Rise to Power*, p. 101. Buchner, the war veteran, one-time Freikorps fighter, 1923 putschist, and local leader in Starnberg, attended this school. He reports that they spoke before audiences of mock Communists, Catholics, Social Democrats, and so forth, each challenging the speakers with appropriate comments, interruptions, catcalls, etc. *Kamerad! Halt aus!*, p. 380.

132. Orlow, *History of the Nazi Party*, pp. 159-160.

133. Pridham, *Hitler's Rise to Power*, p. 101.

134. Noakes, *The Nazi Party*, p. 143. By 1932, the basic fee for speakers had been increased to fifteen marks.

135. Ibid.

136. Ibid., pp. 144-145. Not too surprisingly, the NSDAP made a very good showing in this village in the May 1928 Reichstag election. One additional observation is deserving of at least passing mention: the DVP speaker reported that he became "quite excited" at the meeting, lost his temper, and accused his audience "of having the manners of Jews."

Propaganda activities in *Gau* Hanover-South Brunswick were extremely well developed. In 1930 the local unit already had a corps of skilled speakers who "could appeal to almost any type of audience." This included numerous *Mittelstand* speakers as well as peasants, artisans, white-collar workers, a few civil servants, and a former leading member of the KPD.

The *Gau* propaganda director, appointed in May that year, organized all aspects of the effort. He had standard application forms printed for requesting speakers. These asked if the speaker was to address a "predominantly peasant" or a "strongly Marxist" population, allowing maximum efficiency in the assignment of speakers. When later on the unit diversified its offerings ("to catch those who are impossible to win with political meetings"), one innovation was the special "Hermann Löns evening." Löns was a popular poet in one area of the *Gau*. The evenings were organized by his brother, a member of the NSDAP, and are reported to have been "very successful." The *Gau* also circulated a how-to-do-it memorandum entitled "Guidelines for Hermann Löns Evenings." Noakes, *The Nazi Party*, p. 146.

137. Cited in Pridham, *Hitler's Rise to Power*, p. 79. Candidates were required to sign a form swearing that they had no Jewish relations and that they would "always act according to the directives of the party leadership, make ruthless use of their legal immunity and energy for the propaganda struggle in the country, give up half their salaries as deputies to the party, and, should they leave the NSDAP, resign their seats." Noakes, *The Nazi Party*, pp. 132-133.

138. Pridham, *Hitler's Rise to Power*, p. 80.

139. When NSDAP representatives did appear in national, state, and local legislative bodies, their behavior was thoroughly disruptive. As one example: "Between 14 September 1930 and 14 September 1931, for example, there were

twenty-eight plenary sessions in the Brunswick *Landtag* in which there occurred 8,446 interruptions. Of these, 4,195 came from the nine Nazi members, an average of 406 each. . . . The Nazis were only outdone by the KPD representatives with 475 each. But the tone of crude brutality which they introduced was unique." Noakes, *The Nazi Party*, p. 133.

140. For example, see the work of Hamilton T. Burden, *The Nuremberg Party Rallies: 1923-39*, New York: Praeger, 1967.

141. Hermann Okrass, *Das Ende einer Parole—"Hamburg bleibt rot,"* Hamburg: Hanseatische Verlagsanstalt, 1934, p. 179.

142. Merkl, *Political Violence*, p. 65 and also p. 14.

143. Abel, *The Nazi Movement*, p. 4. There is a serious discrepancy between Abel's and Merkl's (*Political Violence*, p. 13) figures. Abel reports 37 percent of the male members as 41 or over in 1934. Merkl reports only 21.3 percent as 41 or over in 1930. They are not precisely the same samples, it will be remembered, since Merkl included the women respondents and is missing the 100 or so confiscated by the Federal Bureau of Investigation. The National Socialists' official publication, the *Partei-Statistik*, on the basis of a large survey of the membership as of January 1935, only shortly after Abel's contest, shows 34.5 percent of the members as being 41 or over. That includes both male and female members, but only 5.5 percent of the members were female. This result, clearly, is more in line with the Abel finding and for that reason I have used his figures. See the *Partei-Statistik*, vol. 1, Munich, 1935.

144. Merkl, *Political Violence*, pp. 384-385.

145. This point is discussed at greater length in my *Class and Politics in the United States*, New York: John Wiley & Sons, 1972, ch. 9 and in my *Restraining Myths*, ch. 5.

146. Merkl, *Political Violence*, p. 263.

147. Ibid., p. 265. The individual who went bankrupt because of party activities, either neglecting the business or giving too much of the profits to the party, is a familiar figure in the NSDAP memoirs; see, for example, Buchner, *Kamerad! Halt aus!*, pp. 35-36.

A study of the party's *Gauleiter* also throws into question the broken-existences hypothesis. The principal conclusion reads as follows: "The typical Nazi leader . . . was in fact a secure, rather successful professional, official, or businessman with a history of considerable upward mobility before he had joined the movement: a person, to be sure, of lower-middle-class or even working-class origins, but one who by individual achievement (often including promotion from the ranks during the war) had risen considerably higher in life; and one to whom motives of economic insecurity can only rarely be credibly attributed." This author also argues that "a significant, if numerically limited, part of the National Socialist *membership and following* is likely to have consisted of persons of this kind." See Ronald Rogowski, "The *Gauleiter* and the Social Origins of Fascism," *Comparative Studies in Society and History*, 19 (1977): 399-430. The quotations are from p. 402.

148. Bracher, *Die Auflösung*, p. 646.

149. Ibid., p. 656; for the Thuringia result, see the *New York Times*, December 5, 1932, p. 6, and the London *Times*, December 6, 1932, p. 13d.

150. Bracher, *Die Auflösung*, p. 701.

151. Ibid., pp. 707 ff.

THIRTEEN. THE CHARACTER OF THE POLITICAL STRUGGLE

1. As of 1933, one-third (33.0 percent) of the German population lived in communities of less than 2,000 persons. The middle-sized communities, those with from 2,000 to 99,999 persons, contained 36.6 percent of the population. And the large cities, the *Grossstädte*, those of 100,000 or more, contained slightly less than a third, 30.4 percent. Although much emphasis is placed on urbanization and its correlates, it is important to note that more people at this point lived in the smaller communities than in the large cities. Many of those living in the large cities, as we have seen, still lived in a village milieu, that being the result of the 1920s annexations. At the same time, one must remember that many of those living in villages were regular commuters to jobs in the larger cities. For details see *Statistik des Deutschen Reichs*, vol. 451, "Volkszählung: Die Bevölkerung des Deutschen Reichs nach den Ergebnissen des Volkszählung 1933." Part 1, from which the above figures are taken, is entitled "Stand, Entwicklung und Siedlungsweise der Bevölkerung des Deutschen Reichs," Berlin, 1935.

Twenty-nine percent of the economically active population in 1933 was engaged in agriculture. Although most of these people would have been located in the smallest communities, it will be remembered that some farmers were found even in the largest cities, up to and including Greater Berlin. Many commentators speak of the rapidity of the social changes under way. Actually the decline of agricultural employment in the previous decades had been rather gradual, falling from 36 percent of the economically active population in 1895 to 29 percent in 1933, a rate of approximately 2 percent a decade. The most rapid changes in the agricultural sector actually occurred prior to 1895 and after 1950. The first third of the twentieth century, in other words, was a period of relatively slow change. For these figures see Fritz Croner, *Soziologie der Angestellten*, Cologne: Kiepenheuer & Witsch, 1962, pp. 197 ff.

2. Some sense of village life may be gained from the following, all of which review the transformations occurring in the course of the century: Herbert Kötter, *Landbevölkerung im sozialen Wandel: Ein Beitrag zur ländlichen Soziologie*, Düsseldorf: Eugen Diederichs Verlag, 1958; Kötter, *Struktur und Funktion von Landgemeinden im Einflussbereich einer deutschen Mittelstadt*, Darmstadt: Eduard Roether Verlag, 1952; K. G. Grüneisen, *Landbevölkerung im Kraftfeld der Stadt*, Darmstadt; Eduard Roether Verlag, 1952; and Gerhard Wurzbacher, *Das Dorf im Spannungsfeld industrieller Entwicklung*, Stuttgart: Ferdinand Enke Verlag, 1961. For a review of political developments among farmers, see Günther Franz, *Der Bauer in der politischen Welt*, Göttingen: Musterschmidt Verlag, 1964. For a comprehensive account of the economic situation of the farm population in the Weimar period, see Max Sering, ed., *Die deutsche Landwirtschaft unter volks- und weltwirtschaftlichen Gesichtspunkten*, Berlin: Paul Parey, 1932. For a brief over-

view of the subject, see Werner T. Angress, "The Political Role of the Peasantry in the Weimar Republic," *Review of Politics*, 21 (1959): 530-549.

3. William Sheridan Allen, *The Nazi Seizure of Power: The Experience of a Single German Town, 1930-1935*, Chicago: Quadrangle Books, 1965. A detailed sociological account of a middle-sized industrial community in the post–World War II period containing also some historical background, is that of Renate Mayntz, *Soziale Schichtung und sozialer Wandel in einer Industriegemeinde*, Stuttgart: Ferdinand Enke Verlag, 1958.

4. The German census does not give figures for religion in terms of these community-size categories. For the smallest communities reported, those under 10,000, the Protestant percentage (62.6) is essentially the same as for the entire nation (62.7). There is a slight (but irregular) decline in the Catholic percentages in the larger cities. The portion with no religious affiliation increased with city size as did the portion of Jews. For details see *Statistik des Deutschen Reichs*, vol. 451, pt. 3, "Die Bevölkerung des Deutschen Reichs nach der Religionszugehörigkeit," Berlin, 1936. The best account of the segregation of the religious communities is to be found in Johannes Schauff, *Die Deutschen Katholiken und die Zentrumspartei: Eine politische-statistische Untersuchung des Reichstagswahlen seit 1871*, Cologne: Verlag J. P. Bachem, 1928, pp. 28 ff.

5. See my *Affluence and the French Worker*, Princeton: Princeton University Press, 1967, pp. 24-31 for discussion of the problem. Aspects of this problem are discussed in the German context in note 75, Chapter 11.

6. For the erosion of SPD strength in the smaller communities, see Rudolf Heberle, *Landbevölkerung und Nationalsozialismus: Eine soziologische Untersuchung der politischen Willensbildung in Schleswig-Holstein 1918 bis 1932*, Stuttgart: Deutsche Verlags-Anstalt, 1963, pp. 87-88. For the Catholic patterns, see Schauff, *Die Deutschen Katholiken*, pp. 74 ff.

7. It is difficult to make precise estimates as to the numbers involved in each of these segments. The real world is not as neatly divided as the text might suggest. Many communities contained a mixture of farm and city (commuting) populations. Some communities were religiously mixed. I would estimate that somewhere between 20 to 25 percent of the total population would be contained in rural Protestant areas. Not all of these persons, of course, would be farmers. Many of the village and small-town populations engaged in trade and commerce were, of course, directly dependent on agriculture. The NSDAP, as noted repeatedly, gained its greatest electoral successes within this context. Heberle comments that in July the voters in many rural places gave that party between 70 and 100 percent of their votes; see *Landbevölkerung und Nationalsozialismus*, pp. 39, 44, 63, 74, and 82.

8. Dietrich Orlow, *The History of the Nazi Party: 1919-1933*, Pittsburgh: University of Pittsburgh Press, 1969, pp. 129, 131-132.

9. From the issue of May 31, 1928, as quoted in Jeremy Noakes, *The Nazi Party in Lower Saxony 1921-1933*, London: Oxford University Press, 1971, p. 123. See also Peter D. Stachura, "Der kritische Wendepunkt? Die NSDAP und die Reichtagswahlen vom 20. Mai 1928," *Vierteljahrshefte für Zeitgeschichte*, 26 (1978): 79-80.

10. Orlow, *The History of the Nazi Party*, p. 137.

11. Max H. Kele, *Nazis and Workers: National Socialist Appeals to German Labor, 1919-1933*, Chapel Hill: University of North Carolina Press, 1972, pp. 168 ff. Orlow provides only a very limited account of the 1928 election result. He focuses on Schleswig-Holstein, Weser-Ems and Hanover-South-Brunswick (parts of present-day Lower Saxony), and on parts of Bavaria. The NSDAP, as noted earlier, actually made gains in nineteen of the thirty-five election districts of Germany, the largest being in the Palatinate where it went from 1.9 to 5.6 percent.

12. Noakes, *The Nazi Party*, pp. 108 ff. For more detail see John B. Holt, *German Agricultural Policy, 1918-1934*, Chapel Hill: University of North Carolina Press, 1936, pp. 93 ff.; Heberle, *Landbevölkerung und Nationalsozialismus*, pp. 118 ff.; and Sering, *Die Deutsche Landwirtschaft*.

13. Holt, *German Agricultural Policy*, pp. 185-187; Noakes, *The Nazi Party*, pp. 124-125; Heberle, *Landbevölkerung und Nationalsozialismus*, p. 163; also, Geoffrey Pridham, *The Nazi Movement in Bavaria, 1923-1933*, New York: Harper & Row, 1973, pp. 224-236.

The NSDAP, as indicated, was slow to implement the rural possibility. Its organization to reach farmers was developed by Walther Darré who did not begin work in Munich until mid-August 1930. His memorandum outlining plans for an organizational branch to reach farmers was not ready until late that month, obviously too late to have any effect on the September Reichstag election. See Horst Gies, "NSDAP und landwirtschaftliche Organisationen in der Endphase der Weimarer Republik," *Vierteljahrshefte für Zeitgeschichte*, 15 (1967): 341-376. An English version appears in Henry Ashby Turner, Jr., ed., *Nazism and the Third Reich*, New York: Quadrangle Books, 1972, pp. 45-88.

14. Noakes, *The Nazi Party*, p. 125.

15. Milton Mayer, *They Thought They Were Free: The Germans 1933-45*, Chicago: University of Chicago Press, 1955, p. 90.

16. These comments are based on the experience of other times and places. For a portrait of the political life of the Federal Republic of Germany in the fifties, see Juan J. Linz, "The Social Bases of West German Politics," Ph.D. dissertation, Columbia University, 1959, ch. 10. And for France in the same period, see my *Affluence and the French Worker*, Princeton: Princeton University Press, 1967, ch. 11. Generally support for the left parties varies directly with city size, while support for the right varies inversely. There is also a general tendency for the "no preference" choices to vary inversely with community size as does also the tendency to have no opinion on political questions. The apolitical character of the smaller communities also appears in the United States; see my *Class and Politics in the United States*, New York: John Wiley & Sons, 1972, pp. 259 ff. A useful account of the activities of local notables in an American village may be found in Arthur J. Vidich and Joseph Bensman, *Small Town in Mass Society*, Princeton: Princeton University Press, 1958. See also the works cited in note 2, this chapter. Günther Franz (*Der Bauer*, p. 9) touches on this same theme when he states that "the farmer was not really conservative but rather was politically uninterested." Another relevant work is that of Sidney

Verba and Norman H. Nie, *Participation in America: Political Democracy and Social Equality*, New York: Harper & Row, 1972. They report (pp. 237 ff.) very low levels of campaign activity in isolated villages and rural areas as well as in small suburbs. The villages and rural areas show high levels of nonconflictful communal activity and of voting participation. Another important work, this because it provides a close parallel to the case under discussion, is that of Maurice Pinard, *The Rise of a Third Party: A Study in Crisis Politics*, Englewood Cliffs: Prentice-Hall, 1971, pp. 201 ff. See especially his discussion of the small communities, pp. 205 ff.

17. The argument goes as follows: the sons of the upper and upper middle classes, the graduates of the gymnasiums and universities, almost automatically became either career officers or reserve officers. They provided the combat leadership (the first and second lieutenants) and, given the characteristics of World War I combat, they sustained the highest losses. Being the first out in attack and the last back in retreat, they were exposed to enemy fire for longer periods than combatants in the lower ranks. In World War I, Germany suffered a loss of 1.8 million men. Of the regular troops, 13.7 percent were killed in combat. The losses among second lieutenants, by comparison, amounted to 31.5 percent. Among those promoted to lieutenant while in combat the figure was 25.5 percent. For first lieutenants and captains the figure was 25.0 percent. Among staff officers (major and above) the rate was somewhat lower at 20.7 percent.

The initial mobilization took those young men already trained and in the reserves, pulling in many who were already established in their careers. With each subsequent year of the war, new recruits were required, these consisting of both younger and older participants. This means that the four years of war caused considerably more than the loss of four years of birth cohorts to the families of the upper and upper middle classes. One can guess that at least ten birth years of the male population in these ranks were decimated.

These observations and figures are taken from Constantin von Altrock, ed., *Vom Sterben des Deutschen Offizierskorps*, Berlin: E. S. Mittler & Sohn, 1921, Appendix; "Die im Weltkrieg Gefallenen nach Alter und Familienstand," *Wirtschaft und Statistik*, 2 (1922): 385-386; Ernst von Kietzell, "Weltkrieg und Bevölkerungspolitik," *Archiv für Rassen- und Gesellschaftsbiologie*, 34 (1940): 26-30. Apart from the *Wirtschaft und Statistik* account, these sources ought to be viewed with more than the usual suspicion. Letters of inquiry directed to several military archives were not able to turn up anything more substantial on this question.

The same pattern of wartime mortality appeared among American troops in World War II. See Samuel Stouffer et al., *The American Soldier*, Princeton: Princeton University Press, 1949, vol. 2, p. 102. Some studies of U.S. combat mortality during the Vietnam War report a different pattern, one that probably stems from the difference between a "world" war and a "limited" one. The former involves a general mobilization whereas the latter requires only a partial and highly selective mobilization. The student deferment allowed many children of the upper and upper middle classes to escape service entirely.

18. The cautionary terms—"seems," "likely," "apparent," and "plausible"—

are there to emphasize that this is how the farmer in that situation probably saw things. For an account of the difference between the NSDAP's promise and the later reality, see David Schoenbaum, *Hitler's Social Revolution: Class and Status in Nazi Germany 1933-1939*, Garden City: Doubleday-Anchor, 1967, ch. 5.

19. Pridham, *The Nazi Movement*, p. 233.

20. Noakes, *The Nazi Party*, p. 127.

21. For a rich array of programmatic statements by the Social Democrats (and later by the Communists) that could not help but alienate farmers, see Günter Franz, *Quellen zur Geschichte des Deutschen Bauernstandes in der Neuzeit*, Munich-Vienna: G.F.R. Oldenbourg, 1963. Heberle sums up as follows: "The Social Democrats, as an urban industrial party of wage workers, were tactically in a very unfavorable position during the rural agitation. The odium of conscious hostility toward farmers was still attached to it from the former times of stronger dogmatic ties." *Landbevölkerung und Nationalsozialismus*, p. 167. Although a significant concession was made to small farmers at the SPD meeting in Kiel in 1927, that late change could not undo the heritage of decades.

For an analysis of Social Democratic performance in Norway that makes specific comparisons with Heberle's study of Schleswig-Holstein, see the work of Sten S. Nilson, "Wahlsoziologische Probleme des Nationalsozialismus," *Zeitschrift für die gesamte Staatswissenschaft*, 110 (1954): 295-311. A more recent account, which undertakes more extended comparison with Scandinavian countries, is that of Timothy Alan Tilton, *Nazism, Neo-Nazism, and the Peasantry*, Bloomington: Indiana University Press, 1975, pp. 47 ff. Gerhard Stoltenberg reviews the post–World War I development in Schleswig-Holstein indicating how all of the established parties ignored the farmers; see his *Politische Strömungen im schleswig-holsteinischen Landvolk 1918-1933*, Düsseldorf: Droste Verlag, 1962, chs. 2 and 3.

22. Everything in this paragraph is speculation or guesswork. There is a need for detailed systematic content analyses of speeches made to audiences in the countryside in this period. This is obviously a difficult task, since it is exactly in this context that written records of speeches or even the notes of police informants are least likely to be found. It would be useful to have analyses based on a sample of speeches given throughout a given region. This would let us know how controlled or directed the effort was, whether it followed a central plan or whether local speakers were free to undertake their own variations on a theme.

23. Pridham, *The Nazi Movement*, pp. 232-233.

24. There is a curiosity about the Weimar literature that one might note at this point. The claims made are typically *general*: the farm problem sweeps Germany from one end to the other. More detailed studies, to be sure, do make some differentiations, for example, by size of farm or product raised. But I have not found any source that differentiates Catholic and Protestant farmers to show that the depression touched them in different ways, this by way of explaining their different responses. It is certainly conceivable that Catholic farmers raised different crops, or, perhaps lacking a "Protestant ethic," were less indebted than Protestant farmers. Given the overall territorial separation of the two, it is cer-

tainly a possibility but, I think, a rather unlikely one. Catholic pockets, no matter where they appeared, tended to vote for the Zentrum, as was the case for example even with one isolated Catholic segment in East Prussia. In some areas of Germany, in the Palatinate for example, Catholic and Protestant villages existed side by side. It seems unlikely that they produced different crops, faced different markets, or would have had markedly different levels of indebtedness. Max Sering presents figures on indebtedness by region and size of farm. These show only very small differences between Catholic and Protestant regions. *Die deutsche Landwirtschaft*, p. 53.

I would like to express my special appreciation to Ernst Wagner who undertook inquiries in various farm communities of the Palatinate. He was not able to discover any clear differences in the economic circumstances of the Catholic and Protestant farm communities in the area.

25. This is speaking of the orientations expressed in the course of elections. In the postelection negotiations of August 1932, the Catholic opposition, as indicated in Chapter 10, was not as overwhelming as before. And also, once Hitler offered the promise of a concordat, the orientations, or at least the behavior of many Zentrum leaders underwent a pronounced change.

26. Pridham, *The Nazi Movement*, p. 149.

27. Ibid., pp. 17, 19; and D. J. Goodspeed, *Ludendorff: Soldier, Dictator, Revolutionary*, London: Rupert Hart-Davis, 1966, p. 245.

28. Pridham, *The Nazi Movement*, pp. 146-183. The triggering event was the publication of Alfred Rosenberg's "heathen views" in his *Der Mythus des 20. Jahrhunderts* (Myth of the Twentieth Century) that work being brought out by Hoheneichen-Verlag in Munich at the same time as the 1930 election. Although the book did not have official NSDAP backing, Rosenberg explaining in the preface that these were his own personal views, not those of the party, that fact made little difference to the church hierarchy which condemned both the book and the party. It says something about the party's internal controls that this book appeared at such a key point. Rosenberg had put the book into Hitler's hands, seeking his approval but the *Führer* never read it. After some delay, however, he told Rosenberg to go ahead with publication.

Hitler did recognize, of course, that anti-Catholic ravings could cost the party support. In 1925, he dissociated himself from the Ludendorff attacks. When the Thuringian *Gauleiter*, Artur Dinter, refused to give up his antichurch attacks, Hitler expelled him from the party, a disciplinary extreme, it should be noted, that was not applied to the "socialist" dissidents within the party. Gregor Strasser, then head of the party's political organization, took the trouble to obtain signed declarations of support for Hitler's policy vis-à-vis Dinter. In later years, the dismissal of Dinter was offered as proof that the party was not antichurch. See J.R.C. Wright, *"Above Parties": The Political Attitudes of the German Protestant Church Leadership 1918-1933*, London: Oxford University Press, 1974, pp. 79-80. See also Klaus Scholder, *Die Kirchen und das Dritte Reich*, vol. 1, *Vorgeschichte und Zeit der Illusionen 1918-1934*, Frankfurt: Propyläen Verlag, 1977, pt. 1.

29. Pridham, *The Nazi Movement*, p. 169.

30. The emphasis is on the *relative* ease, as opposed to the near impossibility of an official rejection of NSDAP claims within the more *laissez aller* Protestant church. The National Socialists again demonstrated their virtuoso provocative style in their relations with the church hierarchy, and the bishops frequently found it difficult to counter their tactical innovations. Pridham's chapter 5 is devoted to this question, that is, to "the problem of Roman Catholic voters." For a portrait of the events facing the Protestant clergy, see Wright, *"Above Parties,"* pp. 74 ff. Wright summarizes the Protestant position as follows (p. 74): "Church leaders regarded the 'national opposition,' as basically sound and blamed its 'faults' on the way Germany had been made to suffer by her former enemies. Church leaders were also afraid that the church would be isolated if it rejected a mass movement of 'national people' and, in addition, they saw in it a powerful defence against Communism. . . . The NSDAP made concessions to the church and exploited its weaknesses. The result was that although church leaders were aware of some of the dangers of the movement, they did not condemn it."

31. Pridham, *The Nazi Movement*, p. 155.

32. This explanation, clearly, is not in accord with the economic determinist or, as it is sometimes put, with the structural argument as to the causes of human behavior. In its place, a rather soft or fuzzy variable, patterns of personal influence, is being suggested. This argument, moreover, is cultural and, even worse, "micro" as opposed to the approved "macro" lines of explanation. But then, this argument, if correct, would provide an explanation for an observed result, that is, for strikingly different patterns of voting behavior on the part of groups sharing similar structural conditions. Economic strain, it will be noted, at best provides a necessary condition for the National Socialist development. But in addition, the efforts of the party's activists were required (and the support of a range of notables) in order to channel voters in the new direction. Economic strain by itself (or even when coupled with the party effort) did not yield the same result. The efforts of the notables in the Catholic farm communities were sufficient to contain any disaffection stimulated by the economic catastrophe.

It goes without saying that much of what has been argued here is no more than speculation. There are few monographic studies of the political developments in the villages during this period. Most information about the late Weimar development moreover, as was noted earlier, is drawn from Protestant communities, not Catholic ones. The best work in this area is that of Günter Plum, *Gesellschaftsstruktur und politisches Bewusstsein in einer katholischen Region 1928-1933. Untersuchung am Beispiel des Regierungsbezirk Aachen*, Stuttgart: Deutsche Verlags-Anstalt, 1972. Plum points out that in the Aachen region, until 1930 the NSDAP was "nearly unknown" (p. 140), having few members and no organization. In part, he adds, this was because of the presence of occupation troops in the region. The Zentrum press, he notes, paid them little attention until the campaign against the Young Plan. Another valuable source for activities in the Catholic countryside is Elke Frölich and Martin Broszat, "Politische und soziale Macht auf dem Lande: Die Durchsetzung der NSDAP im Kreis Memmingen," *Vierteljahrshefte für Zeitgeschichte*, 25 (1977): 546-572.

33. Pridham, *The Nazi Movement*, p. 172. Put in somewhat different terms, this is to say that the local notables were the Zentrum's (or the BVP's) militants within these communities. Although the Zentrum is sometimes referred to as a party of integration, the integration in this case was into the local community, not into an extensive or well-developed party apparatus. As for the possibility of media impact, Pridham (speaking once again of Bavaria) says (p. 172) that farmers "were not in the habit of reading newspapers." That might well have been the case although one must also consider the possibility of a two-step flow of influence; the notables would read newspapers (the local Catholic press), passing on elements of the content to others.

The Protestant and Catholic areas of Germany were differentiated also in terms of the presence of Jews, who were disproportionately located in Protestant areas. Some 60 percent of the 42,000 Jews living in Bavaria in 1933, for example, were found in the Protestant corner of that largely Catholic state, that is, in Franconia, which contained only about a third of the Bavarian population. Although generally located in the larger cities, the affiliation with Protestant regions was also noted in the countryside, Pridham reporting that Jewish cattle dealers and creditors "were particularly common [in rural Franconia], more so than in Southern Bavaria." That could possibly have meant that the NSDAP made use of economic anti-Semitism there as one of its demagogic themes. In Catholic areas, which lacked the visible target of the local cattle dealer, the party would have had to rely on cultural anti-Semitism. See Pridham, *The Nazi Movement*, pp. 237, 240 and 244. For an account of circumstances in rural Hesse, see John K. Dickinson, *German and Jew: The Life and Death of Sigmund Stein*, Chicago: Quadrangle Books, 1967. For a more general account, see Marvin Lowenthal, *The Jews of Germany: A Story of Sixteen Centuries*, Philadelphia: The Jewish Publication Society of America, 1936. The Protestant states of Germany provided for the emancipation of Jews early in the nineteenth century; in the Catholic states the legal disabilities remained; see especially, pp. 248-249, and 262.

34. Allen, *The Nazi Seizure*, p. 133.

35. Ibid., p. 134.

36. Ibid., pp. 76-77.

37. Ibid., p. 26.

38. Ibid., p. 77.

39. Ibid., p. 79.

40. Ibid., p. 12.

41. Ibid., pp. 23-24. See also note 22, Chapter 2.

42. Ibid., p. 102.

43. Ibid., p. 132.

44. Ibid., p. 69. Given all the stress put on the theme, it may come as a surprise to learn that fewer than 1 percent of Germany's retail shops went bankrupt in 1932. And, moreover, for all the talk about *worsening* conditions, the number of such bankruptcies in 1932 was 26 percent *below* the figure for 1931.

See Heinrich August Winkler, *Mittelstand, Demokratie und Nationalsozialismus: Die politische Entwicklung von Handwerk und Kleinhandel in der Weimarer Republik,* Cologne: Kiepenheuer & Witsch, 1972, p. 34 and p. 206, n. 72.

45. Allen's book, it will be noted, was published in 1965. Despite the serious challenge contained therein, there have been, to the best of my knowledge, no subsequent studies of this question.

Some relevant evidence appears in the *Statistisches Jahrbuch für das Deutsche Reich*. The number of savings accounts, for example, increased steadily from 1924 to 1932. It is to be expected that there would be very few such accounts immediately after the great inflation. One could easily anticipate the steady growth that, in fact, went from 1,723,436 accounts in 1924 to over 16 million in 1929. What is completely unexpected, given the assumptions of the traditional line of argument, is that this number would increase again by one-third, to 21,585,299 accounts in 1932. One might well expect the increase in savings from a modest 24.5 million Reichsmark in 1924 to the 7,227.5 million of 1929. But then one would presumably expect a decline as the depressed middle classes were forced to draw on their savings. But total savings increased again in 1930, to 9,302.1 million RM, and continued to increase until May of 1932. There was some falloff through to July 1932, but then deposits showed a steady growth once again through the rest of the year and throughout 1933. See the yearbooks for 1932, p. 334; 1933, pp. 344, 348; and 1934, pp. 344 and 348.

The number of automobiles in Germany in 1931 (522,943) was 20 percent greater than in 1929. In 1932 there was a modest fall in the number, by some 25,000. The actual deprivation involved a decline in the number of large vehicles and an increase in the number of smaller ones. See the yearbooks for 1932, p. 145; and for 1933, p. 157.

Another indicator of well-being may be found in insurance payments. The yearbooks report increases in the premiums paid for life insurance through 1931, the figure in that year being about 20 percent above that of 1929. The first decline occurred in 1932. The value of premiums for home insurance, theft, and auto declined earlier. But this may not indicate any "immiseration" of the middle class. With a general decline in price levels, one would not need as much of these kinds of insurance as in the previous good times.

46. For anti-Semitic incidents, see Allen, *The Nazi Seizure*, pp. 51-52, 74, and 119. The quotation appears on p. 77. Similar statements appear on pp. 135 and 210.

Since this conclusion is rather unexpected (and to many may seem rather unlikely), it is perhaps of some interest to consider the comment made by the American newspaperman (and later dramatist) Ben Hecht, who reported on Germany in the years immediately after World War I. He states that "in my two years in Germany, I, a Jew, saw and heard no hint of anti-Semitism. Not once in the time I spent in Germany did I hear the word Jew used as an epithet. No Radical or Capitalist was 'accused' of Jewishness in the many wild political debates I heard. I, the only Jewish correspondent at the time covering Germany from the outside world, was never called Jew by the government officials who denounced and barred me from their offices. There was less anti-Semitism to be heard, seen, felt or smelled in that postwar Germany than at any time in the U.S.A. Berlin was as innocent of aversion or even consciousness of Jews as had been Racine, the city of my boyhood. . . . there was no voice in Germany to be heard blaming the Jews for anything." See his *A Child of the Century*, New York: Simon and Schuster, 1954, p. 317.

A similar and even more surprising conclusion was made by Franz Neumann. Writing in the early 1940s, he stated that "spontaneous, popular Anti-Semitism is still weak in Germany. This assertion cannot be proved directly, but it is significant that despite the incessant propaganda to which the German people have been subjected for many years, there is no record of a single spontaneous anti-Jewish attack committed by persons not belonging to the Nazi party. The writer's personal conviction, paradoxical as it may seem, is that the German people are the least Anti-Semitic of all." From *Behemoth: The Structure and Practice of National Socialism, 1933-1944*, New York: Oxford University Press, 1944, p. 121.

A considerable amount of anti-Semitism is reported in Noakes's account: it figured prominently in Oldenburg and in neighboring East Friesland. This region, unlike Thalburg, had a flourishing tradition of anti-Semitism which meant the NSDAP had something it could work with. Those sentiments were found in the holiday resort areas on the coast of East Friesland where, beginning in the 1890s, some effort had been made to exclude Jews. Elsewhere, among the farm populations, a source of strain existed in that many of the cattle dealers of the area were Jewish. There was a tradition of complaining about alleged unfair business practices, and, in a period of falling prices, the Jews became an easy target for attacks.

The NSDAP efforts in this region were organized by an ex-clergyman, one who had been active in anti-Semitic demagogy there in the early twenties. Defrocked for slander, he engaged in propaganda work throughout the area for a *völkische* group between 1926 and 1928, in the latter year joining the NSDAP. His reputation was such that the party made him its leading Reichstag candidate in the Weser-Ems district. The local political police attributed the party's early success in 1928 to his effort. His typical performance would last four hours, interrupted only for the distribution of printed materials. Noakes says that according to the police reports, his audience "remained enthralled to the end. His combination of crude wit, sentimental recollection of past imperial glories, sensational conspiracy stories, and simple remedies for specific grievances proved irresistible." In the more isolated villages and small towns, apart from anything else, Noakes says, "his meetings provided entertainment, an exciting alternative to the cinema." *The Nazi Party*, p. 123.

How can one account for this disparity between Thalburg and the effort in these towns and villages? Does this represent a contradiction? Basically, the answer to the latter question is a simple no. It reflects rather the standard NSDAP operating practice—to make use of anything that worked. If anti-Semitism was not a viable theme in a given area, it was played down or abandoned. If it was viable, it was given considerable play. The basic operational principle is best expressed by Joseph Goebbels who declared that a National Socialist must "be able to ride in all saddles." On the regional variation in propaganda, see Pridham, *The Nazi Movement*, pp. 136-137.

Noakes supports Allen with respect to the primacy of the anti-Marxism theme. "The main target for propaganda," he says, "was 'Marxism.' " He does report anti-Semitism to have been a constant theme; it appeared as a major theme, he says (p. 209), only between 1925 and 1930, that is during the *Mittelstand* campaign, but after 1930 "it was used more as a background to appeals to economic interest and general political propaganda."

Kele cites some instances of National Socialists asking that anti-Semitism be played down, their argument being that "the topic was not popular among workers." *Nazis and Workers*, p. 77. Noakes touches on a similar case: in June 1924, Josef Terboven, the later *Gauleiter* of Essen, called for at least a shift in emphasis saying that "particularly here in an industrial area, it is extremely important that our völkisch press should contain fewer anti-semitic tirades in which it happily forgets that we are also socialists . . . [the press] with ruthless clarity should continually stress the socialist part of our ideology." From p. 17 of his "Conflict and Development in the NSDAP 1924-1927," *Journal of Contemporary History*, 1 (1966): 3-36.

Another relevant source is Peter H. Merkl, *Political Violence under the Swastika*, Princeton: Princeton University Press, 1975. This work, it will be remembered (see note 54, Chapter 12), is based on 581 biographical statements written by early NSDAP activists and collected by Theodore Abel in the early 1930s. A summary tabulation of the "chief objects of hostility" found 63.3 percent focusing on Socialists, trade union leaders, Communists, and "Marxists in general," most of them making the last choice. By comparison, 2.1 percent targeted Jewish Marxists or Communists while another 12.5 percent focused exclusively on "Jews, the 'conspiracy,' " These figures appear on p. 522, but see also pp. 33, 172, and 288.

47. Allen, *The Nazi Seizure*, p. 84.

48. Ibid., p. 80. The support by upper-and upper-middle-class notables reported by Allen was also found elsewhere. In Lower Franconia, in the Protestant corner of Bavaria, government officials "expressed alarm" at the wide support the party was gaining, this even before the September 1930 election. A report described matters as follows: "In wide circles, especially among the better classes, open and hidden sympathies prevail. Every preventive measure of the police authorities is met with sharp criticism. Altogether, the movement nowadays seems to enjoy considerable attention. . . . What is exceedingly critical is the important role that younger university-educated people play to an increasing extent in the movement." From Pridham, *The Nazi Movement*, p. 134.

49. Allen, *The Nazi Seizure*, p. 95.

50. Ibid., pp. 98-99.

51. Ibid., pp. 21, 20.

52. Ibid., p. 98.

53. See the quotation in the section on Hanover in Chapter 8. For a discussion of the same process in Bavaria, see Pridham, *The Nazi Movement*, pp. 249-250. A liberal journal in the city of Kassel was hard hit both by the inflation and by

the depression and, later, by an NSDAP boycott. Its last issue was published on September 30, 1932. It was then merged with a local National Socialist newspaper. See Frieda H. Sichel, "The Rise and Fall of the *Kasseler Tageblatt*," *Leo Baeck Institute Yearbook: 1974*, vol. 19, pp. 237-243.

54. Allen, *The Nazi Seizure*, p. 21.

55. These numbers and facts are deceptive and, moreover, contain an important lesson. The SA had less than 50 members within the town itself but had approximately 2,000 in the district. Its were mobile forces; they could be assembled and moved about the district with relative ease. The statement about the Reichsbanner, in contrast, indicates that its members came on foot and, effectively, could be assembled in only one place, Thalburg itself. The point appears regularly in the literature, albeit somewhat cryptically: the SA was organized for offensive actions, the Reichsbanner for defensive ones.

56. Allen, *The Nazi Seizure*, pp. 130-131.

57. Ibid., p. 137.

58. Ibid.

59. Ibid, p. 275.

60. Ibid., p. 121. The few Socialists living in the surrounding villages, Allen reports, "felt terrorized" (p. 96).

61. Ibid., pp. 131-132.

62. Pridham, *The Nazi Movement*, pp. 108 ff. The election results are from the *Zeitschrift des Bayerischen Statistischen Landesamts*, "Die Reichstagswahl vom 31. Juli 1932 in Bayern," pp. 458-459.

63. Pridham, *The Nazi Movement*, p. 110.

64. Ibid., p. 111.

65. Ibid., p. 114.

66. Ibid., p. 190. The NSDAP took 35.0 percent of the vote in Memmingen in July 1932.

67. Ibid., pp. 144-145.

68. See, for example, the work of Toni Sender, *The Autobiography of a German Rebel*, New York: Vanguard Press, 1939. In rebellion against her well-off bourgeois family, she joined the Social Democrats and, among other things, represented "the workers" in the Reichstag during the Weimar period. With rare exceptions, the faces and voices given attention in the text are those of intellectuals and party leaders. She does, of course, have contact with workers, but these relationships appear to have been rather distant ones. She first escaped her home by going to a business school and then taking a job in a real estate office in Frankfurt. The latter experience she describes as follows (p. 18): "The atmosphere in the office was not on a high intellectual level. There I had my first close contact with people of the working class. None of them was a member of a union, or in any way connected with the labor movement. Their desire seemed to be to rise into the middle class, which I considered an unworthy ambition. I had just left that class and didn't like it."

69. One empirically based portrait of considerable interest, this drawn from the Austrian experience, is provided by Marie Jahoda, Paul F. Lazarsfeld, and Hans Zeisel, *Die Arbeitslosen von Marienthal*, Leipzig: S. Hirzel Verlag, 1933.

70. This argument is based on the assumptions found in the political socialization literature; see Herbert Hyman, *Political Socialization*, Glencoe: The Free Press, 1959; and Kenneth P. Langton, *Political Socialization*, New York: Oxford University Press, 1969. In addition it makes use of the assumptions of the group-bases tradition. For this see Bernard R. Berelson, Paul F. Lazarsfeld, and William N. McPhee, *Voting: A Study of Opinion Formation in a Presidential Campaign*, Chicago: University of Chicago Press, 1954. For a general discussion of this latter tradition, see my *Class and Politics*, ch. 2.

Some recent studies have found the intergenerational political linkages to be not as close as many have assumed. The best available evidence, however, indicates that in earlier decades, parents and teachers were less likely to accept any questioning of their authority, or, more precisely, children believed that to be the case, and they did not openly question. This would suggest closer linkages in the past, if not of specific party choices, then at least of general position on the left-right political spectrum. For some relevant evidence from the Federal Republic of Germany (evidence that reaches back to the Weimar period and earlier), see Gabriel A. Almond and Sidney Verba, *The Civic Culture: Political Attitudes and Democracy in Five Nations*, Princeton: Princeton University Press, 1963, p. 339.

A useful and suggestive study, which reviews a wide range of relevant studies and provides data from one American city, is Rodger Huckfeldt, "Political Behavior and the Social Context of Urban Neighborhoods," Ph.D. dissertation, St. Louis: Washington University, 1977. See also note 81, this chapter.

71. See particularly Hans Neisser, "Sozialstatistische Analyse des Wahlergebnisse," *Die Arbeit*, 7 (1930): 654-659; and Heinz Hamm, *Die wirtschaftlichen und sozialen Berufsmerkmale der kaufmännischen Angestellten, (im Vergleich mit denjeniger der Arbeiter)*, Borna-Leipzig: Universitätsverlag von Robert Noske, 1931 (originally a doctoral dissertation, University of Jena). See also note 35, Chapter 3.

72. There are many references in the literature to what we might call left to right shifts, that is, of Communists shifting to the National Socialists. While such changes did no doubt occur, there is a question to be raised about their frequency. The biographical statements collected by Theodore Abel indicate that the overwhelming majority of these early activists came out of nationalist, patriotic, militarist, and *völkische* backgrounds; see Merkl, *Political Violence*, p. 295.

73. This discussion is based on the analogous case of the British workers; see Robert T. McKenzie and Allan Silver, *Angels in Marble*, Chicago: University of Chicago Press, 1968; and Eric Nordlinger, *Working Class Tories*, Berkeley: University of California Press, 1968.

74. One might ask how these workers could have survived in the face of such opposition. Again one can only speculate. Conservative workers are more likely to be found in small shops, which, ordinarily, are much less politicized and less likely to be unionized. Even within the large firms, it is possible for workers, over time, to locate themselves within congenial work groups. Such "deferential" workers would, presumably, also receive the favor and support of em-

610 Notes, Chapter Thirteen

ployers who valued their loyalty. One does, in addition, have some choice with respect to housing location. Where we have precinct data for working-class areas (as, for example, in Mannheim), it is clear that significant variations existed from one subarea to the next. Conservative workers could, therefore, to some extent at least, find supportive subcommunities even within the urban metropolis. It seems likely that many of the Tory workers would be linked to at least one formal organization, namely to a church, and there too they may have found support for their outlooks. These speculations are based largely on postwar studies of West German workers. See Juan J. Linz, "The Social Bases of West German Politics," Ph.D. dissertation, Columbia University, 1959, especially chs. 10 and 11.

75. Some relevant instances appear in Merkl. A Catholic farmer, "finding no place at home" after the war, went to work in the Ruhr. *Political Violence*, p. 82. There "he experienced the Communist uprising of 1920 when machine guns and hand grenades inside the mine stopped him from going to work and he nearly joined the Free Corps, which put the insurgents down. According to his own account he was almost thrown down a 120-foot mine shaft during a political argument with Communist fellow workers underground." Another worker (p. 212) was in a Communist union in the same post-Kapp uprising. He quit in reaction to their behavior and joined the SPD and, still later, joined the NSDAP. A nationalist woman worker reported (p. 374) attending meetings of all parties in the first months of the republic. The SPD and DNVP meetings "bored [her] to tears." Then she "went to Communist rallies where Karl Liebknecht and Rosa Luxemburg spoke." Her reaction was anything but favorable: "My innermost feelings revolted." Another respondent who worked for the NSDAP "among Communists" made some comments with respect to what Merkl calls (p. 407) the "recruiting function of political violence." "After every Marxist attack," this person reported, "we got new recruits."

Merkl summarizes as follows (p. 366): "The workers in the sample . . . were more often motivated to join by the rough opposition of the Communists, economic troubles, two experiences close to their lives, or by their sense of being repressed."

76. It should be noted that the same processes were probably operating within the smaller communities. The workers there would probably have been more deferential than the big-city workers. They would probably have been more responsive to the cues provided by community notables. And they would have been more easily reached by NSDAP activists. There too, much of the loss suffered by the middle-class parties must have been a loss of working-class voters.

The discussion in the text has focused on voting and party membership. It would also seem likely, especially for younger Tory workers, that the Sturmabteilung would provide an outlet for their anger and frustrations.

77. Kele, *Nazis and Workers*. Kele's demonstration of the NSDAP's continued use of leftist themes and his discussion of the factional dynamics are important contributions. His argument about the impact of the leftist themes on workers in general is much less convincing.

Goebbels's socialism, incidentally, is described by Kele (p. 89) as being "a strange mixture of realism and economic nonsense." Some writers suggest that through this demagogic practice, the NSDAP acquired the support of *leftist* workers. But the specific character of the conversions, the fact that it was *Tory* workers, strongly suggests that it was not leftist themes that attracted them. One of Hitler's definitions of the term "socialist" would only have attracted the good nationalist: he was using the term to mean nationalist. This definition reads as follows: "Whoever is prepared to make the national cause his own to such an extent that he knows no higher ideal than the welfare of his nation; whoever has understood our great national anthem, *Deutschland, Deutschland über Alles*, to mean nothing in the wide world surpasses in his eyes this Germany, people and land, land and people—that man is a Socialist." From Alan Bullock, *Hitler: A Study in Tyranny*, rev. ed., New York: Harper & Row, 1964, p. 76. Schoenbaum quotes Hans Frank as saying National Socialist leaders supplied their own meanings to that term as they saw fit. "There were as many National Socialisms," Frank reports, "as there were leaders." *Hitler's Social Revolution*, p. 41.

78. Kele's discussion of the Bamberg meeting is to be found in *Nazis and Workers*, pp. 83-99. An influential statement of the original position on the Strasser faction and the Bamberg meeting is that of Bullock, *Hitler*, pp. 135-141. Other criticisms of that original position, which incidentally are based on the writings of Otto Strasser, may be found in Orlow, *The History of the Nazi Party*, pp. 66-72; and in Jeremy Noakes, "Conflict and Development in the NSDAP 1924-1927," *Journal of Contemporary History*, 1 (1966): 3-36.

79. For an extended discussion of the background, the announcement, and the effort to disseminate this program, see the important work by Udo Kissenkoetter, *Gregor Strasser und die NSDAP*, Stuttgart: Deutsche Verlags-Anstalt, 1978, especially ch. 4, and, for the use of the program in the key Reichstag election, pp. 134-141. A key slogan in this campaign was "*Arbeit und Brot*" (work and bread).

80. See Chapters 4-6. The results for the other cities are not easily summarized. Some of the voting results were reported for precincts, some for the larger city districts. In no *district* was majority support for the NSDAP discovered. Majority support did appear in some precincts, as, for example, in some of the best areas of Nuremberg and also in a working-class precinct of Mannheim. If percentages for these smaller cities were systematically computed, one would, no doubt, find other instances of majority support in some precincts. The only urban community giving an outright majority to the NSDAP was upper-class Blankenese in the Hamburg metropolitan area.

One would undoubtedly find majorities in many districts in still smaller cities, especially in those with high overall percentages for the NSDAP (in Darmstadt, for example, with 47 percent in July 1932; or Pforzheim, 48 percent; Giessen, 49 percent; Pirmasens, 49 percent; or Marburg, 53 percent). One would have to inquire as to whether the lower-middle-class districts there were distinctive, or whether the "infection" was found throughout the nonmanual ranks.

81. Huckfeldt is one of the few researchers who has addressed this question

with any kind of data. The basic question is whether, in the mixed districts, people's politics will reflect their class or the dominant tendency of the neighborhood. His evidence, from Buffalo, New York, in the late 1960s, shows that people, on the whole, went with the neighborhood. High-, medium-, and low-income respondents in low-income neighborhoods all gave heavy support to the Democrats while the same categories of respondents in high-income neighborhoods all leaned toward the Republicans. "Political Behavior," pp. 106-109. The picture is somewhat more complex when one examines the pattern by occupation. Still, in one key comparison, the assumptions outlined in the text are generally borne out. Four out of five (79.8 percent, N = 109) of those from the blue-collar families in the heavily working-class districts identified themselves as Democrats. Among those families in the same neighborhoods with a white-collar head of household (specifically in clerical, service, or sales), the Democratic identifications were still very high, at 72.7 percent (N = 55). In a more mixed context, only very small differences appeared between those segments.

One sharp exception to this pattern involved the managerial-professional group in the working-class neighborhoods. A small group, they were the most heavily Republican of all twelve categories in Huckfeldt's table (p. 110). That might be a function of the small number of cases involved (N = 19). Or, they could have been older, possibly even retired populations, who remained in the district after its population composition had changed.

The workers in the heavily middle-class districts tended to match their class, showing a strong Democratic tendency. This finding would be consonant with what has been observed in German cities where even in the best areas some SPD-KPD vote was found.

82. Lamar Cecil, *Albert Ballin: Business and Politics in Imperial Germany, 1888-1918*, Princeton: Princeton University Press, 1967, p. 93.

83. Ibid., pp. 32 ff.

84. Gerald D. Feldman, "German Business between War and Revolution: The Origins of the Stinnes-Legien Agreement," pp. 312-341 of Gerhard A. Ritter, ed., *Entstehung und Wandel der moderne Gesellschaft*, Berlin: Walter de Gruyter, 1970. See especially pp. 316-317. For more detail see Feldman's *Army, Industry and Labor in Germany, 1914-1918*, Princeton: Princeton University Press, 1966, chs. 1-5; and his "Economic and Social Problems of the German Demobilization, 1918-19," *Journal of Modern History*, 47 (1975): 1-47. For Ballin's reaction to this state intervention, see Cecil, *Albert Ballin*, pp. 324 ff.

85. These summary sentences cannot come near to describing the complexities of each event. Feldman's "German Business" provides the best overview of the entire new development. The opposition to Stinnes's arrangement is discussed on pp. 334 and 339. Some big business leaders were also annoyed by the fact that Stinnes had bypassed the established business organizations, using his personal contacts to accomplish his aim. Some felt that the effort was a reaction to the more extreme Berlin circumstances; in the calm of the provinces, they argued, such concessions were not necessary.

A brief summary history of German business organizations may be found in

Gerard Braunthal, *The Federation of German Industry in Politics*, Ithaca: Cornell University Press, 1965, ch. 1. Braunthal describes (p. 9) the newly formed RDI as "a superassociation of 26 trade groups, subdivided into 400 national associations and cartels, 58 regional and 70 local associations, over 1,000 individual members and firms, and 70 chambers of industry and commerce."

86. Feldman, "German Business," pp. 314-315.

87. Ibid., p. 318. Stinnes is described by Cecil as a friend of Ballin's. The relationship, especially in the wartime years, must have been a difficult one. Cecil notes that "Stinnes was a member of the HAPAG board during the war and had ambitions of entering the shipping business on his own. Ballin found the Rhinelander an entrepreneurial genius, but also crafty, grasping, and offensive. 'As some children cannot let alone a piece of cake, or some men a beautiful woman,' Ballin warned, 'so Stinnes cannot let business alone; he wants to make everything his own, even if it should happen to belong to someone else.'" *Albert Ballin*, p. 130.

88. Gerald D. Feldman, "The Social and Economic Policies of German Big Business, 1918-1929," *American Historical Review*, 75 (1969-1970): 47-55. The quotations are from p. 48.

One might easily assume that big business would have been satisfied with the old regime. But that was not entirely the case as these quotations indicate. Ballin was most contemptuous of the German Foreign Office, claiming among other things that it had no awareness of economic factors. His efforts to improve Anglo-German relations were sidetracked by Chancellor Bethmann-Hollweg because they went outside of the established chain of command. Ballin also complained bitterly that business had not been consulted about the war. See Cecil, *Albert Ballin*, pp. 123-126, 167-173, 244, and 295-296.

89. Feldman, "Social and Economic Policies," p. 48.

90. Gerald D. Feldman, "Big Business and the Kapp Putsch," *Central European History*, 4 (1971): 99-130. The quotations are from pp. 101-102.

91. Ibid., p. 102. For other similar views, see pp. 128 and 130.

92. Ibid., p. 105.

93. Ibid., p. 106.

94. Ibid., pp. 103, 106-107.

95. Ibid., pp. 108-111, 117.

96. Ibid., pp. 119 ff., 129.

97. Ibid., p. 128.

98. Henry Ashby Turner, Jr., "Big Business and the Rise of Hitler," *American Historical Review*, 75 (1969-1970): 56-70. The quotation appears on p. 57. For a summary discussion of big business gains and losses under the republic, see Feldman, "Social and Economic Policies," pp. 54-55.

99. Turner, "Big Business," p. 57.

100. Ibid., p. 62.

101. Ibid., p. 66. The bulk of the party's funds came from the monthly membership dues (graduated according to ability to pay), collections, and local money-raising activities, plus the entrance fees charged at meetings. A part of the money was retained at the local level, but the bulk of it was passed upward to the *Gau*

and Reich headquarters. For details about the early years of the party (based on documents made available at the time of Hitler's trial in March 1924), see Georg Franz-Willing, *Die Hitlerbewegung: Der Ursprung, 1919-1922*, Hamburg-Berlin: Decker's Verlag, 1962, pp. 177-198. For the comments of the one-time *Gauleiter* of Hamburg, see Albert Krebs, *Tendenzen und Gestalten der NSDAP: Erinnerungen an die Frühzeit der Partei*, Stuttgart: Deutsche Verlags-Anstalt, 1959, pp. 61, 174, and 183. The best available source on the party finances is Horst Matzerath and Henry A. Turner, "Die Selbstfinanzierung der NSDAP 1930-1932," *Geschichte und Gesellschaft*, 3 (1977): 59-92. This account is based on very detailed police reports dealing with the finances of the Rhineland *Gau* (including the city of Cologne). In the period from August 1930 to May 1931, the *Gau* took in 652,600 RM, 333,800 of which were passed on to Munich headquarters. Using Rhineland *Gau* figures as the basis for rough national estimates, Matzerath and Turner conclude that approximately 11.7 million RM were passed on to NSDAP national headquarters between June 1930 and May 1931. There was a slight decline in receipts in the following year, associated no doubt with the worsening depression, but even then the estimate is a sizable one, approximately 10.5 million RM.

The ghostwritten Thyssen memoir (to be discussed immediately in the text) has heavy industry contributions in this period running at two million marks a year. According to the stenographic record on which the book was based, however, what Thyssen actually said was that these contributions amounted to about one to two million marks. Furthermore, he gave no indication of the time span involved. Thus, even if the two-million annual support figure were correct (which is not the case), heavy industry's contributions to the party's national headquarters would have only amounted to about one-sixth of the total budget. Even the lower of Thyssen's figures, which would reduce heavy industry's contribution to one-twelfth of the party's budget, would overstate the contribution for any given year. In addition, one must remember, that at least as judged by the Rhineland *Gau*, there was no significant big business contribution to the local operation. That operation was entirely self-financed.

102. For this entire question see Turner's article, "Fritz Thyssen und 'I Paid Hitler,' " *Vierteljahrshefte für Zeitgeschichte*, 19 (1971): 225-244. The ghostwriters have Thyssen giving huge sums to the NSDAP over an extended period. Turner indicates that the sums were unrealistically large and that the period in question must have been much shorter than the book claims. Thyssen was a member of the DNVP, attending the party convention in September 1931, and was a DNVP city councilor in Mühlheim/Ruhr until January 1932. He did become a member of the NSDAP, but not until May of 1933 (p. 239).

One incident deserves special consideration. Sometime in the spring or summer of 1932, Thyssen arranged to have some 100,000 marks taken from the strike fund of one of the iron and steel industry's organizations and given to the National Socialist Walther Funk, neglecting to tell the other members of the organization of his action. Ernst Poensgen, a member of the board of the organization (and also a member of the board of Thyssen's firm) was outraged by this action, as was Krupp von Bohlen und Halbach. The end result was that

Thyssen was forced to pay the money back out of his own pocket (p. 236). The "Thyssen" work was published in New York in 1941 by Farrar and Rinehart. A British edition came out at the same time.

103. For Kirdorf, see Turner's article, "Emil Kirdorf and the Nazi Party," *Central European History*, 1 (1968): 324-344. Kirdorf was 80 years old when he joined the party. He no longer held office in any firms, hence, contrary to many claims, was not in a position to direct money from corporations to the NSDAP treasury. His personal fortune was limited, and his income declined with the onset of the depression. At that point he was giving his money to the DNVP.

104. Turner, "Big Business," pp. 59-60. See also John A. Leopold, *Alfred Hugenberg: The Radical Nationalist Campaign against the Weimar Republic*, New Haven: Yale University Press, 1977. Leopold's treatment of this question is somewhat equivocal. He does appear, nevertheless, to be in substantial agreement with Turner on the lack of documentary evidence showing financial support; see for example, p. 81.

105. See Turner, "Big Business," pp. 62-63. The cases mentioned are those of Friedrich Flick, a leader in Thyssen's firm, the Vereinigte Stahlwerke, and some officials of I.G. Farben. Both firms were particularly vulnerable to government actions, the former because of some questionable dealings, the Farben concern because of heavy investment in synthetic gasoline, the success of which depended on the maintenance of a high protective tariff. For further discussion of these cases, see Turner's essay, "Das Verhältnis des Grossunternehmertums zur NSDAP," in Hans Mommsen, Dietmar Petzina, and Bernd Weisbrod, eds., *Industrielles System und politische Entwicklung in der Weimarer Republik*, Düsseldorf: Droste Verlag, 1974, pp. 919-931. The complexities of business-government relations cannot be adequately dealt with in these few pages. Some of the complexities are considered in other articles in the Mommsen et al. volume. See also note 119, this chapter.

106. Turner, "Big Business," pp. 64-65. One of those supported for this reason was Gregor Strasser who, as previously noted, is generally viewed as a leading figure in the left wing of the party. This money was donated by the coal cartel, the man handling this matter being August Heinrichsbauer, the cartel's public relations man. In an account published in 1948, Heinrichsbauer reported that Strasser "enjoyed a splendid reputation" in the Ruhr. The cartel's aim was that of "strengthening the hands of persons and offices within the Party whose views were in contradiction to those of men like Goebbels and Göring." Cited in Louis P. Lochner, *Tycoons and Tyrant: German Industry from Hitler to Adenauer*, Chicago: Henry Regnery, 1954, p. 102. For the original, see August Heinrichsbauer, *Schwerindustrie und Politik*, Essen/Kettwig: West-Verlag, 1948, pp. 39-40.

Alfred Hugenberg was also favorably disposed toward Strasser, seeing him as the only "useful personality" in the NSDAP. See Kurt Koszyk, *Deutsche Presse 1914-1945*, Berlin: Colloquium Verlag, 1972, p. 235. Fritz Thyssen's original arrangement for the Düsseldorf Industrieklub speech involved an invitation to Strasser. Hitler then intervened and declared he would make the speech. Hugo Stinnes, Jr., considered Strasser the most promising candidate for the position of Prussian minister president and discussed the matter with him at some length in April of 1932; see Wolfgang Ruge, "Die 'Deutsche Allgemeine Zeitung' und die Brüning-Regierung," *Zeitschrift für Geschichtswissenschaft*, 16 (1968): 52n. The ultraconservative Berlin newspaper, the *Kreuzzeitung*, favored Strasser over Hitler in the internal struggle of December 1932; see Eva Pfeifer, *Das Hitlerbild im Spiegel einiger konservativen Zeitungen in den Jahren 1929-1933*, Munich: UNI-Druck, 1966 (originally a doctoral dissertation, University of Heidelberg, 1965), p. 136. The close links between Strasser and Ruhr industrialists are also indicated in Kissenkoetter, *Gregor Strasser*, pp. 124-127.

107. All the information presented here comes from Turner's article, "The *Ruhrlade*, Secret Cabinet of Heavy Industry in the Weimar Republic," *Central European History*, 3 (1970): 195-228.

108. Ibid., p. 210.

109. Ibid., pp. 212 ff. The newspaper in question was the *Deutsche Allgemeine Zeitung* (Berlin). There had been a possibility of the paper's coming into Hugenberg's possession at an earlier point, in 1927. To prevent that, a business consortium dominated by heavy industry bought it from the then owner, the German government, the matter being arranged by Foreign Minister Stresemann (p. 212). The other daily in which the Ruhrlade had an interest was the *Rheinisch-Westfälische Zeitung* of Essen. See Chapter 7 for information on its political direction and the discussion below for further details on its ownership and control.

110. Ibid., p. 215.

111. Ibid., pp. 216-217. For the parallel relationship of the Bergbau-Verein (the coal side) and the NSDAP, see Heinrichsbauer, *Schwerindustrie*, pp. 42 ff. Funk was placed in the party through Strasser to serve as a financial adviser to Hitler and other top party leaders. To provide him with the necessary freedom of action, he was supported by them to the extent of 1,000 marks a month. The Bergbau-Verein, according to Heinrichsbauer, gave 100,000 marks to the party for the July Reichstag election, this, he says, being especially for the purpose of strengthening Funk's position. Simultaneously, sums two and three times larger were given by that group to the three large bourgeois parties. Its dissatisfaction with the NSDAP caused the group to withhold all support for the party in the November election that year (p. 48). See also Kissenkoetter, *Gregor Strasser*, p. 126.

112. Turner, "The *Ruhrlade*," pp. 217-218. See also Kurt Koszyk, "Paul Reusch und die 'Münchner Neuesten Nachrichten,' " *Vierteljahrshefte für Zeitgeschichte*, 20 (1972): 75-103, especially pp. 79 ff.

113. Turner, "The *Ruhrlade*," pp. 219-220.

114. Ibid., p. 220.

115. See Kissenkoetter, *Gregor Strasser*, pp. 162 ff.

116. Turner, "The *Ruhrlade*," p. 223.

117. Ibid., p. 224.

118. Ibid., p. 225.

119. Ibid., p. 226. Not too surprisingly, the Turner findings have generated considerable controversy. Possibly the leading counterstatement is that of Dirk

Stegmann, "Zum Verhältnis von Grossindustrie und Nationalsozialismus 1930-1933," *Archiv für Sozialgeschichte*, 13 (1973): 399-482. Turner's response appears in his "Grossunternehmertum und Nationalsozialismus 1930-1933," *Historische Zeitschrift*, 221 (1972): 18-68.

Much of the evidence Stegmann presents is in substantial agreement with Turner's conclusion. This is especially the case with regard to the business role in political events up to the time of the November 1932 election. The two major areas of dispute involve their assessments of the role and significance of the Keppler circle and their judgments as to the meaning of a petition sent to Hindenburg by the Keppler group in support of Hitler's claim to the chancellorship.

Since members of the Keppler circle arranged the key meetings in January 1933 that brought about Hitler's accession, this group understandably has been the object of considerable attention. Hjalmar Schacht had organized a "work group," with industry support, at about the same time as the Keppler circle made its appearance, the latter being sponsored by the NSDAP. The basic point at dispute is whether the two were merged or coordinated. If they were merged, it would support the agent theory, that they were acting at the behest of big business. If not, then the circle was an agency of the party. In his comments, Turner provides a convincing case that they had *not* merged. "The *Ruhrlade*," pp. 30 ff., and 50 ff.

Moreover Turner shows that Keppler and his people were not representative of big business and that they in fact had very distant relations with the leading businessmen of the Ruhr. The presence of two key linking figures, Schacht and Vögler, does not contradict this conclusion. Schacht was in poor standing with industry at this point, and Vögler, who attended irregularly, appears to have played no serious role in the Keppler group. The arrangements for the Hitler-Papen meeting, moreover, were not made by the group but, with at least an attempt at secrecy, by two of its members, Keppler and Schroeder, two persons having very distant relationships with the upper echelons of the business world.

Stegmann stresses the number and prominence of those persons signing the petition. Turner notes the paucity of industrial leaders among those who signed. "The *Ruhrlade*, pp. 58 ff. Moreover, the original list of suggested or hoped-for signers is available, and the difference between the aspiration and the achievement is such as to support Turner. There is no question that the petition contained a wide range of prominent signators. That is consistent with the conclusion of this work, namely, that Hitler and the NSDAP had considerable support in upper- and upper-middle-class circles, but that was not the case within the executive committee of the bourgeoisie, even in late November.

Another work criticizing Turner is that of George Hallgarten and Joachim Radkau, *Deutsche Industrie und Politik von Bismarck bis Heute*, Cologne: Europäische Verlagsanstalt, 1974. But see the review by Kenneth D. Barkin, *Journal of Modern History*, 49 (1977): 512-516.

It is obviously impossible to provide a complete discussion of this complicated issue in these few pages. Stegmann has made another contribution to the subject in his "Antiquierte Personalisierung oder sozialökonomische Faschismus-Analyse?" *Archiv für Sozialgeschichte*, 17 (1977): 275-296. Another relevant source is the memoir of Otto Wagener (edited by Turner), *Hitler aus nächster Nahe: Aufzeichnungen eines Vertrauten, 1929-32*, Berlin: Ullstein Verlag, 1978. Turner's forthcoming book, *Big Business and the Rise of Hitler*, will treat all of the matters touched on here, plus many more, in considerable detail.

120. See, for example, Seymour Martin Lipset's early summary in *Political Man: The Social Bases of Politics*, Garden City: Doubleday, 1960, pp. 148-149.

121. Turner, "The *Ruhrlade*," p. 228.

122. Turner, "Big Business," p. 58.

123. In a letter of July 11, 1928, Reusch expressed his judgment of Hugenberg as follows: "I have followed the activities of this man for more than twenty years. [They] have not in any way been fruitful or useful for his party or for industry. On the contrary, I am and have always been of the opinion that Hugenberg's activity has caused enormous damage to western [i.e. Ruhr] industry. . . . If he nevertheless uses the platform of the *Bergbau* [coal] Association or of another western [i.e. Ruhr] economic organization, the impression would be [that] Hugenberg was the representative of the western industry. . . . I beg [you] to take into consideration that the appearance of Hugenberg at the present moment in a nonpolitical economic organization in all likelihood will have a harmful effect on such [an] organization." From Koszyk, *Deutsche Presse*, p. 223. A summary history of the Hugenberg operation is contained there on pp. 219-239.

Hugenberg had challenged Reusch (and the Haniel family) in 1925 in an attempt to gain control of the *Münchner Neueste Nachrichten*. Two years of struggle ensued. See Leopold, *Alfred Hugenberg*, pp. 16-17. For additional information on the attitudes of business leaders toward Hugenberg, see his pp. 80-81, 89, and 116-117. See also the Turner quotation in Chapter 2.

124. Turner, "The *Ruhrlade*," pp. 212-213. Even this means of communications was soon lost to the group. As noted earlier, the deficits were heavy, and they were seeking some solution to this continuing problem. In July 1932, the *DAZ* came into the hands of Hugo Stinnes, Jr. Turner says it was bestowed as a gift, the journal once having been owned by Stinnes's father. Stinnes, too, pressed the opposition to Brüning, and at this point there was nothing Klein could do but go along. For additional details on the *DAZ*, see Koszyk, *Deutsche Presse*, pp. 135-159. The business of Klein versus the Ruhrlade appears on pp. 158-159. For still more details, see Ruge, "Die 'Deutsche Allgemeine Zeitung.' " The name *Deutsche Allgemeine*, incidentally, was first adopted on November 12, 1918. Before then it was the *Norddeutsche Allgemeine Zeitung*. That newspaper had been a front for the government since Bismarck's time. See Robert H. Keyserlingk, *Media Manipulation: A Study of the Press and Bismarck in Imperial Germany*, Montreal: Renouf, 1977.

125. Ruge, "Die 'Deutsche Allgemeine Zeitung,' " p. 31. The same editorial is discussed by Koszyk, *Deutsche Presse*, p. 155. Nothing is indicated as to the source of this new supportive direction, that is, whether it was asked for by the owners or originated at the editorial level. There is also nothing reported as to whether the owners approved or disapproved of the solicitude for Hitler. For a more detailed review of the *DAZ*'s treatment of the NSDAP see Pfeifer, *Das*

Hitlerbild. For a brief summary of the *DAZ*'s (and three other conservative Berlin newspapers') treatment of the National Socialists, see the discussion in Chapter 4.

For evidence on press support and approval as it appeared in a smaller city, one not considered previously, see Klaus Kaiser, *Braunschweiger Presse und Nationalsozialismus. Der Aufstieg der NSDAP im Lande Braunschweig im Spiegel der Braunschweiger Tageszeitungen 1930 bis 1933*, Brunswick: Waisenhaus–Buchdruckerei und Verlag, 1970.

The leading bourgeois newspaper of Brunswick was the *Braunschweigische Landeszeitung.* It provided the strongest support for the National Socialists of any of the newspapers reviewed in this study. In the presidential election of 1932, it declared itself as an "enemy of the system" and as unable to support Hindenburg. Kaiser, *Braunschewiger Presse*, pp. 92-93. The front-page recommendation was: "Do Your National Duty: Vote Adolf Hitler." Hitler did rather well in this city, gaining 46.3 percent (as against 36.8 percent in the nation). It will be remembered that he and his party generally did less well in the cities. These figures are from Ernst-August Roloff, *Bürgertum und Nationalsozialismus 1930-1933: Braunschweigs Weg ins Dritte Reich*, Hanover: Verlag für Literatur und Zeitgeschehen, 1961, p. 103.

126. Koszyk, *Deutsche Presse*, pp. 190 ff. See also Koszyk's article "Paul Reusch," which contains some relevant documents; and Turner, "The *Ruhrlade*," pp. 217-218.

127. See Turner, "The *Ruhrlade*," p. 218; Koszyk, *Deutsche Presse*, pp. 195 ff.

128. Reusch requested that the newspaper work out directives for the treatment of news stories. This request was ignored with the result that Reusch developed his own proposals. An alternative version was then worked up by the newspaper, a proposal that omitted reference to many of Reusch's most pressing concerns. The final version, from May of 1932, may be found in Koszyk, "Paul Reusch," pp. 90-93. This document states very explicitly what a key figure of German industry demanded at this time. The *MNN* should conduct itself as objectively as possible with respect to all national parties; it should attack Marxism with all means (*auf das Schärfste*); it should cultivate the monarchist tradition (although not an immediate restoration). The key demands with regard to constitutional arrangements were the following: "The democratic parliamentary system of Weimar is the last root of many evils. It is to be rejected as unsuited for Germany." And, as an alternative: "The *MNN*, seeks therefore: (a) a considerable strengthening of the position of the president of the Reich; (b) a strengthening of the government of the Reich in the sense that the fall of the government through the Reichstag be made considerably more difficult." As for their position vis-à-vis parties, he demanded that "coalitions with the Social Democrats . . . be rejected on principle, those with the National Socialists . . . encouraged on principle. From the National Socialists it is to be demanded that they console themselves with the recognition of the political necessities and not make any excessive demands." It will be noted that the newpaper violated Reusch's demand with respect to constitutional reform in the following month.

129. Koszyk, *Deutsche Presse*, pp. 197, 200. In the following weeks, it should be noted, although he no longer had any official connection with the newspaper, Reusch did intervene on behalf of *MNN* staff members who had been arrested by the new government.

One factor making it difficult for Reusch to maintain supervision of the newspaper's editorial content was the sheer amount of time it took. With all his other obligations, he could not find the time to read the newspaper on a regular basis. He depended on one of his correspondents, Oswald Spengler, to keep him informed about the *MNN*'s performance. In May of 1932, Spengler wrote to tell him that hardly a day went by without the *MNN* bringing some nasty (*abfällige*) comment about the NSDAP and that there was no equivalent treatment of the SPD.

130. See Turner, "Das Verhältnis," p. 930.

131. The independence is unexpected from the perspective of those who see bureaucratic structures having monocratic control. The image of editors and journalists as helpless pawns may be set in contrast to other possibilities, the most important of which is the notion of the professional journalist with at least some degree of autonomy and personal integrity. This is not to suggest that all journalists were engaged in an underground campaign against the demands of their conservative owners. Reusch had problems with the *MNN*, a journal with at least some elements of a left liberal tradition. No problems of this sort appear to have arisen in his relations with the *Schwäbischer Merkur* or the *Fränkischer Kurier*.

132. In the 1890s, Reismann-Grone had merged some Ruhr dailies to form the *RWZ* and, as of 1903, was sole owner of the newspaper. He was an ardent nationalist, and was early involved in the Alldeutscher Verband (Pan German Association). In the twenties he served as a political adviser to the Bergbau-Verein.

Reismann-Grone's personal links to the National Socialists are well established (although the extent of the connection was not generally known at the time). He was in correspondence with Hitler from about 1926 and met him for the first time either in 1928 or, more likely, in 1930. In December 1927, his daughter married a young journalist, Otto Dietrich, who later became Hitler's press secretary. Otto Wagener, moreover, relates his discussions with Reismann-Grone in connection with the launching of an NSDAP newspaper, the *Essener National-Zeitung*, where Dietrich was for a time employed. Henry A. Turner, who brought these facts to my attention (letters of July 9 and September 1, 1975), reports that Reismann-Grone is listed as an NSDAP party member in the files of the Berlin Document Center. That membership, dated January 1, 1930, was not in the local group but rather in an arrangement called Ortsgruppe Braunes Haus, a fiction that allowed "fine" people to join the party without having contact with its local members. It could also be used to keep memberships hidden. Turner reports that he has found nothing in the papers of the Ruhrlade members to indicate that they knew Reismann-Grone to be a party member. Even Wagener, who was negotiating with him later in 1930, indicates no awareness that he was a member.

Reismann-Grone's firm experienced financial difficulties in the twenties, and it was then that the Bergbau-Verein bought into it, leaving him with only a minority of the shares and his continuing position as business manager. Early in 1930, over his objections, these owners brought a new editor-in-chief, Eugen Mündler, to the newspaper. The new owners imposed other demands on Reismann-Grone, among these that the paper support the moderate Konservative Volkspartei (a split-off from the DNVP) in the September 1930 Reichstag election. In mid-year, 1932, a serious conflict arose between Reismann-Grone and Mündler over the question of support for the Papen government. Reismann-Grone, obviously, opposed that commitment. The discussion came to the newspaper's board (*Beirat*), and the two members of the Bergbau-Verein present sided with Mündler. A few days later, Reismann-Grone severed all connections with the newspaper.

Reismann-Grone's "expropriation" has been mentioned in several sources. The best account, however, is that by Klaus Werner Schmidt, "Die 'Rheinisch-Westfälische Zeitung' und ihr Verleger Reismann-Grone," *Beiträge zur Geschichte Dortmunds und der Grafschaft Mark*, 69 (1974): especially 356-364.

133. The Hohenzollern involvements are reviewed in Karl Dietrich Bracher, *Die Auflösung der Weimarer Republik*, Villingen/Schwarzwald: Ring-Verlag, 1964, pp. 120 and 546. See also pp. 114, 714, and 715. Erich Eyck also reports on the crown prince's solicitude for the National Socialists, *Geschichte der Weimarer Republik*. Erlenbach-Zurich: Eugen Rentsch Verlag, 1956, vol. 2, p. 458.

134. Most discussions of deference voting are focused on working-class populations, specifically on the so-called Tory workers, those with a trained (or irrational) respect for the symbols and persons of traditional or established authority; see, for example, McKenzie and Silver, *Angels in Marble*; or Nordlinger, *Working Class Tories*. But the same kinds of training occur elsewhere in the society; not all upper- and upper-middle-class voters, after all, are rational, aware, and issue oriented.

135. Much of the literature cited in connection with the cultural argument about the origins of National Socialism is of such an abstruse character that it would have been accessible only to highly literate segments of the population. That would ordinarily mean persons in the upper and upper middle classes. This is a difficult conclusion for some people to accept, especially for those who came of age after World War II. It seems almost unnatural that a highly educated segment of the population could be taken in by such patent nonsense. But that reaction is based on later experience, on the North American experience of the 1950s and 1960s where many studies have shown education and tolerance to be closely related. But in Weimar Germany, and possibly in the entire previous century, the educated classes appear to have been very *intolerant* classes. This has been indicated, at many points in the present text, by the linkage of anti-Semitism with the universities and the fraternities. For some fragmentary evidence showing the presence of anti-Semitic literature and enthusiasm among well-off segments of the population, see George Mosse's work, *The Crisis of German Ideology: Intellectual Origins of the Third Reich*, New York: Grosset and Dunlap, 1964. Although this work speaks repeatedly of lower-middle-class sus-

ceptibilities, the hard evidence cited there shows links to the better-off populations; see pp. 143-144, 196-197.

136. Many Jewish voters, those who had previously supported the German
Democrats, would also have been motivated to find a second-best option. Some
survivors and exiles from Hitler's Germany report shifts to the Zentrum.

137. See Heinrichsbauer, *Schwerindustrie*, p. 36 on this point.

138. See Kele, *Nazis and Workers*, especially ch. 6. for discussion of the NSDAP's
antibourgeois effort. See also Hitler's definition of socialism in note 77, this
chapter.

Some of Hitler's antibourgeois vituperation appears in David Schoenbaum,
Hitler's Social Revolution, p. 19. This begins with his statement that "our
bourgeoisie is already worthless for any noble human endeavor." Goebbels (on
p. 29 of this work) is said to have referred to his bourgeois opponents as a
"stinking dung heap."

139. The observations made in this paragraph are based on conversations with
various people who had lived in the "better" districts in the Weimar period.
Most of them were in their seventies when I spoke with them. There would,
of course, have been differences in their awareness of events taking place when
they were coming of age. And there must also have been some difficulties or
distortion in recollection. There was, however, a general agreement on the points
reported here. The radio would have provided only a limited alternative source
of information for most people at that time. See Hans Bausch, *Der Rundfunk im
politischen Kräftespiel der Weimarer Republik, 1923-1933*, Tübingen: J.C.B. Mohr-
Paul Siebeck, 1956.

140. A slogan repeated with considerable frequency when people were asked
about this subject was: *Ein politisches Lied, ein garstiges Lied* (a political song, a
loathsome song).

141. The meetings in the upper- and upper-middle-class districts would have
had a different character from those in the working-class districts. Where the
latter were intended as provocations leading to fights that in turn would gain
the party newspaper attention, direct communication seems to have been the
intent in the former. See, for example, Krebs's description of the local group in
well-off Rotherbaum in Hamburg in "The Question of Linkages," Chapter 5.

142. This notion is taken from Berelson, Lazarsfeld, and McPhee, *Voting*, pp.
109-114.

143. One such high-status notable who gave his approval to National Socialist
aspirations was General Hans von Seeckt, the former commander in chief of the
Reichswehr. Shortly after the September 1930 election, the *Deutsche Allgemeine
Zeitung* asked a number of leading personalities how they viewed the possibility
of Hitler's participation in a government. Seeckt indicated strong support for
the suggestion: "That which forms the true center in this movement," he stated,
"the national feeling, the fighting spirit [*Wehrwille*], the social understanding,
all carried with a youthful reform-seeking enthusiasm, all these elements are an
essential part of the government of the future." Quoted in Pfeifer, *Das Hitlerbild*, p. 16.

144. National Socialist histories focus on the struggle against Marxists as the

center of their activities. See J. K. von Engelbrechten on Berlin, *Eine braune Armee Entsteht: Die Geschichte der Berliner-Brandenburger SA*, Munich: Zentralverlag der NDSAP, 1940. For Hamburg, see Hermann Okrass, *Das Ende einer Parole—"Hamburg bleibt rot,"* Hamburg: Hanseatische Verlagsanstalt, 1934.

145. This sense of threat infected other observers as well. Louis Lochner, head of the Berlin office of the Associated Press at the time, later commented that "Communism was dangerously on the increase." *Tycoons and Tyrants*, p. 5.

FOURTEEN. THE WEIMAR CATASTROPHE

1. See Chapters 1 and 2. The most self-assured statement of this position I have yet encountered is provided by a Polish historian, Jakub Banaszkiewicz, who declares that "the association of the petty bourgeois with the Nazi movement is a generally known and recognized fact. . . . all prominent historians and sociologists of the fascist movement agree that the social base of the Nazi party consisted of various segments of the petty bourgeois. . . . This subject has . . . been almost completely exhausted and it would be difficult to advance any new facts or propositions." His statement is quoted from J. Paul Madden, "The Social Composition of the Nazi Party, 1919-1930," Ph.D. dissertation, University of Oklahoma, 1976, p. 9. The original source is given as: "German Fascism and People on the Social Fringe," *Polish Western Affairs*, 8 (August 1967): 251-288. Madden notes that Banaszkiewicz "does not define 'petty bourgeois' or offer any proof for his contentions. Rather, he attempts to analyze the social structure of the Nazi party through speculation, without the benefit of original research." Madden's own review of the literature on the lower-middle-class thesis concludes with these words (p. 14): "Of all the 'common knowledge' about the Nazis, the lower-middle class hypothesis is the most popular, the most enduring, and the most convincing. However, it has yet to be proven conclusively."

2. This summary conclusion overlooks one rather striking exception, namely, the free port area of the Hamburg harbor. But no generalization can be based on that experience, and, as we have seen, the district went heavily to the Social Democrats.

3. The pattern in Düsseldorf appears to be one of no difference between nonmanual districts although some additional research on the rather heterogeneous subareas there would be useful. Wuppertal too appears to be a case of no difference. For the complexities of that case, see Chapter 7.

4. For more detailed consideration of this argument, see my *Class and Politics in the United States*, New York: John Wiley & Sons, 1972, pp. 46-49; and my *Restraining Myths: Critical Studies of U.S. Social Structure and Politics*, New York: Sage-Halsted-Wiley, 1975, chs. 5 and 6.

5. When the implications are put this directly, it is easy to claim that the theory was never intended to be quite so sweeping in its coverage: of course, there would be some exceptions, some other factors operating. But the telling point about the intentions of these theorists is the absence of any discussion of specifications. One looks far and wide to find consideration of differentiations; there are, typically, no specifications by ethnicity, by religion, by class origins,

by geographic origins; there is no discussion of age or sex. For these theorists class position is *the* decisive factor. The power of the class determinant outweighs all those other factors; it eradicates whatever importance those other factors might have had.

C. Wright Mills offered a brief discussion of social origins, noting that many white-collar workers came from working-class backgrounds. But having made the observation, he just as quickly left it; he made no suggestion that they might be different from other white-collar workers. In some unspecified way, they presumably picked up that distinctive middle-class psychology and thus acquired the same feeling of loss and stress felt by those born and raised in the class. There is an obvious omission here; it is not clear how—or why—they would have adopted this new and different outlook. See Mills's *White Collar*, New York: Oxford University Press, 1951, pp. 272-273, 297.

6. See, for example, that presented by David Schoenbaum, *Hitler's Social Revolution: Class and Status in Nazi Germany 1933-1939*, Garden City: Double-day-Anchor, 1967, pp. 3-4. The two tables contained there provide data covering the period from 1882 to 1933. Unambiguous declines of the farm sector and the independent category are indicated over the entire period, the latter falling from 38 percent to 20 percent over the half-century. While this is a dramatic long-term shift, it is easy to overlook the more relevant detail. The rate of change had slowed down toward the end of that period; between 1925 and 1933, the decline amounted to a single percentage point.

7. Ibid., pp. 166 ff.

8. These arguments are elaborated in more detail and backed with supporting evidence from the United States in my article: "The Marginal Middle Class: A Reconsideration," *American Sociological Review*, 31 (1966): 192-199. See also my *Class and Politics*, chs. 4, 9, and 10. For some consideration of these points in the context of post–World War II Germany, see my "Einkommen und Klassenstruktur: Der Fall der Bundesrepublik," *Kölner Zeitschrift für Soziologie und Sozialpsychologie*, 20 (1968): 250-287.

9. Consider the following example drawn from the United States. A study of the incomes of one segment of the lower middle class, New York City high school teachers, found their incomes in 1934, when corrected for changes in the consumer price levels, had increased by more than 25 percent over 1929 earnings. This gain in real income occurred at a time when their nominal salaries, as in Germany, had declined. The author concludes that "employed teachers were unlikely to be dissatisfied with their salaries." He quotes one teacher as follows: "Most of us were brought up in a period when we were very grateful to have a job. In the depression . . . a teacher on maximum earning $4,500 a year was a prince or a princess. Nobody earned that sort of money. When I got my job in 1937, the top salary of a teacher was $4,500. There were no taxes. It was a great deal of money. I didn't know anybody at that time earning that kind of money." That is a far cry from the assumption of imminent proletarianization and consequent anxiety. It is one case, to be sure, but the real income figures have general relevance, extending as we have seen also to the German scene. This example in addition makes clear the need for another very important

line of differentiation in any discussion of the lower middle class, the distinction between the employed and those not so fortunate. This case study is taken from Stephen Cole, *The Unionization of Teachers*, New York: Praeger, 1969, pp. 22-25. For relevant German data, see note 22, Chapter 2.

10. The paucity of direct evidence on people's reactions to their conditions is indicated in one of the leading dissertations dealing with changes in the white-collar ranks. The author reported a conversation of salesgirls that was overheard by a professor. In the dissertation, that would amount to a second-hand report of a casual conversation. See note 31, Chapter 3.

11. This finding was clear in the earliest published results. Still, apart from an occasional passing recognition of the fact, there has been little integration of that finding in the analyses. The religious factor disappears once again in favor of a general treatment of lower-middle-class distress.

12. Some readers will remember Heberle's finding of extremely high NSDAP support in Schleswig-Holstein's Geest district, a district of small farms, that being contrasted with the Marsch districts, an area with larger farms, a larger Conservative vote, and lower NSDAP voting. But it will also be remembered (see Chapter 3) that the NSDAP vote in the latter areas still ran at a high 67.2 percent and the Conservative vote amounted to only 6.1 percent. One cannot assume that the Conservative vote, in its entirety, came from the larger farmers.

13. Here too the argument involves the imposition of a framework on rather recalcitrant data. In this case the read-in is even more surprising since the logic of the argument would entail upper- and upper-middle-class support for the party. Although the urban evidence is certainly consonant with that logic, most formulations of the left view continue to lay the blame on the lower middle class. One modest exception to this generalization is the rarely cited work of S. Erkner, "NSDAP und die Klassen," *Die Internationale*, 14 (1931): 323-333.

14. Two cases tending to challenge this generalization were those of the *Rheinisch-Westfälische Zeitung* (Essen) and the *Bergisch-Märkische Zeitung* (Wuppertal), both of which were then under the direction of Theodor Reismann-Grone (see the discussion in Chapter 13). The latter newspaper was not ambiguous in its recommendation, only indirect; the recommendation "No Vote for Hindenburg," given the alternatives, could only be taken as a recommendation for Hitler. Reismann-Grone, as we have seen, was later removed by the big business owners of the enterprise.

The only city newspaper discovered in my review of the literature that made a direct recommendation for Hitler was the *Braunschweigische Landeszeitung*; see note 125, Chapter 13. There were, no doubt, others that did so, especially in smaller communities.

15. Henry Ashby Turner, Jr., "Big Business and the Rise of Hitler," *American Historical Review*, 75 (1969): 66; and his "Grossunternehmertum und National-sozialismus 1930-1933: Kritisches und Ergänzendes zu zwei neuen Forschungs-beiträgen," *Historische Zeitschrift*, 221 (1975): 58-60.

16. On Schröder, Schacht, and the Keppler circle, see Turner, "Grossunternehmertum," pp. 30 ff.

17. Karl Dietrich Bracher, *The German Dictatorship: The Origins, Structure, and*

Effects of National Socialism, New York: Praeger, 1970, p. 218. This event is discussed at greater length in Louis P. Lochner, *Tycoons and Tyrant: German Industry from Hitler to Adenauer*, Chicago: Henry Regnery, 1954, pp. 143-147. Two first-hand accounts of the meeting appear in Dirk Stegmann, "Zum Verhältnis von Grossindustrie und Nationalsozialismus 1930-1933," *Archiv für Sozialgeschichte*, 13 (1973): 477-481.

18. This process is treated at some length in Lochner, *Tycoons and Tyrant*, ch. 8. See also Karl Dietrich Bracher, Wolfgang Sauer, and Gerhard Schulz, *Die nationalsozialistische Machtergreifung*, 2d ed., Cologne/Opladen: Westdeutscher Verlag, 1962, pp. 186 ff., 199-214.

19. From Reusch's letter to Jakob Herle, dated July 20, 1933. This excerpt appears in Stegmann, "Zum Verhältnis," p. 482. An excerpt from Herle's reply also appears there, a reply that paints a more optimistic picture of the recent changes. But for the rest of the history, see the following paragraphs of the text.

Additional details on the *Gleichschaltung*, on the subordination of big business, appear in Udo Wengst, "Der Reichsverband der deutschen Industrie in den ersten Monaten des Dritten Reiches: Ein Beitrag zum Verhältnis von Grossindustrie und Nationalsocialismus," *Vierteljahrshefte für Zeitgeschichte*, 28 (1980): 94-110.

20. Schoenbaum, *Hitler's Social Revolution*, pp. 143-144.

21. Ibid. The role of armaments in Germany's economic recovery in 1933-1938 is frequently exaggerated. One leading work on the subject states that "the scale of Germany's economic mobilization for war was quite modest. . . . A basic reason . . . is simply that their war plan did not require such a large effort." The plan called for piecemeal acquisitions (not a general war), those to be accomplished by the blitzkrieg. See Burton H. Klein, *Germany's Economic Preparation for War*, Cambridge, Mass.: Harvard University Press, 1959, p. 78; and Alan S. Milward, *The German Economy at War*, London: Athlone Press, 1965.

22. Schoenbaum, *Hitler's Social Revolution*, p. 145.

23. Ibid., p. 128. A much more detailed account appears in Matthias Riedel, *Eisen und Kohle für das Dritte Reich*, Göttingen: Musterschmidt, 1973. Much of Schoenbaum's account, incidentally, is based on René Erbe, *Die nationalsozialistische Wirtschaftspolitik im Lichte der modernen Theorie*, Zurich: Polygraphischer Verlag, 1958.

The conclusion that business was not in control does not mean that it was to be counted among the victims of the National Socialist regime. Big business leaders did better economically than farmers, workers, or small businessmen. They most certainly fared better than the enemies of National Socialism. The key to success in the regime was cooperation, the will (and the ability) to "be of service," The giant of the chemical industry, I.G. Farben, had very good relations with the government. With its ability to manufacture synthetic products, it was the key agency in the plans to achieve autarchy. For the most part, it was very cooperative, unlike the sometimes recalcitrant steel industry. When business opposed the government, as with the steel industry or as was ultimately the case with Fritz Thyssen, it was helpless. For an account of the chemical combine's activities see Joseph Borkin, *The Crime and Punishment of I.G. Farben*, New York: The Free Press, 1978.

24. T.W. Mason, "The Primacy of Politics—Politics and Economics in National Socialist Germany," in Henry Ashby Turner, Jr., ed., *Nazism and the Third Reich*, New York: Quadrangle Books, 1972, p. 190. Also of some relevance is the essay by Alan Bullock, "Hitler and the Origins of the Second World War," pp. 219-246 of the same volume.

25. The whole concept of rootedness, the beginning point of the mass-society analysis, lacks a solid empirical basis. One typically begins with the plausible assumption that small-town and rural conditions mean rootedness and that big cities mean uprootedness. But that, as we have seen, is open to some question. Only 25 percent of Thalburg's population of 10,000, for example, had been born there. A 1905 census found that 45.6 percent of the population of Essen, which grew rapidly in the nineteenth century, had been born there. That still left a majority who came from some other place. But it is not as if all of those migrants were recent arrivals totally lacking personal contact. Clearly, many of them might have rerooted themselves within the metropolis.

A large part of the people coming from outside the city came from the immediately surrounding countryside. It seems likely that they would not only have maintained contact with friends and kinsmen there, but migrated to the city with friends and kinsmen. Much of the specter of urban growth, moreover, did not involve uprooting at all; it stemmed from annexation, a process that does not disturb existing social networks. See note 3, Chapter 7, for discussion of the Essen case.

26. The likely media effects have been covered in the previous chapters, particularly Chapters 4-8. Some other likely effects are indicated in Modris Eksteins, *The Limits of Reason: The German Democratic Press and the Collapse of Weimar Democracy*, London: Oxford University Press, 1975. The collapse of the old regime in the fall of 1918, frequently laid to the efforts of left activists, may also have been aided by the comments of the *Berliner Tageblatt*, the third largest newspaper in the nation. Conservatives (and anti-Semites) placed a large share of the blame for the stab in the back on the *Tageblatt*.

The German Democratic party, we have seen, began its brief history with a stunning victory in the January 1919 election. That has been explained in terms of the personal reactions of many voters, who wished an insurance policy against the forces of the left. But that avoids the question of why hundreds of thousands of voters saw the DDP as providing that insurance policy. Eksteins indicates that many former right liberal newspapers shifted position, some immediately after the collapse, and supported this new party. The *Münchner Neueste Nachrichten* was among the journals making the shift, abandoning its former National Liberal position (pp. 334-339).

The subsequent decline of the DDP is then linked to the subsequent defection of many of these same journals. Some returned to their former right liberal position, this time to the DVP. Others, recognizing a decline of both liberal parties, backed off and adopted an above-party stand, this so as to not offend any advertisers. DDP party leaders attributed their loss in the May 1924 Reichstag election to their loss of press support. They had lost almost all newspaper backing in the areas east of the Elbe. The party leaders placed a heavy emphasis on the press role because their best showings came in those cities with a reliable press (pp. 77-78, and 87-90).

Eventually, even prominent left liberal journals came to criticize the party, at best providing it with rather disdainful *faute de mieux* support. Party leaders were very bitter about this, especially in the case of the *Berliner Tageblatt* and its famed editor, Theodor Wolff. His criticism was all the more painful because he was a brilliant stylist and political commentator and because he was, for all practical purposes, the founder of the party.

Stresemann's party suffered much the same fate as the DDP. It found itself with no representation in much of east Elbian Prussia, either through defection or through neutralization of the once supportive press (p.87).

Eksteins also reiterates a conclusion stressed at numerous points throughout this work when he says that "the Nationalist press . . . provided a great service to Hitler" (p. 86). It is rather surprising, in view of these observations, that Eksteins later rejects the conclusion that the press was an "independent political power" (p. 137). His reasons for that conclusion are far from convincing. He has provided a plausible case *for* the press-influence hypothesis. If there were serious grounds for doubt, a more appropriate conclusion would be that the case has not been adequately established. In any event, his review of party-press relations in Weimar does provide a set of hypotheses that could be taken as a beginning point for a more definitive research effort.

27. Most leftist readings of contemporary capitalist societies assume a bureaucratic chain of command. Newspaper owners control or dominate their subordinate employees. The *Frankfurter Zeitung* provides an interesting contrary case. The principal editors formed a collegial body that controlled all editorial matters. Unexpectedly (at least from the left or critical vantage point), the *Frankfurter Zeitung* accepted the 1918 revolution and called on the progressive bourgeoisie to join with it. The new Germany, they argued, "must be radical and socialist to the core!" Viewing Theodor Wolff and the DDP as not radical enough, they demanded "extensive socialization." The owners of the newspaper did recognize that this *Revolutionsschwärmerei* (revolutionary enthusiasm) was detrimental to the newspaper's interests (and to those of the entire bourgeoisie). But their talents and interests lay in other fields and nothing was done to control those tendencies. As one person put it, the whole Simon family was "far too good-natured" to be good businessmen. Eksteins, *The Limits of Reason*, pp. 122 ff.

28. Even Hugenberg, who had a much better financial position than most publishers, we are told, "continually expounded the theme that the press had to be viewed as a business enterprise and could not function as an appendage of the party and thus run the risk of 'squandering money unnecessarily.' " See John A. Leopold, *Alfred Hugenberg: The Radical Nationalist Campaign against the Weimar Republic*, New Haven: Yale University Press, 1977, p. 192.

29. On occasion, one finds differentiation within the same organization. The Leonhardt concern owned three newspapers in Brunswick. One of these (see

note 125, Chapter 13) was openly pro-Hitler. The other two, with larger circulations, were anti-Marxist in orientation, but otherwise above party.

30. The phrases quoted here are from Hannah Arendt, *The Origins of Totalitarianism*, New York: World-Meridian, 1958, pp. 317-318.

31. This is not to say that the elements of the school position are wrong. The problem is one of rigid or inappropriate application. The position has both static and dynamic elements. Those commentators discounting the possibility of significant media impacts have focused only on the static elements, neglecting the conditions or situations that would lead to change or realignment. The balance of forces in Weimar Germany appear to have been very different from those in the United States with the destabilizing (or realigning) factors having much greater importance. Almost the entire fourteen years of the Weimar history were characterized by events that would severely test any party loyalties. For some sense of the differences, one might contrast the events facing Germany's chancellors in the early twenties with those facing the American presidents Harding and Coolidge.

The school position on media effects is stated in Joseph T. Klapper, *The Effects of Mass Communication*, Glencoe: The Free Press, 1960. The related political studies, those associated with Paul F. Lazarsfeld and Bernard Berelson, are discussed immediately in the text. For discussion of electoral changes, see V. O. Key, Jr., "A Theory of Critical Elections," *Journal of Politics*, 17 (1955): 3-18; and his "Secular Re-alignment and the Party System," *Journal of Politics*, 21 (1959): 198-210. Also of some interest in this connection, discussing changes in the American party system, is the work of William Nisbet Chambers and Walter Dean Burnham, eds., *The American Party Systems: Stages of Political Development*, New York: Oxford University Press, 1967. The German situation in the twenties was probably much more akin to that of France in the Fourth Republic. Most of the parties there were new, and there were many disrupting events. Voters appeared to be guided more by a general *tendance* than by specific party loyalties. See Philip E. Converse and Georges Dupeux, "Politicization of the Electorate in France and the United States," ch. 14 of Angus Campbell, Philip E. Converse, Warren E. Miller, and Donald E. Stokes, *Elections and the Political Order*, New York: John Wiley & Sons, 1966.

32. This by no means exhausts the theories that have been used to account for the development of National Socialism. In terms of importance or influence, the fourth theory would have to be the cultural explanation. This position argues that Germany had a uniquely poisonous culture. Significant portions of the nation's population were trained in ways that ultimately led to Hitler and to the later crimes. Many authors are named and discussed in such accounts, the influence of one being added to that of another in a later generation with the entire process culminating in the Third Reich. Among those typically reviewed in the process are: Luther, Fichte, Hegel, Treitschke, Wagner, and Nietzsche. A host of lesser figures, literati of a second rank, also appears.

The principal difficulties with this argument are the same as those afflicting the previous theories. There is, first of all, a lack of fit between the requirements of this theory and the actual voting results. Overlooked in most of these accounts is the fundamental division between Protestant and Catholic Germany, the assumption being that German culture had a uniform influence throughout the society. One could save the theory, at least temporarily, by noting that few of these figures were Catholics, almost all of them being either closely linked to Protestant Germany or renegades from the Catholic ranks.

But even with that correction, the theory does not stand up well. In a very general way, it will be noted that, both then and now, literacy and its correlates vary directly with city size while support for National Socialism, as we have seen, varied inversely with size of place. The National Socialist impact, in short, was greatest in those areas where this culture was likely to have had least influence. From one perspective that is in no way surprising. A farmer who was desperately concerned with the price of potatoes was hardly likely, under any circumstances, to be concerned with a crisis of culture. It is not as if, after putting in a day's work plowing the fields, he would come home to an evening's reading of, say, *Rembrandt als Erzieher*.

Ordinarily, one would not assume the urban lower middle class to be major consumers of this somewhat recherché culture. But some proponents of the cultural theory have argued a lower-middle-class attraction to the NSDAP because of some such cultural stimulus. That argument, however, given the urban voting results, appears to be mistaken. The most appropriate setting for cultural arguments, in most times and places, would be among the urban educated upper and upper middle classes. And there, perhaps unbeknown to many of the exponents of this position, the theory does appear to have considerable relevance, because in that setting, as we have seen, one found the greatest attraction to National Socialism (see note 135, Chapter 13).

One does not have to assume that the more limited move to the NSDAP among the lower middle classes was due to cultural causes. That might or might not have been the case. Like the farmers, they too were probably moved by much more pressing issues. But, in any event, it is an empirical question, one to be researched (as best one can at this late date), rather than one to be simply declared. The research here has indicated a frequency distribution, with most of the mixed districts providing only minority support for the NSDAP. One would, accordingly, have to explain why the culture moved some and left others, possibly the majority, unmoved. A key problem for the cultural argument, in short, is to explain the limits of its impact.

33. The leading work in this tradition is that of Bernard R. Berelson, Paul F. Lazarsfeld, and William N. McPhee, *Voting: A Study of Opinion Formation in a Presidential Campaign*, Chicago: University of Chicago Press, 1954; see especially ch. 6. Another important work in this tradition is that of Elihu Katz and Paul F. Lazarsfeld, *Personal Influence*, Glencoe: The Free Press, 1955. The works cited in note 31, this chapter, are also relevant. A major historical study written from this perspective is that of Lee Benson, *The Concept of Jacksonian Democracy: New York as a Test Case*, Princeton: Princeton University Press, 1961. For further discussion of this position, including consideration of its relationship to the mass-society theory, see my *Class and Politics* pp. 49-63.

34. Some theorists, especially those in the pluralist tradition, make much of

the mixing processes of modern society and of the cross-pressures that result. But most of the misplacement that occurs in the society would occur when children first leave the parental family. At that point they have low incomes and only limited ability to choose their environment. The rest of their lives, however, allows for a sorting out, for the choosing of friends and of "better" neighborhoods. The original Berelson, Lazarsfeld, and McPhee study provides some data consonant with this assumption. In a chart entitled "Political Homogeneity Increases with Age," they show that 53 percent of the respondents of ages 21 to 25 had the same politics as their three closest friends. Among those age 26 to 34, the percentage was up to 69; it rose still higher in the older age categories. *Voting*, p. 97.

35. Such micro studies are very rare. One brilliant study of such events is that of Sven Rydenfelt, *Kommunismen i Sverige. En Samhällsvetenskaplig Studie*, Lund: Gleerupska Universitetsbokhandeln, 1954. An English-language summary by W. Phillips Davison appears in the *Public Opinion Quarterly*, 18 (1954): 375-388.

36. Henry Valen and Daniel Katz, *Political Parties in Norway*, London: Tavistock Publications, 1964, pp. 29-30.

37. Sten S. Nilson, "Wahlsoziologische Probleme des Nationalsozialismus," *Zeitschrift für die gesamte Staatswissenschaft*, 110 (1954), particularly pp. 295-311. See also Timothy Alan Tilton, *Nazism, Neo-Nazism, and the Peasantry*, Bloomington: Indiana University Press, 1975, pp. 46-50, for comparison also with Denmark and Sweden.

38. S. M. Lipset, *Agrarian Socialism: The Cooperative Commonwealth Federation in Saskatchewan*, Berkeley: University of California Press, 1950.

The importance of the personal-influence factor in Germany is attested to by still another consideration. In the small and (presumably) well-integrated communities, one would ordinarily expect continuity of the everyday personal influences and, correspondingly, of the political content flowing through those personal channels. It is conceivable that the changes observed in the Protestant communities could have been stimulated by changes in the content of the local press. Indeed, the press content has been stressed in the discussion of urban politics as a key factor at least facilitating the change to the NSDAP. One important consideration, however, casts doubt on the possibility of such a media influence in the villages. The report of a National Socialist from rural Franconia in July 1933, six months after the NSDAP came to power, notes that "many villages" were "so poor that they did not even read newspapers." "Many," the report continued, "did not even have a radio in the village." In those contexts then, the most likely source of the change would be the personal influence of the National Socialist activists. See Edward N. Peterson, *The Limits of Hitler's Power*, Princeton: Princeton University Press, 1969, p. 418.

39. See Berelson, Lazarsfeld, and McPhee, *Voting*, chs. 8 and 11, in which they, with evidence, discount the role of party and media in the community studied.

40. The Versailles treaty also detached various areas from Germany, giving (or returning) them to other nations. This created additional uprooted popula-

tions as Germans left those areas. But they, unlike the military, at least had the possibility of continuing in their chosen professions. The source of their uprootedness too, it will be noted, was political, not social structural.

If the career military men had been allowed to remain in the army, they still would have had some impact on civilian society. They would, no doubt, have been used in the course of the various left uprisings. But that would have involved the insertion of *regular* army units as opposed to the irregular units of the Freikorps or other free-lance movements. Regular units are generally more easily controlled by the legitimate authorities than are irregular ones. Regular units are also under more insistent pressure to refrain from direct political activity. And also, as indicated, they would have had less incentive to involve themselves in politics. Some of the rightist military involvement was intended to forestall dissolution of their units.

41. See Kenneth M. Stampp, *The Era of Reconstruction, 1865-1877*, New York: Alfred. A. Knopf, 1965; and C. Vann Woodward, *Reunion and Reaction: The Compromise of 1877 and the End of Reconstruction*, Boston: Little, Brown, 1951. For an account of the violence associated with the redemption effort, see Francis Butler Simkins, *Pitchfork Ben Tillman: South Carolinian*, Baton Rouge: Louisiana State Univ. Press, 1944, pp. 57-67. The most important work on the South's paramilitary units is that of Allen W. Trelease, *White Terror: The Ku Klux Klan Conspiracy and Southern Reconstruction*, New York: Harper & Row, 1971.

42. See the brilliant work of John Steward Ambler, *The French Army in Politics, 1945-1962*, Columbus: Ohio State University Press, 1966. The novel is that of Jean Lartéguy, *Les Centurions*, Paris: Presses de la Cité, 1960. I have cited from the English language edition, *The Centurions*, London: Hutchinson, 1961, pp. 198-199. This novel shows striking similarities to that of Ernst von Salomon, *Die Geächteten*, Reinbek bei Hamburg: Rowohlt Verlag, 1962, which deals with Freikorps fighters. Salomon's work was first published in 1930.

43. Thomas C. Bruneau, "Portugal: Problems and Prospects in the Creation of a New Regime," *Naval War College Review*, 29 (Summer 1976): 65-82.

44. Ambler notes that in France in 1815 "the army was despised and feared by most [of the restored] conservatives, but cherished by republicans as their best hope for restoration of a republic." *The French Army*, p. 27.

45. World War II provided an obvious parallel to its 1914-1918 predecessor, and yet, the outcome has been markedly different. Despite the long and frequently vicious struggle, there has been no parallel to the developments occurring after 1918. Where Weimar was convulsed with crisis after crisis in its brief fourteen-year existence, the Bonn Republic has flourished economically and had very stable politics in the first decades of its existence. Weimar saw twenty-two governments, the Bonn Republic, on the occasion of its thirtieth anniversary in 1979, had seen only six, and three of them had continued the same coalition of parties, only the chancellor being changed.

In this case, the moral equation was completely different; given the location and state of the contending forces at the end of the war (and given the condition of German cities) there was no question as to the outcome of the war: the defeat was total. There was, in short, no possible basis for a stab in the back (or an undefeated in the field) legend on this occasion. And, given its origins, there could be few illusions about Germany's "sole guilt" in causing the war. Even if some participants had carried notions of national renewal with them through to 1945, the evidence of the concentration camps rather definitively removed any lingering aura of National Socialist "idealism."

Under the occupation, *all* German military formations were disbanded; again military personnel were turned out of their careers and forced into civilian life. But here one finds some key differences. First, there had been a gap, an interruption of the military tradition. The expansion of the army came only after Hitler's accession in 1933; the same lifetime commitments would have been lacking. Second, as just indicated, the entire venture was discredited both by defeat and by the magnitude of the attendant crimes. And third, the occupation powers forbade all military formations; unlike Weimar, there was no army, no Freikorps, and no paramilitary outfits. There were no organizations to maintain either the fighting capacities or the orientations of the militant nationalists. Moreover, again unlike 1919, without those organizations, there was no possibility of educating and training younger cohorts; the generational links were broken. When a viable successor to the NSDAP appeared in the mid-sixties in the form of the National Democratic party, it was an organization of middle-aged men, younger generations (including possibly the party members' own children) having decisively rejected that political direction. It scarcely needs mentioning that the economic wonder that characterized postwar Germany made it difficult to sustain any antiregime movement.

46. Jeremy Noakes, "Conflict and Development in the NSDAP 1924-1927," *Journal of Contemporary History*, 1 (1966): 12. The coalition in Mecklenburg was led by an aristocrat, von Lessel, and he opted for the DVFB (German People's Freedom Movement). The minority of Hitler supporters were led by a young agricultural laborer. The DVFB, incidentally, to touch on a previously discussed theme, had its base within the "anti-semitic upper and upper middle classes." Ibid., p. 12.

47. This account is drawn from Gerhard Stoltenberg, *Politische Strömungen im schleswig-holsteinischen Landvolk 1918-1933*, Düsseldorf: Droste Verlag, 1962, pp. 147-151. The same events are also discussed in Rudolf Heberle, *Landbevölkerung und Nationalisozialismus: Eine soziologische Untersuchung der politischen Willensbildung in Schleswig-Holstein 1918 bis 1932*, Stuttgart: Deutsche Verlags-Anstalt, 1963. A novel dealing with some of the Landvolk history is that of Hans Fallada, *Bauern, Bonzen und Bomben*, Berlin: Vier Falken Verlag, 1931. See also Tilton, *Nazism*, pp. 67-71.

48. Heberle, *Landbevölkerung und Nationalsozialismus*, pp. 78-79. See also Stoltenberg, *Politische Strömungen*, p. 149.

The personal-influence factor also operated in rural Catholic communities. In Warmisried (Bavaria), the National Socialists faced the determined opposition of a devout mayor and the local priest. The priest, Andreas Rampp, is described as "a large, intelligent, powerful man, able and willing to save his flock from any godless philosophy such as the Nazi one." He is also described as "the only educated resident" of the village. When National Socialist speakers appeared there, they had to deal with the priest's provocative questions and challenging comments. The mayor later recalled "how the younger people cheered at every victory their priest scored over the imported speakers." It was a remarkable tribute, Peterson notes, "to Rampp's control over the village, [that] the NS vote in Warmisried dropped from 30 in 1932 to 12 in March 1933." See Peterson, *The Limits of Hitler's Power*, p. 411.

49. This subject is reviewed at length in Stoltenberg, *Politische Strömungen*, ch. 3.

50. Ibid., pp. 161-162, 174-175. Bruno von Salomon was the brother of the Freikorps fighter and chronicler Ernst von Salomon. Another brother, Franz Pfeffer von Salomon, also fought in the Freikorps. Better known as Franz Pfeffer (the name Salomon apparently being too Semitic for his tastes), he was the SA leader in Westphalia and later, the SA's national leader. He was also an NSDAP Reichstag deputy.

51. Ernst-August Roloff, "Wer wählte Hitler? Thesen zur Sozial- und Wirtschaftsgeschichte der Weimarer Republik," *Politische Studien*, 15 (1964): 300. See also Roloff's *Braunschweig und der Staat von Weimar: Politik, Wirtschaft und Gesellschaft 1918-1933*, Brunswick: Waisenhaus-Buchdruckerei und Verlag, 1964, chs. 3 and 6.

In the late 1880s, a political movement appeared in Germany that, in many ways, clearly foreshadowed the later NSDAP electoral style. Essentially, it was a movement of *political* anti-Semitism, its leaders running for Reichstag and state legislative offices. The leader of this effort, and its most successful practitioner, was one Otto Böckel. He was well educated, the holder of a doctorate; his field of interest was modern languages and, later on, folklore. He was employed as a librarian at the University of Marburg and, in pursuit of his folkloric interests, made frequent journeys into the Hessian countryside collecting songs and stories.

Böckel was much given to *völkische* ideas and "discovered" the peasantry of Hesse being "destroyed" by Jewish exploiters. In 1887, he announced his candidacy for the Reichstag in the Marburg-Frankenberg-Kirchhain district, one that had been safely Conservative since 1871. Following traditional practice, the incumbent made a single appearance there and addressed the district's leading citizens. Böckel and his supporters, meanwhile, systematically canvassed the other three-quarters of the district's population, the peasantry. Böckel, we are told, "worked the district. Speaking at open air mass meetings, presiding at peasant fairs, everywhere demonstrating his impressive knowledge of peasant lore, he devoted his full energy to the task." He won the seat by a substantial margin.

Some of the tactics used in his subsequent campaigns foreshadowed the NSDAP's inventiveness. When a local government official refused him the use of a public hall, Böckel "spoke from the window of a peasant hut or resorted to open air meetings. When officials prohibited the use of marching bands, Böckel substituted torchlight processions which marched from village to village singing Lutheran hymns and patriotic songs. Mounted peasant youths guarded

his wagon while hosts of followers, all wearing the blue cornflower as an identifying party badge, trailed along behind."

Another striking feature of his organization, one that will seem familiar, involved his cadres; he "relied on the students of Marburg and Giessen universities
to carry on the agitation." One of the Giessen volunteers was Heinrich Class,
later to be leader of the Pan German Association and a close associate of Alfred
Hugenberg.

The intensity of his electoral activity also has a familiar ring. Personal contact,
we are told, "replaced lengthy manifestoes and abstract principles for party
action. He and his colleagues visited the towns and villages continuously. In the
first four months of 1890, he held sixty-three rallies. For most of 1892-1894 his
party conducted an average of twenty-five to thirty 'major political gatherings'
a month. Many of these meetings were devoted to election agitation, which
usually began a full year in advance. Mass meetings featured lectures, discussions, and entertainment, all of which aimed at 'enlightening' the peasant about
the Jewish question."

Like the National Socialists, Böckel too had a radical stress, his leading slogan naming two targets: *"gegen Junker und Juden"* (against Junkers and Jews).
The established anti-Semites disliked him for his egalitarianism, for his anti-
Conservative stands, and for his sensationalism. From the time of Böckel's first
success up to the First World War, about ninety anti-Semites successfully contested Reichstag seats. Of these, thirty-five came from rural Hesse.

This account is based on the work of Richard S. Levy, *The Downfall of the
Anti-Semitic Political Parties in Imperial Germany*, New Haven: Yale University
Press, 1975, ch. 2. The quotations are from pages 55-56, 58-59, and 62. See also
the work of Paul Massing, *Rehearsal for Destruction: A Study of Political Anti-
Semitism in Imperial Germany*, New York: Harper Brothers, 1949, pp. 87-91.

52. Even the obvious cases have some not-too-obvious exceptions. The
daughters of very well-to-do parents attending Bennington College in the 1930s
shifted markedly to the left in the course of their stay there, the percentages
supporting the Socialist and Communist parties showing steady and sizable increases with each year of attendance. See Theodore M. Newcomb, *Personality
and Social Change: Attitude Formation in a Student Community*, New York: Dry-
den, 1943.

One of England's richest men, Waldorf Astor, a long-time Conservative,
came to accept socialism in the course of World War II; that is to say, he accepted the conclusions of the Beveridge report, seeing "socialism" as "a natural
development of British history." He and his children determined that their influential journal of opinion, the *Observer*, would be used to support that option.
The decision came at great personal cost to him. See Christopher Sykes, *Nancy:
The Life of Lady Astor*, London: Collins, 1972, pp. 451, 490, 508.

In the United States, recently a group of bourgeois children, feeling guilty
about their unearned wealth, have set about to give it away. See the *New York
Times* article, "Reluctantly Wealthy, They Fund Radical Groups," March 4,
1977.

53. Ernst Toller, a leading participant in the revolutionary events of Munich

in 1919, commented on the later Communist rising in central Germany and on the Munich struggle as follows:

> What tragedy in Central Germany. These tactics of revolt cannot be justified. It is a policy of catastrophe which will drive the country into the arms of uncontrolled reaction.
>
> There are radicals now who, for the sake of a phrase, sacrifice the blood of the workers as they did in those April days in Munich when they called on them to fight on the barricades, a fight that had no sense and no prospect of success; because "bloody defeat" helps the proletariat to reach maturity and because "to negotiate is treason." (But the same people who called for the fight could not be found the day before the fight started.)

From *Look Through the Bars*, New York: Farrar & Rinehart, 1937, p. 80. In Great Britain the work is entitled *Letters from Prison*.

54. See Stanley G. Payne, *The Spanish Revolution*, New York: Norton, 1970, pp. 189-190; and also by Payne, "Spanish Fascism in Comparative Perspective," pp. 142-169 of Henry Ashby Turner, Jr., ed., *Reappraisals of Fascism*, New York: Franklin Watts, 1975. See also Juan J. Linz, "The Party System of Spain: Past and Future," pp. 197-282 of Seymour M. Lipset and Stein Rokkan, eds., *Party Systems and Voter Alignments: Cross-National Perspectives*, New York: The Free Press, 1967.

55. Most of the following account, beginning with this quotation, is drawn from F.L. Carsten, *The Rise of Fascism*, Berkeley: University of California Press, 1967, ch. 2. See also Salvatore Saladino's chapter on Italy in Hans Rogger and Eugen Weber, eds., *The European Right: A Historical Profile*, Berkeley: University of California Press, 1966: Ernst Nolte, *Three Faces of Fascism*, New York: Holt, Rinehart and Winston, 1966, pt. 3 (the original German edition is entitled *Der Faschismus in seiner Epoche*); and, for a more detailed account, Denis Mack Smith, *Italy: A Modern History*, Ann Arbor: University of Michigan Press, rev. ed., 1969, pp. 211-372.

56. Carsten, *The Rise of Fascism*, p. 55.

57. Ibid., pp. 55-56; see also Nolte, *Three Faces*, p. 197.

58. Carsten, *The Rise of Fascism*, p. 58.

59. Ibid., p. 57.

60. Ibid., p. 66. The expression "march on Rome" suggests an actual invasion by the insurgent units followed by some struggle with defending forces. But that never happened, the event being an appearance cultivated by Mussolini and his propagandists. Some 25,000 Fascists had been mobilized and were stationed about sixty-five kilometers from Rome. They were poorly organized and ill equipped for any serious military venture, many being unarmed. Most authorities are of the opinion that the government troops in the city could "easily have dominated such a motley collection." But through the continued use of force and with some well planned deception, any will to resist was broken, and the king sent Mussolini a telegram *inviting* him to Rome. On receipt of the invitation, Mussolini boarded a train and "crossed the Rubicon in a sleeping car." After being given power, his columns arrived in the city to be photographed and to give the "semblance of a dictator's private army overpowering the con-

stituted authorities of the state." These details (and the quotations) are from Smith, *Italy*, p. 372.

61. Carsten, *The Rise of Fascism*, p. 59; see also Nolte, *Three Faces*, pp. 197-198.

62. Carsten, *The Rise of Fascism*, pp. 61-62.

63. Some later authorities have questioned the action-reaction analysis, noting that the Socialist actions came in 1919-1920 and, effectively, were ended with the August wave of factory occupations. In that period, except for isolated actions (such as their destruction of the *Avanti* offices), the Fascists made very few moves, mainly because their forces were so minuscule. Their growth, and violence, came largely in 1921 as it became clear that the Socialists were unable to mount a serious defense. As one author has put it, "The Fascist jackal strikes only the already wounded proletarian lion." But that does not challenge the action-reaction claim. It substitutes moral evaluation for analysis saying that the Fascists took unfair advantage, hitting a downed opponent. One can easily agree with the evaluation, but that does nothing to help one's understanding of the factors moving the participants. The quotation is from R. Palme Dutt, *Fascism and Social Revolution: A Study of the Economics and Politics of the Extreme Stages of Capitalism in Decay*, New York: International Publishers, 1935, p. 119.

64. Carsten, *The Rise of Fascism*, p. 54. An entire paragraph is devoted to this theme.

This statement comes without any specific supporting evidence or references, which means it has the same standing as those statements about the German lower middle class discussed in Chapter 2. Considering only the logic of the situation, one might note the following: first, there would be much greater reason to speak of the aroused "fears and the hatred" of the upper and upper middle classes. They, after all, were the prime targets of the left insurgency, and yet no such statement appears. Second, it would seem doubtful that the lower middle class, even if it did fiercely oppose the left insurgency, would be enthusiastic about the fascist counteroffering. Would those farmers who had had their prices forcibly reduced be enthusiastic supporters? Or those Naples restaurant owners? They, obviously, were the targets (or victims) of Fascist actions. If anything, there would be better reason for seeing them as a helpless third party in the struggle, identifying with neither of the contenders. Third, there is the technical question raised earlier about Germany. Would the typical petty bourgeois, hardly able to manage his very marginal shop, have the talents for organizing highly mobile and obviously capable fighting forces? Or would that not involve a different kind of talent, one trained and developed in the military?

There is a question of evidence to be raised about all of the principal claims offered in the text and, similarly, about those appearing in the original sources cited here. In general the Italian case is not as well researched as the German. It is best, therefore, that these statements be viewed as hypotheses rather than as firmly supported conclusions. They constitute a summary of the best available knowledge on the subject. The point is that that knowledge accords better with the analysis offered here than it does with the centrist position.

65. There are other parallels one might mention. As in Germany, the religious

factor cut across the society, making a pure class analysis at least somewhat misleading. In Italy the distinction was between the Catholics, many of whom supported the *populari*, a late-appearing liberal Catholic party with similarities to the Zentrum, and the secularized, unchurched, or anticlerical populations, most of whom, of course, would have been baptized Catholics. As in Germany there was a striking age relationship, the *fasci* being made up of young men, their most famous song being *Giovinezza* (meaning youth). The last prime ministers were in their seventies, Giolitti being 79 as against Mussolini's mere 39 years on his accession. Many of Italy's leading notables provided legitimation for Mussolini's movement. In addition to the business and political leaders, this included Italy's leading poet, Gabriele D'Annunzio. Italy's most famous living composer, Giacomo Puccini, welcomed the movement. The young conductor Arturo Toscanini was a Fascist candidate in 1919. Italy's leading philosopher and historian, Benedetto Croce, a member of Giolitti's cabinet, explained that "Fascism was safe because it had no program." And many of Italy's leading newspapers were more than generous in their words of approval, among these being the leading Milan daily, the *Corriere della Sera*. On Toscanini and Puccini, see Smith, *Italy*, pp. 324-325 and for the comment by Croce, p. 341.

This history may sound as if it more clearly accords with the leftist reading, that is, with fascism as the last stage of capitalism. On this question, however, see Roland Sarti, *Fascism and the Industrial Leadership in Italy, 1919-1940*, Berkeley: University of California Press, 1971. Sarti reports (p. 112) that Italian businessmen had "never really internalized the warlike ethic of fascism [and they] soon discovered that, in their determination to mobilize the country for war, the Fascist leaders were ready to hedge on the unspoken terms of their partnership with business: the politicians challenged the autonomy of business as they had never done before." See also pp. 125, 127-128, and 138. It would appear that Italian businessmen had paid the piper and then danced to the piper's tune. Put differently, it indicates that here, too, there is much to be said for the Caesarist argument. For a more general consideration of Mussolini's impact, see the collection edited by Sarti, *The Ax Within: Italian Fascism in Action*, New York: New Viewpoints-Franklin Watts, 1974.

Renzo De Felice, probably the leading expert on Italian Fascism, rejects the claim that business wished to give Mussolini power. In one summary statement he declares it to be "unthinkable that Italy's great economic forces wanted to bring fascism to power. . . . The industrialists certainly had no thought of giving fascism exclusive power." From his *Fascism: An Informal Introduction to Its Theory and Practice*, New Brunswick, N.J.: Transaction Books, 1976, p. 63.

66. Juan J. Linz, "Political Space and Fascism as a Latecomer: Conditions Conducive to Success or Failure of Fascism as a Mass Movement in Inter-War Europe," pp. 153-189 of Stein Ugelvik Larsen, Bernt Hagtvet, and Jan Petter Myklebust, *Who Were the Fascists: Social Roots of European Fascism*, Bergen: Universitetsforlaget, 1980. See also Linz's "Totalitarian and Authoritarian Regimes," pp. 175-411 of Fred I. Greenstein and Nelson W. Polsby, eds., *Handbook of Political Science: Macropolitical Theory*, vol. 3, Reading, Mass.: Addison-Wesley, 1975; and his essay, "Some Notes toward a Comparative Study of

Fascism in Sociological Historical Perspective," pp. 3-121 of Walter Laqueur, ed., *Fascism: A Reader's Guide*, Berkeley: University of California Press, 1976. For general reviews of positions on the subject, see A. James Gregor, *Interpretations of Fascism*, Morristown, N.J.: General Learning Press, 1974; and, more recently, Gilbert Allardyce, "What Fascism Is Not: Thoughts on the Deflation of a Concept," *American Historical Review*, 84 (1979): 367-388. For a review of Marxist analyses, see Anson G. Rabinbach, "Toward a Marxist Theory of Fascism and National Socialism," *New German Critique*, 3 (1974): 127-153.

67. This entire question has been neglected in the contemporary social sciences. Most works on elites and upper classes dwell on their power, effectively being extended accounts of the resources they have at their disposal. One resource they do not have is numbers. Faced with overwhelming odds against them, one possibility is to simply give up, to abandon the field. This was essentially what happened in November 1918 in Germany.

Some members of the established elites have not seen themselves as all that powerful. We have the following account from the early nineteenth century. Lord Liverpool, upon being congratulated by Chateaubriand for the solidity of British institutions, pointed out his windows and replied, "What can be stable with these enormous cities? One insurrection in London and all is lost." From Val Lorwin, "Working Class Politics and Economic Development in Western Europe," *American Historical Review*, 63 (1957-1958): 341.

More research should be done in the area of ruling-class reactions, that is, rather than simply assuming the logical response. The business classes of Sweden, Norway, and Denmark do not appear to have turned to the fascists with the rise of socialism. If they did so, their support had no evident result. The British ruling classes seem to have accepted MacDonald and the Labour party (and later, Clement Attlee) without making use of fascist weaponry.

68. The Freikorps, it will be noted, was organized by Social Democrats in conjunction with the general staff. Once the units were set up, some capitalists helped finance them, again simply responding to initiatives taken by others. National Socialist memoirs reporting on the period of Freikorps activities contain frequent complaints about the absence of the bourgeoisie. When the need was pressing, the bourgeoisie was nowhere to be seen. The Béla Kun regime in Hungary was overturned by Romanian troops. Some defense formations were organized by Hungarian aristocrats. There seems to have been no business role worthy of note.

69. In 1932, at the moment of crisis in the United States, the Republican party, the chosen agency of the established upper class, was voted out of office. By 1935, many of the leaders of this "establishment" were convinced that Franklin Delano Roosevelt was their archenemy, aiming to overthrow the republic and undermine their position. To oppose these ambitions they organized a countering pressure group, the Liberty League. Despite their money and influence, the league was a complete failure. Eventually, in the course of a wartime alliance, they made their peace with Roosevelt. The important point to be noted is that they accepted and joined someone else's agency.

The party of the establishment lost all presidential elections from 1932 to

1948. Its preferred party scored impressive wins in 1952 and 1956 with a charismatic military hero, although in only two of the eight Eisenhower years did the Republicans gain a majority in the Senate and House. The establishment certainly did not favor Goldwater as the nominee of "its" party in 1964, and there was much unhappiness with Nixon in those circles in 1968. The Republicans did win the presidency in the latter year, on the basis of a minority vote and with the Democratic party in great disarray. Nixon won a major victory in 1972 over a very unpopular Democrat. The establishment had even more reason to be unhappy with Nixon by 1974, the losses stemming from the Watergate episode being enormous. Although business leaders were generally satisfied with President Ford, he lost to Jimmy Carter. The Republicans gained the presidency again in 1980, with just over 50 percent of the vote in an election in which only 54 percent voted. The majority gained in the Senate in 1980 was based on equally thin margins, the Democratic vote having been pulled down by a not too popular president. Republicans have controlled the Senate for only six of the fifty years between 1932 and 1982.

While it is clear that money counts for a lot, and that it is certainly better to have it than not, still, in many struggles business is the loser. As noted in Chapter 13, business lacks one key resource needed for contention in democratic struggles—large numbers of voters.

70. As in the case of Paul Reusch or that of Emil Kirdorf. The Munich publisher J.F. Lehmann had negotiated with Hitler in the anti–Young Plan effort. He declared that "he was completely convinced that Hitler and Hitler alone would save Germany." But then he added that "we must not forget that Hitler is a dangerous, asocial fool." Heinrich Class, the leader of the Pan Germans, replied: "My dear Lehmann, you are and will remain a child. You manage in one and the same breath to describe a man as the savior of the country and as a danger to society!" From Fabian von Schlabrendorff, *The Secret War against Hitler*, London: Hodder and Stoughton, 1966, p. 352.

71. See the works cited in note 66, this chapter.

72. Allardyce, "What Fascism Is Not," pp. 382, 384.

73. Ibid., p. 396. See also the articles by Deák and Weber in Rogger and Weber, *The European Right*. Some sense of the complexities involved may be gained by Carsten's comment that in Hungary, the illegal Communist party, "had advised their followers to vote Arrow Cross." *The Rise of Fascism*, p. 178.

74. There is obviously good reason to agree with Allardyce in his recommendation that we "declassify fascism altogether as a generic concept." "What Fascism Is Not," p. 378. The important task is to explain or account for the manifest differences in the various fascisms. In this case the preference for generalization has meant a misdirection of effort, leading commentators to find, or more specifically, to impose some framework. The presumed common features have yet to be revealed. Stanley Payne, in a comment on Allardyce's "What Fascism Is Not," which appears in the same issue of the *American Historical Review*, indicates that much of the later similarity resulted from an important "outside influence." "Ultimately," he says, "such unity as was achieved stemmed from Nazi influence, which grew with the German imperium. It is not an ex-

aggeration to speak of the Nazification of radical nationalist or fascist movements in Europe after 1937-38" (p. 390).

75. Robert K. Merton et al., *Sociology Today: Problems and Prospects*, New York: Basic Books, 1959, p. xiii.

76. Eksteins, *The Limits of Reason*, pp. 203, 241. Another such statement appears in the liberal *Berliner Morgenpost* of March 10, 1932.

77. Karl Marx and Frederick Engels, *Selected Works*, Moscow: Foreign Languages Publishing House, 1951, vol. 1, pp. 39-40.

78. Ibid., pp. 41-42. See, for example, the recent restatement of the standard claims in the article by Arno Mayer, "The Lower Middle Class as Historical Problem," *Journal of Modern History*, 47 (1975): 409-436.

The text and the Mayer article argue the dominant position with respect to the petty bourgeoisie (*Kleinbürgertum*) or lower middle class. There is a second position on the subject, to be found in the sentence of the *Manifesto* immediately following the one cited in the text. It states that "if by chance they [the members of the lower middle class] are revolutionary, they are so, only in view of their impending transfer into the proletariat, they thus defend not their present, but their future interests, they desert their own standpoint to place themselves at that of the proletariat." The lower middle class, it should be noted, comes to this position "by chance." It arrives in the revolutionary camp to defend its interests, not as the bringer of "enlightenment and progress." This emphasis on "interest" as the motive means that this class is volatile; that is, its members will go wherever their interests demand. This is clearly a very different position from the view that "they *are* reactionary." This second position has been picked up from time to time by various commentators on the subject; see, for example, Jonathan Wiener, "Marxism and the Lower Middle Class: A Response to Arno Mayer," *Journal of Modern History*, 48 (1976): 661-671, but it remains a minority position among Marxists. Both positions, it should be noted, are very much in need of empirical assessment.

79. A parallel to this selectivity may be noted with respect to the second most popular explanation of National Socialism, that is, the mass-society viewpoint. The focus on gullible masses and the clever demagogue has roots that extend back well before 1848. The origins of this view are to be found in ancient Greece and Rome, the prime models being the irresponsible sophists and demagogues out wooing the masses in the agora of Athens or in the Roman forum. Where successful, they overthrew the democracy (or the responsible aristocrats), the end result being, as all good classical scholars know, that things were made worse. It is no accident, to borrow the Marxist cliché, that this view has found greatest favor among the upper- and upper-middle-class populations of the world. Trained in the gymnasium, or in the lycée, or the best schools anywhere, they were predisposed toward this "model" through years of study of classical languages. For the new analytic task, that basic image required only slight modification, the mass media taking the place of the demagogue's personal appearance in the public forum. For those who eventually chose a left or critical direction, it was only necessary to make the established elites the demagogic manipulators, and one had a viable framework. A key element in all versions of this position,

ancient and modern, right and left, is an obvious distance between the analyst-critic and the masses. The latter do not appear with individual faces; they have no individual feelings, nor do they make their own unique judgments; they appear only in stereotypic form.

Although Caesarism and praetorianism are also both very much a part of classical experience, the mass-society adherents appear to have been operating with blinders, focusing on one option, the role of the demagogue, and neglecting this obvious alternative.

80. Speaking of France in the period following World War I, David Caute says that Marxism there, "despite the teachings of Jules Guesde and the writings of Paul Lafargue, was much less widely understood or assimilated than in Germany." There is a strong suggestion, too, that the ideas of Marx played less of a role in French universities than was the case in Germany. See his *Communism and the French Intellectuals, 1914-1960*, London: André Deutsch, 1964, pp. 13 and 363 ff. The leading school of sociology in the United States at that time, the Chicago school, saw "the city" as made up of diverse ethnic groups, all struggling for urban space. Within the cities one saw a continuous sequence of invasion and succession as one group pushed into another's territory. Most of this was discussed within the framework of social Darwinism.

81. On the early relations of the liberals and the left, see the important work by Roger Morgan, *The German Social Democrats and the First International: 1864-1872*, London: Cambridge University Press, 1965, pp. 14 ff., 19 ff., 147 ff. Morgan discusses the importance of *Das Kapital* on pp. 132 ff. Although not widely read when it first appeared, even in socialist circles, it had considerable symbolic importance. It was a scholarly scientific justification of socialism; that made it distinctive among the socialist publications of the age, most of them being crude propagandistic tracts, many of them utopian, many of them written by self-educated artisans. The author of *Das Kapital*, it will be remembered, was Dr. Karl Marx. Few socialists in the 1870s bore that title. That direction became ever more important in the German left, one of Marx's most famous followers being Dr. Rosa Luxemburg. Half of the members of the first central committee of the KPD had doctorates.

Friedrich Naumann, the leader of the left liberal Progressive party from 1906, was very much influenced by Marxism. Marianne Weber says he saw himself as a "workers' lawyer" (*Anwalt der Proletarier*) and that only his religiosity kept him from joining the ranks of the Social Democrats. Pinson reports that he "led German progressive liberalism away from dogmatic *laissez faire*." In the 1890s, Naumann had already argued "the need of infusing social content into middle-class liberalism and creating a bridge to the working classes and the Social Democrats." Among his many illustrious followers were Max Weber and Theodor Heuss. The centrality of Marxist concerns in Weber's work scarcely needs mention. It is of interest to note that his great French contemporary Emile Durkheim concerned himself primarily with problems posed by the liberal world view. For him, socialism was a very peripheral concern. See Marianne Weber, *Max Weber: Ein Lebensbild*, Heidelberg: Verlag Lambert Schneider, 1950, p. 155 and passim; Koppel S. Pinson, *Modern Germany: Its History and Civilization*, 2d ed., New York: Macmillan, 1966, p. 170; and also William O. Shanahan, "Friedrich Naumann: A Mirror of Wilhelmian Germany," *Review of Politics*, 13 (1951): 267-301.

Franz Neumann expresses the same point, along with some other relevant observations, as follows: "The German scholar generally came under three intellectual influences: German idealism, Marxism, and historicism. All three have in common that they are comprehensive systems of thought claiming to fit every phenomenon into a system. All three express the extraordinary weight of historical tradition. Thus the thought of German scholars was primarily theoretical and historical—rarely empirical and pragmatic. . . . it always makes for a certain rigidity bordering on dogmatism." He also speaks of a general "contempt for empiricism" found among these scholars. See Franz L. Neumann et al., *The Cultural Migration: The European Scholar in America*, Philadelphia: University of Pennsylvania Press, 1953, p. 19.

82. This precise development was predicted by Alexis de Tocqueville writing in the 1830s. Historians in democracies, he said, "assign great general causes to all petty incidents." He proceeds to explain the intellectual reasons for the choice of such a "paradigm." He also mentions the consolations that approach provides for second-rate historians. They are thus furnished with "a few mighty reasons to extricate them from the most difficult part of their work . . . it indulges the indolence or incapacity of their minds while it confers upon them the honors of deep thinking." See his *Democracy in America*, New York: Alfred A. Knopf, 1963, vol. 2, pp. 85-88, a brief chapter entitled "Some Characteristics of Historians in Democratic Times."

Another characteristic of the struggle between Marxists and liberals involves an aesthetic component: the one appears tough, dealing with the big or hard events of history; the other appears soft, dealing with a sea of petty and seemingly irrelevant detail. The one is determinant, offering certainty about both the course of history and its causes; the other offers chance or whimsy, at times seeming almost frivolous. In the competition with tough-talking Marxists, it must have seemed surer ground for many liberals to be arguing about the immanent forces of history rather than the fact that a Herr Schulz and some other members of his faction missed the caucus meeting one day, allowing the vote to go against them, which event in turn changed the course of the nation's history.

83. The National Socialist literature is filled with Marxist vocabulary. The same delineation of the classes is to be found. There is much discussion of the exploitation of various segments of the population, workers, middle classes, farmers. Seldom does one find a good word there about the bourgeoisie. As indicated previously, the National Socialist literature is filled with hostility and contempt for that class, which is seen as self-interested, as incompetent, and worse, as cowardly, as unwilling to fight to defend its own, let alone Germany's, interests. The exploited classes in the National Socialist literature are portrayed as in the grips of Jewish or foreign capital (with hard-working Germans paying reparations, and so on). Some accounts, anticipating contemporary analyses of imperialism, speak of exploited proletarian nations, such as Ger-

many, being done in by decadent capitalist nations, by England, France, and the United States. In a Sorelian variation, Ernst von Salomon developed some themes from the Marxian theory of increasing misery. The worse things were for the farmers, he said, the more they would awaken politically. If only the government would exercise the sharpest terror—prohibitions, repression, machine guns—one might thank them for it. A central theme in the NSDAP's "Marxism" is its *voluntarist* challenge to inevitability; one might call it the principal point of the NSDAP repertory. The major claims of the centrist theory, perhaps understandably, are not prominent anywhere in the National Socialist literature. Von Salomon's Marxism appears in Stoltenberg, *Politische Strömungen*, p. 132.

84. See Heberle's foreword, *Landbevölkerung und Nationalsozialismus*, pp. 7-8. The Siegfried work referred to is his *Tableau politique de la France de l'Ouest sous la Troisième Republique*, Paris: Armand Colin, 1913.

85. A brief one-page account, accompanied by six colored maps of the city, appeared in *Aus Hamburgs Verwaltung und Wirtschaft* (From Hamburg's Administration and Economy, a monthly publication of the city-state's statistical office), 8:6 (1931): 177. Various shadings indicated the strength of the major parties in the precincts of the city for the September 1930 Reichstag election. Anyone knowing that city would recognize one distinctive and perhaps unexpected peculiarity in the map showing National Socialist strength—there was a brown ring around the Alster, indicating that the NSDAP had a considerable following among the city's best-off populations. The single page of text does not point up this fact, nor obviously, does it indicate its significance. The publication is rarely cited, even today, in sources dealing with the NSDAP. It first came to my attention in the work of Rudolf Heberle, *Social Movements: An Introduction to Political Sociology*, New York: Appleton-Century-Crofts, 1951, p. 259.

This division in approaches to human affairs had its origins in the compartmentalization of German universities. From an early point statistics was an independent field taught in most German universities. Those departments, not too surprisingly, trained people for the statistical offices of federal, state, and local governments (all major cities already had such an agency by the turn of the century). The various social sciences emerged and gained acceptance (i.e. professional positions) at a later point. Rivalries and open hostility developed, the end result being that very separate and distinct paths were followed. For the details of this history see Susanne Petra Schad, *Empirical Social Research in Weimar-Germany*, Paris-The Hague: Mouton, 1972, pp. 18-35.

Not all knowledge contained in these statistical office publications was lost through compartmentalization. The outstanding work of Erwin Lind in the statistical office of Hesse (Darmstadt) did make its way into the pages of the leading liberal daily, the *Frankfurter Zeitung* (see note 11, Chapter 3). But one finds little suggestion that it had any further impact.

86. Paul Lazarsfeld, as a young man, heard the leader of the Young Socialist Workers Movement reading individual quotations from questionnaires he had distributed, this to show the misery of factory life. When Lazarsfeld asked why he "did not make counts." the leader expressed "surprise at the idea." During

the First World War, when still in his teens, he was living "in the custody of" Rudolf Hilferding, the noted Socialist leader. Lazarsfeld asked him to explain "what this election business was all about." Hilferding discouraged the interest, recommending that he should "first know what the Socialist program was all about." A compromise was eventually reached: Lazarsfeld would read a book by Kautsky in exchange for one on elections. Later, in exile from his native Austria, Lazarsfeld was to found an important school of voting studies, discussed earlier in this chapter. See his "An Episode in the History of Social Research: A Memoir," pp. 270-337 of Donald Fleming and Bernard Bailyn, eds., *The Intellectual Migration: Europe and America, 1930-1960*, Cambridge, Mass.: Harvard University Press, 1969. The above episodes appear on pp. 284-285.

The active denigration of empirical research serves a rather important function for some intellectuals; it protects the claims of speculative commentators, removing them from the threat of independent and possibly damaging assessment.

For an account of the neglect and hostility shown social research in an earlier period, see Anthony Oberschall, *Empirical Social Research in Germany, 1848-1914*, New York: Basic Books, 1965. Max Weber supported empirical studies, doing many himself and founding the German Sociological Society to encourage the conduct of surveys, but even he had little success. Subsequent generations of scholars have neglected his empirical studies and have turned him into a theorist. See also the article by Paul F. Lazarsfeld and Anthony R. Oberschall, "Max Weber and Empirical Social Research," *American Sociological Review*, 30 (1965): 185-199; and Schad, *Empirical Social Research*. She reports that during the first twenty years of the German Sociological Society (that is, from 1910 to 1930), "not *one* paper delivered at the meetings was actually based on an empirical study" (p. 1). See also the Neumann quotation in note 81, this chapter.

Some basic position papers written by the German intellectual community's leading contenders of a later period are collected in Theodor W. Adorno et al., *Der Positivismusstreit in der deutschen Soziologie*, Neuwied and Berlin: Luchterhand, 1969. (There is an English translation, *The Positivist Dispute in German Sociology*, London: Heinemann, 1976.) An approving review of their efforts is to be found in Martin Jay, *The Dialectical Imagination: A History of the Frankfurt School and the Institute of Social Research 1923-1950*, London: Heinemann Educational Books, 1973.

87. For the history of this institute, see Jay, *The Dialectical Imagination*. For a brief but very useful summary of the school's intellectual contribution, see Lewis S. Feuer, "The Preconceptions of Critical Theory," *Jewish Journal of Sociology*, 16 (June 1974): 75-84.

The most significant work dealing with National Socialism produced by a member of this group was, of course, Franz Neumann's *Behemoth*. Another member wrote an important work on political anti-Semitism in Germany; see Paul Massing, *Rehearsal for Destruction*. For Theodor Adorno's intellectual efforts during Hitler's reign over Europe, see his contribution in Fleming and Bailyn, *The Intellectual Migration*, especially pp. 351-352.

88. This is not to say that social determination operates at all times and places

among intellectuals. Nor is it intended to suggest that there are no substantial differences between gossips and scholars. Some part of any serious intellectual's work will be intellectually determined, that is to say, will depend on original investigation. But since no one can investigate all things, much of any person's knowledge will come to depend on the handed-down, on passed-on truths. And the acceptance or rejection of handed-down wisdom will in most cases depend on some interpersonal dynamics, on one's previous intellectual training, on the approval or disapproval of a given claim provided by trusted or respected associates. This point is neither new nor particularly surprising. De Tocqueville expressed it as follows: "There is no philosopher in the world so great but that he believes a million things on the faith of other people and accepts a great many more truths than he demonstrates." "This," he adds, "is not only necessary but desirable." *Democracy in America*, vol. 2, p. 9.

Intellectuals differ considerably in their orientations to empirical investigation. Among those heavily committed to research, group dynamics would probably play a less prominent role. Among those refusing the use of empirical methods, those preferring free speculation or those preferring a deductive approach, the group dynamics factor would probably have considerable importance. It seems likely that German scholarship with its idealist heritage and its emphasis on reason (frequently seen as *opposed* to investigation), would tend in the latter direction. For a summary of the vast literature on conformity, see Edwin P. Hollander, *Principles and Methods of Social Psychology*, 3rd ed., New York: Oxford University Press, 1976, ch. 13, "Being Independent: Conformity and Nonconformity."

It is easy to assume that conformity is a characteristic of someone else's behavior. The very talented, the best and the brightest, are surely exempt from that kind of human failing. But some relevant studies support de Tocqueville's purely theoretical claim. For an impressive analysis of group dynamics processes in operation among top-level decision makers, many of them very capable intellectuals, see Irving L. Janis, *Victims of Groupthink: A Psychological Study of Foreign-Policy Decisions and Fiascoes*, Boston: Houghton Mifflin, 1972. Some researchers, hypothesizing that academics responded as much to form or appearance as to content, concocted a meaningless lecture and trained an actor to give it in the best academic style. They also prepared him with responses to likely questions, providing him with appropriate academic witticisms, irrelevant asides, and so forth. The lecture was ultimately presented before some seventy persons, all of whom possesed some kind of advanced academic degree. Not one of them, in the subsequent evaluation, indicated that the lecture was without substantial content. See Donald H. Naftulin, John E. Ware, Jr., and Frank A. Donnelly, "The Doctor Fox Lecture: A Paradigm of Educational Seduction," *Journal of Medical Education*, 48 (January 1973): 630-635.

89. There are many works available dealing with the out-migration (and subsequent reimplantation) of Germany's intelligentsia. We have: Franz Neumann et al., *The Cultural Migration*; Donald Peterson Kent, *The Refugee Intellectual: The Americanization of the Immigrants of 1933-1941*, New York: Columbia University Press, 1953; Helga Pross, *Die Deutsche Akademische Emigration nach den*

Vereinigten Staaten, 1933-1941, Berlin: Duncker und Humblot, 1955; Fleming and Bailyn, *The Intellectual Migration*; Robert Boyers, ed., "The Legacy of the German Refugee Intellectuals," special number of *Salmagundi*, 10-11 (Fall 1969-Winter 1970). This collection also appears, with the same title, in book form, New York: Schocken Books, 1969; H. Stuart Hughes, *The Sea Change: The Migration of Social Thought, 1930-1965*, New York: Harper & Row, 1975; and Laura Fermi, *Illustrious Immigrants: The Intellectual Migration from Europe, 1930-1941*, Chicago: University of Chicago Press, 1968.

One of the most insightful accounts is that by Henry Pachter, "On Being an Exile: An Old-Timer's Personal and Political Memoir," pp. 12-51 of the *Salmagundi* volume. While there was certainly much tragedy associated with exile, the history was not entirely bleak. He states (p. 31) that "thanks to benevolent committees, general prosperity and the war, many of us were able to join the social class we had left in Europe. This was particularly true of intellectuals. In the beginning, many of us had to take positions that might be described as 'academic proletariat'; but eventually many reached positions they might not have obtained in the old country . . . despite a few cases of failure the percentage of successful careers is truly astounding." See also Pachter's review of Hughes's *The Sea Change*, in *Political Science Quarterly*, 90 (Summer 1975): 406-407.

90. C. Wright Mills, *White Collar*. Hans Gerth, a student of Karl Mannheim, worked as a journalist for the *Berliner Morgenpost* and later as an assistant to Rudolf Heberle in the Schleswig-Holstein study. He was the author of an important article on the NSDAP leadership, "The Nazi Party: Its Leadership and Composition," *American Journal of Sociology*, 45 (1940): 517-541. In exile, he taught at the University of Wisconsin where Mills was his student.

91. See my *Restraining Myths*, chs. 2 and 3. Those chapters also contain some discussion on the sociology of knowledge question, that is, on the reasons for the persistent error.

A similar intellectual pathology was observed on a previous occasion, this, too, involving German émigrés in America. Friedrich Engels, on the basis of his observations there, wrote the following: "The German socialists in America are an annoying business. . . . each new arrival feels himself called upon to turn everything he finds upside down, turning it into something *new*, so that a new epoch may date from himself. Moreover, most of these greenhorns remain stuck in New York for a long time or for life, continually reinforced by new additions and relieved of the necessity of learning the language of the country or of getting to know American conditions properly. All of that certainly causes much harm." From a letter to Friedrich Sorge (December 2, 1893), cited in Karl Marx and Friedrich Engels, *Basic Writings on Politics and Philosophy*, ed. Lewis S. Feuer, Garden City: Doubleday-Anchor, 1959, pp. 457-458.

92. One instance of the ethereal character of the thought produced in such circles is reported by Henry Pachter. "Ernst Cassirer, the philosopher . . . once expressed it in a classical way which I repeat every year for my undergraduates' edification: 'You know, Mr. Pachter, this Hitler is an error (Irrtum) of History; he does not belong in German history at all. And therefore he will perish.'"

From Pachter, "On Being an Exile," p. 16; see also p. 38 for his account of the relationship of writers and "real people."

One outstanding work that is very much focused on the price of bread is Alexander Gerschenkron's *Bread and Democracy in Germany*, Berkeley: University of California Press, 1943. Although frequently cited in other contexts, for example, in the literature of economic development, it only rarely appears in literature dealing with the origins of National Socialism. My students are amused or made uneasy by discussion of such things, some asking for assurance that the discussion of bread is not some kind of joke. The same reaction appears when I discuss gardens (that is, vegetable gardens) in connection with working-class politics. It is part of the same syndrome, the trained inability to deal with the facts of everyday life.

93. Joseph Roth, *Das Spinnennetz*, Frankfurt am Main: Fischer Bucherei, 1970. The postscript is by Peter W. Jensen. The expression "wild gewordene Klein-bürger" of the original is a frequent cliché in the literature. The *Vossische Zeitung*, it will be remembered, used the phrase in July 1929 to describe the National Socialist development.

94. Herbert E. Krugman, "The Role of Hostility in the Appeal of Communism in the United States," *Psychiatry*, 16 (1953): 253-261. See also his "The Appeal of Communism to American Middle Class Intellectuals and Trade Unionists," *Public Opinion Quarterly*, 16 (1952): 331-355.

Krugman's observations in the first of these articles are based on a small (N = 35) and unscientific sample (Communists or ex-Communists who were psychoanalysts' patients). They may, therefore, only be taken as suggestive, that is, as a beginning point for further work. The article contains some hypotheses to account for the origins of the hostility. It also reports on another kind of appeal or need. In addition to the highly active, almost compulsive, expressers of hostility, Krugman found some passive recessive members. They, too, had some guilt feelings over their extreme passivity, which, like hostility, also gives rise to some concern. The Communist party served their psychic needs or purposes also; again it provided moral justification for their passivity, or in this case, for their submission to the party's directives. The coupling of these motivations, the expresser of hostility directing the compulsive conformist, would give considerable force to any movement. Their special needs however, would make it difficult for others to chart and maintain a rational political direction.

The presence of a fringe group of such moralizers has long been noted in the parties of the left. Engels commented on it (see the quotation and discussion in my *Class and Politics*, pp. 548 ff., and 573). See also Robert Michels, *Political Parties*, Glencoe: The Free Press, 1949, p. 101 ("socialism exercises a natural force of attraction for cranks of all kinds") and p. 280. He quotes Franz Mehring to the same effect on p. 342. It should be clear that both types, the politically concerned and the psychologically concerned, are present in varying numbers in many movements and parties. Engels notes this and argues that the role of the latter would be greatest early in a party's history. But with growth and maturity, their impact would be contained and the party's course assured.

For those having a need to express hostility, the petty bourgeoisie would provide little more than a convenient target. There is no intrinsic reason why that group should be chosen from among the world's possible scapegoats. When a party or movement declined, as with the American Communist party, those persons would have to look elsewhere for gratificaton of their needs. This psychological need might explain the ease with which some people shift from one moralizing movement to another.

95. The comments in this and the following paragraphs are not meant to indicate agreement with an extreme relativist position, nor are they meant as an ad hominen argument. The sense of that everyday demand is a legitimate scientific one; it is a request for alternative hypotheses and for neglected (or hidden) evidence.

96. As quoted in Israel Shenker, "Weimar Intellectuals in New York," *New York Times Book Review*, November 28, 1971, pp. 2 and 20. It appears also in *Social Research*, 39 (Summer 1972): 253.

97. Pachter, "On Being an Exile," p. 14.

98. See Jean-François Revel, *The Totalitarian Temptation*, Garden City: Doubleday, 1977, the original, *La Tentation Totalitaire*, Paris: R. Laffont, 1976; and Walter Laqueur, *Terrorism*, London: Weidenfeld and Nicolson, 1977.

APPENDIX A

1. These are: Erich Eyck, *Geschichte der Weimarer Republik*, Erlenbach-Zurich: Eugen Rentsch Verlag, 1956; Arthur Rosenberg, *Geschichte der Weimarer Republik*, Frankfurt: Europäische Verlagsanstalt, 1961; and S. William Halperin, *Germany Tried Democracy: A Political History of the Reich from 1918 to 1933*, New York: Norton, 1965.

2. There was nothing in the previous electoral history to suggest any such underlying support for left liberalism. The Progressives, the clearest precedessor of the Democrats in the old regime, had taken only 12.3 percent in the 1912 election, that being their highest figure since 1893. The National Liberals, the predecessor to the right liberal German People's party (DVP) had taken between 13 and 15 percent of the total in the three elections before the war, whereas in 1919 they had only 4.4 percent of the total. The 1920 result seems to reflect their basic strength more accurately. In 1919, then, it would appear that many of their voters had made this tactical shift to the left liberals.

3. This point is discussed at some length in Johannes Schauff, *Die Deutschen Katholiken und die Zentrumspartei: Eine politisch-statistische Untersuchung der Reichstagswahlen seit 1871*, Cologne: Verlag J.P. Bachem, 1928, pp. 49 ff.

4. The vote was postponed to 1921 in three areas, Schleswig-Holstein, Pomerania, and Silesia. Plebescites were scheduled to take place there, following Wilsonian and Versailles principles, which were to determine what areas would be separated from the Reich.

5. This is, of course, a simplification. Some voters would have disappeared from the electorate (through death or indifference). Some others would have been added. It is not as if there had been a constant staff of voters.

6. This is again hypothetical. Many writers have commented on the fact.

Whether it was a concern to workers, and if so, whether it was a serious one, are questions that can hardly be answered at this point. There were no public opinion polls to probe mass sentiment in those elections.

7. Here there is a need for detailed study. The struggle over the Dawes Plan and the split within the conservative DNVP in the final vote on the plan were given considerable attention in the press at this time. One of the leading monographic studies of Weimar politics describes the electoral developments in Schleswig-Holstein without finding it necessary to make any mention of this controversy. Heberle links the Conservative growth rather to a tradition of opposition that characterized the region. See Rudolf Heberle, *Landbevölkerung und Nationalsozialismus: Eine soziologische Untersuchung der politischen Willensbildung in Schleswig-Holstein 1918 bis 1932*, Stuttgart: Deutsche Verlags-Anstalt, 1963, p. 33. Another line of explanation for the increase in Conservative strength leads in a different direction. The National Socialists had done rather well in the three election districts (*Wahlkreise*) of Bavaria in the first of the 1924 elections. In December voters turned away from that party and were thus free to choose another. The greatest percentage increases for the DNVP were found in these three Bavarian districts. In most of the other districts the changes were marginal, a good many of them even involving losses.

8. Here again one finds complexities. Halperin (*Germany Tried Democracy*) sees the defeat on the education question as providing a "pretext" for the Zentrum. Another source reports that the Zentrum leaders felt it to be close to the heart of their interests. Although the school issue brought down the government, the pocket battleship question seems to have been the more important theme in the election campaign. For some detail see Ellen L. Evans, "The Center Wages *Kulturpolitik*: Conflict in the Marx-Keudell Cabinet of 1927," *Central European History*, 2 (1969): 139-158.

9. Helge Timm, *Die deutsche Sozialpolitik und der Bruch der grossen Koalition im März 1930*, Düsseldorf: Droste Verlag, 1952.

10. S. William Halperin, *Germany Tried Democracy: A Political History of the Reich from 1918 to 1933*, New York: Norton, 1965, p. 431.

LIBRARY OF CONGRESS CATALOGING IN PUBLICATION DATA

Hamilton, Richard F.
  Who voted for Hitler?

  Includes bibliographical references and index.
    1. Elections—Germany—History.   2. Germany—Politics
and government—1918-1933.   3. Social classes—Germany
—Political activity—History.   4. National socialism—
History.   5. Hitler, Adolf, 1889-1945.   I. Title.
JN3838.H35   324.943'085   81-17811

ISBN 0-691-09395-4   AACR2
ISBN 0-691-10132-9 (ltd. pbk.)